BLACKSTONE'S GUIDE TO

THE CRIMINAL JUSTICE ACT 2003

Richard Taylor
Professor of English Law and Head of Lancashire Law School
University of Central Lancashire

Martin Wasik
Professor of Criminal Justice, Keele University
Chairman, Sentencing Advisory Panel

Roger Leng
Reader in Law, University of Warwick

OXFORD
UNIVERSITY PRESS

OXFORD
UNIVERSITY PRESS

Great Clarendon Street, Oxford OX2 6DP

Oxford University Press is a department of the University of Oxford.
It furthers the University's objective of excellence in research, scholarship,
and education by publishing worldwide in

Oxford New York

Auckland Bangkok Buenos Aires Cape Town Chennai
Dar es Salaam Delhi Hong Kong Istanbul Karachi Kolkata
Kuala Lumpur Madrid Melbourne Mexico City Mumbai Nairobi
São Paulo Shanghai Taipei Tokyo Toronto

Oxford is a registered trade mark of Oxford University Press
in the UK and in certain other countries

Published in the United States
by Oxford University Press Inc., New York

Database right Oxford University Press (maker)

First published 2004

British Library Cataloguing in Publication Data

Data available

Library of Congress Cataloging in Publication Data

Data available

ISBN 0-19-926725-1

3 5 7 9 10 8 6 4

Typeset by Newgen Imaging Systems (P) Ltd., Chennai, India
Printed in Great Britain
on acid-free paper by
Ashford Colour Press Limited, Gosport, Hampshire

Contents—Summary

Contents

Preface

The Criminal Justice Act 2003 is the longest Act any of us has had to grapple with, weighing in at 339 sections, 38 Schedules and over 450 pages in the Stationery Office version. Trying to be positive about it, the best one might say is that it is good in parts. It is so wide ranging that it is difficult to identify a coherent theme. Implementing the Report of Lord Justice Auld (*Review of the Criminal Courts of England and Wales*, September 2001) and the Halliday Report (Home Office, *Making Punishments Work: Report of a Review of the Sentencing Framework for England and Wales*, July 2001), might be the simplest way to put it, although not everything in Auld nor even in Halliday was accepted by the government in the subsequent White Paper *Justice for All* (July 2002, Cm 5563), on which much of the Act is based. Many provisions of the Act were highly controversial to the extent that the whole Act was very nearly lost right at the end of the Parliamentary session late in the evening of 20 November 2003 because of an impasse between the Lords and the Commons over the provisions restricting jury trial in certain situations (see further 4.2 below). One suspects that the fact that the most intense opposition was focused on issues such as jury trial meant that other controversial, or simply unduly complex, provisions slipped through with less opposition or scrutiny than they would have received if contained in a smaller Bill with fewer obviously controversial issues to hog the limelight. Whatever one's views of the substance of the changes introduced, its style of drafting, often involving detailed piecemeal amendments to existing complex provisions, does little to make the Criminal Justice system any easier to understand. The fact that the provisions are all being brought into force at different times over a period of two to three years further complicates the situation. We have done our best to make sense of this gargantuan Act and to set out the reasoning behind the new provisions as well as to point out the difficulties. Whatever the difficulties we have encountered in setting out and explaining the provisions, our sympathies lie with those who actually have to implement them and work with them on a daily basis and we hope that this book will be of some assistance to them in that task as well as to those involved in studying the Act or its place in the Criminal Justice system as a whole. Our thanks go to all at OUP for their assistance and patience with us throughout this project and to our families who have borne with equanimity the strange moods into which we have no doubt descended at times as we grappled with some of the more intractable parts of the Act, ie with substantial parts of it.

June 2004

Richard Taylor
Martin Wasik
Roger Leng

Abbreviations

ASBO	anti-social behaviour order
BA 1976	Bail Act 1976
CDA 1971	Criminal Damage Act 1971
CDA 1998	Crime and Disorder Act 1998
CEA 1898	Criminal Evidence Act 1898
CISA	Convention Implementing the Schengen Agreement
CJA 1987	Criminal Justice Act 1987
CJA 1988	Criminal Justice Act 1988
CJA 1991	Criminal Justice Act 1991
CJA 1993	Criminal Justice Act 1993
CJA 2003	Criminal Justice Act 2003
CO	custody officer
CPIA 1996	Criminal Procedure and Investigations Act 1996
CPS	Crown Prosecution Service
DPP	Director of Public Prosecutions
ECHR	European Convention on Human Rights
ECtHR	European Court of Human Rights
HDC	home detention curfew
HRA 1998	Human Rights Act 1998
ISO	individual support order
MCA 1980	Magistrates' Courts Act 1980
MDA 1971	Misuse of Drugs Act 1971
NCIS	National Criminal Intelligence Service (NCIS)
NCS	National Crime Squad
NOMS	national offender management service
OAPA 1861	Offences Against the Person Act 1861
PACE 1984	Police and Criminal Evidence Act 1984
PCC(S)A 2000	Powers of Criminal Courts (Sentencing) Act 2000
TA 2000	Terrorism Act 2000
YJCEA 1999	Youth Justice and Criminal Evidence Act 1999

Table of Cases

Table of Statutes

Table of Secondary Legislation

Table of International Legislation

1

POLICE POWERS

1.1 INTRODUCTION

The scheme for regulating police powers in relation to suspected persons in the Police and Criminal Evidence Act 1984 (PACE 1984) is amended by Part 1 of the Criminal Justice Act 2003 (CJA 2003). These reforms are largely inspired by the *Report of the Joint Home Office/Cabinet Office Review of the Police and Criminal Evidence Act 1984* (hereafter PACE Review) which was published in 2002 (available at http://www.homeoffice.gov.uk/docs/pacereview2002.pdf). The Review's focus on efficiency gains was founded on an unsupported assumption that PACE 1984, as currently operated, adequately protects human rights and minimizes the risk of miscarriages of justice. Thus, in its terms of reference, the purpose of the Review was described as to identify possible changes to the rules that could:

- simplify police procedures;
- reduce procedural or administrative burdens on the police;
- save police resources;
- speed up the process of justice.

These purposes to be pursued '[w]ithout compromising the rights of those that the Act protects.'

The Review focused not only on the primary legislation, but also on the Codes of Practice made under it. Although the Codes were revised from April 2003, further revisions took effect from August 2004, with yet further revisions anticipated. The PACE Review recommends that the Codes should be reworked to provide greater clarity and that this might be achieved by creating a framework of key principles with more detailed guidance moving to National Standards. This more radical reform of the Codes is to follow the revision of the procedures relating to the making of the Codes which is now accomplished in s 11 of the current Act.

The following measures came into force on 20 January 2004: s 1 (power to stop and search); s 2 (warrants to enter and search), s 4 (bail); s 6 (telephone reviews); s 8 (suspect's property); s 11 (codes of practice); and s 12 (consequential amendments) by Commencement Order No 2 (SI 2004/81). Section 3 (arrestable offences) was brought into force on 29 January 2004 (SI 2004/81). The following measures came into force on 5 April 2004: s 9 (taking fingerprints without consent), s 10 (taking non-intimate samples without consent) (SI 2004/829). It is anticipated that s 5 (drug testing) will be brought into force in pilot areas in June 2004.

For convenience, this chapter also includes discussion of two related matters found in other parts of the Act. The first of these is an amendment to the Terrorism Act 2000 which extends the period during which a terrorist suspect may be detained without charge (1.7.3 below). This measure came into force on 20 January 2004. Secondly, a new power to impose bail conditions for a suspect's protection or welfare is considered (1.5.5 below). This is expected to come into force during 2005 or 2006.

Readers are also referred to amendments to PACE 1984 to accommodate new charging procedures which are discussed below at 2.4.

1.2 STOP AND SEARCH POWERS

Section 1 makes a minor amendment to the powers to stop and search persons or vehicles in public by adding criminal damage to the list of offences (in PACE 1984, s 1(8)) in relation to which these powers may be exercised. Following this amendment, any article made or adapted for use in, or in connection with, a criminal damage offence or where the person having the article with him, intends it for such use, whether by himself or anybody else, will be a 'prohibited article'. Examples might include spray paint cans, or even coins to be used for scratching cars. Thus, if a constable suspects with reasonable grounds that he will find such an article, he is empowered to search a person or vehicle (PACE 1984, s 1(3)). If in the course of a lawful search (whether or not in relation to criminal damage), the constable may seize any article which he reasonably suspects to be prohibited (PACE 1984, s1(6)).

The search power will extend to cases of criminal damage being reckless or intentional as to endangering life (Criminal Damage Act 1971 (CDA 1971), s 1(2)) and arson (CDA 1971, s 1 (3)), but not to offences of threatening criminal damage (CDA 1971, s 2); or going equipped for criminal damage (CDA 1971, s 3). The exclusion of the going equipped offence is curious because if a person carries an article to which the new power of search applies he would commit the going equipped offence, subject to proof of the necessary intent to use the article for the purpose of criminal damage. In cases in which the search pre-empts a proposed offence, the most likely charge to follow will in fact be going equipped.

The new power is intended to increase significantly police powers in relation to street disorder. It will have this effect because of the breadth of the criminal damage offence, which may involve painting signs on pavements or walls (*Hardman v Chief Constable of Avon and Somerset* [1986] Crim LR 330), soiling something so that it requires cleaning (*Roe v Kingerlee* [1986] Crim LR 735), disassembly of a machine requiring work to put it right (*R v Tacey* (1821) Russ & Ry 452), and erasing a computer program (*Cox v Riley* (1986) 83 Cr App R 54). In its broadest forms criminal damage may cover activities associated with political demonstrations, or youth culture (eg graffiti). The Home Office have recognized that the power may generate difficult confrontations and have expressed an intention to issue guidance as to its use.

1.3 SEARCH WARRANTS

A search warrant may authorize other persons to accompany the constable who executes the warrant (PACE 1984, s 16(2)). However, until now the legal status of the accompanying person has been in doubt, and whereas she or he would clearly have a defence to an action for trespass, it was not clear if there would be a defence if the accompanying person took an active part in search and seizure. The position is now clarified by s 2 which adds a new s 16(2A) to PACE 1984, and which provides that a person authorized to accompany a constable in executing a warrant shall have the same search and seizure powers as the constable whom he accompanies, but may exercise these powers only in the company and under the supervision of a constable.

1.4 ARRESTABLE OFFENCES

Section 3 adds three new offences to the list of arrestable offence in PACE 1984, Sch 1A. The three offences are:

- making an untrue statement for the purpose of procuring a passport under Criminal Justice Act 1925, s 36;
- possession of cannabis or cannabis resin under Misuse of Drugs Act 1971, s 5(2);
- making a false statement or withholding material information, under Road Traffic Act 1988, s 174.

The rationale for each of these additions to the list of arrestable offences is fairly apparent. The need to regulate and monitor persons entering and leaving this and other countries is becoming increasingly important in view of current terrorist threats. False passports are key factors in illegal immigration and people trafficking, the drug trade and international money laundering. False passports may also be used as proof of identity in a wide range of frauds. Although the basic false statement offence is not treated as a very serious offence in its own right, it is made arrestable by virtue of its links to other, more serious offending.

In relation to the possession of cannabis, as is well known, cannabis was demoted from Class B to Class C status by Misuse of Drugs Act 1971 (Modification)(No 2) Order 2003 (SI 2003/3201). The effect of this was to reduce the maximum sentence for simple possession under Misuse of Drugs Act 1971, s 5(2) from five years' imprisonment to two years. A consequence of that change was that the offence ceased to be arrestable. The measure came into operation on 29 January 2004.

The offence of making a false statement or withholding material information in relation to obtaining driving licences and insurance certificates is an offence which, like the passport offence above, may be committed in order to create a false identity and may be associated with more serious criminality. Hence the need to make it arrestable.

1.5 POLICE BAIL

1.5.1 Background

A key principle propose by the Royal Commission on Criminal Procedure (1981, Cmnd 8092, London: HMSO) was that coercive police powers should be exercised subject to the necessity principle: ie no power should be used unless it was necessary to do so. As envisaged by the Commission, this would have significantly diminished the numbers of suspects taken to the police station under arrest, since in many cases the objective of having the suspect available for interview might be achieved by consent or by an appointment system. In this respect, the Commission's aspiration foundered for two main reasons. Firstly, it was always doubtful whether simply changing the rules would alter long-entrenched police practices and habits. Secondly, the rules which emerged in PACE 1984 militated against the Commission's favoured necessity principle. In particular, under s 30, as originally drafted, once a person was under arrest, they had to be taken to a designated police station as soon as practicable, there being no power to de-arrest on the street, or to make alternative arrangements to secure the attendance of the suspect at a police station. An advantage of the approach under the original version of s 30 was that suspects generally had to be dealt with in the controlled, supervised and relatively visible environment of the police station rather than on the street. A disadvantage was that some citizens might be taken to the police station for mere 'processing' before being released either to return or to appear in court, on a later occasion. This requirement of instant attendance may be inconvenient and disruptive for suspects and is a significant drain on the human resources of the police because an arresting officer has to attend with the suspect. A particular problem is that the need to take suspects to the police station, book them in and then proceed with the interview as soon as possible, may have the effect of removing officers from the streets at peak offending times when they are most needed.

1.5.2 New Provisions on Police Bail

These problems are addressed by s 4, which creates a new power for constables to grant street bail. Section 30 of PACE 1984 is amended by the insertion of four new sections: 30A, 30B, 30C and 30D. In its original form, PACE 1984, s 30 created a duty for a constable to take an arrested person to a police station as soon as practicable. Section 4(2) amends PACE 1984, s 30A, and makes this duty subject to the constable's discretion to release the suspect on bail in certain circumstances under PACE 1984, s 30A and adds a new power to 'de-arrest' under a new sub-s 30(7A). Section 4(5) also modifies the duties of a constable in relation to an arrested person by providing that it is permissible to delay conveying the arrestee to a police station, or the grant of bail, if his presence at a particular place is necessary in order to carry out reasonable investigations. These measures are now found in a substituted s 30(10) and a new PACE 1984, s 30(10A). A substituted PACE 1984, s 30(11) requires that the reason for any delay in taking a suspect to a police station is recorded on arrival or, as the case may be, when he is granted bail. These provisions probably reflect the existing position. It seems likely that in interpreting the former require-ment to take the suspect to a police station as soon as practicable, the courts would have considered that 'practicability' might be judged with reference to the needs of the investigation.

1.5.3 A Power to De-arrest

No doubt, on occasions in the past, police officers have released an arrested person when it became clear that suspicion had been unfounded. However, this practice did not have a foundation in law, at least since PACE 1984 came into force. The primary duty following arrest was to deliver the arrested person to a police station, and to do otherwise would, at least in theory, expose an officer to the risk of complaint or legal action. Now, under new s 30(7) and (7A) of PACE 1984, as inserted by s 4(4) of the present Act, a person arrested on the street (ie not in a police station) must be released if the constable is satisfied that there are no grounds for keeping the arrested person under arrest or releasing him on bail. It may be noted that this provision will not justify an officer de-arresting a suspect in order to embark upon an interview on the street, and to do so would normally contravene Code C. 11.1, and run the risk evidence obtained might be excluded under PACE 1984, s 78. The government hopes that this provision will lead to fewer pointless trips to the station and will serve to keep officers on the street. This aspiration may be defeated by the lure of the police station canteen and the fact that 'wasted' shift time may not be seen as a bad thing on a cold winter's night.

1.5.4 Street Bail

Section 30A PACE 1984, as inserted by s 4(7), permits an arrested person to be released on bail at any time before reaching the police station. The only duty attached to bail is to attend a specified police station at a stated time. The station in question may be any station and the nominated station may be varied if convenient. When given bail, the arrestee must be given a notice indicating the offence for which the arrest was made and the grounds on which it was made (s 30B(2)). The notice must state the duty to attend and state the police station and the relevant time (s 30B(3) and (4)). These duties may be changed or discharged, but such changes must be notified in writing (s 30B(6) and (7), s 30C(1)). Where a person is required to attend a station which is not designated as a custody station, he must be taken to a designated station if not released before six hours have elapsed (s 30C(2)). By way of clarification, it is provided that the Bail Act 1976 has no application to street bail (s 30C(3)).

It is also stated that release on bail does not preclude re-arrest without warrant 'if new evidence justifying arrest has come to light since his release' (s 30C(4)). It is arguable that this subsection is superfluous, since the question of re-arrest is already dealt with by PACE 1984, s 47(2). However, although sub-s (4) adopts the wording of s 47(2) and was probably inserted for the avoidance of doubt, it may have precisely the opposite effect. By apparently restricting the power of re-arrest to cases of new evidence, the provision may: (i) invite detailed consideration of the circumstances in which evidence can be said to be new (as for appeals on new evidence under Criminal Appeal Act 1968, s 23); and (ii) may be taken implicitly to prohibit re-arrest in other circumstances. It is submitted that both issues are unfortunate red herrings: nothing in s 30C should be understood to cut down the general power of arrest without warrant on reasonable suspicion under PACE 1984, s 24, or other cognate powers. Thus, it should be possible to re-arrest where, for instance, the implications of existing evidence become apparent at a later review or where new information (which is not strictly evidence) has a bearing on the issue whether it is desirable as a matter of policy to proceed with the case.

The only sanction for failure to attend a police station as required, following street bail, is that the suspect may be re-arrested. This is provided for by s 30D, although this provision is probably also superfluous because this situation would appear to be covered by the re-arrest power in s 47(2).

1.5.5 Police Bail with Conditions for the Suspect's Welfare or Protection

Section 13(2) extends the power to impose conditions on police bail, consequent on a similar extension to the court's power to impose bail conditions (discussed in 2.2.3). Section 13(2) amends the Bail Act 1976, s 3A. This provision currently permits a custody officer to grant police bail with conditions where it appears to the officer that it is necessary to do so for the purpose of preventing the suspect from (a) failing to surrender to custody, or (b) committing an offence whilst on bail, or (c) interfering with witnesses or otherwise obstructing the course of justice. A new paragraph (d) is now added which permits the imposition of conditions if it appears to the officer to be necessary for the protection of the bailed person, or, if he is a child or young person, for his own welfare or in his own interests. The new provision should prevent unnecessary refusals of bail where a perceived problem could be averted by a condition, which typically might require the suspect's residence at a particular place.

1.6 DRUG TESTING FOR UNDER 18s

Section 5 extends the drug testing regime for adult suspects, introduced by the Criminal Justice and Courts Services Act and currently provided for in PACE 1984, s 63B, to young people between 14 and 18 years old. It is anticipated that this provision will be piloted in particular areas from June 2004. However, practitioners should note that even after the provision is in force, it will not apply in a particular police force area until the relevant chief constable has notified the Home Secretary that arrangements for taking samples from under-18s have been made in the police force area as a whole or in particular police stations (s 63B(9)). The power is to test for Class A drugs, and is available only where a person is under arrest for a 'trigger offence' involving either drugs directly or forms of acquisitive dishonesty associated with funding a drug habit. The list of trigger offences currently includes: theft, robbery, burglary, aggravated burglary, taking a conveyance without consent, aggravated vehicle taking, going equipped for stealing, and offences under the Misuse of Drugs Act 1971 committed in respect of Class A drugs.

Section 5 makes necessary amendments to PACE 1984, ss 38 and 63B. The minimum age applicable to drug testing is lowered to 14 (s 63B(3)). The custody officer may order the detention of an arrested person where he has reasonable grounds for believing that the detention of the person is necessary for the purpose of taking a sample.

A number of amendments are made necessary by the fact that the drug testing regime will now extend to juveniles under 17 who are subject to special safeguards under PACE 1984. Thus, the making of the request to provide a sample, the warning in relation to the consequences of refusal and the act of taking the sample, may not take place except in the presence of an appropriate adult (s 63(5A)). Until now, references to the attendance of appropriate adults have been confined to the Codes of Practice made under PACE 1984, s 67. It is not clear why it has been deemed necessary to provide for this particular function of the appropriate adult in the primary legislation as opposed to the Codes. The definition for appropriate adult in newly inserted s 63B(1) is '[the child's] parent or guardian, or if he is in the care of a local authority or voluntary organisation, or person representing that authority or organisation; or local authority social worker; or if no such person is available, any responsible person aged 18 or over who is not a police officer or person employed by the police'.

1.7 DETENTION PERIODS AND REVIEWS

1.7.1 Extended Detention for Non-serious Offences

By s 7, the procedure for extending detention from a maximum of 24 hours to 36 hours on the authority of a superintendent, formerly available only for serious arrestable offences, is now extended to all arrestable offences, as defined by PACE

1984, s 24. The change is made by substituting a new sub-s 42(1)(b) to PACE 1984. As before, the grounds for authorizing continued detention under s 42 will be that the superintendent has reasonable grounds to believe that the detention of the suspect without charge is necessary to secure or preserve evidence or to obtain evidence by questioning, and that the investigation is being conducted diligently and expeditiously. The change will have a significant impact on the balance between citizen's rights and police powers struck by PACE 1984. In guidance contained in Home Office Circular 60 of 2003, the new provision is described as a 'significant additional power for the police . . . which should be used sparingly and only where there is full justification' (paras 4.3, 4.4). Unusually, it appears that in this case 'strict justification' is not a matter of law but is trusted to police discretion. The Circular advises that the authorizing officer must be satisfied that alternatives to continued detention, such as bail and 'restorative justice' have been considered and that the reasons why these measures are inappropriate must also have been considered (para 4.7). It is apparent that the government, in pursuit of investigative convenience, chose to keep these issues out of the primary legislation. However, they will be directly relevant to the legal test to be applied under s 42. In the light of the guidance, it would be difficult for an officer to claim that she had reasonable grounds to believe that further detention was necessary for the stated objectives without also being able to demonstrate why non-custodial alternatives were inappropriate. This is an issue which should be raised by defence lawyers making representations on continued detention, who should insist that reasons why non-custodial measures are inappropriate are given and recorded.

The Circular also advises that detaining a juvenile or mentally vulnerable person without charge for more than 24 hours will normally be justifiable only in relation to a serious arrestable offence. Before departing from this principle, the authorizing officer would need to have regard to the suspect's special vulnerability, the need to provide an opportunity to the suspect, legal representative and appropriate adult to make representations, and possible alternatives to police custody (para. 4.8). It seems very unlikely that the police would wish to use the power for vulnerable suspects in relation to non-serious offences but, if this is proposed, defence lawyers should insist that full reasons for doing so are given and recorded.

1.7.2 Periodic Reviews by Telephone

Section 6 provides that periodic detention reviews may be routinely carried out by telephone. The requirement to hold such reviews is found in PACE's s 40 which provides that the first review of the detention of a person in custody must be held six hours after the beginning of the detention period, and subsequent reviews held at intervals of no more than nine hours. The reviews must be carried out by an inspector in relation to a person who has not been charged, and by the custody officer in relation to persons detained after charge. Section 40A of PACE 1984 provides for such reviews to be carried out by telephone. Formerly this was permissible only where it was not reasonably practicable for an officer of at least inspector rank to be present. Section 6 substitutes s 40A(1) and (2) and has the effect of removing the practicability test and permitting telephone reviews to be carried out 'by means of a discussion conducted by telephone with one or more persons at the police station' where the detained person is held. Where fax or computer email facilities are available, these may be used for the purpose of making representations to the reviewing officer (s 40A(4)); however, in the absence of such facilities, the defendant's rights to make representations or to have representations made on his behalf will be limited to oral representations (s 40A(4)). The duty to make a record of the review, however, remains except that the duty must be delegated to an officer at the station where the detainee is being held (s 40A(3)).

The only circumstances in which it will not be possible to use telephone reviews routinely will be where a station is equipped and authorized to hold reviews using video conferencing technology under PACE 1984, s 45A, which was inserted by Criminal Justice and Police Act 2001, s 73, and which has yet to be brought into force. Where this is the case, a telephone review should not be conducted unless it is not reasonably practicable to conduct the review by video-conference (substituted s 40A(2)). An important limitation on the use of telephone reviews should be noted. The procedures for periodic review of detention (s 40) and the power to authorize continued detention (s 42) are separate powers and the decision by a superintendent to extend detention beyond 24 hours must always be made in person.

1.7.3 Extended Detention without Charge for Terrorist Offences

Section 306 extends the period during which a person suspected of a terrorist offence may be held, under a warrant for further detention under powers in the TA 2000 from 7 to 14 days.

Under the Terrorism Act, anybody arrested on reasonable suspicion of being a terrorist under s 41 is subjected to a special regime of police powers and procedures prescribed in Part V and Sch 8 of that Act, instead of the regime under PACE which applies to other categories of offence. Under s 41(3), any person arrested under s 41 must be released no later than 48 hours from the time of his arrest. However, if it is intended to make an application for further detention under TA 2000, Sch 8, para 29, the suspect may be detained pending the making of the application (TA 2000, s 41(5)) or, where an application has been made, he may be detained pending the outcome of the proceedings to determine that application (TA 2000, s 41(6)). Under para 29 an officer of at least the rank of superintendent may apply to a judicial authority (normally a specially designated District Judge) for a warrant of further detention. The application must be made within 6 hours of the expiration of the initial period of detention of 48 hours (ie within a total period of 54 hours). The grounds for issuing an extension are similar to those under PACE 1984, s 42, ie that: (a) there are reasonable grounds for believing that the further detention is necessary to obtain relevant evidence by questioning or otherwise or to preserve relevant evidence; and (b) that the investigation is being conducted diligently and expeditiously. The initial warrant must specify a period no longer than 7 days from the time of the arrest under s 41. In the original version of the Terrorism Act, further warrants could be applied for but subject to an overall limit of 7 days. However, by virtue of CJA 2003, s 306 that time limit is now subject to a new para 29(3A) which permits second and subsequent warrants to extend the total period of detention to 14 days from the time of the initial arrest under s 41.

It seems likely that government policy in relation to terrorism is likely to be expressed in yet more legislation in the near future. A discussion paper, *Counter-terrorism Powers: Reconciling Security and Liberty in an Open Society*, was published by the Home Office in February 2004. The paper is largely concerned with the workings of the Anti-terrorism, Crime and Security Act 2001 which deals with foreign terrorist suspects and provides a power of indefinite detention followed by deportation. One of the issues debated in that paper is whether similar rules should apply to terrorist suspects, whatever their origin, ie including those arrested within the UK. If this approach were adopted, the periods during which terrorist suspects could be detained might rise dramatically.

1.8 PROPERTY OF DETAINED PERSONS

Section 8 amends PACE 1984, s 54 by abolishing the custody officer's duty to make a record of everything which a detained person has with him. The duty of the custody officer to 'ascertain' such possessions remains, coupled with a three-stage discretion to to record: (i) all of the things which are 'ascertained'; or (ii) any of such things; and (iii) to make any such record as part of the custody record (or not).

The provision arises from the government review of the operation of PACE and, as with other such reforms, its mission is simply to cut down unnecessary bureaucracy. However, whereas it is beyond doubt that painstakingly recording all possessions of a detained person would be both time-consuming and irritating, it is not clear whether the new provision will lead to a significant reduction in workload. An advantage of the former position was that it involved a clear, easily followed rule. A new para 4.4 of Code C, effective 1 August 2004, provides: 'It is a matter for the custody officer to determine whether a record should be made of the property a detained person has with him or had taken from him on arrest. Any record made is not required to be kept as part of the custody record but the custody record should be noted as to where such record exists.' Notwithstanding this broad discretion, custody officers will no doubt recognize that, if in doubt, the safest course will be to record the suspect's property as before.

1.9 FINGERPRINTS AND NON-INTIMATE SAMPLES

Sections 9 and 10 extend, respectively, police powers to take fingerprints and non-intimate samples to all persons who are detained at a police station following an arrest for a recordable offence. Prior to this, the law had embodied a balance between the interests of investigating offences and the citizen's interest in privacy and not being molested. Whereas both fingerprints and non-intimate samples could be taken lawfully following charge or after the suspect had been told that he may be charged or convicted for a recordable offence, prints and samples could be taken without consent prior to charge only if authorized by a superintendent, where that officer had reasonable grounds to suspect involvement in a recordable offence and for believing that the prints or sample would tend to confirm or disprove his involvement. Formerly, it was also the case that samples and prints were required to be destroyed if the suspect was ultimately acquitted or if no further action was taken. That rule was abrogated in the Criminal Justice and Police Act 2001, s 81 (see now PACE 1984, s 63A). The rationale of the pre-existing law was that a citizen should not be obliged to provide these forms of information about himself unless a realistic investigative purpose could be demonstrated, and had a right that such samples should not be retained once he ceased to be a suspect. By way of contrast, the new provisions clearly reflect the interests of efficiency in investigations, since prints and samples may now taken (and retained) routinely in investigations of recordable offences. The new powers will also facilitate the rapid development of the Police National Crime Database.

1.9.1 Fingerprinting

Section 9 amends PACE 1984, s 61 by substituting new sub-ss (3) and (4) which together prescribe the two circumstances in which fingerprints may be taken without appropriate consent (fingerprints not having been taken previously in the course of the investigation). The two circumstances are:

• where a person is detained in consequence of arrest for a recordable offence (s 61(3)(a));
• where a person is charged, or informed that he will be reported, for a recordable offence (s 61(4)(a)).

A minor amendment is also made to the provision which permits repeat fingerprinting where the first prints taken were incomplete or unsatisfactory. This is dealt with by s 61(3A), which formerly permitted repeat fingerprinting only where a person is charged with, or informed that he may be reported for, a recordable offence. This barred the police from putting right a deficiency in prints during the investigation before the decision to charge or report. That gap is now filled by a new s 61(3A) which allows repeat fingerprinting where the prints taken under s 61 are incomplete or unsatisfactory, at any stage either during the investigation or after the decision to charge or to report.

An opportunity is also taken to put right a former anomaly in the fingerprinting scheme. Section 61(7) requires that where fingerprints are taken without consent, a reason should be given to the suspect and that reason should be recorded as soon as practicable after the prints are taken. This formerly applied when fingerprints had been taken after arrest, under sub-s (3) or after conviction, caution, reprimand or warning under sub-s (6). There was no requirement to inform of the reasons where fingerprints were taken after charge or when a person was informed that he would be reported. The omission of a requirement to give reasons during the investigation contradicted the fundamental constitutional principle that a citizen should not be required to submit to the coercive power of the state without being informed why (cf *Christie v Leachinsky* [1947] AC 573). That defect is now corrected by an amendment to s 61(7) to include fingerprinting after charge or report under s 61(4) in the list of circumstances in which reasons must be given and recorded.

1.9.2 Non-intimate Samples

It will be recalled that non-intimate samples comprise hair (other than pubic hair), samples taken from a nail or under a nail, swabs taken from the body or mouth but not other orifices, saliva and skin impressions. Section 10 amends PACE 1984, s 63 by inserting new sub-ss (2A), (2B) and (2C). Taken together the new subsections provide that non-intimate samples may be taken without consent if a person is in detention following arrest for a recordable offence and that he has either not already had an intimate sample taken from the same part of the body or, if he has had such a sample taken, it has proved to be insufficient.

Section 10(3) and (4) contains some minor consequential amendments to PACE 1984, s 63. Formerly, it was possible to take samples from persons in police detention under s 63(3)(a). That subsection is now amended to remove the reference to persons in police detention. However, the power to take samples from persons in police custody under the authority of the court, under that subsection, remains. Also retained is the power under s 63(3A) to take a sample from a person after he has been charged, or informed that he will be reported, for a recordable offence. A minor amendment is made to that provision to make clear that the power under sub-s (3A) may be exercised notwithstanding that the person might be subject to another sample-taking power by virtue of either being in police detention or being in police custody by authority of the court.

Where the new sample-taking power is exercised the suspect must be told of the reason before the sample is taken and that reason must be recorded as soon as practicable after the sample is taken. This is provided for by addition of a reference to sub-s (2A) in s 63(8A), which similarly requires that reasons are given in relation to other circumstances in which non-consensual samples may be taken.

1.10 PACE CODES

PACE 1984 confers power on the Home Secretary to issue Codes of Practice relating to the tape recording of interviews (s 60), the visual recording of interviews (s 60A), the search of persons and vehicles without arrest; the detention, treatment, questioning and identification of suspects; searches of premises and the seizure of property found on premises (s 66(1)); and drug testing under s 63B of those under arrest (s 66(2)). Procedures relating to all of these Codes are governed by s 67.

Section 11(1) CJA 2003 overhauls the Home Secretary's powers in relation to the Codes by substituting a number of subsections of s 67. The overhaul reflects the view expressed in the PACE Review that the procedure for revising the Codes was too cumbersome and time-consuming. In particular, the former requirement under s 67(1) that the Home Secretary should first publish a draft of any modifications, invite representations from interested parties, consider those representations and amend the draft Code if necessary, is abolished. In place of that provision is a requirement that before making any revisions the Home Secretary must consult representatives of the police authorities and of chief officers of police, the General Council of the Bar, the Law Society of England and Wales, the Institute of Legal Executives, and any other persons as he thinks fit (s 67(4)). This permits the Home Secretary to take advice in advance of the detailed drafting of the revisions to the Codes and avoids the need for the Home Office to invite detailed criticism of the actual Code to be published.

The Home Secretary may revise any of the Codes at any time (s 67(1)) and revisions may apply only in relation to specified areas or for specified periods or in relation to specified offences or descriptions of offender (s 67(3)). Codes may include transitional provisions. Codes or revised codes come into operation on a date ordered by the Home Secretary by statutory instrument (s 67(5), (6)). The Code cannot be brought into effect until the required consultation with professional bodies under s 67(4) has taken place. An order bringing a Code or a revision of a Code into operation (or a draft of such an order), plus the Code or revised Code, must be laid before Parliament and approved by a resolution of both houses before it can take effect (s 67(7), (7A), (7B)).

Similar amendments are applied to Codes applicable to military law under PACE 1984, s 113(3) and (4), as amended by CJA 2003, s 11(3) and (4).

2

BAIL, CAUTIONS, AND CHARGING

2.1 INTRODUCTION

This chapter considers substantial revisions of the Bail Act 1976 (BA 1976), a new procedure for conditional cautions for adult offenders and a simplification of the process of initiating criminal proceedings, coupled with a strengthening of the supervisory role of the Crown Prosecution Service (CPS) in relation to decisions concerning charges and cautions.

The bail measures in the Criminal Justice Act 2003 (CJA 2003), ss 13, 15(3), 16, 17, 19, 20 and 21 were brought into force on 5 April 2004 by SI 2004/829. The new bail scheme for drugs users under s 19 will first be piloted in various areas of the country before general implementation. The remaining bail provisions are expected to be brought into force in 2005/06.

The provision which empowers the Home Secretary to publish a Code of Practice relating to conditional cautions came into force on 29 January 2004 (SI 2004/81). The Code of Practice *Conditional Cautions* has now been published and the new scheme was brought into force on 3 July 2004 by SI 2004/1683.

The new structure for making charging decisions under Police and Evidence Act 1984 (PACE 1984), which is introduced by s 28 and Sch 2, largely came into force on 29 January 2004 (SI 2004/81) except for some particular PACE amendments which refer to the new procedures for initiating criminal proceedings in s 29, for which no implementation date has been announced.

2.2 BAIL FROM COURT

2.2.1 Background

This chapter deals with bail issues in criminal proceedings which fall to be decided in court and are governed by the BA 1976. The more formal court procedures may be contrasted with police bail under PACE 1984, Pt IV which may be more properly considered an aspect of police powers. Reforms relating to police bail are accordingly found in 1.5 above.

The current reforms are in part based on recommendations of the Law Commission Report No 269 *Bail and the Human Rights Act 1998* and the more fully argued Consultation Paper No 157, which preceded it, and also on recommendations made by Lord Justice Auld in the *Review of the Criminal Courts of England and Wales* (2001). In neither case did the government accept every recommendation made.

2.2.2 The Human Rights Context

A major concern of the current legislation is to ensure that BA 1976 procedures are in compliance with the European Convention on Human Rights (ECHR), in particular Article 5, which guarantees the right to liberty and security. The relevant parts of Article 5 are as follows:

5(1) Everyone has the right to liberty and security of person. No one shall be deprived of his liberty save in the following cases and in accordance with a procedure prescribed by law:

. . .

(c) the lawful arrest or detention of a person effected for the purpose of bringing him before a competent legal authority on reasonable suspicion of having committed an offence or when it is reasonably considered necessary to prevent his committing an offence or fleeing after having done so.

. . .

(3) Everyone arrested or detained in accordance with the provisions of para 1(c) of this Article shall be brought promptly before a judge or other officer authorised by law to exercise judicial power and shall be entitled to trial within a reasonable time or release pending trial. Release may be conditioned by guarantees to appear for trial.

(4) Everyone who is deprived of his liberty by arrest or detention shall be entitled to take proceedings by which the lawfulness of his detention shall be decided speedily by a court and his release ordered if the detention is not lawful.

Paragraph (3) would appear to legitimate pre-trial detention which is not unreasonably prolonged. In fact, the paragraph has been interpreted by the European Court of Human Rights (ECtHR), in the light of the presumption of innocence, as requiring the release of a suspect in the absence of a reasonable justification (*Neumeister v Austria* (1968) 1 EHRR 91). Where the ECtHR has been called upon to consider the legitimacy of a reason for detention it has required that the reason must be justified by evidence in the case, rather than by speculation about possibilities. Among the grounds for refusing bail which have been held to be reasonable are: risk of failure to attend trial (*Stogmuller v Austria* (1969) 1 EHRR 155); risk of interference with the course of justice (*Wemhoff v Germany* (1968) 1 EHRR 25); and a risk that the accused may commit further offences (*Letellier v France* (1991) 14 EHRR 83). For a fuller discussion of these issues the reader is referred to J Wadham and H Mountfield, *Blackstone's Guide to the Human Rights Act 1998* (Blackstone Press, 1999, 9.5).

2.2.3 Bail with Conditions

Section 13(1) makes changes to the power of a court to impose conditions when granting bail under BA 1976, s 3(6). A new sub-s (6)(ca) is inserted which permits conditions to be imposed for the protection or welfare of the suspect. Some further necessary textual changes are also made. For convenience the new version of s 3(6) is set out in full:

3(6) He (the suspect) may be required to comply, before release on bail or later, with such requirements as appear to the court to be necessary

(a)   to secure that he surrenders to custody,

(b)   to secure that he does not commit an offence while on bail,

(c)   to secure that he does not interfere with witnesses or otherwise obstruct the course of justice whether in relation to himself or any other person,

(ca) for his own protection, or if he is a child or young person, for his own welfare or in his own interests,

(d)   to secure that he makes himself available for the purpose of enabling enquiries or a report to be made to assist the court in dealing with him for the offence,

(e)   to secure that before the time appointed for him to surrender to custody, he attends an interview with an authorised advocate or authorised litigator, as defined by s 119(1) Courts and Legal Services Act 1990.

A corresponding change is made to BA 1976, Sch 1, Pt 1, para 8(1) by CJA, s13(3) to add 'for the defendant's own protection or if he is a child or young person, for his own welfare or in his own interests' to the list of grounds on which bail conditions may be imposed.

This provision corrects an anomaly in the law, under which formerly a person could be refused bail for his own protection under BA 1976, Sch 1, Pt 1 but, if granted bail, conditions could not be imposed for the same purpose. Thus, a suspect might have been detained needlessly for his own protection in circumstances where the perceived problem might have been dealt with by conditions. This was an area in which the Law Commission feared that a bail refusal could be found to breach ECHR, Article 5(3).

Section 13(2) makes a similar change to BA 1976, s 3A, which permits a custody officer to grant police bail with conditions where it appears to the officer that it is necessary to do so for the purpose of preventing the suspect (a) failing to surrender to custody, or (b) committing an offence whilst on bail, or (c) interfering with witnesses or otherwise obstructing the course of justice. A new paragraph (d) is now added which permits the imposition of conditions if it appears to the officer to be necessary for the protection of the bailed person, or if he is a child or young person, for his own welfare or in his own interests.

2.2.4 Consequences of Bail Breaches

The Law Commission identified a potential human rights problem with the rules relating to the consequences of breaching bail by not surrendering to custody, breaching bail conditions or committing further offences whilst on bail. Under various rules in the Bail Act, these factors are relevant to the decision whether bail should be continued or granted following the alleged breach or further offence. In each case the fact or suspicion of the breach or further offence was ground for refusal of bail, without the court being required to consider closely whether it was necessary to refuse bail because of some continuing future risk. Thus, for instance, a court could have refused bail to a man charged with a non-serious offence where there had been a minor breach of a bail condition, which was not likely to be repeated. It could be argued that a decision to refuse bail in such circumstances would breach ECHR Article 5.3. Accordingly, the CJA 2003 makes a number of changes to the Bail Act, to require that courts address the question of justification in such cases and do not simply refuse bail as a knee-jerk reaction to non-attendance or allegations of further offending or breach of conditions.

Defendants Charged with Non-imprisonable Offences, Re-arrested for Breach
The first such change relates to defendants accused or convicted of imprisonable offences who, having been released on bail, are then either re-arrested under BA 1976, s 7 for failing to appear at court, or who absent themselves from court, or who are suspected on reasonable grounds of either breaking bail conditions or being likely to do so, or where there are reasonable grounds to believe that the defendant is not likely to surrender to custody. Section 13(4) of CJA 2003 substitutes a new para 5 to BA 1976, Sch 1, Pt 2, as follows:

The defendant need not be granted bail if—

(a) having been released on bail in or in connection with the proceedings for the offence, he has been arrested in pursuance of s 7 of this Act; and

(b) the court is satisfied that there are substantial grounds for believing that the defendant if released on bail (whether subject to conditions or not) would fail to surrender to custody, commit an offence on bail, or interfere with witnesses or otherwise obstruct the course of justice (whether in relation to himself or any other person).

The simple point of the reform is to require courts to satisfy themselves that there is a substantial relevant future risk which justifies a refusal of bail. As is appropriate where the charge is itself non-imprisonable, the presumption remains in favour of bail. If the prosecution seek to have the defendant remanded in custody it is for them to satisfy the court, presumably on a balance of probabilities, of the grounds in (b).

Re-offending whilst on Bail

Section 14 provides new tests for determining whether bail should be granted to a person who is charged with an indictable (including triable either way) offence where it appears to the court that the defendant was on bail on the date of the offence. Separate tests are provided for defendants who are respectively over or under 18 years of age. Formerly, BA, Sch 1, Pt 1, para 2A provided simply that such defendants need not be granted bail.

Section 14(1) of CJA substitutes a new para 2A, which relates to a defendant over 18 who is arrested for an offence, apparently committed while the defendant was already on bail. Under the new test in para 2A(1), the defendant may not be granted bail unless the court is satisfied that there is no significant risk of his committing an offence whilst on bail. In this case, the presumption is that bail will be refused and, if bail is sought, the burden of proof on the issue lies on the defendant. It should also be borne in mind that in any event, in these circumstances the court would be free to refuse bail on one of the generally applicable grounds.

Section 14(2) of CJA inserts a new para 9AA, BA, Sch 1, Pt 1 which applies to defendants under 18 who are arrested for offences apparently committed whilst on bail. The test to be applied in determining whether bail should be granted remains that under Sch 1, para 2. That test is whether the court is satisfied that there are substantial grounds for believing that the defendant, if released on bail would: (a) fail to surrender to custody; or (b) commit an offence whilst on bail; or (c) interfere with witnesses or otherwise obstruct the course of justice. However, by virtue of the new para 9AA(2), in considering whether there are substantial grounds for believing that the defendant might commit a further offence whilst on bail, the court shall give particular weight to the fact that the defendant was on bail on the date of the offence alleged against him.

By making separate provision for those over and those under 18, it is presumably intended that different tests will apply to the two age groups. Whether there will be much difference in practice is a moot point. Whereas for over-18s the presumption is against bail and the burden of proof on the defendant, for those under 18, the presumption remains technically in favour of bail, with particular weight being given to the alleged offending whilst on bail. A fair assumption is that by giving particular weight to the alleged offending on bail, the court will effectively reverse the presumption and burden of proof. If that is correct, there may be little difference in substance between the positions of the two age groups.

Absconding

Section 15 of CJA 2003 makes new provisions in relation to defendants aged, respectively, over and under 18 who are charged with imprisonable offences and abscond whilst on bail. Formerly, BA, Sch 1, Pt 1, para 6, provided simply that a bailed defendant who was re-arrested for absconding or breach of conditions under BA 1976, s 7 'need not be granted bail'.

By s 15(1) a new para 6 to Pt 1, is substituted. This applies to over-18s arrested under BA 1976, s 7 where it appears to the court that, having been released on bail, the defendant has failed to surrender to custody. Under the new para 6(1), the defendant need not be granted bail unless the court is satisfied that there is no significant risk that, if released on bail (whether subject to conditions or not), he would fail to surrender to custody. The court is bound to consider whether any risk might be averted by the imposition of bail conditions. However, overall this change does few favours to the defendant. Although the court cannot simply refuse bail without adverting to the issue of risk, the test of 'no significant risk' is a stringent one which would be very hard to satisfy in practice.

The position of the defendant is, however, slightly mitigated by new para 6(3) which holds that para 6(1) should not apply where it appears to the court that the defendant had a reasonable excuse for the initial failure to surrender and then surrendered to custody at the appointed place as soon as reasonably practicable after the appointed time. This corresponds to the defence to the charge of absconding under BA 1976, s 6(1).

The position of absconding under-18s is dealt with in a new para 9AB to BA 1976, Sch 1, Pt 1, which is inserted by CJA 2003, s14(2). This will apply to a defendant who has failed to surrender to custody, except where it also appears that he had a reasonable excuse for failing to surrender but then surrendered as soon as it was reasonably practicable to do so (para 9AB(2)). The test to be applied in the same as applies to Sch 1, Pt 1, para 2(1). However, in considering whether there are substantial grounds for believing that if the defendant were released on bail he would not surrender to custody, the court must give particular weight to the fact of failure to surrender (unless he had reasonable cause for not doing so), or if he did have reasonable cause, the fact that he then failed to surrender as soon as reasonably practicable (para 9AB(3)).

In relation to both age groups, the commonly heard excuse, that the court had failed to provide the defendant with a copy of the court record of the bail decision, does not amount to a defence to the charge of absconding under BA 1976, s 6(4), and neither will it constitute a reasonable cause for failing to surrender for purposes of avoiding the adverse consequences of bail breach on later bail determinations (Sch 1, Pt 1, para 6(4) and para 9AB(4)).

2.2.5 Laying an Information for Absconding

The offence of absconding, or failure to surrender to custody without reasonable cause is triable either summarily or as a contempt of court. Since magistrates' courts have no inherent powers to punish contempt, absconding from the magistrates' court must be dealt with summarily. A problem arises as a consequence of the rule in s 127 Magistrates' Courts Act 1980 (MCA 1980), that an information relating to a summary offence must be laid within six months of its commission. As a result of this, where an absconder has succeeded in staying at large for six months, a prosecution would become time-barred. This issue is now addressed by CJA 2003, s 15(3) which inserts new sub-ss (10)–(14) in BA 1976, s 6. Subsection (10) disapplies MCA 1980, s 127 in relation to absconding offences under s 6(1) and (2). In its place a new sub-s 6(11) provides that a magistrates' court shall not try a person for an absconding offence unless either, the information is laid within six months of the alleged offence (sub-s (12)), or the information is laid no later than three months from the time that the defendant (a) surrenders to custody at the appointed place, (b) is arrested or attends a police station in connection with either the original offence with which he was charged or the absconding offence, or (c) the defendant appears or is brought before the court in relation to either the original offence or the absconding offence (s 6(13) and (14)).

2.2.6 Bail Appeals by the Defendant

Sections 16 and 17 are broadly designed to implement proposals made in the Auld report which had described the existing procedures for appeal as a 'bit of a muddle' (Auld, *Review of the Criminal Courts of England and Wales* (2001) para 84). The current reform seeks to create a rational appeal system and in particular to abolish the inherent jurisdiction of the High Court to hear bail appeals where this was concurrent with the jurisdiction of the Crown Court. The effect is to avoid the duplication of hearings and to concentrate bail appeals in the Crown Court.

In the following cases the inherent jurisdiction of the High Court to hear bail appeals is abolished:

- appeals from the magistrates' court relating to granting or withholding of bail (CJA 2003, s 17(2));
- appeals from the magistrates' court relating to variation of bail conditions (s 17(2));
- appeals from the Crown Court, where that court has determined an application to vary bail conditions, or impose bail conditions where unconditional bail was originally granted (ie the Crown Court has already acted in an appellate capacity) (s 17(3)(a));
- appeals from the Crown Court where that court has determined a bail issue which the magistrates' court had previously determined (eg where a defendant is committed or transferred to the jurisdiction of the Crown Court) (s 17(3)(b));
- appeals from the Crown Court where that court has heard an appeal on the facts against a remand in custody, with full argument certificate, in the magistrates' court (s 17(3)(g)).

In each of the above cases, the Crown Court has effectively already heard an appeal, and the reason for the change in the law is to avoid multiple hearings of the same issue. The High Court's inherent appeal jurisdiction is also abolished for appeals from the Crown Court in relation to a person who is in the custody of the Crown Court pending disposal of the case (eg during a short adjournment in the trial) (s 17(3)(c)). The rationale for this restriction is simply that on pragmatic grounds it avoids the High Court interfering with current proceedings in the Crown Court.

For the avoidance of doubt it is also provided that the High Court has no power to entertain appeals from the appellate jurisdiction of the Crown Court in bail cases under s 16 or in relation to bail determinations made by the Crown Court under ss 88 and 89 of the present Act, relating to the procedure for retrials in serious offences under Part 10 of the Act.

However, the High Court retains its powers to determine bail in relation to applications to state a case for the consideration of the High Court (s 17(1)).

The pre-existing powers of the Crown Court under s 81 Supreme Court Act 1981 to hear an appeal against a refusal of bail remain. These are: (a) where a defendant is committed in custody to the Crown Court for either trial or sentence; (b) where a case is to be tried in the magistrates' court and the magistrates have refused bail after hearing full argument; (c) where the defendant has been convicted in the magistrates' court and seeks bail pending his appeal to the Crown Court.

The Crown Court's powers to hear appeals concerning bail conditions are set out in s 16. No appeal may be brought until either the person granted bail or a constable or prosecutor has made and had determined an application to vary the bail conditions imposed, under BA 1976, s (8)(a) or (b) or s 5B(1) (CJA 2003, s 16(4)). The power to hear an appeal arises when a defendant is granted bail during an adjournment in one of the circumstances listed in s 16(1)(a)–(f). The power to appeal is limited to the types of bail condition listed in s 16(3), which are: (a) to reside away from a particular area; (b) to reside in a particular place other than a bail hostel; (c) to provide surety or sureties or to give some security; (d) to remain indoors; (e) relating to electronic monitoring; (e) not to contact named individuals (s 16(3)).

The Crown Court has power to vary any of the types of condition listed in s 16(3). Once an appeal against bail conditions has been determined by the Crown Court, no further appeal may be brought unless following that appeal there has been an application or a further application under BA 1976, s 3(8)(a) has been made and determined in the magistrates' court (s 17(8)).

2.2.7 Bail Appeals by the Prosecution

Section 18 significantly widens the prosecution's right of appeal against the grant of bail. When originally introduced in the Bail (Amendment) Act 1993, the prosecution power to appeal was restricted to offences punishable by 5 years' imprisonment or more. By virtue of a substitution of s 1(1) of the 1993 Act, that restriction is removed and henceforth the power to appeal will apply to all imprisonable offences. It should be noted, however, that the prosecutor has no power to appeal a refusal to impose conditions which the prosecutor has requested. Certain types of condition such as those relating to residing away from a victim or avoiding certain places may reflect important community interests. It is arguable that if the defendant is to have a right of appeal on such issues under s 16, a similar right should be afforded the prosecution.

This measure is clearly a response to concerns about the high proportion of offenders absconding or committing further offences whilst on bail. Figures quoted in the White Paper *Justice for All* (2002), p 24 suggest that 12% abscond whilst almost a quarter commit further offences. However, although some prosecutors may express frustration when bail is granted in the face of their opposition, it must be accepted that the price we as a society pay for respecting liberty is some degree of risk. It remains to be seen whether prosecutors will wish to expend resources appealing bail decisions and whether the courts, mindful of prison overcrowding, will want to make greater use of custody in marginal cases.

2.2.8 Drug Users—Restrictions on Bail

Section 19 amends the BA 1976 to place special restrictions on the grant of bail to drug users who decline to take part in a programme to address their drug abuse. This measure is part of a broad criminal justice initiative which seeks to respond to the links between serial acquisitive crime and expensive drug habits. Other examples of this policy include the introduction of drug treatment and testing orders under ss 61–68 of the Crime and Disorder Act 1998 (CDA 1998), the introduction of pre-charge drug testing under the Criminal Justice and Courts Services Act but currently found in PACE 1984, s 63B, the extension of that scheme to children as young as 14 in s 5, and the provision for drug testing after conviction under s 161 of the present Act.

The operation of the scheme under s 19 will depend upon the availability of suitable drug testing equipment and personnel in particular areas. As such, the introduction of the scheme in any particular area will be dependent upon the prior establishment of pre-charge drug testing for juveniles in the area. Accordingly, new s 3(6C) and para (6C) in BA, Sch 1, Pt 1 provide that the scheme will only operate in a particular petty session area where the court has been notified by the Home Secretary that necessary arrangements for testing and follow-up have been made in that area. The scheme will require drug testers who are suitably qualified according to standards to be specified by the Home Secretary. However, at the time of writing, a specification of the necessary qualifications to perform this task has not been made. Bail conditions which may be imposed under s 19 will not be available for grants of police bail (CJA 2003, s 19(3)).

The new scheme is outlined in a number of new paragraphs inserted in BA, Sch 1, Pt 1, which contains supplementary provisions about bail in relation to imprisonable offences. The scheme will apply defendants aged 18 or over who have provided a sample under PACE 1984, s 63B or CJA 2003, s 161 and have tested positive for a specified Class A drug (para 6B). The offence for which the defendant has been either charged or convicted must be either an offence of possession relating to the specified Class A drug under s 5(2) of the Misuse of Drugs Act 1971 (MDA 1971), or possession with intent to supply of such a drug under MDA, s 5(3). Alternatively, the court must be satisfied that there are substantial grounds for believing either: (i) that misuse of the specified drug caused or contributed to the offence; or (ii) that the offence was motivated wholly or partly by his intended misuse of the drug. Where these conditions are met, the defendant should be offered a 'relevant assessment', meaning a test conducted by a suitably qualified person to determine whether the defendant is either dependent upon or has a propensity to misuse any specified Class A drugs. If it is concluded that the defendant has such a dependence or propensity, he should be offered a 'follow-up' involving further assessment, assistance or treatment as is considered appropriate (para 6E).

For defendants who have initially tested positive and who have undertaken or agreed to undertake the assessment and follow-up, bail may be granted in the normal way, but if granted this must be subject to the condition that he must undergo the relevant assessment and follow-up, or just any follow-up where the relevant assessment has already been completed (BA 1976, s 3(6D)).

Defendants who have tested positive but have refused either to participate in the assessment or to participate in the proposed follow-up, will presumptively be refused bail. Bail may be granted only if the court is satisfied that there is 'no significant risk of his committing an offence while on bail (whether subject to conditions or not)'. In view of the pre-conditions for the operation of this scheme and the defendant's refusal to co-operate with the assessment and treatment measures offered to him, it would be very unusual for a defendant to receive bail in these circumstances (BA 1976, Sch 1, Pt 1, para 6A).

2.3 CONDITIONAL CAUTIONS

2.3.1 Background

Cautioning as a response to offending by all age groups of offenders has a long history in England. It has been largely practised without legislative warrant. An early exception to this was the mention in s 2 of the Street Offences Act 1959 of the special cautioning scheme for soliciting for prostitution, introduced by agreement between the chief constables at the same time as the 1959 Act. The foundation for the practice of cautioning is the principle that it is neither necessary nor desirable to prosecute every instance of offending. A prosecution may be unnecessary if a caution in will serve the objective of deterring future offending equally well. It is also recognized that there are circumstances in which a prosecution would be disproportionately harmful, for instance in relation to the old or the young or other vulnerable persons. Although cautioning is frequently described in terms of 'diversion' from the formal criminal justice process, this is to misunderstand the practice. Forms of cautioning have been explicit policy for regulatory enforcement agencies such as those policing factory safety and pollution. Cautioning by the police has also been conducted under government guidelines, the most recent version of which are found in Home Office Circular 18/1994, *The Cautioning of Offenders*. More recently, a formal cautioning scheme, described in terms of reprimands and warnings, was introduced for children and young persons under CDA 1998, ss 65 and 66 (see R Leng, R Taylor and M Wasik, *Blackstone's Guide to the Crime and Disorder Act 1998* (Blackstone Press, 1998, pp 75–83)). Thus, cautioning (or whatever label is attached to it) is diversionary only in the sense that a case which results in a caution is removed (or diverted) from the caseload of the court. Nevertheless, a caution, whether administered under government guidelines or legislation, is clearly a response of the criminal justice system. Cautioning may therefore be best viewed not as a diversionary measure but as the criminal justice system's preferred response to offending in certain circumstances.

Cautioning has a number of real advantages over prosecution: it is very cheap and efficient, it provides a very immediate response to offending, it is not vindictive and may leave the offender feeling fairly dealt with by the criminal justice system. It avoids the uncertainty inherent in litigation. However, the practice is also subject to a number of criticisms: it is a low visibility procedure (compared with court proceedings) and therefore may be subject to abuse; because it does not involve formal adjudication there is a danger that it may be used where offending cannot be proved; police decision-makers may act as judge and jury; it may involve 'net-widening' by which individuals who have not committed a crime or do not deserve to be proceeded against are brought into the criminal justice system. It may be seen as an inappropriately lenient 'slap on the wrist' which fails to adequately condemn offending behaviour.

Because cautioning has traditionally been non-statutory it has been possible for radically different cautioning practices and cultures to develop in different areas. Prior to the introduction of the reprimand and warning scheme in 1998, some of the most imaginative schemes aimed at juveniles involved what is known as 'caution plus'. Under these schemes, cautioned juveniles would also be offered the chance to participate in some further activity designed to address their offending behaviour, sometimes involving reparation to the victim. Thus, a young burglar might be given the opportunity to discuss the impact of his crime with the victim, or a joy-rider might be given training in driving and motor maintenance in order to engender a responsible attitude to driving. A problem with these schemes was that it was not possible to formally link the 'plus' element to the caution. It was considered that the effects of the positive activity would be undermined if an offender were coerced into participation by the threat of prosecution. Thus, the caution and the 'plus' element were freestanding, and if having accepted the caution the offender refused to participate in the plus activity, no sanction would follow.

The staged reprimand and warning scheme introduced for children and young persons under CDA 1998, ss 65 and 66, was in effect a national system of caution plus, in which the plus element, attached to a warning, is a referral to a youth offending team for assessment, with a view to participating in a rehabilitation programme. Although records are kept of any refusal to be assessed or failure in relation to a rehabilitation programme, a perceived weakness of the scheme is that a youngster can refuse to co-operate with impunity.

The idea of a conditional caution goes a step beyond the reprimand and warning scheme. The caution is conditional in the sense that it will be given only if the offender complies with specified conditions, whereas a refusal to do so would lead to prosecution. The introduction of conditional cautions was strongly mooted in the Auld review of the criminal courts. The report noted that in 1999 cautions amounted to about 25% of all disposals (convictions and cautions) for criminal offences. While noting that cautions were an efficient method of enhancing a police force's clear-up rate, the report noted that there was concern that cautions might be perceived as let-offs which showed little regard for the injury or insult done to victims of crime. Having considered the experience of other countries, including Scotland and Germany, the report recommended the introduction of a new form of conditional caution under which a caution might be administered for a minor offence, with the consent of the victim and approval of the court, and subject to the offender's agreeing to comply with specified conditions. In the event of failure to comply, the offender could be brought to court and might be punished for the original offence (Auld, *Review of the Criminal Courts of England and Wales* (2001), paras 42–47). The government has been pleased to accept this recommendation which complements a broad policy initiative concerning victim's rights and restorative justice.

2.3.2 Conditional Cautions under s 22

Section 22(1) empowers constables, other investigating officers and prosecutors to administer conditional cautions to apparent offenders aged over 18. A draft code of practice on the workings of the scheme has also been published by the Home Office which, subject to revisions, will be brought into force by the Home Secretary by order, in due course.

It might be assumed that the 'investigating officers' referred to are the same as the now familiar 'persons other than police officers who are charged with the duty of investigating offences' who must comply with the PACE Codes under PACE 1984, s 67(8). In fact the term 'investigating officer' does not refer to this broad group of investigators, but rather to a more limited class of persons who are employed either by a police force or by the National Crime Squad (NCS) or the National Criminal Intelligence Service (NCIS), and who have been designated as an 'investigating officer' by either their chief constable or the relevant director-general in the cases of the NCS and the NCIS (CJA 2003, s 27, Police Reform Act 2002, s 38).

Formerly, cautioning was seen as a diversion from the court system: it was the responsibility of the police rather than the prosecutor. The new power extends to a wide range of prosecuting authorities as listed in s 27. These are: (a) the Attorney-General; (b) the Director of the Serious Fraud Office; (c) the Director of Public Prosecutions (DPP); (d) the Home Secretary; (e) the Commissioners of Inland Revenue; (f) the Commissioners of Customs and Excise; or (g) any other person specified in an order made by the Home Secretary. As well as having a new power to administer conditional cautions, the prosecuting bodies are entrenched in the scheme by virtue of the requirement in s 23(2) that a prosecutor must determine whether that there is sufficient evidence to charge the offender and that a caution should be administered instead of charging. It is not clear why some well-established prosecutors, such as local authorities or the Health and Safety Executive, are excluded from this list and it may be that they will be added in due course by order.

Conditional cautions may be administered only to persons aged 18 or over (s 22(1)). This has the effect of delineating the conditional cautions from the scheme for reprimands and warnings under the CDA 1998, ss 65 and 66. A similar strict dividing line will not apply between cases which can be dealt with by the pre-existing simple caution procedure and the new conditional cautions. As the recently published draft Code of Practice makes clear, when deciding how to proceed with a particular case, prosecutors should consider both types of caution on their merits and it should not be assumed that the two measures represent any sort of hierarchy (para 3.3).

'Conditional caution' is defined as a caution which is given to an offender in respect of an offence, where the caution has conditions attached to it, with which the offender must comply (s 22(2)). The conditions to be attached to the caution must be for the purpose of facilitating the rehabilitation of the offender and/or ensuring that he makes reparation for the offence (s 22(3)). The draft Code of Practice indicates that conditions must be proportionate, achievable and appropriate (para 5.1) and suggests that in setting conditions the prosecutor might first interview the victim and refer to any Victim Personal Statements (which victims have been able to submit on a voluntary basis since October 2001) (paras 7.1, 7.2). The Code does not set any time limits for conditions and indeed points out that a realistic drug rehabilitation programme would take more than twelve months. However, the Code does suggest that prosecutors should think carefully about whether imposing a condition which would take more than six months to fulfil, would be realistic (para 6.2).

It is envisaged that in relation to complying with conditions, offenders may be supervised by the local probation service. The probation service is accordingly placed under duties to assist prosecutors or police forces in determining whether conditional cautions should be imposed and which conditions should be attached to cautions (s 26(2)). The draft Code recommends 'robust monitoring of compliance and that in some cases it may be a good idea to include within the conditions a requirement that the offender should demonstrate that his obligations have been fulfilled' (para 10.1).

2.3.3 The Five Requirements

A conditional caution may be administered only where each of five requirements are satisfied (s 22(1)). The five requirements are set out in subsections of s 23 as follows.

Evidence Sufficient to Charge—s 23(1) and (2)(a)
Under sub-s (1) the person who intends to caution must have evidence that the 'offender' has committed the offence. Where this person is a constable or investigating officer, the case must then be referred to a prosecutor to decide that there is sufficient evidence to charge sub-s (2)(a). The test of sufficiency to charge suggests the rule as applied by the Crown Prosecution Service, that if the offender were prosecuted there would be a realistic prospect of conviction (which is the express test for reprimand under CDA 1998, s 65(b)). This test, known as the 51%

27

rule, is interpreted as requiring that, on the evidence, a conviction would be more likely than not. The prosecutor does not have to satisfy herself of guilt to the criminal standard of beyond reasonable doubt. It is to be hoped that the requirement of scrutiny by a prosecutor will avoid problems which have been identified in the past, such as children being cautioned on the basis of evidence of presence at the scene of a crime, rather than participation in it (R Evans, 'Police cautioning and the young offender' [1991] Crim LR 598).

That a Conditional Caution should be Given—s 23(2)(b)

The prosecutor must also decide whether a conditional caution 'should' be given to the offender. The draft Code of Practice prepared by the Home Office provides guidance on the circumstances in which conditional cautions 'may' be given as required by (s 25(2)(a)). This contrasts with the former Home Office guidance and the test for administering a reprimand under CDA 1998, s 65(1(e)), both of which refer to whether it is in the public interest that the offender should not be prosecuted. The current draft Code suggests that prosecutors should have regard to the serious-ness of the offence and ACPO's 'gravity factors' and that a conditional caution may be indicated where there is some act which the offender is willing and able to under-take which might be conducive to reparation or rehabilitation. It is further suggested that where the performance of this condition would be a preferable alternative to a prosecution then a conditional caution would be appropriate (paras 3.1 and 3.2). Thus, although the Act eschews the terminology of public interest, its test of preferred alternative may amount to much the same thing.

An interesting issue will be how the new scheme will relate to other cautioning systems. For instance, it is generally understood that cautions are not appropriate for those who have re-offended after earlier cautions. Will a conditional caution be ruled out where an offender has received both a reprimand and warning as a youth, or has been cautioned under Home Office guidelines?

That the Offender Admits the Offence—s 23(3)

An admission is required to ensure that cautions are not simply used by suspects as a means of avoiding prosecution and by officers as means of clearing up a crime. The admission must also be confirmed by the form which the offender must sign under sub-s (5) below. Notwithstanding this safeguard, it is important that prosecutors check the suspect's interview tape, and do not rely upon police summaries, to confirm that he admits all elements of the offence, including *mens rea*, and that he does not claim any defence. The need to do this is indicated by empirical research, which demonstrates that police summaries of taped interviews are frequently partial, misleading and may selectively disregard exculpatory claims (J Baldwin, 'Summarising tape recordings of police interviews' [1991] Crim LR 671). The draft Code of Practice requires a 'clear and reliable admission to all of the elements of the offence' and that the defendant must maintain his admission at the time when the caution is administered to him (para 4.1).

Explanation and Acknowledgement—s 23(4) and (5)

The fourth and fifth requirements are that the effects of a conditional caution are explained to the offender, and that he is warned that a failure to comply with any of the conditions attached to the caution may result in him being prosecuted for the offence. Amongst the effects which should be explained are the fact that a caution may be disclosable in relation to certain forms of employment and that a caution for a sex offence, may be attended by the duties consequent on registration as a sex offender under the Sex Offender Act 1997. Finally, the offender is required to sign a document which contains details of the offence, an admission by him that he committed the offence, his consent to being given a conditional caution, and a note of the conditions that are attached to the caution. There is no mention in the primary legislation of the need for an appropriate adult to be present, but no doubt this will be required in relation to mentally vulnerable adults, under the forthcoming Code of Practice.

Particular care must be taken by the suspect and any legal adviser prior to signing the form which the police will present. Not only, must consideration be given to whether the defendant realistically will be able to fulfil the conditions, but the suspect should be advised that the signed admission could itself be evidence against him in the event of prosecution following breach of condition. This in turn will require careful consideration of the statement to ensure that it does not misrepresent what the defendant admits.

An unrepresented suspect in the police station may not receive this advice. At present there is no duty on the police to warn the suspect of the consequences of signing the statement, apart from the standard caution with which all periods of investigative interview with a suspect must begin. Whether or not such a warning will be required under the forthcoming Code of Practice, the police would be well advised to deliver such a warning. It is submitted that in the absence of a warning a court may well exclude the signed admission in the caution acknowledgement, under PACE 1984, s 78 as being unfair, if the accused was not made aware of the potential evidential significance of the statement.

2.3.4 Failure to Comply with Conditions

Under s 24(1), if the offender fails, without reasonable excuse, to comply with any of the conditions attached to the caution, he may be prosecuted for the offence in question, and the initial caution ceases to have effect (sub-s (3)). This apparently straightforward provision will be problematic. The difficulty is that no mechanism for adjudicating the question whether there has been a breach of the conditions, has been provided. This may be contrasted with, for instance, the procedure relating to breach of the conditions contained in an anti-social behaviour order under CDA 1998, s 1. In that situation, the prosecution which follows under CDA 1998, s 1(10) will be for the breach itself, and it will be for the court to determine the issues of breach and reasonable excuse. By contrast in relation to conditional cautions, it will be the prosecutor who must decide on the question of breach, with no formal opportunity provided for the defendant to challenge the decision or the evidence on which it is based, or to present evidence of reasonable excuse. The draft Code of Practice (para 10.5) treats this as being quite unproblematic: the caution is terminated and the prosecutor initiates proceedings. But decisions which have a significant impact on a citizen cannot be taken so lightly. Arguably, the decision should be treated as a determination of a citizen's rights and obligations and as such would attract the right to a fair and public hearing by an impartial tribunal under ECHR, Article 5. As public authorities, the courts are bound to honour this right under the Human Rights Act 1998 (HRA 1998), s 6, and indeed under HRA 1998, s 3(1) the provision should be interpreted so as to permit issues surrounding breach to be properly litigated. How this should be done is another matter.

One possibility would be that the court could consider the question whether there had been a breach and, if so, whether there was a reasonable excuse at a preliminary hearing. The Act appears to contemplate that the issue of breach would be considered in the consequential criminal proceeding. This is implicit in s 24(2), under which the document by which the offender acknowledged his guilt and which records the conditions attached to the caution, would be admissible in the criminal proceedings. But it would be inappropriate for a criminal court to become involved in judicially reviewing an executive decision to prosecute. Nor would the normal channels of judicial review be appropriate in view of the principle that decisions to prosecute should not normally be subject to judicial review (*DPP, ex p Kebilene* [2000] AC 326). This would suggest that the only option open to a defendant who considered that he had been unfairly prosecuted following a conditional caution would be an application to stay the proceedings as an abuse of process.

2.3.5 Code of Practice

Section 25(1) requires the Home Secretary to prepare a Code of Practice relating to conditional cautions. The Home Secretary is obliged to publish a draft of the Code and to consider any representations made to him and if necessary amend the draft (sub-s (2)). The Code must then be laid before both Houses of Parliament, but may be brought into force by order without the need for any form of parliamentary resolution (sub-ss (4) and (5)). Amendments may be made in the same manner as the original Code (sub-s (7)). At the time of writing, a draft Code has been circulated and a draft order to bring the Code into operation was laid before Parliament on 18 April 2004.

Section 25(2) lists a number of matters which the Code may provide for. These are: (a) the circumstances in which conditional cautions may be given; (b) the procedure to be followed in administering the cautions; (c) the conditions which may be attached to cautions and the time for which they may have effect; (d) the category of constable or investigating officer by whom cautions may be given, (e) the persons who may be authorized by the relevant prosecuting bodies to administer cautions; (f) the form which such cautions are to take and the manner in which they are to be given and recorded; (g) the places where such cautions may be given; and (h) the monitoring of compliance with the conditions attached to cautions.

2.4 CHARGING PROCEDURE

2.4.1 Proceedings to be Instituted by Written Charge

Section 29(1) introduces a new method of instituting criminal proceedings by written charge, which will apply to prosecutions by listed public prosecutors but not to private prosecutions. The public prosecutors who must use the new procedure listed in s 29(5) are: police forces, the Serious Fraud Office, the DPP, the Attorney-General, a Secretary of State, the Commissioners of the Inland Revenue, the Commissioners of Customs and Excise, or any other person specified by the Home Secretary. In the case of each of the prosecuting organizations, any person authorized to prosecute on their behalf will be covered by the provision.

Although the old procedure for initiating proceedings by laying an information will remain for private prosecutors, the listed prosecutors will be barred from using the old procedure. It will remain possible, however, for the listed public prosecutors to lay an information for the purpose of obtaining the issue of a summons or warrant under MCA 1980, s 1. The power to charge a person in custody is also preserved (s 30(4)).

At the same time as issuing the written charge, the prosecutor must also issue a second document called a requisition which requires the person charged to attend a specified magistrates' court to answer the charge (s 29(2)). Both documents must be served on the person charged and also on the court (s 29(3)). Generally, any reference in an Act to an information will be read as referring also to a written charge, and references in Acts to summons will include requisitions (s 30(5)).

2.4.2 Removal of Requirement of Oath

The Act also makes a minor change in the interests of administrative convenience, by removing the requirement that all informations laid in the magistrates' courts should be substantiated on oath (s 31).

2.4.3 Charge or Release following Police Detention

By s 28 and Sch 2, revisions are made to PACE, Pt IV for the purpose of structuring decision-making relating to charging, release and bail of detained suspects. In particular, the Act creates a structure in which charging decisions in more difficult cases are likely to be made by the CPS. The new decision-making structure will be more formal than the old procedure under which the police were free to seek advice or not at their own discretion. In particular the DPP will be required to issue guidance on categories of case which should always be referred to the CPS. Also, because once a case is referred, the charging decision will be made by the CPS, there is no scope for the police to choose to disregard a CPS recommendation relating to a file sent for advice. The power of the CPS to initiate charges is complemented by a power to take decisions in relation to cautioning under s 22(1). In this context the term 'caution' includes simple cautions, conditional cautions under CJA 2003, Pt 3 and also reprimands and warnings under CDA 1998, ss 65 and 66 (new PACE 1984, s 37B(9)).

Section 37 of PACE 1984, which prescribes the custody officer's duties before charge, is amended by Sch 2, para 2. Under s 37(7), where the custody officer (CO) determines that she has before her sufficient evidence to charge, she has the following options: (a) to release the suspect without charge on bail in order to refer the decision to the CPS, in which case the suspect must be so informed (s 37(7A)); (b) to release on bail without charge (ie where further investigation is required); (c) to charge the suspect directly. Interestingly, although the CO retains the power to charge immediately there is no similar power to administer an immediate caution.

A new sub-s (7A) confirms that the decision under s 37 is to be that of the custody officer. However, this should be read in the context of a new s 37A (inserted by Sch 2, para 3) by which the DPP may issue guidance to custody officers in relation to decisions under s 37, and to indicate what information would be required in relation to any cases to be referred to the CPS. Custody officers are instructed to have regard to any such guidance, which must be published and set out in the DPP's annual report to the Attorney-General.

Where a person is released on bail pending a decision of the CPS (under s 37(7)(a)), the custody officer may vary the arrangements for the suspect to attend the police station, without affecting any conditions to which the bail is subject and must give the suspect appropriate notice in writing (PACE 1984, s 37D(1), (2) and (3) as inserted by CJA 2003, Sch 2, para 3). Where such a released person returns to answer bail he may be kept in custody as necessary according to the action (eg charging or cautioning) being taken in respect of him, unless he is unfit (eg drunk), in which case he may also be kept until he is fit enough for the relevant procedures to be carried out (s 37D(4) and (5)).

The role of the DPP (in practice this means the CPS) is set out in a new s 37B. Where the custody officer decides to release a suspect on bail to enable the prosecution decision to be taken, a report must be sent to the CPS as soon as practicable, including the information to be specified in the DPP's guidance (sub-s (1)). It will then fall to the CPS to decide whether there is sufficient evidence to charge and whether the suspect should accordingly be charged or cautioned (sub-s (3)). The decision must then be notified in writing to the investigating officer (sub-s (4)). Where the decision is either that there is insufficient evidence to charge or, that notwithstanding sufficient evidence the suspect should be neither charged nor cautioned, the custody officer must give the suspect an appropriate notice in writing (sub-s (5)). Where the decision is to charge, that may be done either by the old method of requiring the suspect to attend the police station to be charged or by the new method of written charge and requisition to attend court under s 29. Where a decision is made to caution, this should be administered by the CPS under guidelines to be issued and where it proves impossible to caution the offender (eg where a conditional caution is proposed but the conditions are refused by the defendant), a charge may be substituted (PACE 1984, s 37B(8)).

Where a person is released on bail pending a decision by the CPS, if he is subsequently re-arrested for failure to answer bail, if the CPS had yet to notify the police of their decision in the case, the custody officer would be free to charge the person (ie without needing to wait for a CPS decision) or to release without charge, either with or without bail. If released on bail, any bail conditions imposed on the earlier occasion would continue (PACE 1984, s 37C inserted by CJA, Sch 2, para 3).

Paragraph 6 of Sch 2 varies PACE 1984, s 47, which deals with bail after arrest. It is provided that where a suspect is granted bail pending a CPS decision whether or not to charge, the CPS have no right to apply to court to have the bail revoked under BA 1976, s 5B. However, where bail conditions are imposed pending a CPS decision, the suspect retains the right to apply to court to have those conditions varied, and if such variance occurs the bail will continue but subject to the conditions as varied.

3

DISCLOSURE PRE-TRIAL

3.1 INTRODUCTION

Since its introduction in 1996, the pre-trial disclosure regime under the Criminal Procedure and Investigations Act 1996 (CPIA 1996) has been controversial. Although substantially modified in practice by guidelines issued by the Attorney-General in 2000, its early reform may have been inevitable in view of the scrutiny and criticism to which it has been subject in its short life. For the empirical research and debates which stimulated the present reform, the reader is directed to: R Leng and R Taylor, *Blackstone's Guide to the Criminal Procedure and Investigations Act 1996* (Blackstone Press, 1996, chapters 1 and 2); J Plotnikoff and R Woolfson, *A Fair Balance? Evaluation of the Operation of Disclosure Law* (Home Office, 2001); Crown Prosecution Service Inspectorate, *Report of the Thematic Review of the Disclosure of Unused Material* (London, 2000); Sir Robin Auld, *A Review of the Criminal Courts of England and Wales* (2000), www.criminal-courts-review.org.uk.

The purpose of the current reform under the Criminal Justice Act 2003 (CJA 2003) is to make the current discredited scheme work. It is sought to achieve this by introducing a single (rather than a staged) test for prosecution disclosure and by emphasizing the prosecutor's continuing duty to disclose. The duties on the defendant are made more burdensome: new duties are created to disclose the identities of proposed witnesses, the fact that expert witnesses have been commissioned, and to give notice of any legal arguments and authorities to be relied on. The circumstances in which evidential inferences may be drawn against the accused in relation to failures in disclosure are extended and clarified, and courts are encouraged to make greater use of their power to draw (or threaten to draw) inferences.

The reforms will disappoint some critics of the current scheme. In particular, the reform aggravates the disparity between the burdens on the prosecution and defence in two respects. Whereas, the defendant will now be required to commit himself to, and disclose, his legal defence at an early stage, the prosecution are placed under no such duty and may reserve their case (apart from its evidential basis) to be disclosed for the first time at trial. In the past when the defendant enjoyed a similar advantage in relation to reserving his factual defence, concerns were raised about the possibility of ambush (Home Office, *Disclosure: A Consultation Paper*, Cm 2864, 1995). It is now the defendant who must risk the possibility of legal ambush in court. Secondly, the CPIA 1996 continues to turn a blind eye to the clear research evidence of disclosure failures by the prosecution, and provides sanctions only for such failures by the accused.

It is anticipated that the disclosure provisions will be brought into force during 2005/2006. As before, the day-to-day operation of the provisions will be mediated by the Disclosure Code under CPIA 1996, Pt II, and it is anticipated that a new version of the Code will be published to coincide with the reforms taking effect. For convenience, the new provisions are described below in the present tense, although they are in fact not yet in force, and the provisions which will be replaced are described in the past tense.

3.2 THE PROSECUTOR'S DISCLOSURE DUTIES

3.2.1 Criticisms of the 1996 Act

A particular criticism of the regime introduced in 1996, as voiced by Sir Robin Auld and others, was that by applying different disclosure duties at the primary and secondary disclosure stages, the Act implied that it was within a prosecutor's duty to withhold material of clear relevance to the case. Under the original scheme, the test for primary disclosure under s 3(1) was whether in the prosecutor's opinion particular material might undermine the case for the prosecution against the accused. The broader test applied at secondary disclosure was whether material might reasonably be expected to assist the accused's defence as disclosed by him. On a narrow reading, the primary disclosure test of undermining the prosecution case might be restricted to material which undermined a particular item of prosecution evidence, and might exclude other material which might support a specific defence or which might suggest new and potentially fruitful lines of inquiry to the defence: matters which would formerly have been disclosable at common law (*Keane* (1994) 99 Cr App R1). This narrow reading of the duties under the 1996 Act would certainly be consistent with the government position, at the time of the passing of the 1996 Act, that the legislation should provide a real incentive for the accused to disclose his defence in order to trigger further disclosure. Whereas, it is arguable that obtaining early informative defence disclosure furthers the interests of justice, the flaw in the scheme was that in some cases it would have legitimated the withholding of material which might have provided the accused with the basis for a defence, unavailable from any other source. In practice it was never clear how prosecutors actually interpreted the undermining test, but what was apparent from empirical research was that there was much dissatisfaction amongst defence lawyers with the quantity and nature of material handed over at primary disclosure (J Plotnikoff and R Woolfson, *A Fair Balance? The Operation of the Disclosure Law* (Home Office, 2001)). In any event, following criticism of the test, the Attorney-General issued guidelines for prosecutors in 2000 which required the disclosure of a wider range of material.

The second criticism was that the test for primary prosecution disclosure appeared to embody a subjective test based on what in 'the prosecutor's opinion might undermine'.

3.2.2 A Single Disclosure Test

These two criticisms are now addressed by Pt 3 of CJA 2003. Section 32 creates a new single test applicable to all stages of prosecution disclosure. The new test will apply to primary prosecution disclosure by virtue of amendments to CPIA 1996, s 3(1)(a), as well as to the prosecutor's continuing duty of disclosure, now found in a new CPIA 1996, s 7A (as inserted by s 37 of the present Act). Under the new test, the prosecutor must disclose any material 'which might reasonably be considered capable of undermining the case for the prosecution against the accused or of assisting the case for the accused'. The same test is also applied to the prosecutor's continuing duty to disclose which is found in a new CPIA 1996, s 7A (as inserted by s 37 of the present Act), and which replaces the former secondary stage of prosecution disclosure (under CPIA 1996, s 7, now repealed by Sch 37, Pt 3).

Although by introducing the new test it is clearly intended that the prosecutor should be making disclosure of all material covered by the test at the primary stage, prior to defence disclosure, this aspiration might be frustrated because the test, like the one it replaces, is susceptible to narrow interpretation. In particular, if the reference to 'the case for the accused' is taken to mean the particular line of argument to be raised in the proceedings, it could be argued that this is unknown until defence disclosure is made. If this interpretation were to prevail, the effect would be to limit the primary disclosure duty to undermining material as under the earlier law. This approach would negate the intended reform. An approach more in line with government intentions would be to treat the reference to the accused's defence as including any defence which might reasonably be considered to be open to the accused.

The new test is objective in form. Whether this makes any difference in practice remains to be seen. Whereas, an objective test is more amenable to judicial review than a subjective one, the structure of the 1996 Act militates against such review. For instance, the Act seeks to pre-empt attempts to review the adequacy of primary disclosure by providing that the duty to serve a defence statement arises where the prosecutor merely 'purports' to comply with his or her duty of primary disclosure (CPI 1996, s 5(1)). It was the government's intention that this would leave no scope for reviewing the primary disclosure duty. However, the court can be ingenious in evading legislative attempts to avoid judicial review, and it would certainly be arguable that if a prosecutor purports to have made primary disclosure, she or he must do so in good faith and therefore must be able to demonstrate the basis for the claim that disclosure has been made.

Whatever the strict legal position, to impose disclosure duties on defendants on the basis of purported disclosure, sends the wrong message about the importance of the disclosure obligation to prosecutors, defendants and the public at large. It is regrettable that the government has not taken the opportunity presented by this legislation to reform this rule in the light of a substantial body of research and anecdotal evidence of insufficient primary prosecution disclosure (Plotnikoff and Woolfson, *A Fair Balance? The Operation of the Disclosure Law* (Home Office, 2001)).

3.2.3 Prosecutor's Continuing Disclosure Duty

The second major change to the prosecutor's disclosure duties is the abolition of secondary disclosure as a particular procedural event, in favour of reliance on a continuing duty to disclose material falling within the new prosecution disclosure test, discussed above. This is achieved by repealing CPIA 1996, s 7 (secondary disclosure) and s 9 (continuing duty to disclose) and replacing them with a new s 7A entitled 'Continuing duty of prosecutor to disclose'—a title confusingly similar to the now repealed s 9. The effect of these changes will leave the CPIA 1996 looking very odd with a s 7A but no s 7 or s 9.

The continuing duty comprises two elements. Firstly, the prosecutor must keep under review the question whether, at any given time, in the light of the current state of affairs and developments in the prosecution case, there is prosecution material fulfilling the general disclosure test and which has not been already disclosed to the accused (s 7A(2) and (4)). Secondly, the prosecutor must make disclosure of any such material as soon as is reasonably practicable (s 7A(3)).

It may be noted that the duty to review relates to the question whether disclosable material exists rather than a duty physically to inspect the material itself. Thus, the Act does not place the prosecutor under any duty to inspect the material and she or he may continue to rely upon descriptions of material in the schedules provided by the disclosure officer.

Although secondary prosecution disclosure is abolished in name, similar duties are imposed on the prosecutor under s 7A(5). These duties apply where the accused has provided a defence statement under s 5 (compulsory defence statement), or s 6 (voluntary disclosure in relation to summary offences), or s 6B (updated disclosure by the accused). In response, the prosecutor must either make any consequential disclosure within the relevant time limit under regulations made under s 12 (currently 14 days) or provide written confirmation that no further disclosure is required, within the same time limit (s 7A (5)).

The new s 7A also re-enacts the following rules from the former s 9. Prosecution material is defined as material which is in the prosecutor's possession and came into his possession in connection with the case for the prosecution against the accused, or which he has inspected in connection with the case against the accused (CPIA 1996, 7A(6)). As for primary disclosure, the means of disclosure is by providing a copy, or if that is not practicable or desirable, by allowing the defence to inspect the material at a reasonable time and place (s 7A(7)). Material may not be disclosed if a court has so ruled on public interest grounds following an application by the prosecutor (CPIA 1996, s 7A(8)) or where disclosure is prohibited by the Regulation of Investigatory Powers Act 2000, s 17 (which covers material obtained by telephone tapping and other methods of intercepting communications) (CPIA 1996, s 7A (9)).

3.2.4 Applications to Court for Further Disclosure to the Defence

In the light of the revisions to the disclosure duties of prosecution and defence, s 38 makes minor consequential amendments to the procedure by which the accused may apply to the court for disclosure under CPIA 1996, s 8. In its original form the procedure sought to reserve judicial intervention until both sides had completed their disclosure duties. The preconditions for an application under s 8 are now that the accused has provided a defence statement under s 5 (compulsory statement in indictable cases), s 6 (voluntary statement in summary only cases), or s 6B (updated defence statement) and that the prosecutor has either responded as required under s 7A(5) or has not done so within the prescribed time limit (s 38(1)). Interestingly, this permits the accused to apply to court prior to fulfilling his disclosure duties by providing an updated statement.

The grounds for making an application for further disclosure are that the accused, at any time, has reasonable cause to believe that there is prosecution material which fulfils the disclosure test under s 7A, that it might reasonably be considered capable of undermining the case for the prosecution or of assisting the case for the accused. It is disappointing that the government did not take the opportunity to remedy some of the defects with this procedure. In particular, the ability of the accused to make an application will depend upon the completeness of the non-sensitive schedule provided by the disclosure officer and the extent to which the descriptions of material 'make clear the nature of the item and contain sufficient detail' (CPIA Code 6.9) to allow judgment of relevance to be made by the prosecutor and defence lawyers. Notwithstanding research evidence indicating that these functions are poorly performed, the government has not considered it necessary to introduce some means to judicially review the schedules.

3.3 DEFENCE DISCLOSURE

When introduced in 1996, the requirement on the accused to provide a defence statement was seen as being almost a revolutionary change in the English system of adversarial justice. As such, it is perhaps not surprising that the disclosure duties imposed on the accused were restricted to an outline of the proposed defence, an indication of the elements of the prosecution case with which the defendant took issue, and the reasons for doing so (CPIA 1996, s 5(6)). Notwithstanding the modesty of these requirements, the reform was demonized by critics as in part reversing the burden of proof; requiring the defendant to assist the better resourced prosecution; and compromising the accused's court strategy by exposing lines of cross-examination in advance. In equal measure, proponents of the reform anticipated criminal justice gains in terms of fewer contested trials, fewer ambush defences in contested trials and ultimately more convictions of the guilty. In retrospect, both sides in the debate expected too much. In reality, defence lawyers have been able to formulate defence statements without greatly prejudicing their chances at trial, and prosecutors and investigators have been frustrated by the sketchiness of defence statements received. Although, in theory, inadequacies in the defence statement may be met with the sanction of evidential inferences under s 11, in practice neither prosecutors nor judges have made much use of the provision to invite the jury to draw inferences from defence disclosure failures. Many prosecutors acknowledge that to invite a jury to consider the possible meaning of some defect in disclosure would unnecessarily extend and complicate the trial and would inevitably distract a jury from their central task of evaluating the positive evidence in the case.

The general consensus is that defence statements have neither presented a great hazard for the defence nor delivered substantial instrumental gains for the criminal justice system. The impetus for the current reform of defence disclosure duties comes partly from the need to deal with some minor problems which had emerged from the case law, but more importantly from a felt need to augment and tighten defence disclosure duties to make them bite. The new provisions are found in ss 33, 34, 35 and 36 which operate to insert a number of new sections and subsections in the CPIA 1996.

3.3.1 Disclosure to Co-accused

In its original form, the CPIA 1996 simply required defence statements to be provided to the court and the prosecutor (s 5(5)) and made no reference to the situation where two or more accused are tried together. The question whether disclosure should also be made to a co-accused was considered in *R v Hillman and Knowles* ([2001] 10 Arch News 4), in which a judge in a joint murder trial at the Central Criminal Court held that the parties should each be allowed access to the court's files in order to get sight of the other party's defence statements. The issue is now governed by new sub-ss 5(5A), (5B) and (5D) inserted by s 33 of the 2003 Act. Where there are two or more accused, each defendant must give copies of his defence statement to the other accused if the court so orders. The court may act of its own motion or on an application by any party. Such disclosure must be made within the period specified by the court. Similarly, an 'updated defence statement' or a statement that the accused has no change to make to the original defence statement (under CPIA 1996, s 6B), must be served on a co-accused within a period to be specified by regulation, if the court so orders (s 6B(5) and (6)).

A more simple approach would have been to require defence statements to be disclosed to any co-accused at the same time as disclosure to the court and prosecution. The government chose not to adopt this approach because there might be some cases in which an accused might be prejudiced by exposing his defence to a co-accused. However, although the new provisions do not indicate that such disclosure will be routine in joint trials, to refuse a defendant's application might run the risk of contravening the right to a fair trial under the European Convention on Human Rights, Article 6. It would be hard to imagine any circumstances in which it would be permissible to permit one only of two co-accused to be provided with the other party's statement.

The timing of disclosure is subject to court order, and it is contemplated that courts will frequently require contemporaneous exchanges to avoid the possibility of one defendant tailoring his statement according to what is disclosed in the co-accused's defence statement.

3.3.2 Contents of Defence Statement

A new s 6A to CPIA 1996, inserted by CJA 2003, s 33(2) deals with the contents of defence statements and effectively replaces s 5(6), (7) and (8) which are repealed by Sch 36, para 23.

The new s 6A(1) specifies the contents of a defence statement. As before, it must set out the nature of the accused's defence, but the phrase 'in general terms' is now excluded, suggesting that courts may require more detail than has hitherto been acceptable. It is also now made clear that the statement must refer to any particular defences on which the accused intends to rely. This apparently straightforward provision may open a doctrinal can of worms since there is no consensus as to what pleas constitute defences. Broadly defined, the term 'defence' might include any plea which, if successful, would lead to an acquittal. This might include pleas involving a denial of one of the elements of an offence, such as causation or *mens rea,* as well as procedural pleas such as applications to exclude evidence or stay proceedings for abuse of process. On the other hand, if a narrower (and doctrinally purer) definition were adopted, the category of defence would be confined to those pleas such as duress, self-defence or diminished responsibility, which might lead to either an acquittal or conviction for a lesser offence, notwithstanding that all of the positive elements of an offence are proven.

Whereas formerly defence statements were largely concerned with factual matters, s 6A(1)(d) now requires the accused to indicate any point of law, to include any point as to the admissibility of evidence or abuse of process, which he wishes to take, and any authority on which he intends to rely for that purpose. This is a significant new burden which will require defence teams to bring forward the detailed preparation of the case to the time when the defence statement is prepared. This work would normally be conducted immediately prior to trial and will therefore require extensive changes to the working practices of defence lawyers. In terms of fair trial, it may be objected that the provision advantages the prosecution which will obtain advance notice of arguments to be raised in court, whereas the defence may be taken by surprise on their day in court. If the defence are required to indicate legal arguments in advance there can be no justification for failing to impose a matching obligation on the prosecution. Without such an obligation, justice could be done to the accused only if adjournments are permitted to allow time to consider legal arguments advanced by the prosecutor in court, but this would hardly be in the interests of efficient judicial administration, particularly in relation to jury trials. Quite apart from the issue of principle, it is far from clear that the defence team will be in a position to fulfil the duty to disclose arguments and authorities without first being informed of the full prosecution case.

Consider the common case of a challenge to the admissibility of an alleged confession under the Police and Criminal Evidence Act 1984 (PACE 1984), s 76(2). In procedural terms all that the accused needs to do in order to raise issue of admissibility is to represent to the court that the confession was obtained by oppression or by anything said or done likely to render it unreliable in the circumstances. It is then for the prosecution to prove beyond reasonable doubt that the confession was not obtained by either means. This may be done by presenting factual evidence and may also involve legal argument. Whereas, in some cases, the accused may have supported the initial representation concerning inadmissibility by legal argument, in many cases legal argument will arise in response to the prosecution case on the issue. In such circumstances, the defence team would be able to anticipate the admissibility challenge, but would not be in a position to disclose in advance relevant legal arguments and authorities.

As before, the defence statements must contain details of proposed alibi witnesses. This is considered below. By s 6A(4) the Home Secretary is empowered to make regulations concerning the details which must be provided in relation to the matters listed in sub-s (1). It should be noted that this is not a power to add new issues to the list of matters which must be addressed in the defence statement.

3.3.3 Defence Witnesses' Details

A major government objective in reforming defence disclosure is to facilitate scrutiny and investigation of the defence case pre-trial. This is reflected in more stringent duties on the defendant in relation to identifying proposed alibi witnesses, a new duty to notify the prosecutor and the court of all witnesses he intends to call in his defence, and a duty to disclose all expert witnesses who have been instructed by the defence, whether the accused intends to call them or not.

The requirement to disclose details of alibis has a long pedigree, having been introduced by the Criminal Justice Act 1967 and subsequently incorporated in the CPIA 1996. The traditional justification for the requirement for advance disclosure of alibi has been the need to investigate alibis in advance to avoid the prosecution being wrong-footed at trial. Although for many years it was widely accepted that alibis were a special case it would seem that prosecutorial convenience and justice might be equally served by early notification of other categories of defence. The logic of this position underpinned the introduction of defence disclosure in 1996, and now the government has taken the next logical step to extend the requirement to disclose to include the identities of all potential defence witnesses. Inconveniently, largely similar rules relating to alibi witnesses and to other defence witnesses are found in separate sections. Disclosure of alibi witnesses must be made as part of the defence statement whereas details of other witnesses are to be notified separately.

The rules relating to alibi witnesses are found in CPIA 1996, s 6A(2), as inserted by CJA 2003, s 33(2). This replaces the former rules in CPIA 1996, s 5(7) and (8), which are repealed. As before, evidence in support of an alibi is defined as evidence tending to show that by reason of the presence of the accused at a particular place or in a particular area at a particular time he was not, or was unlikely to have been, at the place where the offence is alleged to have been committed at the time of its commission (s 6A(3)). Where the defence statement discloses an alibi, the defendant is required to disclose not only the names and addresses of any alibi witnesses (as before) but also their dates of birth, or as many of these details as are know to the accused at the time when the statement is given (s 6A(2)(a)). If any of these details are not known to the accused, he is required to disclose any details in his possession which might be of material assistance in identifying or finding the proposed alibi witnesses.

The rules relating to other defence witnesses are found in CPIA 1996, s 6C, as inserted by CJA 2003, s 34. The accused is required to give to the court and prosecutor a notice indicating whether he intends to call any witnesses at trial, other than himself, and as for alibi witnesses, must provide names, addresses and dates of birth, or other identifying information if any of these details are not known to the accused (s 6C(1)). There is no requirement to repeat information already provided under the alibi scheme (s 6C(2)). Notice of an intention to call a particular witness must be given within a period to be prescribed by order under CPIA 1996, s 12. Where, after giving notice, the accused decides not to call a witness or to call a further witness, or discovers relevant identifying information about a proposed witness, the accused must give an appropriately amended notice to the court and the prosecutor (s 6C(4)). Although, there is no similar provision for amending information provided about alibi witnesses, this is covered by the new procedure for updated disclosure by the accused, considered below.

3.3.4 Expert Witnesses

It is currently the law that both prosecution and defence are required to disclose in advance any expert reports which are intended to be adduced at trial (Crown Court (Advance notice of expert evidence) Rules 1987, SI 1987/716). The new provision in CPIA 1996, s 6D (inserted by CJA 2003, s 35) deals with the rather different issue of expert reports, commissioned by the defence, which are not subsequently used. Whereas, the prosecution would be required to disclose any unused expert report which might reasonably be expected to undermine the prosecution or assist the defence, the accused has been free to 'lose' any expert evidence which did not suit his case. Should the prosecution become aware of an expert report commissioned by the defence, it was always free to subpoena the expert to give evidence, on the basis of the common law principle that there is no ownership in a witness (*Harmony*

Shipping Co SA v Saudi Europe Line Ltd [1979] 1 WLR 1380); however, the ability to do so depended upon knowing that such a witness actually existed. The new provision seeks to arm the prosecution in this respect.

Under s 6D(1) if the accused instructs a person with a view to providing an expert opinion for possible use as evidence at trial, he must notify the court and the prosecutor of the putative expert's name and address. Time limits for the provision of this information will be set by regulation (s 6D(3)). A notice need not be given if relevant details have been provided under s 6C, because the expert is an intended witness (s 6D(2)).

The intent of the provision is twofold: (i) to deter the practice of 'expert shopping' whereby an accused instructs a number of expert witnesses until one is found who will provide a satisfactory report; (ii) to make the unused report potentially available as evidence for the prosecution. The precise scope of the duty to disclose is unclear. Whereas the use of the phrase 'with a view to his providing an expert opinion' suggests that speculative enquiries or early negotiations might be covered by the duty, on the other hand, the use of the word 'instruction' suggests a firm commission to carry out the necessary work. In any event, the scope of what is disclosable will be limited by litigation privilege by which documents brought into existence in connection with obtaining advice about anticipated criminal proceedings cannot be disclosed without a waiver of privilege by the accused (*Re Barings plc* [1998] 1 All ER 673).

The duty on the accused is simply to disclose the name and address of the instructed expert. This may be of little value to the prosecution in the absence of any duty on the expert or the accused to record and preserve any expert opinion obtained, as would apply to expert evidence collected by the prosecution by virtue of the CPIA code of practice. Thus an accused who had commissioned an unfavourable expert report would generally be free to destroy his own copy and also able to instruct the expert to destroy the report and any material on which it was based. Such an instruction may produce moral and legal dilemmas for the expert.

A number of offences may be in issue where an expert destroys material under instructions from the accused. If the expert report is positively inculpatory in relation to a particular offence, to destroy it may run the risk of liability for the offence of assisting an arrestable offender to avoid apprehension or prosecution under the Criminal Law Act 1967, s 4. However, that offence does not include an intent that the offender should avoid conviction, and it is therefore arguable that an expert who assists an offender who has already been apprehended and prosecuted, does not commit an offence. The expert would also avoid liability if he lacked the necessary *mens rea* element of knowing or believing that the person assisted had committed an arrestable offence. Arguably, this will often be the case, since normally the expert will not have access to all of the evidence in the case, the accused would be unlikely to have admitted his own guilt to the expert, and in any event it would not be the expert's business to form an opinion on the ultimate issue of guilt.

The expert may also run the risk of liability under the Criminal Law Act 1967, s 5 for accepting or agreeing to accept consideration for not disclosing information which might be of material assistance in securing the prosecution or conviction of an offender. Because the offence targets circumstances in which a person is specifically rewarded for non-disclosure, it would seem that no liability would attach where there is no specific payment for non-disclosure. Once again the expert would also escape liability if he lacked knowledge or belief that an offence had been committed.

Finally, the expert might incur liability under the common law offence of perverting the course of justice which overlaps considerably with the two statutory offences discussed above. This offence may be committed by destroying or concealing potential evidence (*R v Vreones* [1891] 1 QB 360), where this is done with the intention to mislead a course of justice. The offence will not be committed if the expert does not appreciate the significance of her report for criminal proceedings. Further, in the absence of any positive duty to make evidence available for the purpose of investigation or prosecution, it is submitted that this offence will not be committed where an expert destroys evidence which he believes would not have been found and utilized by the prosecution in any event.

3.3.5 Updated Defence Disclosure

A criticism of the original regime under the CPIA 1996 was that defence disclosure was a once and for all event, which was required to be completed within 14 days. Whereas the prosecutor was required to revisit the disclosure issue after the issue of a defence statement, and thereafter to keep the question of whether further disclosure was required under review, for the defence team disclosure was a one-off event. This issue is now addressed by a new CPIA 1996, s 6B (inserted by CJA 2003, s 33(3)) which creates a duty to provide a further 'updated defence statement', or a statement indicating that the accused has no change to make to the initial defence statement (s 6B(1) and (4)). The defence statement must be given to the court and the prosecutor within a period specified by regulations to be made under s 12 (s 6B(2)). The court has power, of its own motion or on application, to order that any updated defence statement is also given to any co-accused (s 6B(5) and (6)).

This new procedure is intended to improve the quantity and quality of defence disclosure. As will be discussed below, this attempt may be frustrated by the inhibiting effect of the sanctions for disclosure failure under CPIA 1996, s 11.

3.3.6 Authorship

When created in 1996, the new scheme of defence disclosure worked on a carrot and stick principle. The carrot was the possibility that the disclosure of a defence might induce further disclosure of material relevant to that defence at secondary prosecution disclosure. The stick was the possibility that failure to fully disclose the defence would be met by the sanction of evidential inferences drawn against the accused at trial. The sanction of inferences will now assume a greater significance in coercing the accused to co-operate with the scheme. The reason for this is that if prosecutors responsibly comply with their new extended disclosure duties from the outset, the incentive to disclose to obtain further disclosure (a key element of the original scheme) will be considerably diluted.

There are a number of theoretical and practical difficulties associated with using the threat of an adverse evidential finding as a sanction for non-cooperation with the process. Most of these issues have yet to be tackled directly by the courts; however, one issue which has been raised is whether it is legitimate to draw an evidential inference against the accused on the basis of a document drafted by her or his lawyer. This issue was raised in *R v Wheeler* (2000) 164 JP 565 in which the accused ran a defence at trial different from that set out in his defence statement, which he disowned. The Court of Appeal held that where such a conflict arose, the trial judge should consider carefully whether or not to leave the possibility of drawing inferences to the jury. If the jury were permitted to draw such inferences they should be directed to do so only if satisfied that the defendant had personally approved the statement provided. The Court further suggested that defence statements should be signed personally by defendants in order to acknowledge their contents and prevent later disputes. However, in a later case, *R (Sullivan) v Crown Court Maidstone* [2002] 1 WLR 2747, the High Court held that a local practice direction requiring that accused persons sign defence statements, was declared to be unlawful as ultra vires.

A new CPIA 1996, s 6E(1), inserted by CJA 2003, s 36, addresses this issue by deeming that where an accused's solicitor purports to give, on behalf of the accused, a defence statement, an updated defence statement, or a statement that there are no changes to be made to the defence statement, the statement shall, unless the contrary is proved, be deemed to be given on the authority of the accused. This provision simply shifts to the accused the burden of proof on the issue of authorship, authorization or acknowledgement of the statement. However, it is unlikely to prevent further problems in this area and cases may still arise where at trial it becomes apparent that a hurriedly prepared defence statement does not fully represent the accused's case. One unfortunate consequence of shifting the burden of proof on the issue is that defendants who claim to have maintained a consistent story throughout the proceedings may be forced to waive legal professional privilege in order to prove this. Problems may also arise where an 'updated' defence statement significantly departs from the earlier statement. In such a case it may be frankly unrealistic to deem that two inconsistent statements were both made with the full authority of the accused.

3.4 FAULTS IN DEFENCE DISCLOSURE—EVIDENTIAL INFERENCES

3.4.1 Power to Draw Inferences

Where a defendant fails to fulfil his duties in respect of providing a defence statement, or where there are substantial differences between the statement and the defence raised in court, a court or jury may draw appropriate inferences under CPIA 1996, s 11. The power to draw inferences may be seen either as simply enabling the tribunal of fact to exercise common sense and to take into account relevant material in reaching their determination, or as an unprincipled use of the process of proof as a means to secure procedural compliance. However the provision is characterized, it has not been a success: neither judges nor prosecutors have shown much enthusiasm for inviting juries to draw such inferences and it has become clear that the accused may frame his statement in broad terms which give little assistance to the prosecution but nevertheless obviate the possibility of inferences being drawn. The present Act makes a number of reforms relating to the circumstances in which inferences may be drawn and the procedure to be used.

3.4.2 Procedural Issues

New s 6E CPIA 1996 (inserted by s 36) makes some minor procedural clarifications. By s 6E(4) and (5), a trial judge on application or of his own motion may direct that the jury may be given a copy of either the initial defence statement or an updated one (if provided). The statement may be edited if necessary to exclude references to inadmissible matters. The statement should be given to the jury only if the judge is of the opinion that seeing the defence statement would help the jury to understand the case or to resolve any issue in the case (sub-s (5)(b)). This test seems to contemplate that a jury might be given access to the defence for purposes other than determining whether inferences would be appropriate. Since the defence statement is essentially an element of pre-trial procedure for the purpose of assisting the opposing legal teams and the court plan for trial, it is not clear why it should ever be desirable for the jury to see the statement unless inferences are in issue.

By CPIA 1996, s 6E(2) (inserted by s 36) the judge, at a pre-trial hearing held under CPIA 1996, s 39, is given the power to comment on the adequacy of any defence statement provided and to warn the accused of the possibility of inferences being drawn. This provision is legally superfluous since this is an issue which a judge would have been free to address at pre-trial hearing in any event. It appears, therefore, that the purpose of the provision is to encourage prosecutors and judges to make greater strategic use of the possibility of inferences being drawn in order to induce guilty pleas, and/or to encourage recalcitrant defendants to provide missing statements or improve statements already provided. Discussion at pre-trial hearing will be helpful in relation to the latter issue since (as discussed below) there is no current consensus as to the degree of detail required in defence statements, and a warning may prevent an accused finding out for the first time at trial that disclosure is inadequate. However, receiving a warning at this stage may not be helpful unless the accused can take remedial measures, such as reaching an agreement that the issue of inferences will not be raised if a fuller updated statement is provided, or at least an understanding that the judge should point out the fact that fuller disclosure was made prior to trial, if the possibility of drawing inferences is left to the jury.

3.4.3 Circumstances in which Inferences may be Drawn

Section 39 substitutes a new s 11 to CPIA 1996. As before, the provision set outs circumstances in which the court and (generally) any other party (ie prosecution or co-accused) may comment on failure to make adequate disclosure, and in which the jury may draw such adverse inferences as appear proper in deciding whether the accused is guilty of the offence concerned (s 11(5)). It would not, however, be proper to infer guilt solely from a disclosure failure and no person may be convicted solely on the basis of such an inference (s 11(10)). It should be noted that inferences may be drawn only at trial and that there is no scope for inferences in determining whether an accused should be committed for trial or on an application to dismiss a charge in a case which has been either transferred to the Crown Court under the Criminal Justice Act 1987, s 4 or the Criminal Justice Act 1991, s 53, or which has been sent to the Crown Court under the Crime and Disorder Act 1998, s 51.

The possibility of inferences being drawn arises in a number of circumstances set out in s 11(2)(3) and (4):

- *No statement.* Where the accused has failed to give an initial statement required under s 5 or an updated defence statement required under s 6B(1), or a statement that no updating is required under s 6B(4), or a notification of defence witnesses required under 6C.

- *Late statement.* Where the accused has given a compulsory statement under s 5, or voluntary statement under s 6, an updated defence statement under s 6B, or a witness notice under s 6C, but does so outside the relevant time limit.

- *Inconsistent statement.* Where the accused sets out inconsistent defences in his defence statement (s 11(2)(e)).

- *Defence at trial goes beyond statement.* Where the accused puts forward a defence which was not mentioned in his defence statement, or relies on any matter (such as a reason for taking issue with a particular item of prosecution evidence) which was not mentioned in the statement but should have been under s 6A, or adduces alibi evidence where particulars of the alibi were not given in the statement, or calls an alibi witness without having given any necessary particulars in the defence statement, or calls a witness not included or not adequately identified in a witness notice.

3.4.4 Comment by Leave of the Court

In certain circumstances, the ability of other parties to comment on the relevant disclosure defect is by leave of the court. This applies where the defect is a failure to mention a point of law or legal authority to be relied upon, or a point relating to the admissibility of evidence or abuse of process (s 11(6)(b)), and also where the defect involves a failure to provide notification of a particular witness or a failure to adequately identify a witness, or providing late notification of a witness.

3.4.5 Guidance concerning Comments and Inferences

In three circumstances the Act gives guidance concerning comments which may be made and inferences which may be drawn under s 11(5). First, where the disclosure defect is that a defence at trial is different from anything mentioned in the defence statement, the court must have regard to the extent of the difference and to whether there is any justification for it, in determining whether comment should be made and inferences may be drawn, and in determining the nature of any comment or inference (s 11(8)). Secondly, where the defect involves failure to include, or to identify a witness properly, the court must have regard to whether or not there was any justification for the failure (s 11(9)).

The reference to justification in both of these provisions is unfortunate and inappropriate. The term 'justification' normally suggests that what was done was right in the circumstances. However, these provisions are concerned with whether evidential inferences can be drawn. There might be many instances where a court could be satisfied that the explanation for a disclosure defect was an error or negligence on the part of a lawyer or the accused, where it would be inappropriate to draw adverse inferences but where there was no question of the disclosure defect being justified. It is to be hoped that courts will interpret 'justification' widely in such cases so as to include credible explanations, whether or not justified.

The third circumstances in which guidance is given in relation to comments and the drawing of inferences is where an accused, having issued a defence statement, then issues a notice under s 6B(4) indicating that no updating is required. By s 11(11) the question whether the accused has failed to include all the necessary elements in the defence statement and whether there has been adequate notice of any alibi and alibi witnesses, shall be determined by reference to the state of affairs existing when the s 6B(4) statement was made and as if the original defence statement had been made at that time.

3.5 POLICE INTERVIEWS WITH DEFENCE WITNESSES

It is contemplated that as a result of the prosecution being notified of proposed alibi and other defence witnesses, these witnesses might be interviewed by the police. This practice could be beneficial in furthering the process of clarifying issues in advance of trial and might lead to cases being dropped pre-trial. However, the practice runs contrary to a long-standing tradition that the police should generally avoid interviewing defence witnesses for fear of being accused of tampering or intimidation. Accordingly, the practice of interviewing defence witnesses will be made subject to a new code of practice to be made by the Home Secretary under a new s 21A CPIA 1996, inserted by s 40.

In preparing the code the Home Secretary will be required to consult with the Association of Chief Police Officers, the Bar Council, the Law Society and Institute of Legal Executives and equivalent bodies in Northern Ireland to the extent that the code will apply in that province. The code must be brought into operation by order, which must be laid with the proposed code before Parliament, and will not come into force until approved by a positive resolution of both houses (s 11(5),(7) and (8)). Revisions to the code may be made from time to time and may be brought into force in the same manner as the code itself (s 11(6)).

The code will apply to any police officer or other person charged with the duty of investigating offences, who must have regard to it (s 21A(3)). However, as with the PACE codes and the general CPIA disclosure code, a failure to have regard to the code shall not in itself give rise to any criminal or civil liability (s 21A(11)). However, the code will be admissible in evidence in civil and criminal proceedings (s 21A(12)) and, if relevant, any failure to abide by the code and the code itself may be taken into account in determining any issue arising in such proceedings (s 21A(13)).

The code will apply to interviews and arrangements for interviews made by investigators with any person named (or otherwise identified) as an alibi witness in a defence statement, or whose particulars are given as a defence witness in a notice of proposed witnesses given by the accused under s 6C (s 21A(1)). A number of matters about which the code must give guidance are listed in s 21A(2). These are: (a) the information that should be provided to the interviewee and the accused in relation to the interview; (b) the notification of the accused's solicitor about the interview; (c) the attendance of a solicitor for the interviewee; (d) the attendance of a solicitor for the accused; (e) the attendance of any other appropriate person at such an interview taking into account the interviewee's age or any disability. It seems fairly clear that a number of other more substantial issues will need to be dealt with in the code if it is to serve its purpose of insulating any police interviews with defence witnesses from criticism or legal challenge. If this purpose is to be achieved, the code must effectively protect both the welfare of witnesses and optimize the quality of their evidence. But these concerns are of general importance in relation to witnesses: they are not particular to interviews between investigators and proposed defence witnesses. It may be that this code will stimulate a more general examination of issues relating to the pre-trial treatment of witnesses, with further legal developments to match those now applying to witnesses in court (see generally D Birch and R Leng, *Blackstone's Guide to the Youth Justice and Criminal Evidence Act 1991* (Blackstone Press, 2002); J McEwan, 'Special measures for victims and witnesses', chapter 14 in M McConville and G Wilson (eds), *The Handbook of the Criminal Process* (Oxford University Press, 2002).

4

JURIES, AND TRIALS ON INDICTMENT WITHOUT JURIES

4.1 INTRODUCTION

There are a number of provisions in the Criminal Justice Act 2003 (CJA 2003) dealing with or impacting on juries and the cases they will or will not try. Some of the provisions which merely impact on these issues are dealt with elsewhere, such as the increase in maximum sentence available to magistrates (see section 10.6 below) which will affect the number of cases which will be sent to the Crown Court. Similarly, s 41 and Sch 3, dealing with the revised procedure for determining mode of trial and for sending cases to the Crown Court, are dealt with in Chapter 5 and 10.6 below. This chapter, however, is concerned with the provisions which directly impinge on jury trial either in terms of the composition of the jury or in terms of the classes of case which, although still assigned to the Crown Court, may in future be tried without a jury. These latter provisions were amongst the most controversial in the Act and indeed nearly resulted in the loss of the whole Act and consequently were subject to significant amendment at the last minute at the very end of the parliamentary session in November 2003. In summary though, in the event, Part 7 of the Act as enacted enables the *prosecution* to apply for a trial in the Crown Court to be conducted without a jury in two types of case:

(a) complex or lengthy fraud cases;
(b) cases where there is a real and present danger of jury tampering.

A third situation whereby the *defence* could apply for trial without jury was in the original Bill but taken out as part of the last minute parliamentary negotiations. Furthermore, as part of the same negotiations, the government agreed that para (a) above would not actually be implemented until further work had been undertaken, looking at possible alternatives, such as an expert panel or assessors, and the Law Commission's recommendations on fraud and multiple offending (Law Com Nos 276 and 277).

In addition to the above rights for the prosecution to *apply* for non-jury trial in the Crown Court, a trial judge can discharge a jury during the *course* of a trial because jury tampering appears to have taken place and may order the trial to continue without a jury (or he may terminate the trial, in which case he may also order that any new trial should be without a jury).

In contrast to these inroads into the rule that trial on indictment means trial by jury, the importance of the jury is paradoxically emphasized by reforms elsewhere in the Act (s 321 and Sch 33) to the rules on jury service which is now subject to far fewer exemptions and exclusions. The basic rule now is that everyone between 18 and 70 qualifies for jury service subject to much more limited categories of ineligibility and disqualification and with there no longer being any excusals as of right as opposed to discretionary excusals or deferrals. The details will be examined later in this chapter but first we will look at the background to the proposals on trials without jury.

4.2 TRIALS ON INDICTMENT WITHOUT JURIES—BACKGROUND

The current proposals to limit the use of juries in trials on indictment can be traced back at least as far as the mid-1980s and the Report of the Roskill Committee (*Fraud Trials Committee Report 1986*) which recommended, amongst other things, that the complexity and length of some fraud trials meant that they would be better tried by a judge sitting not with a jury but with a smaller number of expert lay members who together would constitute a Fraud Trials Tribunal. Although many of the Committee's proposals were enacted in the Criminal Justice Act 1987 (CJA 1987), this particular proposal was never acted upon; however, the idea of a specialist panel for fraud trials has been mooted in debates about jury trial ever since. The issue was formally raised again in a Home Office Consultation document in February 1998 (*Juries in Serious Fraud Trials*) and the Auld Report subsequently picked up the issue again in its recommendations.

The Report came down firmly in favour of reform and of empowering trial judges in serious and complex frauds to try cases with lay members rather than a jury, or if the defendant so chose, simply to sit alone. This change has been estimated to have been likely to affect between 15 and 20 cases a year (White Paper, para 4.30) but the Auld Report envisaged that if the non-jury trial provisions worked well for fraud cases, they could subsequently be extended to other serious and complex cases. The White Paper endorsed the Auld Committee recommendations but removed any reference to sitting with lay members and specifically invited views as to whether 'the court should have power to direct trial by judge alone in *any* case that involves such a lengthy and complex hearing that justice would be better served by this alternative' (emphasis added).

The White Paper also recommended that cases where a trial has been stopped because of jury intimidation or bribery ('jury tampering') should be dealt with by empowering the judge to continue the trial alone without a jury or alternatively to stop the trial and order a fresh trial without a jury. It also invited views on whether trial by judge alone should be an option even before any actual jury tampering has taken place where there is a serious risk of it and police protection for the jury over a lengthy period would be disruptive and unreasonably intrusive.

In addition, the White Paper took up the Auld recommendation of giving the defendant the option (subject to the consent of the court) of trial on indictment without jury. It was recognized that issues such as 'judge shopping' and joint trials where only one, or not all, of the defendants choose trial without jury would need to be addressed.

As has been outlined above, all three of the situations canvassed for non-jury trial found their way into the Bill despite strong opposition to the White Paper proposals from a number of groups including the Bar Council, the Law Society, Justice, Liberty, and others.

Objections were wide ranging and included the fact that with no research permitted into what goes on in the jury room, assertions about difficulties experienced by juries largely amounted to speculation. Juries, it is argued, maintain a democratic input into the administration and application of the criminal law and keep it in touch with popular mores and standards. The requirement to be able to explain a case, and the legal issues to be decided, to a jury forces the law to remain comprehensible to the layman, a requirement which is particularly important in the field of criminal law. The selection or appointment of a particular judge to try a case, irrespective of the true reasons or indeed randomness of the decision, would be capable of being misinterpreted as being designed to produce a particular outcome and judges may become tarred, justifiably or not, as prosecution- or defence-minded in a way which is much less likely currently where the final decision on the facts is with a jury. Juries are anonymous and can return back into the community from which they came and therefore cannot develop an individual reputation and are less likely to have continuing protection needs. Any option given to defendants to choose non-jury trials may be most likely to be exercised by defendants lacking in public sympathy such as in paedophile or egregious fraud cases or where a technical defence might be thought likely to succeed. Judges might find themselves trying a limited sub-class of cases which the public would come to associate unfavourably with judge-only trials, and acquittals might be in danger of being seen as cases of unmeritorious defendants being acquitted by the legal establishment and evading true justice at the hands of a jury. Furthermore, a defendant who acquiesces in jury trial where he could have opted for non-jury trial may also have his motives unfairly impugned on the basis that he is trying to gain an emotive and unjustified acquittal that a less easily swayed judge might be unlikely to give.

Savings in time and complexity of trials might be largely illusory as judges would still have to apply the same rules of evidence, few of which are nowadays based on the need to prevent prejudicial inferences being drawn by untrained jurors and the complexities of the summing-up would not go away but would simply re-emerge in the form of the detailed reasoning and finding of facts that a single judge's judgment would have to rehearse. In so far as a criterion for non-jury trials would be length and complexity, experience shows that advance estimates of length are not very reliable and the problems for juries dealing with long and complex frauds may be somewhat exaggerated, with most professionals in such cases being of the view that, generally speaking, the juries 'get it right'. A final issue worth mentioning peculiar to the proposal on jury tampering is that of the judge who has to attempt to give a fair hearing to a defendant in a trial where he has already found that the jury has been or is likely to be bribed or intimidated, most likely on behalf of or with the knowledge of the defendant. More generally, non-jury trials require the judge who rules on the admissibility of evidence to have to put out of his mind evidence that he has seen and excluded rather than being able to leave the fact-finding to a jury that has never seen the evidence and thus does not have to perform these mental gymnastics.

For reasons such as the above, the provisions on non-jury trial were given a very rough ride in Parliament and particularly at Committee Stage in the House of Lords (15 July 2003), at which point they were defeated and removed from the Bill. Although some former judges spoke in favour of the provisions and pointed to the fact that similar provisions appeared to have worked perfectly well in New Zealand and in certain other jurisdictions, the overall mood (including that of most former judges and practitioners) was hostile to a set of provisions which were seen as objectionable in principle and as being the thin end of the wedge even though they may not at this stage impact on a large number of trials. The mood was undoubtedly partly influenced by the fact that the provisions were seen as part of a continuing strategy of the government to restrict the role of the jury, a strategy with which the House had in recent years done battle in rejecting two Mode of Trial Bills which sought to limit the defendant's right to elect Crown Court trial for indictable offences.

Having been removed from the Bill in the Lords in July, the non-jury trial proposals reappeared only when the Bill returned to the Commons for consideration of Lords amendments at the very end of its passage when the government reinstated the provisions which meant that they had to go back to the Lords for their approval. As a result, the Bill went backwards and forwards in the final days and hours of the parliamentary session as the government and those opposed to the provisions tested each other's nerve. The government was in danger of losing the Bill altogether although it made it clear finally that it would be prepared to extend the parliamentary session into the following week (during which the Queen's Speech at the start of the new session was due) in order to get the Bill passed in an acceptable form. Eventually, as already indicated, the Act was passed with hours to spare within the original time frame, with two out of the three main provisions on non-jury trial in place but without the third provision. That is with no provision for defendants to opt for non-jury trial and with one of the other two provisions, complex frauds, emasculated by a commitment not to implement without an affirmative resolution of both Houses (see s 330 (5)(b)).

A flavour of the drama and complexity of that final day of the Bill's passing can perhaps be gained from the following extract from Hansard, HL col 2105 (20 November 2003) as the Bill was returned from the Commons to the Lords for the last time:

The Sitting was suspended from 3.29 to 8.10 p.m.

Criminal Justice Bill

A message was brought from the Commons, That they agree to a Lords amendment to the Criminal Justice Bill; they do not insist on an amendment to which the Lords have disagreed; they have made a consequential amendment to which they desire the agreement of your Lordships; and they insist on their disagreement with your Lordships to the remaining amendments, in which the Lords insisted, but have made amendments to the words so restored to the Bill to which they desire the agreement of your Lordships.

Having set out this chequered background to Part 7 of the Act, we can now turn to examining the details of the provisions as enacted.

4.3 APPLICATIONS FOR NON-JURY TRIAL IN FRAUD CASES—S 43

Section 43 is a curious provision, largely as a result of the machinations described above, in that it is highly unlikely that it will be brought into force in the short or medium term and it is quite likely that it will never be brought into force at all. One would not guess this looking at s 43 itself, or even if one looked at s 336 of the Act dealing with commencement. Section 336 does not specifically mention s 43 so it would appear to, and indeed does, fall under s 336(3) as one of the 'remaining provisions' which come into force by order of the Secretary of State. That, however, is not the whole story because carefully tucked away in s 330(5)(b) it is stated that 'an order under section 336(3) bringing section 43 into force . . . may only be made if a draft of the statutory instrument [containing the order] has been laid before, and approved by a resolution of, each House of Parliament'. Hence s 43 will require an affirmative resolution of both Houses to come into force and there is little chance of the House of Lords so resolving in its present mood, quite apart from the possibility that the government may now choose to adopt another strategy in relation to fraud trials. Nevertheless, we will proceed to analyse s 43 despite the somewhat academic status it is likely to enjoy for some time as it provides a useful comparison to s 44 which will be brought into force at a relatively early date.

Section 43 depends (see s 43(1)) for its operation on there being a trial on indictment for an offence under which notice has been given under the Crime and Disorder Act 1998, s 51B (replacing by virtue of Sch 3 of the 2003 Act provisions previously found in CJA 1987) because the evidence 'reveals a case of fraud of such seriousness or complexity that it is appropriate that the management of the case should without delay be taken over by the Crown Court'. If this condition is satisfied, the prosecution may by virtue of s 43(2) apply to a judge of the Crown Court for the trial to be conducted without a jury. On such an application, under s 43(3) the judge *may* make the order requested if he 'is satisfied that condition in subsection (5) is fulfilled', otherwise 'he *must* refuse the application'. Even where he may make the order, he may not do so 'without the approval of the Lord Chief Justice or a judge nominated by him' (s 43(4))—a safeguard added during the last fevered week of the

Bill's passage.) Subsection (5) sets out the condition of which the Crown Court judge has to be satisfied before he can consider making the order:

that the complexity of the trial or the length of the trial (or both) is likely to make the trial so burdensome to the members of a jury hearing the trial that the interests of justice require that serious consideration should be given to the question of whether the trial should be conducted without a jury.

Subsection (6) requires the judge to take into account 'any steps which might reasonably be taken to reduce the complexity or length of the trial' (such as, for example, limiting the number of counts etc) but sub-s (7) provides that steps which 'significantly disadvantage' the prosecution are not to be regarded as reasonable.

Returning to the condition in sub-s (5), two points may be noted. Firstly, the focus is on how burdensome to members of a jury the trial may be (and the impact of that on the interests of justice) as a result of the *complexity or length* of the trial. This is slightly different from the trigger in sub-s (1) of 'serious or complex fraud', the formula in use since CJA 1987 to provide different procedures in fraud cases. There is obviously an overlap between the two tests in that they both are satisfied by complexity but the alternative in sub-s (5) is not the *seriousness* of the fraud but the *length* of the trial (which of course may be thought to be more relevant to the issue of how practical it may be for a jury to try it). Serious cases often turn out to be long ones but not necessarily so and the difference between the two sets of criteria should be noted. The emphasis on the burden to the jury reflects the justification increasingly emphasized by the government in the debates in order to counter opposition to the changes. This opposition was based on the fact that jury trials in serious fraud actually work perfectly well currently, at least in terms of a conviction rate of over 80%. The government's response to this argument of 'the system works' was that it was concerned with the burden on the jury of long and complex trials, the consequent distortion of the types of juror who would be likely to be able to sit in such cases and the danger that some cases were simply not brought to trial in the first place because of the impossibility of getting a jury to sit through it and understand it by the end.

The second notable feature of sub-s (5) is that it does not say that the interests of justice require non-jury trial, merely that they require that 'serious consideration' should be given to it. This is consistent with the fact that where the condition in sub-s (5) is satisfied, the judge, under sub-s (3), *may* but does not have to order a non-jury trial. Given the hurdles in the way of commencement, the main interest of the above is to compare and contrast it with s 44 to which we next turn.

4.4 APPLICATIONS FOR NON-JURY TRIAL WHERE DANGER OF JURY TAMPERING—S 44

4.4.1 Mischief

The opposition to this clause gradually weakened as opponents of the provisions recognized that, relatively speaking, this was less objectionable and that there are very real problems in the relatively small number of cases where jury tampering is attempted.

These real problems were evidenced in Hansard, HL col 1963 (19 November 2003) quoting:

...a letter to ... the Lord Chancellor, [in which] Ian Blair, Deputy Commissioner of the Metropolitan Police, and John Burbeck, head of criminal justice at ACPO, outlined their fears ...

'There is a tier of criminals in this country who are prepared to go to any lengths to evade justice. It is a fact that jury intimidation exists as a consequence of those people. If the current system cannot cope with the threat, and if the system is not improved, there will be a group of violent, sophisticated and dangerous criminals who may truly become untouchable.'

Two examples were then given:

In August 2002, at Liverpool Crown Court, the trial of six defendants for serious drug offences collapsed because of jury tampering. Two jurors were threatened and a third juror was offered £10,000 to return a verdict of not guilty. The trial was in its fifth week and is estimated to have cost in excess of £1 million. In autumn 2001 at Kingston Crown Court, jurors hearing a case had their cars sprayed with paint stripper. The jury was discharged and special protection was given to the retrial jury. During a trial in the West Midlands in July 1999, in which several witnesses were physically assaulted, three members of the jury were threatened on their way home from the court. The jury foreman was approached by a man who gestured that he was going to shoot him. Those are not fanciful cases; they are real, pressing and pernicious.

It was also accepted that where a defendant had abused the right to jury trial by seeking to tamper with the jury, there was less objection to taking away the very right that he had abused.

4.4.2 Details

As a result of the above, there are no special provisions for commencement of this section, it merely requires an Order of the Secretary of State (which however is not expected until 2005). Once in force, s 44(1) merely requires a trial on indictment 'for one or more offences' (i.e. for *any* offence). Again it is for the prosecution to apply to a judge of the Crown Court (sub-s (2)) but under sub-s (3) there are not one, but two conditions to be fulfilled and, in another significant difference from s 44, if the conditions are fulfilled, the judge *must* (not may) make the order for non-jury trial (and, again, otherwise must refuse the application).

The two conditions are as follows:

(a) 'evidence of a real and present danger that jury tampering would take place' (s 44(4));

(b) '*so substantial a likelihood* [that jury tampering would take place] *as to make it necessary in the interests of justice for the trial to be conducted without a jury*, notwithstanding any steps (including the provision of police protection) which might reasonably be taken to prevent jury tampering' (s 44(5)—emphasis added and wording reordered to bring out the essence of the test).

Suggestions that the degree of likelihood should be expressed more strongly were resisted by the government but in recognition of the concern that non-jury trial should only be ordered in exceptional circumstances, sub-s (6) was added in the final stages of the Bill's passage to give examples of what may satisfy the test of 'a real and present danger':

(a) a case where the trial is a retrial and the jury in the previous trial was discharged because jury tampering had taken place,
(b) a case where jury tampering has taken place in previous criminal proceedings involving the defendant or any of the defendants,
(c) a case where there has been intimidation, or attempted intimidation, of any person who is likely to be a witness in the trial.

These are, of course, only examples and are not exhaustive but what they share in common is the fact that jury tampering (or witness intimidation) has actually taken place or been attempted. The implication may be drawn that 'a real and present danger' should not be found to exist merely on the basis of supposition, perhaps based on the violent or corrupt methods alleged to have been used by the defendants in their alleged criminal activities, but should be based on actual evidence of attempts to interfere with the administration of justice. These examples are given in terms of cases where the first condition of a 'real and present danger' may be satisfied. Even if this test is satisfied as a result of such hard evidence, there is the second test which demands, over and above this minimum, such a 'substantial' likelihood that it is necessary in the interests of justice to have the trial without a jury. Furthermore, as the opening words of s 44(5) make clear, the possibility of (and by implication, the degree of effectiveness of) police protection or other possible measures has to be considered in assessing the likelihood and impact of jury tampering. The section is not intended to be an automatic alternative to police protection where that can reasonably be used to obviate the risk of jury tampering although one wonders how the courts will deal with issues about the impact of the cost of police protection on the question of reasonableness.

As regards cost, the following information was given in Hansard, HL col 1963 (19 November 2003):

Police protection is available when the court considers that there is a substantial risk that the jury may be subject to intimidation. In the most serious cases, 24-hour police protection may be ordered, with officers accompanying jurors to their homes and other places outside the court. Over the past three years, that level of jury protection has been provided in approximately four to five trials per year. The cost to the Metropolitan Police over the past two years for full jury protection has been £9 million. That is equivalent to 26,627 police days a year diverted from mainstream policing in London, or an additional 130 officers on the beat.

What level of cost will the courts regard as reasonable and how will they measure that against the merits of maintaining jury trial and how will they assess the likely effectiveness of police protection? One factor which is not mentioned now in s 44 (contrast s 43(5)) is whether 'the level and duration of [police] protection would be likely to place an excessive burden upon the life of a typical juror', a question included in the original Bill as a third condition but dropped during the course of its passage. The section as enacted does not therefore concern itself with the *burden* on the typical juror but is more concerned with the interests of justice which one would expect would be more directly concerned with whether the jury will be likely to return a true verdict. Nevertheless the burden on the jury can probably be brought into the interests of justice test in so far as it impacts on the jury's ability to return a true verdict in the situation in which they would find themselves, including police protection.

Returning to the examples given in s 44(6), it should be noted firstly, that only two out of the three are examples of jury tampering (the third is witness intimidation), and, secondly, none of them expressly requires the jury tampering or intimidation of witnesses to have been done by the defendant or even on his behalf. Section 44(6)(b) might at first glance seem to imply the tampering has been done by the defendant ('involving the defendant or any of the defendants') but on examination this phrase refers merely to previous criminal proceedings involving them, where jury tampering has actually taken place, irrespective of by whom. Indeed, the reference to 'defendant or any of the defendants' potentially covers a situation where A and B are jointly charged and an application for non-jury trial is made on the basis that B was on a former occasion jointly charged with C, and C, quite independently of B, arranged jury tampering in those proceedings. The relationship between A and C may effectively be non-existent but C's past jury tampering may affect A's right to jury trial. This is just an extreme example of the fact that there seems little overt protection for defendants in joint trials where the jury tampering is nothing do with the first defendant (or indeed in trials of a single defendant where the accused is not responsible for the jury tampering). Of course, in some of the above cases (eg that involving A, B and C) the court may feel that the past jury tampering by C is of little relevance to A and B's current trial and may conclude there is not 'real and present danger'. Furthermore, it may be said that the question of who is responsible for the jury tampering is (a) not always easy to know and (b) not strictly relevant since the ultimate issue is whether the jury is likely to be able to return a true verdict. However, it does somewhat undercut the justification for the provision in terms of the defendant having abused his right to jury trial since it may not be the defendant or this particular defendant who has done so.

Discussion of who has been responsible for the jury tampering leads on to the question of what exactly is meant by 'jury tampering'. The Act provides no definition but it seems clear that the expression includes both attempted, and successfully completed, acts of jury intimidation, harm or bribery (compare s 44(6)(c) 'intimidation, or attempted intimidation'). Besides threats etc to actual jury members, the Home Office envisaged that it 'could also include improper approaches to a juror's family or friends, or threats etc in respect of a juror's property' (Home Office Notes on the Bill, November 2002). The example in s 44(6)(c) is interesting in that it is not a case of jury tampering at all but deals with witness intimidation. There are of course other measures in the criminal justice system to try to deal with witness intimidation but this subparagraph is not aimed directly at witness intimidation but is rather using its occurrence as an example of legitimate *evidence* that there is a real and present danger of jury tampering. A court may need some further evidence or persuasion to make the jump from witness intimidation to jury tampering although it is accepted that in some cases, the jump may not be a hard one to make.

The fact that jury tampering is not defined and is not in itself a specific criminal offence (of course conduct which amounts to jury tampering will virtually automatically always be criminal on a number of grounds, not least attempting to pervert the course of justice) does create some potential problems for the assessment of 'real and present danger' and for the examples in s 44(6)(a) and (b). Paragraph (a) is not too much of a problem since the example is one of a retrial where the jury in the previous trial was discharged because of jury tampering. That is simply a question of the grounds on which the trial judge actually discharged the previous jury. Paragraph (b) is not so straightforward as there may not be specific finding in the previous criminal proceedings that jury tampering took place, or at least not in such terms. What sort of evidence the courts will require or accept of previous jury tampering is no doubt a question to which answers will evolve in the course of time as practice and experience develops.

4.4.3 Procedure for an Application for Non-jury Trial—s 45

Section 45 deals with the procedure for applications whether they are under s 43 relating to complex or lengthy frauds (if ever implemented) or under s 44 because of jury tampering. We will focus here on the latter possibility given its more likely practical relevance. The application is to be determined at a preparatory hearing ordered under s 29 of the Criminal Procedure and Investigations Act 1996 (CPIA 1996) as amended by s 45(6) to (8) of the 2003 Act (or under CJA 1987 in the case of complex and lengthy frauds). The application for non-jury trial can only be made by the prosecution (s 44(2)) to a judge of the Crown Court who may order a preparatory hearing (s 45(6)) at which the application will be determined (s 45(7)). The parties (i.e. the defence as well as the prosecution) must be given at the preparatory hearing 'an opportunity to make representations with respect to the application' (s 45(3)). The main criterion for preparatory hearings is normally that it is a case of such complexity or length that substantial benefits will accrue from such a hearing, but this is obviously not required where a non-jury trial is being applied for on the grounds of jury tampering. Section 45(6) adds a new s 29(1A) to CPIA 1996 to allow for this totally separate purpose and s 45(7) adds the determination of a non-jury application to an amended permissible list of purposes of such a hearing.

This raises the question of whether, once a preparatory hearing has been ordered under new s 29(1A), that preparatory hearing can also consider issues under the amended s 29(2)(a) and (b) in addition to determining the non-jury application under what is now s 29(2)(c). The sensible answer would appear to be yes—that once a preparatory hearing is ordered, whether under s 29(1) or s 29(1A), it may as well deal with any issues that can usefully be dealt with at that stage, for example as to admissibility of evidence, even though the preparatory hearing could not have been ordered except for the non-jury trial application. Whether a judge is making an order 'for the purposes of the preparatory hearing' can be an important issue in determining whether there is a right of appeal under CPIA 1996 (both for the prosecution and the defence) an issue which now has also to be looked at in the light of the new prosecution rights of appeal discussed in Chapter 6 below. Despite the complexities which might arise as to the permissible purposes of preparatory hearings generally and/or of the permissible purposes of a particular preparatory hearing ordered specifically because of a non-jury trial application, there are a number of advantages in making the application one that is governed by the preparatory hearing regime. The advantages arise from the fact that this brings with it all the other ancillary provisions relating to preparatory hearings including, for example, reporting restrictions and Procedure Rules which therefore do not have to be replicated in the 2003 Act or in rules made under it. Section 49 of the 2003 Act does provide a power to make rules for the purposes of Part 7 if necessary or expedient but this power may be largely redundant as far as concerns preparatory hearings determining non-jury trial applications. The power to make rules might, however, be needed in relation to cases dealt with in the next section.

4.5 DISCHARGE OF JURY BECAUSE OF JURY TAMPERING—S 44

This section is concerned with the situation where, rather than there being an *application* (in advance of the trial) for non-jury trial under s 44, there is instead an issue about discharging a jury because of jury tampering *part way through a trial* and a related question about continuing without a jury or terminating the trial (followed normally by a retrial).

Such issues are dealt with under s 46 in a series of graduated steps.

Firstly, under s 46(1), the judge is simply 'minded' during a trial on indictment to discharge the jury because jury tampering 'appears to have taken place'.

Secondly, under sub-s (2), *before* taking any steps to discharge the jury, the judge '*must*':

(a) inform the parties he is minded to discharge the jury;
(b) inform the parties of the grounds on which he is so minded;
(c) allow the parties an opportunity to make representations.

This second stage is effectively the in-trial equivalent to the preparatory hearing that is held where the prosecution apply in advance for non-jury trial because of jury tampering.

The third stage comes under sub-s (3) where the judge, having heard the representations, if he decides to and does discharge the jury, then *may* make an order that the trial is to continue without a jury.

He may order the trial to continue:

if, but only if, he is satisfied

(a) that jury tampering has taken place, and
(b) that to continue the trial without a jury would be fair to the defendant or the defendants.

Consistently with the examples in s 44(6) discussed above, this requires actual jury tampering to have taken place but in addition expressly considers fairness to the defendant or defendants given that the trial is part way through. Other than fairness to the defence there is no mention of the interests of justice in s 46(3) as being one of the conditions for ordering the trial to continue without a jury. The implication may be drawn that in the typical case, the interests of justice would mean that the trial should continue without a jury provided that would be fair to the defendant or defendants (presumably if it is not fair in respect of just one of them, the judge cannot continue).

However, the interests of justice test is mentioned in s 46(4) where the judge *must* terminate the trial if he considers this necessary in the interests of justice. This is consistent with the inference above that normally the continuation of the trial will be in the interests of justice if it can in fairness to the defence continue but if, because of unfairness to the defendant, or for any other reason, the judge considers it necessary in the interests of justice to terminate the trial rather than continue with it, he *must* terminate it.

It may have been noted that before taking steps to discharge the jury, the judge is required under sub-s (2) to allow the parties to make representations. The subsection is not explicit on this but the implication would normally be that the representations would be about whether the jury should be discharged and there is no subsequent mention in sub-s (3) of representations relating to the question of whether it is fair to the defendant to continue without a jury or as to whether the interests of justice require the termination of the trial. Clearly both parties would want to and should be heard on these issues and it may be that the most sensible course would be for them to address these questions alongside the primary issue of discharging the jury in the course of their representations under s 46(2)(c).

If the jury is discharged and the trial terminated, rather than continued without a jury, under s 46(5) the judge may make an order (again, presumably having hear both sides on the issue) that any new trial should be without a jury if he is satisfied that the two conditions required for a successful application under s 44 are likely to be satisfied. The first condition will almost by definition be likely to be satisfied because the situation corresponds to the first example given in s 44(6) of a retrial where the first jury was discharged because of jury tampering. The only issue therefore will be whether s 44(5) is likely to be satisfied (jury tampering likelihood so substantial that necessary in the interests of justice to have non-jury trial). Even if the trial judge does not make an order under s 46(5) in respect of any new trial, s 46(7) allows a fresh application for non-jury trial to be made under s 44 (or indeed s 43 if relevant and brought into force).

4.6 APPEAL RIGHTS

Section 47 provides for a right of appeal (with leave) to the Court of Appeal (Criminal Division) from orders under s 46(3) (to continue the trial without a jury) or under s 46(5) (for any new trial to be without a jury). Such orders are to have no effect pending the appeal (and the appeal may ultimately go on to the House of Lords under s 33 of the Criminal Appeal Act 1968 if the usual conditions are satisfied). It is not necessary to give rights of appeal in relation to applications under ss 43 or 44 as they are covered by rights of appeal under the existing preparatory hearing regimes. There is no right of appeal given under s 46 against the first decision to be made under that section, ie the decision to discharge the jury. This is consistent with the common law whereby such a decision is a matter entirely for the judge's discretion and cannot be the subject of an appeal—see *Winsor v R* (1866) LR1 QB 390 and *R v Gorman* [1987] 1 WLR 545. The common law authorities of course relate to potential appeals by the defence but s 57(2) of the 2003 Act (see Chapter 6) also excludes rulings 'that a jury be discharged' from the new rights of appeal for the prosecution. It is of course more likely to be the defence that might want to appeal against the discharge of a jury where they disagree about the fact or extent of any jury tampering and want the trial to continue in front of the same jury. It would appear that they cannot appeal the decision to discharge as opposed to being able to appeal against the subsequent decision to continue without a jury or to order any future trial to be without a jury.

Paradoxically, the prosecution may wish to be able to appeal where the trial judge decides, having heard the representations under s 46(2), *not* to discharge the jury. (Although there is no specific provision or procedure under s 46 for the prosecution to raise with the trial judge the issue of discharge because of jury tampering, normally it will be the prosecution who will alert him to the evidence that there has been jury tampering and thus cause him initially to be minded to discharge the jury under s 46(1).) If the trial judge ultimately decides not to discharge the jury, that appears to be a ruling within the meaning of that word in s 74(1) of CJA 2003 and the prosecution could seemingly appeal under s 58 because the exclusion of the new appeal rights in s 57(2)(a) applies to 'rulings that a jury be discharged', not to rulings that the jury should not be discharged. Having said that, the prosecution can only appeal under s 58 if they are prepared to accept that the failure or abandonment of the appeal will result in an acquittal (see Chapter 6 below). The prosecution will not normally want to risk an immediate acquittal in order to challenge a decision not to discharge a jury unless, either because of the alleged jury tampering or for some other reason, they are convinced that they have very little or no chance of a conviction before this particular jury.

4.7 TRIALS WITHOUT JURY—MISCELLANEOUS

Section 48 contains a number of deeming provisions and provisions which generally state the blindingly obvious such as s 48(1) which illuminatingly tells us that 'the effect of an order under s 43, 44, or 46(5)' [which sections already tell us that the application is for an order that the trial be conducted without a jury] is 'that the trial to which the order relates is to be conducted without a jury'. More helpfully, sub-ss (3) and (4) effectively deem that the powers of courts sitting without juries shall be the same as if it had been sitting with a jury, and references to juries, their verdicts or findings, except where the context otherwise requires, shall be treated as references to the court or its verdict or finding. One express exception to this is to be found in sub-s (6) which preserves the exclusive jurisdiction of a jury to determine the question of fitness to be tried under s 4 of the Criminal Procedure (Insanity) Act 1964 or the issue under s 4A of the same Act (whether the accused 'did the act or made the omission charged against him . . .').

Section 48(5) provides that where a non-jury trial results in a conviction, a judgment stating the reasons for the conviction, at, or as soon as reasonably practical after, the time of the conviction, is required. It goes on to provide for the 28-day period for giving notice of appeal etc to begin to run from the date of the judgment rather than the date of the conviction where the two differ. What is not mentioned in s 48 is what is to happen if the non-jury court acquits. There is certainly no express requirement to give a reasoned judgment and, given there is no right of appeal for the prosecution, there is no need. Furthermore there is a question as to whether a reasoned judgment should be given in the case of acquittals as otherwise different classes of acquittal may develop depending on the reasons given. There is nothing in the Act to prohibit the giving of a reasoned judgment in the case of an acquittal but it would be possible to prohibit it in the procedure rules or by means of a practice direction. It would be an exceptional case where there would be any merit in having a reasoned judgment which would outweigh the interest in maintaining the position that it should not be possible to go behind the verdict of acquittal.

Section 50 applies the non-jury trial provisions to Northern Ireland with appropriate modifications including, of course, the saving in s 50(2) of s 75 of the Terrorism Act 2000 which is the current provision for the long-established so-called Diplock courts (non-jury trials in Northern Ireland in certain types of terrorism-linked cases). The details of the Northern Ireland situation are beyond the scope of this work.

4.8 JURY SERVICE

Restrictions in terms of gender, property ownership, and age affecting who can serve on a jury were gradually removed or eased during the 19th century with the result that the Juries Act 1974, as amended (prior to CJA 2003), provided that all registered electors between the ages of 18 and 70 who have been ordinarily resident in the UK for at least five years since the age of 13 are qualified to serve. However, the 1974 Act went on to provide for a number of persons who are ineligible (eg members of the legal profession or others associated with the administration of justice) or who are disqualified (those with certain types of criminal record) or who are excusable as of right (eg MPs, medical professionals, members of armed services, over 65s and others). Furthermore, individual jurors can apply for discretionary excusal on the basis of personal circumstances or hardship or can apply for deferral of jury service if the summons clashes with, for example, professional, personal or business commitments. Jury service thus cast a wide net but one very much full of holes.

This was well illustrated from figures quoted in the Auld Report (para 5.12). In total around a quarter of a million people are summoned for jury service every year but 'in a sample of 50,000 people summoned for jury service in June and July 1999, only one-third was available for service, about half of whom were allowed to defer their service until a later date. Of the remaining two-thirds, 13% were ineligible, disqualified or excused as of right, 15% either failed to attend on the day or their summonses were returned as "undelivered" and 38% were excused.'

Sanctions against those who ignore the summons are not regularly enforced and jury service was fast acquiring a characteristic often ascribed to inheritance tax: easily avoided by anyone sufficiently well advised. As a consequence the burden of jury service was tending to fall more heavily (just as with taxation) on those who actually perform their duty. As Lord Justice Auld put it:

... it is unfair to those who do their jury service, not least because, as a result of others' avoidance of it, they may be required to serve more frequently and for longer than would otherwise be necessary. Most of the exclusions or scope for excusal from jury service deprive juries of the experience and skills of a wide range of professional and otherwise successful and busy people. They create the impression, voiced by many, . . . that jury service is only for those not important or clever enough to get out of it.

Auld was unimpressed with arguments that the legal profession and others associated with the administration of justice should be ineligible and was sceptical about claims of undue deference that other jurors might give them. He also challenged the excusal as of right of persons such as medical professionals and felt that their needs could be equally well met through discretionary excusal where their duties at the time of the summons warranted it.

In the light of this, Auld recommended that everyone should be eligible for jury service, save for the mentally ill, and no one should be excusable from jury service as of right, only on showing good reason for excusal (save for those who have recently undertaken, or have been excused by a court from jury service). His proposals were endorsed in the White Paper (although his tentative proposals for ethnic minority representation on juries in certain types of case were not taken up by the government as it would undermine the fundamental principle of randomness and lead to other complications).

Section 321 of CJA 2003 implements the reforms to jury service by means of amendments to the Juries Act 1974 which are contained in Sch 33 of the 2003 Act. The new s 1 repeats the same basic positive test of qualification as in the old law of being a registered elector between 18 and 70 with at least five years' residence since the age of 13. It then adds only two much more limited negative tests of being mentally disordered or disqualified. The negative criterion of ineligibility has thus disappeared entirely save for the single category that was formerly merely a part of it, that of mentally disordered persons. These are defined in Part 1 of the new Sch 1, Part 2 of that Schedule deals with the disqualified which consists solely of an almost unchanged list of those with criminal records or who are on bail .

In addition to the disappearance of the category of ineligibility (save for the mentally disordered), the category of excusable as of right, formerly s 9(1) of the Act, is abolished (Sch 33, para 3). Instead, those previously entitled to excusal as of right (including the

65

over 65s) will now have to take their chance on gaining discretionary excusal under s 9(2) or discretionary deferral under s 9A. However, just as was the case previously under the old Sch 1, Pt 3 of the 1974 Act, a full-time serving member of the armed services is entitled to be deferred or excused where the commanding officer certifies that it would be prejudicial to the efficiency of the service if the member was to be required to be absent from duty—see Sch 33, paras 5–11. More generally, in relation to discretionary excusals and deferrals, Sch 33, para 12 inserts a new s 9AA requiring the Lord Chancellor to lay before Parliament and to publish guidance as to the manner in which the appropriate officer of the Crown Court will exercise his power to defer or excuse persons seeking such deferral or excusal from jury service— see the Practice Direction [2002] 1 WLR 2870, para 42 for guidance issued under the old law.

The overall result of the changes wrought by s 321 and Sch 33 is a considerable narrowing of the exemptions from jury service and a potential broadening of the pool of persons who will actually make up juries. Clergymen, judges, lawyers, police officers, prison and probation officers, doctors and dentists, MPs and peers are amongst those who will no longer be ineligible or able to claim excusal as of right. It remains to be seen how many of them will wish to or be able to successfully seek discretionary excusal and the 'appropriate officer' of the Crown Court may be in for a busy time.

Recent research published on the Home Office website on 26 January 2004, 'Jurors' perceptions, understanding, confidence and satisfaction in the jury system: a study in six courts', found that:

The majority of respondents had a more positive view of the jury trial system after completing their service than they did before. Confidence in the jury system was closely associated with the perceived fairness of the process, adherence to due process, respect for the rights of defendants and above all the diversity of the jury and its ability to consider evidence from different perspectives.

Provided that discretionary excusal is not too widely sought or given, the changes to jury service are capable of further strengthening the credibility of the jury system at a time when it has only recently survived a number of attempts to curtail or reduce its role. Fittingly, some of those who have most vociferously come to its defence, including members of the House of Lords, will now become eligible to serve as jurors and can help to maintain its vitality and credibility.

5

ALLOCATION AND TRANSFER OF EITHER WAY CASES AND LIVE LINKS

5.1 INTRODUCTION

Section 41 and Schedule 3 of the Criminal Justice Act 2003 (CJA 2003) significantly change the initial stages of criminal proceedings for offences triable either way and the nature of mode of trial proceedings and plea before venue. For those either way offences which continue to go to the Crown Court for trial, it adopts the procedure introduced in s 51 of the Crime and Disorder Act 1998 for offences triable only on indictment whereby such offences are sent straight to the Crown Court without any need for committal proceedings. Committal proceedings for triable either way offences were retained in the Crime and Disorder Act 1998 but CJA 2003 now effectively abolishes committal proceedings for all offences as once the decision has been made that the case is suitable for trial in the Crown Court (or the defendant has decided to elect for such trial) the case will be sent to the Crown Court without further ado. Furthermore, committals for sentence to the Crown Court following summary trial will also virtually disappear (subject to very limited exceptions) as the general principle will be that magistrates will know of the defendant's record when they decide on whether to accept jurisdiction and so there will be normally be no justification for trying the accused summarily and then deciding that their sentencing powers are insufficient. Coupled with the fact that their sentencing powers are being increased to 12 months (for the time being) for an individual offence and together with a new power to give an indication of sentence to the defendant, this should result in magistrates being able to retain a larger proportion of cases with correspondingly fewer cases going to the Crown Court for trial (or for sentence). These changes are effected by amendments made by Sch 3 to a number of Acts, principally the Magistrates' Courts Act 1980 (MCA 1980), the Crime and Disorder Act 1998 (CDA 1998) and the Powers of Criminal Courts (Sentencing) Act 2000 (PCC(S)A 2000).

Note should also be taken here of s 320 of the 2003 Act which makes the offence of outraging public decency triable either way whereas previously it was triable only on indictment. This chapter will also deal with ss 51–56 of the Act which provide a more general power to direct evidence to be given via a live link.

5.2 BACKGROUND

The initial stages of criminal proceedings for indictable offences and the mechanisms for deciding which cases should actually be tried on indictment and which could, despite their indictable status, be tried summarily have seen a large number of changes in the past forty years. At the start of the period there was a very complicated fivefold division of offences each of which had different rules about how the case could or should be tried, and in virtually all cases where a case went for trial before a jury, full committal proceedings were held at which the prosecution evidence was given in full for the first time. The period since then has been one of rationalization and change following a number of major reports (some of which of course went well beyond the questions being discussed here) including the James Committee in 1975, the Runciman Royal Commission in 1993, the Narey Report in 1997 and most recently the Auld Report. Two main issues have been central concerns almost throughout the period and have driven the changes:

(a) the need to make the system more efficient and to avoid unnecessary delays;
(b) the need to stop too many inappropriate cases going to the Crown Court for trial and taking up unnecessary time and resources there.

Inappropriate here has meant at various times that at one extreme, the cases going to the Crown Court are too weak and should have been weeded out earlier, alternatively that they are too trivial and therefore inappropriate on that ground, or, at the other extreme, inappropriate because they are clear-cut and the defendant should have pleaded guilty at an earlier stage rather than delaying the guilty plea to the start of proceedings in the Crown Court. It is the latter problem that has come to dominate in recent years as the role of committal proceedings as a means of filtering weak cases has become less and less significant as the Crown Prosecution Service has been entrusted with the task of ensuring that weak cases do not get through and the Crown Court itself has become more proactively involved in pre-trial scrutiny and management. The process of erosion of committal proceedings has been a gradual but steady one since the introduction of paper committals in 1967, the advent of the Notice of Transfer procedure for serious or complex fraud in 1987 and for certain child-related cases in 1991 and, most recently, the enactment of the automatic sending provisions for indictable only offences in 1998. The process of removing reliance on committal proceedings has not been without its setbacks such as the ill-fated transfer for trial provisions in the Criminal Justice and Public Order Act 1994 which were never brought into force and indeed were repealed in the Criminal Procedure and Investigations Act 1996 (CPIA 1996), but the abolition of committal proceedings in the 2003 Act can be seen as the end of a process of gradually finding other more effective ways of preventing weak cases coming to trial in the Crown Court.

However, the issue about preventing cases which are not appropriate (either in terms of arguable seriousness or to which the accused eventually pleads guilty), clogging up the Crown Court trial lists has become more and more of a political hot potato. The James Committee back in 1975 simplified the categories of offences into the familiar threefold division of indictable only, either way, and summary which is currently to be found in the MCA 1980 and in so doing shifted the boundaries slightly and moved some offences from indictable only to either way and some from either way to summary. It also considered removing the right of the accused to claim and insist on jury trial in the middle category and to make the decision one for the magistrates but rejected this option because of the complexities and controversy that they very presciently thought it would create. The Runciman Commission however recommended that the accused should not be able to insist on jury trial:

Under our proposed scheme the defendant would have the right to urge any considerations supporting jury trial that he or she wished. If the CPS were persuaded, that would be the end of the matter. If the CPS wished nevertheless to propose summary trial, it would be for the bench to weigh up all the factors and determine the mode of trial. (Ch 6, para 18)

This again proved too controversial as had earlier suggestions, for example that theft below a certain amount should not attract a right to jury trial for that offence. The suggestion that magistrates, if the decision was for them, should take into account the effect of the offences on the defendant's reputation led to criticisms that this would lead to two-tier justice—jury trial for the respectable with no previous convictions and summary justice for the poor and disadvantaged. The CPIA 1996 therefore eschewed, for the time being, the removal of the defendant's option and focused instead on discouraging the defendant from initially claiming jury trial in cases where ultimately he was going to plead guilty anyway. It did so by introducing the plea before venue procedure (inserted in MCA 1980, s17A et seq) whereby the defendant is given an opportunity to indicate his likely plea before venue is considered (and to get the benefit of a greater sentence discount for doing so). If he takes up this opportunity he can then be convicted in the magistrates' court without ever troubling the Crown Court (he cannot claim jury trial if he does not intend there to be a trial at all) whereas if he intends to plead not guilty, his right to Crown Court trial is retained should he wish to exercise it. If the defendant indicated a guilty plea and the magistrates felt that their powers of sentencing were adequate (taking into account also the guilty plea discount), the sentence could also be dealt with in the magistrates' court. The plea before venue procedure has helped to reduce the number of cases going unnecessarily to the Crown Court (35,000 estimate in Runciman nearly halved to 18,500 per annum in Auld) although its biggest weakness has perhaps been that the defendant is not going to offer an early plea if he thinks he may still be sent to the Crown Court for a (potentially heavy) sentence.

Even before the plea before venue reform had been given chance to work, the then Conservative government started canvassing further restrictions on the defendant's right of election in either way cases. The Narey Review into delays followed and amongst its recommendations was a firm proposal to give the decision solely to the magistrates (albeit having heard representations from both sides). The recommendation was taken up by the government (a Labour one this time despite having been unenthusiastic about the idea in opposition). Ill-fated Mode of Trial Bills were introduced in successive years in 1999 and 2000, each of which failed in the face of stiff opposition in the House of Lords on the grounds that the proposals were an unwarranted attack on jury trial and that they were also potentially discriminatory in application.

Although Auld followed Runciman and Narey in recommending removing the defendant's right of election, the government shied away from this (for the time being at least) in the light of the opposition which it knew it would encounter. In the absence of a realistic prospect of curbing the right of election, the government has therefore returned to the plea before venue procedure and the thinking behind its introduction in 1996 and in doing so has also adopted some of the other proposals of Auld (Ch 5, para 172), ie that:

the procedure of committal of 'either-way' cases to the Crown Court for trial should be abolished and, . . . such cases should be 'sent' to the Crown Court in the same way as indictable-only cases; and . . . the procedure of committal for sentence should be abolished.

The consequent changes in the 2003 Act therefore seek to increase the incentives for the defendant to indicate an early plea and to accept the jurisdiction of the magistrates by removing the threat (in most cases) of being committed thereafter for sentence. They also increase the ability of the magistrates to accept jurisdiction by increasing their own powers of sentencing and giving them better information about the antecedents of the defendant. Further encouragement to the defendant to indicate an early plea (or at least to enable the defendant to make an informed decision) is provided by enabling magistrates to give an indication of whether any sentence is likely to be custodial or not. The changes also attempt to speed up the sending to the Crown Court of cases where the defendant does claim jury trial (or where the magistrates decline jurisdiction) by abolishing committal proceedings and in so far as they reduce any delay in cases going to the Crown Court, they also remove or reduce one of the reasons that defendants sometimes are said to elect for jury trial: the desire to postpone the date of their trial.

5.3 THE SCHEDULE 3 AMENDMENTS

Schedule 3 is in two parts. The principal amendments are in Part 1 whilst Part 2 contains minor and consequential amendments. The amendments are extremely complicated and are almost impossible to explain fully without setting out all the details of the initial stages of criminal proceedings and the various statutory provisions associated with them. The discussion below attempts to explain the principal features of the main amendments and how they effect the changes already discussed above.

5.3.1 Mode of Trial—The Allocation Decision

Although the Schedule starts with some relatively minor amendments to the plea before venue provisions (in MCA 1980, s 17A to which is also added new ss 17D and 17E) it makes more sense to start with the principal changes effected to mode of trial determination by new ss 19 to 21 of MCA 1980 which are substituted by paras 5–9 of Sch 3 of the 2003 Act.

The new MCA 1980, s 19 (now headed 'Decision as to Allocation') contains in - sub-s (2)(a), a new requirement to give the prosecution an opportunity to inform the court of the accused's previous convictions (if any). Previous convictions are defined in sub-s (5) and include any conviction by a court anywhere in the United Kingdom. Under sub-s (3), in making the allocation decision, the Court has to consider (a) the adequacy of the sentence it could impose and (b) any representations by the prosecution or accused. Gone are the other factors specifically mentioned in the old sub-s (3) (nature of case and circumstances making it of a serious character and other circumstances). Instead, however, the new sub-s (3) goes on to require the court to have regard to any allocation guidelines issued as definitive guidelines under s170 of the 2003 Act by the Sentencing Guidelines Council (see Chapter 11 below for further information about the Council). The question of the adequacy of the magistrates' sentencing powers and sentencing considerations are thereby much more clearly prominent in the new section and the thrust of the provisions seems to be very much that if the magistrates consider their own sentencing powers to be adequate (taking into account the information provided about previous convictions and the allocation guidelines) they will normally decide the case is suitable for summary trial (subject to the accused's right to claim jury trial).

The former sub-ss (4) and (5) of MCA 1980, s19, dealing with cases carried on by the Attorney-General, Solicitor-General or DPP, where the court was formerly required to move straight to committal proceedings, have disappeared, no doubt partly because of the abolition of committal proceedings (see CJA 2003, Sch 3, Pt 2, para 51(3)).

However, the new s 19(6) provides for an analogous (but different) by-passing of the allocation decision in cases subject to what used to be the notice of transfer procedure (serious or complex fraud or certain cases involving children) which are now to be 'sent' straight to the Crown Court under new ss 51B and 51C of the CDA 1998 (see CJA 2003, Sch 3, para 18).

The new s 20 MCA 1980 deals, as before, with what is to happen if the magistrates' court decides that the case is indeed suitable for summary trial. Subsection (1) is unchanged and the old sub-ss (2)(a) and (2)(b) are effectively subsumed into the new sub-s (2)(a) whereby the court explains to the accused his basic options. The major difference comes in the new sub-s (2)(c) which replaces the former explanation required in old sub-s (2)(b) about the possibility of being committed for sentence to the Crown Court even if he consents to summary trial. The important thing about s 20(2)(c) is that it no longer includes a requirement to warn the accused about the general power to commit for sentence following conviction on summary trial because that general power no longer exists. Unfortunately, in many cases it cannot be presented to the accused quite as simply as this since sub-s (2)(c) does still refer to an exceptional power to commit for sentence. Under the new sub-s (2)(c) the only surviving possibility of committal for sentence following summary trial which still needs to be explained to the accused is in relation to a 'specified' offence within s 224 of CJA 2003, ie an offence listed in Sch 15 relating to the provisions dealing with dangerous offenders (see Chapter 14 below).

The list of offences in Sch 15 is quite long but many of them are indictable only so no question of committal for sentence following summary trial can arise as they will be sent straight to the Crown Court. Quite apart from this, even as regards either way offences to which it can apply, the retained power to commit for sentence following summary trial is to be found in a new s 3A of PCC(S)A 2000 and requires in effect either that the specified offence is a 'serious' one (ie punishable by a least ten years in prison: see s 224(2) and 225(1) of CJA 2003) or that the conditions in s 227(1) are satisfied (significant risk to the public of serious harm from commission of further specified offences by offender). In the House of Commons Standing Committee there was considerable anxiety about the retention of this power still to commit to the Crown Court for sentence which undermines the whole point of allowing the magistrates to be told about the previous convictions of the accused. The government was unwilling to take out the exceptional power still to commit to the Crown Court which it felt might still be required to protect the public in exceptional cases where information about the dangerousness of the accused emerged after the summary trial (eg in a pre-sentence report), and the power (and the duty to warn the accused about it) was therefore retained. It will only be in exceptional cases that it will be needed or exercised but it will be interesting to see how the mere fact of giving a warning about it affects decisions of accused persons to accept summary trial. MCA 1980, s 20(2)(c) only appears to require the warning to be given in relation to those cases where it is at all remotely possible to be applicable, ie 'specified' but triable either way offences which is not a simple list to compile from the long list of specified offences in Sch 15 but it includes, for example, ss 20 and 47 of the Offences Against the Persons Act 1861 (OAPA 1861), and burglary with intent to do unlawful damage.

5.3.2 Indication of Sentence

After the court has explained to the accused his options (including the remote possibility of committal for sentence where appropriate), s 20(4) now enables the accused to ask for an 'indication of sentence', ie an indication of whether a custodial or non-custodial sentence would be likely to be imposed 'if he were to be tried summarily and to plead guilty'. The court may, but does not have to, give such an indication despite attempts during the passage of the Bill to make it compulsory for an indication to be given. The indication is merely as to whether custodial or non-custodial, ie whether or not custodial, not an indication as to length of custody or as to type of non-custodial sentence. If the court does give an indication of custodial or non-custodial, the accused can reconsider any indication of plea already given under the plea before venue procedure (ie can change an indication of not guilty plea to a guilty plea). If the accused changes his plea to guilty he is treated under s 20(7) as though he had pleaded guilty. Under sub-s (8), if no request for indication of sentence is made or granted, and the accused's previous indication of a not guilty plea remains unchanged (to summarize a masterfully convoluted subsection), under sub-s (9) the court must ask him whether he wishes to be tried summarily or on indictment. In the former case, it shall proceed to summary trial and in the latter it shall send him forthwith to the Crown Court under s 51(1) CDA 1998 (as amended). Section 21 MCA 1980 is amended so that once the court has decided that the case is more suitable for trial on indictment, the reference to proceedings as examining justices is replaced by proceeding in accordance with s 51(1) CDA 1998.

If after an indication of sentence under the previous paragraph the accused changes his indication of plea to guilty under MCA 1980, s 20(7), a new MCA 1980, s 20A prevents a custodial sentence being given by any court unless such a sentence had been indicated. This is by s 20A(2) subject only to the power to commit for sentence for dangerous offenders in PCC(S)A 2000, s 3A or as a result of the power to commit for sentence under PCC(S)A 2000, s 4. If, on the other hand, the accused does not change his plea to guilty following an indication of plea, the indication of sentence is not binding on any court (MCA 1980, s 20A(3))—the bargain, in other words, is off.

5.3.3 Crime and Disorder Act Amendments

Paragraphs 15–20 of Sch 3 bring together all the various provisions relating to transfer of cases from the magistrates' court to the Crown Court by amending and inserting new sections into ss 50–52 of CDA 1998.

A new s 51 is substituted into CDA 1998 by para 18 so that it applies to either way cases allocated for trial on indictment as it does to indictable only offences. A new s 51A is inserted dealing with cases where a defendant under 18 may be sent to the Crown Court for trial and new ss 51B and 51C cover the notice of transfer provisions previously to be found in CJA 1987, s 4 (serious fraud cases) and CJA 1991, s 53 (child witness cases).

Paragraph 17 creates a new s 50A which sets out the order in which a magistrates' court is to apply various procedures in respect of an either way offence (the relevant offence). Essentially this provides for the following order to be adopted:

(a) Under s 50A(2), where there is a notice of transfer for the offence under s 51B or 51C, it is sent to the Crown Court forthwith.

(b) Under s 50A(3)(a), where the defendant or someone charged jointly already has been or is being sent to the Crown Court for some *other offence* (being an indictable only offence or one sent to the Crown Court under a notice of transfer).

In this case the magistrates' court will consider the relevant either way offence under s 51(3) to (6) and will (in some instances mandatorily, in some as a result of discretion, see, for example s 51(4)) *either* send it to the Crown Court under those provisions by virtue of its relationship with that other offence *or*, if not, will proceed under ss17A to 23 of MCA 1980, ie to consider plea before venue and mode of trial. Of course the upshot may be that the offence is still sent to the Crown Court in its own right if the offence is not suitable for summary trial or if the defendant refuses to consent to summary trial.

(c) Under s 50A(3)(b), 'in all other cases' (ie where the magistrates are not actually required to send the relevant offence to the Crown Court because of a notice of transfer or have not been required or decided to do so because of its relationship with another offence already sent), the court shall first proceed under MCA 1980, s 17A, ie consider plea before venue. If there is an indication of guilty plea, then the court proceeds to summary trial as on a guilty plea. If there is not an indication of a guilty plea, the court then proceeds to consider the either way offence under ss 51 and 51A and, if the defendant does not consent to be tried summarily or the magistrates do not consider summary trial to be suitable, will send the case to the Crown Court.

5.3.4 Miscellaneous Amendments

By virtue of paras 3 and 4 of Sch 3 the plea before venue and allocation procedures may take place at a hearing before a single justice who may also take a guilty plea, but a single justice cannot impose a sentence on the offender or conduct a contested trial. Paragraph 3 also continues the limitation (under MCA 1980, s 33(1)(a)) on the sentence that may be imposed (limited to 3 months or £2,500 fine) where a person pleads guilty to a low-value scheduled offence (of criminal damage).

To avoid cases involving young defendants being sent to the Crown Court unnecessarily, including where the young defendant is charged jointly with an adult offender but the young defendant may be willing to plead guilty, Sch 3, para 10 adds four new ss (24A–24D) to the Magistrates' Courts Act 1980 which apply a procedure analogous to the plea before venue procedure to defendants who are under 18.

The former power under MCA 1980, s 25 to switch between summary trial and committal proceedings (and vice versa) is abolished by Sch 3, para 11 and instead a new power is provided in an amended s 25 for the prosecution to apply for an either way case which has been allocated for summary trial to be sent to the Crown Court to be tried on indictment. Unlike the old provision, the new s 25 only applies to applications by the prosecution, not the defence, and furthermore, under new s 25(2A), such an application must be made before the summary trial begins. That the real purpose of the new provision is to deal with cases where the prosecution become aware of information making the offence more serious than was first realized is evident from new s 25(2B) which states that the application can only be granted if the court is satisfied that 'the sentence which a magistrates' court would have power to impose for the offence would be inadequate'.

Where a defendant pleads guilty to one either way offence at plea before venue but is sent to the Crown Court to be tried for other related either way offences, there is still a power in s 4 of the Powers of Criminal Courts (Sentencing) Act 2000 (as amended in Sch 3, para 24) to commit for sentence for the offence to which he has pleaded guilty.

Section 42 of the 2003 Act (which by SI 2004/81 came into force on 22 January 2004), makes specific transitory arrangements by means of amendments to MCA 1980, s 24 to ensure that defendants under 18 will be sent to the Crown Court for trial (in the same way as homicide cases would previously be sent) where they have committed certain firearms offences (and were aged 16 or over at the time). These transitory arrangements will become redundant once the new allocation and sending procedure for all offences is introduced (see new s 51A(12) to CDA 1980).

5.4 LIVE LINKS

The giving of evidence by video link was initially introduced by CJA 1988 for child witnesses in prosecutions for sexual offences and offences of violence and cruelty, and the current provision are to be found in s 24 of the Youth Justice and Criminal Evidence Act 1999 as one of the 'special measures' available to vulnerable witnesses to protect them from the ordeal of giving evidence in open court. The main purpose behind ss 51 to 56 of the 2003 Act are quite different. They appear to derive from chapter 11 of the Auld Report (para 148) and the discussion therein of expert witnesses:

Other facilities of modern technology that are already well established are video-conferencing and the giving of evidence by video-link or, increasingly, via the internet. As they become more widely available, these new techniques should be used wherever possible for instructing and conferring with experts. And the law should be developed and facilities provided nationally to enable experts in appropriate cases to give evidence via one or other of these technologies at locations remote from the court and more convenient to them, for example, where their evidence is self-contained and does not turn on possible developments in other evidence in the course of the trial. Expert witnesses are particularly exposed to the vagaries of our listing system, which result in them committing themselves to court fixtures that are cancelled or delayed at the last moment, or which require them to spend much wasted time waiting around at court to give evidence. Anything that can be done, by more efficient preparation of cases for trial, greater use of fixed listing dates and by shorter or alternative ways of giving evidence will make for better use of busy professionals' time and a more respectable trial process.

Section 51 is not limited to expert witnesses but applies to any witness 'other than the defendant' and the criterion for giving a direction under the section is not the vulnerability of the witness but whether, under s 51(4)(a) 'the court is satisfied that it is in the interests of the *efficient or effective administration of justice* for the person concerned to give evidence in the proceedings through a live link' (emphasis added).

Attempts to introduce an express interests of justice test were resisted at the Lords Committee Stage by reference to what is now s 51(6) requiring the court to consider all the circumstances of the case in deciding whether to give a direction. Subsection (7) gives a non-exhaustive list of relevant circumstances, including '(d) the views of the witness' which perhaps might be thought to betray the expert witness origins of the proposal but is not necessarily that closely related to the interests of justice which is perhaps more directly reflected in (f): 'whether a direction might tend to inhibit any party to the proceedings from effectively testing the witness's evidence'.

Under s 51(2) a direction can be given in relation to quite a wide range of criminal proceedings, including both trials on indictment and summary trials (and also appeals therefrom and hearings following a guilty plea). Live link facilities are not yet available in all magistrates' courts so s 53 provides for magistrates' courts to be able to sit for the whole or part of its proceedings in a place appointed for such purposes where such facilities are available (even if this is outside its own petty sessions area).

The government was keen to emphasize the normality of giving evidence via video link. Under s 51(8), 'the court must state in open court its reasons for refusing an application for a direction under this section . . . '. Baroness Scotland said (Hansard, HL col 839 (15 July 2003)) that this requirement 'will focus the court's mind on whether any reasons put forward for refusing to use live links are sufficient for the direction not to be granted and therefore should encourage courts to make use of live link directions where they are appropriate'. Furthermore, under s 54, where the trial is one on indictment before a jury, the judge may give 'such direction as he thinks necessary to ensure that the jury gives the same weight to the evidence as if it had been given by the witness in the courtroom or other place where the proceedings are held'. This was explained by Baroness Scotland (Hansard, HL col 845 (15 July 2003)) as necessary because:

. . . there is no reason why evidence given through a live link may not be accorded the same weight as evidence given in court. The clause does not oblige the court to give any direction; the judge will do so only if he or she considers it necessary. The judge may decide because of the way in which the trial has proceeded that it might be helpful to reiterate or re-emphasize that the evidence should be treated absolutely the same. However, the clause is a useful guide as to the weight that should be accorded to evidence over live link.

The different purposes behind the current provisions as compared with those for vulnerable witnesses can be seen by contrasting the relevant definitions of 'live link'. Section 56(2) of CJA 2003 Act provides:

'live link' means a live television link or other arrangement by which a witness, while at a place in the United Kingdom *which is outside the building where the proceedings are being held*, is able to see and hear a person at the place where the proceedings are being held and to be seen and heard by . . .

whereas s 24(8) of the Youth Justice and Criminal Evidence Act 1999 defines live link to mean:

a live television link or other arrangement whereby a witness, *while absent from the courtroom or other place where the proceedings are being held*, is able to see and hear a person there and to be seen and heard by the persons specified in s 23(2)(a) to (c). (emphasis added in both instances)

Generally, for vulnerable witnesses, the live link will be to a room elsewhere in the same building, the important thing being that the witness is not exposed to the ordeal of the courtroom, whereas for the 2003 Act provisions, the whole point is that the witness is not readily available in the location of the courtroom and he or she will normally be many miles away. Indeed it is a requirement that the witness is outside the building since, if he or she is present at it, there is no justification for not giving evidence in the courtroom (unless the witness comes within the special measures provisions of the 1999 Act). Under s 52(2), once a direction has been given for a witness to give evidence via a live link, 'the person concerned may not give evidence in those proceedings . . . otherwise than through a live link', but the section does go on to give power for a direction to be rescinded either of the court's own motion or 'on an application by a party to the proceedings', but in the latter case, only if 'there has been a material change of circumstances since the direction was given' (s 52(6)).

The live links provisions are expected to be phased in as from April 2005.

6

PROSECUTION APPEALS AGAINST JUDGES' RULINGS

6.1 INTRODUCTION

The prosecution has very limited rights of appeal in relation to trials on indictment and even the broader general right of appeal by way of case stated in relation to summary trial is limited to errors of law or excess of jurisdiction. Prosecution rights of appeal in relation to trials on indictment have been recognized in recent times:

(a) in relation to rulings in *preparatory hearings* in serious fraud cases (CJA 1987 s 9) or long and complex cases (CPIA 1996, ss 35 and 36), and

(b) in effect by means of the procedure created in CJA 1988, ss 35 and 36 whereby the Attorney-General can refer to the Court of Appeal unduly lenient *sentences* in relation to offences triable only on indictment and certain other specified offences.

This latter procedure can and does affect the sentence served by the offender in contrast to the Attorney-General reference on points of law procedure instituted in CJA 1972, s 36 which has no effect on the acquitted person.

Part 9 of CJA 2003 now provides in s 58 a much wider basis for prosecution appeals (with leave) against judges' rulings in relation to *all* trials on indictment and at any stage 'whether before or after the commencement of the trial', prior to the start of the judge's summing up. The most significant limitation (apart for the requirement of leave) on this very wide right of appeal is that the prosecution have to accept that if the appeal is unsuccessful (either because the ruling is confirmed on appeal or leave is refused or the appeal is abandoned) then the accused will be acquitted of the relevant offence (see ss 58(12) and 61(3)).

Section 62 provides a separate right of appeal against 'evidentiary rulings' which is more limited in that it applies only to 'qualifying offences' specified in Sch 4, Pt 1 of the Act and applies only to rulings prior to the opening of the case for the defence. It is of wider utility, however, in the sense that an unsuccessful appeal does not automatically lead to the acquittal of the accused and indeed can only do so if the prosecution indicates that it does not intend to proceed with the prosecution (s 66(3)).

6.2 BACKGROUND

In the Tom Sargant Memorial Lecture, 29 November 1999, the Attorney-General rehearsed some of the arguments for reviewing the question of prosecution rights of appeal.

My concern is simply this: that there is an imbalance in the system. If a judge decides to stay a prosecution on the ground of abuse of process, or to direct the jury to acquit a defendant, or to make a ruling concerning the admissibility of evidence which has the effect of depriving the prosecution of a crucial plank in its case—ought not the prosecution to be able to test that decision on appeal? If it cannot, are we not allowing in fact a system in which judges are unaccountable to the appeal courts as to a crucial aspect of their responsibilities, at the very time that we are providing them with greater powers through the implementation of the Human Rights Act?

I recognise that there are a large number of issues involved in this suggestion. We must not over correct the imbalance, so that the defence are left at a disadvantage. We must not introduce unnecessary delay into the system. If new rights are given to the prosecution, we must take care to ensure that they are not greater than those available to the defence. There is a case for considering some filter in the system, for instance ensuring that no appeal is brought without the consent of the DPP or the Law Officers. Practical and resource issues would need to be addressed. But I strongly suspect that the mere existence of a prosecution right of appeal, even if only sparingly used, could lead to a significant and beneficial change in the culture of practice in the criminal courts.

In January 2000 the Law Commission agreed to start work on the question and, in May 2000, the Home Secretary formally asked it to undertake a review of the law governing prosecution appeals against judge-directed acquittals in criminal proceedings and other adverse rulings by a judge which may lead to the premature ending of the trial.

The terms of reference given were:

To consider

(1) whether any, and if so what, additional rights of appeal or other remedies should be available to the prosecution from adverse rulings of judge in a trial on indictment which

the prosecution may wish to overturn and which may result, or may have resulted, whether directly or indirectly, in premature termination of the trial;

(2) to what, if any, procedural restrictions such appeals would be subject; and to make recommendations.

The Law Commission's Consultation Paper (No 158) was published in July 2000 provisionally proposing that the prosecution should be given a right of appeal against rulings, made before the trial or during it up to the close of the prosecution case, which bring the proceedings to an end ('terminating rulings'). Their notion of terminating rulings included not only those that of their nature automatically terminate the prosecution (eg a stay on the grounds of abuse of process) but also those which do so because of consequent election by the prosecution to offer no further evidence so that the judge orders or directs a verdict of not guilty (eg where crucial evidence has been ruled to be non-admissible).

In its final report, *Double Jeopardy and Prosecution Appeals* (Law Com No 267), the Law Commission noted a broad range of support for the general thrust of its proposals and confirmed its recommendation about terminating rulings and slightly extended it so as to go just beyond the close of the prosecution case and to include appeals against rulings of no case to answer, at least where these were based on the first limb of *R v Galbraith* [1981] 1 WLR 1039 (ie on the basis that the Crown has not adduced any evidence of one or more elements of the offence—a ruling on a point of law) as distinct from the second limb (namely that the evidence adduced is such that a jury could not properly convict on it—a ruling based on the court's view of the evidence).

The Law Commission recommended that the new rights of appeal against acquittal be limited to the more serious cases, ie those same offences in respect of which the Attorney-General has a power to refer the sentence to the Court of Appeal if it appears to him to be unduly lenient.

The Law Commission did not think that there should be any new rights of appeal against what it called non-terminating rulings (as opposed to such rights of appeal as already exist within the preparatory hearing regimes where the rights of appeal do not distinguish between terminating and non-terminating rulings). The result envisaged would be that rulings in pre-trial hearings (which unlike preparatory hearings are not part of the trial itself) would become appealable for the first time, but only if they were terminating rulings, and so too would terminating rulings during the course of the trial itself (whether one following on from a pre-trial hearing or a preparatory hearing) but only rulings up to and including a no case to answer ruling would be appealable. As far as preparatory hearings themselves are concerned, although these already had, in one sense, broader rights of appeal than what was being proposed, in that rulings could be appealed whether or not they were terminating, the problem was that the legislation has been interpreted to mean that only rulings which were made for the very purposes for which the preparatory hearing was itself held could be appealed. This limitation has been starkly illustrated recently by the case of *R v Hoogstraten* [2003] EWCA Crim 3642 where the Court of Appeal held that it could not entertain an appeal against the trial judge's ruling, at a preparatory hearing, accepting an application from the defence that the case against the defendant for manslaughter should not proceed to trial, because even if the prosecution proved their facts, the jury would not in law be able to convict the defendant of manslaughter. The ruling was not for the 'purposes' of the preparatory hearing since the application was designed to (and did) prevent the case going to trial rather being to clarify the issues at a trial which was to take place. The Court found itself reluctantly having to come to this conclusion because of earlier authorities under the serious fraud regime under CJA 1987. The irony is that this means that the rulings which are appealable under the preparatory hearing regime tend to be non-terminating rulings or at least do not include those which automatically terminate the trial. In the light of this, the Law Commission recommended that the preparatory hearing regime, in both fraud and non-fraud cases, should be extended to include rulings on potentially terminating matters such as severance, joinder of counts, or defendants' applications to quash the indictment or stay the proceedings on the grounds of abuse of process. As will be seen, the 2003 Act now effectively provides a right of appeal against such rulings independently of the preparatory hearing rights of appeal (although as to questions relating to joinder and severance, s 309 of the 2003 Act now in any event includes those as within the purposes of a preparatory hearing in the classes of case where such hearing can be held. Furthermore, s 309 widens the classes of case in which such a hearing can be held by adding seriousness as a third alternative criterion alongside complexity and length within s 29 CPIA 1996).

More generally, it should be noted that the Law Commission's approach, in relation to prosecution appeals generally, assumes that the appealable ruling, being a terminating one, has actually resulted in an acquittal or termination of the prosecution and that therefore ultimately the issue before the Court of Appeal would be, if it considered the ruling to be wrong, whether to order a retrial. As will be seen, under the 2003 Act this is only one of the alternatives, the other being the resumption of the original trial. In other words, the Law Commission did not really see its new rights of appeal as being in effect interlocutory or as suspending the original trial or the effect of the ruling appealed against (as it will be seen to be how the new Act operates) but rather saw them as appeals against actual acquittals leading potentially to retrials.

The Auld Report in October 2001 accepted the Law Commission's recommendations, and the White Paper *Justice for All*, in para 4.68, also went along with the Law Commission's proposals save that it dropped their restrictions in terms of the range of the offences in respect of which the right of appeal would be adopted and proposed that it should apply to all cases in the Crown Court.

6.3 THE PROVISIONS OF THE ACT

The Bill as introduced into the House of Commons reflected the White Paper approach in that whilst it applied to the whole range of offences tried on indictment, it in effect only applied to terminating rulings as understood by the Law Commission. Curiously, it did so by making provision both for 'terminating' rulings and 'other' rulings but defined terminating rulings more narrowly than the Law Commission as those that 'without any further action by the prosecution' will result in termination of the offence. However, 'other' rulings were limited to those where the prosecution agrees that an unsuccessful appeal against the ruling should result in the acquittal of the defendant. The net effect was thus similar to the Law Commission's understanding of 'terminating rulings' which included rulings which automatically terminate the proceedings and also those which cause the prosecution to concede that if the ruling is correct, there is no point carrying on.

The Bill also followed the Law Commission in including rulings that there is no case to answer amongst those that can be appealed but went further in extending this to both branches of the *Galbraith* Rule (see above). The Bill also differed from the Law Commission in a more fundamental respect in that it expressly provided for a terminating ruling to be suspended and to have no effect for the period during which the prosecution can appeal or during any such appeal. It thus gave the appeal more of an overtly interlocutory flavour and consequently also provided for expedited and non-expedited appeals and these are features which are to be found in the provisions as ultimately enacted and will be discussed in more detail later.

However, the structure of the provisions as they appeared in the initial version of the Bill, and indeed as they appeared in later versions, was significantly changed when the Bill reached its later stages in the Lords. The relevant amendments were initially introduced at House of Lords Report stage and ultimately agreed to at the 3rd reading.

These amendments replaced the two categories of rulings in the original version of the Bill ('terminating' rulings and 'other' rulings) with a general right of appeal in relation to 'rulings'. Although these rulings are no longer described as 'terminating' they are in effect limited to 'terminating rulings' in the wider sense used by the Law Commission in that the prosecution have to accept that if they appeal unsuccessfully, the result will be the acquittal of the defendant (see now ss 58(9) and 61(3)).

Having conflated automatically terminating rulings and 'other' rulings which result in termination into a single category in what is now s 58 (and which also now goes right up to any stage prior to the start of summing up to the jury), a new second category of evidentiary rulings (which are not terminating in any sense) is created against which the prosecution may appeal. Whilst not 'terminating', these rulings must 'significantly weaken the prosecution case' and must relate to one of the offences listed in Sch 4, Pt 1 and they must be made before the opening of the defence case.

Lord Goldsmith for the government concluded his explanation of the evidentiary rulings provisions as follows:

Finally—this matter arises from detailed discussions with the senior judiciary in the Court of Appeal—the evidentiary appeal regime will be implemented later than, and separately from, the terminating rulings appeals. That will give an opportunity to see how the terminating appeal works in practice and give us advance warning of any unexpected resource implications of the evidentiary regime. (Lord Goldsmith, Hansard, HL col 1787 (17 November 2003) (3rd Reading))

At the same time that these changes were made to the structure of the prosecution appeals provision, the government took the opportunity to clarify, in what has now become s 67 of the Act, what tests the Court of Appeal would apply in determining such appeals that come before them. This was in response to concerns expressed that the prosecution appeals would provide a routine opportunity for the prosecution to try to get an appeal court to reverse the discretion exercised by the trial judge. Section 67 limits the power to reverse any ruling under Part 9 to where the ruling was wrong in law or involved an error of law or principle or was one which was not reasonable for the judge to have made. Whilst this is perhaps not quite as restrictive as judicial review grounds, it certainly makes it clear that the Court of Appeal should not reverse a decision simply because it would have come to a different decision itself.

Having outlined the main structure of the rights of appeal in the Act and how they evolved in the way that they did, we can now examine each of the rights in a little more detail.

6.4 GENERAL RIGHT OF APPEAL IN RESPECT OF RULINGS—S 58

As has already been mentioned, this is wide enough to cover both rulings which of their very nature terminated the proceedings, eg stay for abuse of the process or ruling of no case to answer, and those which do not do so of themselves but may mean the prosecution feel it is pointless or hopeless to carry on (eg a ruling about the inadmissibility of an essential piece of evidence).

6.4.1 Timing

Section 58(1) makes the section applicable to a 'ruling in relation to a trial on indictment', ie any trial, 'at an applicable time' relating to 'one or more offences included in the indictment'. By s 58(13) applicable time means 'any time (whether before or after the commencement of the trial) before the start of the judge's summing-up to the jury'. The words in brackets mean that it applies to rulings in pre-trial hearings as well as to rulings in preparatory hearings as much as to rulings during the course of the trial proper. A curiosity which may give rise to difficulties in relation to preparatory hearings arises from the fact that there are already certain rights of appeal in relation to preparatory hearings as discussed above. Section 57(2) of the 2003 Act provides that there is 'no right of appeal under this Part in respect of . . . a ruling from which an appeal lies to the Court of Appeal by virtue of any other enactment'. This would seem to mean that in order to determine whether the 2003 Act procedure applies in relation to a ruling in a preparatory hearing one has first of all to decide whether there is a right of appeal under either CPIA 1996 or CJA 1988, which is not itself a straightforward question. Most terminating rulings will not be appealable under those provisions, at least where they automatically involve terminating, because they will not be within the purposes of the preparatory hearing (but note the extension of the purposes of such a hearing in s 310 to include questions as to joinder and severance). However, rulings which are not in themselves terminating but which are likely to induce the prosecution to terminate may well be appealable under the existing legislation: compare the discussion by the Law Commission in their Report (Law Com No 267) at para 7.21. Nice questions could arise as to which is the correct basis for any particular appeal and it would perhaps have been better if the existing appeal provisions relating to prosecution appeals in preparatory hearings had been repealed rather than being left as a ground for excluding the operation of the new provisions. Of course, repealing them would have been messy since the existing provision provided for both the defence and the prosecution to appeal and it would have been necessary to repeal the prosecution appeal whilst leaving the provision in force in relation to appeals by the defence.

The vast majority of the rulings likely to be appealed against are those prior to the trial or during it, but before the defence opens its case. As has been seen, the proposals all along had been limited to rulings prior to this point and indeed did not initially include rulings against submissions of no case. However, the final stage of the Bill extended the timescale right up to the point 'before the start of the judge's summing up to the jury' (s 58(13)) so that it includes rulings during the defence case which terminate the trial. These will be comparatively extremely rare and the most likely example envisaged seems to be where a ruling on public interest immunity is made, which can happen during the defence case, and which means that the prosecution is going to have to reveal sources or other information which it is not prepared to do and therefore decides to terminate the prosecution at that time. The extension of the ability to appeal means that the prosecution does not have to immediately withdraw rather than disclose the material but can appeal against the ruling. If successful, it can continue without disclosing, but if unsuccessful it has to accept that the appellant will be acquitted, which is of course the situation under the current law if the prosecution is not prepared to disclose.

6.4.2 Suspensory Effect

The suspensory aspect of the new rights of appeal is brought out in s 58(3) which states that 'the ruling is to have no effect whilst the prosecution is able to take any steps under subsection (4)'.

Subsection (4) essentially refers to the prosecution *'following the making of the ruling'* either

(a) informing the court that it intends to appeal *or*

(b) requesting an adjournment to consider whether to do so AND, in the case of such an adjournment, informing the court 'following the adjournment' that it intends to appeal.

These are essential prerequisites to the prosecution appealing and the ruling is of no effect, and is thus suspended, whilst they can be still carried out. The curious thing is that the statute makes the ruling suspensory for what looks like an indefinite or at least a not clearly finite period. This appears to be the case because the steps referred to in sub-s (4) have to be done following the ruling (or following the adjournment) which of course describes the start of a period rather than the end of a period. There is no express indication of how soon, following the ruling, these steps have to be taken and thus at what point the ruling ceases to be suspended. The point was pressed during Committee stage in the Commons (HC Standing Com B col 1125 (25 February 2003)) and the reassurance was given that the prosecution were expected to act fairly quickly and that detailed provision would be made in the rules of court which would be issued (see s 73(2)(a)). It seems to be envisaged that the prosecution would either have to indicate its intention to appeal immediately following the ruling or would have to request an adjournment to give itself time to consider whether to indicate its intention to appeal. Of course, the issue of timing is in one sense a non-issue if the ruling is one that automatically brings the prosecution to an end. The prosecution need to indicate an intention to appeal, or request an adjournment, more or less straight away otherwise it will be too late. Indeed its seems to have been envisaged, judging from the Solicitor-General's statements in Committee that rather than actually issue a ruling against the prosecution, the judge would indicate that he is minded to make a ruling and then the prosecution could indicate its intention to appeal. However, that is not how the Act is expressed and it speaks of a ruling being made but it being of no effect whilst the prosecution can still appeal. The difference may be more semantic than real, especially where the ruling is in itself terminating. If the judge makes a ruling, for example of no case to answer, the prosecution will be likely either to indicate an intention to appeal or to seek an adjournment except in cases where it is absolutely clear that there is no prospect of a successful appeal.

The more interesting question will arise where the ruling does not of itself automatically mean the case will end but is so damaging to the prosecution case that they may feel they will or may have to discontinue. In such a case the trial will continue until the prosecution decide what to do. The prosecution may not wish to indicate an intention to appeal straight away because there is an important precondition to so doing. The precondition is that to be found in s 58(4) which requires the prosecution to indicate its agreement that, if the appeal is abandoned or leave is not granted, the defendant should be acquitted. (If the appeal goes ahead and is unsuccessful, s 61(3) requires an acquittal anyway.) If the prosecution need time to consider either the question of whether the ruling is so damaging that they are prepared to risk an acquittal if the appeal fails or, alternatively, the question of whether there is a real prospect of succeeding in the appeal in any event (or, most likely, both questions), then they will apply for an adjournment. From the discussions at Committee stage above, it would seem that such an adjournment would be at most an overnight adjournment, following which the trial would continue if no intention to appeal was indicated. So in the normal case, the prosecution will either indicate an intention to appeal straight after the ruling or after an adjournment of no more than a day. If it does not indicate an intention to appeal and does not seek an adjournment, the trial would continue and it would seem that the prosecution cannot come back a day or two later and say, 'remember that ruling a couple of days ago, we have now decided we intend to appeal against it'. There is nothing expressly in the Act to stop this as the Act merely says 'following the ruling', but it is perhaps implicit in the fact that the ruling is of no effect whilst the prosecution can still indicate its intention to appeal. This in itself suggests that the period of time in which this can happen is limited, and if the trial has continued for some time after the ruling, it will often be difficult to say that the ruling has been of no effect if the prosecution (or defence) have meantime acted in reliance on it or in conformity with it. In any event, the rules when made are likely to preclude an appeal several days later subject to the possibility discussed in the next paragraph.

6.4.3 Combining Appeals against No Case Rulings with Other Rulings

Section 58(7) specifically deals with rulings of no case to answer.

Such a ruling is of course in itself a terminating one and as discussed above the prosecution either has to accept that it has lost the case or it indicates an intention to appeal. If it chooses to appeal, by s 58(7)(b), it can indicate not only an intention to appeal against the no case ruling but it can also 'nominate one or more other rulings' made earlier in relation to the same offence to be included in the appeal. Thus if there have been one or a number of rulings made against the prosecution which have weakened its case but not self-evidently in a fatal manner and which the prosecution have therefore not challenged because to do so would have put their whole case at risk in accordance with sub-s (8), the earlier ruling or rulings can still be appealed against as part of the appeal against the no case to answer. This makes sense in that if there have been earlier rulings excluding various pieces of evidence and then the no case submission succeeds because the evidence that has been allowed does not at its highest establish a case, it may be pointless challenging the no case ruling unless one can also challenge the earlier submissions and thereby let in the previously excluded evidence (which if admitted will obviously strengthen the prosecution case and undermine the no case ruling). In the light of this, if the prosecution is unsure about whether to appeal at the earlier stage because it is not sure whether the ruling is fatal, its best policy may be to err on the side of caution and proceed as best it can knowing that if there is a no case submission which goes against it, it can still appeal against those earlier rulings. This may create a paradoxical situation where the defence may be tempted not to make a no case submission since that would give the prosecution an opportunity to appeal against what may be vulnerable earlier rulings in favour of the defence. Instead the defence may decide its best course is to let the weakened prosecution case go to the jury who may well acquit in which case the prosecution will have no right of appeal at all. Of course this is dependent on the prosecution having chosen not to appeal in the first place at the time the ruling was made. Having said that, the prosecution has a separate right of appeal (at least in relation to offences in Sch 4) in respect of evidentiary rulings under s 62 and this appeal can be exercised any time prior to the opening of the case for the defence so the prosecution may still be able to appeal under s 62 against previous evidentiary rulings even if there is no submission of no case if it acts quickly before the defence case opens. However, it is intended that s 62 should not be brought into force until a significantly later stage than s 58 and until it has been seen how s 58 operates in practice (see Lord Goldsmith quoted above at Lords 3rd reading) so, initially at least, the final point at which previous rulings can be challenged will be after a successful submission of no case. This will normally of course be prior to the defence case opening but it should be remembered that submissions of no case can exceptionally be made at a later stage. The defence will have to bear in mind, in cases where the case has been weakened by earlier rulings in its favour, that in making a no case submission (at any stage) it opens up the possibility of the prosecution also challenging those earlier rulings along with the no case ruling.

6.4.4 Expedited and Non-expedited Appeals

Once the prosecution do indicate an intention to appeal against a ruling, the ruling continues to have no effect whilst the appeal is being pursued. The trial of the relevant offence will therefore be suspended whilst the appeal is ongoing. However, this does not mean that the whole trial will stop. The ruling may only affect one or a limited number of offences in an indictment containing a larger number of offences. Section 58(6) makes it clear that the prosecution can indicate an intention to appeal against a ruling only in so far as it affects a particular offence or offences. The trial may well be able to continue (see s 60(2)) uninterrupted as far as the offences not involved in the appeal are concerned. Indeed there may be cases, where the ruling affects two separate counts against the same defendant (eg Offences Against the Persons Act 1861 (OAPA 1861), ss 18 and 20), in which the prosecution decides to hedge its bets and appeal against the ruling in so far as it affects s 18 whilst continuing with the prosecution under s 20, despite being handicapped by the ruling in relation to the later offence. Even for the offence in respect of which the appeal is to be made, the trial may not be held up for too long if the judge decides that the appeal can be expedited under s 59. This would apply where the Court of Appeal is likely to be able to hear and decide the appeal within a few days. The judge in such a case may order an adjournment (s 59(2)) which would mean the jury is not discharged (and one presumes that the trial of any other offences in the indictment would normally be adjourned otherwise the same evidence may have to be given twice). If the appeal is not to be expedited (eg because the Court of Appeal is unlikely to be able to hear it quickly or because there is less point because the jury has not yet been sworn or the trial has only just started), by s 59(3) the judge may still order an adjournment (although this is going to be less likely except in pre-trial or preparatory hearings) or 'he may discharge the jury (if one has been sworn)'. Thus, depending on all the circumstances, the appeal may be a fully interlocutory one after which, if the appeal is successful, the trial may resume in front of the original jury or it may be one which brings the proceedings in front of that particular jury to an end (at least as far as concerns the offence or offences in respect of which the appeal is brought) even though (again only if the appeal is successful) it may then be followed by a fresh trial with a new jury.

6.4.5 Determination by the Court of Appeal

By s 61, the Court of Appeal (Criminal Division—s 74(6)) may confirm, reverse or vary any ruling to which the appeal relates.

Where the appeal is against a single ruling (as opposed to against a no case ruling plus other nominated rulings), sub-ss (3) to (5) apply.

If the Court of Appeal *confirms* a ruling, sub-s 3 requires the court to order the acquittal of the defendant in relation to each offence which is a subject of appeal against that ruling.

If the Court of Appeal reverses or varies a ruling (ie if the prosecution are wholly or partly successful in their appeal against the ruling) the Court of Appeal must do one of the following in relation to each offence subject of the appeal:

(a) order proceedings to resume in the Crown Court (this would be possible only if the case had been adjourned rather than the jury discharged);
(b) order a fresh trial in the Crown Court (eg where the original jury had been discharged in a non-expedited appeal);
(c) order the acquittal of the defendant (this would seem more likely if the ruling was only varied rather than reversed but it is certainly not limited to this situation).

The real test is the interests of justice as by sub-s (5) resumption of proceedings or a fresh trial can only be ordered if the Court of Appeal 'considers it necessary in the interests of justice to do so'. If for any reason the Court of Appeal considers that it is not in the interests of justice for the accused to be tried, then it has to order an acquittal under s 61(4)(c).

Subsections (7) and (8) provide for a similar regime in relation to appeals against no case rulings. They are separately provided for, it seems, to make it clear that it is what happens to the no case ruling that matters. If the no case ruling is confirmed, the defendant must be acquitted. What is left unsaid, but seems implicit and is uncontroversial, is that the fact that earlier rulings are reversed or varied is immaterial if the Court of Appeal thinks that nevertheless, the no case ruling is still correct. The corollary, however (which is equally unstated), is that if the earlier rulings are reversed or varied and these reversals or variations *do* undermine the no case ruling and mean that there is now a case to answer, then the no case ruling itself can be reversed even if it would have been correct in the light of the other rulings as they initially stood. In this situation, by sub-s (8), the court must order either a fresh trial or resumption of proceedings, subject again to the interests of justice test or alternatively it must again order an acquittal. Although sub-s (8) refers to reversing or varying a ruling of no case, it is difficult to see how such a ruling can itself be varied—either there is a case to answer in respect of a particular offence or there is not; there seems no room for any intermediate position.

6.5 EVIDENTIARY RULINGS—S 62

The prosecution right of appeal against (non-terminating) evidentiary rulings was only added at a late stage in the passage of the Bill and is to be found in s 62. The *modus operandi* of this right of appeal is not dissimilar in many respects to that which applies to terminating rulings under s 58 but there are also some significant differences. Principally these differences are that s 62 only applies to Sch 4 offences, the intention to appeal must be notified to the court (s 62(5)) before the opening of the defence case (s 62(8)) and the ruling (or combination of rulings) must 'significantly weaken' (s 63) the prosecution case even though not fatal to it. Another major practical point to note is that the evidentiary rulings regime will not be brought into force until after it has been seen how the s 58 regime is working in relation to in effect 'terminating' rulings. One should not let the title of s 62 referring to 'evidentiary rulings' mislead one into thinking that s 58 itself cannot or will not often apply to evidentiary rulings—it will and this is expressly confirmed by s 58(11). But s 58 will only apply, as we have seen, if the prosecution are prepared to accept that the failure or abandonment of the appeal will lead to acquittal. The advantage of s 62 for the prosecution, if and when it comes into force, will be that there will be an opportunity to appeal without risking an immediate acquittal. The meaning of 'evidentiary ruling' might seem fairly self-evident but s 62(9) defines it as (and limits it to) 'a ruling which relates to the admissibility or exclusion of any prosecution evidence'. So rulings relating to defence evidence do not qualify which is perhaps not surprising given that the intention to appeal has to come before the opening of the defence case. Having said that, issues about defence evidence can arise before that point, especially in pre-trial or preparatory hearings, but as a result of s 62(9) there is no possibility, where the ruling relates to defence evidence, of a prosecution right of appeal under s 62 (as opposed to under s 58 if the conditions for s 58 are met).

Another difference is that under s 58, generally a ruling is appealed against 'following' the time it is made and rulings will be appealed individually (albeit possibly in relation to more than one offence in the indictment) as and when they are made (except where the appeal is following a no case ruling and the appeal then also nominates other past adverse rulings). Under s 62(1), by contrast, an appeal may always be against a 'single' ruling or 'two or more' rulings. The reasons for this would appear to be related to the requirement of 'significantly weakening' the prosecution case under s 63. A single ruling on its own may weaken the prosecution case but not always 'significantly'. In such a case the prosecution cannot appeal against the ruling. There may then be a second ruling which again, in itself, weakens the prosecution case but not, in isolation significantly. So individually the rulings would not be appealable. However if the combined effect of the two is to significantly weaken the prosecution case, the prosecution can appeal against both together. The idea is not to allow appeals on relatively trivial issues but to recognize the cumulative effect of a number of small reverses for the prosecution and to give a right of appeal once the cumulative effect adds up to a significant weakening. Under s 63 it is for the trial judge or the Court of Appeal, in giving leave, to be satisfied that the 'relevant condition is fulfilled', ie that there is a significant weakening of the prosecution case in relation to the offence or offences which are the subject of the appeal.

There is no provision under s 62 for suspending the effect of an evidentiary ruling whilst it is still possible to appeal but there are similar provisions to the s 58 procedure as regards expedited and non-expedited appeals (s 64) so that once an intention to appeal has been announced, the trial of the offences to which it relates may be adjourned or, if appropriate, the jury may be discharged. Although one of the offences which is the subject of the appeal must be a qualifying offence (ie one listed in Sch 4, Pt 1), that is by way of a triggering requirement and if the ruling is appealed in relation to at least one qualifying offence, it seems that other offences in the indictment to which the ruling relates, but which are not qualifying offences, can be included in the appeal if the prosecution wish to do so (see s 62(6)(b)). Section 65 again provides for proceedings to be able to continue if appropriate in relation to any offence in the indictment not the subject of appeal.

Section 66 sets out the options which the Court of Appeal has when it hears a s 62 appeal, which are again to confirm, vary or reverse the ruling. These echo the options set out in s 61 on a s 58 appeal but there is a significant difference in that there is no requirement to acquit the defendant if the ruling is confirmed (which follows because the prosecution have not treated the ruling as a terminating one in choosing to appeal). Section 66(2) does, however, set out three similar potential outcomes to s 61 in terms of resuming the trial, ordering a fresh trial or acquitting. Again, however, there is a significant difference in that there is no interests of justice test to be satisfied before the resumption of the trial or a fresh trial can be ordered, and, in addition, an acquittal can only be ordered if the prosecution indicates that they do not intend to continue with the prosecution. This emphasizes the difference between s 58 and s 62 appeals. In the former the prosecution have to concede that failure of the appeal automatically leads to acquittal and they lose control of the prosecution in that sense. Under s 62, it effectively remains the prosecution's decision whether the prosecution can continue and thus they retain control although, of course, the prosecution may be severely compromised if the appeal has been unsuccessful.

6.6 MISCELLANEOUS AND SUPPLEMENTAL

Sections 68 to 74 deal with various supplementary issues common to both types of appeal.

Section 68 provides for a further appeal from the Court of Appeal to the House of Lords on the usual terms as to leave, point of law etc (and effectively for either party). Section 69 provides for costs out of central funds or for costs against the accused where appropriate. Section 70 provides for the suspension of the running of time limits, including custody time limits, during any period of adjournment for an appeal under Part 9. This will normally be of significance where the appeal is made in the course of a pre-trial hearing, ie before the trial has started for the purposes of the running of time limits.

Section 71 provides for restrictions on reporting of prosecution appeals until after the conclusion of the trial (subject to the usual powers to lift the restriction provided it is in the interests of justice). The obvious danger is that the jury may read reports which may be prejudicial during the period of any adjournment, or members of a future jury may be prejudiced if the appeal is followed by a fresh trial. Section 72 provides for various offences in connection with reporting in contravention of s 71.

Section 73 provides for rules of court to be made which it has already been noted will, inter alia, have to make provision in relation to time limits for appealing (see s 73(2)(a)) and s 74 deals with a number of matters of interpretation for Part 9.

The most significant definition, other than those which merely refer to definitions already set out in earlier sections of the Act, is that of a 'ruling'. Section 74(1) defines this very widely to include 'a decision, determination, direction, finding, notice, order, refusal, rejection or requirement'. It is wide enough to cover, and this was con- firmed in debates on the Bill, a decision about whether a particular question can be asked of a witness. Of course, the question would have to be a highly significant one, either to the extent under s 58 that the prosecution were willing to accept an acquittal if they lost the appeal or, under s 62, that the court giving leave was satisfied that the ruling met the test of significantly weakening the prosecution case. But subject to those tests and the other conditions under the two species of prosecution appeal, the definition of ruling is wide enough to cover virtually anything that the judge does or says in the course of the trial (or before it) prior to the summing up (or the opening of the defence as far as s 62 is concerned). Apart from the summing up (and the jury's verdict), the only other thing which is expressly excluded is 'a ruling that a jury be discharged'—see s 57(2)(b).

Other points of interest under s 74 include sub-s (3) which effectively means that once a ruling has been subject to one appeal under Part 9 (in the sense that the prosecution has informed the court of its intention to appeal), it cannot be subject to any further appeal under Part 9. Thus if, for example, a ruling is appealed under s 62 as an evidentiary ruling and that appeal is unsuccessful, the prosecution cannot then have another go at the same ruling by nominating it as one of the rulings to be considered alongside an appeal against a ruling of no case to answer under s 58. Subsection (4) deals with the situation where a ruling affects a number of offences but the prosecution only appeal the ruling in so far as it relates to some (or one) of them. In such a case 'nothing in this Part is to be regarded as affecting the ruling' in so far as it relates to the offence or offences not the subject of appeal. If an appeal is successful this could cause some anomalous results in terms of a ruling continuing to hamper the prosecution on one charge but having been overturned in relation to another. The anomaly is of course to some extent of the prosecution's own making in choosing not to appeal in relation to all offences, but it is an anomaly nonetheless which the legislation, in providing for selective rights of appeal, contemplates and creates. Subsection (5) makes it clear that where defendants are charged jointly, each defendant is regarded as charged with a separate offence which can therefore be separately appealed against (or not appealed against). The anomaly referred to above will seem even more striking if the prosecution choose to appeal a ruling in relation to D1 as charged under, for example, OAPA 1861, s 20, but not to appeal in relation to D2 charged with the same s 20 offence. If the appeal is successful it will affect D1 adversely (ie it will help the prosecution against D1) but will have no effect in relation to D2. This may look very odd but again it is dependent on the prosecution having chosen not to appeal in relation to D2's offence and they would only do so presumably for a good reason which may explain away the anomaly which they ought to have realized would be a consequence of their selective appeal against the ruling.

6.7 CONCLUSIONS

The new rights of appeal for the prosecution are designed to avoid mistaken rulings at first instance in favour of the defence leading to injustice in the form of acquittals of the palpably guilty and the consequent public disquiet and loss of confidence which that can cause. Prosecution rights of appeal have been severely limited in the past because of the potential oppressive effect of allowing the prosecution to appeal and the reluctance to be seen to give the prosecution two bites at the cherry. By and large the new rights of appeal avoid any such criticisms by allowing an interlocutory appeal before the challenged ruling has had full effect or resulted in an acquittal. Understandable concerns about equality of arms are countered by pointing out that the defence have a right of appeal against conviction at the end of the process which the prosecution do not have. To give the defence an interlocutory right of appeal is both unnecessary and undesirable and might lead to every single adverse ruling being challenged by the defence. It would be impossible to have an equivalent to the sanction, that applies to prosecution appeals under s 58, of saying that the person appealing must accept that if their appeal fails, they lose the whole case, ie one could not say to the defence, you can appeal the ruling, but if you lose, you must accept a guilty verdict. And in effect the defence already can (and sometimes do) create that situation if they wish by changing the plea to guilty in the light of a ruling and then appealing on the basis that the ruling which caused the change of plea was wrong.

The more difficult question to answer at this stage is whether the new rights of appeal will work smoothly in practice without unduly complicating or prolonging criminal proceedings. Much will depend on the rules of court to be made under s 73 and on the extent to which appeals can be expedited. There will also be issues about how long a jury can be expected to remain empanelled whilst a case is adjourned or, where the jury is discharged, how quickly a fresh trial can be organized where this is in the interests of justice. There have undoubtedly been a number of high profile cases where prosecutions have failed as a result of

apparently mistaken rulings, often after considerable expense has been incurred on the trial and its preparation to date. The new rights will be useful in providing a mechanism for resolving or remedying such cases and for allowing the prosecution to continue if the Court of Appeal finds there has been a mistake by the trial judge (or for vindicating the trial judge and preventing public disquiet where the trial judge has in fact got it right and there has merely been the appearance or the allegation of a mistaken ruling). It is to be hoped that the new rights of appeal are not pressed into service too frequently in situations where the delay involved in the cure is worse than the perceived defect, and the prosecution will need to be disciplined in the use of their new rights (which of course are subject to leave). The requirement under s 58, which will be the only type of appeal allowed initially, that the prosecution accept that the failure of their appeal results in an acquittal is perhaps the best guarantee that the new rights will be used only where the situation warrants it.

7

DOUBLE JEOPARDY

7.1 INTRODUCTION

A classic statement of the double jeopardy rule is to be found in Hawkins' Pleas of the Crown, Chap 35, s 1 as cited by Lord Hodson in *Connelly v DPP* [1964] AC 1254 at 1330:

That a man shall not be brought into danger of his life for one and the same offence more than once. From whence it is generally taken, by all the books, as an undoubted consequence, that where a man is once found 'not guilty' on an indictment or appeal free from error, and well commenced before any court which hath jurisdiction over the cause, he may, by the common law, in all cases whatsoever plead such acquittal in bar of any subsequent indictment or appeal for the same crime.

The rule against double jeopardy is given effect to by the ancient pleas in bar of *autrefois acquit*, ie 'previously acquitted' and *autrefois convict* ('previously convicted') which prevent a retrial for the same offence (or any alternative verdict offence of which the accused could have been convicted on the first indictment). These pleas are also supplemented by other rules such as abuse of process which may prevent, for example, the subsequent trial of the accused for *any* offence founded on substantially the same facts as the first—see *Connelly v DPP* (above) and *R v Beedie* [1998] QB 356. The focus of this chapter and of the Civil Justice Act 2003 is on the narrow *autrefois acquit* rule although it will be necessary at times to refer to the wider protection available via abuse of process (sometimes referred to as the *Connelly* rule). To avoid confusion, double jeopardy will be taken in this chapter to refer to the narrower *autrefois* rule which is subjected to exception by the Act, and the Connelly principle will be treated as the distinct but related form of discretionary protection which in truth it is.

The double jeopardy rule is sufficiently fundamental that in the United States it is enshrined in the Fifth Amendment to the Constitution and has there been described in the Supreme Court as a 'guarantee that the State with all its resources and power [shall] not be allowed to make repeated attempts to convict an individual for an alleged offence, thereby subjecting him to embarrassment, expense and ordeal and compelling him to live in a continuing state of anxiety and insecurity' [Brennan J in *Ashe v Swenson* 397 US 435 at 451 (1970) quoting from *Green v US* 355 US 184 at 187 (1957)].

Nevertheless, Part 10 of CJA 2003 controversially introduces a substantial exception to the double jeopardy rule and specifically to the *autrefois acquit* rather than *autrefois convict* branch of it. It makes it possible for the Court of Appeal to quash a person's previous acquittal in relation to a wide range of offences and to order him to be retried for the offence of which he has already been acquitted once. The power to quash the acquittal and order a retrial is not based on any defect or irregularity in the original trial but is founded on the existence of 'new and compelling evidence against the acquitted person' and a retrial being in 'the interests of justice'. The exception is much more substantial than the first true exception introduced in the Criminal Procedure and Investigations Act 1996 (CPIA 1996) which dealt with 'tainted acquittals' which at least were based on defects in the original trial such as jury nobbling or witness tampering. We described those more limited exceptions in 1996 as being 'important more for their symbolic significance rather than for their potential practical impact', a comment borne out by the fact that no acquittals have so far been quashed under the 1996 procedure. That may to some extent be simply a question of time due to the 1996 procedure having had no element of retrospectivity built into it, but the provisions in the 2003 Act are by contrast fully retrospective which is itself another matter of controversy. Despite no action having been taken under the 1996 procedure we predicted that it would:

stand as a symbol of the vulnerability of principles such as those underpinning the double jeopardy rule, which are designed to protect the individual against potential oppression by the State, in an age when a Government Minister can describe acquittals, equally as well as convictions, as 'unsafe' and the acquittal of a guilty person is regarded by some as an injustice equal to that involved in the conviction of the innocent.

How, then, have we come to the situation where only seven years later the vulnerability of such principles has been so quickly taken advantage of by the enactment of this much more substantial exception to the double jeopardy rule?

7.2 BACKGROUND

7.2.1 The Macpherson Report

The initial catalyst for a further tilt at the double jeopardy rule came in the shape of the Macpherson report into the matters arising from the death of Stephen Lawrence (Cm 4262–I) which was published in February 1999.

Although the report was primarily concerned with wide-ranging failures of the investigative process into the murder of a black youth by a group of white racist youths, one unsatisfactory aspect of the whole affair lay in the fact that three prime suspects were tried in 1996 in a private prosecution which resulted in directed acquittals because of the absence of any firm and sustainable evidence.

At para 7.46 the Report states:

[w]e . . . have considered, in the context of this case, whether the law which absolutely protects those who have been acquitted from any further prosecution for the same or a closely allied offence should prevail. If, even at this late stage, fresh and viable evidence should emerge against any of the three suspects who were acquitted, they could not be tried again however strong the evidence might be. We simply indicate that perhaps in modern conditions such absolute protection may sometimes lead to injustice. Full and appropriate safeguards would be essential. Fresh trials after acquittal would be exceptional. But we indicate that at least the issue deserves debate and reconsideration perhaps by the Law Commission, or by Parliament.

Recommendation 38 states:

That consideration should be given to the Court of Appeal being given power to permit prosecution after acquittal where fresh and viable evidence is presented.

7.2.2 The Law Commission Consultation Paper

Although it is now generally accepted that in the light of the barrage of publicity generated in the Stephen Lawrence case it would be almost impossible to have a fair trial of the individuals concerned and that the real problem was not so much the double jeopardy rule but the fact that a private prosecution was brought with little prospect of success, the Home Secretary acted upon recommendation 38 and referred the double jeopardy (after acquittal) rule to the Law Commission. The Law Commission published a detailed Consultation Paper (No 56) which provisionally proposed that:

(1) the rule against double jeopardy should be retained;
(2) the rule should be extended so as to prohibit the prosecution of a person not only
  (a) for any offence of which he or she has previously been acquitted or convicted, but also
  (b) for any offence founded on the same or substantially the same facts as such an offence; and
  (c) the rule as thus extended, and any exceptions to it, should be stated in statutory form.

However, the consultation paper also provisionally proposed that the rule against double jeopardy should be subject to an exception for certain cases where new evidence is discovered after an acquittal. The exception was not to apply to all offences and the Law Commission tendered for consideration the rather vague test of offences likely to result in three years in prison on conviction following a not guilty plea.

It should be noted that the proposal in the Consultation Paper would have broadened the double jeopardy rule to include the situations previously covered by the discretionary 'Connelly rule' which of course makes the case for an exception to the proposed composite broader rule somewhat easier to make.

Appendix B provided summaries of the law on double jeopardy in eleven other jurisdictions including Australia, New Zealand, Canada and Scotland, in none of which can a person be retried for the same offence following a final acquittal. In only three of the eleven (none of the three being common law jurisdictions) was this even a possibility (the three being Germany, Denmark and Finland) and in the latter two the procedure was expressly noted to be 'rarely' or 'very rarely' used. Despite this the Law Commission's case for some degree of relaxation of the double jeopardy rule was found to be justified in principle by some commentators (eg Dennis (2000) Crim LR 933) although others were less sanguine about the proposals (see Roberts (2002) 65 MLR 393 and [2002] *International Journal of Evidence and Proof* 199).

7.2.3 The Home Affairs Select Committee

The Home Affairs Select Committee examined the issue next and reported in May 2000 (*3rd Report 1999–2000* (HC Paper No 190)) in which they summed up the arguments for and against providing any further exception to the double jeopardy rule.

It identified the following key questions:

- Does the public interest in convicting the guilty outweigh the long-standing principle of double jeopardy?
- Does the availability of new evidence based on scientific advance create a new situation in which the old principle ought to be re-examined?
- Are the proposed safeguards set at such a level that the new procedure would be used only in exceptional cases?
- If the rule were changed, is it likely in practice that fair second trials would be held and that people would be convicted?

It also outlined potential best and worst scenarios if the law were to be changed.

Best scenario
- Most applications for retrials are based on scientific advance—rather than on changes to the rule of admissibility or previously reluctant witnesses coming forward.
- The procedure is invoked only in relation to very serious cases.
- Three acquittals are quashed each year.
- Two retrials a year result in conviction—with the third case resulting in acquittal by the second jury rather than the trial being stopped on legal grounds.
- No retrials are abandoned on account of pre-trial publicity.

Worst scenario
- An unexpected acquittal in a high profile case leads to immediate pressure for the police to collect further evidence for a retrial.
- The High Court dashes expectations of quashing an acquittal in a serious case on the grounds that the original police investigation was incompetent and the 'new' evidence could have been produced for the first trial.

- A retrial is ordered in a prominent case but at the retrial the defendant argues successfully that all the publicity surrounding his first trial and subsequently will make it impossible for him to receive a fair trial.
- Someone originally acquitted and then convicted at the retrial subsequently has his case reviewed by the Criminal Cases Review Commission on the grounds that the police evidence at the retrial was perjured, is released and wins substantial compensation.

Paragraph 65 accepted:

that the public interest in convicting and punishing the guilty fully justifies a re-examination of the double jeopardy rule. The possibility of scientific advance making available new evidence not considered at the first trial is particularly attractive. On the other hand, a change to the double jeopardy rule is not necessarily the best solution to perceived faults in the admissibility of evidence at the first trial (or in the police investigation). These issues should be addressed in other ways, not least the possibility of prosecution appeals on legal issues during a trial. A change in the rule subject to very tight conditions may end up, like the tainted acquittals exception, not being used at all. Alternatively a large number of investigations may, like the investigations following the War Crimes Act 1991, produce very few actual cases, disappointed expectations and concerns about publicity impugning a fair trial.

Paragraph 66 concluded that:

there is a strong case for relaxation of the double jeopardy rule to allow re-trials in the following circumstances:

- there is new evidence that makes the previous acquittal unsafe
- the offence is sufficiently serious for a life penalty to be available to the judge on conviction.

It will be noted in passing that the notion of an 'unsafe acquittal' reared its head again here and unfortunately illustrates the dangers and difficulties inherent in seeking to identify and describe those cases which should be liable to being reopened. Questionable *convictions* can be described as unsafe because of the criminal burden and standard of proof beyond a reasonable doubt. If there is a reasonable doubt, the conviction is unsafe. Acquittals cannot be required to be safe since the criminal standard of proof dictates an acquittal even though there are substantial doubts about the accused's innocence and perhaps even a probability that he is guilty. Our criminal justice system is committed to accepting that there will be 'unsafe acquittals' in this sense because it puts a greater weight on the prevention of the conviction of the innocent rather than precluding the acquittal of the guilty where the two aims are in conflict. The broader the interference with the double jeopardy rule, the more such values are likely to be undermined, especially if the language of 'unsafeness' is used. Fortunately, the legislation does not use this term although, as we shall see, the formulation of a test for those acquittals which should be reopened has proved problematic.

7.2.4 The Law Commission Final Report, the Auld Report and the White Paper

The next stage in the evolution of the proposals came in March 2001 when the Law Commission published its final report (Law Com No 267) which took a more conservative stance than its Consultation Paper. Although it still recommended an exception to the double jeopardy rule (which it now defined more restrictively in line with the *autrefois* rule), it considered that it had given insufficient weight to the value of finality and thus recommended that the exception should only apply to murder (or genocide involving killing or any new offence of reckless killing). Given this more restricted list of offences, the Commission thought that the new exception could be retrospective but on the other hand was now clear that the fact that evidence which was not admissible at the original trial had now become admissible because of a change in the law would not be a permissible reason for allowing a retrial.

The Auld Report in October 2001 found the Law Commission's final position to be unduly cautious and recommended that the exceptions should not be limited to murder offences but should extend to other grave offences punishable with life and/or long terms of imprisonment as Parliament might specify.

However, in response to concerns that police authorities, disappointed with acquittals, might harass acquitted persons with further investigations, it further recommended that there should be no reopening of an investigation of a case following an acquittal without the Director of Public Prosecution's prior personal consent and recommendation.

The White Paper *Justice for All* in para 4.64 preferred the Auld variation of the Law Commission proposal and decided that the change should extend beyond murder 'to a number of other very serious offences such as rape, manslaughter and armed robbery. We do not expect these procedures to be used frequently, but their existence will benefit justice.'

The result was ss 75 to 97 of the Act to which we will now turn.

7.3 CASES THAT MAY BE RETRIED

Section 75 and Schedule 5 set out the types of cases which can potentially be ordered to be retried.

7.3.1 Qualifying Offences

A key concept is the notion of a qualifying offence which by s 75(8) means an offence listed in Sch 5, Pt 1. As has already been discussed, the Law Commission narrowed its initial view of the range of offences which should qualify for being liable for retrial following acquittal and in its final report restricted it in essence to murder which it regarded as qualitatively different from other offences. The Home Affairs Select Committee and the Auld Report preferred a broader approach essentially based on offences carrying a maximum of life imprisonment and the Bill as introduced into the Commons specified a long list of 30 separate offences. At each stage of its parliamentary passage attempts were made by those opposed to such a wide derogation from the double jeopardy rule to cut back this list to murder or homicides or some other limited subset of offences. The point was repeatedly made that the most notorious cases where serious injustice seemed to be done, because double jeopardy prevented the retrial of someone who had since publicly admitted responsibility despite their acquittal, were cases of murder. However, the response was that serious sexual and paedophile offences could also give rise to equal public disquiet where acquittals are subsequently shown very likely to have been wrong. Furthermore it was said that the safeguards in the Act which had to be met before a previous acquittal could be reopened meant that there was no need to worry unduly about the breadth of the notion of a qualifying offence. Better to include acquittals for offences that might give rise to a serious affront to justice than to have too narrow a definition that meant the procedure, with all its safeguards, was not available at all. Eventually at one of the last stages of the Bill's progress, Report stage in the House of Lords, the government made limited concessions on this point and substituted a revised list in Sch 5 which still nevertheless comprised 29 offences.

One offence omitted in the new schedule which was originally included was wounding with intent contrary to the Offences Against the Person Act 1861 (OAPA 1861), s 18 in relation to which it had been pointed out that there are approximately 1,000 acquittals per year and that to include such an offence would create a very large number of 'provisional acquittals' which might subsequently be reopened. It would thus expose a large number of people to the risk and worry that one day their acquittals might be looked into again, something which could not be justified by the relatively small number of serious cases where there may on any view be thought to be good reason to look again at the acquittal. Similar arguments were raised in relation to the original inclusion of robbery in possession of a firearm which also no longer appears in the Schedule. Critics of Part 10 of the Act would argue that all acquitted persons are entitled to know that they will never be subjected to a prosecution for the same offence and that even the theoretical risk that they might be puts them at risk of harassment by the police or the media. However, even if one accepts the principle of a limited derogation from double jeopardy protection in the most serious cases such as homicide, rape, terrorism etc, it is then a question of judgment of where to strike the balance between the legitimate interests of the acquitted and the public interest in resolving troublesome cases of apparently unjustified acquittals (of which some will of course still result in acquittals even following a second trial). Whilst wounding with intent and robbery were taken out, as were various offences of hijacking and other offences in relation to ships and aircraft, hostage taking remains in the list which is still 29 offences long due to the inclusion of 8 offences under the Sexual Offences Act 2003 which of course did not exist in November 2002 when the Bill was first introduced.

Although the list of qualifying offences is quite wide, the notion of a qualifying offence does have built into it one restriction which is to be found in s 75(3) which effectively provides that an offence is not qualifying if the acquittal was one following an order for retrial under the new procedure. Thus an acquittal for a qualifying offence does not preclude a second trial but if there is a second trial and a second acquittal then there cannot be a third prosecution. So whilst double jeopardy protection is compromised, there can be no triple jeopardy. Or at least not under these provisions, but one must not forget the tainted acquittals exception in CPIA 1996. If there is a retrial under the 2003 Act but subsequently someone is convicted of an administration of justice offence in relation to that second trial, there seems nothing to stop a third set of proceedings being permitted under the 1996 procedure although the interests of justice test would have to be satisfied and the fact that it was a third trial might well be a highly relevant factor. At least one would hope so although it would no doubt be argued on the other hand that if the second acquittal was only due, for example, to jury nobbling, then the accused should still stand trial again and indeed the Law Commission Report at para 5.33(2) supports such a possibility. Furthermore paras 4.97 and 5.31 expressly contemplate the converse case of a second trial under the tainted acquittal procedure (resulting in a second acquittal) being followed by a third trial under the new evidence (now the 2003 Act) process.

For Northern Ireland, the list of Qualifying Offences is to be found in Part 2 of Sch 5 and it covers largely the same ground as Part 1 does for England and Wales except that it does not include the offences under the Sexual Offences Act 2003 (which under that Act are not extended to Northern Ireland). It will be noted that there are no provisions dealing with qualifying offences in Scotland as criminal justice is a matter for the Scottish Parliament, and the Scottish authorities have decided against any relaxation of the double jeopardy rule in Scotland. Not only does this mean that there will be no orders for retrials in Scotland following an acquittal there but, as we shall see, it has also been decided that an acquittal in Scotland will *remain* as a bar to retrial in England and Wales whereas in similar circumstances an acquittal for the same offence in any country of the world outside the United Kingdom will *now not* be an absolute bar to a retrial in England and Wales (the assumption being in both cases that the offences are such that the English courts would normally have jurisdiction). This is the strange by-product of s 75(4) which leads us into the next section dealing with the meaning of acquittals.

7.3.2 Acquittals

Acquittals are defined in s 75(7) as referring to acquittals in circumstances within s 75(1) and (4). Section 75 (1) provides for the Act to apply to acquittals (of qualifying offences) following proceedings on indictment in England and Wales and that is the main type of case to which the new procedure will apply.

However, pursuing for the moment the less common type of case touched upon above where there has been a previous acquittal abroad, s 75(4) also provides:

This Part also applies where a person has been acquitted, *in proceedings elsewhere than in the United Kingdom*, of an offence under the law of the place where the proceedings were held, if the commission of the offence as alleged would have amounted to or included the commission (in the United Kingdom or elsewhere) of a qualifying offence. (emphasis added)

Thus if D, a British citizen (even if from Scotland), is charged with murder in France (or with some other qualifying offence for which the English courts also have jurisdiction) and is acquitted in France, he may now still be at risk of being retried in England or Wales for the same alleged murder since the 'commission of the offence as alleged would have amounted to . . . a qualifying offence' (the offence of murder by a British citizen overseas being still murder under English law and thus amounting to a qualifying offence).

If, however, the acquittal took place in Scotland or Northern Ireland, s 75(4) would not apply as D would not have been acquitted 'in proceedings elsewhere than in the United Kingdom'. In this instance there can be no question of retrial in England although an acquittal in Northern Ireland could lead to a retrial in Northern Ireland (s 96 provides for the application of the retrial provisions to Northern Ireland). However, for an acquittal in Scotland (of an offence which would amount to a qualifying offence triable also in England—murder is not the best example here because of the peculiar position in English law of murders in Scotland: see *Blackstone's Criminal Practice* B1.9 and Hirst [1995] CLJ 488), there is no possibility of a retrial in England or Scotland or anywhere else. Scottish acquittals have as a result been given an elevated 'first class' status since they appear to be the only ones in the world which the Act regards as untouchable (and that would appear paradoxically to include their rarely used 'not proven' verdict). There will of course be only limited scope for retrying in England persons acquitted abroad because there are a limited number of cases where the English courts would have jurisdiction in the first place and persons at risk may be reluctant to enter the jurisdiction voluntarily and extradition attempts may run into difficulty where the person has already been acquitted in the country from which extradition is sought. The ease with which a person acquitted in Scotland might be brought back over the border was one of the reasons for not allowing a retrial in England in relation to Scottish acquittals since this would too readily undermine the decision in Scotland to retain the double jeopardy rule fully intact.

Returning to the main provision relating to acquittals 'in proceedings in England and Wales', under s 75(1) this applies to acquittals

(a) on indictment in England and Wales,
(b) on appeal against a conviction, verdict or finding in proceedings on indictment in England and Wales, or
(c) on appeal from a decision on such an appeal.

Thus it applies to acquittals of qualifying offences on indictment in the Crown Court or following appeal to the Court of Appeal or to the House of Lords. The reference to 'verdict' in para (b) is apt to cover the situation where a special verdict of not guilty by reason of insanity is initially returned and there is a successful appeal against that verdict by the defence to the Court of Appeal or House of Lords resulting in a full acquittal (which is thus susceptible to being quashed). The implication of this (and s 75(2)(b)) is that the special verdict *itself* is not an acquittal for the purposes of s 75(1) and cannot itself be later quashed under the Act in order to lead to a retrial. Similarly, a full acquittal resulting from an appeal against a finding that the accused is unfit to plead *is* an acquittal but the original finding *is not*.

The restriction to acquittals on indictment is important as not all the qualifying offences in Sch 5 are triable only on indictment (eg importation of Class A drugs) which is a further illustration of the breadth of the notion of a qualifying offence.

7.3.3 Alternative Verdict Acquittals

The meaning of acquittal for the purposes of s 75(1) is extended by s 75(2).

A person acquitted of an offence in proceedings mentioned in subsection (1) is treated for the purposes of that subsection as also acquitted of any qualifying offence of which he could have been convicted in the proceedings because of the first-mentioned offence being charged in the indictment, except an offence—

(a) of which he has been convicted,

(b) of which he has been found not guilty by reason of insanity, or

(c) in respect of which, in proceedings where he has been found to be under a disability (as defined by section 4 of the Criminal Procedure (Insanity) Act 1964 (c. 84)), a finding has been made that he did the act or made the omission charged against him.

The first half of this provision reflects the part of the double jeopardy rule which prevents retrial for an offence of which the accused could have been convicted on the original indictment as an alternative verdict (eg manslaughter on a murder indictment). The purpose of s 75(2), however, is not to prevent retrial of such an offence (the common law already does that) but quite the opposite—to provide power to quash, for example, the implicit manslaughter acquittal so that a retrial can be ordered. This could be done either with a view to making an order for a retrial for manslaughter (if that is all that the new evidence supports) or to making an order for retrial for murder, at which retrial manslaughter would still be an alternative verdict (provided of course the acquittal for manslaughter has actually been quashed, a point to which we shall return).

The second half of s 75(2) contains three exceptions.

Subparagraph (a) makes it plain that if the accused was actually convicted of the alternative verdict offence that alternative verdict conviction stands and he is not to be nonsensically deemed to have been acquitted of that offence. So if D is found not guilty of murder but guilty of manslaughter there is no manslaughter acquittal to quash and he cannot be retried for manslaughter because of the *autrefois convict* branch of the double jeopardy rule. The interesting question which arises from this example is whether the acquittal for murder can be quashed (even though there is a manslaughter conviction) and a retrial ordered for murder where there is new evidence that the accused was guilty of that offence rather than manslaughter. This would be contrary to the so-called principle in *R v Elrington* (1861) 121 ER 170 that one should not be serially charged with offences of ascending order of severity. As against that, if the Act can authorize an exception to the strict *autrefois acquit* rule, it can surely override the *Elrington* principle; but even if in theory an order for retrial for murder could be sought, one would expect it normally to be refused on interests of justice grounds (cf *Hoogstraten* [2003] EWCA 3642)

Subparagraph (b) clarifies that a special verdict of not guilty by reason of insanity in relation to an alternative verdict offence is not to be regarded as an acquittal (thus such a verdict is not susceptible to quashing).

Subparagraph (c) similarly clarifies that where there has been a finding of unfitness to plead, a finding that the accused did the act deemed to be charged in an alternative verdict offence is not to be treated as an acquittal (and thus is also not susceptible to quashing).

7.3.4 Retrospectivity

Controversially, and as has been noted already, in contrast to the non-retrospective nature of the tainted acquittals procedure enacted in 1996, the new exception to the double jeopardy rule is made fully retrospective by means of s 75(6) which simply states: 'This part applies whether the acquittal was before or after the passing of this Act'. The arguments against retrospectivity are to some extent the same as the arguments against the amendment of the rule in the first place—that acquitted persons are entitled to be able to put their prosecution behind them and to get on with the their lives, arrange their affairs and enter into personal and other commitments knowing they will not be put in peril for that offence again. Those favouring this argument pour double scorn on making the change retrospective since that affects people who at the time of their acquittal could regard themselves as acquitted absolutely and for ever. A prospective amendment to double jeopardy would at least not interfere with these existing legitimate expectations whereas the people affected by a *prospective* exception to double jeopardy protection would at least know at the time of their acquittal that retrial on fresh evidence was now a possibility. Such arguments are often met by the assertion that only the guilty need genuinely fear that their previously unassailable acquittal may be reopened but that assertion misses the point—both because it assumes (contrary to the presumption of innocence) that only the guilty will be selected for retrial and also because it ignores the fact that even those innocents against whom there is never likely to be any 'new and compelling' evidence will live in fear that they might unjustifiably one day be embroiled in a retrial.

One of the arguments in favour of making the change retrospective on the other hand has been that it is the striking improvements in recent years in the technology of forensic evidence such as DNA profiling that have made retrial on fresh evidence viable in a number of notorious cases and that not to apply the reform retrospectively would unjustly mean that these existing cases could not be reopened. This argument on occasions implies that such dramatic technological breakthroughs are not likely to be repeated in future so there is only any real point in reform if it is going to be retrospective, to which the response might be that if we are only legislating for a largely temporary phenomenon, should we be doing it at all? Of course there are other types of fresh evidence besides DNA profiling and the like, not least subsequent confessions by the acquitted person (which may or may not be truthful or reliable) and there are a number of high profile cases where the media have named individuals who in their view ought to be retried and there are many victims, and relatives of victims, who are keen to see retrials where they hope that justice (as they understandably see it) will be done. The paradox is that the more notorious the case has become over a period of years, the less likely is it that a fair retrial can be secured. Some of the individual cases are mentioned in the parliamentary debates, including one involving a subsequent confession where the minister said that he could not look the murder victim's mother in the eye if the reform was not made retrospective, but it would be inappropriate (if not potentially prejudicial) to further rehearse the details of such cases here.

There is clearly a danger that the retrospective nature of the provisions will give rise to false hopes in those who have long believed in the guilt of those who have been acquitted of grave offences against them or their loved ones. The government only expects a handful of existing acquittals cases to be susceptible to being retried, and even if one put aside the problems of prejudicial publicity, the new provisions can only operate where there is new evidence not used in the first trial and can have no real application where the problem is an inadequate initial investigation which can never realistically be remedied as is generally agreed to be the case in examples such as the Stephen Lawrence and Damilola Taylor cases. Quite apart from the raising of false hopes in victims and their families (which is an issue not just in relation to retrospectivity) there is also the dangerously strong temptation for the police, where they feel, as they sometimes have been known to do, that they got the right man despite his acquittal, to find some reason for seeking to reopen the investigation.

7.3.5 Retrospectivity and the European Convention on Human Rights

Compatibility with the European Convention on Human Rights (ECHR) was raised at various stages in the Bill's passage by opponents of retrospectivity.

Article 7 of the Convention provides:

No one shall be held guilty of any criminal offence on account of any act or omission which did not constitute a criminal offence under national or international law at the time when it was committed. Nor shall a heavier penalty be imposed than the one that was applicable at the time the criminal offence was committed.

The Law Commission was confident that Article 7 was not a problem:

The objective of this guarantee is to ensure that a person should be able to judge, at the time of engaging in particular conduct, whether or not it amounts to a crime.

The article does not, however, prohibit retrospective changes in the rules of criminal procedure so as to remove a bar or obstacle to a prosecution. The requirements of Article 7 are, in our view, satisfied if the conduct in question constituted a crime at the time when the offence was committed: it is immaterial that the procedural rules in existence at the time of an acquittal or conviction prevented it from being reopened. Article 7 would not prevent the reopening of such an acquittal or conviction under provisions subsequently coming into force. (Report, para 4.52)

The Joint Committee on Human Rights came to a similar conclusion in para 44 of its report on the Bill, subject to the proviso that:

the applicable law relating to the offence for which the retrial is ordered is the same as that in force at the time of the offence and any sentence which could be imposed on conviction following retrial would be no more severe than that which might have been imposed at the time of the offence.

The Law Commission (whose recommendation for retrospectivity was made in the context of the change in the law being restricted to murder offences) also recognized the need to take care with the retrospective application of the new rules:

. . . we recognised in CP 156 that acquitted defendants will have organised their lives on the justified basis that they would not be troubled by criminal proceedings a second time. This is a serious concern, the more so in the light of our revaluation of the importance of finality in criminal proceedings. Although, in our view, the arguments in favour of retrospective effect are compelling, we accept the force of this particular concern, and we seek in our recommendations to provide some recognition of their force. Where the new evidence is already in the hands of the authorities at the time when the new exception comes into force, we would expect an application for a retrial to be made with all reasonable despatch or not at all. If the prosecution were unduly dilatory in making such an application, under our recommendations the court hearing the application would be required to take account of that delay in deciding whether to order a retrial. If, moreover, the court hearing the application thought it would be unjust to reopen the acquittal because the defendant had acted in reliance on the assumption that it could not be challenged, that is an argument which a defendant might wish to advance in order to persuade the court to refuse a retrial on the grounds that it would not be in the interests of justice, or thereafter at the retrial to seek to persuade the court to stay the proceedings as an abuse of process.

These sentiments are to some extent reflected in s 79(2)(d) making failure to act with due diligence or expedition since commencement of the relevant Part of the Act, in relation to acquittals before commencement, a relevant factor for the Court of Appeal in determining whether it is the interests of justice to make an order quashing such an acquittal and ordering a retrial. So too with s 79(2), making the length of time since the qualifying offence was allegedly committed a relevant factor since such a factor is likely to be more pronounced with retrospective cases.

The existence of the interests of justice test and the mention of the above specific factors will no doubt be used to counter the argument (which is almost bound to be made) that the retrospective aspect (in particular) of the new rules is contrary to the right to a fair trial enshrined in Article 6 of the ECHR.

7.4 APPLICATION FOR A RETRIAL

Having looked at the circumstances in which an acquittal is at risk of being quashed giving rise to a retrial, we turn now to the procedure for doing so. Section 76(1) provides for a prosecutor to apply to the Criminal Division (see s 95(2)) of the

Court of Appeal (contrast the tainted acquittal procedure where it is to the High Court) for an order

(a) quashing a person's acquittal in proceedings within section 75(1), and
(b) ordering him to be retried for the qualifying offence.

In the case of acquittals outside the United Kingdom, the English courts do not have any jurisdiction to quash an acquittal but s 76(2) enables them to achieve within the jurisdiction the same effect by providing a procedure for enabling a further trial of the same offence in England an Wales. In this instance the prosecutor may apply to the Court of Appeal for

(a) a determination whether the acquittal is a bar to the person being tried in England and Wales for the qualifying offence, and
(b) if it is, an order that the acquittal is not to be a bar.

This latter procedure brings out starkly the nature of the exception now being enacted since it involves the Court of Appeal first of all determining that a previous acquittal *is* a bar and then immediately ordering that the acquittal is *not* to be a bar.

By s 76(3) any application under sub-s (1) or (2) requires the written consent of the DPP. Given the serious nature of the step being taken in seeking to quash an acquittal and the relatively few cases where it will be appropriate, the DPP's written consent will normally have to be given personally. Section 92 thus disapplies the rule whereby many of the DPP's functions can be exercised by a Crown Prosecutor. Section 92(2) and (3) allows some delegation by the DPP to a person or persons authorized by him, but the opening words of s 92(2) only permit this 'in the absence of the DPP', which is intended to cover the situation where he is out of the country or not available due to illness etc. It was recognized that it is important to have a rigorous filter on applications to quash a conviction since even an application, quite apart from any subsequent retrial, will be potentially oppressive and unsettling to a person who has already once been acquitted of the offence in question.

With this in mind, for the DPP to give his consent he must be satisfied under s 76(4) of three things:

(a) there is evidence as respects which the requirements of section 78 appear to be met,
(b) it is in the public interest for the application to proceed, and
(c) any trial pursuant to an order on the application would not be inconsistent with obligations of the United Kingdom under Article 31 or 34 of the Treaty on European Union relating to the principle of *ne bis in idem*.

Paragraph (a) relates to the requirement that there is new and compelling evidence which will be discussed below at 7.5.1 and it is also something that the court will have to be satisfied of itself before making an order.

Paragraph (b) is not something that the court itself has to be satisfied of but it will often overlap with the interests of justice test in s 79 which is something the court will ultimately have to be satisfied on. It was made clear in the debates that the public interest test includes the interests of justice but that it is wider than that. This presumably means wider in the sense that whilst it may be in the interests of justice for a trial to take place, there may still be some wider and overriding public interest *against* proceeding. It can hardly be the case that public interest could be wider in the sense that it overrides a situation where it is not in the interests of justice to proceed because that would be to permit an application where the DPP does not expect the Court to make the order because the interests of justice test will not be satisfied.

Paragraphs (a) and (b) appeared in the Bill as originally drafted. Paragraph (c) was added at a late stage and is interesting not just as an illustration that the use of Latin is not yet completely redundant. *Ne bis in idem*—'not twice at the same thing'—is the continental equivalent of the prohibition on double jeopardy.

Article 31 of the Treaty on European Union does not itself mention *ne bis in idem* but it does provide, inter alia, that:

1. Common action on judicial cooperation in criminal matters shall include:

. . .

preventing conflicts of jurisdiction between Member States;

The Convention Implementing the Schengen Agreement (CISA) (OJ 2000 L239 22.09.2000 p 19) contains various provisions by which such co-operation is implemented. Although the United Kingdom is not a Schengen state it is bound by Articles 54–58 of CISA (see Fletcher (2003) 66 MLR 769 at 772) which specifically guarantees *ne bis in idem* (double jeopardy protection) in the following terms:

Article 54
A person whose trial has been finally disposed of in one Contracting Party may not be prosecuted in another Contracting Party for the same acts provided that, if a penalty has been imposed, it has been enforced, is actually in the process of being enforced or can no longer be enforced under the laws of the sentencing Contracting Party.

The protection is qualified by a limited power to provide for exceptions as follows:

Article 55
1. A Contracting Party may, when ratifying, accepting or approving this Convention, declare that it is not bound by Article 54 in one or more of the following cases:

(a) where the acts to which the foreign judgment relates took place in whole or in part in its own territory; in the latter case, however, this exception shall not apply if the acts took place in part in the territory of the Contracting Party where the judgment was delivered;

(b) where the acts to which the foreign judgment relates constitute an offence against national security or other equally essential interests of that Contracting Party;

(c) where the acts to which the foreign judgment relates were committed by officials of that Contracting Party in violation of the duties of their office.

2. . . .

Thus s 76(4)(c) of CJA 2003 will require the DPP to certify that a retrial will not involve trying a person for any offence for which he has already been tried (and sentenced etc) in an EU Member State (other than for offences for which a valid reservation under Article 55 has been made).

There are proposals to replace Articles 54–58 of CISA with a new Framework Directive which would provide a somewhat more rigorous application of the *ne bis in idem* principle and, beyond that, the proposed Charter of Fundamental Rights has an even more stark statement of the principle in Article 50 which proposes

Right not to be tried or punished twice in criminal proceedings for the same criminal offence
No one shall be liable to be tried or punished again in criminal proceedings for an offence for which he or she has already been finally acquitted or convicted within the Union in accordance with the law.

These European developments make the English reform of the double jeopardy rule appear even more ill-timed and anomalous, but for the time being they would only appear to have any bite where there is an international element and there is a proposed retrial of an offence alleged to have already been dealt with in another EU state in which case it is for the DPP to certify whether any retrial would be contrary to the United Kingdom's EU obligations.

Once the DPP has given consent for an application for an order under s 64 and an application has been made, by virtue of s 76(5) no further application may be made in relation to that acquittal. If the application is unsuccessful (following any appeal to the House of Lords as provided for by s 81(2)), that is the end of the matter, the prosecution cannot try a second time to get the conviction quashed on the basis of new evidence. To do otherwise would be (even more) unduly oppressive. Note, however, that s 76(5) only applies to the current new evidence provisions. It would not prevent a separate application under the tainted acquittals procedure under the 1996 Act.

One final but important point in relation to applications for a retrial means harking back to the extended definition of 'acquitted' in s 75(2) which provides for this Part of the Act to apply also where a person is acquitted of alternative verdict offences. Thus if D is tried for murder and is acquitted altogether he is treated inter alia as being acquitted of manslaughter. Suppose then that new and compelling evidence emerges and an order for him to be retried for murder is sought and obtained. D's acquittal for murder is quashed and he is tried for murder, but whilst the jury are now sure that he did the fatal act, they conclude that he only acted with sufficient intent for manslaughter. Can the jury convict D of manslaughter at the retrial as would normally be the case on an indictment for murder? On the face of it, the answer would appear to be no as D has a good plea of *autrefois acquit* as far as manslaughter is concerned since the original acquittal of that offence has not been quashed. It was his murder acquittal which was quashed and there appears to be nothing in the Act explicitly providing for an order 'quashing an acquittal' to extend to quashing all acquittals of alternative verdict offences. Section 75(2) merely extends the meaning of where a person is to be treated as being acquitted and not of which acquittals shall be regarded as quashed. If this argument were to be accepted, it would seem that the prosecution would have to apply in advance for a quashing order in relation to all or any alternative verdict acquittals of which they wish the jury at the retrial to be able to convict.

The contrary argument would point to s 75(7) providing that 'references in this part to acquittal are to acquittal in circumstances within subsection 1 or 4.' The order applied for under s 76 'quashing a person's acquittal' would be regarded as effective to quash all and any alternative verdict acquittals under s 75(2) which is effectively a deeming provision for s 75(1). This is almost certainly what the draftsman intended and is certainly much more convenient for the prosecution but it is a pity it was not made clearer in s 75(7) that s 75(2) is also relevant and in s 76(1) that a single order is effectively quashing more than one acquittal in alternative verdict cases (it is noticeable also that s 76(1) refers to quashing an acquittal (singular) rather than acquittals (plural)).

7.5 DETERMINATION BY THE COURT OF APPEAL

In considering an application the Court of Appeal has to consider two sets of requirements and, if they are met, 'must make the order applied for'. The two sets of requirements are:

(a) new and compelling evidence under s 78; and
(b) the interests of justice under s 79.

7.5.1 New and Compelling Evidence—How Compelling?

Originally this requirement was that 'there is new and compelling evidence *that the acquitted person is guilty* of the offence' and which was compelling in the sense that 'when it is considered in the context of the outstanding issues, it is *highly probable* that the person is guilty of the offence' (emphases added).

These tests were objected to as being judicial findings that would be too highly prejudicial to any eventual retrial. Section 78(1) now simply requires there to be new and compelling evidence 'against the acquitted person in relation to the qualifying offence' and the notion of compelling now includes under s 78(3) (in addition to its being (a) reliable and (b) substantial) that, (c) 'it appears highly probative of the case against the accused person'. This test is regarded as less prejudicial as it speaks to how the evidence appears rather than states a conclusion that the accused is probably guilty. The provision is really caught in a Catch 22 situation. There is a desire to avoid a finding that is too pre-emptive of the verdict of the jury at any subsequent retrial but at the same time there is a desire to set a reasonably high threshold before subjecting anyone to a retrial for an offence for which he or she has already been acquitted. The existing tainted acquittal procedure avoids confronting this issue head on by focusing on the initial acquittal and whether it appears to have been caused by the interference or intimidation of a juror or witness.

111

At para 4.61 of the Law Commission Report this backward looking approach was rejected for the following reasons:

We do not think that this approach would be appropriate in the context of new evidence. The tainted acquittal procedure focuses on the legitimacy of the first trial. What happened at the first trial, and what might have happened at the first trial but for the conduct complained of, is of the essence of the exercise. The justification for that procedure is that there has not yet been a proper trial. By contrast, the new evidence exception applies where there has been a proper first trial at which a legitimate verdict was reached. Thus the focus of the question should be whether the effect of the new evidence is such that the first jury's verdict (legitimately reached after a proper trial) cannot in the interests of justice be allowed to stand. What the first jury would, or might, have done if the case presented to it had been different is neither here nor there. Its task is done.

Instead the Law Commission proposed:

that the *strength* of the new evidence be considered *in the context of* issues that arose at the trial (whether or not matters of dispute between the prosecution and defence), thus enabling its *probative force* properly to be judged. (para 4.63) (emphases added)

This approach is reflected in s 78(3)(c) but 'outstanding issues' appears to be a more limited concept in that by s 78(4) it 'means the issues in dispute in the proceedings in which the person was acquitted' whereas the Law Commission referred to 'issues that arose at the trial (whether or not matters of dispute …)'.

This seems a clearer way of articulating the correct approach to the Law Commission's own example which was given at para 4.64 as follows:

Where the only issue at trial is identity but after D's acquittal further evidence of D's involvement is discovered (for example, the weapon, bearing D's fingerprints is found in D's house or garden; or DNA evidence showing that D had contact with the victim; or the victim's blood on D's clothing; or CCTV footage showing D at the scene of the crime) it would not be realistic to ask whether such new evidence is *in itself* compelling evidence of guilt, in isolation from the issues raised at the trial. The probative value of the new evidence will vary according to the matters that are and are not in dispute. For example, it may be the case that in interview or in evidence at the first trial D had denied knowing or having any contact with the victim, or being anywhere near the scene of the crime at the relevant time. Seen in that context, the new evidence may acquire the quality of being compelling. On the other hand D may already have accepted, in interview or in evidence, that he knew the victim, or had been at the scene and come into contact with her and/or was the owner of the weapon (but had lent it to another). In such a case the context within which the new evidence is considered may deprive it of any great significance.

Despite the above reference to 'probative value of the new evidence', the Law Commission still expressed its conclusion at para 4.67 in terms of the Court concluding that there is a high probability of guilt:

Our recommendation is that a successful application to quash the acquittal on the ground of new evidence must satisfy the test that the new evidence is such, when taken in the context of the issues at the trial, that it appears at that stage to be compelling, in that it drives the court to the conclusion that it is *highly probable* that the defendant is guilty.

112

Given that the Act eventually eschewed this approach, one is left wondering how substantial a limitation is the test of being 'highly probative of the case against the acquitted person'. Is there now the danger spoken of by the Law Commission in para 4.65, ie the risk of cases being 'reopened merely because there is a bit more to boost what had been a strong case and a surprising verdict'? The answer to this is hopefully to be found in the s 78(3)(b) requiring the evidence to be 'substantial' which, unlike reliability in s 78(3)(a), was not specifically mentioned in the Law Commission's report.

7.5.2 New and Compelling Evidence—New in what Sense?

Under the Bill as originally drafted, evidence was new 'if it was not available or known to an officer or prosecutor at or before the time of the acquittal'. Section 78(2) allows for a much broader notion of 'new' evidence simply on the basis that 'it was not adduced in the proceedings in which the person was acquitted'. Whilst this test is much simpler to apply it seems at first sight to admit evidence which the prosecutor had available and knew about but chose not to use for some reason. One way to exclude such evidence would be to rely on the court ruling under s 79 that it is not in the interests of justice to order a retrial. Section 79(2)(c) specifically makes a failure 'by a prosecutor to act with due diligence or expedition' but this does not naturally cover a tactical decision not to use certain evidence first time around. However, Lord Goldsmith for the government (Hansard, HL col 710 (4 November 2003)) gave the House

an undertaking, which I have agreed with the Director of Public Prosecutions, that where evidence was not adduced for tactical reasons, it would not be right to use it as a basis for an application. . . . I hope that that will give some comfort. It will be reflected in guidance.

The broad notion of 'new evidence' meaning simply evidence not adduced in the original trial also opened up the possibility of including evidence which *could* not be adduced at the first trial because it was not admissible *then* although it has *now* become admissible because of a change in the law. The Law Commission in its Consultation Paper had contemplated such evidence being admissible but in its report (at para 4.94) had a change of mind, noting that 'this proposal was comprehensively rejected by respondents, largely through fears that the law might be changed *in order* to secure a second trial'. Even though changing the law with this *purpose* was considered 'far fetched', the Law Commission thought there were sufficient dangers (associated with retrospective *effect*) to recommend

that it should not be possible to apply for a retrial on the basis of evidence which was in the possession of the prosecution at the time of the acquittal but could not be adduced because it was inadmissible, even if it would now be admissible because of a change in the law.

Despite this, s 78(5) does exactly the opposite and provides: 'For the purposes of this section, it is irrelevant whether any evidence would have been admissible in earlier proceedings against the acquitted person.' Again, protection against any unjust consequences of this rule are left to the requirement of the interests of justice test, to which we now turn.

7.5.3 The Interests of Justice

The basic requirement under s 79(1) is that:

in all the circumstances it is in the interests of justice for the court to make the order under section 77.

Section 79(2) provides that this question is to be determined

having regard in particular to—

(a) whether existing circumstances make a fair trial unlikely;

(b) for the purposes of that question and otherwise, the length of time since the qualifying offence was allegedly committed;

(c) whether it is likely that the new evidence would have been adduced in the earlier proceedings against the acquitted person but for a failure by an officer or by a prosecutor to act with due diligence or expedition;

(d) whether, since those proceedings or, if later, since the commencement of this Part, any officer or prosecutor has failed to act with due diligence or expedition.

Paragraph (a) is particularly relevant to whether highly publicised or notorious cases can fairly be retried. This is an issue which the Court of Appeal has to consider already in the slightly different context of whether to order a retrial under the Criminal Appeal Act 1968 s 7 where an appeal against conviction has been allowed. In *R v Taylor* (1994) 98 Cr App R 361, sensational and inaccurate publicity at the first trial was partly responsible for quashing the conviction in the first place and it also made a fair retrial impossible. On the other hand in *R v Stone* [2001] Crim LR 465, the court was not satisfied on the balance of probabilities that exceptional and possibly inaccurate publicity was such as to make a retrial oppressive or unfair. Kennedy LJ in *Stone* commented on *Taylor* as follows:

Plainly the decision in *Taylor* is authority for the proposition that this court can, in an appropriate case, regard past press coverage as a sufficient reason not to order a re-trial, but otherwise, as it seems to us, it must be regarded as a decision on its own facts. ([2001] EWCA Crim 297, para 44)

This suggests that it will not be easy to establish in advance that existing circumstances make 'a fair trial unlikely' even though fairness must surely be influenced by the fact one is dealing here with a retrial following an acquittal rather than a retrial following a quashed conviction. In practice there may be exceptional cases where a fair trial is found to be unlikely, but in general terms the Court of Appeal is quite likely to reason that the time gap between the publicity and the actual trial will militate against any unfairness or prejudice due to previous publicity and be prepared leave it to the trial judge to determine whether a the time of the actual trial a fair trial is in fact possible and to direct the jury in such a way as to guard against allegations of unfair prejudice.

Paragraph (b) refers to the length of time since the alleged offence 'for the purposes of that question and otherwise'. The 'question' seems to be the question in para (a) of 'whether existing circumstances make a fair trial unlikely'. It cannot simply refer to the question of 'the interests of justice' since in that case it would be unnecessary to mention it. So the notion of a fair trial and the potential impact of the lapse of time is central to para (b) even though the word 'otherwise' allows more general considerations relevant to the interests of justice to be considered as well. Perhaps the most likely sense in which a trial might be unfair after a long laps of time would be where the accused is no longer in as good a position to defend himself and offer explanations for his conduct as he would have been at the earlier time.

The impact of delay on the right to a fair trial 'within a reasonable time' under Article 6 of the ECHR has been discussed at length by the House of Lords recently in *Attorney-General's Reference (No 2 of 2001)* [2004] 2 WLR 1. The majority held that criminal proceedings were only required to be stayed, on the ground that there had been a violation of the requirement that a hearing should be held within a reasonable time under the ECHR, if (but only if) a fair hearing was no longer possible or it was for any compelling reason unfair to try the defendant. The breach resulting from a failure to hold the trial within a reasonable time was said to consist in the delay which had accrued and not in the prospective hearing. The appropriate ordinary remedy for the delay might be a public acknowledgement of the breach, a reduction in the penalty imposed on a convicted defendant or the payment of compensation to an acquitted defendant. Only if the delay made the trial unfair should there be granted a stay.

Although this decision was made after the passing of the Act it is largely consistent with it since s 79(2)(b), as analysed above, makes the length of time relevant for the purposes of the question of whether a fair trial is unlikely. However, the word 'otherwise' does let in other considerations relevant to the interests of justice even thought they would not be likely to affect the fairness of the trial (or as it is under the 2003 Act, the retrial). The most likely of these considerations might be that it would not be in the interests of justice to order a retrial where the provision was being applied retrospectively to an offence for which a person was acquitted many years ago. Such a trial might be unfair anyway because, for instance, as suggested above, the accused may no longer be in a position to answer as readily or convincingly questions that might be put to him about his conduct. But even apart from this it might be thought to be not in the interests of justice to reopen a case a long time after an acquittal simply because of the oppressiveness involved in doing so such a long time after the event, when the accused has organized his life and entered into personal and financial commitments on the assumption that he has been finally acquitted. This factor could indeed be relevant not just to retrospective applications of the new procedure but to any application where there has been a long interval between the original acquittal and the new application, but in the short term it is most likely to be a factor in retrospective applications.

Paragraph (c) referring to evidence that might have been adduced in the earlier trial if there had been due diligence or expedition by an officer or prosecutor, was at one time canvassed as an absolute bar to a retrial on that evidence. However, the Law Commission Report thought that on balance it was inappropriate to have it as a mandatory bar since any disciplinary or incentive effect on the original investigation was likely to be rather remote and, as a mandatory bar, it would distract attention from the real issue of whether adhering to the original acquittal is in the interests of justice, as to which issue it should merely be a factor. One wonders, however, how often, if at all, it will be a significant factor. As the Law Commission itself put it in para 4.84:

The practical effect of including this as a relevant factor would probably be limited. If the case satisfies our criteria in other respects, it is perhaps unlikely that the court would refuse a retrial solely on the grounds of a want of due diligence in the original investigation. As in the case of fresh evidence relied upon by the defence in an appeal against conviction, the want of due diligence will often be of marginal importance by comparison with the other considerations involved; but in certain borderline cases it may be right that it should tip the balance. The Court of Appeal is well used to applying this factor in the context of defence appeals.

The same comments can be made in relation to para d) which deals with due diligence etc *since* the earlier proceedings (or since the commencement of this part of the Act in the case of retrospective application to acquittals before that time). The most likely application of this paragraph is to acquittals prior to the passing of the Act where the evidence is already well known to the authorities and to the public. A failure to act on this within a reasonable time of the Act's passing will surely be frowned upon and any inappropriate delay would be a good reason for refusing to make an order as not being in the interests of justice. For future acquittals, it may in practice be more difficult for the defence to show that an officer or prosecutor has failed to act with due diligence, apart from cases where it is obvious that the new evidence has fallen into the hands of the authorities at a much earlier date. Even here, given that a retrial can be ordered even where the evidence was available at the date of the original trial, the impact of para (d) may in practice not be that great unless the courts decide, contrary to the Law Commission's expectations, to operate it very proactively, which perhaps they may choose to do given that the Law Commission's views were premised on the new procedure's applying only to murder cases.

7.5.4 Procedure for Applying to the Court of Appeal

Section 80 provides for notice to be given to the Court of Appeal of an application, and within two days a notice must be served on the acquitted person charging him with the offence, although this time can be extended if the person to be charged is absent from the United Kingdom. The Court of Appeal must consider the application at a hearing at which the appellant is entitled to be present and represented. The Court may order the production of any document or exhibit etc which appears to be necessary for the determination of the application and may order to attend for examination any witness who would be compellable in any retrial that might result from the application. The hearing in the Court of Appeal may consider more than one application (whether or not relating to the same person) but only if the offences concerned could be tried on the same indictment. Although the Law Commission did not think it appropriate for an appeal to lie from the Court of Appeal to the House of Lords in relation to an application because 'the success of the application is unlikely to turn on an issue of law suitable for consideration by the House of Lords', s 81 of the Act in the event provides such a right of appeal (subject to leave etc), either for the acquitted person or the prosecutor, by means of a new subsection 1B inserted into s 33 of the Criminal Appeal Act 1968.

Section 82 of the Act provides for the Court of Appeal to, in effect, prohibit the publication or re-publication of matter 'which would give rise to a substantial risk of prejudice to the administration of justice in a retrial'. Such a prohibition can be made *in advance* of an application to quash a conviction only where the DPP applies for such a prohibition and an investigation into the qualifying offence has been commenced since the acquittal. An advance application of this sort must specify the time when it cease to have effect (s 82(8)). *After* notice of an application to quash a conviction has been given under s 80, a prohibition can also be made of the Court's own motion or on application by the DPP (but there is curiously no provision for an application by the acquitted person). The prohibition may subsequently be revoked or varied on application either by the DPP or the acquitted person or of the Court's own motion. Any prohibition order made will cease in any event once it becomes impossible for there to be retrial pursuant to the application or at the conclusion of any such retrial. Section 83 provides for summary offences in relation to publication 'in any part of the United Kingdom' punishable by a fine up to level 5 on the standard scale and requiring the Attorney-General's consent for prosecution. This offence-creating section is not strictly necessary for England and Wales given that a breach of an order made by the Court of Appeal prohibiting publication would be punishable in England and Wales as a contempt of court but the offence was included to ensure that the prohibition was enforceable in Scotland as well.

7.6 RETRIAL

Section 84 provides that retrials following an order under s 77 must be on indictment (remember that some Sch 5 offences are triable either way) and the indictment is to be 'preferred by direction of the Court of Appeal'. To minimize the length of time that the previously acquitted person is exposed to the risk and anxiety of the retrial, normally he cannot be arraigned more than two months after the order quashing his acquittal and ordering a retrial 'unless the Court of Appeal gives leave' (s 84(2)). Such leave must not be given unless the Court of Appeal is satisfied under s 84(3) that (a) there has been due expedition and (b) there is good and sufficient cause for the trial despite the lapse of time. If (a) is satisfied, (b) will not often be much of a barrier given that the Court has already taken the drastic step of ordering an acquittal to be quashed. Once the two months period is up and thus the opening words of s 84(4) apply in that now he 'may not be arraigned without leave', the previously acquitted person can apply to the Court of Appeal to set aside the order quashing his acquittal and for a direction restoring an earlier judgment and verdict of acquittal or, in the case of foreign acquittals, a declaration that the acquittal is a bar to his being tried for the qualifying offence.

Under s 84(5) an indictment pursuant to an order for a retrial may relate to more than one offence or person and those other offences or persons need not themselves be retried. Thus if X is tried and acquitted of murder jointly with a person unknown and then that other (Y) is apprehended and (perhaps as a consequence) new and compelling evidence against X also emerges, X may find his acquittal quashed and an order for retrial made and the indictment may be preferred charging both X (previously acquitted) and Y (not previously charged). In mentioning indictments being possible for multiple offences, the point made above at the end of 7.4 should not be forgotten: that it is possible to argue that the accused can only be convicted of alternative verdict offences which he is deemed to have been acquitted of in a previous trial if an order has been obtained explicitly quashing those acquittals—otherwise he might argue that he still has a valid plea of *autrefois acquit* in relation to those alternative verdict acquittals.

On a retrial there might be a temptation to rely on a written transcript of evidence given at the first trial, particularly where the witness is vulnerable or traumatized by an incident which he or she wished to forget. However, s 84(6) provides that evidence must be given orally if it was given orally at the first trial unless:

(a) all the parties to the trial agree otherwise,
(b) section 116 applies, or
(c) the witness is unavailable otherwise than under s116(2) and s114(1)(d) applies.

Section 116 is discussed in Chapter 9 but is essentially concerned with witnesses who are dead, unfit, outside the United Kingdom, untraceable or in fear. Paragraph (c) above is concerned with witnesses whose unavailability does not fall under s 116 (and hence are not covered by para (b) and allows the evidence at the first trial under the new hearsay rule (s 114) but only if para (d) of s 114 applies, ie 'the court is satisfied that it is in the interests of justice for it to be admissible'. A non-exhaustive list of factors relevant to this test are set out in s 114 and discussed in Chapter 9. Putting aside these exceptions to the principle that the evidence at the retrial should be given orally, s 84(7) means that even though depositions from certain witnesses may have been admissible at the original trial where the person was sent for trial under s 51 of the Crime and Disorder Act 1998, such depositions may not be used at the retrial.

7.7 INVESTIGATIONS

7.7.1 Authorization of Investigations

One of the benefits of the current rules on double jeopardy is that an acquitted person is not subject to harassment by the police seeking fresh or further evidence that he committed the offence of which he has been acquitted. Once there is the potential for an acquittal to be reopened, there is a need to protect the acquitted person from unnecessary harassment or intrusion by the police into his personal life. Sections 85 and 86 seek to provide a modicum of protection in this regard. Section 85 is headed, slightly misleadingly, 'authorisation of investigations' but in fact only requires the written authorization of the DPP before the taking of certain types of step in an investigation, ie those listed in s 85(3) involving arresting, questioning searching or seizing the acquitted person or his property or taking his fingerprints or samples, 'with or without his consent'. Other steps in an investigation do not appear to require any authorization so there appears to be nothing preventing the police trawling for information about an acquitted person even without an authorization from the DPP provided they do not involve the accused himself in any of the ways mentioned in sub-s (3). That it is not the commencement of the investigation which has to be authorized is implicitly confirmed by s 85(2), where, in requiring the DPP's consent to the investigation before acts under sub-s (3) can be performed, it adds in parentheses 'whether before or after the start of the investigation'. This makes it clear an investigation can be started without the DPP's consent provided none of the acts under sub-s (3) are undertaken.

The DPP may give his consent only if the application for it is made by a high ranking officer (Assistant Chief Constable or, in London, Commander or above). Such an application may only be made if either:

(a) the high ranking officer concerned is satisfied that new evidence has been obtained which would be relevant to an application to quash the acquittal and order a retrial; or

(b) he has reasonable grounds for believing that such evidence is likely to be obtained as a result of the investigation.

The curious thing is that the focus is on the results of the investigation rather than what is likely to be produced by the particular steps mentioned in sub-s (3), which are the things that cannot be done without the authorization. It is the investigation which has to be consented to by the DPP, not the particular steps involving the acquitted person, even though the investigation may well already have begun. This curiosity is also exhibited in sub-s (6) setting out what the DPP has to be satisfied about when giving his consent, which again focuses on the result of the investigation overall and whether it is in the public interest for it to proceed rather than on the particular steps outlined in sub-s (3) relating to the accused. Subsection (6) sets the DPP a somewhat circular, almost clairvoyant, task of deciding whether 'there is likely as a result of the investigation to be sufficient new evidence to warrant the conduct of the investigation' Subsection (7) recognizes the potential danger of allowing a police force to investigate someone they strongly believe got away with it the first time round by allowing the DPP to recommend that the investigation be conducted by officers other than officers of a specified police force etc. Although this may be a little late if the investigation is already well under way, at least it means that any further steps in the investigation which involve the accused personally will not involve the specified police force.

7.7.2 Urgent Investigative Steps

Section 86 allows steps involving the acquitted person under s 85 to be undertaken even without the DPP authorizing the investigation if 'the action is necessary as a matter of urgency to prevent the investigation being substantially and irrevocably prejudiced' and certain other conditions in sub-s (2) *plus either* sub-s (3) *or* (5) are met. These other conditions are essentially that there has been no undue delay in applying for the DPP's consent and in view of the urgency it is not reasonably practical to get his consent first. In addition a superintendent or above has to authorize *the action* (note not the investigation) *or* it must be not reasonably practicable to obtain such authorization. The upshot is that if the police need to arrest etc an acquitted person urgently to prevent irrevocable prejudice to the investigation, they will be able to do so if they go about it in the right way.

7.7.3 Arrest, Custody and Bail

Sections 87–91 make provision for arrest custody and bail and for the application of the Police and Criminal Evidence Act 1984 and the Bail Act 1976 to a person arrested in relation to an offence for which he has been acquitted. Appropriate modifications are made to reflect, for example as in s 87(4), that the question is not whether there is evidence sufficient to charge but whether it is sufficient for the case to be referred to a prosecutor to consider whether consent should be sought for an application to quash the acquittal and order a retrial.

7.8 CONCLUSIONS

The reform to double jeopardy is complex and controversial and, as even its supporters admit, unlikely to be used in very many cases. To cause acquittals for such a wide range of offences to become in effect only provisional, with the potential to be reopened in the future on the discovery of apparently compelling new evidence, seems a high price to pay for the limited benefits in the small number of cases where the provisions may be used to correct what may seem to have been a flagrant injustice. It is doubly unfortunate that we should be making this change when other jurisdictions and the European Union appear to be moving in the opposite direction, and to be unashamedly doing so retrospectively adds another layer of unease for those opposed to the change. Defenders of the new provisions will say that they will only be used in clear or flagrant cases, but apart from the damage to the presumption of innocence involved in designating a case as a clear or flagrant one, the real damage may not be found primarily in those limited instances where a retrial is actually sought or ordered. The real damage may lie in the apprehension felt by a much larger number of genuinely innocent people, quite properly acquitted of offences, who fear, perhaps unreasonably, that their cases may be reopened. Some of these may be individuals who may be vulnerable to insinuations or pressure from the police (who themselves may genuinely feel they have a chance of quashing what seems to them to be an unjustified acquittal) to the effect that their acquittal will be reopened unless they co-operate in relation to some other matter. However, it is the impact on the values underpinning the criminal justice system which may be the most lasting and significant legacy of the changes rather than the effects on particular cases.

8

EVIDENCE OF BAD CHARACTER

8.1 INTRODUCTION

Traditional criminal justice rhetoric suggest that evidence of bad character, in the sense of criminal convictions or other misconduct of a defendant, is a distraction to truth finding and should be kept from the tribunal of fact as far as possible to enable a proper focus on the question whether the defendant committed the particular crime charged. This principle has never been seen as a justification for the exclusion of evidence of prior wrongdoing in all cases and over the years important exceptions have been developed at common law and under statute. Thus, rebuttal evidence could be adduced where a defendant chooses to adduce evidence of his own good character; evidence of prior misconduct of particular probative force, whether because of the similarity of two events or for other reasons, is admitted; and under the Criminal Evidence Act 1898 (CEA 1898) rebuttal evidence may be admitted where the accused has put his character in issue, or made imputations against prosecutors, witnesses or deceased victims. More recently, the courts have recognized an exception for background evidence which proves little but merits admission by virtue of its ability to put in context the other evidence in the case. By the end of the twentieth century, the state of the law on bad character apparently suited no one: prosecutors and investigators railed at a law which kept from a jury the very evidence which might dispel any final qualms about convicting; practising lawyers despaired at the muddle which the law had become; academics queried the premise that criminal history was prejudicial and not probative, and civil libertarians criticized the crudity of the tit-for-tat procedure under the Criminal Evidence Act.

The fact that reform was due was signalled by a Law Commission Report, *Evidence of Bad Character in Criminal Proceedings* (Law Com No 273, 2001), calls for reform from Sir Robin Auld's *Review of the Criminal Courts of England and Wales*, published in 2001 and a White Paper, *Justice for All*, published in 2002. The various reports generated much debate and a huge raft of proposals and counter proposals (see for instance P Mirfield 'Bad character and the Law Commission' (2002) 6 E&P 141–162; M Redmayne 'The Law Commission's character convictions' (2002) 6 E&P 71–93). But that debate is now ended and the reform enacted. The common law rules governing the admissibility of bad character evidence (of accused persons and others) will be abolished, as will s 1(3) (formerly s 1(f)) of the Criminal Evidence Act 1898, when the new provisions found in Part 11 of the Criminal Justice Act 2003 (CJA 2003) are brought into force. However enticing the debate which preceded the reform, the purpose of this chapter is to get to grips with the new law.

For convenience, the new law is described in the present tense and the law which is replaced is described in the past tense. Readers are, however, asked to bear in mind that for the present the 'old' law persists until this part of the Act is brought into force, probably in 2005 or 2006.

8.2 BAD CHARACTER

8.2.1 Definition of Bad Character

For the purposes of CJA 2003, 'bad character' means evidence of misconduct or evidence of a disposition towards misconduct (s 98), with 'misconduct' defined as 'the commission of an offence or other reprehensible behaviour' (s 112(1)). The inclusion of reprehensible behaviour within misconduct will serve the useful purpose of avoiding collateral arguments about whether or not conduct alleged against a non-defendant amounted to an offence where this has not resulted in a charge or conviction. However, the inclusion of reprehensible behaviour will also cause problems because of its vagueness. Presumably, it is intended that the issue whether behaviour is reprehensible should be judged according to a community, rather than personal, standard. But apart from behaviour which is contrary to the criminal law, there is no reliable means of determining what conduct is considered reprehensible. A reasonably clear example is suggested by the facts of *R v Marsh* ((1994) Crim LR 52). That case was a decision under s 1(3)(b) of the Criminal Evidence Act 1898, in which it was held that a defendant who had claimed good character could be cross-examined about his bad disciplinary record as a rugby player. Comparable circumstances would include where an employee had been warned or dismissed for misconduct at work, where a parent has had a child taken into care or where a council tenant had been subject to formal complaint or civil proceedings in relation to the tenancy. Much more problematic would be circumstances in which there is neither an agreed code of conduct nor an authoritative mechanism of adjudication. How should a court determine what is reprehensible in relation to sexual conduct, drunkenness, discourtesy or whatever? It would not be possible to rely upon the social awareness of the jury, as is done in determining dishonesty (*R v Ghosh* [1982] QB 1053), because issues of admissibility of evidence are for the judge. But nor would a judge appear to be the most appropriate person to determine an issue of this sort.

8.2.2 Exceptions to Bad Character

This definition of bad character in s 98 is subject to exceptions in relation to two categories of evidence which at common law were not subject to the same restrictions as general bad character evidence. The two exceptions are, under para (a), evidence which has to do with the alleged facts of the offence with which the defendant is charged and, under para (b), evidence of misconduct in connection with the investigation or prosecution of that offence. The clumsy phrase 'has to do with' in the first exception is intended to mean 'directly relevant to' and would encompass both direct evidence which tends to prove a matter in issue and background evidence without which a court or jury might have difficulty fully understanding the case. These categories of evidence directly relevant to the alleged offence were admissible against the accused at common law and will continue to be so by virtue of falling outside the definition of bad character evidence.

Rather different considerations apply to evidence of misconduct relating to the investigation or prosecution covered by exception (b). Clearly, where the relevant misconduct is by somebody other than the accused it may well be admissible. For instance, misconduct by a police officer in the course of interview may be relevant to the question of the admissibility of a confession. However, where misconduct of the accused in the course of the investigation is alleged, this is a category of evidence which has never been subject to a general rule of admissibility at common law. Rather, evidence of such misconduct may be admissible only if relevant to a particular issue. Thus, for instance, evidence of resisting arrest by running away may be admissible because in law the attempt to escape may imply an acknowledgement of guilt. Similarly, evidence that a suspect struck an interviewing officer and was then restrained might be used to rebut the accused's allegation of oppression in interview. However, unless admissible as relevant to a particular issue in the proceedings, evidence of misconduct will not generally be admissible. By excepting investigative misconduct from the general abolition of bad character rules, s 99(b) leaves this category of evidence in exactly the same position as it was at common law, ie generally inadmissible unless made admissible by virtue of its relevance to a live issue at trial.

A further exception to the abolition of the common law rules is found in s 99(2) which refers to the common law exception preserved by s 118(1) under which in criminal proceedings a person's reputation is admissible for the purposes of proving his bad character. This exception should be treated with considerable caution. In particular it must be borne in mind that it applies only to the extent that such a common law rule exists. In fact, although evidence of *good* reputation may be admissible to prove good character, there appears to be no reliable authority to suggest that evidence of bad reputation may be admissible for a similar purpose.

8.2.3 Exception for Defendant's Childhood Offending

By s 108(2), where a defendant is aged 21 or over, any offences committed by him when under 14 are disregarded in relation to proof of bad character unless both the current offence and the historic offence are indictable only or the court is satisfied that the interests of justice require the evidence to be admissible. The former rule under which all offences committed when a person was under 14 were to be disregarded for character purposes (Children and Young Persons Act 1963, s 16(2) and (3)) now ceases to have effect.

The rationale of the new provision is that an offence committed as a youngster becomes less significant as a guide to character by passage of time. However, it may be noted that the new provision will work in a very arbitrary manner. For instance, it would be possible to admit a theft conviction as a 12-year-old at the trial of a man of 20, but not a conviction as a 13-year-old at the trial of a man of 21. It is difficult to understand the justice of treating these two cases differently.

8.3 BAD CHARACTER OF NON-DEFENDANTS

8.3.1 Background

The common law relating to the character of non-defendants consisted of a body of rules relating to witnesses, but no particular rules, other than relevance, applied to the bad character of other persons. Even the general principle of relevance was not applied rigorously because in the absence of a requirement for leave and without anybody to champion the interests of a third party, such evidence might often be heard by the court unchallenged. That position is now consigned to history, with the admissibility of evidence of character of all non-defendants strictly governed by s 100. This provision makes no distinction between non-defendants who are witnesses and others who are strangers to the proceedings. This is odd in view of the current climate in which it is recognized that the criminal justice system must respect the human rights of witnesses and in which it is recognized that issues relating to the welfare of witnesses may impact upon the reporting of offences, the availability of witnesses, the quality of evidence at trial and ultimately on whether justice is achieved. It is also odd because some special rules relating to witnesses remain, notably the rule in s 6 of the Criminal Procedure Act 1865 that a witness may be questioned about previous convictions, and that any such convictions may be proved in evidence if the witness denies or does not admit them, or refuses to answer.

8.3.2 Leave required for Admission

The new regime for character evidence of non-defendants requires that in all cases, except where all parties agree, evidence of the bad character of a non-defendant must not be given except with leave of the court (s 100(1)(c) and (4)). The exception for agreement by the parties makes clear that the rationale of this measure is not to protect the reputations or feelings of third parties, but rather to avoid distracting the tribunal of fact from the issues in the case.

In deciding to grant leave, the court must be satisfied that the evidence of bad character is either: (a) important explanatory evidence, or (b) that it has substantial probative value in relation to a matter in issue in the proceedings, or a matter which is of substantial importance in the context of the case as a whole (s 100(1)).

8.3.3 Important Explanatory Evidence

The term 'important explanatory evidence' in para (a) imports the concept of background evidence. This is a category of evidence which has probably always been admissible but which has only recently been acknowledged and labelled by the courts (*R v Pettman* (CA, 2 May 1985 (5048/C/82)); *R v Sawoniuk* [2000] 2 Cr App R 220). Evidence will be important explanatory evidence if (a) without it, the court or jury would find it impossible or difficult properly to understand other evidence in the case, and (b) its value for understanding the case as a whole is substantial (s 100(2)).

8.3.4 Substantial Probative Value

In relation to the substantial probative value test, s100(3) sets out a non-exhaustive list of factors in paras (a) to (d) for the court to consider. The first two factors are as follows:

(a) the nature and number of the events or other things to which the evidence relates;
(b) when those events or things are alleged to have happened or existed;

The links between these factors and probative value are reasonably self-evident. Factors (c) and (d) however require a little more explanation.

(c) where—
    (i) the evidence is evidence of a person's misconduct, and
    (ii) it is suggested that the evidence has probative value by reason of similarity between that misconduct and other alleged misconduct,

the nature and extent of the similarities and the dissimilarities between each of the alleged instances of misconduct; . . .

Factor (c) typically deals with the case where the accused seeks to use 'similar fact' evidence in his defence. Thus, the accused alleges that a third party has, or may have, committed the crime charged, and that this is evidenced by other similar misconduct by that third party. In this situation, in applying the 'substantial probative value test' to determine whether to admit evidence of misconduct by the third party, the court must consider 'the nature and extent of the similarities and dissimilarities between each of the alleged instances of misconduct'. Although, the typical case described above involves the accused seeking to rely on similar misconduct of another, there may be instances in which the prosecution seek to rely on such evidence. This may be the case, for instance, where it is necessary for the prosecution to prove the involvement of an alleged accomplice in this way, where the accomplice is still at large and has not been charged.

(d) where—

    (i)   the evidence is evidence of a person's misconduct,

    (ii) it is suggested that that person is also responsible for the misconduct charged, and

    (iii) the identity of the person responsible for the misconduct charged is disputed,

the extent to which the evidence shows or tends to show that the same person was responsible each time.

Factor (d) deals with the situation where the accused denies the offence and wishes to adduce evidence of a different offence (or other misconduct) committed by another to support his suggestion that that other person committed the offence with which he is charged. Normally, in this type of situation there would be some evidence to link the two offences together and to suggest that each was committed by the same person. In deciding whether to admit evidence of the other offence, the court is directed to consider the extent to which the evidence shows or tends to show that the same person was responsible for both offences. Thus, at D's trial for robbery A, D should be able to lead evidence of similarities between robberies A and B, and evidence that X committed robbery B, in order to support a suggestion that X was also responsible for robbery A (cf *R v McGranaghan* [1995] Cr App R 559). In deciding whether to admit evidence of the other offence, the court is directed to consider the extent to which the evidence shows or tends to show that the same person was responsible for both offences.

It may be noted that there will be a substantial overlap between situations in which factor (c) (similarity) and factor (d) (linked offences) are relevant. For instance, in applying factor (d), the evidence which tends to show that the same person was responsible for each incident may be the similarity of the incidents or of some aspect of them.

8.3.5 Evidence Presumed True for Assessment of Probative Value

In line with normal practice where a court must determine either the relevance of a piece of evidence or its probative value in relation to the admission of evidence of bad character of non-defendants or of defendants, that evidence will be assumed to be true solely for the purpose of determining the admissibility issue (s 109(1)). However, a court need not assume that a piece of evidence is true if it appears to the court, on the basis if any material before it or of any evidence it decides to hear, that no court or jury could reasonably find it to be true (s 109(2)).

8.3.6 Assessment of Provisions relating to Non-defendants

It cannot be predicted that s 100 will deliver any benefits for justice. At root, the provision is simply concerned with restricting evidence to that which is relevant. But this is the first principle of admissibility at common law and it is very doubtful that anything is to be gained by setting out in detail some, but not all, factors which may be relevant to the assessment of evidence. The requirement to apply for leave before adducing bad character evidence of a non-defendant will in many cases lengthen proceedings needlessly. Consider a typical case in which a wounding results from a pub closing time disturbance. In order to set the incident in context, the prosecution might properly lead evidence of abuse, threats and aggression by a number of people present. In the past this would have been absolutely routine and it is difficult to see what advantage will be served by requiring a separate application to admit such evidence.

It will also be significant that the majority of applications to admit evidence under s 100(4) are likely to be by the defence. Inevitably, if in any doubt, judges will admit the evidence, anticipating that a refusal to do so may furnish grounds for an appeal after conviction. It will also be important for judges to be mindful of the differential burdens of proof on prosecution and defence. For the prosecution, the test of substantial probative value must be assessed against the task of the prosecutor to prove the case beyond reasonable doubt. For the defence, however, the task is merely to raise a reasonable doubt. Evidence which is far from persuasive may still be capable of raising such a doubt and should accordingly be considered to have substantial probative value in the context of the defence case.

8.4 DEFENDANT'S BAD CHARACTER

8.4.1 Evidence of Propensity and Untruthfulness

Section 101 and supplementary sections dealing with the defendant's character represent a revolution in the principles of criminal justice. Traditionally, the focus of the criminal trial has been on whether the accused committed a particular offence on a particular occasion. Accordingly, evidence relating to similar wrongdoing on other occasions has been excluded. Whereas it is hard to deny that a proven propensity to commit a particular sort of offence has some probative force, the criminal courts have eschewed such evidence as tending to distract the tribunal of fact from an assessment of the direct evidence (or lack of it) of wrongdoing on the particular occasion in question. It has always been considered that the risk that juries might reason directly from propensity: 'If he did it once he probably did it again', was sufficient to bar the use of such evidence in the interests of fairness to the accused and ensuring that guilty verdicts were well founded. The basis principle that bad character should be kept from the jury was subject to important exceptions, notably the rule that evidence of previous wrongdoing would be admissible if it had particular probative force in relation to the charge under consideration, and the rules permitting a defendant to be cross-examined about previous wrongdoing where direct evidence of this would be admissible (ie under the particular probative value rule) (CEA 1898, s 1(3)(a)); where the accused by evidence or questioning sought to establish his own good character, or where the conduct of his defence involved casting imputations on the character(s) of the prosecutor, witnesses or a deceased victim of the alleged offence (CEA 1898, s 1(3)(b)); or where he gives evidence against a co-accused in the same proceedings (CEA 1898, s 1(3)(c)).

Whereas the Act does not completely lift the general bar on the admission of evidence of the accused's bad character, it reverses the presumptions against admitting evidence of propensity to commit a particular type of crime and evidence of propensity to untruthfulness. Now evidence of propensity to commit a particular type of crime (s 103(1)(a)) and evidence of the defendant's past untruthfulness (s 103(1)(b)), may be admitted. This significant extension to the admissibility of character evidence is balanced by two new measures. First, a power to exclude such evidence, on application by the accused on the ground that the admission of the evidence would have such an adverse effect on the fairness of the proceedings that the court ought not to admit it (s 101(4)). Secondly, a judicial power to stop the case where character evidence is admitted which is contaminated and where the court is of the view that as a result of the contamination, any conviction obtained in the proceedings would be unsafe (s 107). Both of these safeguards will be considered in greater detail below.

Section 101(1) effectively abrogates any relevant common law rules on evidence of the bad character of the defendant, and holds that such evidence may be admissible but only in specified circumstances.

8.4.2 Applications to Admit

A provision restricting admissibility in this way would normally require that affected evidence should not be admitted without leave of the court and that it should be for the party proposing to adduce the evidence who should seek leave. Indeed, this is the model applied in relation to bad character evidence of a non-defendant under s 100. However, in relation to defendant's character evidence there is no procedure for seeking leave. Instead, under rules of court to be made under s 111, if the prosecution proposes to adduce evidence of a defendant's bad character, or proposes to cross-examine a witness with a view to eliciting such evidence, the rules will require that a notice is served on the defendant containing such particulars as *may* be prescribed (s 111(2)). The section also indicates that the notice requirement may be applied by the rules where the party seeking to adduce or elicit the evidence is a co-defendant. In fact it is hard to imagine any reason why notice should not be given in the case of the co-accused and it is therefore anticipated that the notice requirement will be the same whoever seeks to adduce the bad character evidence. In relation to the rule-making power, there is no mention of a duty to notify the court at the same time as the defendant. This is a curious omission since the court would normally wish to be forewarned if a party is seeking to adduce potentially inadmissible evidence. It is to be hoped that this omission will be rectified under the general rule-making power to 'make such provision as appears to the rule-making authority to be necessary or expedient' (s 111(1)). It is also provided that the court or defendant may, in prescribed circumstances, dispense with a notice requirement (s 111(3)), although it is not indicated in what circumstances such a dispensation may be made.

Once notice has been given that the prosecution or a co-accused plans to adduce or elicit bad character evidence, the defendant would have a right to challenge it on the ground that the proposed evidence does not fall within the specified categories of admissibility in s 101(1) (considered below). It is implicit that such a right of challenge exists although not not mentioned in the legislation, for in the absence of a procedure for obtaining leave to admit the evidence, there would otherwise be no mechanism for giving effect to the general bar on evidence of the defendant's bad character (s 101(1)). The existence of a mechanism for challenge is also implicit in s 110 which requires courts to make any rulings as to admissibility under ss 100 and 101, in open court.

As well as the general right to challenge the grounds of admissibility, s 101(3) confers on the defendant a special right to challenge evidence which goes to an important matter in issue between the defendant and the prosecution or character evidence which is admitted in response to an attack on another person's character. Where an application is made, the court must exclude the evidence if it appears that the admission of the evidence would have such an adverse effect on the fairness of the proceedings that the court ought not to admit it. (This is also considered in greater detail below.)

8.4.3 Grounds for Admitting Defendant's Bad Character

The grounds for admitting evidence of the defendant's bad character are set out in s 101(1)(a)–(g), as follows:

(a) all parties to the proceedings agree to the evidence being admissible,
(b) the evidence is adduced by the defendant himself or is given in answer to a question asked by him in cross-examination and intended to elicit it,
(c) it is important explanatory evidence,
(d) it is relevant to an important matter in issue between the defendant and the prosecution,
(e) it has substantial probative value in relation to an important matter in issue between the defendant and co-defendant,
(f) it is evidence to correct a false impression given by the defendant, or
(g) the defendant has made an attack on another person's character.

8.4.4 Waiver by the Defendant

The general rule excluding bad character evidence is treated as a procedural benefit for the accused which he may waive if he so wishes. Thus, character evidence is admissible by agreement of all parties (including the defendant) under (a), or where the evidence is adduced or intentionally elicited by the defendant in cross-examination under (b). Implicitly, evidence of the defendant's bad character elicited accidentally by defence counsel during cross-examination, will not be admissible. The practical significance of this rule will not be great. There will be no scope for the leave requirement once the evidence has been given although the defendant will be entitled to a jury direction to ignore the rogue evidence. In extreme cases where the inadmissible character evidence is highly prejudicial, the trial judge could dismiss the jury and order a retrial or the Court of Appeal could quash a resulting conviction as unsafe. However, the problem of a defendant accidentally eliciting evidence of his own bad character is not new, and since courts have not responded to the problem in these ways in the past, it seems unlikely that they would choose to do so under the new legislation.

8.4.5 Important Explanatory Evidence

The definition of important explanatory evidence is the same as applies to the admissibility of a non-defendant's bad character. Under s 102, evidence is important explanatory evidence if (a) without it, the court or jury would find it impossible or difficult properly to understand other evidence in the case, and (b) its value for understanding the case as a whole is substantial.

8.4.6 Relevance to Issue between Defendant and Prosecution

Perhaps the most revolutionary change in the law relating to the defendant's character is brought about by para (d) which makes admissible, evidence which is relevant to an important matter at issue between the prosecution and defence. Logically, only the prosecution can rely upon this exception (s 103(6)).

The new rule sweeps away a century or more of the similar fact doctrine and the modern rule which it has evolved into. The similar fact doctrine permitted the admission of evidence of previous misconduct by the accused, whose probative value stemmed from striking similarity with some aspect of the charged offence (*Boardman v DPP* [1975] AC 421) as well as the broader modern doctrine that evidence of other misconduct may be admissible if its probative force is sufficiently great to make it just to admit the evidence notwithstanding its prejudicial effect (per Lord Mackay LC, *DPP v P* [1991] 2 AC 47 at 462). The test in *P* was generally understood as embodying a high threshold of relevance or probative value—indicating that the default position of English law was that the interest in avoiding prejudice to the defendant outweighed evidential value, unless the latter was very strong. The new test in para (d) requires relevance to an important issue, but the requirement of 'importance' probably adds little since any issue which may affect the outcome of the case would surely qualify. Thus, the new test based on simple relevance suggests a much lower threshold than at common law. It should however be noted that the second part of the *P* test, requiring a consideration of the justice of admitting the evidence, will continue to be an issue in relation to the court's power to exclude character evidence under s 101(3).

The view that s 101(1)(d) imports a revolutionary change is compounded by s 103(1), which provides that the matters in issue between prosecution and defendant will include the question whether the defendant has a propensity to commit offences of a kind with which he is charged, and whether the defendant has a propensity to be untruthful. Thus, on a trial for burglary, the fact that the defendant has previously been tried, pleaded not guilty and then been convicted of burglary, will be potentially admissible, first to demonstrate a relevant propensity to commit burglary, secondly to demonstrate a propensity to untruthfulness. The general rule is subject to two factual exceptions: where as a matter of fact having the propensity to commit such offences makes it no more likely that he committed the offence in question; and (in the case of alleged propensity to untruthfulness), where it is not alleged that the defendant's case is untruthful in any respect.

8.4.7 Meaning of Propensity

Until now the courts have had no cause to define propensity. Nor is a definition of propensity offered in s 112, the interpretation section for Part 11 of the Act. However s 103(2) suggests one way in which propensity may be established.

. . . a defendant's propensity to commit offences of the kind with which he is charged may (without prejudice to any other way of doing so) be established by evidence that he has been convicted of—

(a) an offence of the same description as the one with which he is charged, or
(b) an offence of the same category as the one with which he is charged.

Subsection (3) further provides that sub-s (2) should not apply if the court is satisfied that by reason of the length of time since the conviction, or for any other reasons, it would be unjust to apply this method of inferring propensity from record.

Earlier offences will be of the same 'kind' as an offence with which the accused is currently charged if they are of the same description or same category. These two terms are explained in sub-s (4)(a) and (b):

(a) two offences are of the same description as each other if the statement of the offence in a written charge or indictment would, in each case, be in the same terms;

Although reference is made to whether the respective statements of offence 'would be' in the same terms, in practice where proceedings have commenced for both the past and current offence, the question will be whether the statements of offence are actually in the same terms. Generally, the issue will be whether the two charges involve the same statutory or common law offence. Difficulties may arise with offences which may be committed in alternative ways. For instance, in relation to two similar damage cases, the respective statements could read: (i) 'Destroying property with intent to endanger life contrary to the Criminal Damage Act 1971, s 1(2)'; or 'Damaging property being reckless as to whether life would be endangered . . .'. In many cases the choice of one form or another will simply be made for tactical reasons or convenience. Whether or not an earlier conviction is available to prove propensity as being 'of the same description' as a current offence, may turn on what may have been a quite arbitrary choice.

(b) two offences are of the same category as each other if they belong to the same category of offences prescribed for the purposes of this section by an order made by the Secretary of State.

Quite unnecessarily, we are further told that a category prescribed by order under sub-s (4)(b) must consist of offences of the same type. There is currently no indication of the contents of any such proposed order. The task of categorizing offences for this purpose may prove extremely complex. It may be queried whether it might have been more satisfactory simply to leave the question of whether a prior record demonstrates a relevant propensity to the good sense of the judges.

A finding of propensity to commit a particular kind of offence will not follow automatically from a record of previous convictions. This is apparent from the wording of s 103(2) which states that propensity 'may' be established in this way, but also from sub-s (3) which provides that a finding of propensity should not be made if it would be unjust to do so on grounds of the length of time since conviction or for any other reason. Other reasons which might militate against a finding of propensity might include particular circumstances surrounding either of the offences. For instance, a court might determine that a person had no general propensity for criminal damage on the basis of an earlier damage offence arising specifically in the context of a neighbour dispute.

8.4.8 The Operation of the Provision

Proponents of more liberal admissibility of bad character evidence perhaps anticipated a simple change in the rules, which would allow a relevant criminal record of the defendant to be put before the court. In fact the operation of this provision will be very complex and will inevitably draw trial judges into the process of evaluating evidence, normally considered the proper function of the jury. The first question for the judge will be to determine prima facie admissibility. The test under s 103(1) is not simply whether the defendant has committed offences or been untruthful in the past, but rather whether he has a (presumably current) propensity to commit such offences or to lie. In cases of a substantial criminal record, the issue of propensity may be easily determined. In other cases the judge may be required to assess historical events, for which evidence may be patchy, in order to determine whether they demonstrate a current propensity. For instance, in the burglary example given above, the defendant might argue that his single burglary conviction is old, and in the light of a clean record over the last few years, does not suggest a propensity to burglary. He might also argue that although he pleaded not guilty to the original burglary charge, he did not testify and simply put the prosecution to proof, thus not demonstrating any propensity to lie.

What this example illustrates is that the issue of propensity may involve difficult questions of fact, which the accused can be expected to contest in view of the impact which admission of the accused's criminal record is likely to have on the case. If the propensity enquiry is likely to involve a consideration of not simply the fact of convictions but also the facts on which the convictions were based, prosecutors may well decide that the process cost in terms of court time outweighs the benefits in adducing the bad character evidence.

8.4.9 Relevance to Issue between Defendant and Co-defendant

The power to admit bad character evidence in respect of an issue between the defendant and co-defendant under s 101(1)(e) is restricted to evidence either adduced by the co-defendant or which the co-defendant intends to elicit in cross-examination (s 104(2)). The test for admissibility is probative value in relation to an important matter in issue. As suggested above, any issue which might affect the outcome of the case must be considered important. The requirement that probative value is substantial is included to avoid unregulated mud-slinging between defendants but probably adds little weight to the test since the normal legal meaning of 'substantial' is 'more than trivial'.

This new provision which regulates not only adducing evidence against the defendant but also cross-examining him about his record, will effectively replace CEA 1898, s 1(3)(c), which is repealed by Sch 37, Pt 5. Whereas the former provision was drafted in terms of 'giving evidence' against a co-defendant, it was interpreted widely to include cases where the defence in court was simply inconsistent with that being run by the co-accused (*Murdoch v Taylor* [1975] AC 474). The new provision, which relates to matters in issue, will thus cover the same ground as the former.

In one important respect, the new provision will be significantly narrower than s 1(3)(c). Under the former provision, once the defendant had given evidence against a co-accused, the power to cross-examine on his character was available to the co-accused without any limitation as to relevance. Under s 101(d), only evidence or cross-examination which is relevant to the matter in issue between the parties will be admissible. Consistent with this, where bad character evidence relates to whether the defendant has a propensity to be untruthful, it is admissible only if the nature and conduct of the defendant's defence are such as to undermine the co-defendant's defence (s 104(1)), ie where the question of D's truthfulness is very relevant to the case for the co-defendant.

8.4.10 Evidence to Correct a False Impression

Section 101(f) permits bad character evidence to be given by the prosecution, but not by a co-accused (s 105(7)), if the defendant is responsible for the making of an express or implied assertion which is apt to give the court or jury a false or misleading impression about the defendant (s 105(1)(a)). This provision effectively replaces CEA 1898, s 1(3)(b) (repealed by Sch 37, Pt 5) which permitted a defendant to be cross-examined on his character if he gave or adduced evidence about his own good character. The defendant is treated as being responsible for the making of an express or implied assertion, not only in his own testimony in court, but also in the following situations:

- when evidence is given of what the defendant said on being questioned under caution, prior to charge (s 105(2)(a));

- when evidence is given of what the defendant said on being charged or officially informed that he might be prosecuted (s 105(2)(b));
- when the assertion is made by a witness called by the defendant (s 105(2)(c));
- when the assertion is made by a witness under cross-examination by the defendant, that is either intended or likely to elicit the assertion (s 105(2)(d));
- the defendant adduces evidence of an assertion made out of court by another (s 105(2)(e));
- where it appears to the court that the defendant by his conduct in the proceedings (including his appearance or dress) is seeking to give the court or jury a false or misleading impression about himself (s 105(4) and (5)).

The most significant change brought about by this provision is that the defendant may lose his shield whether or not he personally testifies. Whereas under CEA 1898, s 1(3)(b) a defendant could avoid being cross-examined by not giving evidence, under s 101 the sanction that bad character evidence may be admitted applies in any case in which the defendant is deemed responsible for an assertion.

The Act seeks to preclude any possibility that the defendant may present himself favourably (or otherwise in a misleading way) without the risk of his bad character becoming admissible. Thus relevant assertions may be express or implied or conveyed by the defendant's conduct in the proceedings, including his appearance or dress. The latter condition might be satisfied if the defendant appeared in court in a cassock or wearing a stethoscope, but it is to be hoped that courts will not seek to apply the provision where the defendant simply presents himself smartly in court, however uncharacteristic this may be. Where such cases of false impression by conduct or appearance occur, there may in fact be no obvious 'remedy' available to the prosecution. Under s 101(1) the permissible response to the false impression is the admission of bad character evidence, but this must be for the purpose of correcting the false impression (s 105(1)(b)) and go no further than to correct the false impression (s 105(6)). In relation to an example given above of a defendant wearing a cassock to court, it seems unlikely that any specific evidence relating to offences or reprehensible behaviour would dispel the impression that the defendant is a cleric. If that were the case, the prosecution would be left without an apparent remedy since evidence of specific misconduct would clearly go beyond what would be necessary to correct the false impression that the defendant is a cleric.

8.4.11 Avoiding Unfairness to the Accused

The Act deems the defendant responsible for making assertions in a number of circumstances in which the production of the evidence in court is not wholly under the defendant's control. Thus, in relation to statements made by the accused in police interview or when charged, the evidence will be adduced by the prosecution. In relation to statements made by defence witnesses or during cross-examination of prosecution witnesses, the words will be uttered by another. In these situations, the defendant is not responsible in the sense of having a power to determine whether the assertion is made: rather the 'responsibility' of the defendant is a legal construct. The Act seeks to overcome unfairness associated with this constructive responsibility in two ways. First, in relation to evidence elicited in cross-examination of prosecution witnesses, the defendant will be responsible only if the question asked was either intended or likely to elicit that assertion (s 105(1)(d)). In some cases this determination may be straightforward. In other cases it would involve a *voir dire*, an examination of defence counsel's intentions, and legal argument. It is doubtful whether justice would be furthered by complicating trials in this way.

8.4.12 Withdrawal and Disassociation

The second method of avoiding unfairness to the accused is even more problematic. Under s 105(3) a defendant who would otherwise be treated as responsible for an assertion shall not be so treated if, or to the extent that, he withdraws it or disassociates himself from it. The mechanism for making any such withdrawal or disassociation is not specified. Since this is an issue relating to the potential admissibility of bad character evidence, it would normally be dealt with on *voir dire* in the absence of the jury. However, since the substance of the issue is whether the court or jury have been given a false impression, clearly a withdrawal or disassociation is pointless unless made before the jury, but this in turn would create a number of difficulties.

Where the relevant assertion is in the defendant's own evidence, it is not clear how and when the defendant should be given the opportunity to withdraw. Should it be for defence counsel to invite a withdrawal in examination in chief, or should the opportunity for withdrawal arise in the course of cross-examination by the prosecutor? If an opportunity for withdrawal is not taken, would the defendant be permitted to withdraw later and would an adjournment be permitted for the defendant to be given advice on the particular significance of the issue? Similar issues arise in relation to statements made by the defendant in interview or upon being charged at the police station.

Where a relevant assertion is elicited from a prosecution witness in cross-examination, an opportunity for the defendant to disassociate himself from it would arise when and if the defendant testifies. Where, however, the defendant has chosen not to testify, as he is entitled to do, it is not clear by what procedure he should disassociate himself from the statement made. There would not seem to be any need for the defendant to be put on oath for this procedure since the jury would not be invited to believe anything he said. However, whether under oath or not, it would seem very strange for an otherwise silent defendant to be called upon to address a single issue in a prosecution witness's statement. More difficult questions would arise where the relevant assertion was adduced from a defence witness. At this stage, the defendant would have either testified or elected to remain silent. In either event, it would be strange for him to be called for the sole purpose of disassociating himself from a positive assertion about himself.

The final difficulty about the disassociation exception is that it is not clear what would be acceptable as disassociation. Would the defendant be required to contradict the statement made, even if this reflected very badly upon himself? Or might the requirement be satisfied by a formalistic recitation of a neutral verbal formula or perhaps the single-word answer 'No' in response to a question from counsel? A further issue which is not addressed in the Act, is whether it would be necessary to provide some form of caution or warning, coupled with an opportunity to withdraw or disassociate, before the judge could give leave to admit bad character evidence. This would be consistent with the approach taken to the drawing of inferences from silence in court under s 35 of the Criminal Justice and Public Order Act 1994 and also with the requirements of fair trial under Article 6 of the European Convention on Human Rights (cf *Murray v United Kingdom* [1996] EHRR 29). Although not mentioned specifically in s 111, it may be necessary for the issues discussed here to be dealt with by rules of court made under that section.

8.4.13 Incidental Misleading Impression

The Act does not answer the question whether the defendant should be exposed to bad character evidence where he makes an assertion necessary for his defence, but which incidentally gives a misleading impression. Under the Criminal Evidence Act 1898, the better view was that if the defendant did no more than assert facts necessary for his defence, he would not be considered to have put his character in issue independently and would not lose his shield under s 1(3)(b) (see eg *Malindi v R* [1967] AC 439). Although ss 101 and 105 are silent on the issue, it would seem to be axiomatic that the defendant must be permitted to put his defence, and this would seem to be implicit in the right of the accused to defend himself under Article 6(3)(c) of the European Convention on Human Rights. Should this issue arise, the court would be bound by s 3 of the Human Rights Act 1998 to interpret the statute so as to be compatible with Article 6.

8.4.14 False and Misleading Assertions

A significant departure from the pre-existing law is that whereas under CEA 1898, s 1(3)(b) it was sufficient if the defendant merely adduced evidence of his own good character, under the new provision, giving evidence of his own good character would cause him to lose his shield only if the evidence adduced were false or misleading. The use of these terms in tandem suggests that evidence may be strictly true and therefore not false, but nevertheless convey a misleading impression. Deciding whether or not this is the case may be problematic. For instance, where a defendant with a criminal record adduces true evidence of his own regular church-going, could it be said that it is misleading because it gives an impression of an overall good person, or should it be simply treated as true and therefore not misleading? The difficulty with the former proposition is that if the jury are misled by the church-going evidence, it is because they have jumped to an unfounded conclusion. In the absence of a specific indication from defence counsel to infer good character from such evidence, it is difficult to see that it would be fair to penalize the defendant by admitting evidence of bad character.

A practical advantage of the rather crude scheme under CEA 1898, s 1(3)(b) was that all parties knew that if a defendant with a record put his character in issue, whether or not his evidence was true, he ran the risk of cross-examination on his record. The new scheme, under which evidence which is neither true nor misleading may be adduced without risk, may encourage defence lawyers to present evidence for the sole purpose of casting their client in a good light. There is authority for the proposition that the defendant can call evidence of a reputation for good character but is barred from adducing evidence of specific good conduct (*R v Rowton* [1865] Le & Ca 520, CCR). Commentators have doubted whether this still represents the law (eg I Dennis, *The Law of Evidence* (2nd edn, 2002, p 652). Whatever the legal status of the proposition, in practice, it is difficult to prevent evidence of this sort being given, particularly if this may now be done without risk in some situations. In any event judges are rightly wary of being seen to interfere with evidence being given by or on behalf of defendants.

An oddity about this provision is that although it has been presented as providing a means of responding to a defendant's claims about himself, under s 101(1)(f) the false impression can relate to anything, and could involve personal issues unrelated to criminality or matters totally unrelated to the defendant. However, in view of the fact that the 'sanction' for the false or misleading assertion is the admissibility of bad character evidence, and this must go no further than is required to correct the false impression (s 105(6)), the provision is likely to be used only for character assertions.

8.4.15 Attack on Another Person's Character

At common law a defendant was free to attack another person's character in the course of his defence without putting his own character in issue (*R v Butterwasser* [1948] 1 KB 4). This rule was favourable to defendants who did not give evidence in their own defence. For defendants who chose to testify, the rule was subject to the important statutory exception under the second limb of CEA 1898, s 1(3)(b). Under that provision a defendant might be cross-examined on his criminal record if the nature and conduct of his defence was such as to involve imputations on the character of the prosecutor, witnesses or deceased victim of the alleged crime. Section 1(3) is now repealed by Sch 37, Pt 5. Under s 101(1)(g) bad character evidence will be admissible against a defendant who has made an attack on any other person's character, whether or not the defendant chooses to give evidence. Only the prosecution can adduce evidence under this provision (s 106(3)). The rationale of the provision is not to protect the reputations of others but rather to provide evidence to balance any attack which the defendant should make.

Evidence attacking another person's character means evidence that the other person has committed an offence or has behaved or is disposed to behave in a reprehensible way (s 106(2)). The allegation made against the other person may relate to the same offence with which the defendant is charged, and therefore the provision may be engaged where the defendant simply blames another for the offence with which he is charged. In this circumstance it is arguable that the provision goes too far since it appears to penalize a simple defence to the charge. Interestingly, it is not necessary that the person attacked should be named and it would seem that the provision would apply if an unnamed or imaginary person is implicated. As with the common law, there is no requirement that the attack should be untrue or unfounded. This is an important rule procedurally because it avoids the court becoming bogged down in the collateral issue of the truth or otherwise of the defendant's allegations. However, it would seem unfair to place any restraint on the defendant making an allegation which was both true and relevant to the proceedings. In such a case the only formal means of protecting the defendant would be an application under s 101(3) to exclude the bad character evidence proposed by the prosecution, on the ground that it would have such an adverse effect on the fairness of the proceedings that the court ought not to admit it.

An attack on another's character may be made by adducing evidence, by asking questions in cross-examination that are intended to elicit such evidence or are likely to do so, or where a relevant imputation about another person is made by the defendant on being questioned under caution or when charged or informed that he might be prosecuted (s 106(1)). An inconsistency in the scheme of the Act is that there is no provision for withdrawing an imputation made during the investigative stage in the police station.

8.5 STOPPING CONTAMINATED CASES

Section 101 provides for a number of circumstances in which a defendant may suffer detriment as a result of the introduction of bad character evidence. To demonstrate a commitment to fairness, s 107 provides a special procedure to protect a defendant who may potentially be prejudiced where such bad character evidence has been interfered with. The power is additional to the court's existing powers to order an acquittal, stay proceedings for abuse of process, or discharge a jury and order a retrial to avoid unfairness (sub-s (4)).

Under s 107 a trial court may stop a case where evidence of bad character has been adduced by the prosecution under s 101 (other than by agreement of all parties) but it later appears that that evidence has been contaminated, such that any resulting conviction would be unsafe. The power applies in relation to trial before judge and jury (sub-s (1)) or where a jury is required to decide whether a person charged on an indictment did the act or omission charged, where the issue of unfitness to plead has been raised under the Criminal Procedure (Insanity) Act 1964 (sub-s (3)). In either case where the power is exercised, the judge has a choice of either directing the jury to acquit or to discharge the jury and order a retrial (sub-s (1)) or rehearing in a case of unfitness to plead (sub-s (3)(c)). In cases where, if the defendant is acquitted of the offence charged, he may be convicted of a lesser offence, the court should consider whether any conviction for the lesser offence would similarly be unsafe and if it would, the jury will be barred from a finding of guilty of that lesser offence (sub-s (2)).

Evidence is contaminated where it is false or misleading or it is different from what it otherwise would have been, (a) as a result of an agreement or understanding between the witness and one or more other persons, or (b) as a result of the witness being aware of anything alleged by another person whose evidence has been or may be given in the proceedings. This test is remarkably wide. Although aimed at witness nobbling by an investigator, victim or co-accused, it might equally apply to the hitherto approved practice whereby police officers who anticipate refreshing their memories from notebooks during testimony, will prepare their notebooks together or share a single record of events (*R v Kelsey* (1982) 74 Cr App R 213). (Note that the common law on refreshing memory is now codified in s 139.)

8.6 PROCEDURE

8.6.1 Court's Duty to give Reasons

Courts will be required to make a number of different sorts of rulings in operating the new bad character provisions. By s 110(1) courts are required to state reasons for certain 'relevant rulings' in open court, in the absence of the jury if there is one, and in the case of a magistrates' court the ruling must be entered on the court register. The relevant rulings to which these requirements apply are: (a) rulings on whether evidence is evidence of a person's bad character; (b) a ruling on whether such evidence is admissible in relation to a non-defendant (under s 100) or a defendant (under s 101); (c) a variety of rulings which may be made under the procedure for stopping cases affected by contaminated evidence under s 107 (s 110(2)).

8.6.2 Rules of Court

Section 111 confers broad powers to make rules for the Crown Court, Court of Appeal and magistrates' courts. The rules must provide for the prosecution to give notice to the defendants if it is proposed to adduce evidence of the defendant's bad character or to elicit such evidence from a witness in cross-examination (s 111(2)). Similar rules may be made where the party proposing to offer bad character evidence is a co-defendant and the rules may also prescribe circumstances in which notice requirements may be dispensed with (s 111(3)). In exercising its powers with respect to costs, a court may take into account any failure by a party to comply with a notice requirement under the rules (s 111(4)).

8.6.3 Application to the Armed Forces

Section 113 gives effect to Sch 6 which applies the provisions of ss 98–112 to criminal procedure in service courts with necessary modifications of terminology.

9

HEARSAY

9.1 INTRODUCTION

9.1.1 Background

Chapter 2 of Part 11 of the Criminal Justice Act 2003 (CJA 2003) is concerned with a wholesale reform of the rule against hearsay. Perhaps the only aspect of hearsay on which there is broad agreement is Sir Rupert Cross's statement of the rule: 'that a statement other than one made by a person while giving oral evidence in the proceedings is inadmissible as evidence of any fact stated' (*Cross and Tapper on Evidence* (9th edn, 1999, p 529)). Although attempts had been made by the Criminal Justice Act 1988 (CJA 1988) to bring the rule up to date by the introduction of an exception for business records and an extension of the exceptions permitted for absent witnesses, the rule has remained a continuing source of uncertainty for practitioners and of illogicality for commentators. Particular issues which have stimulated considerable debate include, whether the rule should be relaxed in favour of defendants, whether it should apply equally to implied and express assertions, and whether the intrinsic reliability of a statement should be a ground for exception from the rule. Reform of the rule has been on the agenda for some time. The virtual abolition of the rule in civil proceedings by the Civil Evidence Act 1995 has provided a stimulus for action. The endeavours of academics (eg P Murphy, 'Practising safe hearsay: Surrender may be inevitable, but shouldn't we take precautions' (1997) 1 E&P 105), the Law Commission in Consultation Paper No 138 (1995) and Report No 245 (1997), the Auld *Review of the Criminal Courts* (2001) and the White Paper *Justice for All* (Cm 5563, 2002) have all provided models for reform—now at last given substance in the Criminal Justice Act 2003.

9.1.2 The Scheme of Hearsay Reform

Ultimately the government has substantially accepted the advice of the Law Commission in Report No 245. The major features of the resulting scheme of hearsay reform are as follows:

• the exclusionary hearsay rule is retained;
• subject to any statutory exceptions, including those found in Act;
• subject to common law rules expressly preserved by the Act;
• hearsay rule not applicable to implied assertions;
• rigidity of the hearsay rule tempered by a new rule to admit hearsay evidence with the consent of all parties;
• new 'safety-valve' discretion to admit hearsay in the interests of justice;
• similar 'safety-valve' discretion to exclude otherwise admissible hearsay in the interests of efficiency;
• statutory exceptions for unavailable witnesses and business documents are reformed and extended;
• previous statements admitted to demonstrate consistency or inconsistency become evidence of any matter stated;
• work preparatory to expert reports to be admissible hearsay;
• clarification of rules relating to admissibility of co-accused's confession;
• power to admit video-recording of eye-witness statement as evidence in chief;
• reform of rules about refreshing memory.

9.1.3 Implementation

It is anticipated that the bulk of the hearsay reforms will be brought into force in 2005/2006. However, the reform of the rules on refreshing memory while giving evidence, found in ss 139–141 were brought into force on 5 April 2004 by SI 2004/829.

9.2 SCOPE OF THE EXCLUSIONARY RULE

9.2.1 The Exclusionary Rule

Section 114 confirms the traditional exclusionary rule of hearsay but also introduces two reforms which will significantly reduce the scope of hearsay and in doing so will remove some criticisms of the rule. First, the hearsay rule ceases to apply to implied assertions; secondly, a broad discretion to admit hearsay in the interests of justice is introduced.

Under s 114, a statement not made in oral evidence in the proceedings is inadmissible as evidence of any matter stated. Hearsay may be admissible under any express statutory provision, including the various rules in Chapter 2 of the Act, or under one of the common law rules expressly preserved by s 118, or where all parties agree to the hearsay statement being admitted or where the court is satisfied that admission is in the interests of justice.

Statements covered by the rule include any representation of fact or opinion, including sketches, photofits and other forms of picture (s 115(2)).

9.2.2 Exclusionary Rule Ceases to apply to Implied Assertions

A major criticism of the scope of the hearsay rule has been its application to implied assertions. Although that term has been conventionally used in this context, it may include circumstances in which it is artificial to suggest that any assertion is being made at all. Thus, in *R v Kearley* ([1992] AC 228) it was held that telephone calls to the defendant's flat, in which the callers requested drugs, were inadmissible hearsay because they contained implied assertions that the defendant was a drug dealer. Another often repeated hypothetical example is that a sea captain who takes his family on a sea journey, impliedly asserts that in his opinion the ship is sound. The objection to including such implied assertions within the hearsay rule is that whereas words may convey lies, conduct which is not intended to convey any message to others is naturally honest. The government, following the Law Commission advice, have accepted this argument.

The removal of implied statements from the hearsay rule is achieved by s 115(3) under which a matter stated is one to which the hearsay provisions apply if (and only if) the purpose, or one of the purposes, of the person making the statement appears to the court to have been (a) to cause another person to believe the matter, or (b) to cause another person to act or a machine to operate on the basis that the matter is as stated. Thus, if the sea captain intended to convey no particular message to anybody else when he embarked with his family, he would make no statement to which the hearsay provisions would apply.

9.2.3 Statements by Machines

The definition of 'statement' in s 115 is limited to 'representations of fact or opinion made by a person by whatever means' (sub-s (2)). The definition follows the common law in excluding from the ambit of 'statement' any purely mechanical output of a machine, such as a read out from an intoximeter or a piece of video footage, both of which are properly classified as real evidence. Difficulties arising in classifying documents or other things which are produced by machines but which may also express a representation made by a person, express or implied. The clearest cases are documents printed out by word-processors which are clearly classified as statements. More difficult are things like airline tickets, which are printed out after some information has been input by a ticket clerk. In *R v Rice* ([1963] 1 QB 857) the Court of Appeal said that an airline ticket could be admitted as real evidence to suggest that the person named on the ticket had taken a particular flight, but that if the document were to be taken as speaking its contents, the resulting statement would be hearsay. This case is generally considered to have been wrongly decided, at least on technical grounds. The only relevance of the ticket to the facts in issue was that the ticket clerk, by typing a name into a machine, had stated that he was issuing the ticket to the named individual.

The issue of documents produced by machines but with some human input is now dealt with by s 129.

(1) Where a representation of any fact—
    (a) is made otherwise than by a person, but
    (b) depends for its accuracy on information supplied (directly or indirectly) by a person,

the representation is not admissible in criminal proceedings as evidence of the fact unless it is proved that the information was accurate.

The paradigm case under s 129 will be the airline ticket, bearing a traveller's name, starting and destination airports, seat number and date and time of travel. It will be noted that s 129 does not itself classify such documents as either hearsay or real evidence. However, the definition of 'statement' in s 115(2) is 'any representation of fact or opinion made by a person by whatever means'. This definition applies in relation to all of the hearsay provisions in Part 11 of the Act. At first glance s 129 and s 115 appear to be mutually exclusive. Section 129 deals with representation made 'otherwise than by a person', whereas s 115 confines statements to representations by persons. However, this approach would probably rob s 129 of any effect. The better view is that s 129 prescribes a rule of admissibility for hearsay representations made by a person via the mechanical agency of a machine. The production of the statement by the machine may be considered as falling within the term 'representation of fact . . . made by whatever means' in s 115(2).

If the argument above is correct, the admissibility rule is very strict indeed. It appears to require proof of accuracy (with no scope for doubt). In the case of *Rice* that test could only be satisfied (if at all) by calling the ticket clerk and examining his sources for the information he typed into the ticket machine. This raises all the difficulties associated with routine information recorded by functionaries which is normally accurate but difficult to verify after the event, which was considered in *Myers v DPP* ([1965] AC 1001). Whereas, the rules relating to the admissibility of business documents (now found in CJA 2003, s 117) were designed to banish those problems, it would appear that s 129, with its strict test for admissibility, has revived them in relation to the numerous business documents produced by computers and other devices.

9.3 THE SAFETY-VALVE DISCRETION TO ADMIT

A persistent criticism of the hearsay rule is that in its categorical rigidity it may exclude some item of evidence which considered individually would warrant admission. This criticism will be largely defused by the various reforms to the rule found in the present Act. However, as a safety valve, a broad discretion to admit otherwise inadmissible hearsay is included in s 114(1)(d). Subsection (2) sets out a non-exhaustive list of factors which the court must have regard to in exercising its discretion. A number of these factors relate to the significance of the evidence in question. These include the statement's probative value or value in assisting understanding of other evidence (background evidence), whether other evidence is available on this issue and how important the relevant matter is in relation to the case as a whole. Other factors relate to the circumstances in which the statement was made, how reliable the maker appears to be, how reliable is the evidence relating to the making of the statement, whether oral evidence of the matter stated can be given and if not why not. The court must also consider adversarial issues including the amount of difficulty which the other party might have in challenging the statement (ie because the witness is not available for cross-examination) and the extent to which that difficulty would be likely to prejudice the party facing it.

The discretion may be significant in a case such as *R v Blastland* ([1986] AC 41) in which hearsay evidence was arguably the only means available to put a particular line of defence before the jury. The discretion may also be significant in cases which fall outside other hearsay exceptions, for instance because the identity of an absent witness is not known. No doubt since the coming into force of the Human Rights Act 1998, the courts will be keen to use the discretion in order to guarantee the fair trial rights of an accused under Article 6 of the European Convention on Human Rights (ECHR). The courts may be less willing to contemplate use of the discretion to admit evidence against the accused for fear of breaching those same fair trial rights (cf *R v Radak* [1999] 1 Cr App R 187).

9.4 THE SAFETY-VALVE DISCRETION TO EXCLUDE

The overriding 'safety-valve' discretion to admit in the interests of justice under s 114(1)(d) is matched by discretion to exclude otherwise admissible hearsay statements in s 126. The extent to which the test confers a broad general discretion is open to question. The overall test is that the court is satisfied that the 'case for excluding the statement' . . . 'outweighs the case for admitting it'. Stated thus, the section appears to confer a broad discretion under which the relative cases for admitting or excluding the statement are at the discretion of the parties and may include any matters. However, this position is called into some doubt by the fact that two particular matters are expressly mentioned as being relevant to the cases for an against admission. These are, the danger that to admit the statement would result in an undue waste of time (against admission) and the value of the evidence (for admission). By mentioning only two relevant factors the provision may be understood as limiting the discretion to these two factors. If that were to be the case the discretion would be remarkably narrow, and in particular would allow exclusion on grounds of resources but not on grounds of injustice. It is submitted that parliamentary intentions could not have been so narrow, particularly in view of the need for 'safety-valve' procedure to protect against breaches of the right to fair trial under ECHR Article 6.

9.5 UNAVAILABLE WITNESSES

9.5.1 Background

English law has included a statutory hearsay exception for absent witnesses since 1925 with the most recent manifestation of the rule being found in CJA 1988, s 23. Two particular criticisms of the rules contained in s 23 were that admissibility was limited to statements in documents and therefore excluded equally reliable accounts of things said by an absent witness, and that the rule was limited to first-hand hearsay. Section 23 will be repealed by Sch 37, Pt 5, and replaced by CJA 2003, s 116 when the hearsay provisions are implemented. Both criticisms mentioned here are met by the new provision.

9.5.2 Admissible Statements of Unavailable Witnesses

Section 116 makes admissible certain statements of absent witnesses. For this purpose, statement is as defined in s 115 and includes any representation of fact or opinion made by a person by whatever means. Thus, oral, documentary and non-verbal statements are included, in contrast to CJA 1988, s 23 which was limited to statements in documents. The breadth of the definition of 'document' will avoid argument in cases like *R v McGillivray* ((1993) 97 Cr App R 232) where a statement from a burns victim was taken down by a police officer and verified by the witness, although not signed because of injuries. The provision is also not limited to first-hand hearsay, although in order for multiple hearsay statements to be admitted the requirements of s 121 must be satisfied.

The characteristics of a prior statement which may be admissible under s 116 are set out in sub-s (1). The first requirement is that oral evidence of the same matter would be admissible if the maker were available to give evidence in person. This rule avoids s 116 being used to admit evidence which is inadmissible for some reason other than its hearsay nature. Secondly, the maker of the statement must be identified to the court's satisfaction. This is a new requirement which was not found in the old s 23. Identity is a difficult concept, with some people being known by different names in different contexts. It will be interesting to see how the phrase 'identified to the court's satisfaction' is interpreted in practice.

9.5.3 New Conditions of Unavailability

Five conditions of unavailability are set out in sub-s (2) all of which correspond to conditions under CJA 1988, s 23. As with the former provision, the conditions are stated as objective facts and no standard of proof is specified. Courts have a tendency to gloss over degrees of uncertainty in these cases, but where the issue of proof is addressed it can cause problems. Thus in *R v Case* ([1991] Crim LR 192) the court refused to accept that the evidence of a robbery victim who was known to be a Portuguese tourist, could be admitted because there was no evidence that the tourist had returned to Portugal. Thus, in theory the apparent requirement that the conditions objectively exist, might make it difficult to apply the provision where, for instance, the court has received evidence of a witness's death but lacks clear proof of this. In this type of situation, it will be convenient to rely upon the broad discretion to admit hearsay under s 114(1)(d). The conditions are as follows:

(a) that the relevant person is dead;

(b) that the relevant person is unfit to be a witness because of his bodily or mental condition;

(c) that the relevant person is outside the United Kingdom and it is not reasonably practicable to secure his attendance;

(d) that the relevant person cannot be found, although such steps as it is reasonably practicable to take to find him have been taken;

(e) that, through fear, the relevant person does not give (or does not continue to give) oral evidence in the proceedings, either at all or in connection with the subject matter of the statement, and the court gives leave for the statement to be given in evidence.

A number of minor differences between these conditions and those they replace may be noted. Condition (b) is updated to take account of the possibility of evidence being given elsewhere than at court (eg by video link) under the Youth Justice and Criminal Evidence Act 1999 (YJCEA 1999), s 19 or by live link from outside the court under Part 8 of the current Act. Thus the test ceases to be whether the witness is 'unfit to attend' and becomes 'unfit to be a witness'. Formerly, for a witness who cannot be found, it was required that 'all reasonable steps' had been taken. This is now replaced with a more realistic test: 'such steps as it is reasonably practical to take', in para (d).

More substantial changes are made to what may be described as the 'intimidation' condition in para (e). Formerly, only statements taken by the police or other persons charged with the duty of investigating offences could be admitted on the basis of the witness's fear of giving evidence (CJA 1988, s 23(3)). This rule no longer applies and any prior statement may be admitted under this head. Also under the old provision, statements were admissible not only for witnesses in fear but also where the witness was 'kept out of the way'. That test was difficult to apply because where a witness is actually kept out of the way, it is difficult to prove. With the abolition of this head, the appropriate conditions will be either that the witness cannot be found under (d) or the fear condition in (e). The formulation of the test in (e) accommodates circumstances in which a witness declines to give evidence on a particular issue or who stops giving evidence after having started to do so. The courts had pragmatically held that the test under s 23 covered both situations (*R v Ashford Justices ex p Hidden* (1993) QB 555; *R v Waters* (1997) 161 JP 249) but it is useful to have the point clarified.

Under the old test in s 23 it was not clear what sorts of harm the fear must relate to. Now s 116(3) provides that in this context 'fear' is to be widely construed and (for example) includes fear of the death or injury of another person or of financial loss. The inclusion of just two examples of a wide construction of fear is not very helpful, because it is not clear whether these examples are meant to indicate the level or type of anxiety which can amount to fear. It might be argued, for instance, that fear of being drenched in cold water would not be included because it is not comparable.

In the past, evidence of fear has been proved by a witness's written statement which is itself hearsay, but which may be admitted under the common law rule (preserved in s 118(1)4(c)) that hearsay evidence is admissible to prove a state of mind or emotion (*R v Bellmarsh magistrates' court ex p Gilligan* [1998] 1 Cr App R 14).

Unlike the other conditions of unavailability, where the fear condition prevents the witness giving evidence, an earlier statement may be admitted only with leave of the court. The court must consider that the statement ought to be admitted in the interests of justice, having regard (a) to the contents of the statement, (b) to any risk that its admission or exclusion will result in unfairness to any party to the proceedings (particularly any difficulties in challenging the evidence), (c) the possibility that a witness might be assisted to give his evidence by a special measures direction under YJCEA 1999, s 19, and (d) any other relevant circumstances.

A limitation on the admission of the statement of an absent witness is made where the absence of the witness can be attributed to the fault of the person in support of whose case it is sought to give the statement in evidence. Thus, if the relevant circum-stances of unavailability are caused by the relevant party (normally the defendant, but this could also apply to the prosecutor) or by someone acting on his behalf, in order to prevent the witness giving oral evidence in the proceedings, the statement should not be admitted (s 117(5)).

9.6 BUSINESS AND OTHER DOCUMENTS

9.6.1 Background

Business documents first became admissible as an exception to the hearsay rule under CJA 1988, s 24. Admissibility under s 24 was not automatic but might be refused by a court in the interests of justice, with regard to a number of considerations set out in CJA 1988, s 25. In reviewing this provision, the Law Commission noted that it had been successful and should be retained, but were of the view that the process of considering whether a particular document should not be admitted in the interests of justice under s 25 was time consuming and wasteful. The Law Commission also considered that the drafting of s 24 could be improved and in particular noted the unhelpful confusion which had arisen over the question of whether the provider of information or its recorder should be considered the 'maker' of a document (*Field* (*Andrew John*) [1993] 97 Cr App R 357). The Commission therefore recommended that the rule should be retained and that any document which fell within the statutory test should be routinely admitted but subject to a power of the court to rule that it should not be admitted. The Commission also considered the presumption against admission of 'business documents' prepared for the purpose of criminal proceedings in CJA 1988, s 26 and the court's power to exercise a discretion to admit under that provision. It was agreed that the maker of such a document should generally be called to give evidence and that the such documents should generally not be admitted except where the witness fulfilled the unavailability criteria. The Commission therefore recommended that the rule should be retained and extended but subject to some redrafting, that any document which fell within the statutory test should be automatically admitted but subject to a power of the court to rule that it should not be admitted, and that documents prepared for the purpose of criminal proceedings should be subjected to a stricter test for admission (Law Comm No 245, paras 8.71–8.83).

9.6.2 Admissibility of Business and Other Documents under s 117

The test for admissibility under s 117 is essentially similar to the former test under CJA 1988, s 24 and applies only to statements which would have been admissible if given as oral evidence (sub-s (1)). The test in sub-s (2) has three components:

(a) the document or the part containing the statement was created or received by a person in the course of a trade, business, profession or other occupation, or as the holder of any paid or unpaid office,

(b) the person who supplied the information contained in the statement (the relevant person) had or may reasonably be supposed to have had personal knowledge of the matters dealt with, and

(c) each person (if any) through whom the information was supplied from the relevant person to the person mentioned in paragraph (a) received the information in the course of trade, business, profession or other occupation, or as the holder of a paid or unpaid office.

The person creating or receiving the information under (a) may be either a different person or the same person as the provider of information under (b) (sub-s (3)). The new provision clears up confusion arising under CJA 1988, s 24 and confirms that it is the supplier of the information who must be reasonably supposed to have personal knowledge of the matters stated. Unlike the absent witnesses provision, the identity of any of the individuals involved in supplying information and generating business documents need not be known. Indeed, the original impetus for admitting business documents arose from a case in which documents were not admitted because it was not possible to trace who had provided relevant information and recorded it in a factory situation in which many different individuals might share particular tasks (*Myers v DPP* [1965] AC 1001). The provision contemplates the admission of multiple hearsay where information is passed through a number of hands before being recorded. The consequential document will be admissible in such a case provided that the original supplier of information may reasonably be supposed to have had personal knowledge of the matters stated and each successive person who handled the information did so in the course of a relevant trade, business, profession etc. Because the issue of multiple hearsay is specifically addressed, the special requirement for multiple hearsay in s 121 will not apply to business documents.

It is not intended that the s 117 will make routine the admission of written statements in place of oral testimony in criminal proceedings. Thus, if a document prepared for the purpose of pending criminal proceedings is sought to be admitted under s 117, a further requirement will apply as set out in sub-s (5). The further requirement is that either the witness must be unavailable and satisfy one of the unavailability conditions in s 116(2) or the original provider of the information cannot be expected to have any recollection of the matters dealt with in the statement, having regard to the time elapsed since the statement was made.

Section 117 is also subject to a long-stop provision which permits a court to direct that a document should be inadmissible in circumstances in which it would otherwise satisfy the criteria for a business document. The ground for making such a direction is that the reliability of a document is doubtful in view of its contents, the source of the information contained in it, the way in which the information was supplied or received, and the way in which the document was created or received (sub-ss (6) and (7)).

9.7 PREVIOUS STATEMENTS OF WITNESSES

9.7.1 Background

The law relating to previous statements made by witnesses, as it applied prior to the current reform, was complex but might be simply summarized. Prior statements which were inconsistent with a witness's testimony were admissible in relation to credibility under statute and similarly prior consistent statements were admissible at common law to rebut allegations of fabrication. Exceptionally, a prior consistent statement in the form of a timely complaint in a case of alleged sexual assault was admissible to prove the complainant's consistency. A number of major issues emerged from the Law Commission's consideration of previous statements (Law Com No 245, 10.2–10.99). First, it was recognized that the rule that previous statements go only to demonstrate credibility and are not evidence of the truth of any matter stated, is unrealistic in terms of the task facing the fact-finder and also undesirable: the Commission could identify no good reason why the fact-finder should not be able to consider the previous statement, for what it was worth, in attempting to discover the truth. Secondly, the rule that oral evidence was always to be preferred to documents made earlier was flawed in principle since there might be many circumstances in which a contemporaneous statement would be much more reliable than a later recollection from memory.

9.7.2 Previous Statements as Evidence of Truth

The Act embodies the Law Commission's view that, once admitted, previous statements should be evidence for all purposes. Under s 119(1), where a witness either admits making a previous inconsistent statement or where such a statement is proved against him under s 3, 4 or 5 Criminal Procedure Act 1865, the statement becomes evidence of any matter stated in it of which oral evidence would have been admissible from him.

Similarly, where a hearsay statement has been admitted in evidence and a previous inconsistent statement is admitted as relevant to the credibility of the maker of the hearsay statement under CJA 2003, s 124(2)(c), the previous inconsistent statement is admissible as evidence of any matter on which oral evidence would have been admissible (s 119(2)). For example, if a document recording an insurance contract were admitted as a business document under s 117, a previous inconsistent statement by the author of the document would be admissible under s 124(2)(c). This previous statement would be admissible in relation to the credibility of its maker, but also as evidence of any fact stated within it.

The same approach is taken to previous consistent statements which are admitted to rebut a suggestion of fabrication and to previous statements which are made admissible following their use to aid a witness to refresh his memory. Under s 120(2), where a previous consistent statement is admitted it will now also be admissible as to the truth of the matter stated. Where a document is admitted after being referred to in cross-examination of a witness who had previously refreshed his memory from that document, the document will also be admissible as to the truth of any matter stated in it under s 120(3).

9.7.3 Admissibility of Certain Previous Statements

Section 120(4) admits previous statements where the witness vouches in court that to the best of his belief he made the statement and that to the best of his belief it states the truth. This applies to three categories of statement detailed in sub-ss (5), (6) and (7).

Under sub-s (5) previous statements identifying or describing a person, object or place are admissible. The rationale for this provision is that a witness is likely to be in a much better position to remember the relevant details sooner, rather than later, after the sighting. This provision may have a very wide application because a huge proportion of witness statements will cover one of these matters at least in part. The subsection does not make clear to what extent a statement should be admissible where only part of it fulfils the condition in sub-s (5). It would be contrary to the apparent intention of this provision if it were used to admit a high proportion of police witness statements. On the other hand, a partial statement might be hard to understand and evaluate if divorced from its context.

Under sub-s (6) a previous statement may be admitted if made by the witness when the relevant matters were fresh in his memory, but he neither remembers them and nor could he reasonably be expected to do so well enough to give oral evidence of them in the proceedings. The test here is a strange one because witnesses frequently give evidence of matters about which they have hazy memories. This suggests that the test of how well one needs to remember an event in order to give oral evidence about it represents a low hurdle. If the test were understood in this way, very little evidence would be admitted under sub-s (6). It is to be hoped that the courts will interpret the provision as importing a relative test which would make a previous statement admissible if it is likely to be substantially more accurate than any evidence which the witness could be expected to give in oral evidence. In any event, it may well be that this test is little used in view of the facility to use previous statements as aids to memory under s 139.

Subsection (7) provides a general rule permitting the admission of recent (timely) complaints by the victims of all classes of offences. The provision applies only to a person who claims to be a person against whom an offence, which is the subject of the proceedings, was committed. The statement must comprise a complaint about the offence, made freely and not under threat or promise, to a person in authority as soon as could reasonably be expected after the alleged offence. It is no objection that the complaint was elicited by a leading question, such as 'Did X hit you?' (sub-s (8)). The complaint will only be admissible if the witness first gives oral evidence in connection with the complaint.

9.8 DOCUMENTS PRODUCED AS EXHIBITS

Section 122 addresses the concern that where previous inconsistent or consistent statements are admitted under the relaxation of the hearsay rule, they may be accorded more relevance or authority than the oral evidence which they supplement. It is provided that when a statement is admitted under s 119 (inconsistent statements) or s 120 (consistent statements) and the document itself or a copy is put before the jury as an exhibit, that exhibit must not accompany the jury when they retire to consider their verdict unless the court considers this appropriate or all parties agree.

9.9 PRESERVATION OF COMMON LAW ADMISSIBILITY RULES

9.9.1 Background

The Law Commission's approach was to build upon the wisdom of the past rather than to place faith in a modern discretion. Accordingly, the Commission recommended retaining a number of common law exceptions to the rule against hearsay, either on the basis of some specific justification or on the basis that the exception fulfilled a useful function and did not apparently cause difficulties (Law Com No 245, 8.114–8.132).

By s 118(1), a number of rules of law concerning the admissibility of hearsay statements are preserved. Whereas, the title of this section refers to the common law, within the section reference is to 'rules of law' and is not restricted to common law rules. The provision will therefore also serve to preserve rules statutory rules, although generally these would be preserved in any event unless abrogated either expressly or by clear implication by a later statute.

Those 'common law rules governing the admissibility of hearsay evidence in criminal proceedings' which are not expressly preserved are abolished by s 118(2). If read literally, the abolition of 'rules governing admissibility' would affect rules providing for both the admissibility and inadmissibility of hearsay statements. If read in this broad sense, the subsection would have the unintended effect of abolishing the common law rule against hearsay and thus, at a stroke rendering nugatory the elaborate reform of the rule in Part 11 of the Act. It appears therefore that s 118(2) should be read as simply abolishing any common law rules rendering hearsay admissible, which are not expressly preserved by s 118.

Although the statements of the preserved rules set out in sub-s (1) are precisely drafted, as they would be for the purpose of creating statutory rules, it must be remembered that these provisions do not create rules but simply preserve existing ones. Thus, if any dispute arises about whether a particular type of statement is preserved, reference must be made to the pre-existing common law rather than to statutory words describing the purported rule. However, problems may arise because the preserved common law rules are described so precisely. The danger is that precise description may stultify development. Whereas normally a valuable feature of the common law is its flexibility, in the future flexibility of these rules may be inhibited because a condition of preservation is that each rule should comply with its description in s 118(1).

9.9.2 Public Information etc

Rules concerning the admissibility of four categories of 'public' documents are preserved by s 118(1)1. As used here, 'public' seems to have two connotations: first, a matter is public if it is a matter of common public knowledge; secondly, a statement is 'public' where it has a degree of inherent reliability because it is made either by a public authority or under a public duty.

Under para (a), published works dealing with matters of a public nature (such as histories, scientific works, dictionaries and maps) are admissible as evidence of facts of a public nature stated in them. Care should be taken with this 'preserved rule' since it is not clear on what authorities it is based. As stated, the rule resembles the rule that a judge may consult a textbook in order to determine a fact to be judicially noticed (*McQuaker v Goddard* [1940] 1 QB 687). However, the rule about judicial notice is a rule about what facts need not be proved by evidence rather than a rule about what categories of evidence are admissible to prove a fact. It should also be noted that under the purported rule only 'public' facts may be evidenced in this way. Thus a history book may be used to provide evidence of the date of the battle of Hastings, but the author's opinion of King Harold's battle strategy would not be similarly admissible.

Under para (b), public documents (such as registers, and returns made under public authority with respect to matters of public interest) are admissible as evidence of facts stated in them. This is a well-established ground for admitting hearsay which relates to documents made under a duty and which are available to the public. Although the rationale for admissibility is inherent reliability, it is not a requirement that the maker should have acted under a duty to verify the information recorded (*R v Halpin* [1975] QB 907).

Under para (c), records (such as records of certain courts, treaties, Crown grants, pardons and commissions) are admissible as evidence of facts stated in them, and under para (d) evidence relating to a person's age or date or place of birth may be given by a person without personal knowledge of the matter. The rule in para (d) is entirely pragmatic: without it an individual would be barred from providing such personal details to the court because of an inability to record such information at the time of his birth.

9.9.3 Reputation as to Character

Paragraph 2 preserves any rule of law under which in criminal proceedings evidence of a person's reputation is admissible for the purpose of proving his good or bad character.

9.9.4 Reputation or Family Tradition to prove Family Matters

Paragraph 3 preserves any rule of law under which in criminal proceedings evidence of reputation or family tradition is admissible for the purpose of proving or disproving (a) pedigree or the existence of a marriage, (b) the existence of any public or general right, or (c) the identity of a person or thing.

9.9.5 *Res Gestae*
In the Law Commission Report on which the current reform is based, it was recognized that the term *res gestae* encompasses a number of different rules about admissibility, each of which had its own preconditions and independent justification (Law Com 245,

8.114). Following the Commission's recommendations, para 4 preserves three distinct rules for admitting *res gestae* statements. They are where: (a) the statement was made by a person so emotionally overpowered by an event that the possibility of concoction or distortion can be disregarded, (b) the statement accompanies an act which can properly be evaluated as evidence only if considered in conjunction with the statement, (c) the statement related to a physical sensation or mental state (such as intention or emotion).

9.9.6 Confessions

Paragraph 3 preserves any rule of law relating to the admissibility of confessions or mixed statements in criminal proceedings. The rules by which a defendant's confession may be admitted for the prosecution as an exception to the hearsay rule is now found in the Police and Criminal Evidence Act 1984 (PACE 1984), s 76(1). Further rules, by which a presumptively admissible confession may be rendered inadmissible for oppression or unreliability, are found in s 76(2). However, a considerable body of law relating to confessions remains subject to the common law (see D Wolchover and A Heaton-Armstrong, *Confession Evidence* (Sweet & Maxwell, 1996)). The most important common law admissibility rule which will be preserved by para 3 is the rule that where an accused's statement is 'mixed' and contains some elements which are incriminating and some which are exculpatory, the whole statement is admissible as evidence of truth (*R v Sharp* [1988] 1 WLR 7). An equally important common law rule, that a co-accused's confession is admissible in evidence for an accused person, even in circumstances when it might be inadmissible for the prosecution (*R v Myers* [1998] AC 124) is now incorporated, in a modified form, in a new s 76A to PACE 1984, inserted by s 128 of the current Act.

9.9.7 Admission by Agents and Referees

Paragraph 6 preserves any rule of law under which in criminal proceedings (a) an admission of an agent of a defendant is admissible against the defendant, or (b) a statement made by a person to whom the defendant refers a person for information is admissible against the defendant. These twin rules are based on old and not very satisfactory authority (see generally *Blackstone's Criminal Practice*, F 16.51). It is clear that the notion of agency used here differs from that applied in civil law, where the interest in commercial certainty is paramount. For the purposes of imputing the agent's admission to the defendant it seems that the admission must be made in the presence of the defendant without any indication of non-acceptance (*R v Turner* (1975) 61 Cr App R 67; *R v Fitzgerald* [1998] 4 Arch News 2). In these cases the admission is imputed to the defendant on the basis of his silence. The Law Commission included this head of admissible hearsay within its category of rules which fulfilled a useful function and did not apparently cause difficulties (Law Com No 245, 8.114–8.132). On the contrary it is submitted that to employ agency notions for this purpose is inherently problematic. In the two cases referred to above, the 'agent' was a lawyer who spoke for the defendant in circumstances in which for the defendant to take issue with his lawyer would have been very difficult. In each of these cases the imputed admission was convenient for the prosecution for the very reason that in reality the defendant had not made a similar personal admission. It seems probable that it would simply not occur to most sensible prosecutors to try to pin the defence brief's careless words on the client. It is to be hoped that dignifying this dubious rule with a mention in the present Act will not spur more prosecutors to employ it.

9.9.8 Common Enterprise

Paragraph 7 preserves the rule under which a statement made by one party to a common enterprise is admissible against another party to the enterprise. The rule applies to conspiracies and also to cases where two or more defendants are jointly charged.

9.9.9 Expert Evidence

It has long been accepted that the role of the expert is to make accessible to the court a body of special expertise or learning. The expert is expected to draw upon the researches and writings of others. Any expert evidence which adopts a scientific view developed by another is hearsay, but is nevertheless traditionally admitted. By para 8, the largely unacknowledged rule of law under which an expert witness may draw upon the body of expertise relevant to his field, is preserved.

9.10 CAPACITY TO MAKE STATEMENT

The general rule relating to competence of a witness to give evidence in criminal proceedings is found in YJCEA 1999, s 53. By s 53(1) all persons of whatever age are presumed to be competent, subject to s 53(3) under which a person is not competent to give evidence in criminal proceedings if it appears to the court that he is (a) not able to understand questions put to him as a witness, and (b) not capable of giving answers to such questions which can be understood. A person will also be incompetent as a witness for the prosecution (whatever his intellectual abilities) in particular criminal proceedings if he is charged as a defendant in those proceedings (s 53(4)). It will be apparent that legal competence is a product of two factors: the putative witness's mental faculties and his status in relation to the proceedings in question. The first element of competence may also be described as capacity.

By s 123 it is provided that hearsay evidence admissible under the 2003 Act must emanate from a person who would have sufficient capacity to give oral evidence in the proceedings. The test for capacity in this context is effectively the same as under YJCEA 1999, s 53, although expressed in different terms. Under sub-s (3) a person has the required capacity if he is (a) capable of understanding questions put to him about the matters stated, and (b) capable of giving answers to such questions which can be understood. The test effectively requires sufficient capacity to play a meaningful role as a witness in the proceedings and in particular in cross-examination. An oddity is that the putative witness must have this capacity at the time when the original statement is made and not at a time when he may be required to submit to cross-examination on it.

Thus, it is provided that nothing in the rules which permits the admission of hearsay in relation to unavailable witnesses, business documents and prior consistent or inconsistent statements, permits the admission of a statement made by a person who lacked the required capacity when the statement was made. In relation to business records, capacity is also a requirement for each person who supplied or received the information, or created or received the completed document under s 117. It will be no objection that it is impossible to identify all of the people who played a role in the creation of a business document. By s 123(2) a business document which otherwise fulfils the necessary legal requirements will be admissible unless a relevant person did not have the required capacity or cannot reasonably be assumed to have had the required capacity. The effect of this is to create a presumption that all persons involved in the making of business documents have the required capacity.

Subsection (4) provides a procedure for determining capacity where this is put in issue. This procedure closely follows the similar procedure for oral witnesses under YJCEA 1999, s 54. Once the capacity of the maker of a statement is questioned, the burden of proof on a balance of probabilities lies on the party seeking to adduce the statement. Proceedings to determine the issue must take place in the absence of the jury (if there is one) and the court may receive expert evidence and evidence from the person to whom the statement in question was made.

9.11 CREDIBILITY OF STATEMENT MAKER

9.11.1 Maker of Hearsay Statement immune from Cross-examination

A very significant difference between live oral evidence and a statement admitted as hearsay is that in the former case the witness may be cross-examined as to his credit, and rebutting evidence brought in a limited range of circumstances, whereas the maker of a hearsay statement, who does not also give oral testimony, is immune from cross-examination. As a result, the court or jury may be deprived of an opportunity to assess the credibility of the hearsay statement. Section 124 seeks to correct this anomaly by permitting evidence to be given concerning the credibility of the maker of the statement in place of the cross-examination.

9.11.2 Evidence Admissible concerning Credit

Section 124 applies where a hearsay statement is admitted in evidence and the maker does not also give oral evidence. Where evidence would have been admissible in relation to credibility of a witness giving oral testimony, such evidence will be similarly admissible in relation to the maker of the hearsay statement (sub-s (2)(a)). Similarly, such evidence will be admissible against any person who supplied or received information which was admitted in a business document under s 117

159

(s 124(4)). The sorts of evidence which may be admitted under this provision are, evidence of general reputation for dishonesty (*R v Richardson: R v Longman* (1968) 52 Cr App R 317) or expert evidence of a medical condition affecting credibility (*Toohey v Metropolitan Police Comr* [1965] AC 595).

Evidence may also be given, with the leave of the court, of any matter which could have been put to the witness in cross-examination as relevant to his credibility, but which would not normally be admissible in evidence (sub-s (2)(b)). This provision makes good the disadvantage of the party against whom hearsay is adduced, by permitting evidence in place of cross-examination. This would apply to any issue on which normally a witness's answer as to credit would have been final. For instance, if it was alleged that a witness against the accused had fabricated evidence in an earlier case, this allegation could be the subject of cross-examination of the witness but not rebutting evidence because the issue goes only to credit (*R v Edwards* [1991] 2 All ER 266). However under s 124 , with the leave of the court, evidence could be adduced relating to the alleged fabrication in an earlier case.

Finally, under sub-s (2)(c) evidence may be admitted which tends to show that the maker of a hearsay statement had at any time made an inconsistent statement. The admission of this evidence would perform the same function as cross-examination on previous inconsistent statements for a live witness.

9.11.3 Attacks on Maker of Hearsay Statement

Section 124(3) deals with the situation in which the accused adduces evidence attacking the character of the maker of a hearsay statement under s 124(3). Under sub-s (3), in such circumstances the court is given a wide discretion to permit a party to lead additional evidence of such description as the court may specify for the purposes of denying or answering the allegation. Although at first glance this looks rather like an application of the tit-for-tat principle, the provision only permits evidence 'denying or answering' the allegation. It is submitted that the term 'answering' should not be interpreted as including a power to adduce evidence of the defendant's bad character, in the absence of words clearly expressing such an intention.

9.12 STOPPING THE CASE WHERE EVIDENCE IS UNCONVINCING

9.12.1 Prosecution Cases based on Unconvincing Hearsay Evidence

Section 125(1) empowers a trial judge to stop a case in which the case against the defendant is based wholly or partly on a hearsay statement and the evidence provided by the statement is so unconvincing that if he were to be convicted of the offence his conviction would be unsafe. In these circumstances the judge must either direct the jury to acquit the defendant or discharge the jury and order a retrial. If the jury is directed to acquit in a case in which the jury could find the defendant guilty of an alternative or included charge, the court must consider whether a conviction for the lesser charge would also be unsafe and, if it would, the jury must be directed that they may not find the defendant guilty of the lesser offence (sub-s (2)).

The power under s 125 is included in the new hearsay scheme as a means of providing a semblance of balance and a protection against any risks which may attend the enhanced power of the prosecution to call hearsay evidence. One may query whether its value is practical or merely symbolic. If the courts sensibly employ the broad power to exclude otherwise admissible hearsay under s 126, cases which need to be stopped because of reliance on unconvincing hearsay evidence should be rare. In any event it is arguable that the new power adds nothing to the court's existing duty to stop a case where the evidence is so tenuous that no jury could responsibly convict, under *R v Galbraith* ([1981] 1 WLR 1039, see also *R v Bron (Davina)* 1 Cr App R 46).

9.12.2 Determinations in Unfitness to Plead Cases

Under s 125(3) a similar procedure applies in a case in which the court must determine under s 4A(2) Criminal Procedure (Insanity) Act 1964 whether or not a person charged on indictment did the act or made the omission charged. If the court is satisfied that the case against the accused is based wholly or partly on a hearsay statement and the evidence provided by that statement is so unconvincing that a finding that the defendant did the act or made the omission would be unsafe, the court must either direct the jury to acquit the defendant of the offence or discharge the jury and order a rehearing if it considers that the appropriate course.

9.13 EXPERT EVIDENCE—PREPARATORY WORK

As discussed above, the common law rule that an expert witness may draw upon the body of expertise in his field, is confirmed by s 118(1)8. Rather different considerations apply where the expert relies also upon specific information, other than general scientific learning, as the basis for evidence to be presented in court. A straightforward example is provided by the doctor who is required to report on the health of somebody injured in an assault. The doctor may properly rely upon a questionnaire, concerning the symptoms, completed by the patient, as well as on a physical examination and accrued medical knowledge. Until now, the evidential status of any statement on which an expert based her opinion was doubtful. This issue is now clarified by s 127.

Section 127 explicitly permits an expert to base her opinion or any inference on a preparatory statement made by another person (sub-s (2)), but subject to the right of any party to the proceedings to object (sub-s (4)). If expert evidence based on the statement is given in court then the preparatory statement will itself be treated as evidence of what it states (sub-s (3)). These rules apply to a statement which has been prepared for the purpose of a criminal proceeding (sub-s (1)(a)) or investigation (sub-s (6)), provided that the person who prepared the statement may reasonably be supposed to have had a personal knowledge of the matter stated (sub-s (1)(b)), and a notice is given which states that the expert will give evidence based on such a report and which identifies the person who prepared the statement and indicates the nature of the matters stated (sub-s (1)(c) and (d)). The required notice must be given in accordance with court rules to be made under PACE 1984, s 81, which deals with advance notice of expert evidence in the Crown Court, and in relation to the magistrates' courts under Magistrates' Courts Act 1980, s 144, which applies by virtue of s 20(3) of the Criminal Procedure and Investigations Act 1996.

A party who objects to the preparatory report being admitted as evidence (in lieu of personal testimony by the person who prepared the statement) may apply under sub-s (4). In considering such an application, the court must consider, among other things, (a) the expense of calling as a witness the person who prepared the statement, (b) whether relevant evidence could be given by that person which could not be given by the expert, and (c) whether the person who prepared the statement can be expected to remember the matters on which the statement was based sufficiently well to justify giving evidence.

9.14 CONFESSIONS ADMISSIBLE FOR CO-ACCUSED

9.14.1 Background—Confessions

Prior to 1986, the law relating to confessions was almost entirely a matter of common law. Generally confessions, typically involving admissions made to the police, were admissible if voluntary, and constituted the most important exception to the general rule excluding hearsay evidence. The admissibility of confessions was justified under the general principle applicable to statements made against the maker's interest, that such a statement was intrinsically reliable because generally a person would not make such a statement unless true. Curiously, however valid that rationale as a general proposition, it does not hold good for confessions emanating from police interviews, which are particularly subject to the risk of unreliability (G Gudjonsson, *The Psychology of Interrogations and Confessions* (Wiley, 2002)).

Under PACE 1984, which came into force in 1986, the term 'confession' is partly defined in s 82(1) as including 'any statement wholly or partly adverse to the person who made it, whether made to a person in authority or not, and whether made in words or otherwise'. Under PACE 1984, s 76(1) such a confession, if relevant, is admissible at the trial of its maker. Admissibility is made subject to twin exclusionary rules applicable where the prosecution proposes to give evidence of a confession against an accused person. The grounds for exclusion are, where the confession was obtained by oppression of the person who made it (s 76(2)(a)) or in consequence of anything said or done which was likely, in the circumstances existing at the time, to render unreliable any resulting confession (s 76(2)(b)). Supplementary provisions concerning confessions are found in the remaining subsections of s 76.

9.14.2 Confessions against Co-accused, the Common Law

However, s 76 deals only with the situation in which the prosecution proposes to rely upon confession evidence and is silent on the issue of admissibility where a co-accused wishes to rely on a confession. This issue has been considered by the courts but the resulting legal position is unclear in some respects and has been subject to criticism for inconsistency with rules under s 76. In the leading case *R v Myers* ([1998] AC 124), the House of Lords held that an accused person could put in evidence an incriminating statement made by her co-accused, even though the trial judge had ruled that that statement should be inadmissible for the prosecution under PACE 1984, s 78 because of unfairness in the circumstances in which it was obtained. The House suggested that such a statement might not be admissible if it were obtained in a manner which would have made it inadmissible at the instance of the Crown under PACE 1984, s 76(2).

The decision in *Myers* is considered unsatisfactory for a number of reasons. The House of Lords did not explain satisfactorily why it should make any difference to admissibility for a co-accused whether the statement would have been inadmissible under s 76 or s 78 PACE if presented by the prosecution. Nor was it explained why the admission of the statement would be any less unfair on its maker if adduced by a co-accused rather than the prosecution (see generally M Hirst, 'Confessions as proof of innocence' [1998] CLJ 146).

Recognizing these difficulties, the Law Commission recommended that in the proposed codification of hearsay, the best way to ensure the harmonious development of the law on the admissibility of confessions, at the instance of either the prosecution or a co-accused, would be to adapt the exclusionary principles of s 76(2) to the case where one defendant seeks to adduce the confession of another. The only suggested difference would be that whereas the prosecution must satisfy the criminal standard of proof in order to have the statement admitted in the face of allegations of oppression or unreliability, a co-accused would have to satisfy a lower standard of proof on the balance of probabilities. The Commission also recommended that where a confession is admitted against one accused on behalf of a co-accused, the fact-finders may consider the admission as exonerating the defendant who did not make it, but may not take it as evidence against the defendant who made it (Law Com No 245, 8.95, 8.96). The Commission's proposals are given effect by CJA 2003, s 128.

9.14.3 Admissibility of Confessions for Co-accused

Section 128(1) inserts a new s 76A in PACE 1984. Under s 76A(1) a confession made by an accused person may be given in evidence for a co-accused in the same proceedings, in so far as it is relevant, and is not excluded by the court. Admissibility under s 76A is only likely to become an issue in a case in which either the prosecution chooses not to rely on the confession, or it is ruled inadmissible for the prosecution under PACE 1984, s 76(2) or s 78. Although, under *Myers*, Lord Slynn had suggested that inadmissibility under s 76(2) would also bar admissibility on behalf of a co-accused, this rule does not apply under s 76A. Instead, similar exclusionary provisions may apply under s 76A(2), which is quoted below:

If, in any proceedings where a co-accused proposes to give in evidence a confession made by an accused person, it is represented to the court that the confession was or may have been obtained—

(a) by oppression of the person who made it; or

(b) in consequence of anything said or done which was likely, in the circumstances existing at the time, to render unreliable any confession which might be made by him in consequence thereof,

the court shall not allow the confession to be given in evidence for the co-accused except in so far as it is proved to the court on the balance of probabilities that the confession (notwithstanding that it may be true) was not so obtained.

This provision mimics s 76(2) under which the prosecution may be barred from admitting a confession. The two differences to note are the substitution of reference to a co-accused for reference to the prosecution, and that the burden of proof on the co-accused to disprove oppression or unreliability is on a balance of probabilities rather than beyond reasonable doubt. Under both provisions the court may act of its own motion to require the party proposing the evidence to prove its admissibility (sub-s (3)). The same partial definition of 'oppression' as including torture and inhuman or degrading treatment, and the use or threat of violence (whether or not amounting to torture) is employed in both provisions (sub-s (7)). Generally, case law concerning s 76 will be applicable to s 76A.

The justification offered by the Law Commission for applying the same exclusionary tests to confessions adduced by the prosecution and by a co-accused was that this would aid the harmonious development of the law. As indicated above, there is every reason to suppose that harmony will prevail since, apart from the differences in the burdens of proof, the same legal tests will apply. However, a question which has not been satisfactorily answered is whether the law in these two area should be harmonious. The two circumstances in which confessions may be adduced are quite different and it is arguable that, accordingly, different principles should apply. There are many reasons for excluding prosecution evidence for oppression and unreliability. Among the most important of these are the need to avoid the risk of a defendant being convicted on the basis of fundamentally flawed and tainted evidence, and the need to protect the perceived integrity of the prosecution process. Different considerations apply where the confession is adduced to support the defence of an accused person. The fact that evidence is flawed and not totally reliable is less of a problem for the defendant, who only needs to raise a reasonable doubt, than it is for the prosecution who must prove its case beyond reasonable doubt. Equally, whereas state criminal justice agencies might be brought into disrepute if the CPS was seen to rely upon evidence obtained by police oppression, the same restraint need not be shown by a defendant who would simply be the innocent beneficiary of police misconduct. Of course, if such tainted evidence were admissible for the defence, it would be necessary to direct the jury very carefully in relation to it and its potential flaws. However, in view of the presumption of innocence, it is difficult to understand why the tribunal of fact should not be given the opportunity to consider what weight could be accorded to such evidence.

An argument which the courts may have to face in the future, is that if the defendant is denied the opportunity to adduce his co-accused's confession because it is excluded under s 76A(2), this would be a breach of his right to a fair trial. Under ECHR, Article 6(3)(d) a defendant in criminal proceedings has a right to obtain the attendance and examination of witnesses on his behalf under the same conditions as witnesses against him. A similar argument was considered by the European Court of Human Rights in *Blastland v United Kingdom* ((1998) 10 EHRR 528). In that case, in a trial for murder, the defendant had been denied the right to adduce evidence of an alleged confession by a third party. It was held that the defendant's right to fair trial had not been violated, but a significant element in the Court's reasoning was that the defendant knew the identity of the third party and was free to call him as a witness if he wished. That reasoning could not apply to a co-accused who would not be a compellable witness. It follows therefore that a defendant in this position might well succeed on a claim of breach of the right to a fair trial.

A co-accused's statement is admissible under s 76A only in so far as it is 'relevant to any matter in issue in the proceedings'. Read literally, this would suggest that a statement could be admitted if relevant to proof of guilt in relation to either the maker of the statement or his co-accused. However, it is submitted that if the statement has already been ruled inadmissible on behalf of the prosecution as against its maker, it should not thereafter be considered relevant to prove the guilt of the maker of the statement, but instead its relevance should be restricted to the issue of the co-accused's innocence or guilt. Because admissibility is restricted to the parts of the statement which are relevant to the guilt of the co-accused it may be necessary to edit the statement to excise any passages which do no more than implicate the maker of the statement. However, clearly in many cases such protective editing will not be an option. Thus, if the co-accused is running a cut-throat defence and claims that the maker of the statement is the guilty party, the parts of the statement which are relevant to the co-accused's defence will also be those which implicate the maker of the statement.

The new s 76A also mimics s 76 in its supplementary rules relating to facts discovered as a result of an excluded confession. Where a confession is wholly or partly excluded this will not affect the admissibility of any facts discovered as a result of the confession (sub-s (4)(a)). However, in order to prevent the excluded confession being effectively admitted by implication, evidence cannot be given to establish the link between the confession and any facts discovered as a result of it. Thus, where any fact is discovered as a result of a part of a co-accused' statement which has been excluded, evidence that the fact was discovered as a result of the statement made by the co-accused shall not be admissible unless evidence of how the fact was discovered is given by the maker of the statement (sub-ss (5) and (6)).

9.15 EVIDENCE BY VIDEO RECORDING

9.15.1 Background

The English adversarial trial has a long tradition of live oral evidence. Many of the justifications offered for the practice do not stand up to scrutiny. Thus arguments that witness testimony in court is the best evidence, that it allows magistrates or jury to judge credibility from demeanour, that it permits forensic testing by cross-examination or that it permits the defendant to confront his or her accuser, can all be either countered, or accommodated by other means of receiving evidence. After substantial debate, measures were first introduced to permit children in very stressful cases to give their evidence by live video link in 1988. This was rapidly followed in 1991 by a more radical power to permit children to give evidence in chief in the form of a video-recorded interview, this power being extended to a broad category of vulnerable witnesses by YJCEA 1999, Pt II (see D Birch and R Leng, *Blackstone's Guide to the Youth Justice and Criminal Evidence Act 1999* (Blackstone Press, 2000, chs 3, 4, 5)). On the basis of developing experience under the 1999 Act, and the acceptance that the sooner a witness gives his evidence the better its quality is likely to be, the government has now grasped the nettle to allow more general admissibility of video-recorded interviews with eye witnesses. The new measure is found in s 138 and should be considered alongside the more realistic approach to refreshing memory under s 139 below, as well as the measures for live links in Part 8. It should also be noted that the new general provision complements, rather than replaces, existing measures to permit video evidence to be admitted (s 138(5)).

9.15.2 Video Recording as Evidence in Chief

Section 137 permits a court to direct that an eye witness to the events immediately surrounding an offence may have a video recording of an earlier account admitted in place of his evidence in chief (sub-s (1)(f)). The new method of receiving evidence will apply only to indictable only cases and either way offences to be prescribed by the Home Secretary (sub-ss (1) and (6)). The procedure can apply to all classes of witnesses and is not linked to particular characteristics like vulnerability or youth. The defendant however is excluded and must give his evidence in chief live. The provision also dispenses with any requirement that the initial statement is made on oath (sub-s (5)), but the recorded account will only be treated as the witness's evidence in the proceedings to the extent that he asserts the truth of the statements made in the recorded account (sub-s (2)).

The pre-conditions for an order under sub-s (1)(f) are that the witness gave a video-recorded account, whether by answering questions or otherwise, at a time when the witnessed events were fresh in his memory (if it is assumed that he was telling the truth) (sub-s (1)). The court may make a direction under s 137 only if satisfied that the witness's recollection of events is likely to have been significantly better when he gave the recorded account than it would be if he gave live evidence in court and that it is in the interests of justice to admit the video recording (sub-s (3)(b)).

Subsection (4) sets out a number of matters which the court should have regard to when considering whether it is in the interests of justice to admit the statement. These are: the time lapse between the events and the recording of the account, any factors which might affect the reliability of the account, the quality of the recording, and any view of the witness as to whether he should give his evidence orally or by means of the recording.

Section 138 deals with a number of issues concerning the video-recorded evidence. A video recording admitted under s 137(1)(f) need not constitute the whole of a witness's evidence in chief, but where live evidence is also given, the court may order that it should not cover matters adequately dealt with in the recording (s 138(1)). Video recordings may be edited so that only part may be admitted as evidence, and in considering whether part of a recording should not be admitted the court must consider whether to admit it would be prejudicial to the defendant and if so whether the interests of justice require that the recording should be shown in its entirety (s 138(2) and (3)).

As with other procedural measures dependent upon available technology, video recordings may not be admitted until the Home Secretary has notified the relevant court that arrangements are in place for implementing the provision (s 138(4)).

9.16 DOCUMENTS TO REFRESH MEMORY

9.16.1 Background—Refreshing Memory and Hearsay Reform

The common law rule which permits a witness to refresh his memory by referring to a document made contemporaneously with the events described, is not strictly an exception to the hearsay rule because the evidence will be the witness's testimony and it is not necessary that the document itself should be put in as evidence. However, as Professor Dennis has observed, 'this aspect of the rule is a benevolent fiction' which effectively permits a witness to give reliable hearsay evidence on the basis that the witness is willing to vouch for the accuracy of the contemporaneous record (I Dennis, *Principles of Evidence* (2nd edn, 2002, p 473)). Where a document is used to refresh memory in this way it must be made available to the other side and may be put in evidence if the other party chooses to cross-examine the witness on any matters in the document which the witness did not mention in oral evidence. In such cases the document would have been admissible as to the consistency and therefore credibility of the witness's testimony but would not have been evidence of the truth of its contents. In many cases the distinction drawn between evidence of truth and evidence of consistency would have been artificial and in any event intrinsically difficult for a jury or magistrates' court to apply in practice. Also, as the Law Commission recognized, the rule served no useful purpose where in reality the best source of the substance of the witness's evidence was the earlier document rather than testimony in court (Law Com No 245, 10.63–10.82).

Accordingly, the Commission recommended that where the earlier statement was a more reliable source than the witness's current recollections, the earlier statement should be admitted as evidence of the truth of what was stated and not simply as evidence of consistency. This recommendation is reflected in the new rule to admit previous statements of witnesses in the proceedings as evidence of anything stated therein under s 120(4). For the Law Commission it followed as a matter of logic that if a witness's earlier documentary statement were to be admitted as free-standing evidence the same rule should apply to a similar documentary statement used to refresh memory. This rule is now found in s 120(3).

9.16.2 Scope of the Refreshing Memory Rule

As indicated above, the question of the admissibility and relevance of previous statements by a witness, whether or not used to refresh memory fell within the scope of general overhaul of hearsay in the present Act. Having dealt with this linked issue, the government took the opportunity to clarify the scope of the rule itself. Some years ago it would have been possible to identify a well-understood rule permitting a witness to refresh his memory during testimony, where the document in question had been made contemporaneously with the events described, where the contents of the statement had been verified at the time when it was made and where the witness swore that it was a truthful account. This was complemented by a rule of practice under which it was acceptable for witnesses generally to consult earlier statements prior to giving evidence. However, a succession of recent decisions have blurred the distinction between the two rules culminating in *R v Ribble magistrates ex p Cochrane* ([1996] 2 Cr App R 544) which indicated a wide judicial discretion to allow witnesses to refer to statements made earlier which were not made contemporaneously with the incidents they described. The logic of this decision was simply that even if not contemporaneous, the earlier statement would be the best evidence available on the point if there was good reason to believe that the witness's recollection at the time of making the statement would have been better than at the time of giving evidence in court. This logic commended itself to Auld LJ who recommended a general clarification of the law along these lines (Auld, *Review of the Criminal Courts of England and Wales* (2001, 551)). Such a clarification is now found in s 139.

9.16.3 Section 139

Section 139 confirms and extends the common law rule under which a witness may refer to a document in order to refresh memory. As indicated above, the rule about refreshing memory at common law is strictly a rule about how ordinary oral testimony may be given and does not necessarily involve the admission of hearsay. The common law rule will this be unaffected by s 114(1) which effectively abolishes common law exceptions to the hearsay rule unless preserved by s 118. It seems therefore that the common law rule on refreshing memory will linger on alongside the new rule in s 139. This is unlikely to be of significance in view of the breadth of the new rule.

Section 139(1) provides for witnesses giving oral evidence in criminal proceedings to refresh their memory while doing so. The term 'oral evidence' is defined in s 140 to include evidence which, by reason of any disability, disorder or other impairment, a person called as a witness gives in writing or by signs or by way of any device. This would includes evidence given by a witness in relation to whom a special measures direction has been made under YJCEA 1999, s 19 and who gives evidence by means of an 'aid to communication' under YJCEA 1999, s 30. Less obviously, s 139 will also include other instances where witnesses are assisted to give their evidence by special measures, including evidence by live link, evidence given in private, evidence given by means of a video recording (YJCEA 1999, ss 24, 25, 27 and 28). The same will apply even in the unusual case of evidence being given by an intermediary under YJCEA 1999, s 29, where the voice heard by the court will not be that of the witness. This follows from YJCEA 1999, s 31 which provides that evidence given in accordance with a special measures direction forms part of the witness's evidence in the proceedings (sub-s (1)) and the statement shall be treated as if made by the witness in direct oral testimony in court (sub-s (2)), even where the statement is not made on oath (sub-s (3)).

Section 139 sweeps away the former distinction drawn between contemporaneous and non-contemporaneous documentary statements and the extent to which reference to the latter was subject to judicial discretion. The provision permits a witness to refresh his memory at any stage in the course of giving evidence by reference to a document which was either made or verified by the witness at an earlier time. The reference to verification imports the former rule that the earlier statement may be made jointly, or by another provided that it is verified by the witness after having read it or having had it read to him (*R v Kelsey* (1982) 74 Cr App R 213). In order for a witness to refresh his memory from a document, two conditions must be satisfied: (a) he must state in oral evidence that the document records his recollection of the matter at that earlier time, and (b) his recollection of the matter is likely to have been significantly better at that time than it is at the time of his oral evidence (sub-s (1)). Consideration of the latter objective test will be little more than a formality since, generally speaking, memory degrades over time.

Section 139(2) confirms, for the avoidance of doubt, that the same rules about refreshing memory will apply to transcripts of earlier sound recordings in the same way as to other written statements. The requirement of a transcript makes clear that a witness will not be able to listen to a recording whilst in the witness box. One drafting oddity is that the requirement that the earlier statement must have been verified at an earlier stage by a witness does not appear to apply where the document to be relied upon is a transcript. This is particularly odd since in relation to statements originating from sound recordings, verification should be an issue at two stages, firstly in relation to the recording itself and secondly in relation to the transcript. However, it is a requirement that the witness should state that the earlier account represented his recollection of the matter at the time when it was made. If cross-examined on this, it might be difficult for a witness to maintain the statement about recollection without indicating to the court that the recording was checked at the time when it was made.

Where a transcript of recording is relied upon, under normal principles the transcript and a copy of the recording should be made available for inspection by the other side and should be put in evidence as an exhibit if the other party chooses to cross-examine the witness on any discrepancies between the oral evidence and the earlier statement.

9.17 RULE-MAKING POWER

Section 132 provides for rules to be made relating to the Crown Court, Court of Appeal and magistrates' courts. In particular the rules may provide for the procedure to be followed, notice to be given and other conditions to be fulfilled by a party proposing to tender a statement under any of the hearsay provisions. The rules will prescribe a procedure by which hearsay evidence may be admitted by agreement under which, where one party has given a prescribed notice to the other, the evidence will become admissible if no counter-notice is received. Where a party proposing to tender evidence fails to comply with a requirement, the evidence will not be admissible without leave of the court. The court or jury having considered whether there is any justification for the failure to comply, may draw such inferences from the failure as appear proper and the failure may also be taken into account in relation to the assessment of costs. However, where an inference is drawn from failure to comply with prescribed requirements in relation to proposed evidence, no person shall be convicted solely on an inference drawn from such failure.

9.18 DEPOSITIONS AS EVIDENCE AT TRIAL

Section 130 amends the procedure whereby depositions of evidence generated for the purpose of transfer to the Crown Court under s 51 of the Crime and Disorder Act 1998 (CDA 1988) may be subsequently used as evidence in the Crown Court. Under CDA 1998, Sch 3, para 5(2) such depositions may, without further proof, be read as evidence at the trial of the accused. Under para 5(3)(c) the accused can object to depositions being read, but this objection might have been overruled by the Crown Court under para 5(4). By CJA 2003, s 130, para 5(3) is now omitted. The effect of this is that the accused will now have an absolute power of veto over the admission of evidence by deposition against him in the Crown Court.

9.19 EVIDENCE AT RETRIAL

Section 131 substitutes a new para 1 for paras 1 and 1A, Sch 2 to the Criminal Appeal Act 1968 which deals with evidence to be admitted at a retrial. The amendments made are consequential to changes to the hearsay rules in the present Act. Under substituted para 1(1) evidence which was given orally at the original trial must be likewise given orally at the retrial unless the parties agree otherwise, but this is now subject to the possibility of the evidence of an unavailable witness being admitted under CJA 2003, s 116 or to the court exercising its 'safety-valve' discretion to admit hearsay evidence under s 114(d) where a witness is unavailable to give evidence but the requirements of s 116 are not satisfied.

9.20 REPEALS AND AMENDMENTS

A number of provisions which are effectively replaced by new rules in the present Act are repealed. By s 136 the whole of Part II and Sch 2 of CJA 1988, which made exceptions to the hearsay rule for absent witnesses and business records, are repealed. A further list of consequential repeals is also found in Sch 37, Part 6.

10

GENERAL SENTENCING PROVISIONS

10.1 INTRODUCTION

Chapter 1 of Part 12 of the Criminal Justice Act 2003 (CJA 2003) contains a number of general provisions relating to sentencing. It is convenient to consider these together at this stage, although it will be necessary to refer back to them later in this book. The general sentencing provisions in the Act are a mix between some genuinely new principles and some restatement of pre-existing sentencing provisions. The new provisions, in the main, have their origin in Home Office, *Making Punishments Work: Report of a Review of the Sentencing Framework for England and Wales* (July 2001), more generally known as the Halliday Report. Key recommendations of Halliday were accepted by the government and restated in their policy document *Justice for All* (Cm 5563, July 2002).

Most of the pre-existing provisions were previously to be found in the Powers of Criminal Courts (Sentencing) Act 2000 (PCC(S)A 2000). That statute, which is referred to throughout CJA 2003 as 'the Sentencing Act', had been intended as a consolidation of sentencing provisions, but now many of that Act's key sections are repealed and replaced by the new arrangements in CJA 2003. The draftsman of this Part of the 2003 Act might have opted simply to amend the relevant provisions of the 2000 Act, but chose rather to repeal them and replace them with, in some cases, almost identical provisions. This dashes any remaining hopes of those who thought that the 2000 Act would bring a pause in the flood of legislation change in sentencing. Having said that, at the time of writing it is unclear when these provisions are likely to be brought into effect. Current information from the Home Office suggests that provisions on general sentencing principles will be among the last of the Act's provisions to be brought into force, and not before 2006/2007. This may seem surprising given that there are no significant cost implications to most of these changes. The new framework does anticipate, however, the bringing into force of the new suspended sentence (termed 'custody minus' by Halliday) and custody plus. The latter is not expected to come into operation until 2005 onwards. Given the pace of legislative change in sentencing, there can be no guarantee that the general provisions on sentencing will be brought into force unamended, and it is possible that some may not become law at all.

10.2 PURPOSES OF SENTENCING

Section 142(1) sets out in legislative form for the first time a list of the purposes of sentencing. The section provides that:

Any court dealing with an offender in respect of his offence must have regard to the following purposes of sentencing—

(a) the punishment of offenders,

(b) the reduction of crime (including its reduction by deterrence)

(c) the reform and rehabilitation of offenders,

(d) the protection of the public, and

(e) the making of reparation by offenders to persons affected by their offences.

Section 142(2) limits the scope of this by stating that subsection (1):

. . . does not apply

(a) in relation to an offender aged under 18 at the time of conviction,

(b) to an offence the sentence for which is fixed by law,

(c) to an offence the sentence for which falls to be imposed under section 51A(2) of the Firearms Act 1968 (minimum sentence for certain firearms offences), under sub-section (2) of section 110 or 111 of the Sentencing Act (required custodial sentences) or under any of sections 225 to 228 of this Act (dangerous offenders), or

(d) in relation to the making under Part 3 of the Mental Health Act 1983 of a hospital order (with or without a restriction order), an interim hospital order, a hospital direction or a limitation direction.

To deal first with the limitations in s 142(2), it is clear that (a) means that the purposes set out in s 142(1) are not applicable to youth courts, where the great majority of offenders aged under 18 when convicted are sentenced. The 2003 Act thereby preserves an important distinction between the sentencing principles applicable to young offenders and those aged 18 and over. By the Crime and Disorder Act 1998 (CDA 1998), s 37, the principal aim of the youth justice system (including the youth court) is 'to prevent offending by children and young persons' and there is also a statutory duty under the Children and Young Persons Act 1933, s 44, to 'have regard to the welfare of the child or young person'. The purposes of sentencing set out in s 142(2) are also inapplicable to those few young offenders who are sentenced in the Crown Court, whether alongside an adult, or after having been convicted in the higher court of a homicide offence or other 'grave crime' under PCC(S)A 2000, s 91. Section 44 of the 1933 Act, and s 37 of the 1998 Act certainly do apply to those young offenders (see the broad definition of 'youth justice system' provided by s 42(1) of the 1998 Act: 'the system of criminal justice in so far as it relates to children and young persons').

The reference in s 142(2)(b) to a sentence 'fixed by law' is customarily taken to refer to a mandatory life sentence imposed for the crime of murder. This includes mandatory life imprisonment for offenders aged 21 and over, custody for life for offenders aged 18, 19 or 20, and detention at Her Majesty's pleasure for offenders aged under 18 at the time of offence. When s 61 of the Criminal Justice and Court Services Act 2000 is brought into force, the sentence of custody for life will be abolished, and murderers aged 18, 19 or 20 will receive imprisonment for life.

The sections referred to in s 142(2)(c) are those which require (subject to the sentencing court finding 'exceptional circumstances' relating to the offender or to the offence) the passing of a minimum sentence of 5 years (or in some cases 3 years) on an offender convicted of one of a range of offences under the Firearms Act 1968 or, subject to the sentencing court finding 'particular circumstances' relating to the offender or to any of the offences, 7 years on an offender convicted for the third time of a Class A drug trafficking offence (s 110 of the Sentencing Act) or the passing of a minimum sentence of 3 years on an offender convicted for the third time of residential burglary (s 111 of the Sentencing Act). It may be noted in passing that there is no reference here to the automatic life sentence for the second serious offence, in s 109 of the Sentencing Act. The CJA 2003, s 303(d)(iv) repeals that section, as part of the general overhaul of sentencing of 'dangerous offenders'. For discussion of these provisions see Chapter 14 below.

Section 142(2)(d) exempts from the general purposes of sentencing in the CJA 2003 cases where the sentencing court chooses to make a disposal of the offender which is directed towards his treatment for a mental disorder.

We turn then to the specified 'purposes of sentencing' in s 142(1). It is hard to know what to make of this provision. There is no proposal in the Halliday Report that such a list of purposes should appear in statute but, in *Justice for All*, the government indicated its intention to 'set out in legislation the purposes of sentencing' (para 5.8), with a requirement that sentencers 'consider these purposes when sentencing and how the sentence they impose will impose the right balance between the purposes' (para 5.9). The list of purposes in *Justice for All* is somewhat different from that which appeared in the Bill as introduced into Parliament, and slightly different again from the list which can now be found in s 142(1). Everyone can agree that these listed purposes may be important, to a greater or lesser extent, in the sentencing of any individual offender. But setting out a 'shopping list' in this way is unhelpful to sentencers. As the learned editor of the *Criminal Law Review* has said, when commenting on the relevant paragraphs of *Justice for All*, 'This list . . . resembles a first year criminal justice student's revision notes. . . . [T]his is not so much a framework as a bran tub'

(Editorial [2002] Crim LR 688). This criticism is surely correct. It is very unsatisfactory to say that sentencers must 'balance' aims which are prima facie conflicting, such as deterrence and reparation, or punishment and rehabilitation. If purposes of sentencing are to be specified in statute, what is required is the setting of priorities amongst those aims. *Justice for All* did hint at this by stating that protection of the public was 'paramount', but the practical implication of this for sentencers was not explained in the document, and all attempt to give priority to a particular purpose or purposes has been abandoned in s 142(1).

There are far more promising models available, which could have been adopted or developed. The Council of Europe in 1993 advocated the selection of a primary rationale in sentencing, for reasons of consistency (Council of Europe, *Consistency in Sentencing*, Recommendation No R(92) 17, 1993, Part A). The Swedish sentencing statute has adopted desert as its primary rationale, but allows for other approaches to be taken in relation to specific offences or offenders (see A von Hirsch and N Jareborg, 'Sweden's sentencing statute enacted' (1989) Crim LR 275). Section 142 is a woeful section. The best that can be hoped for is that nobody refers to it, because it is of little theoretical value and has no practical relevance. There must be concern, however, that the section will create mischief in the future, especially for those bodies charged by the Act with the drafting of guidelines to enhance greater consistency in sentencing (see Chapter 11, below). The section, if taken seriously, makes consistency much harder to achieve.

10.3 OFFENCE SERIOUSNESS

10.3.1 Harm and Culpability

The Criminal Justice Act 1991 was based on the principle of 'desert', or proportionality between offence seriousness and sentence severity. One of the criticisms of that Act was that the legislation provided little help in interpreting the key notion of 'seriousness'. See for example, D Thomas, 'The Criminal Justice Act 1991: custodial sentences' (1992) Crim LR 232, who asked when, exactly, was an offence 'serious enough' to justify a community sentence, or 'so serious' that only custody can be justified? As Professor Ashworth has said, it is unfortunate that the Act did not make clear enough its commitment to the principle of proportionality, and instead proceeded by 'allusion and implication' (A Ashworth, *Sentencing and Criminal Justice* (2000, p 85)). These were the threshold tests provided by the 1991 Act. The lack of clarity in the Act allowed rationales such as general deterrence, which conflicts with proportionality, back in to the equation. So, in *R v Cunningham* (1993) 14 Cr App R (S) 444, at 447, Lord Taylor CJ stated that ' "commensurate with the seriousness of the offence" must mean "commensurate with the punishment and *deterrence* which the seriousness of the offence requires" ' (emphasis added). Whilst Lord Taylor did go on to say that the 1991 Act now prevented the passing of a deterrent sentence to make an example of a particular offender, deterrence had been read back into a statutory sentencing scheme which had been intended to marginalize or exclude it.

The 2003 Act retains the threshold tests of 'serious enough' and 'so serious', but has a little more to say about the meaning of 'serious'. Section 143(1) provides that:

In considering the seriousness of any offence, the court must consider the offender's culpability in committing the offence and any harm which the offence caused, was intended to cause or might foreseeably have caused.

This provision is a welcome attempt to clarify the concept of offence seriousness. It may be compared with the words of Professor Andrew von Hirsch, the leading proponent of desert theory in sentencing. After stating that the major components of offence seriousness are harm and culpability, von Hirsch explains that: 'Harm refers to the injury done or risked by the criminal act. Culpability refers to the factors of intent, motive and circumstance that determine how much the offender should be held accountable for his act' (A von Hirsch, *Past or Future Crimes* (1986, p 64). The relationship *between* harm and culpability is an important, but complex, issue. Sometimes the harm caused by an offence is very great, but the culpability of the offender is low (some cases of causing death by dangerous driving provide examples). Sometimes the culpability is high but, by good fortune, the harm does not occur at all, or is much less than might have been expected (some cases of attempted crime provide examples). Von Hirsch suggests that: 'The consequences that should be considered in gauging the harmfulness of an act should be those that can fairly be attributed to the actor's choice. This militates, for example, against including in harm the unforeseeable consequences of the act . . .'. Section 143 is silent on the relationship between harm and culpability, so this may be a question for the Sentencing Guidelines Council to give guidance on in due course. See 11.3 below.

Unfortunately, the relationship, if any, between s 143(1) and s 142 is obscure. These adjacent sections jar against each other. If culpability and harm are the key considerations of offence seriousness, as s 143 declares, what role is to be played by the other objectives of sentencing listed in s 142? What, for example, is the role of general deterrence? One way of interpreting the relationship between the provisions would be to say that proportionality provides the principal rationale for sentence selection, and that the other sentencing aims can be pursued only within that constraint. So, for example, a sentence can properly be imposed with a view to reforming the offender, or making reparation to the victim of the offence, provided that the severity of the sentence remains in proportion with the seriousness of the offence which was committed. This would be a coherent scheme but, if that was what was intended by the legislation, one would have expected s 142 to have said so.

10.3.2 Previous Convictions

The relevance and weight to be attributed to an offender's previous convictions when imposing sentence for a new offence has been an issue which has caused particular difficulty in the English sentencing legislation. The original version of the rather restrictive provision in CJA 1991 was repealed and replaced by a much more loosely worded provision in CJA 1993. This latter version was consolidated into the

Sentencing Act and is now, in its turn, repealed and replaced by s 143(2) of CJA 2003.

The Halliday Report made it clear that the treatment of persistent offenders in sentencing legislation was 'unsatisfactory because it is not as clear as it might be and has unpredictable results . . .' (para 1.15). Halliday accordingly recommended that: 'The existing "just deserts" philosophy should be modified by incorporating a new presumption that severity of sentence should increase when an offender has sufficiently recent and relevant previous convictions', but precisely how this should be done should be spelt out in sentencing guidelines rather than in primary legislation.

Section 143(2) states that:

In considering the seriousness of an offence ('the current offence') committed by an offender who has one or more previous convictions, the court must treat each previous conviction as an aggravating factor if (in the case of that conviction) the court considers that it can reasonably be so treated having regard, in particular, to—

(a) the nature of the offence to which the conviction relates and its relevance to the current offence, and
(b) the time that has elapsed since the conviction.

This is a highly controversial provision, in terms of both the underlying philosophy of the Act and its likely impact on the custodial population which, at the time of writing, stands at the record level of 74,500, an increase of 25,000 over the last ten years. It is assumed by most commentators that, once this provision is in force, there will be enhanced 'sentencing on the record'. See, for example, A von Hirsch, 'Record enhanced sentencing in England and Wales: reflections on the Halliday Report's proposed treatment of prior convictions' in S Rex and M Tonry (eds), *Reform and Punishment: The Future of Sentencing* (2002, ch 10). Much will depend, however, on the way in which the Sentencing Guidelines Council chooses to interpret the subsection. On the one hand, future sentencing guidelines could reflect the criminal records of offenders in a stepped and inevitable way, reminiscent of American sentencing guideline grids which adopt record as a prime driver of sentence. On the other hand, the Council might take the important proviso in the subsection, 'if . . . the court considers that it can reasonably be so treated', to mean that there will, in fact, be no sharp change in sentencing policy. The subsection requires the court to consider the 'relevance' of any previous convictions to the current offence, and a sentencer may properly conclude that a previous conviction does not aggravate the current offence, especially where it is old and quite different from the current offence. Lord Woolf CJ (who in March 2004 became the chairman of the Council) has in *R v McInerney* [2003] 1 Cr App R 627 already set his face against stepped increases in sentencing for burglary to reflect criminal record. In recommending community sentence starting points for a range of burglary cases, his Lordship's view was that community sentences with appropriate conditions can provide greater protection for the public than custodial sentences of up to 12 or 18 months. This was in the context of a judgment in which his Lordship had already agreed that record was of more importance in sentencing for burglary than in some other crimes.

Section 143(4) states that 'previous conviction' in this context means 'a previous conviction by a court in the United Kingdom or a previous finding of guilt in service disciplinary proceedings', but s 143(5) states that the sentencing court *may* treat a previous conviction by a court outside the United Kingdom as an aggravating factor if it appears appropriate to do so. The term 'service disciplinary proceedings' is defined in s 305(1) of the Act. As originally introduced into the House of Commons, the Criminal Justice Bill had provisions which restated the law in s 151(5) and (6) of PCC(S)A 2000, that absolute and conditional discharges and some probation orders, which by law count as convictions for limited purposes only, do count as convictions for the purposes of s 136(2). These provisions were removed during the passage of the Bill through Parliament, and do not reappear in the 2003 Act. The whole of s 151 of PCC(S)A 2000 has nonetheless been repealed. This may leave room for argument over whether previous discharges, or probation orders imposed before October 1992, do count as 'previous convictions' for these purposes.

10.3.3 Offending on Bail

Offending on bail was previously dealt with in PCC(S)A 2000, s 151(2). Section 143(3) replaces s 151(2) with an almost identically worded provision. The only difference is the substitution of the word 'shall' by the word 'must'. The provision makes it clear that when considering the seriousness of an offence committed whilst the offender was on bail, the court must treat that fact as an aggravating factor. The new Act therefore makes no change in this area.

10.3.4 Reduction for Guilty Plea

Sentence reduction for guilty plea was previously dealt with in s 152 of PCC(S)A 2000. Section 144 replaces s 152(1) and (3) of that Act with an almost identically worded provision. The only difference in s 144(1) is the substitution of the word 'shall' by the word 'must'.

Subsection 144(2) refers to the two pre-existing examples of presumptive minimum sentences (for third time traffickers in Class A drugs in s 110 of the 2000 Act, and third time domestic burglars in s 111 of the 2000 Act). In those two cases the discount for guilty plea can be no more than 20% of the sentence. Surprisingly, however, s 144(2) makes no reference to the operation of the guilty plea in cases where the new minimum sentences for certain firearms offences apply (these are considered at 11.7 below). The lack of such a provision might be construed to mean that in the relevant firearms cases no discount for guilty plea may be given by the sentencing court at all. This interpretation would be highly anomalous, however, and it is submitted that the sentencing court might properly discount sentence for an offence under s 51A in accordance with the normal principles. Nothing in s 152 of the 2000 Act or in s 144 of the 2003 Act which replaces it, prevents that conclusion.

Section 152(2) of the 2000 Act, which was the subsection requiring the sentencer to state in open court that a reduction in sentence had been made to take into account the offender's guilty plea, is replaced, in almost identical terms, by s 174(2)(d) of CJA 2003. Section 174 is a compendious section listing a range of requirements for sentencers to give reasons for, and explain the effects of, sentence. The new Act therefore makes no change in this area. It may be noted in passing that the Sentencing Advisory Panel issued a consultation paper on reduction in sentence for guilty plea towards the end of 2003, and that the Sentencing Guidelines Council may be expected to issue sentencing guidelines on that matter during 2004. In October 2003 the High Court of Justiciary in Scotland, in *Du Plooy v HM Advocate* 2003 SLT 1237, issued sentencing guidance on the guilty plea reduction.

10.3.5 Increase in Sentence for Racial or Religious Aggravation

Provisions dealing with racial or religious aggravation in sentencing were previously found in s 153 of PCC(S)A 2000, as amended by the Anti-terrorism, Crime and Security Act 2001, s 39 (which extended 'racial aggravation' to 'racial and religious aggravation'). Section 145 of the 2003 Act replaces s 153 with an almost identically worded provision. The only difference is the substitution (in two places) of the word 'shall' by the word 'must'. The new Act therefore makes no changes in this area. The definition of racial or religious aggravation can be found in the Crime and Disorder Act 1998 (CDA 1998), s 28.

Guidelines for sentencers dealing with an offence committed in circumstances involving racial aggravation were issued by the Court of Appeal in *R v Saunders* [2000] 1 Cr App R (S) 458 and *R v Kelly* [2001] 2 Cr App R (S) 341. The guidelines were issued prior to the amendment made by the Anti-terrorism, Crime and Security Act 2001, s 39. They apply both to the special group of 'racially aggravated offences' created by CDA 1998 (for example, racially aggravated criminal damage, racially aggravated harassment, and racially aggravated assault occasioning actual bodily harm) which carry higher maximum sentences than the equivalent basic offences, and to offences in general. It could perhaps be assumed that the existing guidelines will be applicable to religious aggravation in the same way as they are to racial aggravation, although there is no authority on the point.

10.3.6 Increase in Sentence for Aggravation related to
Disability or Sexual Orientation

Introduced at a late stage into the Bill, s 146 of the 2003 Act adds two further considerations to those of racial and religious aggravation which must be treated by the sentencing court as an aggravating factor in the case. These are where, at the time of committing the offence, the offender demonstrated hostility towards the victim based on the victim's sexual orientation or their disability, or where the offence is shown to have been motivated wholly or partly by hostility towards persons who are of a particular sexual orientation or who have a disability or particular disability. The wording of the section, with its reliance on evidence of demonstrated hostility or evidence of motivation, reflects the wording of s 28 of CDA 1998 on racial or religious aggravation.

Section 146 is concerned to specify in statute a general aggravating factor in sentencing, which the courts almost certainly had been taking into account anyway when weighing offence seriousness. Its inclusion within the statute is symbolic, however, as underlining its importance, and in requiring the sentencer to make reference to the fact that the offence was committed in aggravating circumstances of that sort. It should be noted that s 146 does not amend the provisions relating to the special group of 'racially or religiously aggravated offences', created by ss 29 to 32 of CDA 1998, which carry higher maximum penalties than the basic offence. It can perhaps be assumed that the sentencing guidelines referred to in 10.3.5 above, relating to sentencing enhancement for offences involving racial (and religious) aggravation, will also be broadly applicable to offences aggravated by hostility based on the disability or sexual orientation of the victim.

10.4 COMMUNITY SENTENCES—GENERAL PROVISIONS

The CJA 2003 recasts the pre-existing range of community orders. In general terms, the range of orders is now subsumed under a generic heading of 'community sentence'. Where, following CJA 2003, a sentencing court passes a community sentence, it may include in that sentence one or more of a menu of requirements. These requirements broadly reflect the nature of the pre-existing community orders. So what, prior to CJA 2003, would have been expressed as a 'community punishment order' now becomes 'an unpaid work requirement' within a community sentence. At the time of writing it is expected that the new provisions on community orders will be brought into force in spring 2005.

The origins of this change are in chapter 6 of the Halliday Report, although Halliday proposed that the generic sentence should be known as a new 'community punishment order' (para 6.6). Halliday justified these reforms by noting the proliferation of community orders in recent years 'which often replicate the virtues and defects of existing orders' (para 6.2). 'New ideas and developments in the supervision of offenders should, where possible, be incorporated into existing sentences without resorting to the regular introduction of entirely new ones', he said (para 6.2). Halliday also suggested that greater consistency in sentencing might be achieved by scrapping a number of distinct orders and rebranding these as requirements within a single generic 'community sentence' (para 6.2). This is optimistic, however, since consistency can hardly be achieved simply by giving all community orders the same name. Consistency will depend upon how the new 'community sentence' is used, and on the number and complexity of requirements which are written into it by sentencers. For a valuable discussion of the Halliday approach to community orders see S Rex, 'Reinventing community penalties: the role of communication' in S Rex and M Tonry, *Reform and Punishment: The Future of Sentencing* (2002, ch 7).

181

The provisions relating to requirements which can be inserted into a community sentence are considered in detail in Chapter 15, below. First, however, it is necessary to examine certain general provisions, including the threshold provisions, on the new community sentence scheme. These are to be found in ss 147–151 of CJA 2003.

10.4.1 Restrictions on imposing a 'Community Sentence'

By s 147, a 'community sentence' means a 'sentence which consists of or includes a community order' or 'one or more youth community orders'. A 'community order' is an order imposed on an offender aged 16 or over, which contains one or more requirements (such as unpaid work, curfew, residence, supervision, drug rehabilitation, etc). A 'youth community order' means (a) a curfew order, (b) an exclusion order, (c) an attendance centre order, (d) a supervision order, or (e) an action plan order. These youth community orders remain as defined in the relevant sections of the 2000 Act. Exclusion orders are not in force.

Section 148(1) provides that:

A court must not pass a community sentence on an offender unless it is of the opinion that the offence, or the combination of the offence and one or more offences associated with it, was serious enough to warrant such a sentence.

The threshold provision for community sentences was previously dealt with in s 35(1) of PCC(S)A 2000. Section 148(1) replaces s 35(1) of that Act with this almost identically worded provision. The only difference is the substitution of the word 'shall' by the word 'must'. Section 148(2) provides that in a community sentence which consists of one or more community orders, the requirements which are imposed must be (a) 'the most suitable for the offender' and (b) the restrictions on liberty imposed by the order must be 'commensurate with the seriousness of the offence, or the combination of the offence and one or more offences associated with it'. These restrictions on imposing community sentences were previously dealt with in s 35(3) of the 2000 Act. Section 148(2) replaces s 35(3) with a similarly worded provision. Section 148(3) applies the same wording to a community sentence consisting of one or more youth community orders. The changes made by the new Act in this area are required to reflect the nature of the new generic 'community sentence' containing one or more requirements.

In his Report, Halliday noted that in the past the community sentence threshold (that the offence must be 'serious enough' to justify a community sentence), 'may have unintentionally created an impression that fines should be reserved for the less serious cases' (para 6.5). Halliday went on to recommend 'a more flexible sentencing framework at the lower end of the seriousness spectrum, in which it would be possible for sentencers to respond more easily to the circumstances of offenders with limited financial means by routinely imposing a community penalty rather than a fine . . . ' (para 6.5). The 'impression', referred to by Halliday, that the threshold for community sentences also serves to mark out offences which are 'too serious' for a fine is, indeed, a mistaken impression, which may have been gained through over-reliance on the idea that the 1991 Act framework was a sentencing 'pyramid' with custody at the top, community orders at the second level, fines at the third, and discharges at the fourth. This is misleading, since all that the pre-existing law said was that an offence had to be of a certain level of seriousness to *justify* a community sentence. It did not say that such level of seriousness automatically ruled out the use of a fine. Indeed, substantial fines are frequently and properly used as a penalty in the Crown Court in cases which are well above the community sentence threshold.

10.4.2 Community Sentence—Offender previously Remanded in Custody

Section 149 deals with the situation where an offender, in respect of whom the court is now proposing to pass a community sentence, was remanded in custody in connection with that offence before being convicted of or pleading guilty to it. The section states that the sentencing court 'may have regard' to any such period of remand when determining the restrictions on liberty to be imposed by a community order or youth community order. This clearly confers a discretion to take account of such period, rather than requiring the court to do so. 'Remanded in custody' is given a wide meaning here, to include remands to local authority accommodation where the offender was kept in local authority secure accommodation or in a secure training centre, or was removed to a hospital: see further CJA 2003, s 242(2).

This section does not have a legislative antecedent. Section 67 of the Criminal Justice Act 1967, which will be repealed and replaced by CJA 2003, deals with the effect of time spent on remand on a subsequent custodial sentence, but not a community sentence. There may be a difficulty in cases where an offender is subsequently in breach of the community sentence. Existing case law in authorities such as *R v McIntyre* (1985) 7 Cr App R (S) 196 and *R v Henderson* [1997] 2 Cr App R (S) 266 indicates that where the court revokes a community sentence on breach, and substitutes a custodial sentence, an adjustment should normally be made to the length of the custodial sentence to reflect any period spent on remand by the offender before the community sentence was passed. In a case where a sentencer exercises the discretion in s 149 and adjusts the community order accordingly, it will be important that this is made clear on the record, to avoid the possibility of a double allowance in the event of revocation of the order.

10.4.3 Community Sentence Not Available

Section 150 provides, for the avoidance of doubt, that the power to make a community order or youth community order is not available where the sentence for the offence is fixed by law (murder), or where it falls to be imposed under s 51A(2) of the Firearms Act 1968, s 110(2) or 111(2) of PCC(S)A 2000, or where it falls to be imposed under ss 225 to 228 of CJA 2003 (dangerous offenders). For further comment on these exceptions see 10.2 above. The section re-enacts the substance of s 34 of the Powers of Criminal Courts (Sentencing) Act 2000.

10.4.4 Community Order—Persistent Offender previously Fined

Section 151 allows for the sentencer to impose a community order on certain offenders aged 16 or over, instead of imposing a fine, if the offender is a 'persistent offender previously fined'. This status requires that the offender has, on three or more previous occasions since attaining the age of 16, been convicted and given 'a sentence consisting only of a fine' (s 151(1)(b)). It is not relevant for these purposes whether he has, on other occasions, been given a custodial sentence or a community order. If, despite the general effect of s 143(2) (aggravation of sentence to reflect previous convictions—see above, 10.3.2) the sentencing court would not (apart from s 151) have regarded the latest offence as being serious enough to justify a community sentence, the court may still pass a community sentence if, having regard to all the circumstances, including the previous convictions, it is in the interests of justice to make such an order.

This section bears a superficial similarity to s 59 of PCC(S)A 2000, which is repealed by CJA 2003. Section 59 was restricted to imposing a curfew order, or a community punishment order, on a 'petty persistent offender' for whom a fine would normally have been the appropriate sentence for the latest offence, but against whom there were outstanding fines which had not been paid. It will be seen that s 151 is more general in its effect, allowing the court to move from a fine to a community sentence in light of all the circumstances of the case, including the offender's record. The courts will need to decide the meaning of the phrase 'a sentence consisting only of a fine'. Would this, for example, include a fine plus an ancillary order, such as compensation or a disqualification?

10.5 CUSTODIAL SENTENCES—GENERAL PROVISIONS

The Criminal Justice Act 2003 recasts the pre-existing arrangements for custodial sentences, by introducing new forms of prison sentence and replacing the old form of suspended sentence with an entirely new version. These new sentences are dealt with in detail in Chapter 13 below. The new suspended sentence (which was termed 'custody minus' by Halliday) is expected to be implemented in two stages, firstly for 18- to 21-year-olds in December 2004, and secondly for those aged 21 and over by 2005/2006. Custody plus is not expected to be implemented before 2005/2006 for 18- to 21-year-olds and not before 2006/2007 for those aged 21 and over. First, however, it is necessary to examine certain general provisions relating to the new scheme of custodial sentences. These are to be found in CJA 2003, ss 152–155.

10.5.1 General Restrictions on imposing Discretionary Custodial Sentences

Section 152 of CJA 2003 is closely similar to PCC(S)A 2000, s 79, which is repealed by the 2003 Act. Section 152(1) provides that the power to impose a discretionary custodial sentence applies where a person is convicted of an offence punishable with imprisonment other than one where the sentence for the offence is fixed by law (murder), or where it falls to be imposed under s 51A(2) of the Firearms Act 1968, s 110(2) or 111(2) of PCC(S)A 2000, or where it falls to be imposed under ss 225 to 228 of CJA 2003 (dangerous offenders). For further comment on these exceptions see 10.2 above.

Section 152(2) states that:

The court must not pass a custodial sentence unless it is of the opinion that the offence, or the combination of the offence and one or more offences associated with it, was so serious that neither a fine alone nor a community sentence can be justified for the offence.

This provision is, of course, similar to the s 79(1)(a) of the 2000 Act, which has provided the custody threshold in the past. There are two main differences. The first is the now familiar substitution of the words 'shall not' in the 2000 Act by the words 'must not'. Secondly, more importantly, the words 'only such a sentence can be justified by the offence' in the 2000 Act are replaced by 'neither a fine alone nor a community sentence can be justified for the offence'. It is unclear what real difference this change will make in practice. The earlier formula required the sentencer to turn to a custodial sentence only when all other sentencing options had been considered and rejected. This clearly made custody a 'last resort'. The new formula requires the sentencer to turn to a custodial sentence only when (i) a fine alone and (ii) a community sentence have been considered and rejected. Logically, this seems to leave open the possibility of the court moving to a custodial sentence in a case where a combination of a community sentence and fine would have sufficed. It is submitted that the earlier wording was clearer, and was to be preferred. 'So serious' must of course be read in the light of s 143, especially s 143(1) on the relevance of previous convictions.

It should be noted that there is no provision in s 152 which is equivalent to s 79(2)(b) of the 2000 Act, which permitted a court to impose a 'longer-than-commensurate' sentence on an offender convicted of a violent offence or a sexual offence and where only a custodial sentence would be adequate to protect the public from serious harm from him. This is because these powers are abolished by CJA 2003, which introduces new provisions for sentencing 'dangerous offenders'. These are considered in Chapter 14, below.

Section 152(3) deals with the exceptional situation where a court may pass a custodial sentence on an offender who has failed to express his willingness to comply with a requirement proposed to be included in a community order and where the requirement requires an expression of such willingness. This subsection has similar effect to s 79(3) of the 2000 Act, with two differences. The first change is that the new provision, reflecting the new generic 'community sentence', refers to compliance with specific requirements in the community order. The requirements which still need the offender's expression of willingness to comply are a mental health treatment requirement (s 207(3)(c)), a drug rehabilitation requirement (s 209(2)(d)), and an alcohol treatment requirement (s 212(3)). The second change is that CJA 2003, s 161 introduces provisions for pre-sentence drug testing (see 10.8 below), and s 152(3) states that the court may impose a custodial sentence if the offender has failed to comply with an order made under s 161.

10.5.2 General Provision on Length of Discretionary Custodial Sentences

Section 153 of CJA 2003 is similar to s 80 of PCC(S)A 2000, which is repealed by the 2003 Act. Section 153(1) states that the section applies where a court passes a custodial sentence other than one fixed by law (murder), or where it falls to be imposed under s 51A(2) of the Firearms Act 1968, ss 110(2) and 111(2) of the Sentencing Act, or s 225 or 226 of CJA 2003 (dangerous offenders). For further comment on these exceptions see 10.2 above.

Section 153(2) states that:

Subject to section 51A(2) of the Firearms Act 1968, sections 110(2) and 111(2) of the Sentencing Act and sections 227(2) and 228(2) of this Act, the custodial sentence must be for the shortest term (not exceeding the permitted maximum) that in the opinion of the court is commensurate with the seriousness of the offence, or the combination of the offence and one or more offences associated with it.

This provision is, of course, similar to s 80(2)(a) of the 2000 Act, which has provided the discretionary custodial sentence length provision in the past. There are two main differences. The first is the now familiar substitution of the words 'shall be' in the 2000 Act by the words 'must be'. Secondly, more importantly, the words 'for such term' in the 2000 Act are replaced by 'for the shortest term'. The new wording is a clearer reflection of the principle that, where it is necessary to impose a custodial sentence that sentence should be as short as possible to achieve the goals of that sentence. It reflects statements of the senior judiciary to the same effect. The leading example is that of Lord Woolf CJ in *R v Kefford* [2002] 2 Cr App R (S) 495, where his Lordship declared (at 499) that 'the message is imprisonment only when necessary and for no longer than necessary . . .'. Recent research shows that judges believe that they are already carrying out this instruction, despite the fact that the custody rate in the Crown Court has increased from 46% to 64% between 1991 and 2001 and, during the same period, the average sentence length in the Crown Court increased from 20.5 months to 26 months (see Hough, Jacobson and Millie, *The Decision to Imprison: Sentencing and the Prison Population* (Prison Reform Trust, 2003)). It seems unlikely, in the absence of any clear political will to 'talk down' the prison population, that this subtle change in wording will make any difference in practice.

It should be noted that there is no provision in s 153 which is equivalent to PCC(S)A 2000, s 80(2)(b), which imposed some constraint on the length of a 'longer-than-commensurate' sentence. Powers to impose such sentences are abolished by CJA 2003, which introduces new provisions for sentencing 'dangerous offenders'. These are considered in Chapter 14, below.

10.6 MAGISTRATES' COURTS' POWERS TO IMPOSE IMPRISONMENT

Potentially, a highly significant change to sentencing arrangements in England and Wales is ushered in by s 154 of the 2003 Act. This section increases substantially the powers of magistrates to impose prison sentences. It is not clear when these provisions are likely to be brought into effect. At the time of writing, the latest indication from the Home Office was that the change would not take place until 2005/2006 at the earliest, to coincide with the introduction of 'custody plus'. It is clear that implementation of 'custody plus' will require very substantial additional funding to be made available to the criminal justice system, especially to the national probation service, or the national offender management service (NOMS) of which it is soon to form part. It may be that the introduction of custody plus will be delayed further beyond these projected dates, the government may change its mind on increasing magistrates' sentencing powers and not bring these provisions into effect at all. It would not be the first time that complex sentencing provisions have appeared in legislation but have never actually been implemented.

10.6.1 The New Provisions

The pre-existing law, set out in PCC(S)A 2000, s 78, was that the maximum prison sentence which could be imposed in a magistrates' court was six months in respect of any one offence, unless a shorter maximum term is provided by statute. Section 154(1) increases that maximum to 12 months. The maximum aggregate term which magistrates could impose was also six months, unless two of the terms were imposed for offences triable either way, in which case the maximum aggregate sentence was 12 months. Section 154(3) and s 155 increase the maximum aggregate term from 6 months to 65 weeks.

These provisions have also applied to the sentence of detention in a young offender institution (custodial sentence for offenders aged 18, 19, 20) and they will continue to do so for long as the sentence of detention in a young offender institution remains. When s 61 of the Criminal Justice and Court Services Act 2000 is brought into force, the sentence of detention in a young offender institution will be abolished. Offenders who would have received such sentences will thereafter be eligible to be sentenced to imprisonment, which will become the standard custodial sentences for those aged 18, 19 and 20 as well as for those aged 21 and over. No date for the implementation of s 61 has yet been set, but by s 333(1) and Sch 38, para 1 of the 2003 Act, if relevant sentencing provisions of the 2003 Act are brought into force before the sentence of detention in a young offender institution is abolished, the sentencing provisions may be modified accordingly. This means that s 154(1) should be read as if it contained the words 'or detention in a young offender institution' after 'imprisonment' until such time as the former sentence is abolished. Section 154(1) does not apply to the detention and training order (standard custodial sentence for offenders under 18), where the maximum sentence which may be imposed by a youth court for a summary offence remains at 6 months, and at 24 months for an offence triable either way.

The minimum prison sentence which may be imposed by a magistrates' court is 5 days (MCA 1980, s 132). Section 154(7) of the 2003 Act makes a rather oblique reference to the existence of that section, but clearly makes no amendment to it.

10.6.2 Background to the Change

In his *Review of the Criminal Courts* published in 2001, Lord Justice Auld could discern 'no wide or well-based support for a change in the general limit of 6 months' custody or £5,000 fine now applicable to District Judges and magistrates alike' (p 101). His Lordship did recognize, however, that there was an anomaly in the fact that the youth court has had power since the Crime and Disorder Act 1998 to impose a detention and training order on an offender aged under 18 for up to a maximum of 2 years (see now PCC(S)A 2000, ss 100–107). He also noted that planned changes emanating from the Halliday Report, especially the introduction of a new kind of prison sentence of less than 12 months to be called 'custody plus', might force a change to the adult jurisdiction. Custody plus is introduced by the 2003 Act, although it is as yet unclear when the relevant provisions will be brought into force. See Chapter 12, below.

In his Report *Making Punishments Work* (July 2001), Halliday proposed that 'custody plus' should normally consist of a period in prison (up to a maximum of 3 months) and then a period of supervision (from a minimum of 6 months and up to a maximum of whatever would take the sentence as a whole to something less than 12 months). Halliday proposed that magistrates (as well as the Crown Court) should be able to pass these sentences up to the 3 months custodial maximum, and that 'it could be argued that magistrates' courts should also be able to pass the new sentences consecutively, so that the custodial period could be up to 6 months and the supervisory period up to 12 months'. In the event, as we have seen, CJA 2003 limits the powers of the magistrates to pass consecutive sentences of imprisonment to a total of 65 weeks. This rather odd-looking number equates to 15 months, calculated on the basis of 52 weeks plus one-quarter of 52 weeks (13 weeks), which is 65 weeks. Fifteen months appears to be a compromise between the new 12 month maximum for a single offence and the 18 months that Halliday envisaged for consecutive sentences.

For further discussion of the future operation of custody plus in magistrates' courts, see 13.2.1.

10.7 PRE-SENTENCE AND OTHER REPORTS

Sections 156 to 160 are concerned with pre-sentence reports and related matters. They re-enact earlier provisions from the 2000 Act, but with some minor amendments.

10.7.1 Pre-sentence Reports: Definition and General Provisions

Section 156 of the 2003 Act substantially re-enacts the definition of 'pre-sentence report', previously to be found in s 162 of the 2000 Act. If the offender is aged 18 or over the report is prepared by an officer of the local probation board, and if the offender is aged under 18 the report is prepared by such an officer, or by a social worker of a local authority social services department, or by a member of a youth offending team. An important difference between the definitions in the two provisions, however, is that the 2000 Act required pre-sentence reports to be 'in writing', while the 2003 Act equivalent does not. This must mean that when the new provisions come into force, an oral 'stand down' report will count for all relevant purposes as a 'pre-sentence report', and a court having heard such an oral report will be taken to have complied with the requirements of section 156. This represents something of a watering down of the earlier law.

Section 156 deals with pre-sentence reports and other requirements, with respect to community and custodial sentences. It substantially re-enacts s 36 of the 2000 Act (community sentences: pre-sentence reports) and s 81 of that Act (custodial sentences: pre-sentence reports). The upshot is that whenever a court is considering whether to impose a discretionary custodial sentence, and considering how long it should be, or is considering whether to impose a community sentence, and what restrictions to put on the offender's liberty as part of that sentence, the court must take into account all the information available to it, including information about the offence and about the offender.

Before imposing a custodial or community sentence the sentencing court must normally obtain a pre-sentence report but, reflecting the earlier provisions, the court need not obtain such a report if it considers it 'unnecessary' to do so. There has been very little case law on the question of what constitutes circumstances sufficient to dispense with the need for a pre-sentence report but where, given the seriousness of the case, a custodial sentence is absolutely inevitable the sentencer might properly regard a pre-sentence report as 'unnecessary'. In *R v Armsaramah* [2001] 1 Cr App R (S) 467 the Court of Appeal approved the decision of the sentencer to pass a custodial sentence of five years on an offender convicted of kidnapping and robbery, without the benefit of a pre-sentence report. The statute indicates that a pre-sentence report is normally required to assist the sentencer in fixing the length of sentence, but it is submitted that the greatest value of such reports is for cases in and around the custody threshold rather than for cases which are clearly well above that threshold. In *R v Gillette* (1999) The Times, 3 December 1999, however, the Court of Appeal said that a sentencer should almost always order a pre-sentence when passing a *first* custodial sentence on an offender. Given the information and specialist advice contained in pre-sentence reports, it is rare for courts to impose a community sentence without first considering such a report. The 2000 Act distinguished between community orders which could not be imposed without the court first considering a pre-sentence report (such as a community punishment order), and those which could be imposed without a report (such as a curfew order). The advent of the new 'generic' community sentence in the 2003 Act (see 10.4 above) brings this formal dichotomy to an end. Henceforth, obtaining a pre-sentence report is a pre-condition for the imposition of *any* community sentence (subject to the rather vague 'unnecessary' exception, referred to above).

The rather different requirements for ordering pre-sentence reports in respect of offenders aged under 18 (and where the offence is summary, or triable either way) are retained in the 2003 Act. The court must not dispense with the requirement to obtain a pre-sentence report in such a case unless there already is one which relates to the offender and the court has had access to it.

10.7.2 Disclosure of Pre-sentence Reports

Section 159 of the 2003 Act deals with disclosure of pre-sentence reports to the defence and the prosecution, and substantially re-enacts s 156 of the 2000 Act. There are two small differences between the provisions. The first is that s 159 specifically states that the disclosure provisions do not apply to pre-sentence reports given orally. The second difference is that s 159(2) requires that 'the court must give a copy of the report . . . to the offender, his counsel or solicitor, and . . . to the prosecutor', while s 156(2) of the 2000 Act required that 'the court shall give a copy of the report . . . to the offender or his counsel or solicitor, and . . . to the prosecutor'. This slight change of wording may mean nothing, or it may mean that *two* copies are now to be given to the defence (the offender receiving his or her own copy), with a further copy for the prosecution.

10.7.3 Mentally Disordered Offenders—Medical Reports

Section 157 of the 2003 Act re-enacts s 82 of the 2000 Act, with minor amendment. It provides that, normally, the sentencing court should order a medical report on an offender, in any case where the offender is or appears to be mentally disordered, before the court passes a custodial sentence on that offender, other than a custodial sentence which is fixed by law (murder cases). This requirement does not apply, however, if the court thinks that in the circumstances it is 'unnecessary' to obtain a medical report. Section 157(6) defines 'medical report'. A medical report is quite different from a pre-sentence report, and s 157(7) clearly states that the ordering of a medical report on an offender does not displace the need to order a presentence report under s 156.

10.7.4 Other Reports

Section 160 of the 2003 Act applies where a report (other than a pre-sentence report) is made by an officer of a local probation board or a member of the youth offending team with a view to assisting any court (except a youth court) in deciding how best to deal with an offender. This section provides for disclosure of the contents of that report to the defence (but not the prosecution), and re-enacts section 157 of the 2000 Act in identical terms. The slight change of wording referred to in 10.7.2 above has not been repeated here, so that it would appear to be necessary to provide only *one* copy of the report, for the offender *or* his legal representative.

The category of 'other reports' provided by the probation service or a youth offending team has previously included 'specific sentence reports', which provide sentencers with required information about the likely suitability in practice of a particular community disposal. Thus, while a court has in the past been able to pass a curfew order without calling for a pre-sentence report on the offender, a curfew order could not be imposed unless the court has 'obtain[ed] and consider[ed] information about the place proposed to be specified in the order (including information as to the attitude of persons likely to be affected by the enforced presence there of the offender'. The introduction of the generic community sentence (see 10.4 above) means that the curfew order is no longer a community sentence in its own right, but becomes a requirement which the court may choose to make part of the community sentence being ordered. A pre-sentence report (including an oral report) will henceforth need to address the detailed suitability issues relating to requirements which the court is proposing to insert.

10.8 PRE-SENTENCE DRUG TESTING

In any case where the court is considering imposing a community sentence, it may make an order that the offender undergo pre-sentence drug testing, to ascertain whether the offender has any specified Class A drug in his body. Section 161 provides for pre-sentence drug testing, and it re-enacts with important modifications, s 36A of the 2000 Act.

Section 36A (which was inserted into the 2000 Act by s 48 of the Criminal Justice and Court Services Act 2000) provided for pre-sentence drug testing of offenders aged 18 and over, while s 161 provides for pre-sentence drug-testing of offenders aged 14 and over. Where the offender is aged 14, 15 or 16, provision must be made for an appropriate adult to be present when the sample is taken. For these purposes an 'appropriate adult' is the offender's parent or guardian or, if the offender is in the care of the local authority or voluntary organization, a person representing that authority or organization, a social worker or (if no person coming within these categories is available) any responsible person aged 18 or over who is not a police officer or employed by the police.

Failure without reasonable excuse to comply with the testing as required by the court is punishable by a fine of an amount not exceeding level 4 (currently £2,500). It should be noted that power to order pre-sentence drug testing is only exercisable in areas where the court has been notified by the Secretary of State that the power is available by that court and the notice has not been withdrawn. At the time of writing it is expected that schemes for pre-sentence drug testing will be piloted in certain court areas starting in June 2004.

10.9 MITIGATION

Section 166 of the 2003 Act re-enacts and modifies s 158 of the 2000 Act (savings for powers to mitigate sentences and deal appropriately with mentally disordered offenders).

10.9.1 Personal Mitigation

Section 166(1) refers to a range of other sections in the Act (s 148 on imposing community sentences, ss 152, 155 and 157 on imposing custodial sentences, s 156 on pre-sentence reports and other requirements, and s 164 on the fixing of fines), and makes it clear that none of these sections should be taken as detracting from the sentencing court's general power to mitigate sentence 'by taking into account any such matters as, in the opinion of the court, are relevant in mitigation of sentence'.

It is submitted that this section is concerned with matters of personal mitigation, rather than with mitigation which affects more directly the harm and culpability dimensions of the seriousness of the offence (such as the fact that the offender was provoked before the assault, or that the property stolen by the offender was of low value). Mitigation affecting seriousness of offence should always be taken into account when deciding whether the offence is 'serious enough' to warrant a community sentence (s 148(1)) or 'so serious that neither a fine alone nor a community sentence can be justified' (s 152(2)). Whether to take account of mitigation which is extrinsic to the offence but personal to the offender has always been a matter within the discretion of the court (see Scarman LJ in *R v Inwood* (1974) 60 Cr App R 70), although the Court of Appeal has from time to time provided guidance on the exercise of that discretion. One example is *R v Bernard* [1997] 1 Cr App R (S) 135, in which the Court considered the relevance to sentence of the fact that the offender is suffering from a serious illness.

Section 166(2) is new, and it provides that, notwithstanding the fact that the seriousness of an offence is such that it crosses the custody threshold, the court may impose a community sentence instead, in light of mitigation personal to the offender. This principle has been clear from the early case law on CJA 1991, especially *R v Cox* [1993] 1 WLR 188. In that case Lord Taylor CJ, in the Court of Appeal, stated that, although 'on all the known facts of the case, we have reached the conclusion that only a custodial sentence could be justified for this offence', a community rehabilitation order was the proper sentence having regard to personal mitigation, in particular the offender's youth and clean record. Section 166(2) helpfully confirms that the *Cox* principle survives the 2003 Act.

Section 166(3) provides that nothing in the sections mentioned in s 166(1) prevents a court:

(a) from mitigating any penalty included in an offender's sentence by taking into account any other penalty included in that sentence, and
(b) in the case of an offender who is convicted of one or more other offences, from mitigating his sentence by applying any rule of law as to the totality of sentences.

This wording simply re-enacts s 158(2) of the 2000 Act, and does not change the law. It does, however, provide a welcome reminder of the continuing importance of the totality principle in sentencing. Whenever a court is imposing a combination of custodial or community sentences on an offender, or a combination of requirements under the umbrella of a community sentence, the court should always consider the overall severity of those sentences, or the overall severity of those requirements, to ensure that they are not disproportionate to the totality of the offending. This concept of 'totality', developed over the years by the Court of Appeal is, however, more appropriately referred to as a 'principle of sentencing' rather than, as the statute does, a 'rule of law'.

10.9.2 Mentally Disordered Offenders—Mitigation

Section 166(5) and (6) provides that nothing in the sections mentioned in s 166(1) is to be taken as requiring a court to pass a custodial sentence on a mentally disordered offender or as restricting any power which enables the court to deal more appropriately with such an offender. In this context, 'mentally disordered' means suffering from a mental disorder within the terms of the Mental Health Act 1983. These subsections simply re-enact sub-ss 158(3) and (4) of the 2000 Act, and do not change the law.

10.10 CHANGES TO MAXIMUM PENALTIES ETC

Sections 280 to 286, taken together with Schs 25 to 28 of the 2003 Act, make a large number of changes to penalties. Sections 280 and 281 and Schs 25 and 26 deal with alteration of penalties for summary offences. Section 282 deals with the maximum term which may be imposed on summary conviction for an offence either way. Section 283 with Sch 27 contains an enabling power to alter maximum penalties. Sections 280 to 283 are necessary to ensure that the maximum penalties available for certain offences are compatible with the new sentencing framework, especially the introduction of custody plus, which will eventually replace all short custodial sentences for those aged 18 and over which are currently available. Custody plus is considered in Chapter 13 below, and it is not yet clear when that sentence will be brought into force. Section 284 with Sch 28 increases the maximum penalty for trafficking in Class C drugs. Section 285 and 286 deal with increases in penalties for certain driving offences. Section 285 (driving offences causing death) is already in force. These matters are dealt with now in turn.

10.10.1 Alteration of Penalties for Summary Offences and Either Way Offences tried Summarily

Section 280 is consequential upon the changes made by the 2003 Act to the structure of short sentences of imprisonment (and, for so long as that sentence continues to exist, detention in a young offender institution) and the corresponding increase in magistrates' courts sentencing powers (see 10.6 above). Detention and training orders are not sentences of imprisonment and are unaffected by these changes (see s 298 of the 2003 Act). Section 280 introduces Schs 25 and 26, which make changes to the maximum penalties for summary only offences that previously carried a maximum penalty of less than 12 months. These offences are either to have their maximum penalty lowered so that they are no longer punishable with imprisonment (see Sch 25) or raised to 51 weeks so that they may be punishable by way of the new custodial sentence, custody plus (see Sch 26). The maximum length of a sentence of custody plus, in relation to a single offence, will be 51 weeks.

There are 105 offences listed in Sch 25 which will become non-imprisonable. Many of these are delightfully obscure. They include sweeping near a dockyard or artillery range, injuring gardens, offences in relation to the control of rams, using an aircraft for advertising, and any offence under para 7 of the schedule to the Polish Resettlement Act 1947. There are numerous offences listed in Sch 26 where the maximum increases to 51 weeks. Some of the more important of these include interference with a motor vehicle under the Criminal Attempts Act 1981, s 9 (formerly 3 months), being in charge of a vehicle when unfit through drink, or with excess alcohol, or some cases of failure to provide a specimen, under the Road Traffic Offenders Act 1988, ss 4(2), 5(1)(b), and s 7) (all formerly 3 months), and resisting or wilfully obstructing a police officer under the Police Act 1996, s 89(2) (formerly one month).

Section 281 enables the Secretary of State to amend by order the maximum penalties for summary only offences which currently carry a maximum custodial penalty of 5 months or less. Such amendments may be made only in relation to offences which are not listed in Sch 25 or 26 and are contained in any Act which was passed before CJA 2003. The Secretary of State may in such a case by order either remove imprisonment as the penalty for the offence or raise the maximum penalty to 51 weeks.

Section 282 makes the equivalent alterations to offences which are triable either way but which, when triable summarily, carry maximum penalties of 6 months' imprisonment or less. These penalties are all increased to the full extent of the new magistrates' courts sentencing powers. Section 283 makes the necessary provisions for offences created under enabling powers in any Act which was passed before CJA 2003 to have their maximum sentences increased so that they may be compatible with the new sentencing framework.

10.10.2 Increase in Penalty for Class C Drug Trafficking

Section 284 and Sch 28 increases the maximum penalty for various offences under the Misuse of Drugs Act 1971 involving Class C drugs from 5 years to 14 years' imprisonment. Fourteen years has generally been the maximum sentence for Class A or Class B drugs, and this change no doubt reflects the alteration in the classification of cannabis from a Class B to a Class C drug. The offences are production under s 4(2), supply under s 4(3), possession with intent to supply under s 5(3), being the occupier of premises and permitting certain activities under s 8. In each case the maximum penalty is increased from 5 years on indictment to 14 years. This brings these maxima into line with the maximum sentence for cultivation of cannabis, which was formerly anomalously high at 14 years. Maximum penalties relating to Class C drugs under the Customs and Excise Management Act 1979 and the Criminal Justice (International Co-operation) Act 1990 are also similarly increased. These changes took effect from 29 January 2004.

10.10.3 Increase in Penalty for Driving Offences

Section 285 increases to 14 years the maximum penalties for the three offences of causing death by dangerous driving, causing death by careless driving under the influence of drink or drugs, and aggravated vehicle-taking where the aggravating feature is that, owing to the driving of the vehicle, an accident occurs and death results. The government published *Review of Road Traffic Penalties* in July 2002. Some concerns were expressed, by respondents to that review, that existing maximum penalties for these offences were too low, mainly on the basis that some sentences had recently been passed at or near the maximum of 10 years, the most obvious example of which was *R v Noble* [2003] 1 Cr App R (S) 213, where a total sentence of 15 years was reduced by the Court of Appeal to 10 years. In its advice to the Court of Appeal on the offence of causing death by dangerous driving, the Sentencing Advisory Panel expressed the view that the maximum for that offence should *not* be increased, since it would widen the gap with the offence of dangerous driving (see *Advice to the Court of Appeal 11: Causing Death by Dangerous Driving*, February 2003). The Court of Appeal endorsed that view in the resulting guideline case of *R v Cooksley* [2003] 2 Cr App R 275, but the maximum sentences have been increased by Parliament in any event. In consequence of this change s 91(2) of PCC(S)A 2000, which deals with long-term detention of juveniles, is repealed. The increase in the relevant maximum penalties for these offences to 14 years brings them squarely within the scope of s 91, and the special reference to those offences in s 91(2) which was formerly required is now removed. These changes took effect from 27 February 2004.

Section 286 increases the maximum penalties for the offences of giving false statements and withholding information in relation to road traffic documentation. For those offences, when tried on indictment the maximum penalty in increased to 2 years, a fine, or both, and when tried summarily the maximum penalty is increased to 6 months or the statutory maximum or both. These changes took effect from 27 February 2004.

11

SENTENCING GUIDELINES AND STANDARDS

11.1 INTRODUCTION

The Criminal Justice Act 2003 (CJA 2003) makes a number of important changes to the way in which sentencing guidelines for the criminal courts in England and Wales are in future to be produced. The provisions are already in force. They centre around the creation of the Sentencing Guidelines Council, a new body to be chaired by the Lord Chief Justice, which will be responsible for creating and issuing sentencing and mode of trial guidelines to the Crown Courts and magistrates' courts. The Sentencing Advisory Panel, which was established by the Crime and Disorder Act 1998 (CDA 1988), will continue its work, but henceforth it will advise and assist the Council, rather than the Court of Appeal. The Court will relinquish its role in setting guidelines. This chapter traces the background to these changes, and examines the future responsibilities of the Council, the Panel, and the Court of Appeal under the new arrangements.

As well as setting up this new machinery for the generation of sentencing guidelines, the Act intervenes more directly in sentencing standards. By s 269 and Sch 21 of the Act, it establishes legislative starting points for the minimum term to be served by a person convicted of murder. This is clearly a response to the decision of the House of Lords in *Anderson v Secretary of State for the Home Department* [2003] 1 AC 837, that the power formerly enjoyed by the Home Secretary to set the 'tariff' in a murder case, contained in s 29 of the Crime (Sentences) Act 1997, was incompatible with the fair trial provisions of the European Convention on Human Rights (ECHR). The legislative scheme for murder is highly controversial for two reasons. First, it sets legislative standards directly by Parliament, rather than by entrusting the task to the Sentencing Guidelines Council. Why create the Council if it cannot be relied upon to produce appropriate sentencing standards for this offence? Secondly, the starting points in the schedule represent a significant increase over the starting points for minimum terms in murder which were laid down by the Lord Chief Justice in a Practice Statement in May 2002, after wide consultation. The Act also creates a new form of presumptive minimum sentence for a range of firearms offences.

11.2 BACKGROUND TO THE CHANGES

11.2.1 Court of Appeal Guideline Judgments

Prior to the Crime and Disorder Act 1998, the Court of Appeal from time to time issued sentencing guidelines in the course of dealing with an appeal, or group of appeals, against sentence. The practice began in the 1980s, and was taken up and developed thereafter. In a typical guideline judgement the Court of Appeal would review the existing sentencing pattern for the offence, consider relevant aggravating and mitigating factors, and generate one or more starting points to assist judges when sentencing for that offence. The particular appeal or appeals before the court would then be disposed of in accordance with the newly produced guidelines.

In their time, guideline judgments of particular importance were *R v Aramah* (1982) 4 Cr App R (S) 407 on drug offences, *R v Barrick* (1985) 7 Cr App R (S) 153 on theft in breach of trust, *R v Billam* (1986) 8 Cr App R (S) 48 on rape, *Attorney-General's Reference (No 1 of 1989)* [1989] 1 WLR 1117 on incest, and *R v Brewster* [1998] 1 Cr App R (S) 181 on domestic burglary. Given the nature of cases which typically come before the Court of Appeal on sentence, the guideline judgments related mainly to offences at the very serious end of the spectrum. In a quite separate development the Magistrates' Association developed with the approval of the higher judiciary their own *Sentencing Guidelines*, covering summary offences and those offences triable either way which come most frequently before the lower courts. The latest edition of the Magistrates' Courts' guidelines was published in 2003, and has been effective since January 2004.

11.2.2 The Work of the Sentencing Advisory Panel

In the Crime and Disorder Act 1998, by section 80, Parliament for the first time placed a statutory duty on the Court of Appeal to produce new sentencing guidelines for criminal offences, and to revise old ones. Section 81 of the Act also established the Sentencing Advisory Panel to act as an independent advisory body to assist the Court of Appeal in framing subsequent guidelines. The Panel currently has 14 members, all appointed on a part-time basis. Four are sentencers. There are four members with current or recent experience of other criminal justice agencies (the police, prosecution, prisons, and the probation service), three academics, and three members with no previous connection with the criminal justice system. For further information on membership, published Annual Reports and other details see the website at www.sentencing-advisory-panel.gov.uk.

The Panel began work in 1999 and, to date, has published 12 sets of Advice. The Court of Appeal, in turn, has acted on 11 of these (all except the first), issuing sentencing guidelines based on the Panel's advice. These have included new sentencing guidelines on racially aggravated offences in *R v Kelly* [2001] 2 Cr App R (S) 341, on handling stolen goods in *R v Webbe* [2002] 1 Cr App R (S) 82, on extended sentences in *R v Nelson* [2002] 1 Cr App R (S) 565, on child pornography offences in *R v Oliver* [2003] 1 Cr App R 463, and causing death by dangerous driving in *R v Cooksley* [2003] 2 Cr App R 275. There have also been revised guidelines on rape in *R v Millberry* [2003] 1 Cr App R (S) 396 and (controversially at the time) domestic burglary in *R v McInerney* [2003] 1 Cr App R 627. Lord Woolf CJ also issued *Practice Statement (Life Sentences)* [2002] 2 Cr App R 287 on minimum terms in murder cases, which was based on the Panel's advice. The setting of minimum terms in murder cases is considered further at 11.8 below.

Two principal defects of the 1998 Act scheme have become apparent. The first was that the advice which the Panel could provide to the Court of Appeal was limited by s 81(3) of that Act to guidelines relating to 'a particular category of offence'. This meant that the Panel could not advise on more general sentencing issues which might cut across a wide range of offences. The second defect was that the approach of the Court of Appeal was to continue its practice of issuing guidelines in the context of a specific appeal. Occasionally, this created a significant time-lag, where the Panel's advice related to an offence which rarely came before the Court of Appeal. An example is possession of an offensive weapon, on which topic the Panel issued its Advice in May 2000 but the first occasion on which the Court of Appeal could consider that advice in the context of an appeal was more than two years later in October 2002: see *R v Celaire and Poulton* [2003] Crim LR 124. The continuation of the case-centred approach, by necessary implication, has removed the opportunity to issue guidelines for common 'low-level' offences and has acted as a barrier to the Panel's work on offences at the less serious end of the range.

11.2.3 The Proposals for Change

In his *Review of the Criminal Courts of England and Wales* (October 2001), Lord Justice Auld proposed (at 655) to remedy these defects by two small legislative amendments: the first to widen the remit of the Panel to include general principles of sentencing, and the second to empower the Court of Appeal to issue guidelines without having to tie them to a specific appeal. However, the Halliday Report, *Making Punishments Work* (July 2001), advocated a much more sweeping reform of the machinery for generating sentencing guidelines, and this is the approach which the government has, with some adaptations, followed in the 2003 Act. Halliday stated that a 'clear code of sentencing guidelines' was required (para 8.7), which 'should be continuously available to all, in up to date form' (para 8.10). The guidelines would include 'descriptions of graded seriousness levels, covering all the main offences', and 'presumptive "entry points" of sentence severity in relation to each level'. The guidelines would deal with community as well as custodial sentences, and cover issues such as relevance of previous convictions, multiple offence sentencing, and grounds for aggravation and mitigation (para 8.9). Halliday proposed three different models for the new machinery to generate these more comprehensive guidelines. The Court of Appeal might continue with the task, or a new judicial body might be established, or there might be an independent body with a mix of sentencers and other people to promulgate the guidelines. That body might be assisted by the Sentencing Advisory Panel, or the Panel might be subsumed within the new arrangements. Parliament should, in any event, be given an opportunity to comment on draft guidelines.

By the time of the White Paper *Justice for All* (July 2002), the government had decided to legislate to establish a Sentencing Guidelines Council, 'which will be responsible for setting guidelines for the full range of criminal offences' (para 5.15), including those offences dealt with primarily or exclusively in the magistrates' courts. The Council was to be made up entirely of sentencers, but drawn from the Court of Appeal, the High Court, the Crown Court and the magistrates' courts. It was to be chaired by the Lord Chief Justice. The Sentencing Advisory Panel would continue in being, but henceforth the Panel would advise the Sentencing Guidelines Council, rather than the Court of Appeal. The Court would be shorn of its responsibility in the development of sentencing guidelines. Parliament would have a role in considering and scrutinizing draft guidelines drawn up by the Council.

11.3 THE COUNCIL AND THE PANEL

11.3.1 Changes to the Bill

The Bill, as first introduced into the Commons, contained provisions designed to implement the proposals in *Justice for All*. The relevant clauses proved to be controversial, especially with regard to the composition and membership of the Sentencing Guidelines Council. Amendments tabled in Committee were designed to broaden representation on the Council, by including a number of non-judicial members. Debate on these amendments was, unfortunately, characterized by a lack of appreciation of the role of the Sentencing Advisory Panel which, as was explained in 11.1.1, has a broad membership in which sentencers are in the minority. The amendments were, however, accepted by the government, and the Bill went forward to the Lords on that basis.

Section 167 of CJA 2003 establishes the Sentencing Guidelines Council, which is to consist of the Lord Chief Justice (as chairman of the Council), seven judicial members and four non-judicial members. The judicial members must, by s 167(3), include a circuit judge, a district judge (magistrates' courts), and a lay justice, with other senior judges being drawn from the Court of Appeal and the High Court. They are to be appointed by the Lord Chancellor. The Lord Chief Justice is able to nominate another judge to attend in his place if he is unable to attend a meeting of the Council, but it appears that all other members of the

Council must appear in person. A person is eligible for appointment as a non-judicial member if, by s 167(4), he or she has experience in policing, criminal prosecution (specifically, by s 167(5), to include the DPP), criminal defence and the promotion of the welfare of victims of crime. They are to be appointed by the Home Secretary. All of these specified areas must be covered by the non-judicial members, but presumably any one such individual might qualify on more than one ground.

An earlier version of the Bill allowed for a person having experience of sentencing policy and the administration of sentences to be eligible for appointment to the Council. It is likely that such a person would have been a serving civil servant, and objection was taken that a serving civil servant might feel bound to convey and reflect the views of the Secretary of State, or at least there would be a perception that such a person would not be independent. The House of Lords Select Committee on the Constitution, in their 7th Report of 2002–03, *Criminal Justice Bill* (HL Paper 129, 25 June 2003), expressed its 'concern at the proposal that a serving civil servant should act as a member of the Sentencing Guidelines Council . . . ' (para 6). In the event the provision was dropped at a late stage, and replaced by what now appears as s 167(9). This subsection permits the Home Secretary to appoint a person with the relevant experience 'to attend and speak at any meeting of the Council', but not to be a member of that Council.

Section 168 contains supplementary provisions dealing with matters of appointment and removal of Council members, payment of remuneration (as appropriate) to non-judicial members. Section 168(1) and (2) came into effect on Royal Assent, which was 20 November 2003 (see CJA 2003, s 336(1)). Advertisements appeared in the national press in December 2003 inviting applications for positions on the Council, other than the *ex officio* appointments. All appointments to the Council were completed in time for the Council to meet for the first time in March 2004.

Section 169 provides that 'there shall continue to be' a Sentencing Advisory Panel. This form of drafting ensures that the Panel continues in being, despite the repeal of ss 80 and 81 of the Crime and Disorder Act 1998 by CJA 2003, Sch 37, Pt 7. It will be constituted as before but, as we have seen, the establishment of the Council now means that the Panel will henceforth assist and advise that body, rather than the Court of Appeal.

11.3.2 The New Arrangements

Sections 170 and 171 set out the legislative arrangements within which the Council and Panel will now operate. By s 170(1) the relevant guidelines incorporate both 'sentencing guidelines' and 'allocation guidelines'. 'Sentencing guidelines' are now defined as 'guidelines relating to the sentencing of offenders, which may be general in nature or limited to a particular category of offence or offender'. This wording is designed to remove the limitation to 'a particular category of offence', which formerly applied (see 11.2.2 above). It does not refer specifically to the production of guidelines on, for example, the proper use of a particular *sentence*, but this might be covered by the reference to guidelines which are 'general in nature'. Section 171(2), which

201

deals with the functions of the Panel, states that the Panel may propose guidelines 'in respect of a particular matter affecting sentencing'. It is unfortunate that the wording is different in the two provisions.

'Allocation guidelines' refers to guidelines for 'mode of trial' for offences triable either way, to assist those courts with allocation of cases between the magistrates' courts and the Crown Court. The existing guidelines date from 1990, though these have since been revised and reissued by the Criminal Justice Consultative Council. The updated version is now to be found in *Practice Direction (Criminal: Consolidated)* [2002] 2 Cr App R 533, para 51. The guidelines include a presumption that cases should be tried summarily unless one or more of the specified offence features is present *and* the magistrates regard their own sentencing powers as inadequate. Allocation guidelines did not form part of the Crime and Disorder Act 1998 provisions, and they are an additional responsibility for the Council and the Panel. No mention of them was made in Halliday, or in *Justice for All*, but their inclusion within the new arrangements makes good sense. Allocation of cases between magistrates' courts and the Crown Court is of course highly relevant to sentence, because of the very different sentencing powers of the two courts. Clearly, the allocation guidelines for individual offences will require a complete overhaul if and when magistrates' courts' sentencing powers are increased from 6 months to 12 months (see 10.6 above).

The initiative to issue new or revised sentencing or allocation guidelines may come from the Council itself (under s 171(1)), or from the Home Secretary (under s 170(2), or from the Panel (under s 171(2)). In any case where the Council decides to frame new guidelines, it must first consider the views of the Panel and the need to promote consistency in mode of trial or sentencing decisions. For sentencing guidelines, the Council must have regard to a range of other considerations, including 'the cost of different sentences and their relative effectiveness in preventing re-offending' and 'the need to promote public confidence in the criminal justice system' (s 170(6)).

Section 170(8) is controversial. It requires that the Council should publish any proposed sentencing or allocation guidelines in draft form and, at that stage, consult the Home Secretary, and such persons as the Lord Chancellor (after consultation with the Home Secretary) may direct, and such other persons as the Council considers appropriate. How the processes of consultation will operate in practice is as yet unclear. The Court of Appeal and the Panel established good working relations, and the Council and the Panel are likely to do the same. There is a risk, however, that the new arrangements will be slower and more cumbersome than before. The Sentencing Advisory Panel will (as before) conduct the relevant research and then issue a public consultation paper on the topic in question. Such consultation, in line with Cabinet Office guidance, must normally last for a minimum of three months. The Panel will no doubt adjust its views in light of the responses it receives. Its advice will then be drafted and tendered to the Council. That advice, with or without adjustment by the Council, will then be published as the Council's draft guidelines. There will then be a further consultation on this draft, as indicated by s 170(8). Arrangements are being put in place to allow a committee of each House of Parliament to consider the guidelines in their draft form, and to make comment upon them. An additional delay must be expected at this stage. While the Home Secretary has no power of veto over the draft guidelines, and a decision of the Council to issue the guidelines 'as definitive guidelines' is final, the potential for unseemly conflict over their content is all too apparent. If, for example, the Home Secretary took strong exception to the draft guidelines, the Council would surely feel the need to reconsider or re-draft, or perhaps re-submit to the Panel for further work to be done. At the end of this process, guidelines will be issued by the Council as 'definitive guidelines'.

Section 171 provides for the functions of the Sentencing Advisory Panel. With necessary adjustments to allow for the creation of the Council, and the broadening of the Panel's remit, the manner in which the Panel will function will be similar to its previous practice. Section 171(4) is, however, new. This provides that the Council may notify the Panel that, in view of 'the urgency of the case', the Panel can dispense with its normal consultation exercise, although it would still be required to tender its own views to the Council. It is thought that this provision will be used only exceptionally, since much of the weight which has traditionally attached to the Panel's advice has derived from information gathered through its consultative process.

11.4 DUTY OF COURTS TO HAVE REGARD TO GUIDELINES

Section 172 of CJA 2003 requires that 'every court must . . . in sentencing an offender, *have regard to* any guidelines which are relevant to the offender's case' (emphasis added). This section seems to be superfluous, since it has long been understood that sentencers must 'have regard to' the sentencing guideline decisions of the Court of Appeal, and the purpose of the legislation is that the pronouncements of the Council should henceforth have at least comparable standing. Guideline judgments have always been regarded as authoritative, but not strictly binding, in the sense that a sentencer may for good reason depart from them. According to Roch LJ in *R v Johnson* (1994) 15 Cr App R (S) 827, at 830:

A judge when passing sentence must pay attention to the guidance given by this court and sentences should be broadly in line with guideline cases, unless there are factors applicable to the particular case which require or enable the judge to depart from the normal level of sentence. In such special cases the judge should indicate clearly the factor or factors which in his judgment allow departure from the tariff set by this Court.

Appellate judges have also stressed that it is the duty of counsel to bring any guideline cases to the attention of the sentencer, in case otherwise they might be overlooked. An example is *R v Panayioutou* (1989) 11 Cr App R (S) 535, where it was said that 'if this Court has laid down guidelines, then the time has come when judges are entitled to have those guideline cases drawn to their attention'. There is, however, evidence to show a failure by counsel in some cases to do so. Sentences have been passed by judges in ignorance of recent (or, sometimes, not so recent) sentencing guidelines. An example is *R v O'Brien* [2003] 2 Cr App R (S) 390, a case on racially aggravated criminal damage. The sentencer dealt with the case on October 25, 2002, but was not made aware of the guideline case of *R v Kelly* [2001] 2 Cr App R (S) 341, which had been handed down on 6 February 2001 and which was prominent in the then current editions of the standard practitioner works, *Blackstone's Criminal Practice* (Oxford University Press, 2004) and *Archbold: Criminal Pleading, Evidence and Practice* (Thomson, 2004). The Court of Appeal dealt with the appeal in *O'Brien* on 9 January 2003, but did not do much better. The Court had been referred by counsel to the Sentencing Advisory Panel's advice on racially aggravated offences, but not to the Court's own guideline judgment which had resulted from it, and which was by now almost two years old. This demonstrates a weakness in the dissemination of sentencing guidelines to practitioners who need to be aware of them. Such problems can only be remedied by better training, and by improving the channels of communication between the appellate courts and sentencers on the ground. There is no reason to think that this section will make any practical difference here.

It seems odd that s 172 is specifically confined to 'sentencing guidelines' and does not include 'allocation guidelines'. The statutory duty laid down by section 172 on the face of it relates only to guidelines issued by the Sentencing Guidelines Council but the Act makes it clear that this does not in any way reduce the standing of sentencing guideline judgments issued before the Council came into being, unless and until those guidelines are revised by the Council (see Sch 38, para 2).

As we have seen, the purpose of the Sentencing Guidelines Council is to take over from the Court of Appeal its traditional function of issuing sentencing guidelines for the courts. The question arises as to the future role of the Court which will, of course, continue to hear large numbers of sentencing appeals from the Crown Court. In a significant number of such appeals there will, as yet, have been no guidelines issued by the Council, and there may be no Court of Appeal guideline judgment either. Lord Woolf CJ has stated that '[O]nce the Council is in existence, I would not expect the Court of Appeal to issue guidelines thereafter, save in exceptional circumstances. It may well, however, have to amplify and explain the guidelines issued by the Council' (reply from the Lord Chief Justice to the House of Lords Select Committee on the Constitution, *Criminal Justice Bill* (HL Paper 129, 25 June 2003, App 3)). A different view has been expressed by Dr David Thomas. He argues that: 'In practice it will be many years before guidelines formulated by the Council will cover a wide range of sentencing questions, and it will be necessary for the Court of Appeal to give guidance, albeit on an interim basis, on those issues on which the Council has not yet had time to pronounce' (ibid, App 5). Dr Thomas predicts that the Court of Appeal will stay active in the business of giving guideline judgments (but perhaps avoiding direct conflict with the legislation by calling them something else, such as 'guidance') and that, for some time at least, sentencing judges may be more ready to recognize the authority of the Court rather than the Council. For further comments along similar lines see the commentary by Dr Thomas at [2003] Crim LR 132.

11.5 DUTY OF COURTS TO GIVE REASONS FOR, AND EXPLAIN EFFECT OF, SENTENCE

Section 174 imposes a general duty on courts to give reasons for, and to explain the effect of, the sentence which is being passed on an offender. The section brings together in one place various obligations to give reasons, and to provide explanations, which a sentencing court already has by virtue of various legislative provisions. It also adds in some new ones. While nobody can doubt the importance of a sentencing court giving reasons for the sentence it has passed on an offender, the onerous nature of these diverse requirements is striking to see, especially now that they are gathered together in one place. It should not be forgotten that these obligations apply to lay magistrates, and to part-time sentencers such as recorders, as much as they do to the full-time judiciary.

11.5.1 What is Required?

The requirements to give reasons extend not only to custodial and community sentences, but to fines, conditional discharges, and the wide range of ancillary orders which are now available to the courts. The court must explain:

- the effect of the sentence (s 174(1)(b)(i));
- the effects of non-compliance with any order (s 174(1)(b)(ii));
- the effect of any power to vary or review the order (s 174(1)(b)(iii)); and
- the effect of failure to pay any fine (s 174(1)(b)(iv)).

It must explain the relevance of any sentencing guidelines applicable to the offender's case and, if the court has departed from those guidelines, explain why (s 174(2)(a)). This requirement is new. It must explain how any custodial sentence or community sentence can be justified in accordance with the relevant statutory criteria (s 174(2)(b) and (c)). It must state, where appropriate, that the offender's plea of guilty has affected the sentence passed (s 174(2)(d)), and it must mention any aggravating or mitigating features of the case which have been regarded as particularly important in the case (s 174(2)(e)). The last of these requirements is new.

The section is not exhaustive. It must, for example, be read alongside the obligations on a sentencer who passes a custodial sentence on an offender, to explain the practical effect of the early release provisions on the duration of that sentence. These requirements are set out in *Practice Direction (Criminal: Consolidated)* [2002] 2 Cr App R 533, para 7. The Practice Direction explains that since the statutory provisions governing the early release of offenders are not widely understood by the general public, whenever a custodial sentence is passed its practical effect should be made clear to the defendant, to any victim, and to any member of the public who is present in court or who reads a full report of the proceedings. Some other provisions, which require a court to explain why it has *not* taken a particular course of action in sentencing, have not been brought within s 174. Failure to re-enact these in the 2003 Act may, perhaps, increase the risk that they are overlooked. Examples are:

(a) the duty imposed by s 130(3) of the Powers of Criminal Courts (Sentencing) Act 2000 to 'give reasons, on passing sentence, if [the court] does not make a compensation order';

(b) the duty imposed under the Criminal Justice and Court Services Act 2000, s 28, to give reasons, when sentencing an offender for an offence against a child, for not disqualifying that offender from working with children;

(c) the duty imposed under the Football Spectators Act 1989, where the offender is convicted of a 'relevant offence', for the court to give reasons why it is not making a banning order; and

(d) the duty imposed under the Crime and Disorder Act 1998, s 9, to impose a parenting order on the parent of a young offender aged under 16, unless the court is not satisfied that such an order would be desirable in the interests of preventing re-offending by the young offender, in which case the sentencer must state in open court that this criterion is not satisfied, and why it is not.

By s 174(1), the court must give the specified explanations, as appropriate, in open court, and it must do so in 'ordinary language and in general terms' which are comprehensible to the offender. Clearly, it is an important function of the sentencing court to communicate the effect of the sentence to an offender, but one may be sceptical of the practical value of such requirements. Take the case of an offender who is waiting with trepidation for the court's decision on whether he or she will be sent to prison. Those are the crucial words that he or she needs to hear, and the offender is unlikely to take in, at that time, a detailed invocation of the statutory reasons which have led the court to make the decision it has made, or to be interested in the details of the consequences of a failure to comply, or an explanation of why the court has not made orders which in other circumstances it would have made. There is an argument for saying that these details are best communicated in written rather than oral form, and by the offender's legal representative rather than by the sentencer, at a more suitable time when the offender is likely to be able to take them in.

11.5.2 Failure to Comply

There remains the question of what happens if the sentencing court fails in some way to carry out any of the responsibilities specified in the section. No consequence is mentioned in s 174.

In the past, the Court of Appeal has taken the view that a failure to comply with procedural requirements in statute cannot invalidate the sentence nor can it, as such, provide the basis for an appeal against sentence. In commenting upon provisions in CJA 1991, requiring sentencers to explain in ordinary language the justification for imposing a custodial sentence on an offender, Lord Taylor CJ said in *R v Baverstock*

(1993) 14 Cr App R (S) 471 at 475 that the statutory provisions were 'not to be treated as a verbal tightrope for judges to walk', and that even if judges made a mistake and failed to explain something they should have explained, the Court of Appeal would not interfere with the resultant sentence 'unless it is wrong in principle or excessive'. It is likely that the Court of Appeal will treat the compendious requirements in s 174 in much the same way.

11.6 DUTY TO PUBLISH INFORMATION ABOUT SENTENCING

Under section 95 of CJA 1991 the Home Secretary is required each year to publish information 'for the purposes of (a) enabling persons engaged in the administration of criminal justice to become aware of the financial implications of their decisions, or (b) facilitating the performance by such persons of their duty to avoid discriminating against any persons on the ground of race or sex or any other improper ground'. Such publications have been produced in hard copy and on the Home Office website and contain useful information about, for example, differential sentencing of men and women by the criminal courts and differential treatment of ethnic minority defendants.

Section 175 of CJA 2003 adds to that requirement the publication of material 'enabling such persons to become aware of the relative effectiveness of different sentences — (i) in preventing re-offending, and (ii) in promoting public confidence in the criminal justice system'. This requirement may be seen alongside the duty imposed on the Sentencing Guidelines Council by s 170(5)(c) to have regard, when framing or revising sentencing guidelines, to 'the cost of different sentences and their relative effectiveness in preventing re-offending'. It may be noted that a review by the Strategy Unit, *Managing Offenders, Reducing Crime: A New Approach* (December 2003) (the 'Carter Report') has proposed that it should be the responsibility of the Panel and the Council to produce and disseminate research data on the efficacy of different sentences.

11.7 FIREARMS OFFENCES

Sections 287 to 293 of the 2003 Act make important changes to the sentencing provisions for various firearms offences. In particular, s 287 provides for minimum sentences for certain serious firearms offences. The government has taken the step of prescribing minimum sentences in such cases following the release of criminal statistics showing an increase in gun-related offences in recent years. Despite some of the rather hysterical media coverage, however, the picture is more complex than it may seem. The *Times* newspaper (generally one of the more responsible in its coverage of crime) proclaimed on 23 January 2004 that 'Gun crime soars in rising tide of violence'. In fact, the crime statistics issued on the previous day and which formed the basis for the story showed that gun-related crime had risen by about 2% between 2002 and 2003, but that robberies involving firearms had fallen by 13%, the use of a handgun to commit an offence had fallen by 6%, and homicides involving firearms had fallen by 16% over that period. The statutory change to the law in this area was closely associated in time with a particular shooting in Birmingham which resulted in the deaths of two young women. The circumstances attracted a great deal of media interest and may well have provided the impetus for government action. The provisions on firearms were brought into force in January 2004.

Initially the change to the law was presented to the media as a minimum sentence which would admit of no exceptions but, shortly afterwards it became clear that sentencers might refrain from imposing the minimum sentence if there were '*exceptional circumstances* relating to the offence or to the offender which *justify* its not doing so' (s 287(2), emphasis added). The 'exceptional circumstances' proviso brings the minimum sentence provision on firearms offences broadly into line with the other two pre-existing examples of minimum sentences. These are the minimum sentence of 7 years for the third Class A drug trafficking offence, and the minimum sentence of 3 years for the third domestic burglary. These provisions originated in the Crime (Sentences) Act 1997 and are now to be found in the Powers of Criminal Courts (Sentencing) Act, ss 110 and 111 respectively. They are slightly differently worded, however, in that they permit the sentencer to avoid the prescribed sentence if there are '*particular circumstances* which relate to any of the offences or the offender which would *make it unjust* to do so in all the circumstances' (emphases added). The Court of Appeal has so far declined to provide guidance on the meaning of this phrase: see, for example Lord Bingham CJ in *R v Harvey* [2000] 1 Cr App R (S) 368. It is hard to know whether the difference in wording is significant. It should be noted, however, that the main distinction between the minimum sentence for firearms offences and the other two examples is that the former applies to *all* such offences whereas the latter apply only to *repeat* offenders.

Also, in contrast to ss 110(2) and 111(2), there is no specific provision in s 51A limiting the extent to which the offender's guilty plea can affect the sentence imposed. The lack of such a provision might be construed to mean that in cases falling within s 51A no discount for guilty plea may be given by the sentencing court at all. This interpretation would be highly anomalous, however, and it is submitted that the sentencing court might properly discount sentence for an offence under s 51A in accordance with the normal principles.

11.7.1 Firearms—Minimum Sentence Provisions

Section 287 of the 2003 Act proceeds by inserting new provisions into the Firearms Act 1968. A new s 51A is created, which prescribes a minimum sentence of 5 years' imprisonment in the case of an offender aged 18 or over, or a minimum sentence of 3 years' detention under s 91 of the Powers of Criminal Courts (Sentencing) Act 2000 (long-term detention), for any offender who was aged at least 16 at the time he committed the offence, and is convicted of an offence under any of the following provisions of the 1968 Act:

- s 5(1)(a), (ab), (aba), (ac), (ad), (ae), (af) or (c): possessing or distributing certain prohibited weapons or ammunition;
- s 5(1A)(a): possessing or distributing firearm disguised as another object.

Section 287 applies to offences committed on or after commencement of this section, which was 22 January 2004 (SI 2004/81). For further information on these offences reference should be made to a specialist work, such as *Blackstone's Criminal Practice* (2004, B12.38).

It will be noted that the specified minimum sentences refer to 'imprisonment' in the case of an offender aged 18 or over. This wording anticipates the projected abolition of the sentence of detention in a young offender institution (the standard custodial sentence for offenders aged 18, 19 or 20), by s 61 of the Criminal Justice and Court Services Act 2000. For transitional provisions, see CJA 2003, Sch 38, para 1. The specified minimum sentence on an offender aged under 18 is the sentence of long-term detention under PCC(S)A 2000, s 91. In general, a sentence under s 91 can be imposed on a young offender only where the maximum penalty for the offence is at least 14 years' imprisonment in the case of an adult. The relevant firearms offences all carry a maximum penalty of 10 years' imprisonment. Section 91 is therefore amended by s 289 of the 2003 Act to bring the relevant firearms offences within its scope. Section 289 came into force on 22 January 2004 (SI 2004/81), together with consequential amendments in Sch 32, paras 48 to 50.

11.7.2 Firearms—Mode of Trial

Section 288 of the 2003 Act, by amending Sch 6 to the Firearms Act 1968 (mode of prosecution) makes the same firearms offences which are listed in 11.7.1 above (and which were formerly triable either way), now triable only on indictment. The maximum penalty for each of these offences is unchanged (10 years). Section 42 of the 2003 Act (mode of trial for certain firearms offences) contains transitory arrangements for sending such cases to the Crown Court prior to implementation of Sch 3 of the 2003 Act (allocation and sending of offences). See Chapter 5 above.

Section 288 applies to offences committed on or after commencement of this section, which was 22 January 2004 (SI 2004/81). Section 42 also came into effect on that date.

11.7.3 Firearms—Maximum Penalties for Importation and Exportation

Section 293 of the 2003 Act increases the maximum penalties available for the improper importation of, improper exportation of, or fraudulent evasion of duty on, any of the weapons or ammunition mentioned in the sections listed in 11.7.1 above. The penalties provided in ss 50(5A), 68(4A) and 170(4A) of the Customs and Excise Management Act 1979 are all increased from 7 years to 10 years.

Section 293 applies to offences committed on or after 22 January 2004 (SI 2004/81).

11.8 MINIMUM TERMS IN MURDER

By s 269 and Sch 21 of the 2003 Act, Parliament has established for the first time legislative starting points for the minimum term to be served by a person convicted of murder. It must be appreciated from the outset that a *minimum term* is quite different from a *sentence*, although the difference is often misunderstood. A *sentence* is subject to the statutory rules on early release, so that an offender serving a long determinate sentence would normally be released at some point between the halfway and two-thirds point of the sentence. Release is subject to supervision and licence. A *minimum term*, however, is the period which must be served *in full* before early release can be ordered. A rough comparison, therefore, is that a minimum term of 12 years is equivalent to a sentence of at least 24 years (assuming early release at the halfway point), and a minimum term of 15 years is equivalent to a sentence of at least 30 years.

11.8.1 Background to the Changes

In order to understand this highly significant development, a brief history of recent change in this area of law is appropriate.

The starting point was the decision of the European Court of Human Rights in *T v K, V v UK* (2000) 30 EHRR 121, the case which concerned the aftermath of the murder of the toddler Jamie Bulger in Merseyside and the subsequent conviction of Venables and Thompson, two 11-year-old boys, of his murder. The mandatory sentence imposed in such cases is the sentence of detention during Her Majesty's pleasure, under s 90 of the Powers of Criminal Courts (Sentencing) Act 2000. That sentence is indeterminate in length but requires the setting of a minimum period of time which must be served by the offender prior to their being considered for release on licence. That task, at the time, was performed by the Home Secretary, after considering informally the views of the trial judge and the Lord Chief Justice. The European Court decided, inter alia, that the Home Secretary's power to set the 'tariff' in cases involving murder committed by offenders aged under 18 at the time of the killing contravened ECHR, Article 6, right to a fair trial. In order to bring English law into line with this decision, therefore, Parliament passed s 60 of the Criminal Justice and Court Services Act 2000, which inserted s 82A into the Powers of Criminal Courts (Sentencing) Act 2000. This section makes it clear that in cases of mandatory life sentences where murder has been committed by a juvenile, the minimum term to be served should be set in open court by the trial judge, bringing the procedure into line with that used where an offender is made subject to a discretionary life sentence or (prior to its abolition by the 2003 Act) an automatic life sentence under s 109 of the 2000 Act.

Following that important development, the Home Secretary invited the Lord Chief Justice to review the minimum terms which had been imposed on young offenders convicted of murder who at the time were still serving their sentences. As part of that exercise, Lord Woolf asked the Sentencing Advisory Panel to consult, and provide advice on, the provision of guidelines for judges required to set minimum terms in such cases in the future. The Panel, in their advice submitted to the Court of Appeal, also considered and tendered advice on the appropriate minimum terms to be served by offenders aged 18 and over convicted of murder, who are subject to the mandatory sentences of custody for life (for those aged 18, 19 or 20) or life imprisonment (for those aged 21 and over). The decision of the European Court did not apply to defendants aged 18 and over. No previous sentencing guidelines existed in this area, save for a general understanding that the 'starting point' for the tariff in cases of murder committed by an adult was 14 years. The Panel's advice proposed a *normal starting point* of 12 years, with higher and lower starting points for different types of murder, and indicated a range of aggravating and mitigating factors. The Panel also observed that the term 'tariff' was widely misunderstood, and was confused with the term 'sentence'. See Sentencing Advisory Panel, *Advice to the Court of Appeal 7: Minimum Terms in Murder Cases* (March 2002). These proposals were substantially adopted by the Lord Chief Justice in a Practice Statement issued in May 2002, which can now be found in *Practice Direction (Criminal: Consolidated)* [2002] 2 Cr App R 533, paras 49.1 to 49.28). For discussion see C Valier, 'Minimum terms of imprisonment in murder' [2003] Crim LR 326.

Then came the decision of the House of Lords in *Anderson v Secretary of State for the Home Department* [2003] 1 AC 837, where the House decided that the equivalent power still enjoyed by the Home Secretary, to set minimum terms in murder cases involving defendants aged 18 and over, after considering informally the views of the trial judge and the Lord Chief Justice, was incompatible with the fair trial provisions of the European Convention on Human Rights. The House therefore made a declaration of incompatibility under s 4 of the Human Rights Act 1998 with respect to the relevant domestic statutory provision, s 29 of the Crime (Sentences) Act 1997. The legislative response has been:

(a) to repeal (by Sch 37, Pt 8) s 29 of the 1997 Act;

(b) to repeal (by Sch 37, Pt 8) the now rarely used power in s 1(2) of the Murder (Abolition of Death Penalty) Act 1965 for the judge to make a recommendation in open court; and

(c) to establish in the 2003 Act a detailed statutory scheme for setting minimum terms in all murder cases, adult and juvenile alike. This is to be found in ss 269 to 277 and Sch 21 of the Act.

11.8.2 The New Scheme

It is difficult to make a direct comparison of the minimum term starting points set out in Sch 21 of the 2003 Act with the minimum term starting points in the Practice Direction (PD). This is because there are some overlapping categories, and categories which are differently described. The interplay between starting points and aggravating/ mitigating factors is also different in the two schemes.

In broad terms, however (and remembering that a minimum term is equivalent to a determinate sentence of *at least* twice that length):

(a) The Act has a minimum term starting point of *15 years* for offenders aged 18 and over (PD = *12 years*, but *8 or 9* years in a number of specified situations to mark significantly reduced culpability).

(b) The Act has a minimum term starting point of *12 years* for offenders aged under 18 (PD = sliding scale depending on age from *12 years down to 5 years*).

(c) The Act has a minimum term starting point of *30 years* which would typically include:

    (i) murder of a police officer or prison officer in the course of duty (PD = *15 or 16 years*, but broader category of 'public servant'),

    (ii) murder involving a firearm or explosive (PD = no equivalent category, but 'use of firearm' general aggravating factor),

    (iii) a murder done for gain (eg in the course of a robbery or burglary) (PD = *15 or 16 years*),

    (iv) a murder intended to obstruct the course of justice (PD = *15 or 16 years*),

    (v) a murder involving sexual or sadistic conduct (PD = *15 or 16 years*),

    (vi) the murder of two or more persons (PD = *15 or 16 years*),

    (vii) a murder racially or religiously aggravated or aggravated by sexual orientation (PD = *15 or 16 years*)

Note: PD provided that 'the most serious cases' could move from a starting point of 15 years to a minimum term of 30 years.

(d) The Act has a minimum term starting point of '*a whole life order*' for murders *committed by a person aged 21 and over* which include:

    (i) the murder of two or more persons, where each murder involved a substantial degree of premeditation or planning, or the abduction of the victim, or sexual or sadistic conduct (PD = no equivalent),

    (ii) the murder of a child (ie person aged under 18) if involving the abduction of the child or sexual or sadistic motivation (PD = no equivalent),

    (iii) a political, religious or ideological murder (PD = no equivalent), or

    (iv) murder by a person with a previous conviction for murder (PD = no equivalent).

Note: PD provided that a whole life minimum term should not be set, but that in 'cases of exceptional gravity' the judge should indicate that no minimum term could properly be set.

Aggravating and mitigating factors listed in the Act are closely similar to those specified in the Practice Direction. Schedule 21, para 12 clearly states that the starting points are subject to appropriate reduction for guilty plea.

The new legislative scheme for murder is highly controversial for two reasons. First, it sets sentencing standards directly through legislation, rather than by entrusting that task to the Sentencing Guidelines Council. It is hard to understand why so much store has been set by the government in establishing the Council if that body cannot be relied upon to produce appropriate sentencing standards for the offence of murder. It is hardly a vote of confidence in the new mechanisms for generating sentencing guidelines. A possible response to this criticism would be that the offence of murder has long been regarded as a special case, at least since the Murder (Abolition of Death Penalty) Act 1965, and that a legislative hand may be appropriate in sentencing for that offence where it would not be appropriate elsewhere. That leads on to the second problem, however. Schedule 21 is based on the structure of the May 2002 Practice Statement, but the starting points are increased sharply from those laid down, after wide consultation, by the Lord Chief Justice. This escalation (in some cases, it would seem, a doubling of the minimum term) is bound to create knock-on problems for sentencing in a range of other serious crimes. The 'punishment gap' between murder and manslaughter has been widened significantly by Sch 21, and the policy implications of that will need to be addressed by the Sentencing Guidelines Council in the months to come.

11.8.3 Fixing the Minimum Term

Section 269 of the 2003 Act sets out the new arrangements for the setting of minimum terms in murder cases. Valuable guidance on the interpretation of this section is provided by *Practice Direction (Mandatory Life Sentences)* of 18 May 2004. This Practice Direction amends the relevant provisions of *Practice Direction (Criminal: Consolidated)* [2002] 2 Cr App R 533, paras 49.1 onwards.

Section 269(1) makes it clear that the provisions apply only to cases where the sentence 'is fixed by law'. It is clear, then, that it applies only to the mandatory sentences of life imprisonment, custody for life, and detention during Her Majesty's pleasure. The setting of the specified period in relation to other forms of life sentence, such as discretionary life sentences and automatic life sentence under s 109 of the Powers of Criminal Courts (Sentencing) Act 2000, continues to be governed by s 82A of the 2000 Act. Section 82A is accordingly amended by Sch 32, para 109, so as to remove sentences of detention during Her Majesty's pleasure from the scope of that section. When s 61 of the Criminal Justice and Court Services Act 2000 is brought into force, the sentence of custody for life will be abolished. In the context of murder, the implication of this will be that offenders aged 18 and over convicted of that offence will be subject to the mandatory penalty of life imprisonment. This change has not yet happened, but transitory provisions in Sch 38, para 1 allow for the bringing into force of the new arrangements for fixing the minimum term in murder cases ahead of that change.

Section 269(2), (3) and (4) then sets out a scheme for setting minimum terms in murder cases which is closely similar to that which is provided under s 82A of the 2000 Act (as amended) to apply in other life sentence cases. The court must select the minimum term which is appropriate, taking into account the seriousness of the offence or the combination of the offence and other offences associated with it, and making allowance for any period which the offender has already spent in custody on remand. Section 269(2) states that the court must fix a minimum term in a murder case, unless it makes an order under s 269(4) that the offender was aged 21 or over when he committed the offence and that 'because of the seriousness of the offence . . . no order should be made . . .'. The function of s 269(4) is to allow for the setting of a 'whole life' term in an appropriate case, such as those which are indicated in Sch 21. Section 269(5) is important. It states that when considering the seriousness of a murder case the court must have regard to (a) the general principles set out in Sch 21, and (b) any guidelines relating to offences in general which are relevant to the case and are not incompatible with the provisions of Sch 21. The terms of Sch 21 were outlined in 11.8.2. It should be noted that these 'general principles' or 'starting points' are *not* mandatory. The sentencing court must 'have regard to' them. Section 270, however, requires a court imposing a minimum term in a murder case to state in open court and in ordinary language the reasons for deciding on the order made, to state which of the starting points in Sch 21 have been chosen and why, and to state reasons for any departure from the stated starting point. Section 270 does appear to tie the court closely to the terms of the schedule. Section 269(6) and (7) provides power for the Secretary of State to amend the terms of Sch 21 by order, but requires him to consult the Sentencing Guidelines Council before doing so.

Section 271 provides that an appeal can be made by an offender, either against the minimum term set by the court in a murder case, or against a decision by that court to set a 'whole life' minimum term. Of course there can be no appeal against a mandatory sentence as such, but s 271(1) inserts a new sub-s (1A) into s 9 of the Criminal Appeal Act 1968, to make it clear that an appeal may lie against the minimum term set by the court.

It follows from this amendment to the 1968 Act that the Attorney-General may, under ss 35 and 36 of the Criminal Justice Act 1988 (reviews of sentencing), refer a minimum term in a murder case to the Court of Appeal as being an example of an unduly lenient sentence. Section 272 of the 2003 Act breaks new ground, however, by providing that if the Attorney-General does refer such a case to the Court of Appeal, and the Court of Appeal is persuaded that the minimum term set by the judge was unduly lenient, the court 'shall not . . . make any allowance for the fact that the person to whom it relates is being sentenced for a second time'. It should be understood that the well-established principle in cases where the Court of Appeal does increase sentence in light of a reference from the Attorney-General is to discount that increase to some extent to allow for the fact that the offender has had the ordeal of being sentenced twice for the offence. The normal practice of the Court of Appeal is to state what the proper sentence should have been, and then to indicate what reduction from that sentence is being made for 'double jeopardy' (see *A-G's Reference (No 4 of 1989)* [1990] 1 WLR 41, followed in many subsequent cases). Section 272 now makes any such adjustment unlawful in murder cases. This creates an obvious disparity in practice between murder and all other offences which the Attorney-General has power to refer in this way. The Sentencing Guidelines Council may need soon to consider the implications of s 272 for the handling of Attorney-General's references in cases other than murder.

11.8.4 Transitional Provisions

The relevant provisions are already in force. Sections 269 to 277 and Schs 21 and 22 to the Act came into effect on 18 December 2003. They apply to all cases in which a court passes a mandatory life sentence for murder (life imprisonment, custody for life, or detention during Her Majesty's pleasure) on or after that date. Valuable guidance on the interpretation of the transitional provisions is provided by *Practice Direction (Mandatory Life Sentences)* of 18 May 2004. This Practice Direction amends the relevant provisions of *Practice Direction (Criminal: Consolidated)* [2002] 2 Cr App R 533, paras 49.1 onwards.

It should be noted that the relevant date is the date of sentence, and not the date of commission of the offence. This open up a possible challenge to these provisions under Article 7 of the European Convention on Human Rights. Article 7 provides 'Nor shall a heavier penalty be imposed than the one that was applicable at the time the criminal offence was committed.' If it could be shown that, in the case of a particular defendant who committed a murder before 18 December 2003, the minimum term imposed under Sch 21 was longer than such term would have been at the time the murder was committed, there would appear to be a breach of Article 7. One response to such a challenge would be that the sentence for murder is, and has been since 1965, a mandatory life sentence and, as such, is no more severe than it was before the 2003 Act changes. It is submitted that such a defence would fail. A number of challenges under Article 7 have come before the English courts already, and the approach has been to consider the substance, rather than the form, of sentence when deciding if the 'penalty' is now 'heavier' than it was before. See, for example, the detailed consideration given to these matters in *R v Field* [2003] 1 WLR 882 and *R (Uttley) v Secretary of State for the Home Department* [2003] EWCA Civ 1130.

The Act itself provides a better reply to challenge under Article 7, however. Schedule 22, paras 9 and 10 of the 2003 Act refer to those cases where sentence is passed on or after the commencement date, in respect of a murder committed before that date. They state that, when dealing with such a case, the court fixing the minimum term must not fix a minimum term which, in the opinion of the court, is greater than that which the Home Secretary would have been likely to have imposed prior to December 2002, and must not make a 'whole life' minimum term in any case where in the opinion of the court the Home Secretary would not have imposed a 'whole life tariff' before December 2002. These paragraphs may meet the potential challenge under Article 7, but they will require that any court sentencing in a murder case be furnished with relevant policy details and statistical materials relating to past practice in tariff-setting by the Home Secretary. Some guidance on this matter is provided by *Practice Direction (Mandatory Life Sentences)* of 18 May 2004, in paras 49.13 to 49.22.

Apart from challenge under Article 7, it seems unlikely that any other challenge to these provisions would succeed. There seems to be no constitutional or human rights infringement in legislating for murder sentencing in this way. It was established in *R v Secretary of State for the Home Department, ex p Hindley* [2001] 1 AC 410 that a 'whole life tariff' imposed under the provisions which preceded the 2003 Act did not infringe Article 3, and it is hard to see that this would be any different after the Act.

Schedule 22 makes provision for transitional cases, where (a) existing mandatory life sentence prisoners have already been notified of their minimum term by the Home Secretary or (b) existing mandatory life sentence prisoners who have not been so notified. In the first case, where an application of the prisoner to a single judge of the High Court, the judge must review the minimum term which has been notified to the prisoner by the Home Secretary and, if appropriate, amend it, but not increase it. In the second case the Home Secretary must refer such prisoners to a single judge of the High Court for the setting of the minimum term by that judge. The minimum term so set must not be greater that than which the Home Secretary would have been likely to have imposed prior to December 2002. Reasons need to be given by the High Court in each case. There is a right of appeal by the defendant to the Court of Appeal against a minimum term set by the judge under either of these procedures, and the Attorney-General may refer a minimum term to the Court of Appeal which he regards as being unduly lenient.

12

NON-CUSTODIAL ORDERS

12.1 INTRODUCTION

This chapter deals with a range of matters in the Criminal Justice Act 2003 (CJA 2003) relating to sentencing, which lie outside the custodial sentence provision. We deal here with the new community sentence scheme, provisions on fines and fine default, on deferment of sentence, on disqualification from working with children, on individual support orders, and on matters relating to community orders which are clearly intended to come into force prior to the main reshaping of the community sentence.

12.2 COMMUNITY SENTENCE

The CJA 2003 recasts the pre-existing range of community orders. In general terms, the range of orders is now subsumed under a generic heading of 'community sentence'. Where, following CJA 2003, a sentencing court passes a community sentence, it may include in that sentence one or more of a menu of requirements. These requirements broadly reflect the nature of the pre-existing community orders. So what, prior to CJA 2003, would have been expressed as a 'community punishment order' now becomes 'an unpaid work requirement' within a community sentence. At the time of writing it is expected that the new provisions on community orders will be brought into force in spring 2005.

The origins of this change are in chapter 6 of the Halliday Report (*Making Punishments Work: Review of the Sentencing Framework for England and Wales* (July 2001)), although it was proposed in that report that the generic sentence should be known as a new 'community punishment order' (para 6.6). Halliday justified these reforms by noting the proliferation of community orders in recent years 'which often replicate the virtues and defects of existing orders' (para 6.2). 'New ideas and developments in the supervision of offenders should, where possible, be incorporated into existing sentences without resorting to the regular introduction of entirely new ones', he said (para 6.2). Halliday also suggested that greater consistency in sentencing might be achieved by scrapping a number of distinct orders and rebranding these as requirements within a single generic 'community sentence' (para 6.2). This is optimistic, however, since consistency can hardly be achieved simply by giving all community orders the same name. Consistency will depend upon how the new 'community sentence' is used, and on the number and complexity of requirements which are written into it by sentencers. For a valuable discussion of the Halliday approach to community orders see S Rex, 'Reinventing community penalties: the role of communication' in S Rex and M Tonry, *Reform and Punishment: The Future of Sentencing* (2002, ch 7).

The provisions relating to requirements which can be inserted into a community sentence are considered next. Certain general provisions, including the threshold provisions relevant to the new community sentence scheme, are to be found in CJA 2003, ss 147–151, and were considered in 10.4 above.

12.2.1 Community Sentence: Requirements Available

Section 177 lists the requirements with which the court may order an offender aged 16 or over to comply during the course of a community sentence. They are:

(a) an unpaid work requirement (as defined in s 199),
(b) an activity requirement (s 201),
(c) a programme requirement (s 202),
(d) a prohibited activity requirement (s 203),
(e) a curfew requirement (s 204),
(f) an exclusion requirement (s 205),
(g) a residence requirement (s 206),
(h) a mental health treatment requirement (s 207),
(i) a drug rehabilitation requirement (s 209),
(j) an alcohol treatment requirement (s 212),
(k) a supervision requirement (s 213), and
(l) in a case where the offender is aged under 25, an attendance centre requirement (s 214).

All of these requirements closely reflect community orders which have existed prior to the 2003 Act, although there are some changes of detail. A number of general provisions apply, which are dealt with now, before turning to the details of the individual requirements.

Any community order must specify the petty sessions area in which the offender resides or will reside (s 216(1)). The court must ensure, so far as practicable, that any requirement imposed in a community sentence is such as to avoid conflict with the offender's religious beliefs, conflict with the requirements of any other order to which the offender may be subject, and avoids interference with the times, if any, at which the offender normally works or attends school or other educational establishment (s 217(1)). The court which makes the relevant order must forthwith provide copies of the order to the offender and to the appropriate responsible officer (s 219(1)), and to certain other persons affected by the order (s 219(2) and Sch 14). There is also a general duty on the offender made subject to a community order to keep in touch with the responsible officer in accordance with such instructions as he may from time to time be given by that officer, and must notify him of any change of address (s 220). A community sentence must specify a date, not more than three years after the date of the order, by which all the requirements in it must have been complied with (s 177(5)). Before making a community sentence which contains one or more requirements the court must consider whether the requirements are compatible with each other (s 177(6)).

The requirements are now considered in turn.

12.2.2 Unpaid Work Requirement

Section 199 re-enacts, with some changes, s 46 of the Powers of Criminal Courts (Sentencing) Act 2000 (PCC(S)A 2000), which deals with community punishment orders (formerly community service orders). The number of hours of unpaid work which may be ordered by the court must be not less than 40 and not more than 300 (s 199(2)). This represents a change, since the maximum number of hours which could be ordered under a community punishment order was 240. No reason is given in the Halliday Report, or in *Justice for All,* for this increase. Before inserting an unpaid work requirement into a community sentence the court must, if it thinks necessary, hear from an appropriate officer that the offender is a suitable person to perform work under the requirement (s 199(3)) and that local arrangements exist for the requirement to be carried out (s 218(1)). The appropriate officer is either an officer of the local probation board (if the offender is aged 18 or over) or an officer of the local probation board, a social worker of a local authority social services department, or a member of a youth offending team (if the offender is aged under 18).

If the court makes community orders on the offender in respect of two or more offences of which the offender has been convicted on the same occasion and includes unpaid work requirements in each of them, the court may direct that the hours of work may run concurrently or consecutively, but the total number of hours must not exceed 300 (s 199(5)). The work required should normally be completed within 12 months (s 200(2)). The Secretary of State may by order amend the maximum number of hours of unpaid work which may be specified under an unpaid work requirement (s 223)(1)(a)).

12.2.3 Activity Requirement

Section 201 is based on the requirements as to activities formerly to be found in Sch 2, para 2 to the 2000 Act. Section 201(1) defines an activity requirement as a requirement that the offender must either present himself to a specified person, at a specified place such as a community rehabilitation centre, for a certain number of days, and/or take part in specified activities for a certain number of days. The aggregate number of days must not exceed 60 (s 201(5)). An activity requirement may include such tasks as receiving help with employment, or group work on social problems. Reparative activities, involving contact between offenders and persons affected by their offences, are also an aim of this requirement (s 201(2)). Before inserting an activity requirement into a community sentence the court must consult an appropriate officer, be satisfied that it is feasible to secure compliance with the requirement (s 201(3)), and be satisfied that local arrangements exist for persons to participate in such activities (s 218(2)). The appropriate officer is either an officer of the local probation board (if the offender is aged 18 or over) or an officer of the local probation board or a member of a youth offending team (if the offender is aged under 18). If the activity requirement would involve the co-operation of a person other than the offender and the responsible officer, the consent of that other person must be obtained before the requirement can be inserted into the order (s 201(4)).

12.2.4 Programme Requirement

Section 202(1) defines a 'programme requirement' as a requirement that the offender must participate in an accredited programme at a specified place on a certain number of days. Such programmes include those which address offending behaviour and cover such topics as anger management, sex offending, substance misuse and so on. The court may not insert a programme requirement into a community sentence unless the relevant accredited programme has been recommended to the court as being suitable for the offender by an officer of the local probation board (if the offender is aged 18 or over) or by an officer of the local probation board or a member of a youth offending team (if the offender is aged under 18), and the court is satisfied that the programme is or will be available at the place specified in the community order (s 202(4)). If the activity requirement would involve the co-operation of a person other than the offender and the responsible officer, the consent of that other person must be obtained before the requirement can be inserted into the order (s 202(5)).

12.2.5 Prohibited Activity Requirement

Section 203(1) defines a prohibited activity requirement. The court can require an offender to refrain from taking part in certain activities, on a certain day or days (such as attending football matches), or over a period of time. The requirement may include forbidding him to contact a certain person, and may be that the offender does not possess, use or carry a firearm (s 203(3)). Before inserting a prohibited activity requirement into a community sentence the court must consult an officer of the local probation board (if the offender is aged 18 or over) or an officer of the local probation board or a member of a youth offending team (if the offender is aged under 18) (s 203(2)).

12.2.6 Curfew Requirement

Section 204 re-enacts, with some changes, PCC(S)A 2000, s 37, which deals with curfew orders. A curfew requirement is a requirement that the offender remain at a place specified by the court for certain periods of time. These periods of time must not be less than 2 hours and not more than 12 hours in any given day (s 204(2)). An order might require the offender to be indoors at home between seven in the evening and seven in the morning. A curfew requirement within a community order must not last for more than six months from the day on which it is made (s 204(3)). The Secretary of State may by order amend the number of hours or the periods of time which can be specified in a curfew requirement (s 223(1)(b) and (3)(a)).

Before inserting a curfew requirement into a community order the court must obtain and consider information about the place proposed to be specified in the order, including information as to the attitude of persons likely to be affected by the enforced presence there of the offender (s 204(6)). Where the court makes a community sentence which includes a curfew requirement, it must normally also impose an electronic monitoring requirement unless the court considers it inappropriate to do so (s 177(3)).

12.2.7 Exclusion Requirement

Section 205 re-enacts, with some changes, s 40A of the 2000 Act, which was inserted by s 46 of the Criminal Justice and Court Services Act 2000. Exclusion orders were not brought into force, but are now translated into exclusion requirements under the 2003 Act. An exclusion requirement is a requirement which prohibits an offender from entering a specified place, or places, or area (such as town centre), during a period specified in the order. The order can exclude the offender from different places for different periods of time. It may also be used as a means of keeping the offender away from a specified person, in which case the person for whose protection the order is made should be given a copy of the requirement made by the court (s 219 and Sch 14). An exclusion requirement cannot last longer than two years. The Secretary of State may by order amend the periods of time which can be specified in an exclusion requirement (s 223(3)(b)). Where the court makes a community sentence which includes an exclusion requirement, it must normally also impose an electronic monitoring requirement unless the court considers it inappropriate to do so (s 177(3)).

12.2.8 Residence Requirement

The residence requirement in s 206 is based on pre-existing requirements as to residence that can be inserted into a community rehabilitation order (formerly a probation order) under Sch 2, para 1 to the 2000 Act. The residence requirement is a requirement that the offender resides at a place specified in the order for a specified period of time (s 206(2)). Before making such a requirement the court must consider the home surroundings of the offender (s 206(3)). A court may not specify residence at a hostel or other institution except on the recommendation of an officer of a local probation board (s 206(4)).

12.2.9 Mental Health Treatment Requirement

The mental health treatment requirement in s 207 is based on pre-existing requirements as to treatment that can be inserted into a community rehabilitation order (formerly a probation order) under Sch 2, para 5 to the 2000 Act. The court may direct an offender to undergo mental health treatment, by or under the direction of a doctor or chartered psychologist. The treatment may take the form of treatment as a resident patient in a hospital or care home, treatment as a non-resident patient, or treatment under the direction of a doctor or chartered psychologist as may be specified (s 207(2)). Before the court can insert a mental health treatment requirement, it must be satisfied on the evidence of a doctor approved for the purposes of s 12 of the Mental Health Act 1983 that the mental condition of the offender is such as requires and may be susceptible to treatment, is not such as to warrant the making of a hospital order or a guardianship order, the court is satisfied that arrangements have been made or can be made for the treatment to be specified in the order, and that the offender has expressed his willingness to comply with such an order (s 207(3)). The supervising officer will supervise the offender only to the extent necessary for revoking or amending the order (s 207(4)).

Section 208 deals with provision for the doctor or chartered psychologist subsequently to change the place at which the offender is to receive treatment, to a place where treatment can be better or more conveniently given. The doctor or registered psychologist must notify the responsible officer in advance, and the offender must consent to any such change.

12.2.10 Drug Rehabilitation Requirement

By s 209 the court may insert into a community sentence a drug rehabilitation requirement, which includes drug treatment and testing. The requirement is closely similar to the pre-existing drug treatment and testing order which can be imposed under s 52 of the 2000 Act and the drug abstinence order which can be imposed under s 58A of the 2000 Act. It requires that during a period specified in the order (the treatment and testing period) the offender must submit to treatment by or under the direction of a specified person having the necessary qualifications or experience and must provide samples, at such times and in such circumstances as are requested, to determine whether he has any drug in his body during that period (s 209(1)). Guidance on the use of drug treatment and testing orders was provided by the Court of Appeal in *R v Robinson* [2002] 2 Cr App R (S) 434, *R v Kelly* [2003] 1 Cr App R (S) 472 and *A-G's Reference (No 64 of 2003)* [2004] Crim LR 241 and commentary. The importance of the sentencing court following the procedural provisions properly before passing such a sentence was stressed in *R (Inner London Probation Service) v Tower Bridge Magistrates' Court* [2002] 1 Cr App R (S) 179.

Before imposing a drug rehabilitation requirement the court must be satisfied that the offender is dependent on, or has a propensity to misuse, any controlled drug (as defined by s 2 of the Misuse of Drugs Act 1971) and that his dependency or propensity is such as requires and may be susceptible to treatment (s 209(2)(a)). The court must also be satisfied that arrangements have been made or can be made for the proposed treatment (s 209(2)(b)), and that the insertion of a drug rehabilitation requirement has been recommended to the court as being suitable for the offender by an officer of the local probation board (if the offender is aged 18 or over) or by an officer of the local probation board or a member of a youth offending team (if the offender is aged under 18) (s 209(2)(c)). The offender must express his willingness to comply with the requirement (s 209(2)(d)). The treatment and testing period must be for at least six months (s 209(3)), and may take the form of treatment as a resident in a specified institution or place, or treatment as a non-resident (s 209(4)). The Secretary of State may by order amend the periods of time which can be specified in a drug rehabilitation requirement (s 223(3)(c)).

Section 210 states that the court may provide for the drug rehabilitation requirement to be reviewed periodically at time intervals of not less than one month, provide for these reviews to be held by the court responsible for the order (a review hearing) and require the offender to attend each review hearing. The responsible officer will provide a written report, which will include the results of the offender's drug tests, on the offender's progress under the requirement in advance of each review hearing (s 210(1)). Section 211 sets out what is to happen at each review of a drug rehabilitation requirement. The court, after considering the report from the responsible officer, may amend the requirement, but cannot do so unless the offender consents. It cannot reduce the term of the treatment and testing period below six months (s 211(2)). If the offender does not consent to the proposed amendment to the requirement, the court may revoke the order and re-sentence the offender as if he had just been convicted (s 211(3)). If it does so, the court must take into account the extent to which the offender has complied with the requirements of the order. If the court wishes it may impose a custodial sentence on the offender, provided the offence was punishable with imprisonment (s 211(4)). If the offender's progress is satisfactory, the court can state that, in future, reviews can be on paper and without a hearing (s 211(6)). If the offender's progress then becomes unsatisfactory and he is not present, the court can require him to attend in future (s 211(7)). The court may also amend the order to provide for future review hearings (s 211(8)).

12.2.11 Alcohol Treatment Requirement

By s 212 the court may insert into a community sentence an alcohol treatment requirement. The requirement is closely similar to the pre-existing alcohol treatment requirement of a community rehabilitation order (formerly probation order) under Sch 2, para 6 of the 2000 Act. It requires that during a period specified in the order the offender must submit to treatment by or under the direction of a specified person having the necessary qualifications or experience with a view to the reduction or elimination of the offender's dependency on alcohol.

Before imposing an alcohol treatment requirement the court must be satisfied that the offender is dependent on alcohol and that his dependency is such as requires and may be susceptible to treatment (s 212(2)). The court must also be satisfied that arrangements have been made or can be made for the proposed treatment. The offender must express his willingness to comply with the requirement (s 212(3)). The alcohol treatment requirement must be in effect for at least six months (s 212(4)), and may take the form of treatment as a resident in a specified institution or place, or treatment as a non-resident or treatment by or under the direction of such person having the necessary qualification or experience (s 212(5)). The Secretary of State may by order amend the periods of time which can be specified in an alcohol treatment requirement (s 223(3)(d)).

12.2.12 Supervision Requirement

Supervision has long been a key component of community rehabilitation orders made under s 41 of the 2000 Act (formerly probation orders). The 2003 Act now makes a supervision requirement available in a community sentence. The supervision requirement is a requirement that, during the relevant period, the offender must attend appointments with the responsible officer or another person determined by the responsible officer at such time and place as may be determined by the officer (s 213(1)), with a view to promoting the offender's rehabilitation (s 213(2)). The 'relevant period' in this context means the full duration of the community sentence.

12.2.13 Attendance Centre Requirement

Attendance centre orders have long been a form of community order for young offenders, made under s 60 of the 2000 Act. These centres offer practical activities, including sport, to occupy offenders for a certain number of hours, especially at weekends. An attendance centre requirement may now, additionally, be inserted as a requirement into a community sentence. The continuing availability of attendance centre orders under s 60 is clear from ss 221 and 222, which set out the powers of the Secretary of State to continue to provide attendance centres and to regulate a number of aspects of their provision. As with attendance centre orders, attendance centre requirements are available only in respect of offenders aged under 25 years.

Under an attendance centre requirement in a community sentence the offender must attend at an attendance centre specified in the relevant order for a specified number of hours which must be not less than 12 nor more than 36 (s 214(2)). The offender must not be required to attend more than once on any single day or for more than three hours on any occasion (s 214(6)). The court cannot make an attendance centre requirement unless satisfied that there is an attendance centre available locally (s 218(3)) and that the attendance centre order specified is reasonably accessible to the offender (s 214(3)). The responsible officer will notify the offender of the date and time required for the first attendance, and subsequent hours are fixed by the officer in charge of the attendance centre (s 214(5) and (6)).

12.2.14 Electronic Monitoring Requirement

Section 215 provides that the court passing a community sentence can order the electronic monitoring of the offender's compliance with any of the other requirements in the sentence. Electronic monitoring has been available throughout England and Wales since 1999, following a series of pilot projects. It has never been used as a sentence in its own right, but was employed initially in conjunction with curfew orders. The use of electronic monitoring has expanded rapidly in recent years, as an element in non-custodial sentencing, as a bail condition for certain young defendants, and as an important part of the home detention curfew scheme where offenders are released from prison in advance of their normal eligibility date for early release from custody.

The sentencing court may set an electronic monitoring requirement to ensure an offender's compliance with other requirements in the community sentence. Where the court makes a community sentence which includes a curfew requirement or an exclusion requirement, it *must* also impose an electronic monitoring requirement, unless the court considers it inappropriate to do so (s 177(3)), and it *may* do so in respect of any other requirement (s 177(4)). The periods of electronic monitoring can be specified by the court in the order, or set by the responsible officer (s 215(1)). If the court is proposing to include such a requirement but there is a person other than the offender without whose co-operation it will not be practicable to secure the monitoring, the requirement cannot be included without that person's consent (s 215(2)). The court must ensure that electronic monitoring arrangements are available in the local area and that the necessary provision can be made under those arrangements (s 218(4)).

12.2.15 Breach, Revocation or Amendment of Community Orders

Section 179 introduces Sch 8 to the 2003 Act which contains provisions dealing with breach, revocation and amendment of community orders, and the effect of the offender being convicted of a further offence.

Paragraphs 5 and 6 of Sch 8 are the key provisions here. By para 5, if the responsible officer is of the opinion that the offender has failed without reasonable excuse to comply with any of the requirements of a community order, the officer must give a *warning* describing the circumstances of the failure, stating that the failure is unacceptable, and informing the offender that if within the next twelve months he again fails to comply with any requirement of the order, he will be brought back before the court. By para 6, if there has been a warning, and within twelve months there is a further failure without reasonable excuse to comply, the responsible officer must cause an information to be laid before a magistrate or before the Crown Court in respect of that second failure. Paragraphs 7 and 8 deal with details with the arrangements for issue of summons or warrant by the justice of the peace or by the Crown Court.

Paragraph 9 describes the powers of a magistrates' court when dealing with a breach of a community order. If it is proved to the satisfaction of the court before which the offender is brought that he has failed without reasonable excuse to comply with any of the requirements of the community order, the court must deal with him in one of the following ways set out in para 9(1):

(a) by amending the terms of the community order so as to impose more onerous requirements (subject to para 9(3)), or

(b) where the community order was made by a magistrates' court, revoke the order and deal with him for the offence in any way in which the court could deal with him if he had just been convicted, or

(c) where the community order was made by a magistrates' court in respect of an offence which was not punishable with imprisonment, and the offender is aged 18 or over, and he has wilfully and persistently failed to comply with the requirements of the order, revoke the order and impose a sentence of imprisonment for a term not exceeding 51 weeks.

When dealing with the offender under para 9(1) the magistrates' court must take into account the extent to which the offender has complied with the requirements of the community order (para 9(2)). If the community order was made by the Crown Court, the magistrates' court may instead commit the offender in custody or release him on bail to appear before the Crown Court (para 9(6)).

Paragraph 10 describes the powers of the Crown Court when dealing with a breach of a community order. If it is proved to the satisfaction of the court before which the offender is brought that he has failed without reasonable excuse to comply with any of the requirements of the community order, the court must deal with him in one of the following ways set out in para 10(1):

(a) by amending the terms of the community order so as to impose more onerous requirements (subject to para 10(3)), or

(b) by revoking the order and dealing with him for the offence in any way in which he could have been dealt with for that offence by the court which made the order, or

(c) where the offence in respect of which the order was made which was not punishable with imprisonment, and the offender is aged 18 or over, and he has wilfully and persistently failed to comply with the requirements of the order, revoke the order and impose a sentence of imprisonment for a term not exceeding 51 weeks.

When dealing with the offender under para 10(1) the Crown Court must take into account the extent to which the offender has complied with the requirements of the community order (para 10(2)).

Paragraphs 13 to 15 deal with revocation of a community order where, on application by the offender or the responsible officer, having regard to changed circumstances since the order was made, it is in the interests of justice to revoke the order or to deal with the offender for the offence in some other way. These circumstances would include the offender making good progress under the order or responding satisfactorily to the requirements in the order.

Paragraphs 16 to 20 deal with various forms of amendment to requirements in a community order which may be made by an appropriate court, on application by the offender or the responsible officer, as to change of residence, change of circumstances of the offender, and other matters.

Paragraphs 21 to 23 deal with the powers of a magistrates' court and the Crown Court in circumstances where an offender subject to a community order has been convicted of a further offence. If a magistrates' court is dealing with the subsequent offence, and the community order was made by a magistrates' court, the magistrates' court may revoke the community order, or revoke it and deal with the offender for that original offence in any way in which he could have been dealt with by the court for that offence (para 21(2)). When dealing with the offender under para 21(2) the magistrates' court must take into account the extent to which the offender has complied with the requirements of the community order (para 21(3)). If the community order was made by the Crown Court, the magistrates' court may instead commit the offender in custody or release him on bail to appear before the Crown Court (para 22(1)). If the Crown Court is dealing with the subsequent offence, it may revoke the community order, or revoke it and deal with the offender for that original offence in any way in which he could have been dealt with for the offence by the court which made the order (para 23(2)). When dealing with the offender under para 23(2) the Crown Court must take into account the extent to which the offender has complied with the requirements of the community order (para 23(3)).

12.3 FINES AND FINE DEFAULT

12.3.1 Fines

Sections 162 to 165 of the 2003 Act contain general provisions on the use of the fine in sentencing. They substantially re-enact ss 126 to 129 of the Powers of Criminal Courts (Sentencing) Act 2000, with a few relatively minor changes.

Section 162 deals with the powers of a court to order a statement as to the offender's financial circumstances. Failure to comply with such an order is an offence punishable by a fine not exceeding level 3. The only change from the earlier law is that the offence of making a false statement in response to financial circumstances order is made non-imprisonable. Previously it was punishable by a term of imprisonment not exceeding three months, a fine at level 4 or both. Now it is punishable simply by a fine at level 4.

Section 163 deals with the general power of the Crown Court to impose a fine on an offender convicted on indictment. The section is slightly different from its earlier version as s 127 of the 2000 Act. In general the Crown Court can impose a fine on an offender either instead of, or in addition to, dealing with him in any other way. There are certain exceptional cases where the imposition of a fine is incompatible with another sentence being passed for the offence. Section 163 removes reference to one such case, s 109 of the 2000 Act (automatic life sentence) because that section is repealed by the 2003 Act. It does, however, include reference to ss 225 to 228 of the 2003 Act, which are the new provisions on dangerous offenders, use of which on sentence is incompatible with the imposition of a fine. Section 163 refers to the fact that there are some sentences which cannot be combined with a fine. These are now rare, but a fine cannot be combined with a hospital order (see Mental Health Act 1983, s 37(8)), nor with a discharge when sentencing for a single offence (*R v McClelland* [1951] 1 All ER 557).

Section 164 is an important section concerned with fixing the level of a fine. The court must enquire into the financial circumstances of an offender before fixing the amount of a fine. When determining the amount of the fine, the court must take the financial circumstances of the offender, the seriousness of the offence and the circumstances of the case into account. The section re-enacts s 128 of the 2000 Act, with minor changes. There is the by now familiar changing of the word 'shall' to the word 'must' at several places in the section. The old sub-s (5)(b)(i) of s 128 has been amended to include reference to the offence of making a false statement as to financial circumstances in CJA 1991, s 20A. Two further matters should be noted, though it is submitted that neither provision actually changes the law. Section 166(1)(d) states the rather obvious point that any matters relevant in mitigation of sentence are material to fixing the level of a fine, and s 151(2) makes it clear that a fine may still be an appropriate sentence even though the offence is 'serious enough' to justify a community sentence. Also, s 151(1) makes special provision for imposing a community sentence on an offender who has received a sentence consisting only of a fine on three or more occasions. Section 151(1) was considered at 10.4.4 above.

Section 165 deals with remission of fines. It re-enacts s 129 of the 2000 Act. If an offender's financial circumstances are made clear to the court after it has fixed a fine, it can reduce the fine or withdraw it completely. If a term of imprisonment has already been fixed in default of payment of the fine, that term must be reduced accordingly.

12.3.2 Fine Default

Sections 300 and 301 of the 2003 Act are concerned with fine default. Section 300 replaces, with some amendments, certain fine default provisions in s 35 of the Crime (Sentences) Act 1997.

Where a magistrates' court has power to commit an offender to prison in default of payment of a fine, the 1997 Act provided that the court may, instead of committing the defaulter to prison, impose a community service order or a curfew order, though subject to special rules about the number of hours which could be ordered or the number of days of curfew. Community service orders and curfew orders are abolished by the 2003 Act, and are replaced by 'unpaid work requirements' and 'curfew requirements' within the new community sentence scheme (see 12.2 above). An order under s 300 is now named a 'default order' by s 300(3). Section 300(4) permits the unpaid work or curfew requirement to be made subject to electronic monitoring. Section 300(5) allows the magistrates' court to postpone making a default order for such period as it thinks fit.

Section 300(6) applies to the new breach provisions of Sch 8 to the 2003 Act, and it applies the new community sentence provisions, subject to Sch 31. Schedule 31 sets out two tables, specifying the number of hours unpaid work, and the number of days of curfew, which may be ordered in respect of various amounts of fine for which the offender is in default. These correspond to the periods which were formerly provided in s 35 of the 1997 Act. If the offender pays the whole or any part of the sum of the fine defaulted, the number of hours of unpaid work or the number of day of curfew are reduced by a corresponding amount (s 300(7)).

Section 301 re-enacts the provisions of s 40 of the Crime (Sentences) Act 1997. As an alternative to committing the offender to custody in default of payment of a fine, it provides the magistrates' court with a power to disqualify the offender from driving for a period of up to 12 months. Under s 301(3) if the fine is repaid the order ceases to have effect, or if it paid in part the period of disqualification is reduced by a corresponding amount. The power in s 301 has always been controversial. No doubt in some cases it will provide an effective threat and thereby force the offender into paying outstanding fines. On the other hand, it employs the driving disqualification as a form of punishment, which seems unsuited to that particular measure. It is submitted that disqualifications are distinct from punishments, and that their use should be confined to cases in which the offender represents a particular risk with respect to the activity from which the court has disqualified him. See, however, s 146 of the Powers of Criminal Courts (Sentencing) Act 2000 (in force from 1 January 2004), which permits a court to impose a driving ban on an offender convicted of any offence, whether or not the offence was related to the offender's use of a motor vehicle.

12.4 DEFERMENT OF SENTENCE

Powers of the criminal courts to defer sentence on an offender were previously to be found in ss 1 and 2 of the Powers of Criminal Courts (Sentencing) Act 2000. They should be distinguished from powers to adjourn prior to sentence, such as for the purposes of obtaining a pre-sentence report (see *R v Fairhead* [1975] 2 All ER 737).

Deferment of sentence provisions are of long standing, and can be found in very similar form in the Powers of Criminal Courts Act 1973. The power to defer sentence has long been recognized as a useful power to be used occasionally where circumstances require. It has provided the Crown Court or a magistrates' court with an opportunity to postpone passing sentence on an offender for a specified period of time of up to six months. The power is meant to be used in cases where some impending change in the offender's life means that it would be in the interests of justice to reconsider the case after a few weeks or months. It should not be used where the court cannot make up its mind what to do, or where the court's requirements could be fulfilled perfectly adequately under the terms of a short community sentence (see the guidance provided by the Court of Appeal in *R v George* [1984] 1 WLR 1082). The court must make clear to the offender the purposes of the deferment, and specify clearly what is required of the offender during that time. There have been limits as to what can be required of the offender. In *R v Skelton* [1983] Crim LR 686, for example, the Court of Appeal said that it was not appropriate to require the offender to go into hospital for treatment for a mental condition during the deferment period. That requirement could only be imposed by passing a community rehabilitation order with an appropriate treatment condition. The offender must consent to the deferment of sentence. At the end of the period of deferment the offender is brought back to court and sentenced for the offence. The court has exactly the same powers available to deal with the offender as it did when it deferred sentence, save that it cannot defer sentence for a second time. It is good practice, where possible, for the offender to be brought before the same sentencer who deferred sentence, since they will be most familiar with the case and the reasons for the deferment. If the offender has wholly or substantially complied (or, at least, has tried to comply) with the requirements of the deferment of sentence, the offender can expect that a non-custodial sentence will be passed (see Lord Lane CJ in *George*). If the sentencer is of the view that the offender has not complied, then the circumstances of non-compliance must be spelled out. Of course, conviction of a further offence during the period of deferment will almost certainly entail a custodial sentence (see, for example, *R v Hope* (1980) 2 Cr App R (S) 6).

By s 278 and Sch 23 of the 2003 Act the provisions on deferment of sentence are recast. At the time of writing it is expected that the new arrangements for deferment of sentence will be piloted in certain courts areas from July 2004, with roll-out of the provisions to all courts by December 2004. There appear to be two main purposes of the new legislation. The first is to include within statute certain procedural matters which are currently in the case law, such as clarifying the conditions of the deferment and reducing them to writing. The second is to formalize and extend the powers of the sentencing court to specify one or more of a range of requirements which are to be undertaken by the offender during the period of the deferment. The offender is still required to consent to deferment of sentence (Sch 23, para 1(3)(a)) and, as before, the court must be satisfied that, having regard to the nature of the offence and the character and circumstances of the offender, it would be in the interests of justice to defer sentence (Sch 23, para 1(3)(c)). Schedule 23 substitutes new ss 1, 1A, 1B, 1C and 1D for ss 1 and 2 of the 2000 Act. In s 1, sub-ss 1(3)(b) and 1(5) are of particular importance. The former makes it clear that deferment can only occur if the offender undertakes to comply with 'any requirements as to his conduct during the period of the deferment as the court considers it appropriate to impose', and the latter states that the details of the deferment must be written down and a copy given to the offender and to any supervisor appointed to oversee a requirement of the deferment. The requirements which may be imposed as conditions of the deferment include requirements as to residence (s 1A(1)), but that is expressly stated to be without prejudice to the 'generality' of sub-s 1(3)(b). Section 1B empowers the court to deal with the offender before the end of the period of deferment where the offender is in breach of any requirement. Section 1C deals with the situation where the offender commits a further offence during the period of deferment.

It should be noted that, under the new s 1(3)(b), the court may specify 'any requirements' as to the offender's conduct during the period of deferment that it considers it appropriate to impose. On the face of it this confers a very broad discretion on the sentencer. It is submitted that vague or unrealistic conditions, or conditions which are only partly within the offender's ability to control, would not be appropriate. A requirement that the offender must make an effort to resolve problems in his marriage, as was imposed in *R v Aquilina* (1989) 11 Cr App R (S) 431, might be thought undesirable on these grounds. There is also the possibility that courts might think up some individualized and ingenious requirements. Some sentencers are known to favour the development of flexible powers of this sort, such as to order an offender convicted of dangerous driving to spend time in the accident unit of a hospital to see the effects of road traffic accidents on victims. While that kind of order might in an individual case have a salutary effect, great care would need to be taken to ensure that the requirement was properly understood, set up and supervised, and that the offender's compliance with it was properly assessed. The range and flexibility of requirements which can now be written into a community sentence under CJA 2003 would seem to make a community sentence in many cases a more attractive option than deferment of sentence.

12.5 DRUG TREATMENT AND TESTING REQUIREMENTS

By CJA 2003, s 279 and Sch 24, it becomes possible to insert a drug treatment and testing requirement into a supervision order or an action plan order. Both of these orders are currently available for offenders aged 10 to 17 inclusive (under ss 63 and 69 of PCC(S)A 2000 respectively). At the time of writing it is expected that power to insert a drug treatment and testing requirement into a supervision order or an action plan order will come into force and be piloted in selected courts from July 2004.

For offenders aged 10 to 15 inclusive, action plan orders and supervision orders will stay in place, and they are unaffected by CJA 2003 apart from being renamed as two of the five available 'youth community orders' (CJA 2003, s 147). Offenders aged 16 or 17 will, however, be affected by the recasting of community sentences generally, as explained at 12.2 above. This change is not expected to take place until spring 2005, but from that time offenders aged 16 and over may receive a community order imposing one or more of a range of requirements, including a 'drug rehabilitation requirement'. See further 12.2.10.

12.6 DISQUALIFICATION FROM WORKING WITH CHILDREN

The Criminal Justice and Court Services Act 2000, ss 26 to 34, introduced a power (and in some cases a duty) for the Crown Court to impose on an offender who has been convicted of an offence committed against a child, and who has received a 'qualifying sentence' for that offence, to be disqualified by the court from working with children in the future. A 'qualifying sentence' is basically a custodial sentence of 12 months or more, or a hospital or guardianship order (for details see s 30 of that

231

Act). According to s 28, if the offender is aged 18 or over the order *must* be made, unless the court is satisfied that it is unlikely that the offender will commit any further offence against a child. This exception needs to be established to the civil standard of proof (*R v MG* [2002] 2 Cr App R (S) 1). According to s 29, if the offender is aged under 18, the court *may* make the order if the court is satisfied that it is likely that the offender will commit a further offence against a child. Again, this seems to be the civil standard of proof. These powers came into force on 11 January 2001, but are applicable whether the offence occurred before or after that date. This is clear from *R v Field* [2003] 1 WLR 882, in which the Court of Appeal stated that such a disqualification was not a 'penalty', and its use in respect of offences committed before 11 January 2001 did not infringe Article 7 of the ECHR.

Schedule 30 to the 2003 Act inserts a new s 29A into the Criminal Justice and Court Services Act 2000. The section adds an extra category of case in which a disqualification *may* be ordered by the Crown Court. This category applies when an individual is convicted of an offence against a child, *whatever* the age of the offender, and where '*no* qualifying sentence is imposed in respect of the conviction' (s 29A(1)(c), emphasis added). This extends the power to make a disqualification order to all cases in the Crown Court involving offences against a child, irrespective of the sentence imposed. There are thus now three categories: (a) where the offender is aged 18 or over and a qualifying sentence has been passed: *duty* to impose order, (b) where the offender is aged under 18 and a qualifying sentence has been passed: *power* to impose order, and (c) offender of any age where a non-qualifying sentence has been passed: power to impose order.

By s 29B (as inserted by Sch 30), if the Crown Court has, in respect of an offender aged 18 or over, not made a disqualification order and has not given reasons for not doing so or, in respect of an offender aged under 18, the Crown Court has not made a disqualification order and it appears to the prosecutor that it has failed to consider whether it should have done so, then in either case the prosecutor may apply to the court for a disqualification to be made. It should be noted that this possibility of involvement by the prosecution in reminding the court of its duty or power to make a disqualification order is limited to cases under s 28 and s 29 of the 2000 Act, but does not apply to the new third category of case introduced by s 29A and discussed in the last paragraph.

The relevant provisions came into force on 1 May 2004 (SI 2004/829). Presumably, following the decision in *R v Field* [2003] 1 WLR 882, these extended powers will be available in respect of an offender convicted of an offence committed against a child, whether that offence was committed before or after the commencement date.

12.7 INDIVIDUAL SUPPORT ORDERS

Section 1 of the Crime and Disorder Act 1998 (CDA 1998) permits the police, local authorities and registered social landlords to apply for anti-social behaviour orders

(ASBOs) in the magistrates' courts. Orders can be issued in respect of defendants of 10 years of age and over, who have acted in an anti-social manner, and where the order is necessary to protect the public from further anti-social acts. Section 1 defines an anti-social manner as that which causes or is likely to cause harassment, alarm or distress to one or more persons not of the same household (s 1(1)(a)). Anti-social behaviour typically includes harassment, noise nuisance, writing graffiti and verbal abuse. An ASBO prohibits the defendant from doing anything described in the order. It should normally last for a period of not less than two years (s 1(9)). Breach of the order is punishable with up to 6 months' imprisonment, a fine, or both summarily, and up to 5 years' imprisonment on indictment (s 1(10)).

Section 292 of the 2003 Act inserts new ss 1AA (individual support orders) and 1AB after s 1A of the 1998 Act. These sections allow for a new order to be made by a magistrates' court aimed at preventing further anti-social behaviour to be available where an anti-social behaviour order has already been granted against a juvenile defendant. Where an ASBO has already been made against a juvenile defendant, the magistrates' court must consider whether an individual support order (ISO) should be made in addition (s 1AA(1)). The ISO requires the defendant to comply, for a period not exceeding six months, with various requirements included in the order (s 1AA(2)). These requirements may directly, or by way of directions given under the order by a responsible officer, require the defendant to participate in specified activities, present themselves to a person specified in the order as and when required, or comply with education requirements (s 1AA(6)). The court should consider whether an ISO would be desirable in the interests of preventing repetition of the kind of behaviour which led to the making of the ASBO, and if the court considers that this is not so it should explain its decision in open court (s 1AA(4)). The legislation envisages that the ISO will be imposed in addition to an ASBO but, limited as it is to a period of six months, it will normally come to an end before the ASBO does. If an ASBO ceases to have effect, the ISO must come to an end as well (s 1AB(5)).

The magistrates' court is required to explain to the defendant in ordinary language the effect of the order and the consequences of failure to comply with it (s 1AB(1)). If the defendant does fail without reasonable excuse to comply with any requirement included in the order, he is guilty of an offence punishable by a fine not exceeding £250 (if he is aged under 14 at the date of conviction) and a fine not exceeding £1,000 (if he is aged 14 or over).

The relevant provisions came into force on 1 May 2004 (SI 2004/829).

12.8 PARENTING ORDERS AND REFERRAL ORDERS

Section 324 of the 2003 Act introduces Sch 34, which makes provision about the interaction between parenting orders (Crime and Disorder Act 1998, ss 8 to 10) and referral orders (Powers of Criminal Courts (Sentencing) Act 2000, ss 16 to 32). Section 324 and Sch 34 are already in force, with effect from 27 February 2004 (see SI 2004/81).

A parenting order requires the parent of the juvenile to attend such counselling or guidance sessions as may be specified, where this would be desirable in the interests of preventing the commission of any further offence by the juvenile. Parenting orders are controversial measures, but it was held in *R(M) v Inner London Crown Court*, The Times, 27 February 2003, that they did not contravene Article 8 of the ECHR. A referral order is an order of the youth court referring a juvenile offender to a youth offender panel for the drawing up of a contract between the panel and the offender, together with the juvenile's parent and, where appropriate, the victim of the offence, which is aimed at tackling the juvenile's future behaviour. The contract may include elements of reparation, counselling and rehabilitation. The referral order is a required disposal for the youth court where the juvenile is a first offender and has pleaded guilty, and where neither an absolute discharge nor a custodial sentence is an appropriate disposal for the offence.

The powers of the youth court to impose other orders at the same time as imposing a referral order are very limited. This is largely because the conditions to be made part of the referral order are a matter to be determined at a subsequent meeting of the youth offender panel to be attended by the juvenile, and so are not a matter for the youth court as such (see PCC(S)A 2000, s 21). Section 8 of CDA 1998 had formerly prevented a youth court from imposing a parenting order on the parent of a juvenile at the same time as making a referral order on the juvenile. That restriction is now removed by paras 1 and 3 of Sch 34. Further, by s 9 of CDA 1998, where the youth court is dealing with an offender under the age of 16, it is under a *duty* to make a parenting order, or to explain why such an order would not help to prevent the offender from committing another offence. That duty, however, does *not* extend to cases where the youth court is combining a referral order with a parenting order (Sch 34, para 2(2), substituting a new sub-s (1A) into the 1998 Act). If the youth court does decide to make a parenting order at the same time as a referral order, the court must obtain a report from an appropriate officer (Sch 34, para 2(3), inserting new sub-ss (2A) and (2B) into s 9 of the 1998 Act).

By s 20 of PCC(S)A 2000 the youth court may, at the time of imposing a referral order, make an order requiring the parent of the juvenile to attend the meeting of the youth offender panel. Section 22 of the Act deals with attendance at meetings of the panel. Schedule 34, para 4 of the 2003 Act amends s 22 by inserting a new sub-s (2A). This provides that if a parent, who has been ordered by the youth court under s 20 to attend, fails to comply with that order the youth offender panel may refer the case back to the youth court. This would then allow the court the opportunity, inter alia, to decide whether it should now make a parenting order. Schedule 34, paras 5 and 6 of the 2003 Act set out the procedural arrangements in a case where the panel has referred such a case back to the youth court, and provide for a right of appeal where a parenting order has been made.

13

CUSTODIAL SENTENCES OF LESS THAN 12 MONTHS

13.1 INTRODUCTION

The Criminal Justice Act 2003 (CJA 2003) makes important changes to the operation of custodial sentences. The new provisions have their origins in Home Office, *Making Punishments Work: Review of the Sentencing Framework for England and Wales* (July 2001), more generally known as 'the Halliday Report'. The key recommendations on custodial sentences were accepted by the government and restated in their policy document *Justice for All* (Cm 5563, July 2002). This chapter considers three new custodial sentences under the Act: sentences of 'custody plus', provisions for 'intermittent custody', and the new suspended sentence (referred to as 'custody minus' by Halliday).

Intermittent custody is already operational, being piloted in selected court areas from 26 January 2004. The implementation date for custody plus is uncertain but, at the time of writing it is expected that custody plus will be brought into effect in two stages, from December 2005 for offenders aged 18, 19 and 20, and from May 2006 for offenders aged 21 and over. The new suspended sentence will also take effect in two stages. The sentence is expected to become available for those aged 18, 19 and 20 from December 2004, with full implementation from June 2005. The special arrangements involving custodial sentences for dangerous offenders are described in Chapter 14.

Sections 152 and 153 of CJA 2003 specify when custodial sentences can be used, and set out general restrictions on their use. These provisions were considered at 10.5 above. It should also be appreciated that ss 154 and 155 of the Act amend the existing limits on the custodial sentencing powers of magistrates' courts dealing with offenders aged 18 and over, increasing the maximum custodial sentence available from 6 months to 12 months. These provisions were considered at 10.6 above. Sections 156 to 160 set out various procedural requirements with respect to the imposition of custodial (and community) sentences, including pre-sentence reports and requirements in respect of mentally disordered offenders. These matters were discussed at 10.7 above.

13.2 CUSTODY PLUS

Halliday was very critical of the use of custodial sentences of less than 12 months, on the basis that such sentences offered little real opportunity for any worthwhile rehabilitative work to be done with offenders, and that the statistics indicated that reconviction rates (measured as the percentage of those so sentenced who are reconvicted within two years) was very high, at 60%. He stated that such sentences were 'one of the most important deficiencies in the present sentencing framework' (para 3.1). It should be appreciated that at the time of the Halliday Report an offender serving a sentence of less than 12 months would be released automatically at the halfway point of the sentence, and although he would be subject to recall during the second half of the sentence, after release there would be no supervision, licence conditions or other control in the community. Halliday stated that custodial sentences of under 12 months are used 'for large numbers of persistent offenders, with multiple problems and high risks of re-offending, whose offences and record are serious enough to justify a custodial sentence but not so serious that a longer prison sentence would be justified. A more effective recipe for failure could hardly be conceived' (para 3.1).

New sentences of less than 12 months' duration are thereby prescribed in the Act, which the government expects will provide a more effective framework within which to address the needs of offenders. In this respect the judiciary appears to be in agreement with the executive. In *R v McInerney* [2003] 1 Cr App R 627, the guideline case on sentencing in cases of domestic burglary, Lord Woolf CJ was also highly critical of short custodial sentences, although he appeared to have in mind sentences of up to 18 months or even 2 years. His Lordship referred to the effects of the home detention curfew (HDC) scheme, which permitted release of some short sentence prisoners at an earlier point than halfway through the sentence, at the discretion of the prison governor. Such offenders are subject to electronic monitoring, or 'tagging'. This scheme, as described by Lord Woolf, was further extended by statutory instruments in 2002 (see SI 2002/1602) and 2003 (see SI 2003/1602) so as to increase substantially the time during which a short sentence prisoner might be released subject to HDC. Underlying this, of course, is pressure of prison overcrowding at a time when the custodial sentenced population is at an all-time high. For a sentence of 6 months' imprisonment, the minimum period which needs to be served before HDC is now 6 weeks, for a 12 month sentence it is 3 months, and for an 18 month sentence it is $4\,^1/_2$ months. See further *R v Al-Buhairi* [2004] 1 Cr App R (S) 496, and for critical comment by David Thomas on the relationship between HDC and sentencing see the commentary to that case at [2004] Crim LR 147.

13.2.1 The Elements of 'Custody Plus'

Sections 181 and 182 make provision for the new sentence (described by Halliday, and by the Act, as 'custody plus') which will, when in force, replace all sentences of imprisonment under 12 months in length (with the exception of intermittent custody). Currently sentences of imprisonment apply only to offenders aged 21 and over, and the equivalent custodial sentence for 18-, 19- and 20-year-olds is detention in a young offender institution. When s 61 of the Criminal Justice and Court Services Act 2000 is brought into force, the sentence of detention in a young offender institution will be abolished, and the sentence of imprisonment will apply to all offenders aged 18 and over. The current provisions must be read with that pending change in mind, but they will not apply to custodial sentences imposed on offenders aged under 18, for whom the detention and training order will continue to be the standard sentence.

Custody plus will comprise a total custodial sentence term, which must be expressed in weeks, of at least 28 weeks but not more than 51 weeks and, of course, must not exceed the maximum term for the offence (s 181(2)). Custody plus comprises two parts. The first part, 'the custodial period' must be for at least two weeks and not more than 13 weeks, in respect of any one offence (s 181(5)). This part is designed to fulfil the punitive element in the sentence. It is followed by a second part, when the offender is released on licence, under supervision in the community, which must be at least 26 weeks in length (s 181(6)). This is designed to fulfil the reparative and crime reduction purposes of the sentence. When imposing a sentence of custody plus, the court will specify the lengths of the two parts of the sentence, and will have power to attach one or more of a range of specific conditions requiring the offender's compliance during the licence. The conditions are designed to address the rehabilitative needs of the offender.

It will be clear that, when custody plus is introduced, the sentencing court will become responsible for setting the content for the whole of the sentence, both the duration of the custodial period and the duration, content and specified conditions of the supervision in the community. It is the length of the overall sentence which must amount to at least 28 weeks but not more than 51 weeks, and which must be proportionate to the seriousness of the offence committed. Additionally, there is provision in the Act for magistrates (at such time as their custodial sentencing powers are increased) to pass a sentence of 12 months' imprisonment. That sentence will not be a sentence of custody plus, since it will be for a period of more than 51 weeks.

13.2.2 Custody Plus—Consecutive Terms

If a court imposes two or more terms of custody plus which are to be served consecutively, the aggregate length of the terms of imprisonment must not exceed 65 weeks (ie 15 months) and the aggregate length of the custodial periods must not exceed 26 weeks (ie 6 months).

13.2.3 Custody Plus—Licence Conditions

Section 182 lists the requirements which the court may attach to the licence period of a custody plus order. These are:

(a) an unpaid work requirement,
(b) an activity requirement,
(c) a programme requirement,
(d) a prohibited activity requirement,
(e) a curfew requirement,
(f) an exclusion requirement,
(g) a supervision requirement, and
(h) in a case where the offender is aged under 25, an attendance centre requirement.

These eight requirements are drawn from a full list of twelve specified requirements which a court may insert into a community sentence. The operational details of these eight requirements were considered at 12.2.2 to 12.2.7 and 12.2.12 to 12.2.13 above.

Whenever the court makes a custody plus order which requires a licence to contain two or more different requirements, it must consider whether, in the circumstances of the case, the requirements are compatible with each other (s 182(5)). Power to insert such conditions into the licence is made subject to the court ensuring, so far as possible, that the condition or conditions avoid conflict with the offender's religious beliefs, the requirements of any other relevant order to which he may be subject, and avoid interference with the offender's work, schooling or other educational commitments (s 217). The court must also be satisfied that local facilities exist, and that local arrangements are in place, for the carrying out of relevant requirements (s 218). A custody plus order must specify the petty sessions area in which the offender will reside during the licence period (s 216(2)(a)).

The court cannot make an unpaid work requirement unless satisfied that the offender is a suitable person to perform such work (s 199(3)). The court cannot impose an activity requirement unless it has consulted an officer of a local probation board or a member of a youth offending team (as appropriate), is satisfied that it is feasible to secure compliance with the requirement (s 201(3)) and has secured the agreement of any person other than the offender and the responsible officer whose co-operation is required (s 201(4)). The court cannot insert a programme requirement unless the relevant accredited programme has been recommended to the court by an officer of a local probation board or a member of a youth offending team (as appropriate) as being suitable for the offender, the court is satisfied that the programme will be available (s 202(4)) and has secured the agreement of any person other than the offender and the responsible officer whose co-operation is required. The court cannot insert a prohibited activity requirement unless it has consulted an officer of a local probation board or a member of a youth offending team (as appropriate) (s 203(2)).

If the custody plus order contains a curfew requirement or an exclusion requirement, the court *must* also require the licence to contain an electronic monitoring requirement, as defined by s 215 of the Act, *unless* the court is unable to do so because there is some person, other than the offender, whose co-operation is required but who does not consent (s 215(2)), or because electronic monitoring arrangements are not available in the local area (s 218(4)), or because in the particular circumstances of the case the court considers it inappropriate to do so.

If the custody plus order contains an unpaid work requirement, an activity requirement, a programme requirement, a prohibited activity requirement, a supervision requirement or an attendance centre requirement, the court *may* also require the licence to contain an electronic monitoring requirement, unless the court is unable to do so because there is some person, other than the offender, whose co-operation is required but who does not consent (s 215(2)), or because electronic monitoring arrangements are not available in the local area (s 218(4)).

13.2.4 Custody Plus—Further Provisions

Section 187 refers to Sch 10 to the Act, which contains provisions relating to the revocation or amendment of custody plus orders. Schedule 10, para 3 allows for the revocation by an appropriate court, on application by the offender or the responsible officer, of the licence period of the custody plus order, 'having regard to circumstances which have arisen since the order was made'. This does not affect the imprisonment part of the order. Paragraph 4 deals with amendment by reason of change of residence. Paragraph 5 allows for the amendment of any requirement in such an order to be made by the appropriate court on application of the offender, the Secretary of State or the responsible officer. Amendment may involve (a) cancelling a requirement, or (b) replacing it with a requirement of the same kind imposing different obligations.

13.3 INTERMITTENT CUSTODY

Halliday noted that 'partial' or 'intermittent' custody has long been advocated by some as a way of imposing a short custodial sentence while avoiding some of the worst adverse effects of imprisonment, such as loss of the offender's job or home, or damage to family or other relationships. 'Intermittence' could cover weekend imprisonment, or imprisonment for parts of the day or night. The prison service already uses release on temporary licence in support of resettlement of offenders nearing the end of the custodial part of their sentences but Halliday noted that this was a process managed by the prison service and was not a form of sentence in its own right.

In his report Halliday was tentative in recommending intermittent custody. A wide range of practical difficulties in operating such a scheme had been drawn to his attention, many of which had been discussed nearly twenty years earlier in Home Office, *Intermittent Custody* (Cmnd 9281, 1984). Halliday notes the misgivings of the prison service who, at a time of gross overcrowding in prison, felt that it could not accommodate prisoners serving such a sentence. Intermittent custody would be served in local prisons, which are already under the greatest pressure of space and staff resources. Holding prison cell space vacant for days, or parts of days, to accommodate intermittent custody prisoners would be 'difficult, disruptive, and potentially wasteful' (para 5.5) and full-time prisoners might have to be dispersed or have their regimes disrupted to ensure that cell space was available for prisoners returning at weekends from licence periods during the week.

More generally, apart from the practical problems in making the scheme work, there are issues of concern about how sentencers might use the new sentence. If intermittent custody is used for offenders who would otherwise have received prison sentences there will some reduction of pressure on the prison service, but if it is used for those now receiving community sentences the pressure on prison places will be made worse. No doubt for a combination of these concerns, intermittent custody has been made available only to certain trial courts on a pilot basis, from January 2004 (see the Intermittent Custody (Transitory Provisions) Order SI 3283/2003).

At the time of writing the Intermittent Custody Pilot Project is under way. There are 12 participating Crown Court centres and 35 magistrates' courts for female offenders only, two Crown Court centres and three magistrates' courts for male offenders only, and two Crown Court centres and one magistrates' court for both female and male offenders. The pilot courts can impose either weekend or weekday custody. The former runs from Friday evening to Sunday evening and the latter for four days each week, either Monday to Thursday or Tuesday to Friday. Travel time is not included in the custody period. As of 4 May 2004, a total of 34 sentences of intermittent custody had been passed. Eleven of the offenders so sentenced were female.

13.3.1 The Elements of Intermittent Custody

Where the Crown Court passes a sentence of at least 28 weeks and not more than 51 weeks, it may impose an 'intermittent custody order'. As with 'custody plus' the sentence must be expressed in weeks and, of course, the court must not exceed the maximum sentence for the offence. The order will specify the total number of custodial days the offender must serve in prison, and at the same time provide for his release on temporary periods of licence, subject to specified conditions, and at set intervals throughout his sentence, until the total number of custodial days has been served (s 183(1)). The number of custodial days where the Crown Court imposes the sentence must be at least 14 and not more than 90 for any one offence (s 183(5)). The offender must consent to serving the custodial part of his sentence intermittently, in the manner prescribed by the court (183(6)). It should be noted (although this is not apparent from the face of the statute) that some of these provisions operate differently when a magistrates' court is imposing an intermittent custody order. By the Intermittent Custody (Transitory Provisions) Order SI 3283/2003, for a magistrates' court the term of the sentence must be for at least 14 weeks (rather than 28), and not more than 26 weeks (rather than 51). The maximum number of custodial days which can be ordered by a magistrates' court is 45 (rather than 90). These differential periods will apply until such time as s 154 of the 2003 Act, which increases the normal maximum term of imprisonment which can be passed by a magistrates' court from 6 months to 12 months, is brought into effect.

The court cannot make an intermittent custody order unless notified by the Secretary of State that arrangements for implementing such orders are in place locally (s 184(1)). The court cannot make an intermittent custody order unless it has consulted an officer of a local probation board to assess whether the offender is suitable for intermittent custody, has received notification from the Secretary of State that suitable prison accommodation is available for the custodial periods, and that the offender will have suitable accommodation available to him during the licence periods of the sentence (s 184(2)).

13.3.2 Intermittent Custody—Consecutive Terms

If the Crown Court imposes two or more terms of intermittent custody which are to be served consecutively, the aggregate length of the terms of imprisonment must not exceed 65 weeks (ie 15 months) and the aggregate of the numbers of the custodial days must not exceed 180 (s 183(7)). It should be noted (although this is not apparent from the face of the statute) that these provisions operate differently when a magistrates' court is imposing an intermittent custody order. By the Intermittent Custody (Transitory Provisions) Order SI 3283/2003, for a magistrates' court the aggregate length of the terms of imprisonment must be not more than 52 weeks, and the aggregate of the number of custodial days must not be more than 90. These differential periods will apply until such time as s 154 of the 2003 Act, which increases the normal maximum term of imprisonment which can be passed by a magistrates' court from 6 months to 12 months, is brought into effect.

13.3.3 Intermittent Custody—Licence Conditions

Section 185 lists the requirements which the court may attach to the licence periods of an intermittent custody order. These are:

(a) an unpaid work requirement,
(b) an activity requirement,
(c) a programme requirement, and
(d) a prohibited activity requirement.

These four requirements are drawn from a full list of twelve specified requirements which a court may insert into a community sentence. The operational details of these four requirements were considered at 12.2.2 to 12.2.5 above.

Whenever the court makes an intermittent custody order which requires a licence to contain two or more different requirements, it must consider whether, in the circumstances of the case, the requirements are compatible with each other (s 185(2)). Power to insert such conditions into licence periods is made subject to the court ensuring, so far as possible, that the condition or conditions avoid conflict with the offender's religious beliefs, the requirements of any other relevant order to which he may be subject, and avoid interference with the offender's work, schooling or other educational commitments (s 217). The court must also be satisfied that local facilities exist, and that local arrangements are in place, for the carrying out of relevant requirements (s 218). An intermittent custody order must specify the petty sessions area in which the offender will reside during the licence periods (s 216(2)(b)).

The court cannot make an unpaid work requirement unless satisfied that the offender is a suitable person to perform such work (s 199(3)). The court cannot impose an activity requirement unless it has consulted an officer of a local probation board or a member of a youth offending team (as appropriate) and is satisfied that it is feasible to secure compliance with the requirement (s 201(3)) and has secured the agreement of any person other than the offender and the responsible officer whose co-operation is required (s 201(4)). The court cannot insert a programme requirement unless the relevant accredited programme has been recommended to the court by an officer of a local probation board or a member of a youth offending team (as appropriate) as being suitable for the offender, and the court is satisfied that the programme will be available (s 202(4)) and has secured the agreement of any person other than the offender and the responsible officer whose co-operation is required. The court cannot insert a prohibited activity requirement unless it has consulted an officer of a local probation board or a member of a youth offending team (as appropriate) (s 203(2)).

Where the intermittent custody order contains one or more of the above requirements, the court *may* also require the licence to contain an electronic monitoring requirement, unless the court is unable to do so because there is some person, other than the offender, whose co-operation is required but who does not consent (s 215(2)), or because electronic monitoring arrangements are not available in the local area (s 218(4)).

13.3.4 Intermittent Custody—Further Provisions

Section 186 provides that payments under s 21 of the Prison Act 1952 (expenses of conveyance to prison) are not available in relation to an intermittent custody order, but that an offender on whom an intermittent custody order has been made may be reimbursed for the whole or part of the cost incurred in travelling to and from prison during the licence periods. An offender who has been temporarily released under an intermittent custody order shall be deemed to be unlawfully at large if he fails to return at the end of his temporary licence period (s 186(3)). Section 186(5) creates an offence of remaining at large after temporary release in pursuance of an intermittent custody order.

Section 187 refers to Sch 10 to the Act, which contains provisions relating to the amendment of intermittent custody orders. Schedule 10, para 3 allows for the revocation by an appropriate court, on application by the offender or the responsible officer, of the licence periods from the intermittent custody order, 'having regard to circumstances which have arisen since the order was made'. This does not affect the imprisonment part of the order. Schedule 10, para 4 allows for amendment by reason of change of residence. Paragraphs 5 and 6 allow for the amendment of any requirement in such an order to be made by the appropriate court on application of the offender, the Secretary of State or the responsible officer. Amendment may involve (a) cancelling a requirement, or (b) replacing it with a requirement of the same kind imposing different obligations. The appropriate court may also, on application (a) vary the licence periods within the order or (b) require the offender to stay in prison to complete the required number of custodial days.

13.4 SUSPENDED SENTENCE

Powers to suspend a sentence of imprisonment have been available to the criminal courts since the Criminal Justice Act 1967. The suspended sentence is a sentence of imprisonment, and it should be imposed only where the offence is serious enough to justify the passing of an immediate custodial sentence of not more than two years, but where the mitigation available to the offender is such as to allow the court to hold that term of imprisonment in suspense for a period of between one year and two years (PCC(S)A 2000, s 118(1) and (2)). If the offender committed a further offence within the operational period of the suspended sentence, the suspended sentence would be activated, normally in full, and normally required to run consecutively to any custodial sentence imposed for the fresh offence (2000 Act, s 119). Custodial sentences other than imprisonment, such as detention in a young offender institution, cannot be suspended, so the suspended sentence has only ever been available to offenders aged 21 and over.

The suspended sentence was at one time a popular sentencing tool, since it offered an opportunity for the sentencer to 'mark out' the seriousness of the offence but, at the same, avoid imposing imprisonment on an offender who could offer significant personal mitigation and for whom there seemed little chance of his reoffending. The anomaly of the sentence, however, was that an offence regarded as so serious that only custody could be justified generally resulted in the offender leaving court with no immediate penalty at all. It is true that a fine could be added to a suspended sentence, and there was also a possibility (rarely used in practice) of adding an element of supervision (2000 Act, s 122). The rationale for the suspended sentence was one of individual deterrence, with the threat of activation of the sentence hanging over the offender's head. The suspended sentence did not fit well within the proportionality framework of the Criminal Justice Act 1991, and the use of the suspended sentence was greatly curtailed by that Act. Its operation was restricted to cases displaying 'exceptional circumstances' only (2000 Act, s 118(4)). Since the 1991 Act the Court of Appeal has steadfastly refused to offer any general guidance on the meaning of 'exceptional circumstances' (see *R v Okinikan* [1993] 1 WLR 173), and those reported appellate cases in which such circumstances have been found are hard to reconcile with other cases in which they have not.

13.4.1 The Elements of the New Suspended Sentence

Section 189(1) provides that where a court passes a sentence of imprisonment of at least 28 weeks but not more than 51 weeks and provided, of course, that the term does not exceed the maximum sentence for the offence, the court may suspend that sentence for a period of between six months and two years while at the same time ordering the offender to undertake one or more of a range of requirements in the community. It is this element of work or supervision in the community which clearly marks out the new form of the suspended sentence from the old form. It should also be noted, however, that the longest sentence which can now be suspended is one of 51 weeks, whereas formerly a prison sentence of up to two years could be suspended. When s 61 of the Criminal Justice and Court Services Act 2000 is brought into force, the sentence of detention in a young offender institution will be abolished. Offenders who would have received such sentences will thereafter be eligible to be sentenced to imprisonment, which will become the standard custodial sentences for those aged 18, 19 and 20 as well as for those aged 21 and over. No date for the implementation of s 61 has yet been set, but by s 333(1) and Sch 38, para 1 of the 2003 Act, if relevant sentencing provisions of the 2003 Act are brought into force before the sentence of detention in a young offender institution is abolished, the sentencing provisions may be modified accordingly. This will mean that the suspended sentence will become available for offenders aged 18, 19 or 20 as well as for those aged 21 and over. The detention and training order, the standard custodial sentence for offenders aged under 18, will not be affected.

The period in the suspended sentence during which the offender is to undertake these specified requirements is called the 'supervision period' of the suspended sentence, and the entire length of the order is called the 'operational period' of the suspended sentence. The supervision period must not last longer than the operational period, but each of the two periods must last between six months and two years (s 189(3) and (4)). The sentence of imprisonment imposed by the court will not take effect unless (a) the offender fails to comply with the requirements imposed by the court, or (b) he commits another offence during the operational period of the suspended sentence. There will henceforth be two ways of 'breaching' a suspended sentence, while formerly there was only one.

Section 189(6) states that a suspended sentence is to be treated as a sentence of imprisonment. This reflects the position in respect of the earlier form of the suspended sentence. It is an important provision, because it means that the threshold provisions and all the other general sentencing provisions which apply to custodial sentences also apply to the suspended sentence. This must mean that a suspended sentence cannot be passed unless the offence is serious enough to justify the imposition of a immediate prison term of the same length. One of the problems with the practical operation of the previous form of the suspended sentence was that sentencers did not always comply with the terms of the statute, and passed suspended sentences in some cases which did not cross the custody threshold but where it was thought that the putative deterrent effect of the suspended sentence might be more appropriate than a community sentence. Using the suspended sentence in such a way clearly does not divert the offender from custody and, given the wording of the provisions on breach, if the offender commits any further offence (or, now, fails to comply with a work or supervision requirement of the order) they are very likely then to receive custody.

13.4.2 Suspended Sentence—Consecutive Terms

Section 189(2) states that where two or more sentences imposed on the same occasion are to be served consecutively, the power to suspend sentence is not exercisable in relation to any of the sentences unless the aggregate of the terms does not exceed 65 weeks (ie 15 months).

13.4.3 Suspended Sentence—Combining with Other Sentences or Orders

Section 189(5) states that a court which passes a suspended sentence on an offender must not on the same occasion impose a community sentence in respect of that offence or any other offence for which he is dealt with by the court. The limitation clearly flows from the fact that requirements of work or supervision in the community are now an essential part of the suspended sentence. To pass a community sentence at the same time would create a confusing duplication. The subsection does not say that a community sentence could not be imposed on an offender who is already subject to a suspended sentence, but that would appear to be an undesirable sentencing combination. There is no restriction on imposing a fine at the same time as a suspended sentence, and ancillary provisions such as compensation orders, restitution orders, or deprivation orders, could also be imposed as appropriate.

13.4.4 Suspended Sentence—Imposition of Requirements

Section 190 lists the requirements with which the court may order the offender to comply during the supervision period of the suspended sentence. These are:

(a) an unpaid work requirement,
(b) an activity requirement,
(c) a programme requirement,
(d) a prohibited activity requirement,
(e) a curfew requirement,
(f) an exclusion requirement,
(g) a residence requirement,
(h) a mental health treatment requirement,
(i) a drug rehabilitation requirement,

(j) an alcohol treatment requirement,

(k) a supervision requirement, and

(l) in a case where the offender is aged under 25, an attendance centre requirement.

These twelve requirements are the same as those which a court may insert into a community sentence. The operational details of these requirements were considered at 12.2.2 to 12.2.13 above.

Whenever the court passes a suspended sentence which contains two or more different requirements, it must consider whether, in the circumstances of the case, the requirements are compatible with each other (s 190(5)). Power to insert such conditions into the licence is made subject to the court ensuring, so far as possible, that the condition or conditions avoid conflict with the offender's religious beliefs, the requirements of any other relevant order to which he may be subject, and avoid interference with the offender's work, schooling or other educational commitments (s 217). The court must also be satisfied that local facilities exist, and that local arrangements are in place, for the carrying out of relevant requirements (s 218). A suspended sentence must specify the petty sessions area in which the offender will reside (s 216(1)).

The court cannot make an unpaid work requirement unless satisfied that the offender is a suitable person to perform such work (s 199(3)). The court cannot impose an activity requirement unless it has consulted an officer of a local probation board or a member of a youth offending team (as appropriate), is satisfied that it is feasible to secure compliance with the requirement (s 201(3)) and has secured the agreement of any person other than the offender and the responsible officer whose co-operation is required (s 201(4)). The court cannot insert a programme requirement unless the relevant accredited programme has been recommended to the court by an officer of a local probation board or a member of a youth offending team (as appropriate) as being suitable for the offender, the court is satisfied that the programme will be available (s 202(4)) and has secured the agreement of any person other than the offender and the responsible officer whose co-operation is required. The court cannot insert a prohibited activity requirement unless it has consulted an officer of a local probation board or a member of a youth offending team (as appropriate) (s 203(2)). The court cannot insert a mental health requirement unless the court is satisfied on the evidence of a registered medical practitioner that the mental condition of the offender is such as requires and is susceptible to treatment, does not warrant the making of a hospital or guardianship order, that arrangements have been made for the treatment to be carried out, and that the offender has consented to the inclusion of the mental health requirement into the suspended sentence (s 207(3)). The court may not insert a drug rehabilitation requirement unless it is satisfied that the offender is dependent on, or has a propensity to misuse a controlled drug and that his dependency or propensity is such as requires and may be susceptible to, treatment, that arrangements can be made for the treatment to be carried out, that the requirement has been recommended by the responsible officer, and that the offender has expressed his willingness to comply with the requirement (s 209(2)). The court may not impose an alcohol treatment requirement unless it is satisfied that the offender is dependent on alcohol, that his dependency is such as requires and may be susceptible to treatment, that arrangements can be made for the treatment to be carried out, and that the offender has expressed his willingness to comply with the requirement.

If the suspended sentence contains a curfew requirement or an exclusion requirement, the court *must* also require the licence to contain an electronic monitoring requirement, as defined by s 215 of the Act, *unless* the court is unable to do so because there is some person, other than the offender, whose co-operation is required but who does not consent (s 215(2)), or because electronic monitoring arrangements are not available in the local area (s 218(4)), or because in the particular circumstances of the case the court considers it inappropriate to do so.

If the suspended sentence contains an unpaid work requirement, an activity requirement, a programme requirement, a prohibited activity requirement, a residence requirement, a mental health treatment requirement, a drug rehabilitation requirement, an alcohol treatment requirement, a supervision requirement or an attendance centre requirement, the court *may* also require the licence to contain an electronic monitoring requirement, unless the court is unable to do so because there is some person, other than the offender, whose co-operation is required but who does not consent (s 215(2)), or because electronic monitoring arrangements are not available in the local area (s 218(4)).

13.4.5 Suspended Sentence—Power to provide for Review

Section 191(1) confers a discretion on the court to provide that a suspended sentence is made subject to periodic review, at review hearings, at specified intervals of time. The court may order the offender to attend those hearings, and it may order the responsible officer, before each review, to provide to the court a report on the offender's progress under the suspended sentence. If the offender is subject to a suspended sentence which contains a drug rehabilitation requirement, such requirement is already subject to court review hearings under s 210 of the 2003 Act, so s 191(2) provides that the suspended sentence itself cannot be subject to review under s 191(1). A review hearing is conducted by the court responsible for the order, and s 191(3) to (5) specifies which court is responsible for review of the suspended sentence in particular situations.

Section 192 describes what is to happen at the review hearings. Section 192(1) permits the court to amend any community requirement of the suspended sentence order, after consideration of the report from the supervising officer. This is limited by s 192(2) which explains that the court cannot amend the order by adding a requirement of a different kind unless the offender consents to that new requirement, but it can impose a requirement of the same kind. The offender's consent is always required before the court amends a drug treatment requirement, an alcohol treatment requirement, or a mental health treatment requirement (s 192(2)(b)), although the reference in this subsection to a drug treatment requirement seems to be inconsistent with s 191(2). The court may also extend the supervision period but not so that it infringes the normal rules on suspended sentences in s 189(3) or (4), by lasting for longer than two years from the date of the original order or ending after the operational period is over.

Under s 192(4) if, on the basis of the report from the responsible officer, the court is of the opinion that the offender is making satisfactory progress it can dispense with the next pending review hearing, or may amend the order so that subsequent reviews can be held by considering the papers rather than by a full hearing. The court may order the offender to attend a review hearing if progress is no longer satisfactory, or it may adjust the intervals of time between review hearings (s 192(5) and (7)).

13.4.6 Suspended Sentence—Breach, Commission of Further Offence, and Amendment

Section 193 refers to Sch 12, which contains provisions relating to the breach, revocation and amendment of the community requirements of suspended sentence orders, and to the effect of the offender being convicted of a further offence.

Paragraphs 4 and 5 of Sch 12 are the key provisions here. By para 4, if the responsible officer is of the opinion that the offender has failed without reasonable excuse to comply with any of the community requirements of the suspended sentence, the officer must give a *warning* describing the circumstances of the failure, stating that the failure is unacceptable, and informing the offender that if within the next 12 months he again fails to comply with any requirement of the order, he will be brought back before the court. By para 5, if there has been a warning, and within 12 months there is a further failure without reasonable excuse to comply, the responsible officer must cause an information to be laid before a magistrate, or before the Crown Court, in respect of that second failure. Paragraphs 6 and 7 deal with details with the arrangements for issue of summons or warrant by the magistrate or by the Crown Court.

Paragraph 8 describes the powers of the court when dealing with a breach of a community requirement in a suspended sentence, or on conviction of a further offence. If it is proved to the satisfaction of the court before which the offender is brought that he has failed without reasonable cause to comply with any of the community requirements or has been convicted of an offence committed during the operational period of the suspended sentence, the court must deal with him in one of the following ways set out in para 8(2):

(a) to order that the suspended sentence takes effect with the original term and custodial period unaltered, or

(b) to order that the suspended sentence takes effect with the substitution of a *lesser term* (which, however, cannot be less than 28 weeks) and/or the substitution of a *lesser custodial period* (which, however, cannot be less than 2 weeks), or

(c) to amend the order by imposing more onerous community requirements or extending the supervision period (but not so that it exceeds two years in total or ends later than the operational period) or extending the operational period (but not so that it exceeds two years in total).

By para 8(3), the court must make an order under para 8(2)(a) or (b) above unless it is of the opinion that it would be unjust to do so in view of all the circumstances. The circumstances include (by para 8(4)), the extent to which the offender has complied with the community requirements of the suspended sentence order, and (where the offender has breached the suspended sentence by committing a further offence) the facts of that subsequent offence. If the court is of the opinion that it would be unjust to order that the suspended sentence should take effect in full, it should state its reasons. It would seem that pre-existing principles derived from case law on breach of community sentences (where the offender has failed to comply with community requirements) and breach of suspended sentence (where the offender has committed a further offence) will be of some value, at least in the short term, in applying these provisions. Their operation will be a crucial factor in determining whether the net impact of the suspended sentence will be to reduce, or increase, the custodial population.

By para 9, if the court makes an order in para 8(2)(a) or (b) that the suspended sentence is to take effect, the court *must* also make a custody plus order and *may* order that the sentence takes effect immediately or on the expiry of another term of imprisonment imposed on the offender.

Paragraphs 13 to 18 deal with various forms of amendment to community requirements in a suspended sentence order which may be made by an appropriate court on application by the offender or the responsible officer, or as to change of residence and other matters.

14

DANGEROUS OFFENDERS

14.1 INTRODUCTION

While, as was explained in Chapter 13, 'custody plus' will in due course become the standard custodial sentence of up to 51 weeks in length, something need to be said briefly by way of explanation in relation to longer custodial sentences under the Criminal Justice Act 2003 (CJA 2003). Determinate custodial sentences of 12 months and upwards (whether of imprisonment, long-term detention under s 91 of the Powers of Criminal Courts (Sentencing) Act 2000 (PCC(S)A 2000) or, for so long as that sentence continues to exist, detention in a young offender institution) will continue to be governed by the general principles on the imposition of custodial sentences and determination of the length of such sentences (see 10.5). Sentences of that length will be the exclusive province of the Crown Court, except that magistrates' courts will (when their powers are in due course so extended) have power to pass a sentence of imprisonment of exactly 12 months. The 12-month sentence will be a sentence of imprisonment, and not a sentence of custody plus, the maximum duration of which is to be 51 weeks.

The main changes to custodial sentences of 12 months or more will be in respect of release on licence. This matter is considered in detail in Chapter 15, but it is worth noting here that, once the relevant provisions are in force, if a court passes a custodial sentence of imprisonment of 12 months or more, the normal rule will be automatic release from custody at the halfway point, although the extesion of the home detention curfew (HDC) scheme to longer sentences may well mean in practice that the offender will leave custody earlier than that (see further 15.3.1). The Parole Board will not be involved in setting a date for release from a determinate sentence, even where the sentence is one of 4 years or more, unless the offender is serving an extended sentence for a specified violent or sexual offence. From the offender's release at the halfway point of the sentence (or for up to 135 days after a quarter of their sentence has been served, on HDC), he or she will be made subject to requirements on licence to be served in the community. This period on licence will operate in a similar manner to a community sentence. Section 238 of CJA 2003 empowers the sentencing court to recommend, when passing a sentence of 12 months or more, particular requirements which in its view ought to be included in the offender's licence once he is released. It is clear from the working of the Act that these are recommendations only, and that the licence conditions will actually be set shortly before release by the prison and probation service (national offender management service, or NOMS, as it is to become). This is because the sentencer will not, in most cases, be well placed to anticipate the most suitable requirements for an offender who will be released months, or years, later.

The provisions in relation to custodial sentences of 12 months or more are expected to be brought into force in spring 2005.

Sections 224 to 236 and Sch 15 to CJA 2003 provide an entirely new set of measures for sentencing 'dangerous offenders'. They are also expected to come into force in spring 2005.

(1) They replace measures in PCC(S)A 2000, s 79(2)(b) and s 80(2)(b), for the imposition of a 'longer than commensurate' determinate custodial sentences, which could be imposed on an offender convicted of a violent offence or a sexual offence, and from whom it is necessary to protect the public from serious harm. These provisions date from the Criminal Justice Act 1991. Sections 79 and 80 are repealed by Sch 37 to the 2003 Act.

(2) They replace Crown Court powers to make an order extending the period of supervision on licence appropriate for an offender convicted of a violent offence or a sexual offence (extended sentence provisions under section 85 of the 2000 Act). Section 85 is repealed by section 303(d)(ii) of the 2003 Act.

(3) They replace the 'automatic' life sentence for the second 'serious offence', under s 109 of the 2000 Act (a sentence which was the subject of restrictive interpretation by the Court of Appeal in *R v Offen (No 2)* [2001] 1 WLR 253). The sentencing court has been required to set a specified minimum period under s 82A of the 2000 Act which the offender must serve before being considered for early release. Section 109 is repealed by s 303(d)(iv) of the 2003 Act.

It should be noted, however, that in any case where the sentence for the offence would otherwise fall within the new provisions for the sentencing of dangerous offenders, nothing shall prevent the sentencing court from imposing a hospital or guardianship order under the Mental Health Act 1983 instead (2003 Act, Sch 32, para 38).

The Home Office report *Making Punishments Work: Review of the Sentencing Framework for England and Wales* (July 2001) (the 'Halliday Report') criticized this disparate set of provisions for sexual and violent offenders and proposed a different sentencing structure to deal with this kind of offender. Halliday proposed that, after release from the custodial part of the sentence, supervision of a dangerous offender should last right up until the end of the sentence, both to improve public confidence in the sentencing system and to increase the likely effectiveness of work to reduce re-offending (para 4.7). There would be liability to recall if conditions of supervision were breached. As well as lasting longer, supervision should be more intensive, with offender programmes begun in prison continuing 'seamlessly' into community supervision and resettlement (para 4.9). In particular, violent or sexual offenders who present a risk of serious harm to the community should be subject to a power of the court to extend the supervisory part of the sentence.

The Act introduces a new scheme of sentences for offenders who have been assessed as dangerous, and who have committed a specified 'sexual offence' or 'violent offence', where the court is of the opinion that 'there is a significant risk to members of the public of serious harm occasioned by the commission by him of further specified offences'. Under the new scheme, dangerous offenders who have been convicted of such a trigger offence (all of which are listed in Sch 15, and for which the maximum penalty is between 2 and 10 years), will be given an 'extended sentence'. The extended sentence will be a determinate sentence, served in custody at least to the halfway point. Release during the whole of the second half of the sentence will be subject to the positive recommendation of the Parole Board. Additionally, extended supervision periods of up to 5 years for violent offenders, and up to 8 years for sexual offenders *must* be added to the sentence.

If an offender has been 'assessed as dangerous' and has been convicted of an offence listed in Sch 15 whose maximum penalty is 10 years or more, he will receive *either* a sentence of imprisonment for public protection under s 225 of the 2003 Act *or* a discretionary life sentence. If the offender has been assessed as dangerous, and has been convicted of an offence listed in Sch 15 which carries a maximum sentence of life imprisonment, the court must consider the seriousness of the offence when deciding which of the two possible sentences to impose. For either sentence the court *must* specify a minimum term which the offender is required to serve in custody. After this point the offender will remain in custody until the Parole Board is satisfied that the risk which the offender represents has diminished, such that they can be released and be supervised in the community. Offenders aged under 18 are made subject to similar provisions.

14.2 DANGEROUS OFFENDERS—SPECIFIED OFFENCES

Section 224 defines 'specified offence', 'serious offence', and 'serious harm' for the purposes of these provisions. 'Specified offences' are those sexual offences or violent offences which are listed in Sch 15 (s 224(1)). It should be appreciated that these offences are quite different from the list of sexual offences and the definition of violent offence which was formerly to be found in s 161 of the 2000 Act. All of the 'sexual offences' or 'violent offences' in Sch 15 carry a maximum penalty of two years' imprisonment or more. A 'serious offence' is defined as a specified sexual or violent offence which carries a maximum penalty of 10 years' imprisonment or more, including life imprisonment (s 224(2)). 'Serious harm' means death or serious personal injury, whether physical or psychological (s 224(3)).

There are no fewer than 65 specified violent offences in Sch 15. It is notable that Parliament has provided a *list* of such offences this time, rather than giving a general definition of 'violent offence', as it has previously done in s 161(3) of the 2000 Act. The former definition stated that a violent offence was an offence 'which leads, or is intended to lead, to a person's death or physical injury to a person . . .'. An offence such as robbery, for example, would normally qualify under this definition, but sometimes would not, depending on the precise facts of the case (see, for example, *R v Khan* (1995) 16 Cr App R (S) 180, compared with *A-G's Reference* (*No 113 of 2001*) [2002] 2 Cr App R (S) 269). Robbery is now *always* a violent offence for these purposes, since robbery is one of the specified offences in Sch 15. Paragraph 64 of that schedule also makes it clear that aiding, abetting, counselling, procuring, inciting, attempting or conspiring to commit any of the specified violent offences is also covered. There are also 88 specified sexual offences in Sch 15. Parliament has provided a list of such offences, as it did under the former provisions in s 161(2) of the 2000 Act. Paragraph 153 of Sch 15 also makes it clear that aiding, abetting, counselling, procuring, inciting, attempting or conspiring to commit any of the specified sexual offences is also covered. The list of sexual offences is such a long list partly because it contains both the sexual offences in the Sexual Offences Act 1956, and the new sexual offences in the Sexual Offences Act 2003 which will replace them. The Sexual Offences Act 2003 came into effect on 1 May 2004. The old 1956 sexual offences continue in place only in respect of offences committed before that date.

14.3 LIFE SENTENCE OR CUSTODY FOR PUBLIC PROTECTION

Section 225(1) applies where:

(a) a person aged 18 or over is convicted of a serious offence [ie which carries a maximum penalty of 10 years or more], which is committed after the commencement of this section, and
(b) the court is of the opinion that there is a significant risk to members of the public of serious harm occasioned by the commission by him of further specified offences.

Then, if the offence with which the person has been convicted carries life as its maximum penalty and 'the court considers that the seriousness of the offence, or of the offence and one or more offences associated with it, is such as to justify the imposition of a sentence of imprisonment for life', the court *must* impose a life sentence (s 225(2)). If the offence of conviction does not carry life imprisonment as its maximum penalty, or if it does but the court considers that the seriousness of the offence does not justify a life sentence, it *must* impose a sentence of public protection (s 225(3)).

This section is bound to attract a fair amount of case law in the first few years, just as the provisions on 'longer than commensurate' sentences under the 1991 Act did. It is difficult to judge how often the courts will invoke s 225 rather than impose a proportionate sentence to reflect the seriousness of the offence. Guidance, whether on a case by case basis from the Court of Appeal, or in the form of more comprehensive guidelines from the Sentencing Guidelines Council, will be needed on the meaning of sub-s 225(1)(b). In particular, the phrases 'significant risk' and 'serious harm', are crucial. Does 'significant risk' mean 'high risk' or 'more than minimal risk'? It should be noted that the 'significant risk' relates to the commission of 'further *specified* violent or sexual offences' and not 'further *serious* violent or sexual offences'. There must, however, be a 'significant risk' of '*serious* harm'. The latter phrase was used in the earlier provisions. But the threshold for 'serious harm' may now be somewhat lower than before, given the inclusion within Sch 15 of offences such as attempted assault occasioning actual bodily harm (paras 20 and 64(c)), or indecent exposure (para 149).

It has been decided under the earlier law that a sentence for public protection could in principle be imposed where only a small group of the public, or perhaps only one person, was at future risk from the offender (*R v Hashi* (1995) 16 Cr App R (S) 121; *R v Nicholas* (1994) 15 Cr App R (S) 381). It is likely that the same approach would be adopted under the new provisions. There is a difficult issue in relation to sexual offences which have been committed by the offender against a child within the family. If there is now no chance that the offender and the victim would ever be in contact again, it would seem that there is no significant risk to members of the public, and the offender would be sentenced on ordinary principles of proportionality and not within s 225 (see, for example, *R v L* (1994) 15 Cr App R (S) 501; *R v S* (1995) 16 Cr App R (S) 303).

Section 226(1) applies where:

(a) a person aged under 18 is convicted of a serious offence [ie which carries a maximum penalty of 10 years or more], which is committed after the commencement of this section, and

(b) the court is of the opinion that there is a significant risk to members of the public of serious harm occasioned by the commission by him of further specified offences.

Then, if the offence with which the person under 18 has been convicted carries detention for life under s 91 of PCC(S)A 2000 as its maximum penalty and 'the court considers that the seriousness of the offence, or of the offence and one or more offences associated with it, is such as to justify the imposition of a sentence of detention for life', the court *must* impose a sentence of detention for life (s 226(2)). If the case does not come within s 226(2), the court must choose between a sentence of detention for public protection and an extended sentence. If the court considers that an extended sentence under s 228 would not be adequate for public protection, the court must impose a sentence of detention for public protection (s 226(3)).

14.4 EXTENDED SENTENCES

Section 227 replaces and extends the previous provisions for extended sentence supervision for sexual and violent offenders contained in s 85 of PCC(S)A 2000. The previous version allowed the court sentencing a violent or sexual offender to make an order which extended the period of supervision on licence which the offender would receive after release from the custodial part of their sentence. The provisions were complex and sometimes misunderstood by sentencers, which prompted the Court of Appeal to issue sentencing guidelines on the proper use of extended sentences under s 85 in *R v Nelson* [2002] 1 Cr App R (S) 565.

The new provisions for extended sentences are applicable to offenders aged 18 and over convicted of a specified violent or sexual offence. Section 227 applies where:

(a) a person aged 18 or over is convicted of a specified offence other than a serious offence [ie which carries a maximum penalty of between 2 years and 10 years], which is committed after the commencement of this section, and

(b) the court is of the opinion that there is a significant risk to members of the public of serious harm occasioned by the commission by him of further specified offences.

In these circumstances the court *must* impose an extended sentence of imprisonment, which is a sentence of imprisonment (not exceeding the maximum for the offence) the term of which is equal to the aggregate of (a) the appropriate custodial term (not exceeding the maximum for the offence) and (b) a further period (the extension period) on licence, of such length as the court considers necessary to protect members of the public from serious harm occasioned by the commission by him of further specified offences (s 227(2)).

The custodial term of the extended sentence is the commensurate sentence appropriate to the offence or (if that commensurate sentence would be less than 12 months), a term of 12 months (s 227(3)). The extension period must not exceed 5 years in the case of a specified violent offence and must not exceed 8 years in the case of a specified sexual offence (s 227(4)). During the second half of the appropriate custodial term the offender may be released on the recommendation of the Parole Board (s 247).

Section 228 applies the extended sentence provisions to young offenders aged under 18, who are convicted of a specified violent or sexual offence. Section 228 applies where:

(a) a person aged under 18 is convicted of a specified offence committed after the commencement of this section, and

(b) the court considers —

(i) that there is a significant risk to members of the public of serious harm occasioned by the commission by him of further specified offences, and

(ii) where the specified offence is a serious offence that the case is not one in which the court is required by section 226(2) to impose a sentence of detention for life or by section 226(3) to impose a sentence of detention for public protection.

In these circumstances the court *must* impose an extended sentence of detention, which is a sentence of detention (not exceeding the maximum for the offence) the term of which is equal to the aggregate of (a) the appropriate custodial term (not exceeding the maximum for the offence) and (b) a further period (the extension period) on licence, of such length as the court considers necessary to protect members of the public from serious harm occasioned by the commission by the young offender of further specified offences (s 228(2)).

The custodial term of the extended sentence is such term as the court considers appropriate which must be at least 12 months (s 228(3)). The extension period must not exceed 5 years in the case of a specified violent offence and must not exceed 8 years in the case of a specified sexual offence (s 228(4)). During the second half of the appropriate custodial term the young offender may be released on the recommendation of the Parole Board (s 247). A person sentenced to be detained under s 228 is liable to be detained in such place as may be determined by the Secretary of State (s 235).

14.5 THE ASSESSMENT OF DANGEROUSNESS

Section 229 is an important section which deals with the necessary evidence base for the assessment of dangerousness required for the court to establish whether, under any of the ss 225 to 228, the offender poses a 'significant risk to members of the public of serious harm occasioned by the commission by him of further specified offences' and therefore whether the offender is eligible for one of the new sentences for dangerous offenders. 'Serious harm' means 'death or serious personal injury, whether physical or psychological' (s 224(3)). The definition of serious harm, and the risk criteria are based on the existing provisions at s 161(4) of PCC(S)A 2000, but with some significant changes, especially the 'assumption' of the offender's dangerousness in s 229(3).

If, at the time the specified offence was committed, the offender had not been previously convicted of any specified offence, or was aged under 18, the court in deciding whether the offender poses a 'significant risk . . .' etc:

(a) *must* take into account all such information as is available to it about the nature and circumstances of the offences,
(b) *may* take into account any information which is before it about any pattern of behaviour of which the offence forms part, and
(c) *may* take into account any information about the offender which is before it (s 229(2)).

It seems that in such a case the court will be relying upon the facts of the offence (especially where these have emerged in some detail during the course of a contested trial), the contents of a pre-sentence report, and the contents of any other relevant report, such as a psychiatric report.

If, at the time the specified offence was committed, the offender was aged 18 or over, or had been previously convicted of one or more specified offence, the court *must assume that* the offender poses a 'significant risk . . .' etc *unless*, after taking into account:

(a) all such information as is available to it about the nature and circumstances of each of the offences,

(b) where appropriate, any information which is before it about any pattern of behaviour of which any of the offences forms part, and

(c) any information about the offender which is before it,

the court considers that it would be unreasonable to conclude that there is such a risk (s 229(3)).

In such a case the court will be relying upon the facts of the offence (especially where these have emerged in some detail during the course of a contested trial), information on the defendant's previous conviction(s), the contents of a pre-sentence report, and the contents of any other relevant report, such as a psychiatric report. It can perhaps be assumed that some of the case law applicable to the imposing of longer than commensurate sentences under the 2000 Act will continue to be relevant under the new scheme. The Court of Appeal has held in *R v Oudkerk* (1995) 16 Cr App R (S) 172 that the court must be sure that it is basing its decision on accurate information. There may be cases involving factual disputes between the prosecution and the defence that a *Newton* hearing will have to be held to see if the prosecution can establish the disputed facts to the criminal standard of proof (see *R v Newton* (1982) 77 Cr App R 13 and numerous authorities following and applying that case).

The need to ensure accuracy is equally important when there is uncertainty about the facts or circumstances of previous convictions of the offender. It may be necessary, according to *R v Samuels* (1995) 16 Cr App R (S) 856, to investigate the circumstances of an earlier offence to see if the offender really does constitute a risk. Section 231 deals with the unusual situation where an offender has been sentenced to imprisonment or detention for public protection and then a previous conviction without which the court would not have been required to make the assumption in s 229(3) is set aside on appeal.

It was held in *R v Baverstock* (1993) 14 Cr App R (S) 471 that a judge should not pass a longer than commensurate sentence without first giving a warning to defence counsel that this is a possibility. This same point applies when the court is considering imposing a discretionary life sentence, and it was applied to extended sentences under s 85 of the 2000 Act by the Court of Appeal in *R v Nelson* [2002] 1 Cr App R (S) 565. It is submitted that this is a valuable principle, and should be taken to apply to the new range of sentences for dangerous offenders under the 2003 Act.

15

RELEASE ON LICENCE

15.1 INTRODUCTION

The last major restructuring of the law on parole and early release was in the 1991 Criminal Justice Act subject to further amendments made by the Crime and Disorder Act 1998 which brought in the additional possibility of discretionary early release, for up to two months prior to the normal release date, on electronically monitored home detention curfew, otherwise known as 'tagging' or HDC. As far as prisoners serving fixed-term sentences were concerned, the basic scheme of the 1991 Act depended on a distinction between short-term and long-term prisoners, the latter covering those serving four years or more. Short-term prisoners were given automatic early release once they had served 50% of the sentence whereas long-term prisoners became eligible for release at that point only if the Parole Board recommended it. However, once a long-term prisoner reached the two-thirds point in the sentence they too became entitled to automatic early release. Except for sentences of less than 12 months, early release was initially on licence and thus subject to supervision up to the three-quarters point of the sentence after which the release became unconditional save for the possibility of being returned to serve the remaining term if there is further offending during the currency of the original sentence. Early release for sentences under 12 months was not on licence or under supervision even up to the three-quarters point because supervision for periods of less than three months was not considered to be meaningful or realistic.

The scheme introduced by Chapter 6 of Part 12 of the Criminal Justice Act 2003 (CJA 2003) for fixed-term prisoners builds upon but has significant differences from the 1991 scheme (the relevant provisions of CJA 1991 are repealed by Sch 37, Pt 7). The new scheme is essentially (and by name) much more a scheme for *release on licence* up to the end of the sentence and as an integral part of it, aiming to minimize the risks of re-offending following release, rather than *early release* as a concession reducing the normal period of custody. Some of the more significant changes from the 1991 scheme are as follows.

Firstly the distinction between long-term and short-term prisoners disappears. Whether the sentence is above or below 4 years, the normal rule will be automatic release on licence halfway through the sentence. The Parole Board will not need to consider release on licence for the normal fixed-term prisoner, even one serving 4 years or more as release on licence will be automatic at the halfway point. Instead the Parole Board's attention will be focused, as far as fixed-term prisoners are concerned, on those given extended sentences for specified violent or sexual offences under s 227 or 228 (see Chapter 14). Such extended sentence prisoners will not be eligible for automatic release either at the halfway point or even at the three-quarters point of their custodial term, but will only be released at its end unless the Parole Board has previously directed early release (on licence) at some point between the halfway point and the end of the custodial term. It should be remembered that even after release at the end of the custodial term, such prisoners' release will be on licence under supervision for the extension period of the sentence which could be up to a further 5 years for violent offences or 8 years for sexual offences.

Secondly, there is a major change for sentences of less than 12 months. Halliday (para 0.10) noted that

One of the most serious deficiencies in the present framework is the lack of utility in prison sentences of less than 12 months. Only half of such sentences are served, less with Home Detention Curfew, and the second half is subject to no conditions whatsoever. The Prison Service has little opportunity to work on the factors which underlie the criminality because the time served in custody is so limited—and yet these sentences are used for large numbers of persistent offenders who are very likely to re-offend. There is a need to provide a structured framework for work with the large number of offenders who persist in criminality at a level of seriousness that does not require longer prison sentences.

The custody plus order (see Chapter 13) was introduced in s 181 of the Act to deal with this issue and the result is that for sentences of less than 12 months, 'early' release on licence is expressly built into the sentence itself which has a maximum custodial period of 13 weeks and a minimum licence period of 26 weeks. So the maximum proportion of the sentence to be served in custody will be one-third of the total and in many cases will be a much smaller proportion (contrast the 50% rule under the previous regime). Equally significantly however, the offender will be on licence once released until the whole of the sentence has expired and subject to the conditions which can be imposed under s 182. Previously, as has been seen, there was no licence or supervision for the second half of sentences of less than 12 months.

The previous point leads on to a third significant change in the new regime which is that licence periods for all offenders now continue to the end of the sentence and do not expire at the three-quarters point as was previously the case. The sentence is served partly in custody and partly in the community on licence. Release on licence is part of the sentence and continues until its end. Hence the title of Chapter 6 of Part 12 of the Act, 'Release on Licence', not 'Early Release'. Release is not early, it comes at the end of the custodial period of the sentence, the remainder of the sentence being served in the community. A fourth significant change is that whereas home detention curfew (which is still a form of 'early' release) was previously only available to short-term prisoners, with the abolition of the short term/long term distinction, it now becomes available for all fixed-term prisoners.

Having set out some of the most significant changes to the system, we can now look at the provisions in more detail.

15.2 CASES WHERE THERE IS A DUTY TO RELEASE PRISONERS—AUTOMATIC RELEASE ON LICENCE

Section 244 sets out the situations where 'it is *the duty* of the Secretary of State to release him' and thus where a prisoner will automatically be entitled to release on licence. It applies by sub-s (1) to 'a fixed-term prisoner' other than one serving an extended sentence under s 227 or s 228. A 'fixed-term prisoner' is defined in s 237 as:

(a) a person serving a sentence of imprisonment for a determinate term, or
(b) a person serving a determinate sentence of detention under section 91 of the Sentencing Act or under section 228 of this Act.

Paragraph (a) covers adult prisoners (other than lifers) whereas para (b) applies to those under 18.

Such a prisoner is entitled to release on licence once he has served '*the requisite custodial period*'.

Section 244(3) then defines the '*requisite custodial period*' for four categories of case at the expiry of which a fixed-term prisoner will be entitled to release:

(a) For sentences of imprisonment of *12 months or more*, the period is *one-half of the sentence*.
(b) For sentences of imprisonment of *less than 12 months* (other than an intermittent custody order), the period is the custodial period within s 181, ie *the period of between 2 and 13 weeks specified in the sentence*.
(c) For *intermittent custody orders*, it is any part of the term which is a licence period under s 183(3)—this seems to mean a separate entitlement to release *after each intermittent custody period*.
(d) For persons serving two or more *concurrent or consecutive sentences*, the period is governed by ss 263(2) and 264(2). These in effect provide that the *period is that required for the longest sentence* (in the case of concurrent terms) *or the aggregate of the custodial periods* (in the case of consecutive terms).

Section 245 provides for a complicated exception to the above for intermittent custody orders where such a prisoner returns to custody after being unlawfully at large. Essentially it provides for the prisoner to be held for 72 hours even though he would otherwise be normally entitled to be released (eg over a weekend) under s 244(3)(c). During that 72 hours, an application to amend the intermittent custody order can be made but if it is not, he will thereafter be eligible for intermittent release in accordance with the original order. If during the 72 hours he actually completes the full number of custodial days specified in his sentence, he is entitled to be released in any event. Section 245(3) deals with the situation where the intermittent custody prisoner has not (voluntarily) returned but rather has been recalled to prison under s 254. In this case, he will not be released again at all unless the Parole Board has directed his further release on licence.

15.3 DISCRETIONARY RELEASE

15.3.1 Home Detention Curfew

Section 246(1) gives the Secretary of State *a power* (rather than imposing a duty) to release a fixed-term prisoner on licence up to 135 days (effectively $4^1/_2$ months) earlier than the expiry of the requisite custodial period (or in the case of intermittent custody with 135 or fewer custodial days still to be served). By subsection (2) this power does not apply unless the requisite custodial period was at least 6 weeks and the prisoner has actually served a minimum of 4 weeks *and* at least half the requisite custodial period. So if the custodial period was 12 weeks and the prisoner has served 5 weeks, he is not eligible for discretionary release until he has served 6 weeks (one half of the custodial period). (Subsection (3) makes equivalent provision for intermittent custody orders.) There is a long list of exclusions from the benefit of s 246 in sub-s (4) including extended sentences under ss 227 or 228, those subject to deportation and those recalled after previous discretionary release during the currency of the sentence. The various periods and proportions specified in the section (including the period of 135 days) can be amended by order (as has been done in the past in the extending the maximum HDC period from the original 2 months to the current $4^1/_2$ months).

Section 246 itself does not specifically mention the electronic curfew condition but s 250(5) requires that a 'licence under section 246 must also include a curfew condition complying with section 253'. Section 253 provides that the curfew condition 'is to remain in force until the date when the released person would (but for his release) fall to be released on licence under section 244'. The most significant change wrought by s 246 is of course the extension of HDC availability to sentences of 4 years or more. Home Office figures show that since HDC first came into operation in 1999 there have been around 3,500 on licence at any one time and over 80,000 in total with a successful completion rate of 90%. The figures seem likely to grow further.

15.3.2 Discretionary Release—Extended Sentences

Section 247 provides for discretionary release on licence once half the custodial term, determined by the court in the original sentence under s 227 or 228, has been served.

However, the decision in this case is not that of the Secretary of State but of the Parole Board. As soon as the Parole Board 'has directed' the prisoner's release under this section, 'it is the duty of the Secretary of State to release him'. However, by sub-s (3) the Parole Board may not give a direction unless it is satisfied 'that it is no longer necessary for the protection of the public that the prisoner should be confined'. If the Parole Board does not give a direction during the currency of the (second half of) the custodial term, the prisoner will become entitled to release at the expiry of the custodial term. As has been commented on above, as far as determinate sentences are concerned, it is on the cases falling under this section that the Parole Board will now be focusing its attention and it will no longer play a role in determining the release date of prisoners serving ordinary sentences of 4 years or more. Section 239 provides for the continued operation of the Parole Board and substantially re-enacts s 32 of the Criminal Justice Act 1991 in this respect.

15.3.3 Discretionary Release on Compassionate Grounds

This section largely re-enacts CJA 1991, s 36 and provides for the release of fixed-term prisoners on compassionate grounds by the Secretary of State if exceptional circumstances exist (for example where the prisoner is suffering from a terminal illness). In the case of prisoners serving extended sentences, the Parole Board must be consulted first unless it is impracticable.

15.4 LICENCE CONDITIONS

15.4.1 Power of Court to recommend Licence Conditions

Section 238 empowers the court to recommend, when passing a custodial sentence of 12 months or more, particular conditions that in its view should be included in the licence to which the offender is subject on release. The Secretary of State, when setting the conditions of the licence, must have regard to any recommendations which the court may have made.

This provision is part of the policy of improving pre-release planning and sentence management discussed in Halliday, ch 7. The pre-sentence report will inform any recommendations which the courts make under the section. Section 238 only applies to sentences of 12 months or more and should be compared with s 181, dealing with sentences of less than 12 months, which requires the court to specify licence conditions falling within s 182. There is no requirement to specify any conditions under s 238, nor do they seem to have to come from the list in s 182 or elsewhere and any that are specified are merely recommendations and by s 238(3), they are not part of the sentence.

15.4.2 Standard Licence Conditions

Section 250 provides for 'standard conditions' to be attached to licences on release. An example would be a requirement that the offender be of good behaviour.

Section 250 (8) requires the Secretary of State to have regard to the following purposes of the supervision of offenders in prescribing such conditions:

(a) the protection of the public;
(b) the prevention of re-offending; and
(c) securing the successful reintegration of the prisoner into the community.

A distinction is then drawn between sentences of less than 12 months and longer sentences. Section 250(2) deals with these and provides that the licence *must* include the conditions required by the relevant court order (usually a custody plus order under s181(3)(b)) and the standard conditions so far as not inconsistent with those earlier conditions. It *may* also include compatible electronic monitoring or drug testing requirements and such other conditions of a kind prescribed by the Secretary of State as necessary for the protection of the public (but seemingly without reference in this case to the prevention of re-offending or securing successful reintegration of the offender). Section 250(3) makes it clear that the period specified in certain licence conditions specified in the original court order will be taken also to include any period for which a person is released on HDC or on compassionate grounds. Under s 251, where a prisoner serving a sentence of less than 12 months is released on licence, recalled and then re-released, his licence conditions may be varied from that in the original court order and he is in effect treated as a prisoner serving 12 months or more as below.

For sentences of 12 months or more, there is no relevant court order specifying conditions (although there may be a recommendation under s 238) so s 250(4) *requires* the licence, which will be set by Prison and Probation Service prior to the prisoner's release, to include the standard conditions as no issue of incompatibility with a court order arises. Again, in addition, the licence may include electronic monitoring or drug testing requirements and such other conditions of a kind prescribed under s 250(4)(b)(ii) (which on this occasion does refer to all three purposes mentioned in s250(8)).

15.4.3 Compliance with Licence Conditions and Recall to Prison

Section 252 imposes a duty to comply with licence conditions. Although no specific sanction is mentioned in s 252, s 254 effectively provides it by authorizing the Secretary of State to revoke a licence and recall a prisoner to prison (although it does not actually make this power conditional on there having been a breach of a licence condition). Section 254(2) entitles a person recalled to make written representations about his recall and to be informed of the reasons for his recall. All cases of persons recalled must be referred to the Parole Board under s 254(3) and if, under 254(4), the Board decides that the person should be immediately released again on licence, the Secretary of State must release him. If the Board does not decide on immediate release, s 256 applies and the Board must either fix a future date for his release or fix a date for the next review of the case, in both instances within the next 12 months unless the prisoner is due in any event to be released within that period at the end of his custodial term. By virtue of s 254(7), offenders recalled from early release home detention curfew under s 246 are to be dealt with separately under s 255 which is of largely similar effect except that:

(a) the power to revoke and recall is expressly dependent on there being a breach of a licence condition (or the electronic monitoring no longer being possible); and

(b) recalls of HDC licensees released early under s 246 are not to be referred to the Parole Board but representations by the recalled prisoner are to be considered by the Secretary of State.

Because prisoners will now be on licence right until the end of their sentences rather than just up to the three-quarters point (see s 249), they are of course liable to recall to prison right up to the end point. There is therefore no need for an equivalent to CJA 1991, s 40 which provided for an order for return to prison where a further imprisonable offence is committed before the sentence is served in full. Such a case can now be dealt with by recall under s 254 up to the end of the sentence and any new offences can be dealt with simply by sentencing for that new offence. This is part of the simplification of the enforcement provision called for in chapter 7 of the Halliday Report. There still remains a need though for sanctions for misbehaviour in prison as opposed to after being released on licence.

Section 257 therefore substantially reproduces, with one or two minor changes of wording, CJA 1991, s 42 and continues to provide for additional days to be added to sentences for disciplinary offences whilst in custody. These not only extend the custodial period but also push back the date at which any licence period will end.

15.5 CREDITING PERIODS OF REMAND

One other matter dealt with in Halliday, chapter 7 was the confused position in relation to the effect of periods of remand in custody on terms of imprisonment and detention:

The present framework has caused great difficulties in relation to sentence calculation (the means of translating the sentence of the court into a period of custody), in particular the counting of remand time. The basic principles—namely that time spent on remand or in police custody reduces any sentence of imprisonment, but must not be counted more than once—are now fairly clear. But the application of these principles has been, and can still be, ambiguous as a result of the successive tranches of legislation and judgements by the courts which overlay the basic statutory provision in Section 67 of the Criminal Justice Act 1967. An attempt to devise a workable system whereby remand time is taken into account by the courts was embodied in section 9 of the Crime (Sentences) Act 1997 (now section 87 of the Powers of Criminal Courts (Sentencing) Act 2000)—but the provision was never brought into force because of the difficulties of calculating police detention and court custody time. (Halliday para 7.2)

Section 240 accordingly re-enacts a modified version of s 87 of PCC(S)A 2000. If the court makes a direction under sub-s (3), time spent remanded in custody (as defined in s 242(2)) is to count as time served by the offender as part of his sentence of imprisonment provided the remand was in connection with the same offence, or a related offence. Normally the court is required to make a direction under sub-s (3), and under sub-s (5) must state in open court the number of days remanded in custody and the number of days which count towards time served under the sentence. Subsection (4) allows the court not to give a direction if and to the extent that rules so provide (in relation to remands concurrent with prison sentences or in relation to concurrent or consecutive sentences) *or* if it is in the interests of justice in all the circumstances not to give a direction. Where no direction is given or a direction is given for a lesser period of days than that spent in custody, s 240(6) requires the reasons under sub-s (4) to be stated in open court.

Section 241 provides for remand time specified in a direction under s 240 to be treated as time served under the sentence for the purposes of calculating whether a prisoner has served a certain proportion of his sentence and whether he is therefore eligible for release under licence. The expression 'remanded in custody' is defined in s 242 and, it should be noted, does not include time spent in police detention so this will not count as time spent on remand for the purposes of s 240. There is said to be an essential difference between time spent on remand, which is preventative and imposed by the courts, and time spent in police custody which is simply a by-product of the investigative process. Section 243 replaces CJA 1991, s 47 for extradited prisoners but is of largely similar effect and it now takes effect so that days kept in custody awaiting extradition are to be treated as though they were days remanded in custody.

APPENDIX

Criminal Justice Act 2003

CONTENTS

PART 1
AMENDMENTS OF POLICE AND CRIMINAL EVIDENCE ACT 1984

PART 2
BAIL

PART 11
EVIDENCE

CHAPTER 1

271

CRIMINAL JUSTICE ACT 2003

PART 1.
AMENDMENTS OF POLICE AND CRIMINAL EVIDENCE ACT 1984

1. Extension of powers to stop and search

(1) In this Part, "the 1984 Act" means the Police and Criminal Evidence Act 1984 (c. 60).

(2) In section 1(8) of the 1984 Act (offences for purpose of definition of prohibited article), at the end of paragraph (d) there is inserted "; and

    (e) offences under section 1 of the Criminal Damage Act 1971 (destroying or damaging property)."

2. Warrants to enter and search

In section 16 of the 1984 Act (execution of warrants), after subsection (2) there is inserted—

    "(2A) A person so authorised has the same powers as the constable whom he accompanies in respect of—

        (a) the execution of the warrant, and

        (b) the seizure of anything to which the warrant relates.

    (2B) But he may exercise those powers only in the company, and under the supervision, of a constable."

3. Arrestable offences

(1) Schedule 1A to the 1984 Act (specific offences which are arrestable offences) is amended as follows.

(2) After paragraph 2 there is inserted—

"Criminal Justice Act 1925

2ZA An offence under section 36 of the Criminal Justice Act 1925 (untrue statement for procuring a passport)."

(3) After paragraph 6 there is inserted—

"Misuse of Drugs Act 1971

6A An offence under section 5(2) of the Misuse of Drugs Act 1971 (having possession of a controlled drug) in respect of cannabis or cannabis resin (within the meaning of that Act)."

(4) After paragraph 17 there is inserted—

    "17A An offence under section 174 of the Road Traffic Act 1988 (false statements and withholding material information)."

4. Bail elsewhere than at police station

(1) Section 30 of the 1984 Act (arrest elsewhere than at police station) is amended as follows.

(2) For subsection (1) there is substituted—

"(1) Subsection (1A) applies where a person is, at any place other than a police station—

(a) arrested by a constable for an offence, or

(b) taken into custody by a constable after being arrested for an offence by a person other than a constable.

(1A) The person must be taken by a constable to a police station as soon as practicable after the arrest.

(1B) Subsection (1A) has effect subject to section 30A (release on bail) and subsection (7) (release without bail)."

(3) In subsection (2) for "subsection (1)" there is substituted "subsection (1A)".

(4) For subsection (7) there is substituted—

"(7) A person arrested by a constable at any place other than a police station must be released without bail if the condition in subsection (7A) is satisfied.

(7A) The condition is that, at any time before the person arrested reaches a police station, a constable is satisfied that there are no grounds for keeping him under arrest or releasing him on bail under section 30A."

(5) For subsections (10) and (11) there is substituted—

"(10) Nothing in subsection (1A) or in section 30A prevents a constable delaying taking a person to a police station or releasing him on bail if the condition in subsection (10A) is satisfied.

(10A) The condition is that the presence of the person at a place (other than a police station) is necessary in order to carry out such investigations as it is reasonable to carry out immediately.

(11) Where there is any such delay the reasons for the delay must be recorded when the person first arrives at the police station or (as the case may be) is released on bail."

(6) In subsection (12) for "subsection (1)" there is substituted "subsection (1A) or section 30A".

(7) After section 30 there is inserted—

"30A Bail elsewhere than at police station

(1) A constable may release on bail a person who is arrested or taken into custody in the circumstances mentioned in section 30(1).

(2) A person may be released on bail under subsection (1) at any time before he arrives at a police station.

(3) A person released on bail under subsection (1) must be required to attend a police station.

(4) No other requirement may be imposed on the person as a condition of bail.

(5) The police station which the person is required to attend may be any police station.

30B Bail under section 30A: notices

(1) Where a constable grants bail to a person under section 30A, he must give that person a notice in writing before he is released.

(2) The notice must state—
    (a) the offence for which he was arrested, and
    (b) the ground on which he was arrested.

(3) The notice must inform him that he is required to attend a police station.

(4) It may also specify the police station which he is required to attend and the time when he is required to attend.

(5) If the notice does not include the information mentioned in subsection (4), the person must subsequently be given a further notice in writing which contains that information.

(6) The person may be required to attend a different police station from that specified in the notice under subsection (1) or (5) or to attend at a different time.

(7) He must be given notice in writing of any such change as is mentioned in subsection (6) but more than one such notice may be given to him.

30C Bail under section 30A: supplemental

(1) A person who has been required to attend a police station is not required to do so if he is given notice in writing that his attendance is no longer required.

(2) If a person is required to attend a police station which is not a designated police station he must be—
    (a) released, or
    (b) taken to a designated police station,
        not more than six hours after his arrival.

(3) Nothing in the Bail Act 1976 applies in relation to bail under section 30A.

(4) Nothing in section 30A or 30B or in this section prevents the re-arrest without a warrant of a person released on bail under section 30A if new evidence justifying a further arrest has come to light since his release.

30D Failure to answer to bail under section 30A

(1) A constable may arrest without a warrant a person who—
    (a) has been released on bail under section 30A subject to a requirement to attend a specified police station, but
    (b) fails to attend the police station at the specified time.

(2) A person arrested under subsection (1) must be taken to a police station (which may be the specified police station or any other police station) as soon as practicable after the arrest.

(3) In subsection (1), "specified" means specified in a notice under subsection (1) or (5) of section 30B or, if notice of change has been given under subsection (7) of that section, in that notice.

(4) For the purposes of—
    (a) section 30 (subject to the obligation in subsection (2)), and
    (b) section 31,
        an arrest under this section is to be treated as an arrest for an offence."

5. Drug testing for under-eighteens

(1) The 1984 Act is amended as follows.

(2) In section 38 (duties of custody officer after charge)—
    (a) in subsection (1)—
        (i) for sub-paragraph (iiia) of paragraph (a) there is substituted—

287

"(iiia) except in a case where (by virtue of subsection (9) of section 63B below) that section does not apply, the custody officer has reasonable grounds for believing that the detention of the person is necessary to enable a sample to be taken from him under that section;",

  (ii) in sub-paragraph (i) of paragraph (b), after "satisfied" there is inserted "(but, in the case of paragraph (a)(iiia) above, only if the arrested juvenile has attained the minimum age)",

(b) in subsection (6A), after the definition of "local authority accommodation" there is inserted— ""minimum age" means the age specified in section 63B(3) below;".

(3) In section 63B (testing for presence of Class A drugs)—

(a) in subsection (3), for "18" there is substituted "14",

(b) after subsection (5) there is inserted—

"(5A) In the case of a person who has not attained the age of 17—

  (a) the making of the request under subsection (4) above;

  (b) the giving of the warning and (where applicable) the information under subsection (5) above; and

  (c) the taking of the sample,

may not take place except in the presence of an appropriate adult.",

(c) after subsection (6) there is inserted—

"(6A) The Secretary of State may by order made by statutory instrument amend subsection (3) above by substituting for the age for the time being specified a different age specified in the order.

(6B) A statutory instrument containing an order under subsection (6A) above shall not be made unless a draft of the instrument has been laid before, and approved by a resolution of, each House of Parliament.",

(d) after subsection (8) there is inserted—

"(9) In relation to a person who has not attained the age of 18, this section applies only where—

  (a) the relevant chief officer has been notified by the Secretary of State that arrangements for the taking of samples under this section from persons who have not attained the age of 18 have been made for the police area as a whole, or for the particular police station, in which the person is in police detention; and

  (b) the notice has not been withdrawn.

(10) In this section—

"appropriate adult", in relation to a person who has not attained the age of 17, means—

  (a) his parent or guardian or, if he is in the care of a local authority or voluntary organisation, a person representing that authority or organisation; or

  (b) a social worker of a local authority social services department; or

  (c) if no person falling within paragraph (a) or (b) is available, any responsible person aged 18 or over who is not a police officer or a person employed by the police;

"relevant chief officer" means—

  (a) in relation to a police area, the chief officer of police of the police force for that police area; or

  (b) in relation to a police station, the chief officer of police of the police force for the police area in which the police station is situated."

6. Use of telephones for review of police detention

For section 40A(1) and (2) of the 1984 Act (use of telephone for review under s.40) there is substituted—

(1) A review under section 40(1)(b) may be carried out by means of a discussion, conducted by telephone, with one or more persons at the police station where the arrested person is held

(2) But subsection (1) does not apply if—

   (a) the review is of a kind authorised by regulations under section 45A to be carried out using video-conferencing facilities; and

   (b) it is reasonably practicable to carry it out in accordance with those regulations."

7. Limits on period of detention without charge

In section 42(1) of the 1984 Act (conditions to be satisfied before detention without charge may be extended from 24 to 36 hours), for paragraph (b) there is substituted—

   "(b) an offence for which he is under arrest is an arrestable offence; and".

8. Property of detained persons

(1) In subsection (1) of section 54 of the 1984 Act (which requires the custody officer at a police station to ascertain and record everything which a detained person has with him), there is omitted "and record or cause to be recorded".

(2) For subsection (2) of that section (record of arrested person to be made as part of custody record) there is substituted—

   "(2) The custody officer may record or cause to be recorded all or any of the things which he ascertains under subsection (1).

   (2A) In the case of an arrested person, any such record may be made as part of his custody record."

9. Taking fingerprints without consent

(1) Section 61 of the 1984 Act (fingerprinting) is amended as follows.

(2) For subsections (3) and (4) (taking of fingerprints without appropriate consent) there is substituted—

   "(3) The fingerprints of a person detained at a police station may be taken without the appropriate consent if—

   (a) he is detained in consequence of his arrest for a recordable offence; and

   (b) he has not had his fingerprints taken in the course of the investigation of the offence by the police.

   (4) The fingerprints of a person detained at a police station may be taken without the appropriate consent if—

   (a) he has been charged with a recordable offence or informed that he will be reported for such an offence; and

   (b) he has not had his fingerprints taken in the course of the investigation of the offence by the police."

(3) In subsection (3A) (disregard of incomplete or unsatisfactory fingerprints) for the words from the beginning to "subsection (3) above" there is substituted "Where a person mentioned in paragraph (a) of subsection (3) or (4) has already had his fingerprints taken in the course of the investigation of the offence by the police".

(4) In subsection (5) (authorisation to be given or confirmed in writing) for "subsection (3)(a) or (4A)" there is substituted "subsection (4A)".

(5) In subsection (7) (reasons for taking of fingerprints without consent) for "subsection (3) or (6)" there is substituted "subsection (3), (4) or (6)".

10. Taking non-intimate samples without consent

(1) Section 63 of the 1984 Act (other samples) is amended as follows.

(2) After subsection (2) (consent to be given in writing) there is inserted—

"(2A) A non-intimate sample may be taken from a person without the appropriate consent if two conditions are satisfied.

(2B) The first is that the person is in police detention in consequence of his arrest for a recordable offence.

(2C) The second is that—

(a) he has not had a non-intimate sample of the same type and from the same part of the body taken in the course of the investigation of the offence by the police, or

(b) he has had such a sample taken but it proved insufficient."

(3) In subsection (3)(a) (taking of samples without appropriate consent) the words "is in police detention or" are omitted.

(4) In subsection (3A) (taking of samples without appropriate consent after charge) for "(whether or not he falls within subsection (3)(a) above)" there is substituted "(whether or not he is in police detention or held in custody by the police on the authority of a court)".

(5) In subsection (8A) (reasons for taking of samples without consent) for "subsection (3A)" there is substituted "subsection (2A), (3A)".

11. Codes of practice

(1) In section 67 of the 1984 Act (supplementary provisions about codes), for subsections (1) to (7C) there is substituted—

"(1) In this section, "code" means a code of practice under section 60, 60A or 66.

(2) The Secretary of State may at any time revise the whole or any part of a code.

(3) A code may be made, or revised, so as to—

(a) apply only in relation to one or more specified areas,

(b) have effect only for a specified period,

(c) apply only in relation to specified offences or descriptions of offender.

(4) Before issuing a code, or any revision of a code, the Secretary of State must consult—

(a) persons whom he considers to represent the interests of police authorities,

(b) persons whom he considers to represent the interests of chief officers of police,

(c) the General Council of the Bar,

(d) the Law Society of England and Wales,

(e) the Institute of Legal Executives, and

(f) such other persons as he thinks fit.

(5) A code, or a revision of a code, does not come into operation until the Secretary of State by order so provides.

(6) The power conferred by subsection (5) is exercisable by statutory instrument.

(7) An order bringing a code into operation may not be made unless a draft of the order has been laid before Parliament and approved by a resolution of each House.

(7A) An order bringing a revision of a code into operation must be laid before Parliament if the order has been made without a draft having been so laid and approved by a resolution of each House.

(7B) When an order or draft of an order is laid, the code or revision of a code to which it relates must also be laid.

(7C) No order or draft of an order may be laid until the consultation required by subsection (4) has taken place.

(7D) An order bringing a code, or a revision of a code, into operation may include transitional or saving provisions."

(2) Section 113 of the 1984 Act (application of Act to armed forces) is amended as follows.

(3) After subsection (3) there is inserted—

"(3A) In subsections (4) to (10), "code" means a code of practice under subsection (3)."

(4) For subsections (5) to (7) there is substituted—

"(5) The Secretary of State may at any time revise the whole or any part of a code.

(6) A code may be made, or revised, so as to—

(a) apply only in relation to one or more specified areas,

(b) have effect only for a specified period,

(c) apply only in relation to specified offences or descriptions of offender.

(7) The Secretary of State must lay a code, or any revision of a code, before Parliament."

12. Amendments related to Part 1

Schedule 1 (which makes amendments related to the provisions of this Part) has effect.

PART 2. BAIL

13. Grant and conditions of bail

(1) In section 3(6) of the 1976 Act (which sets out cases where bail conditions may be imposed)—

(a) the words "to secure that" are omitted,

(b) the words "to secure that" are inserted at the beginning of each of paragraphs (a) to (e),

(c) after paragraph (c) there is inserted—

"(ca) for his own protection or, if he is a child or young person, for his own welfare or in his own interests,",

(d) for "or (c) " there is substituted ", (c) or (ca)".

(2) In section 3A(5) of the 1976 Act (no conditions may be imposed under section 3(4), (5), (6) or (7) unless necessary for certain purposes) —

(a) the words "for the purpose of preventing that person from" are omitted,

(b) the words "for the purpose of preventing that person from" are inserted at the beginning of each of paragraphs (a) to (c),

(c) after paragraph (c) there is inserted "or

(d) for that person's own protection or, if he is a child or young person, for his own welfare or in his own interests."

(3) In paragraph 8(1) of Part 1 of Schedule 1 to the 1976 Act (no conditions may be imposed under section 3(4) to (7) unless necessary to do so for certain purposes) for the words from "that it is necessary to do so" onwards there is substituted "that it is necessary to do so—

(a) for the purpose of preventing the occurrence of any of the events mentioned in paragraph 2(1) of this Part of this Schedule, or

(b) for the defendant's own protection or, if he is a child or young person, for his own welfare or in his own interests."

(4) For paragraph 5 of Part 2 of that Schedule (defendant need not be granted bail if having been released on bail he has been arrested in pursuance of section 7) there is substituted—

"5 The defendant need not be granted bail if—

(a) having been released on bail in or in connection with the proceedings for the offence, he has been arrested in pursuance of section 7 of this Act; and

(b) the court is satisfied that there are substantial grounds for believing that the defendant, if released on bail (whether subject to conditions or not) would fail to surrender to custody, commit an offence on bail or interfere with witnesses or otherwise obstruct the course of justice (whether in relation to himself or any other person)."

14. Offences committed on bail

(1) For paragraph 2A of Part 1 of Schedule 1 to the 1976 Act (defendant need not be granted bail where he was on bail on date of offence) there is substituted—

"2A (1) If the defendant falls within this paragraph he may not be granted bail unless the court is satisfied that there is no significant risk of his committing an offence while on bail (whether subject to conditions or not).

(2) The defendant falls within this paragraph if—

(a) he is aged 18 or over, and

(b) it appears to the court that he was on bail in criminal proceedings on the date of the offence."

(2) After paragraph 9 of that Part there is inserted—

"9AA (1) This paragraph applies if—

(a) the defendant is under the age of 18, and

(b) it appears to the court that he was on bail in criminal proceedings on the date of the offence.

(2) In deciding for the purposes of paragraph 2(1) of this Part of this Schedule whether it is satisfied that there are substantial grounds for believing that the defendant, if released on bail (whether subject to conditions or not), would commit an offence while on bail, the court shall give particular weight to the fact that the defendant was on bail in criminal proceedings on the date of the offence."

15. Absconding by persons released on bail

(1) For paragraph 6 of Part 1 of Schedule 1 to the 1976 Act (defendant need not be granted bail if having been released on bail he has been arrested in pursuance of section 7) there is substituted—

"6 (1) If the defendant falls within this paragraph, he may not be granted bail unless the court is satisfied that there is no significant risk that, if released on bail (whether subject to conditions or not), he would fail to surrender to custody.

(2) Subject to sub-paragraph (3) below, the defendant falls within this paragraph if—

(a) he is aged 18 or over, and

(b) it appears to the court that, having been released on bail in or in connection with the proceedings for the offence, he failed to surrender to custody.

(3) Where it appears to the court that the defendant had reasonable cause for his failure to surrender to custody, he does not fall within this paragraph unless it also appears to the court that he failed to surrender to custody at the appointed place as soon as reasonably practicable after the appointed time.

(4) For the purposes of sub-paragraph (3) above, a failure to give to the defendant a copy of the record of the decision to grant him bail shall not constitute a reasonable cause for his failure to surrender to custody."

(2) After paragraph 9AA of that Part (inserted by section 14(2)) there is inserted—

"9AB (1) Subject to sub-paragraph (2) below, this paragraph applies if—

    (a) the defendant is under the age of 18, and

    (b) it appears to the court that, having been released on bail in or in connection with the proceedings for the offence, he failed to surrender to custody.

(2) Where it appears to the court that the defendant had reasonable cause for his failure to surrender to custody, this paragraph does not apply unless it also appears to the court that he failed to surrender to custody at the appointed place as soon as reasonably practicable after the appointed time.

(3) In deciding for the purposes of paragraph 2(1) of this Part of this Schedule whether it is satisfied that there are substantial grounds for believing that the defendant, if released on bail (whether subject to conditions or not), would fail to surrender to custody, the court shall give particular weight to—

    (a) where the defendant did not have reasonable cause for his failure to surrender to custody, the fact that he failed to surrender to custody, or

    (b) where he did have reasonable cause for his failure to surrender to custody, the fact that he failed to surrender to custody at the appointed place as soon as reasonably practicable after the appointed time.

(4) For the purposes of this paragraph, a failure to give to the defendant a copy of the record of the decision to grant him bail shall not constitute a reasonable cause for his failure to surrender to custody."

(3) In section 6 of the 1976 Act (offence of absconding by person released on bail) after subsection (9) there is inserted—

"(10) Section 127 of the Magistrates' Courts Act 1980 shall not apply in relation to an offence under subsection (1) or (2) above.

(11) Where a person has been released on bail in criminal proceedings and that bail was granted by a constable, a magistrates' court shall not try that person for an offence under subsection (1) or (2) above in relation to that bail (the "relevant offence") unless either or both of subsections (12) and (13) below applies.

(12) This subsection applies if an information is laid for the relevant offence within 6 months from the time of the commission of the relevant offence.

(13) This subsection applies if an information is laid for the relevant offence no later than 3 months from the time of the occurrence of the first of the events mentioned in subsection (14) below to occur after the commission of the relevant offence.

(14) Those events are—

    (a) the person surrenders to custody at the appointed place;

    (b) the person is arrested, or attends at a police station, in connection with the relevant offence or the offence for which he was granted bail;

    (c) the person appears or is brought before a court in connection with the relevant offence or the offence for which he was granted bail."

16. Appeal to Crown Court

(1) This section applies where a magistrates' court grants bail to a person ("the person concerned") on adjourning a case under—

    (a) section 10 of the Magistrates' Courts Act 1980 (c. 43) (adjournment of trial),

    (b) section 17C of that Act (intention as to plea: adjournment),

    (c) section 18 of that Act (initial procedure on information against adult for offence triable either way),

(d) section 24C of that Act (intention as to plea by child or young person: adjournment),

(e) section 52(5) of the Crime and Disorder Act 1998 (c. 37) (adjournment of proceedings under section 51 etc), or

(f) section 11 of the Powers of Criminal Courts (Sentencing) Act 2000 (c. 6) (remand for medical examination).

(2) Subject to the following provisions of this section, the person concerne may appeal to the Crown Court against any condition of bail falling within subsection (3).

(3) A condition of bail falls within this subsection if it is a requirement—

(a) that the person concerned resides away from a particular place or area,

(b) that the person concerned resides at a particular place other than a bail hostel,

(c) for the provision of a surety or sureties or the giving of a security,

(d) that the person concerned remains indoors between certain hours,

(e) imposed under section 3(6ZAA) of the 1976 Act (requirements with respect to electronic monitoring), or

(f) that the person concerned makes no contact with another person.

(4) An appeal under this section may not be brought unless subsection (5) or (6) applies.

(5) This subsection applies if an application to the magistrates' court under section 3(8)(a) of the 1976 Act (application by or on behalf of person granted bail) was made and determined before the appeal was brought.

(6) This subsection applies if an application to the magistrates' court—

(a) under section 3(8)(b) of the 1976 Act (application by constable or prosecutor), or

(b) under section 5B(1) of that Act (application by prosecutor), was made and determined before the appeal was brought.

(7) On an appeal under this section the Crown Court may vary the conditions of bail.

(8) Where the Crown Court determines an appeal under this section, the person concerned may not bring any further appeal under this section in respect of the conditions of bail unless an application or a further application to the magistrates' court under section 3(8)(a) of the 1976 Act is made and determined after the appeal.

17. Appeals to High Court

(1) In section 22(1) of the Criminal Justice Act 1967 (c. 80) (extension of power of High Court to grant, or vary conditions of, bail)—

(a) after "Where" there is inserted "(a)", and

(b) after "proceedings,", in the second place where it occurs, there is inserted "and

(b) it does so where an application to the court to state a case for the opinion of the High Court is made,".

(2) The inherent power of the High Court to entertain an application in relation to bail where a magistrates' court—

(a) has granted or withheld bail, or

(b) has varied the conditions of bail,
is abolished.

(3) The inherent power of the High Court to entertain an application in relation to bail where the Crown Court has determined—

(a) an application under section 3(8) of the 1976 Act, or

(b) an application under section 81(1)(a), (b), (c) or (g) of the Supreme Court Act 1981 (c. 54), is abolished.

(4) The High Court is to have no power to entertain an application in relation to bail where the Crown Court has determined an appeal under section 16 of this Act.

(5) High Court is to have no power to entertain an application in relation to bail where the Crown Court has granted or withheld bail under section 88 or 89 of this Act.

(6) Nothing in this section affects—

    (a) any other power of the High Court to grant or withhold bail or to vary the conditions of bail, or

    (b) any right of a person to apply for a writ of habeas corpus or any other prerogative remedy.

(7) Any reference in this section to an application in relation to bail is to be read as including—

    (a) an application for bail to be granted,

    (b) an application for bail to be withheld,

    (c) an application for the conditions of bail to be varied.

(8) Any reference in this section to the withholding of bail is to be read as including a reference to the revocation of bail.

18. Appeal by prosecution

(1) Section 1 of the Bail (Amendment) Act 1993 (c. 26) (prosecution right of appeal) is amended as follows.

(2) For subsection (1) (prosecution may appeal to Crown Court judge against bail in case of offence punishable by imprisonment for five years or more etc) there is substituted—

    "(1) Where a magistrates' court grants bail to a person who is charged with, or convicted of, an offence punishable by imprisonment, the prosecution may appeal to a judge of the Crown Court against the granting of bail."

(3) In subsection (10)(a) for "punishable by a term of imprisonment" there is substituted "punishable by imprisonment".

19. Drug users: restriction on bail

(1) The 1976 Act is amended as follows.

(2) In section 3 (general provisions), after subsection (6B) there is inserted—

    "(6C) Subsection (6D) below applies where—

        (a) the court has been notified by the Secretary of State that arrangements for conducting a relevant assessment or, as the case may be, providing relevant follow-up have been made for the petty sessions area in which it appears to the court that the person referred to in subsection (6D) would reside if granted bail; and

        (b) the notice has not been withdrawn.

    (6D) In the case of a person ("P")—

        (a) in relation to whom paragraphs (a) to (c) of paragraph 6B(1) of Part 1 of Schedule 1 to this Act apply;

        (b) who, after analysis of the sample referred to in paragraph (b) of that paragraph, has been offered a relevant assessment or, if a relevant assessment has been carried out, has had relevant follow-up proposed to him; and

        (c) who has agreed to undergo the relevant assessment or, as the case may be, to participate in the relevant follow-up,

    the court, if it grants bail, shall impose as a condition of bail that P both undergo the relevant assessment and participate in any relevant follow-up proposed to him or, if a relevant assessment has been carried out, that P participate in the relevant follow-up.

    (6E) In subsections (6C) and (6D) above—

(a) "relevant assessment" means an assessment conducted by a suitably qualified person of whether P is dependent upon or has a propensity to misuse any specified Class A drugs;

(b) "relevant follow-up" means, in a case where the person who conducted the relevant assessment believes P to have such a dependency or propensity, such further assessment, and such assistance or treatment (or both) in connection with the dependency or propensity, as the person who conducted the relevant assessment (or conducts any later assessment) considers to be appropriate in P's case,

and in paragraph (a) above "Class A drug" and "misuse" have the same meaning as in the Misuse of Drugs Act 1971, and "specified" (in relation to a Class A drug) has the same meaning as in Part 3 of the Criminal Justice and Court Services Act 2000.

(6F) In subsection (6E)(a) above, "suitably qualified person" means a person who has such qualifications or experience as are from time to time specified by the Secretary of State for the purposes of this subsection."

(3) In section 3A(3) (conditions of bail in case of police bail), for ", (6A) and (6B)" there is substituted "and (6A) to (6F)".

(4) In Schedule 1 (which contains supplementary provisions about bail), in Part 1 (imprisonable offences)—

(a) after paragraph 6 there is inserted—

"6A Exception applicable to drug users in certain areas

Subject to paragraph 6C below, a defendant who falls within paragraph 6B below may not be granted bail unless the court is satisfied that there is no significant risk of his committing an offence while on bail (whether subject to conditions or not).

6B (1) A defendant falls within this paragraph if—

(a) he is aged 18 or over;

(b) a sample taken—

(i) under section 63B of the Police and Criminal Evidence Act 1984 (testing for presence of Class A drugs) in connection with the offence; or

(ii) under section 161 of the Criminal Justice Act 2003 (drug testing after conviction of an offence but before sentence),

has revealed the presence in his body of a specified Class A drug;

(c) either the offence is one under section 5(2) or (3) of the Misuse of Drugs Act 1971 and relates to a specified Class A drug, or the court is satisfied that there are substantial grounds for believing—

(i) that misuse by him of any specified Class A drug caused or contributed to the offence; or

(ii) (even if it did not) that the offence was motivated wholly or partly by his intended misuse of such a drug; and

(d) the condition set out in sub-paragraph (2) below is satisfied or (if the court is considering on a second or subsequent occasion whether or not to grant bail) has been, and continues to be, satisfied.

(2) The condition referred to is that after the taking and analysis of the sample—

(a) a relevant assessment has been offered to the defendant but he does not agree to undergo it; or

    (b) he has undergone a relevant assessment, and relevant follow-up has been proposed to him, but he does not agree to participate in it.

  (3) In this paragraph and paragraph 6C below—

    (a) "Class A drug" and "misuse" have the same meaning as in the Misuse of Drugs Act 1971;

    (b) "relevant assessment" and "relevant follow-up" have the meaning given by section 3(6E) of this Act;

    (c) "specified" (in relation to a Class A drug) has the same meaning as in Part 3 of the Criminal Justice and Court Services Act 2000.

6C Paragraph 6A above does not apply unless—

    (a) the court has been notified by the Secretary of State that arrangements for conducting a relevant assessment or, as the case may be, providing relevant follow-up have been made for the petty sessions area in which it appears to the court that the defendant would reside if granted bail; and

    (b) the notice has not been withdrawn.",

    (b) in paragraph 8(1), for "(4) to (7)" there is substituted "(4) to (6B) or (7)"

20. Supplementary amendments to the Bail Act 1976

(1) In Part 1 of Schedule 1 to the 1976 Act (supplementary provisions relating to bail of defendant accused or convicted of imprisonable offence) the existing text of paragraph 2 is to be sub-paragraph (1) of that paragraph, and after that sub-paragraph (as so re-numbered) there is inserted—

"(2) Where the defendant falls within one or more of paragraphs 2A, 6 and 6B of this Part of this Schedule, this paragraph shall not apply unless—

    (a) where the defendant falls within paragraph 2A, the court is satisfied as mentioned in sub-paragraph (1) of that paragraph;

    (b) where the defendant falls within paragraph 6, the court is satisfied as mentioned in sub-paragraph (1) of that paragraph;

    (c) where the defendant falls within paragraph 6B, the court is satisfied as mentioned in paragraph 6A of this Part of this Schedule or paragraph 6A does not apply by virtue of paragraph 6C of this Part of this Schedule."

(2) In paragraph 9 of that Part (matters to be taken into account in making decisions under paragraph 2 or 2A of that Part) for "2 or 2A" there is substituted "2(1), or in deciding whether it is satisfied as mentioned in paragraph 2A(1), 6(1) or 6A,"

21. Interpretation of Part 2

In this Part—

"bail" means bail in criminal proceedings (within the meaning of the 1976 Act),

"bail hostel" has the meaning given by section 2(2) of the 1976 Act,

"the 1976 Act" means the Bail Act 1976 (c. 63),

"vary" has the same meaning as in the 1976 Act.

PART 3. CONDITIONAL CAUTIONS

22. Conditional cautions

(1) An authorised person may give a conditional caution to a person aged 18 or over ("the offender") if each of the five requirements in section 23 is satisfied.

(2) In this Part "conditional caution" means a caution which is given in respect of an offence committed by the offender and which has conditions attached to it with which the offender must comply.

(3) The conditions which may be attached to such a caution are those which have either or both of the following objects—

(a) facilitating the rehabilitation of the offender,

(b) ensuring that he makes reparation for the offence.

(4) In this Part "authorised person" means—

(a) a constable,

(b) an investigating officer, or

(c) a person authorised by a relevant prosecutor for the purposes of this section.

23. The five requirements

(1) The first requirement is that the authorised person has evidence that the offender has committed an offence.

(2) The second requirement is that a relevant prosecutor decides—

(a) that there is sufficient evidence to charge the offender with the offence, and

(b) that a conditional caution should be given to the offender in respect of the offence.

(3) The third requirement is that the offender admits to the authorised person that he committed the offence.

(4) The fourth requirement is that the authorised person explains the effect of the conditional caution to the offender and warns him that failure to comply with any of the conditions attached to the caution may result in his being prosecuted for the offence.

(5) The fifth requirement is that the offender signs a document which contains—

(a) details of the offence,

(b) an admission by him that he committed the offence,

(c) his consent to being given the conditional caution, and

(d) the conditions attached to the caution.

24. Failure to comply with conditions

(1) If the offender fails, without reasonable excuse, to comply with any of the conditions attached to the conditional caution, criminal proceedings may be instituted against the person for the offence in question.

(2) The document mentioned in section 23(5) is to be admissible in such proceedings.

(3) Where such proceedings are instituted, the conditional caution is to cease to have effect.

25. Code of practice

(1) The Secretary of State must prepare a code of practice in relation to conditional cautions.

(2) The code may, in particular, include provision as to—

(a) the circumstances in which conditional cautions may be given,

(b) the procedure to be followed in connection with the giving of such cautions,

(c) the conditions which may be attached to such cautions and the time for which they may have effect,

(d) the category of constable or investigating officer by whom such cautions may be given,

(e) the persons who may be authorised by a relevant prosecutor for the purposes of section 22,

(f) the form which such cautions are to take and the manner in which they are to be given and recorded,

(g) the places where such cautions may be given, and

(h) the monitoring of compliance with conditions attached to such cautions.

(3) After preparing a draft of the code the Secretary of State—

(a) must publish the draft,

(b) must consider any representations made to him about the draft, and

(c) may amend the draft accordingly,

but he may not publish or amend the draft without the consent of the Attorney General.

(4) After the Secretary of State has proceeded under subsection (3) he must lay the code before each House of Parliament.

(5) When he has done so he may bring the code into force by order.

(6) The Secretary of State may from time to time revise a code of practice brought into force under this section.

(7) Subsections (3) to (6) are to apply (with appropriate modifications) to a revised code as they apply to an original code.

26. Assistance of National Probation Service

(1) Section 1 of the Criminal Justice and Court Services Act 2000 (c. 43) (purposes of Chapter 1) is amended as follows.

(2) After subsection (1) there is inserted—

"(1A) This Chapter also has effect for the purposes of providing for—

(a) authorised persons to be given assistance in determining whether conditional cautions should be given and which conditions to attach to conditional cautions, and

(b) the supervision and rehabilitation of persons to whom conditional cautions are given."

(3) After subsection (3) there is inserted—

"(4) In this section "authorised person" and "conditional caution" have the same meaning as in Part 3 of the Criminal Justice Act 2003."

27. Interpretation of Part 3

In this Part—

"authorised person" has the meaning given by section 22(4),

"conditional caution" has the meaning given by section 22(2),

"investigating officer" means a person designated as an investigating officer under section 38 of the Police Reform Act 2002 (c. 30),

"the offender" has the meaning given by section 22(1),

"relevant prosecutor" means—

(a) the Attorney General,

(b) the Director of the Serious Fraud Office,

(c) the Director of Public Prosecutions,

(d) a Secretary of State,

(e) the Commissioners of Inland Revenue,

(f) the Commissioners of Customs and Excise, or

(g) a person who is specified in an order made by the Secretary of State as being a relevant prosecutor for the purposes of this Part.

PART 4. CHARGING ETC

28. Charging or release of persons in police detention

Schedule 2 (which makes provision in relation to the charging or release of persons in police detention) shall have effect.

29. New method of instituting proceedings

(1) A public prosecutor may institute criminal proceedings against a person by issuing a document (a "written charge") which charges the person with an offence.

(2) Where a public prosecutor issues a written charge, it must at the same time issue a document (a "requisition") which requires the person to appear before a magistrates' court to answer the written charge.

(3) The written charge and requisition must be served on the person concerned, and a copy of both must be served on the court named in the requisition.

(4) In consequence of subsections (1) to (3), a public prosecutor is not to have the power to lay an information for the purpose of obtaining the issue of a summons under section 1 of the Magistrates' Courts Act 1980 (c. 43).

(5) In this section "public prosecutor" means—

    (a) a police force or a person authorised by a police force to institute criminal proceedings,

    (b) the Director of the Serious Fraud Office or a person authorised by him to institute criminal proceedings,

    (c) the Director of Public Prosecutions or a person authorised by him to institute criminal proceedings,

    (d) the Attorney General or a person authorised by him to institute criminal proceedings,

    (e) a Secretary of State or a person authorised by a Secretary of State to institute criminal proceedings,

    (f) the Commissioners of Inland Revenue or a person authorised by them to institute criminal proceedings,

    (g) the Commissioners of Customs and Excise or a person authorised by them to institute criminal proceedings, or

    (h) a person specified in an order made by the Secretary of State for the purposes of this section or a person authorised by such a person to institute criminal proceedings.

(6) In subsection (5) "police force" has the meaning given by section 3(3) of the Prosecution of Offences Act 1985 (c. 23).

30. Further provision about new method

(1) Rules under section 144 of the Magistrates' Courts Act 1980 may make—

    (a) provision as to the form, content, recording, authentication and service of written charges or requisitions, and

    (b) such other provision in relation to written charges or requisitions as appears to the Lord Chancellor to be necessary or expedient.

(2) Without limiting subsection (1), the provision which may be made by virtue of that subsection includes provision—

    (a) which applies (with or without modifications), or which disapplies, the provision of any enactment relating to the service of documents,

    (b) for or in connection with the issue of further requisitions.

(3) Nothing in subsection (1) or (2) is to be taken as affecting the generality of section 144(1) of that Act.

(4) Nothing in section 29 affects—

    (a) the power of a public prosecutor to lay an information for the purpose of obtaining the issue of a warrant under section 1 of the Magistrates' Courts Act 1980 (c. 43),

    (b) the power of a person who is not a public prosecutor to lay an information for the purpose of obtaining the issue of a summons or warrant under section 1 of that Act, or

    (c) any power to charge a person with an offence whilst he is in custody.

(5) Except where the context otherwise requires, in any enactment contained in an Act passed before this Act—

    (a) any reference (however expressed) which is or includes a reference to an information within the meaning of section 1 of the Magistrates' Courts Act 1980 (c.43) (or to the laying of such an information) is to be read as including a reference to a written charge (or to the issue of a written charge),

    (b) any reference (however expressed) which is or includes a reference to a summons under section 1 of the Magistrates' Courts Act 1980 (or to a justice of the peace issuing such a summons) is to be read as including a reference to a requisition (or to a public prosecutor issuing a requisition).

(6) Subsection (5) does not apply to section 1 of the Magistrates' Courts Act 1980.

(7) The reference in sub section (5) to an enactment contained in an Act passed before this Act includes a reference to an enactment contained in that Act as a result of an amendment to that Act made by this Act or by any other Act passed in the same Session as this Act.

(8) In this section "public prosecutor", "requisition" and "written charge" have the same meaning as in section 29.

31. Removal of requirement to substantiate information on oath

(1) In section 1(3) of the Magistrates' Courts Act 1980 (warrant may not be issued unless information substantiated on oath) the words "and substantiated on oath" are omitted.

(2) In section 13 of that Act (non-appearance of defendant: issue of warrant) in subsection (3)(a) the words "the information has been substantiated on oath and" are omitted.

(3) For subsection (3A)(a) of that section there is substituted—

    "(a) the offence to which the warrant relates is punishable, in the case of a person who has attained the age of 18, with imprisonment, or".

PART 5. DISCLOSURE

32. Initial duty of disclosure by prosecutor

In the Criminal Procedure and Investigations Act 1996 (c. 25) (in this Part referred to as "the 1996 Act"), in subsection (1)(a) of section 3 (primary disclosure by prosecutor)—

(a) for "in the prosecutor's opinion might undermine" there is substituted "might reasonably be considered capable of undermining";

(b) after "against the accused" there is inserted "or of assisting the case for the accused".

33. Defence disclosure

(1) In section 5 of the 1996 Act (compulsory disclosure by accused), after subsection (5) there is inserted—

"(5A) Where there are other accused in the proceedings and the court so orders, the accused must also give a defence statement to each other accused specified by the court.

(5B) The court may make an order under subsection (5A) either of its own motion or on the application of any party.

(5C) A defence statement that has to be given to the court and the prosecutor (under subsection (5)) must be given during the period which, by virtue of section 12, is the relevant period for this section.

(5D) A defence statement that has to be given to a co-accused (under subsection (5A)) must be given within such period as the court may specify."

(2) After section 6 of that Act there is inserted—

"6A Contents of defence statement

(1) For the purposes of this Part a defence statement is a written statement—

    (a) setting out the nature of the accused's defence, including any particular defences on which he intends to rely,

    (b) indicating the matters of fact on which he takes issue with the prosecution,

    (c) setting out, in the case of each such matter, why he takes issue with the prosecution, and

    (d) indicating any point of law (including any point as to the admissibility of evidence or an abuse of process) which he wishes to take, and any authority on which he intends to rely for that purpose.

(2) A defence statement that discloses an alibi must give particulars of it, including—

    (a) the name, address and date of birth of any witness the accused believes is able to give evidence in support of the alibi, or as many of those details as are known to the accused when the statement is given;

    (b) any information in the accused's possession which might be of material assistance in identifying or finding any such witness in whose case any of the details mentioned in paragraph (a) are not known to the accused when the statement is given.

(3) For the purposes of this section evidence in support of an alibi is evidence tending to show that by reason of the presence of the accused at a particular place or in a particular area at a particular time he was not, or was unlikely to have been, at the place where the offence is alleged to have been committed at the time of its alleged commission.

(4) The Secretary of State may by regulations make provision as to the details of the matters that, by virtue of subsection (1), are to be included in defence statements."

(3) After section 6A of that Act (inserted by subsection (2) above) there is inserted—

"6B Updated disclosure by accused

(1) Where the accused has, before the beginning of the relevant period for this section, given a defence statement under section 5 or 6, he must during that period give to the court and the prosecutor either—

    (a) a defence statement under this section (an "updated defence statement"), or

    (b) a statement of the kind mentioned in subsection (4).

(2) The relevant period for this section is determined under section 12.

(3) An updated defence statement must comply with the requirements imposed by or under section 6A by reference to the state of affairs at the time when the statement is given.

(4) Instead of an updated defence statement, the accused may give a written statement stating that he has no changes to make to the defence statement which was given under section 5 or 6.

(5) Where there are other accused in the proceedings and the court so orders, the accused must also give either an updated defence statement or a statement of the kind mentioned in ssubsection (4), within such period as may be specified by the court, to each other accused so specified.

(6) The court may make an order under subsection (5) either of its own motion or on the application of any party."

34. Notification of intention to call defence witnesses

After section 6B of the 1996 Act (inserted by section 33 above) there is inserted—

"6C Notification of intention to call defence witnesses

(1) The accused must give to the court and the prosecutor a notice indicating whether he intends to call any persons (other than himself) as witnesses at his trial and, if so—
   (a) giving the name, address and date of birth of each such proposed witness, or as many of those details as are known to the accused when the notice is given;
   (b) providing any information in the accused's possession which might be of material assistance in identifying or finding any such proposed witness in whose case any of the details mentioned in paragraph (a) are not known to the accused when the notice is given.

(2) Details do not have to be given under this section to the extent that they have already been given under section 6A(2).

(3) The accused must give a notice under this section during the period which, by virtue of section 12, is the relevant period for this section.

(4) If, following the giving of a notice under this section, the accused—
   (a) decides to call a person (other than himself) who is not included in the notice as a proposed witness, or decides not to call a person who is so included, or
   (b) discovers any information which, under subsection (1), he would have had to include in the notice if he had been aware of it when giving the notice,
   he must give an appropriately amended notice to the court and the prosecutor."

35. Notification of names of experts instructed by defendant

After section 6C of the 1996 Act (inserted by section 34 above) there is inserted—

"6D Notification of names of experts instructed by accused

(1) If the accused instructs a person with a view to his providing any expert opinion for possible use as evidence at the trial of the accused, he must give to the court and the prosecutor a notice specifying the person's name and address.

(2) A notice does not have to be given under this section specifying the name and address of a person whose name and address have already been given under section 6C.

(3) A notice under this section must be given during the period which, by virtue of section 12, is the relevant period for this section."

36. Further provisions about defence disclosure

After section 6D of the 1996 Act (inserted by section 35 above) there is inserted—

"6E Disclosure by accused: further provisions

(1) Where an accused's solicitor purports to give on behalf of the accused—
    (a) a defence statement under section 5, 6 or 6B, or
    (b) a statement of the kind mentioned in section 6B(4), the statement shall, unless the contrary is proved, be deemed to be given with the authority of the accused.

(2) If it appears to the judge at a pre-trial hearing that an accused has failed to comply fully with section 5, 6B or 6C, so that there is a possibility of comment being made or inferences drawn under section 11(5), he shall warn the accused accordingly.

(3) In subsection (2) "pre-trial hearing" has the same meaning as in Part 4 (see section 39).

(4) The judge in a trial before a judge and jury—
    (a) may direct that the jury be given a copy of any defence statement, and
    (b) if he does so, may direct that it be edited so as not to include references to matters evidence of which would be inadmissible.

(5) A direction under subsection (4)—
    (a) may be made either of the judge's own motion or on the application of any party;
    (b) may be made only if the judge is of the opinion that seeing a copy of the defence statement would help the jury to understand the case or to resolve any issue in the case.

(6) The reference in subsection (4) to a defence statement is a reference—
    (a) where the accused has given only an initial defence statement (that is, a defence statement given under section 5 or 6), to that statement;
    (b) where he has given both an initial defence statement and an updated defence statement (that is, a defence statement given under section 6B), to the updated defence statement;
    (c) where he has given both an initial defence statement and a statement of the kind mentioned in section 6B(4), to the initial defence statement."

37. Continuing duty of disclosure by prosecutor

Before section 8 of the 1996 Act there is inserted—

"7A Continuing duty of prosecutor to disclose

(1) This section applies at all times—
    (a) after the prosecutor has complied with section 3 or purported to comply with it, and
    (b) before the accused is acquitted or convicted or the prosecutor decides not to proceed with the case concerned.

(2) The prosecutor must keep under review the question whether at any given time (and, in particular, following the giving of a defence statement) there is prosecution material which—
    (a) might reasonably be considered capable of undermining the case for the prosecution against the accused or of assisting the case for the accused, and
    (b) has not been disclosed to the accused.

(3) If at any time there is any such material as is mentioned in subsection (2) the prosecutor must disclose it to the accused as soon as is reasonably practicable (or within the period mentioned in subsection (5)(a), where that applies).

(4) In applying subsection (2) by reference to any given time the state of affairs at that time (including the case for the prosecution as it stands at that time) must be taken into account.

(5) Where the accused gives a defence statement under section 5, 6 or 6B—
    (a) if as a result of that statement the prosecutor is required by this section to make any disclosure, or further disclosure, he must do so during the period which, by virtue of section 12, is the relevant period for this section;

(b) if the prosecutor considers that he is not so required, he must during that period give to the accused a written statement to that effect.

(6) For the purposes of this section prosecution material is material—

  (a) which is in the prosecutor's possession and came into his possession in connection with the case for the prosecution against the accused, or

  (b) which, in pursuance of a code operative under Part 2, he has inspected in connection with the case for the prosecution against the accused.

(7) Subsections (3) to (5) of section 3 (method by which prosecutor discloses) apply for the purposes of this section as they apply for the purposes of that.

(8) Material must not be disclosed under this section to the extent that the court, on an application by the prosecutor, concludes it is not in the public interest to disclose it and orders accordingly.

(9) Material must not be disclosed under this section to the extent that it is material the disclosure of which is prohibited by section 17 of the Regulation of Investigatory Powers Act 2000 (c. 23)."

38. Application by defence for disclosure

In section 8 of the 1996 Act (application by accused for disclosure), for subsections (1) and (2) there is substituted—

"(1) This section applies where the accused has given a defence statement under section 5, 6 or 6B and the prosecutor has complied with section 7A(5) or has purported to comply with it or has failed to comply with it.

(2) If the accused has at any time reasonable cause to believe that there is prosecution material which is required by section 7A to be disclosed to him and has not been, he may apply to the court for an order requiring the prosecutor to disclose it to him."

39. Faults in defence disclosure

For section 11 of the 1996 Act there is substituted—

"11 Faults in disclosure by accused

(1) This section applies in the three cases set out in subsections (2), (3) and (4).

(2) The first case is where section 5 applies and the accused—

  (a) fails to give an initial defence statement,

  (b) gives an initial defence statement but does so after the end of the period which, by virtue of section 12, is the relevant period for section 5,

  (c) is required by section 6B to give either an updated defence statement or a statement of the kind mentioned in subsection (4) of that section but fails to do so,

  (d) gives an updated defence statement or a statement of the kind mentioned in section 6B(4) but does so after the end of the period which, by virtue of section 12, is the relevant period for section 6B,

  (e) sets out inconsistent defences in his defence statement, or

  (f) at his trial—

    (i) puts forward a defence which was not mentioned in his defence statement or is different from any defence set out in that statement,

    (ii) relies on a matter which, in breach of the requirements imposed by or under section 6A, was not mentioned in his defence statement,

    (iii) adduces evidence in support of an alibi without having given particulars of the alibi in his defence statement, or

       (iv) calls a witness to give evidence in support of an alibi without having complied with section 6A(2)(a) or (b) as regards the witness in his defence statement.

(3) The second case is where section 6 applies, the accused gives an initial defence statement, and the accused—

    (a) gives the initial defence statement after the end of the period which, by virtue of section 12, is the relevant period for section 6, or

    (b) does any of the things mentioned in paragraphs (c) to (f) of subsection (2).

(4) The third case is where the accused—

    (a) gives a witness notice but does so after the end of the period which, by virtue of section 12, is the relevant period for section 6C, or

    (b) at his trial calls a witness (other than himself) not included, or not adequately identified, in a witness notice.

(5) Where this section applies—

    (a) the court or any other party may make such comment as appears appropriate;

    (b) the court or jury may draw such inferences as appear proper in deciding whether the accused is guilty of the offence concerned.

(6) Where—

    (a) this section applies by virtue of subsection (2)(f)(ii) (including that provision as it applies by virtue of subsection (3)(b)), and

    (b) the matter which was not mentioned is a point of law (including any point as to the admissibility of evidence or an abuse of process) or an authority,

comment by another party under subsection (5)(a) may be made only with the leave of the court.

(7) Where this section applies by virtue of subsection (4), comment by another party under subsection (5)(a) may be made only with the leave of the court.

(8) Where the accused puts forward a defence which is different from any defence set out in his defence statement, in doing anything under subsection (5) or in deciding whether to do anything under it the court shall have regard—

    (a) to the extent of the differences in the defences, and

    (b) to whether there is any justification for it.

(9) Where the accused calls a witness whom he has failed to include, or to identify adequately, in a witness notice, in doing anything under subsection (5) or in deciding whether to do anything under it the court shall have regard to whether there is any justification for the failure.

(10) A person shall not be convicted of an offence solely on an inference drawn under subsection (5).

(11) Where the accused has given a statement of the kind mentioned in section 6B(4), then, for the purposes of subsections (2)(f)(ii) and (iv), the question as to whether there has been a breach of the requirements imposed by or under section 6A or a failure to comply with section 6A(2)(a) or (b) shall be determined—

    (a) by reference to the state of affairs at the time when that statement was given, and

    (b) as if the defence statement was given at the same time as that statement.

(12) In this section—

    (a) "initial defence statement" means a defence statement given under section 5 or 6;

    (b) "updated defence statement" means a defence statement given under section 6B;

    (c) a reference simply to an accused's "defence statement" is a reference—

       (i)   where he has given only an initial defence statement, to that statement;

       (ii) where he has given both an initial and an updated defence statement, to the updated defence statement;

    (iii) where he has given both an initial defence statement and a statement of the kind mentioned in section 6B(4), to the initial defence statement;

  (d) a reference to evidence in support of an alibi shall be construed in accordance with section 6A(3);

  (e) "witness notice" means a notice given under section 6C."

40. Code of practice for police interviews of witnesses notified by accused

In Part 1 of the 1996 Act after section 21 there is inserted—

"21A Code of practice for police interviews of witnesses notified by accused

(1) The Secretary of State shall prepare a code of practice which gives guidance to police officers, and other persons charged with the duty of investigating offences, in relation to the arranging and conducting of interviews of persons—

  (a) particulars of whom are given in a defence statement in accordance with section 6A(2), or

  (b) who are included as proposed witnesses in a notice given under section 6C.

(2) The code must include (in particular) guidance in relation to—

  (a) information that should be provided to the interviewee and the accused in relation to such an interview;

  (b) the notification of the accused's solicitor of such an interview;

  (c) the attendance of the interviewee's solicitor at such an interview;

  (d) the attendance of the accused's solicitor at such an interview;

  (e) the attendance of any other appropriate person at such an interview taking into account the interviewee's age or any disability of the interviewee.

(3) Any police officer or other person charged with the duty of investigating offences who arranges or conducts such an interview shall have regard to the code.

(4) In preparing the code, the Secretary of State shall consult—

  (a) to the extent the code applies to England and Wales—

    (i)   any person who he considers to represent the interests of chief officers of police;

    (ii) the General Council of the Bar;

    (iii) the Law Society of England and Wales;

    (iv) the Institute of Legal Executives;

  (b) to the extent the code applies to Northern Ireland—

    (i)   the Chief Constable of the Police Service of Northern Ireland;

    (ii) the General Council of the Bar of Northern Ireland;

    (iii) the Law Society of Northern Ireland;

  (c) such other persons as he thinks fit.

(5) The code shall not come into operation until the Secretary of State by order so provides.

(6) The Secretary of State may from time to time revise the code and subsections (4) and (5) shall apply to a revised code as they apply to the code as first prepared.

(7) An order bringing the code into operation may not be made unless a draft of the order has been laid before each House of Parliament and approved by a resolution of each House.

(8) An order bringing a revised code into operation shall be laid before each House of Parliament if the order has been made without a draft having been so laid and approved by a resolution of each House.

(9) When an order or a draft of an order is laid in accordance with subsection (7) or (8), the code to which it relates shall also be laid.

(10) No order or draft of an order may be laid until the consultation required by subsection (4) has taken place.

(11) A failure by a person mentioned in subsection (3) to have regard to any provision of a code for the time being in operation by virtue of an order under this section shall not in itself render him liable to any criminal or civil proceedings.

(12) In all criminal and civil proceedings a code in operation at any time by virtue of an order under this section shall be admissible in evidence.

(13) If it appears to a court or tribunal conducting criminal or civil proceedings that—

    (a) any provision of a code in operation at any time by virtue of an order under this section, or

    (b) any failure mentioned in subsection (11),

is relevant to any question arising in the proceedings, the provision or failure shall be taken into account in deciding the question."

PART 6. ALLOCATION AND SENDING OF OFFENCES

41. Allocation of offences triable either way, and sending cases to Crown Court

Schedule 3 (which makes provision in relation to the allocation and other treatment of offences triable either way, and the sending of cases to the Crown Court) shall have effect.

42. Mode of trial for certain firearms offences: transitory arrangements

(1) The Magistrates' Courts Act 1980 is amended as follows.

(2) In section 24 (summary trial of information against child or young person for indictable offence)—

    (a) in subsection (1), for "homicide" there is substituted "one falling within subsection (1B) below",

    (b) in subsection (1A)(a), for "of homicide" there is substituted "falling within subsection (1B) below",

    (c) after subsection (1A), there is inserted—

        "(1B) An offence falls within this subsection if—

            (a) it is an offence of homicide; or

            (b) each of the requirements of section 51A(1) of the Firearms Act 1968 would be satisfied with respect to—

                (i) the offence; and

                (ii) the person charged with it, if he were convicted of the offence."

(3) In section 25 (power to change from summary trial to committal proceedings and vice versa), in subsection (5), for "homicide" there is substituted "one falling within section 24(1B) above".

PART 7. TRIALS ON INDICTMENT WITHOUT A JURY

43. Applications by prosecution for certain fraud cases to be conducted without a jury

(1) This section applies where—

    (a) one or more defendants are to be tried on indictment for one or more offences, and

(b) notice has been given under section 51B of the Crime and Disorder Act 1998 (c. 37) (notices in serious or complex fraud cases) in respect of that offence or those offences.

(2) The prosecution may apply to a judge of the Crown Court for the trial to be conducted without a jury.

(3) If an application under subsection (2) is made and the judge is satisfied that the condition in subsection (5) is fulfilled, he may make an order that the trial is to be conducted without a jury; but if he is not so satisfied he must refuse the application.

(4) The judge may not make such an order without the approval of the Lord Chief Justice or a judge nominated by him.

(5) The condition is that the complexity of the trial or the length of the trial (or both) is likely to make the trial so burdensome to the members of a jury hearing the trial that the interests of justice require that serious consideration should be given to the question of whether the trial should be conducted without a jury.

(6) In deciding whether or not he is satisfied that that condition is fulfilled, the judge must have regard to any steps which might reasonably be taken to reduce the complexity or length of the trial.

(7) But a step is not to be regarded as reasonable if it would significantly disadvantage the prosecution.

44. Application by prosecution for trial to be conducted without a jury where danger of jury tampering

(1) This section applies where one or more defendants are to be tried on indictment for one or more offences.

(2) The prosecution may apply to a judge of the Crown Court for the trial to be conducted without a jury.

(3) If an application under subsection (2) is made and the judge is satisfied that both of the following two conditions are fulfilled, he must make an order that the trial is to be coducted without a jury; but if he is not so satisfied he must refuse the application.

(4) The first condition is that there is evidence of a real and present danger that jury tampering would take place.

(5) The second condition is that, notwithstanding any steps (including the provision of police protection) which might reasonably be taken to prevent jury tampering, the likelihood that it would take place would be so substantial as to make it necessary in the interests of justice for the trial to be conducted without a jury.

(6) The following are examples of cases where there may be evidence of a real and present danger that jury tampering would take place—
(a) a case where the trial is a retrial and the jury in the previous trial was discharged because jury tampering had taken place,
(b) a case where jury tampering has taken place in previous criminal proceedings involving the defendant or any of the defendants,
(c) a case where there has been intimidation, or attempted intimidation, of any person who is likely to be a witness in the trial.

45. Procedure for applications under sections 43 and 44

(1) This section applies—
(a) to an application under section 43, and
(b) to an application under section 44.

(2) An application to which this section applies must be determined at a preparatory hearing (within the meaning of the 1987 Act or Part 3 of the 1996 Act).

(3) The parties to a preparatory hearing at which an application to which this section applies is to be determined must be given an opportunity to make representations with respect to the application.

(4) In section 7(1) of the 1987 Act (which sets out the purposes of preparatory hearings) for paragraphs (a) to (c) there is substituted—

"(a) identifying issues which are likely to be material to the determinations and findings which are likely to be required during the trial,

(b) if there is to be a jury, assisting their comprehension of those issues and expediting the proceedings before them,

(c) determining an application to which section 45 of the Criminal Justice Act 2003 applies,"

(5) In section 9(11) of that Act (appeal to Court of Appeal) after "above," there is inserted "from the refusal by a judge of an application to which section 45 of the Criminal Justice Act 2003 applies or from an order of a judge under section 43 or 44 of that Act which is made on the determination of such an application,"

(6) In section 29 of the 1996 Act (power to order preparatory hearing) after subsection (1) there is inserted—

"(1A) A judge of the Crown Court may also order that a preparatory hearing shall be held if an application to which section 45 of the Criminal Justice Act 2003 applies (application for trial without jury) is made."

(7) In subsection (2) of that section (which sets out the purposes of preparatory hearings) for paragraphs (a) to (c) there is substituted—

"(a) identifying issues which are likely to be material to the determinations and findings which are likely to be required during the trial,

(b) if there is to be a jury, assisting their comprehension of those issues and expediting the proceedings before them,

(c) determining an application to which section 45 of the Criminal Justice Act 2003 applies,"

(8) In subsections (3) and (4) of that section for "subsection (1)" there is substituted "this section"

(9) In section 35(1) of that Act (appeal to Court of Appeal) after "31(3)," there is inserted "from the refusal by a judge of an application to which section 45 of the Criminal Justice Act 2003 applies or from an order of a judge under section 43 or 44 of that Act which is made on the determination of such an application,".

(10) In this section—

"the 1987 Act" means the Criminal Justice Act 1987 (c. 38),

"the 1996 Act" means the Criminal Procedure and Investigations Act 1996 (c. 25).

46. Discharge of jury because of jury tampering

(1) This section applies where—

(a) a judge is minded during a trial on indictment to discharge the jury, and

(b) he is so minded because jury tampering appears to have taken place.

(2) Before taking any steps to discharge the jury, the judge must—

(a) inform the parties that he is minded to discharge the jury,

(b) inform the parties of the grounds on which he is so minded, and

(c) allow the parties an opportunity to make representations.

(3) Where the judge, after considering any such representations, discharges the jury, he may make an order that the trial is to continue without a jury if, but only if, he is satisfied—
   (a) that jury tampering has taken place, and
   (b) that to continue the trial without a jury would be fair to the defendant or defendants;
   but this is subject to subsection (4).
(4) If the judge considers that it is necessary in the interests of justice for the trial to be terminated, he must terminate the trial.
(5) Where the judge terminates the trial under subsection (4), he may make an order that any new trial which is to take place must be conducted without a jury if he is satisfied in respect of the new trial that both of the conditions set out in section 44 are likely to be fulfilled.
(6) Subsection (5) is without prejudice to any other power that the judge may have on terminating the trial.
(7) Subject to subsection (5), nothing in this section affects the application of section 43 or 44 in relation to any new trial which takes place following the termination of the trial.

47. Appeals

(1) An appeal shall lie to the Court of Appeal from an order under section 46(3) or (5).
(2) Such an appeal may be brought only with the leave of the judge or the Court of Appeal.
(3) An order from which an appeal under this section lies is not to take effect—
   (a) before the expiration of the period for bringing an appeal under this section, or
   (b) if such an appeal is brought, before the appeal is finally disposed of or abandoned.
(4) On the termination of the hearing of an appeal under this section, the Court of Appeal may confirm or revoke the order.
(5) Subject to rules of court made under section 53(1) of the Supreme Court Act 1981 (c. 54) (power by rules to distribute business of Court of Appeal between its civil and criminal divisions)—
   (a) the jurisdiction of the Court of Appeal under this section is to be exercised by the criminal division of that court, and
   (b) references in this section to the Court of Appeal are to be construed as references to that division.
(6) In section 33(1) of the Criminal Appeal Act 1968 (c. 19) (right of appeal to House of Lords) after "1996" there is inserted "or section 47 of the Criminal Justice Act 2003".
(7) In section 36 of that Act (bail on appeal by defendant) after "hearings)" there is inserted "or section 47 of the Criminal Justice Act 2003".
(8) The Secretary of State may make an order containing provision, in relation to proceedings before the Court of Appeal under this section, which corresponds to any provision, in relation to appeals or other proceedings before that court, which is contained in the Criminal Appeal Act 1968 (subject to any specified modifications).

48. Further provision about trials without a jury

(1) The effect of an order under section 43, 44 or 46(5) is that the trial to which the order relates is to be conducted without a jury.
(2) The effect of an order under section 46(3) is that the trial to which the order relates is to be continued without a jury.
(3) Where a trial is conducted or continued without a jury, the court is to have all the powers, authorities and jurisdiction which the court would have had if the trial had been conducted

or continued with a jury (including power to determine any question and to make any finding which would be required to be determined or made by a jury).

(4) Except where the context otherwise requires, any reference in an enactment to a jury, the verdict of a jury or the finding of a jury is to be read, in relation to a trial conducted or continued without a jury, as a reference to the court, the verdict of the court or the finding of the court.

(5) Where a trial is conducted or continued without a jury and the court convicts a defendant—

(a) the court must give a judgment which states the reasons for the conviction at, or as soon as reasonably practicable after, the time of the conviction, and

(b) the reference in section 18(2) of the Criminal Appeal Act 1968 (c. 19) (notice of appeal or of application for leave to appeal to be given within 28 days from date of conviction etc) to the date of the conviction is to be read as a reference to the date of the judgment mentioned in paragraph (a).

(6) Nothing in this Part affects—

(a) the requirement under section 4 of the Criminal Procedure (Insanity) Act 1964 (c. 84) that a question of fitness to be tried be determined by a jury, or

(b) the requirement under section 4A of that Act that any question, finding or verdict mentioned in that section be determined, made or returned by a jury.

49. Rules of court

(1) Rules of court may make such provision as appears to the authority making them to be necessary or expedient for the purposes of this Part.

(2) Without limiting subsection (1), rules of court may in particular make provision for time limits within which applications under this Part must be made or within which other things in connection with this Part must be done.

(3) Nothing in this section is to be taken as affecting the generality of any enactment conferring powers to make rules of court.

50. Application of Part 7 to Northern Ireland

(1) In its application to Northern Ireland this Part is to have effect—

(a) subject to subsection (2), and

(b) subject to the modifications in subsections (3) to (16).

(2) This Part does not apply in relation to a trial to which section 75 of the Terrorism Act 2000 (c. 11) (trial without jury for certain offences) applies.

(3) For section 45 substitute—

"45 Procedure for applications under sections 43 and 44

(1) This section applies—

(a) to an application under section 43, and

(b) to an application under section 44.

(2) An application to which this section applies must be determined—

(a) at a preparatory hearing (within the meaning of the 1988 Order), or

(b) at a hearing specified in, or for which provision is made by, Crown Court rules.

(3) The parties to a hearing mentioned in subsection (2) at which an application to which this section applies is to be determined must be given an opportunity to make representations with respect to the application.

(4) In Article 6(1) of the 1988 Order (which sets out the purposes of preparatory hearings) for sub-paragraphs (a) to (c) there is substituted—

"(a) identifying issues which are likely to be material to the determinations and findings which are likely to be required during the trial;

(b) if there is to be a jury, assisting their comprehension of those issues and expediting the proceedings before them;

(c) determining an application to which section 45 of the Criminal Justice Act 2003 applies; or".

(5) In Article 8(11) of the 1988 Order (appeal to Court of Appeal) after "(3)," there is inserted "from the refusal by a judge of an application to which section 45 of the Criminal Justice Act 2003 applies or from an order of a judge under section 43 or 44 of that Act which is made on the determination of such an application,".

(6) In this section "the 1988 Order" means the Criminal Justice (Serious Fraud) (Northern Ireland) Order 1988."

(4) For section 47(1) substitute—

"(1) An appeal shall lie to the Court of Appeal—

(a) from the refusal by a judge at a hearing mentioned in section 45(2)(b) of an application to which section 45 applies or from an order of a judge at such a hearing under section 43 or 44 which is made on the determination of such an application,

(b) from an order under section 46(3) or (5)."

(5) In section 47(3) after "order" insert "or a refusal of an application"

(6) In section 47(4) for "confirm or revoke the order" substitute—

"(a) where the appeal is from an order, confirm or revoke the order, or

(b) where the appeal is from a refusal of an application, confirm the refusal or make the order which is the subject of the application".

(7) Omit section 47(5)

(8) For section 47(6) substitute—

"(6) In section 31(1) of the Criminal Appeal (Northern Ireland) Act 1980 (right of appeal to House of Lords) after "1988" there is inserted "or section 47 of the Criminal Justice Act 2003"."

(9) For section 47(7) substitute—

"(7) In section 35 of that Act (bail) after "hearings)" there is inserted "or section 47 of the Criminal Justice Act 2003"."

(10) In section 47(8) for "Criminal Appeal Act 1968" substitute "Criminal Appeal (Northern Ireland) Act 1980"

(11) In section 48(4) after "enactment" insert "(including any provision of Northern Ireland legislation)"

(12) For section 48(5)(b) substitute—

"(b) the reference in section 16(1) of the Criminal Appeal (Northern Ireland) Act 1980 (c. 47) (notice of appeal or application for leave) to the date of the conviction is to be read as a reference to the date of the judgment mentioned in paragraph (a)."

(13) In section 48(6)—

(a) for "section 4 of the Criminal Procedure (Insanity) Act 1964 (c. 84)" substitute "Article 49 of the Mental Health (Northern Ireland) Order 1986",

(b) for "section 4A of that Act" substitute "Article 49A of that Order", and

(c) for "that section" substitute "that Article".

(14) After section 48 insert—

"48A. Reporting restrictions

(1) Sections 41 and 42 of the Criminal Procedure and Investigations Act 1996 (c. 25) are to apply in relation to—

(a) a hearing of the kind mentioned in section 45(2)(b), and

(b) any appeal or application for leave to appeal relating to such a hearing,

as they apply in relation to a ruling under section 40 of that Act, but subject to the following modifications.

(2) Section 41(2) of that Act is to have effect as if for paragraphs (a) to (d) there were substituted

"(a) a hearing of the kind mentioned in section 45(2)(b) of the Criminal Justice Act 2003;

(b) any appeal or application for leave to appeal relating to such a hearing."

(3) Section 41(3) of that Act is to have effect as if—

(a) for "(2)" there were substituted "(2)(a) or an application to that judge for leave to appeal to the Court of Appeal", and

(b) after "matter" in the second place where it occurs there were inserted "or application".

(4) Section 41 of that Act is to have effect as if after subsection (3) there were inserted—

"(3A) The Court of Appeal may order that subsection (1) shall not apply, or shall not apply to a specified extent, to a report of—

(a) an appeal to that Court, or

(b) an application to that Court for leave to appeal.

(3B) The House of Lords may order that subsection (1) shall not apply, or shall not apply to a specified extent, to a report of—

(a) an appeal to that House, or

(b) an application to that House for leave to appeal."

(5) Section 41(4) of that Act is to have effect as if for "(3) the judge" there were substituted "(3), (3A) or (3B), the judge, the Court of Appeal or the House of Lords".

(6) Section 41(5) of that Act is to have effect as if for "(3) the judge" there were substituted "(3), (3A) or (3B), the judge, the Court of Appeal or the House of Lords"."

(15) For section 49(2) substitute—

"(2) Without limiting subsection (1), rules of court may in particular make provision—

(a) for time limits within which applications under this Part must be made or within which other things in connection with this Part must be done;

(b) in relation to hearings of the kind mentioned in section 45(2)(b) and appeals under section 47."

(16) In section 49(3)—

(a) after "section" insert "or section 45(2)(b)", and

(b) after "enactment" insert "(including any provision of Northern Ireland legislation)".

PART 8. LIVE LINKS

51. Live links in criminal proceedings

(1) A witness (other than the defendant) may, if the court so directs, give evidence through a live link in the following criminal proceedings.

(2) They are—

Criminal Justice Act 2003, s 52

(a) a summary trial,

(b) an appeal to the Crown Court arising out of such a trial,

(c) a trial on indictment,

(d) an appeal to the criminal division of the Court of Appeal,

(e) the hearing of a reference under section 9 or 11 of the Criminal Appeal Act 1995 (c. 35),

(f) a hearing before a magistrates' court or the Crown Court which is held after the defendant has entered a plea of guilty, and

(g) a hearing before the Court of Appeal under section 80 of this Act.

(3) A direction may be given under this section—

(a) on an application by a party to the proceedings, or

(b) of the court's own motion.

(4) But a direction may not be given under this section unless—

(a) the court is satisfied that it is in the interests of the efficient or effective administration of justice for the person concerned to give evidence in the proceedings through a live link,

(b) it has been notified by the Secretary of State that suitable facilities for receiving evidence through a live link are available in the area in which it appears to the court that the proceedings will take place, and

(c) that notification has not been withdrawn.

(5) The withdrawal of such a notification is not to affect a direction given under this section before that withdrawal.

(6) In deciding whether to give a direction under this section the court must consider all the circumstances of the case.

(7) Those circumstances include in particular—

(a) the availability of the witness,

(b) the need for the witness to attend in person,

(c) the importance of the witness's evidence to the proceedings,

(d) the views of the witness,

(e) the suitability of the facilities at the place where the witness would give evidence through a live link,

(f) whether a direction might tend to inhibit any party to the proceedings from effectively testing the witness's evidence.

(8) The court must state in open court its reasons for refusing an application for a direction under this section and, if it is a magistrates' court, must cause them to be entered in the register of its proceedings.

52. Effect of, and rescission of, direction

(1) Subsection (2) applies where the court gives a direction under section 51 for a person to give evidence through a live link in particular proceedings.

(2) The person concerned may not give evidence in those proceedings after the direction is given otherwise than through a live link (but this is subject to the following provisions of this section).

(3) The court may rescind a direction under section 51 if it appears to the court to be in the interests of justice to do so.

(4) Where it does so, the person concerned shall cease to be able to give evidence in the proceedings through a live link, but this does not prevent the court from giving a further direction under section 51 in relation to him.

(5) A direction under section 51 may be rescinded under subsection (3)—

(a) on an application by a party to the proceedings, or

(b) of the court's own motion.

(6) But an application may not be made under subsection (5)(a) unless there has been a material change of circumstances since the direction was given.

(7) The court must state in open court its reasons—

(a) for rescinding a direction under section 51, or

(b) for refusing an application to rescind such a direction,

and, if it is a magistrates' court, must cause them to be entered in the register of its proceedings.

53. Magistrates' courts permitted to sit at other locations

(1) This section applies where—

(a) a magistrates' court is minded to give a direction under section 51 for evidence to be given through a live link in proceedings before the court, and

(b) suitable facilities for receiving such evidence are not available at any petty–sessional court–house in which the court can (apart from subsection (2)) lawfully sit.

(2) The court may sit for the purposes of the whole or any part of the proceedings at any place at which such facilities are available and which has been appointed for the purposes of this section by the justices acting for the petty sessions area for which the court acts.

(3) A place appointed under subsection (2) may be outside the petty sessions area for which it is appointed; but (if so) it shall be deemed to be in that area for the purpose of the jurisdiction of the justices acting for that area.

54. Warning to jury

(1) This section applies where, as a result of a direction under section 51, evidence has been given through a live link in proceedings before the Crown Court.

(2) The judge may give the jury (if there is one) such direction as he thinks necessary to ensure that the jury gives the same weight to the evidence as if it had been given by the witness in the courtroom or other place where the proceedings are held.

55. Rules of court

(1) Rules of court may make such provision as appears to the authority making them to be necessary or expedient for the purposes of this Part.

(2) Rules of court may in particular make provision—

(a) as to the procedure to be followed in connection with applications under section 51 or 52, and

(b) as to the arrangements or safeguards to be put in place in connection with the operation of live links.

(3) The provision which may be made by virtue of subsection (2)(a) includes provision—

(a) for uncontested applications to be determined by the court without a hearing,

(b) for preventing the renewal of an unsuccessful application under section 51 unless there has been a material change of circumstances,

(c) for the manner in which confidential or sensitive information is to be treated in connection with an application under section 51 or 52 and in particular as to its being disclosed to, or withheld from, a party to the proceedings.

(4) Nothing in this section is to be taken as affecting the generality of any enactment conferring power to make rules of court.

56. Interpretation of Part 8

(1) In this Part—

"legal representative" means an authorised advocate or authorised litigator (as defined by section 119(1) of the Courts and Legal Services Act 1990 (c. 41)),

"petty-sessional court-house" has the same meaning as in the Magistrates' Courts Act 1980 (c. 43),

"petty sessions area" has the same meaning as in the Justices of the Peace Act 1997 (c. 25),

"rules of court" means Magistrates' Courts Rules, Crown Court Rules or Criminal Appeal Rules,

"witness", in relation to any criminal proceedings, means a person called, or proposed to be called, to give evidence in the proceedings.

(2) In this Part "live link" means a live television link or other arrangement by which a witness, while at a place in the United Kingdom which is outside the building where the proceedings are being held, is able to see and hear a person at the place where the proceedings are being held and to be seen and heard by the following persons.

(3) They are—

(a) the defendant or defendants,

(b) the judge or justices (or both) and the jury (if there is one),

(c) legal representatives acting in the proceedings, and

(d) any interpreter or other person appointed by the court to assist the witness.

(4) The extent (if any) to which a person is unable to see or hear by reason of any impairment of eyesight or hearing is to be disregarded for the purposes of subsection (2).

(5) Nothing in this Part is to be regarded as affecting any power of a court—

(a) to make an order, give directions or give leave of any description in relation to any witness (including the defendant or defendants), or

(b) to exclude evidence at its discretion (whether by preventing questions being put or otherwise).

PART 9. PROSECUTION APPEALS

Introduction

57. Introduction

(1) In relation to a trial on indictment, the prosecution is to have the rights of appeal for which provision is made by this Part.

(2) But the prosecution is to have no right of appeal under this Part in respect—

(a) a ruling that a jury be discharged, or

(b) a ruling from which an appeal lies to the Court of Appeal by virtue of any other enactment.

(3) An appeal under this Part is to lie to the Court of Appeal.

(4) Such an appeal may be brought only with the leave of the judge or the Court of Appeal.

General right of appeal in respect of rulings

58. General right of appeal in respect of rulings

(1) This section applies where a judge makes a ruling in relation to a trial on indictment at an applicable time and the ruling relates to one or more offences included in the indictment.

(2) The prosecution may appeal in respect of the ruling in accordance with this section.

(3) The ruling is to have no effect whilst the prosecution is able to take any steps under subsection (4).

(4) The prosecution may not appeal in respect of the ruling unless-
    (a) following the making of the ruling, it—
        (i) informs the court that it intends to appeal, or
        (ii) requests an adjournment to consider whether to appeal, and
    (b) if such an adjournment is granted, it informs the court following the adjournment that it intends to appeal.

(5) If the prosecution requests an adjournment under subsection (4)(a)(ii), the judge may grant such an adjournment.

(6) Where the ruling relates to two or more offences—
    (a) any one or more of those offences may be the subject of the appeal, and
    (b) if the prosecution informs the court in accordance with subsection (4) that it intends to appeal, it must at the same time inform the court of the offence or offences which are the subject of the appeal.

(7) Where—
    (a) the ruling is a ruling that there is no case to answer, and
    (b) the prosecution, at the same time that it informs the court in accordance with subsection (4) that it intends to appeal, nominates one or more other rulings which have been made by a judge in relation to the trial on indictment at an applicable time and which relate to the offence or offences which are the subject of the appeal,
that other ruling, or those other rulings, are also to be treated as the subject of the appeal.

(8) The prosecution may not inform the court in accordance with subsection (4) that it intends to appeal, unless, at or before that time, it informs the court that it agrees that, in respect of the offence or each offence which is the subject of the appeal, the defendant in relation to that offence should be acquitted of that offence if either of the conditions mentioned in subsection (9) is fulfilled.

(9) Those conditions are—
    (a) that leave to appeal to the Court of Appeal is not obtained, and
    (b) that the appeal is abandoned before it is determined by the Court of Appeal.

(10) If the prosecution informs the court in accordance with subsection (4) that it intends to appeal, the ruling mentioned in subsection (1) is to continue to have no effect in relation to the offence or offences which are the subject of the appeal whilst the appeal is pursued.

(11) If and to the extent that a ruling has no effect in accordance with this section—
    (a) any consequences of the ruling are also to have no effect,
    (b) the judge may not take any steps in consequence of the ruling, and
    (c) if he does so, any such steps are also to have no effect.

(12) Where the prosecution has informed the court of its agreement under subsection (8) and either of the conditions mentioned in subsection (9) is fulfilled, the judge or the Court of Appeal must order that the defendant in relation to the offence or each offence concerned be acquitted of that offence.

(13) In this section "applicable time", in relation to a trial on indictment, means any time (whether before or after the commencement of the trial) before the start of the judge's summing-up to the jury.

59. Expedited and non-expedited appeals

(1) Where the prosecution informs the court in accordance with section 58(4) that it intends to appeal, the judge must decide whether or not the appeal should be expedited.

(2) If the judge decides that the appeal should be expedited, he may order an adjournment.

(3) If the judge decides that the appeal should not be expedited, he may—

(a) order an adjournment, or

(b) discharge the jury (if one has been sworn).

(4) If he decides that the appeal should be expedited, he or the Court of Appeal may subsequently reverse that decision and, if it is reversed, the judge may act as mentioned in subsection (3)(a) or (b).

60. Continuation of proceedings for offences not affected by ruling

(1) This section applies where the prosecution informs the court in accordance with section 58(4) that it intends to appeal.

(2) Proceedings may be continued in respect of any offence which is not the subject of the appeal.

61. Determination of appeal by Court of Appeal

(1) On an appeal under section 58, the Court of Appeal may confirm, reverse or vary any ruling to which the appeal relates.

(2) Subsections (3) to (5) apply where the appeal relates to a single ruling.

(3) Where the Court of Appeal confirms the ruling, it must, in respect of the offence or each offence which is the subject of the appeal, order that the defendant in relation to that offence be acquitted of that offence.

(4) Where the Court of Appeal reverses or varies the ruling, it must, in respect of the offence or each offence which is the subject of the appeal, do any of the following—

(a) order that proceedings for that offence may be resumed in the Crown Court,

(b) order that a fresh trial may take place in the Crown Court for that offence,

(c) order that the defendant in relation to that offence be acquitted of that offence.

(5) But the Court of Appeal may not make an order under subsection (4)(a) or (b) in respect of an offence unless it considers it necessary in the interests of justice to do so.

(6) Subsections (7) and (8) apply where the appeal relates to a ruling that there is no case to answer and one or more other rulings.

(7) Where the Court of Appeal confirms the ruling that there is no case to answer, it must, in respect of the offence or each offence which is the subject of the appeal, order that the defendant in relation to that offence be acquitted of that offence.

(8) Where the Court of Appeal reverses or varies the ruling that there is no case to answer, it must in respect of the offence or each offence which is the subject of the appeal, make any of the orders mentioned in subsection (4)(a) to (c) (but subject to subsection (5)).

Right of appeal in respect of evidentiary rulings

62. Right of appeal in respect of evidentiary rulings

(1) The prosecution may, in accordance with this section and section 63, appeal in respect of—

(a) a single qualifying evidentiary ruling, or

(b) two or more qualifying evidentiary rulings.

(2) A "qualifying evidentiary ruling" is an evidentiary ruling of a judge in relation to a trial on indictment which is made at any time (whether before or after the commencement of the trial) before the opening of the case for the defence.

(3) The prosecution may not appeal in respect of a single qualifying evidentiary ruling unless the ruling relates to one or more qualifying offences (whether or not it relates to any other offence).

(4) The prosecution may not appeal in respect of two or more qualifying evidentiary rulings unless each ruling relates to one or more qualifying offences (whether or not it relates to any other offence).

(5) If the prosecution intends to appeal under this section, it must before the opening of the case for the defence inform the court—

    (a) of its intention to do so, and

    (b) of the ruling or rulings to which the appeal relates.

(6) In respect of the ruling, or each ruling, to which the appeal relates—

    (a) the qualifying offence, or at least one of the qualifying offences, to which the ruling relates must be the subject of the appeal, and

    (b) any other offence to which the ruling relates may, but need not, be the subject of the appeal.

(7) The prosecution must, at the same time that it informs the court in accordance with subsection (5), inform the court of the offence or offences which are the subject of the appeal.

(8) For the purposes of this section, the case for the defence opens when, after the conclusion of the prosecution evidence, the earliest of the following events occurs—

    (a) evidence begins to be adduced by or on behalf of a defendant,

    (b) it is indicated to the court that no evidence will be adduced by or on behalf of a defendant,

    (c) a defendant's case is opened, as permitted by section 2 of the Criminal Procedure Act 1865 (c. 18).

(9) In this section—

    "evidentiary ruling" means a ruling which relates to the admissibility or exclusion of any prosecution evidence,

    "qualifying offence" means an offence described in Part 1 of Schedule 4.

(10) The Secretary of State may by order amend that Part by doing any one or more of the following—

    (a) adding a description of offence,

    (b) removing a description of offence for the time being included,

    (c) modifying a description of offence for the time being included.

(11) Nothing in this section affects the right of the prosecution to appeal in respect of an evidentiary ruling under section 58.

63. Condition that evidentiary ruling significantly weakens prosecution case

(1) Leave to appeal may not be given in relation to an appeal under section 62 unless the judge or, as the case may be, the Court of Appeal is satisfied that the relevant condition is fulfilled.

(2) In relation to an appeal in respect of a single qualifying evidentiary ruling, the relevant condition is that the ruling significantly weakens the prosecution's case in relation to the offence or offences which are the subject of the appeal.

(3) In relation to an appeal in respect of two or more qualifying evidentiary rulings, the relevant condition is that the rulings taken together significantly weaken the prosecution's case in relation to the offence or offences which are the subject of the appeal.

64. Expedited and non-expedited appeals

(1) Where the prosecution informs the court in accordance with section 62(5), the judge must decide whether or not the appeal should be expedited.

(2) If the judge decides that the appeal should be expedited, he may order an adjournment.

(3) If the judge decides that the appeal should not be expedited, he may-

    (a) order an adjournment, or

    (b) discharge the jury (if one has been sworn).

(4) If he decides that the appeal should be expedited, he or the Court of Appeal may subsequently reverse that decision and, if it is reversed, the judge may act as mentioned in subsection (3)(a) or (b).

65. Continuation of proceedings for offences not affected by ruling

(1) This section applies where the prosecution informs the court in accordance with section 62(5).

(2) Proceedings may be continued in respect of any offence which is not the subject of the appeal.

66. Determination of appeal by Court of Appeal

(1) On an appeal under section 62, the Court of Appeal may confirm, reverse or vary any ruling to which the appeal relates.

(2) In addition, the Court of Appeal must, in respect of the offence or each offence which is the subject of the appeal, do any of the following—

    (a) order that proceedings for that offence be resumed in the Crown Court,

    (b) order that a fresh trial may take place in the Crown Court for that offence,

    (c) order that the defendant in relation to that offence be acquitted of that offence.

(3) But no order may be made under subsection (2)(c) in respect of an offence unless the prosecution has indicated that it does not intend to continue with the prosecution of that offence.

67. Reversal of rulings

The Court of Appeal may not reverse a ruling on an appeal under this Part unless it is satisfied—

(a) that the ruling was wrong in law,

(b) that the ruling involved an error of law or principle, or

(c) that the ruling was a ruling that it was not reasonable for the judge to have made.

Miscellaneous and supplemental

68. Appeals to the House of Lords

(1) In section 33(1) of the 1968 Act (right of appeal to House of Lords) after "this Act" there is inserted "or Part 9 of the Criminal Justice Act 2003".

(2) In section 36 of the 1968 Act (bail on appeal by defendant) after "under" there is inserted "Part 9 of the Criminal Justice Act 2003 or".

(3) In this Part "the 1968 Act" means the Criminal Appeal Act 1968 (c. 19).

69. Costs

(1) The Prosecution of Offences Act 1985 (c. 23) is amended as follows.

(2) In section 16(4A) (defence costs on an appeal under section 9(11) of Criminal Justice Act 1987 may be met out of central funds) after "hearings)" there is inserted "or under Part 9 of the Criminal Justice Act 2003".

(3) In section 18 (award of costs against accused) after subsection (2) there is inserted—

"(2A) Where the Court of Appeal reverses or varies a ruling on an appeal under Part 9 of the Criminal Justice Act 2003, it may make such order as to the costs to be paid by the accused, to such person as may be named in the order, as it considers just and reasonable."

(4) In subsection (6) after "subsection (2)" there is instered "or (2A)".

70. Effect on time limits in relation to preliminary stages

(1) Section 22 of the Prosecution of Offences Act 1985 (c. 23) (power of Secretary of State to set time limits in relation to preliminary stages of criminal proceedings) is amended as follows.

(2) After subsection (6A) there is inserted—

"(6B) Any period during which proceedings for an offence are adjourned pending the determination of an appeal under Part 9 of the Criminal Justice Act 2003 shall be disregarded, so far as the offence is concerned, for the purposes of the overall time limit and the custody time limit which applies to the stage which the proceedings have reached when they are adjourned."

71. Restrictions on reporting

(1) Except as provided by this section no publication shall include a report of—
   (a) anything done under section 58, 59, 62, 63 or 64,
   (b) an appeal under this Part,
   (c) an appeal under Part 2 of the 1968 Act in relation to an appeal under this Part, or
   (d) an application for leave to appeal in relation to appeal mentioned in paragraph (b) or (c).

(2) The judge may order that subsection (1) is not to apply, or is not to apply to a specified extent, to a report of—
   (a) anything done under section 58, 59, 62, 63 or 64, or
   (b) an application to the judge for leave to appeal to the Court of Appeal under this Part.

(3) The Court of Appeal may order that subsection (1) is not to apply, or is not to apply to a specified extent, to a report of—
   (a) an appeal to the Court of Appeal under this Part,
   (b) an application to that Court for leave to appeal to it under this Part, or
   (c) an application to that Court for leave to appeal to the House of Lords under Part 2 of the 1968 Act.

(4) The House of Lords may order that subsection (1) is not to apply, or is not to apply to a specified extent, to a report of—
   (a) an appeal to that House under Part 2 of the 1968 Act, or
   (b) an application to that House for leave to appeal to it under Part 2 of that Act.

(5) Where there is only one defendant and he objects to the making of an order under subsection (2), (3) or (4)—

    (a) the judge, the Court of Appeal or the House of Lords are to make the order if (and only if) satisfied, after hearing the representations of the defendant, that it is in the interests of justice to do so, and

    (b) the order (if made) is not to apply to the extent that a report deals with any such objection or representations.

(6) Where there are two or more defendants and one or more of them object to the making of an order under subsection (2), (3) or (4)—

    (a) the judge, the Court of Appeal or the House of Lords are to make the order if (and only if) satisfied, after hearing the representations of each of the defendants, that it is in the interests of justice to do so, and

    (b) the order (if made) is not to apply to the extent that a report deals with any such objection or representations.

(7) Subsection (1) does not apply to the inclusion in a publication of a report of—

    (a) anything done under section 58, 59, 62, 63 or 64,

    (b) an appeal under this Part,

    (c) an appeal under Part 2 of the 1968 Act in relation to an appeal under this Part, or

    (d) an application for leave to appeal in relation to an appeal mentioned in paragraph (b) or (c),

at the conclusion of the trial of the defendant or the last of the defendants to be tried.

(8) Subsection (1) does not apply to a report which contains only one or more of the following matters—

    (a) the identity of the court and the name of the judge,

    (b) the names, ages, home addresses and occupations of the defendant or defendants and witnesses,

    (c) the offence or offences, or a summary of them, with which the defendant or defendants are charged,

    (d) the names of counsel and solicitors in the proceedings,

    (e) where the proceedings are adjourned, the date and place to which they are adjourned,

    (f) any arangemnts as to bail,

    (g) whether a right to representation funded by the Legal Services Commission as part of the Criminal Defence Service was granted to the defendant or any of the defendants.

(9) The addresses that may be included in a report by virtue of subsection (8) are addresses—

    (a) at any relevant time, and

    (b) at the time of their inclusion in the publication.

(10) Nothing in this section affects any prohibition or restriction by virtue of any other enactment on the inclusion of any matter in a publication.

(11) In this section—

"programme service" has the same meaning as in the Broadcasting Act 1990 (c. 42),

"publication" includes any speech, writing, relevant programme or other communication in whatever form, which is addressed to the public at large or any section of the public (and for this purpose every relevant programme is to be taken to be so addressed), but does not include an indictment or other document prepared for use in particular legal proceedings,

"relevant time" means a time when events giving rise to the charges to which the proceedings relate are alleged to have occurred,

"relevant programme" means a programme included in a programme service.

72. Offences in connection with reporting

(1) This section applies if a publication includes a report in contravention of section 71.

(2) Where the publication is a newspaper or periodical, any proprietor, editor or publisher of the newspaper or periodical is guilty of an offence.

(3) Where the publication is a relevant programme—

    (a) any body corporate or Scottish partnership engaged in providing the programme service in which the programme is included, and

    (b) any person having functions in relation to the programme corresponding to those of an editor of a newspaper,

is guilty of an offence.

(4) In the case of any other publication, any person publishing it is guilty of an offence.

(5) If an offence under this section committed by a body corporate is proved—

    (a) to have been committed with the consent or connivance of, or

    (b) to be attributable to any neglect on the part of,

an officer, the officer as well as the body corporate is guilty of the offence and liable to be proceeded against and punished accordingly.

(6) In subsection (5), "officer" means a director, manager, secretary or other similar officer of the body, or a person purporting to act in any such capacity.

(7) If the affairs of a body corporate are managed by its members, "director" in subsection (6) means a member of that body.

(8) Where an offence under this section is committed by a Scottish partnership and is proved to have been committed with the consent or connivance of a partner, he as well as the partnership shall be guilty of the offence and shall be liable to be proceeded against and punished accordingly.

(9) A person guilty of an offence under this section is liable on summary conviction to a fine not exceeding level 5 on the standard scale.

(10) Proceedings for an offence under this section may not be instituted—

    (a) in England and Wales otherwise than by or with the consent of the Attorney General, or

    (b) in Northern Ireland otherwise than by or with the consent of-

        (i) before the relevant date, the Attorney General for Northern Ireland, or

        (ii) on or after the relevant date, the Director of Public Prosecutions for Northern Ireland.

(11) In subsection (10) "the relevant date" means the date on which section 22(1) of the Justice (Northern Ireland) Act 2002 (c. 26) comes into force.

73. Rules of court

(1) Rules of court may make such provision as appears to the authority making them to be necessary or expedient for the purposes of this Part.

(2) Without limiting subsection (1), rules of court may in particular make provision—

    (a) for time limits which are to apply in connection with any provisions of this Part,

    (b) as to procedures to be applied in connection with this Part,

    (c) enabling a single judge of the Court of Appeal to give leave to appeal under this Part or to exercise the power of the Court of Appeal under section 58(12).

(3) Nothing in this section is to be taken as affecting the generality of any enactment conferring powers to make rules of court.

74. Interpretation of Part 9

(1) In this Part—

"programme service" has the meaning given by section 71(11), "publication" has the meaning given by section 71(11), "qualifying evidentiary ruling" is to be construed in accordance with section 62(2),

"the relevant condition" is to be construed in accordance with section 63(2) and (3),

"relevant programme" has the meaning given by section 71(11),

"ruling" includes a decision, determination, direction, finding, notice, order, refusal, rejection or requirement,

"the 1968 Act" means the Criminal Appeal Act 1968 (c. 19).

(2) Any reference in this Part (other than section 73(2)(c)) to a judge is a reference to a judge of the Crown Court.

(3) There is to be no right of appeal under this Part in respect of a ruling in relation to which the prosecution has previously informed the court of its intention to appeal under either section 58(4) or 62(5).

(4) Where a ruling relates to two or more offences but not all of those offences are the subject of an appal under this Part, nothing in this Part is to be regarded as affecting the ruling so far as it relates to any offence which is not the subject of the appeal.

(5) Where two or more defendants are charged jointly with the same offence, the provisions of this Part are to apply as if the offence, so far as relating to each defendant, were a separate offence (so that, for example, any reference in this Part to a ruling which relates to one or more offences includes a ruling which relates to one or more of those separate offences).

(6) Subject to rules of court made under section 53(1) of the Supreme Court Act 1981 (c. 54) (power by rules to distribute business of Court of Appeal between its civil and criminal divisions)—

(a) the jurisdiction of the Court of Appeal under this Part is to be exercisd by the criminal division of that court, and

(b) references in this Part to the Court of Appeal are to be construed as references to that division.

PART 10. RETRIAL FOR SERIOUS OFFENCES

Cases that may be retried

75. Cases that may be retried

(1) This Part applies where a person has been acquitted of a qualifying offence in proceedings—

(a) on indictment in England and Wales,

(b) on appeal against a conviction, verdict or finding in proceedings on indictment in England and Wales, or

(c) on appeal from a decision on such an appeal.

(2) A person acquitted of an offence in proceedings mentioned in subsection (1) is treated for the purposes of that subsection as also acquitted of any qualifying offence of which he could have been convicted in the proceedings because of the first-mentioned offence being charged in the indictment, except an offence—

(a) of which he has been convicted,

(b) of which he has been found not guilty by reason of insanity, or

(c) in respect of which, in proceedings where he has been found to be under a disability (as defined by section 4 of the Criminal Procedure (Insanity) Act 1964 (c. 84)), a finding has been made that he did the act or made the omission charged against him.

(3) References in subsections (1) and (2) to a qualifying offence do not include references to an offence which, at the time of the acquittal, was the subject of an order under section 77(1) or (3)

(4) This Part also applies where a person has been acquitted, in proceedings elsewhere than in the United Kingdom, of an offence under the law of the place where the proceedings were held, if the commission of the offence as alleged would have amounted to or included the commission (in the United Kingdom or elsewhere) of a qualifying offence.

(5) Conduct punishable under the law in force elsewhere than in the United Kingdom is an offence under that law for the purposes of subsection (4), however it is described in that law

(6) This Part applies whether the acquittal was before or after the passing of this Act.

(7) References in this Part to acquittal are to acquittal in circumstances within subsection (1) or (4).

(8) In this Part "qualifying offence" means an offence listed in Part 1 of Schedule 5.

Application for retrial

76. Application to Court of Appeal

(1) A prosecutor may apply to the Court of Appeal for an order—
  (a) quashing a person's acquittal in proceedings within section 75(1), and
  (b) ordering him to be retried for the qualifying offence.

(2) A prosecutor may apply to the Court of Appeal, in the case of a person acquitted elsewhere than in the United Kingdom, for—
  (a) a determination whether the acquittal is a bar to the person being tried in England and Wales for the qualifying offence, and
  (b) if it is, an order that the acquittal is not to be a bar.

(3) A prosecutor may make an application under subsection (1) or (2) only with the written consent of the Director of Public Prosecutions.

(4) The Director of Public Prosecutions may give his consent only if satisfied that—
  (a) there is evidence as respects which the requirements of section 78 appear to be met,
  (b) it is in the public interest for the application to proceed, and
  (c) any trial pursuant to an order on the application would not be inconsistent with obligations of the United Kingdom under Article 31 or 34 of the Treaty on European Union relating to the principle of ne bis in idem.

(5) Not more than one application may be made under subsection (1) or (2) in relation to an acquittal.

77. Determination by Court of Appeal

(1) On an application under section 76(1), the Court of Appeal—
  (a) if satisfied that the requirements of sections 78 and 79 are met, must make the order applied for;
  (b) otherwise, must dismiss the application.

(2) Subsections (3) and (4) apply to an application under section 76(2).

(3) Where the Court of Appeal determines that the acquittal is a bar to the person being tried for the qualifying offence, the court—
  (a) if satisfied that the requirements of sections 78 and 79 are met, must make the order applied for;
  (b) otherwise, must make a declaration to the effect that the acquittal is a bar to the person being tried for the offence.

(4) Where the Court of Appeal determines that the acquittal is not a bar to the person being tried for the qualifying offence, it must make a declaration to that effect.

78. New and compelling evidence

(1) The requirements of this section are met if there is new and compelling evidence against the acquitted person in relation to the qualifying offence.

(2) Evidence is new if it was not adduced in the proceedings in which the person was acquitted (nor, if those were appeal proceedings, in earlier proceedings to which the appeal related).

(3) Evidence is compelling if—

    (a) it is reliable,

    (b) it is substantial, and

    (c) in the context of the outstanding issues, it appears highly probative of the case against the acquitted person.

(4) The outstanding issues are the issues in dispute in the proceedings in which the person was acquitted and, if those were appeal proceedings, any other issues remaining in dispute from earlier proceedings to which the appeal related.

(5) For the purposes of this section, it is irrelevant whether any evidence would have been admissible in earlier proceedings against the acquitted person.

79. Interests of justice

(1) The requirements of this section are met if in all the circumstances it is in the interests of justice for the court to make the order under section 77.

(2) That question is to be determined having regard in particular to—

    (a) whether existing circumstances make a fair trial unlikely;

    (b) for the purposes of that question and otherwise, the length of time since the qualifying offence was allegedly committed;

    (c) whether it is likely that the new evidence would have been adduced in the earlier proceedings against the acquitted person but for a failure by an officer or by a prosecutor to act with due diligence or expedition;

    (d) whether, since those proceedings or, if later, since the commencement of this Part, any officer or prosecutor has failed to act with due diligence or expedition.

(3) In subsection (2) references to an officer or prosecutor include references to a person charged with corresponding duties under the law in force elsewhere than in England and Wales.

(4) Where the earlier prosecution was conducted by a person other than a prosecutor, subsection (2)(c) applies in relation to that person as well as in relation to a prosecutor.

80. Procedure and evidence

(1) A prosecutor who wishes to make an application under section 76(1) or (2) must give notice of the application to the Court of Appeal.

(2) Within two days beginning with the day on which any such notice is given, notice of the application must be served by the prosecutor on the person to whom the application relates, charging him with the offence to which it relates or, if he has been charged with it in accordance with section 87(4), stating that he has been so charged.

(3) Subsection (2) applies whether the person to whom the application relates is in the United Kingdom or elsewhere, but the Court of Appeal may, on application by the prosecutor, extend the time for service under that subsection if it considers it necessary to do so because of that person's absence from the United Kingdom.

(4) The Court of Appeal must consider the application at a hearing.

(5) The person to whom the application relates—

(a) is entitled to be present at the hearing, although he may be in custody, unless he is in custody elsewhere than in England and Wales or Northern Ireland, and

(b) is entitled to be represented at the hearing, whether he is present or not.

(6) For the purposes of the application, the Court of Appeal may, if it thinks it necessary or expedient in the interests of justice—

(a) order the production of any document, exhibit or other thing, the production of which appears to the court to be necessary for the determination of the application, and

(b) order any witness who would be a compellable witness in proceedings pursuant to an order or declaration made on the application to attend for examination and be examined before the court.

(7) The Court of Appeal may at one hearing consider more than one application (whether or not relating to the same person), but only if the offences concerned could be tried on the same indictment.

81. Appeals

(1) The Criminal Appeal Act 1968 (c. 19) is amended as follows.

(2) In section 33 (right of appeal to House of Lords), after subsection (1A) there is inserted—

"(1B) An appeal lies to the House of Lords, at the instance of the acquitted person or the prosecutor, from any decision of the Court of Appeal on an application under section 76(1) or (2) of the Criminal Justice Act 2003 (retrial for serious offences)."

(3) At the end of that section there is inserted—

"(4) In relation to an appeal under subsection (1B), references in this Part to a defendant are references to the acquitted person."

(4) In section 34(2) (extension of time for leave to appeal), after "defendant" there is inserted "or, in the case of an appeal under section 33(1B), by the prosecutor"

(5) In section 38 (presence of defendant at hearing), for "has been convicted of an offence and" substitute "has been convicted of an offence, or in whose case an order under section 77 of the Criminal Justice Act 2003 or a declaration under section 77(4) of that Act has been made, and who".

82. Restrictions on publication in the interests of justice

(1) Where it appears to the Court of Appeal that the inclusion of any matter in a publication would give rise to a substantial risk of prejudice to the administration of justice in a retrial, the court may order that the matter is not to be included in any publication while the order has effect.

(2) In subsection (1) "retrial" means the trial of an acquitted person for a qualifying offence pursuant to any order made or that may be made under section 77.

(3) The court may make an order under this section only if it appears to it necessary in the interests of justice to do so.

(4) An order under this section may apply to a matter which has been included in a publication published before the order takes effect, but such an order—

(a) applies only to the later inclusion of the matter in a publication (whether directly or by inclusion of the earlier publication), and

(b) does not otherwise affect the earlier publication.

(5) After notice of an application has been given under section 80(1) relating to the acquitted person and the qualifying offence, the court may make an order under this section only—

     (a) of its own motion, or

     (b) on the application of the Director of Public Prosecutions.

(6)   Before such notice has been given, an order under this section—

     (a) may be made only on the application of the Director of Public Prosecutions, and

     (b) may not be made unless, since the acquittal concerned, an investigation of the commission by the acquitted person of the qualifying offence has been commenced by officers.

(7)   The court may at any time, of its own motion or on an application made by the Director of Public Prosecutions or the acquitted person, vary or revoke an order under this section.

(8)   Any order made under this section before notice of an application has been given under section 80(1) relating to the acquitted person and the qualifying offence must specify the time when it ceases to have effect.

(9)   An order under this section which is made or has effect after such notice has been given ceases to have effect, unless it specifies an earlier time—

     (a) when there is no longer any step that could be taken which would lead to the acquitted person being tried pursuant to an order made on the application, or

     (b) if he is tried pursuant to such an order, at the conclusion of the trial.

(10) Nothing in this section affects any prohibition or restriction by virtue of any other enactment on the inclusion of any matter in a publication or any power, under an enactment or otherwise, to impose such a prohibition or restriction.

(11) In this section—

     "programme service" has the same meaning as in the Broadcasting Act 1990 (c. 42),

     "publication" includes any speech, writing, relevant programme or other communication in whatever form, which is addressed to the public at large or any section of the public (and for this purpose every relevant programme is to be taken to be so addressed), but does not include an indictment or other document prepared for use in particular legal proceedings,

     "relevant programme" means a programme included in a programme service.

83. Offences in connection with publication restrictions

(1)   This section applies if—

     (a) an order under section 82 is made, whether in England and Wales or Northern Ireland, and

     (b) while the order has effect, any matter is included in a publication, in any part of the United Kingdom, in contravention of the order.

(2)   Where the publication is a newspaper or periodical, any proprietor, editor or publisher of the newspaper or periodical is guilty of an offence.

(3)   Where the publication is a relevant programme—

     (a) any body corporate or Scottish partnership engaged in providing the programme service in which the programme is included, and

     (b) any person having functions in relation to the programme corresponding to those of an editor of a newspaper,

     is guilty of an offence.

(4)   In the case of any other publication, any person publishing it is guilty of an offence.

(5)   If an offence under this section committed by a body corporate is proved—

     (a) to have been committed with the consent or connivance of, or

     (b) to be attributable to any neglect on the part of,

an officer, the officer as well as the body corporate is guilty of the offence and liable to be proceeded against and punished accordingly.

(6) In subsection (5), "officer" means a director, manager, secretary or other similar officer of the body, or a person purporting to act in any such capacity.

(7) If the affairs of a body corporate are managed by its members, "director" in subsection (6) means a member of that body.

(8) Where an offence under this section is committed by a Scottish partnership and is proved to have been committed with the consent or connivance of a partner, he as well as the partnership shall be guilty of the offence and shall be liable to be proceeded against and punished accordingly.

(9) A person guilty of an offence under this section is liable on summary conviction to a fine not exceeding level 5 on the standard scale.

(10) Proceedings for an offence under this section may not be instituted—
  (a) in England and Wales otherwise than by or with the consent of the Attorney General, or
  (b) in Northern Ireland otherwise than by or with the consent of—
    (i) before the relevant date, the Attorney General for Northern Ireland, or
    (ii) on or after the relevant date, the Director of Public Prosecutions for Northern Ireland.

(11) In subsection (10) "the relevant date" means the date on which section 22(1) of the Justice (Northern Ireland) Act 2002 (c. 26) comes into force.

Retrial

84. Retrial

(1) Where a person—
  (a) is tried pursuant to an order under section 77(1), or
  (b) is tried on indictment pursuant to an order under section 77(3),
  the trial must be on an indictment preferred by direction of the Court of Appeal.

(2) After the end of 2 months after the date of the order, the person may not be arraigned on an indictment preferred in pursuance of such a direction unless the Court of Appeal gives leave.

(3) The Court of Appeal must not give leave unless satisfied that—
  (a) the prosecutor has acted with due expedition, and
  (b) there is a good and sufficient cause for trial despite the lapse of time since the order under section 77.

(4) Where the person may not be arraigned without leave, he may apply to the Court of Appeal to set aside the order and—
  (a) for any direction required for restoring an earlier judgment and verdict of acquittal of the qualifying offence, or
  (b) in the case of a person acquitted elsewhere than in the United Kingdom, for a declaration to the effect that the acquittal is a bar to his being tried for the qualifying offence.

(5) An indictment under subsection (1) may relate to more than one offence, or more than one person, and may relate to an offence which, or a person who, is not the subject of an order or declaration under section 77.

(6) Evidence given at a trial pursuant to an order under section 77(1) or (3) must be given orally if it was given orally at the original trial, unless—
  (a) all the parties to the trial agree otherwise,
  (b) section 116 applies, or

   (c) the witness is unavailable to give evidence, otherwise than as mentioned in subsection (2) of that section, and section 114(1)(d) applies.

(7) At a trial pursuant to an order under section 77(1), paragraph 5 of Schedule 3 to the Crime and Disorder Act 1998 (c. 37) (use of depositions) does not apply to a deposition read as evidence at the original trial.

Investigations

85. Authorisation of investigations

(1) This section applies to the investigation of the commission of a qualifying offence by a person—
   (a) acquitted in proceedings within section 75(1) of the qualifying offence, or
   (b) acquitted elsewhere than in the United Kingdom of an offence the commission of which as alleged would have amounted to or included the commission (in the United Kingdom or elsewhere) of the qualifying offence.

(2) Subject to section 86, an officer may not do anything within subsection (3) for the purposes of such an investigation unless the Director of Public Prosecutions—
   (a) has certified that in his opinion the acquittal would not be a bar to the trial of the acquitted person in England and Wales for the qualifying offence, or
   (b) has given his written consent to the investigation (whether before or after the start of the investigation).

(3) The officer may not, either with or without the consent of the acquitted person—
   (a) arrest or question him,
   (b) search him or premises owned or occupied by him,
   (c) search a vehicle owned by him or anything in or on such a vehicle,
   (d) seize anything in his possession, or
   (e) take his fingerprints or take a sample from him.

(4) The Director of Public Prosecutions may only give his consent on a written application, and such an application may be made only by an officer who—
   (a) if he is an officer of the metropolitan police force or the City of London police force, is of the rank of commander or above, or
   (b) in any other case, is of the rank of assistant chief constable or above.

(5) An officer may make an application under subsection (4) only if—
   (a) he is satisfied that new evidence has been obtained which would be relevant to an application under section 76(1) or (2) in respect of the qualifying offence to which the investigation relates, or
   (b) he has reasonable grounds for believing that such new evidence is likely to be obtained as a result of the investigation.

(6) The Director of Public Prosecutions may not give his consent unless satisfied that—
   (a) there is, or there is likely as a result of the investigation to be, sufficient new evidence to warrant the conduct of the investigation, and
   (b) it is in the public interest for the investigation to proceed.

(7) In giving his consent, the Director of Public Prosecutions may recommend that the investigation be conducted otherwise than by officers of a specified police force or specified team of customs and excise officers.

86. Urgent investigative steps

(1) Section 85 does not prevent an officer from taking any action for the purposes of an investigation if—

    (a) the action is necessary as a matter of urgency to prevent the investigation being substantially and irrevocably prejudiced,

    (b) the requirements of subsection (2) are met, and

    (c) either—

        (i) the action is authorised under subsection (3), or

        (ii) the requirements of subsection (5) are met.

(2) The requirements of this subsection are met if—

    (a) there has been no undue delay in applying for consent under section 85(2),

    (b) that consent has not been refused, and

    (c) taking into account the urgency of the situation, it is not reasonably practicable to obtain that consent before taking the action.

(3) An officer of the rank of superintendent or above may authorise the action if—

    (a) he is satisfied that new evidence has been obtained which would be relevant to an application under section 76(1) or (2) in respect of the qualifying offence to which the investigation relates, or

    (b) he has reasonable grounds for believing that such new evidence is likely to be obtained as a result of the investigation.

(4) An authorisation under subsection (3) must—

    (a) if reasonably practicable, be given in writing;

    (b) otherwise, be recorded in writing by the officer giving it as soon as is reasonably practicable.

(5) The requirements of this subsection are met if—

    (a) there has been no undue delay in applying for authorisation under subsection (3),

    (b) that authorisation has not been refused, and

    (c) taking into account the urgency of the situation, it is not reasonably practicable to obtain that authorisation before taking the action.

(6) Where the requirements of subsection (5) are met, the action is nevertheless to be treated as having been unlawful unless, as soon as reasonably practicable after the action is taken, an officer of the rank of superintendent or above certifies in writing that he is satisfied that, when the action was taken—

    (a) new evidence had been obtained which would be relevant to an application under section 76(1) or (2) in respect of the qualifying offence to which the investigation relates, or

    (b) the officer who took the action had reasonable grounds for believing that such new evidence was likely to be obtained as a result of the investigation.

Arrest, custody and bail

87. Arrest and charge

(1) Where section 85 applies to the investigation of the commission of an offence by any person and no certification has been given under subsection (2) of that section—

    (a) a justice of the peace may issue a warrant to arrest that person for that offence only if satisfied by written information that new evidence has been obtained which would be relevant to an application under section 76(1) or (2) in respect of the commission by that person of that offence, and

    (b) that person may not be arrested for that offence except under a warrant so issued.

(2) Subsection (1) does not affect section 89(3)(b) or 91(3), or any other power to arrest a person, or to issue a warrant for the arrest of a person, otherwise than for an offence.

(3) Part 4 of the 1984 Act (detention) applies as follows where a person—

    (a) is arrested for an offence under a warrant issued in accordance with subsection (1)(a), or

    (b) having been so arrested, is subsequently treated under section 34(7) of that Act as arrested for that offence.

(4) For the purposes of that Part there is sufficient evidence to charge the person with the offence for which he has been arrested if, and only if, an officer of the rank of superintendent or above (who has not been directly involved in the investigation) is of the opinion that the evidence available or known to him is sufficient for the case to be referred to a prosecutor to consider whether consent should be sought for an application in respect of that person under section 76.

(5) For the purposes of that Part it is the duty of the custody officer at each police station where the person is detained to make available or known to an officer at that police station of the rank of superintendent or above any evidence which it appears to him may be relevant to an application under section 76(1) or (2) in respect of the offence for which the person has been arrested, and to do so as soon as practicable—

    (a) after the evidence becomes available or known to him, or

    (b) if later, after he forms that view.

(6) Section 37 of that Act (including any provision of that section as applied by section 40(8) of that Act) has effect subject to the following modifications—

    (a) in subsection (1)—

        (i) for "determine whether he has before him" there is substituted "request an officer of the rank of superintendent or above (who has not been directly involved in the investigation) to determine, in accordance with section 87(4) of the Criminal Justice Act 2003, whether there is";

        (ii) for "him to do so" there is substituted "that determination to be made";

    (b) in subsection (2)—

        (i) for the words from "custody officer determines" to "before him" there is substituted "officer determines that there is not such sufficient evidence";

        (ii) the word "custody" is omitted from the second place where it occurs;

    (c) in subsection (3)—

        (i) the word "custody" is omitted;

        (ii) after "may" there is inserted "direct the custody officer to";

    (d) in subsection (7) for the words from "the custody officer" to the end of that subsection there is substituted "an officer of the rank of superintendent or above (who has not been directly involved in the investigation) determines, in accordance with section 87(4) of the Criminal Justice Act 2003, that there is sufficient evidence to charge the person arrested with the offence for which he was arrested, the person arrested shall be charged.";

    (e) subsections (7A), (7B) and (8) do not apply;

    (f) after subsection (10) there is inserted—

        "(10A) The officer who is requested by the custody officer to make a determination under subsection (1) above shall make that determination as soon as practicable after the request is made."

(7) Section 40 of that Act has effect as if in subsections (8) and (9) of that section after "(6)" there were inserted "and (10A)"

(8) Section 42 of that Act has effect as if in subsection (1) of that section for the words from "who" to "detained" there were substituted "(who has not been directly involved in the investigation)"

88. Bail and custody before application

(1) In relation to a person charged in accordance with section 87(4)—

    (a) section 38 of the 1984 Act (including any provision of that section as applied by section 40(10) of that Act) has effect as if, in subsection (1), for "either on bail or without bail" there were substituted "on bail",

    (b) section 47(3) of that Act does not apply and references in section 38 of that Act to bail are references to bail subject to a duty to appear before the Crown Court at such place as the custody officer may appoint and at such time, not later than 24 hours after the person is released, as that officer may appoint, and

    (c) section 43B of the Magistrates' Courts Act 1980 (c. 43) does not apply.

(2) Where such a person is, after being charged—

    (a) kept in police detention, or

    (b) detained by a local authority in pursuance of arrangements made under section 38(6) of the 1984 Act,

he must be brought before the Crown Court as soon as practicable and, in any event, not more than 24 hours after he is charged, and section 46 of the 1984 Act does not apply.

(3) For the purpose of calculating the period referred to in subsection (1) or (2), the following are to be disregarded—

    (a) Sunday,

    (b) Christmas Day,

    (c) Good Friday, and

    (d) any day which is a bank holiday under the Banking and Financial Dealings Act 1971 (c. 80) in the part of the United Kingdom where the person is to appear before the Crown Court as mentioned in subsection (1) or, where subsection (2) applies, is for the time being detained.

(4) Where a person appears or is brought before the Crown Court in accordance with subsection (1) or (2), the Crown Court may either—

    (a) grant bail for the person to appear, if notice of an application is served on him under section 80(2), before the Court of Appeal at the hearing of that application, or

    (b) remand the person in custody to be brought before the Crown Court under section 89(2).

(5) If the Crown Court grants bail under subsection (4), it may revoke bail and remand the person in custody as referred to in subsection (4)(b)

(6) In subsection (7) the "relevant period", in relation to a person granted bail or remanded in custody under subsection (4), means—

    (a) the period of 42 days beginning with the day on which he is granted bail or remanded in custody under that subsection, or

    (b) that period as extended or further extended under subsection (8).

(7) If at the end of the relevant period no notice of an application under section 76(1) or (2) in relation to the person has been given under section 80(1), the person—

    (a) if on bail subject to a duty to appear as mentioned in subsection (4)(a), ceases to be subject to that duty and to any conditions of that bail, and

    (b) if in custody on remand under subsection (4)(b) or (5), must be released immediately without bail.

(8) The Crown Court may, on the application of a prosecutor, extend or further extend the period mentioned in subsection (6)(a) until a specified date, but only if satisfied that—

(a) the need for the extension is due to some good and sufficient cause, and

(b) the prosecutor has acted with all due diligence and expedition.

89. Bail and custody before hearing

(1) This section applies where notice of an application is given under section 80(1).

(2) If the person to whom the application relates is in custody under section 88(4)(b) or (5), he must be brought before the Crown Court as soon as practicable and, in any event, within 48 hours after the notice is given.

(3) If that person is not in custody under section 88(4)(b) or (5), the Crown Court may, on application by the prosecutor—

(a) issue a summons requiring the person to appear before the Court of Appeal at the hearing of the application, or

(b) issue a warrant for the person's arrest,

and a warrant under paragraph (b) may be issued at any time even though a summons has previously been issued.

(4) Where a summons is issued under subsection (3)(a), the time and place at which the person must appear may be specified either—

(a) in the summons, or

(b) in a subsequent direction of the Crown Court.

(5) The time or place specified may be varied from time to time by a direction of the Crown Court

(6) A person arrested under a warrant under subsection (3)(b) must be brought before the Crown Court as soon as practicable and in any event within 48 hours after his arrest, and section 81(5) of the Supreme Court Act 1981 (c. 54) does not apply.

(7) If a person is brought before the Crown Court under subsection (2) or (6) the court must either—

(a) remand him in custody to be brought before the Court of Appeal at the hearing of the application, or

(b) grant bail for him to appear before the Court of Appeal at the hearing.

(8) If bail is granted under subsection (7)(b), the Crown Court may revoke the bail and remand the person in custody as referred to in subsection (7)(a).

(9) For the purpose of calculating the period referred to in subsection (2) or (6), the following are to be disregarded—

(a) Sunday,

(b) Christmas Day,

(c) Good Friday, and

(d) any day which is a bank holiday under the Banking and Financial Dealings Act 1971 (c. 80) in the part of the United Kingdom where the person is for the time being detained.

90. Bail and custody during and after hearing

(1) The Court of Appeal may, at any adjournment of the hearing of an application under section 76(1) or (2)—

(a) remand the person to whom the application relates on bail, or

(b) remand him in custody.

(2) At a hearing at which the Court of Appeal—

(a) makes an order under section 77,

(b) makes a declaration under subsection (4) of that section, or

    (c) dismisses the application or makes a declaration under subsection (3) of that section, if it also gives the prosecutor leave to appeal against its decision or the prosecutor gives notice that he intends to apply for such leave,

the court may make such order as it sees fit for the custody or bail of the acquitted person pending trial pursuant to the order or declaration, or pending determination of the appeal.

(3) For the purpose of subsection (2), the determination of an appeal is pending—

    (a) until any application for leave to appeal is disposed of, or the time within which it must be made expires;

    (b) if leave to appeal is granted, until the appeal is disposed of.

(4) Section 4 of the Bail Act 1976 (c. 63) applies in relation to the grant of bail under this section as if in subsection (2) the reference to the Crown Court included a reference to the Court of Appeal.

(5) The court may at any time, as it sees fit—

    (a) revoke bail granted under this section and remand the person in custody, or

    (b) vary an order under subsection (2).

91. Revocation of bail

(1) Where—

    (a) a court revokes a person's bail under this Part, and

    (b) that person is not before the court when his bail is revoked,

the court must order him to surrender himself forthwith to the custody of the court.

(2) Where a person surrenders himself into the custody of the court in compliance with an order under subsection (1), the court must remand him in custody.

(3) A person who has been ordered to surrender to custody under subsection (1) may be arrested without a warrant by an officer if he fails without reasonable cause to surrender to custody in accordance with the order.

(4) A person arrested under subsection (3) must be brought as soon as practicable, and, in any event, not more than 24 hours after he is arrested, before the court and the court must remand him in custody.

(5) For the purpose of calculating the period referred to in subsection (4), the following are to be disregarded—

    (a) Sunday,

    (b) Christmas Day,

    (c) Good Friday,

    (d) any day which is a bank holiday under the Banking and Financial Dealings Act 1971 (c. 80) in the part of the United Kingdom where the person is for the time being detained.

Part 10: supplementary

92. Functions of the DPP

(1) Section 1(7) of the Prosecution of Offences Act 1985 (c. 23) (DPP's functions exercisable by Crown Prosecutor) does not apply to the provisions of this Part other than section 85(2)(a).

(2) In the absence of the Director of Public Prosecutions, his functions under those provisions may be exercised by a person authorised by him.

(3) An authorisation under subsection (2)—

(a) may relate to a specified person or to persons of a specified description, and

(b) may be general or relate to a specified function or specified circumstances.

93. Rules of court

(1) Rules of court may make such provision as appears to the authority making them to be necessary or expedient for the purposes of this Part.

(2) Without limiting subsection (1), rules of court may in particular make provision as to procedures to be applied in connection with sections 76 to 82, 84 and 88 to 90.

(3) Nothing in this section is to be taken as affecting the generality of any enactment conferring power to make rules of court.

94. Armed Forces: Part 10

(1) Section 31 of the Armed Forces Act 2001 (c. 19) (provision in consequence of enactments relating to criminal justice) applies to an enactment contained in this Part so far as relating to matters not specified in subsection (2) of that section as it applies to a criminal justice enactment.

(2) The power under that section to make provision equivalent to that made in relation to qualifying offences by an enactment contained in this Part (with or without modifications) includes power to make such provision in relation to such service offences as the Secretary of State thinks fit.

(3) In subsection (2) "service offence" means an offence under the Army Act 1955 (3 & 4 Eliz. 2 c. 18), the Air Force Act 1955 (3 & 4 Eliz. 2 c. 19) or the Naval Discipline Act 1957 (c. 53).

95. Interpretation of Part 10

(1) In this Part—

"the 1984 Act" means the Police and Criminal Evidence Act 1984 (c. 60),

"acquittal" and related expressions are to be read in accordance with section 75(7),

"customs and excise officer" means an officer as defined by section 1(1) of the Customs and Excise Management Act 1979 (c. 2), or a person to whom section 8(2) of that Act applies,

"new evidence" is to be read in accordance with section 78(2),

"officer", except in section 83, means an officer of a police force or a customs and excise officer,

"police force" has the meaning given by section 3(3) of the Prosecution of Offences Act 1985 (c. 23),

"prosecutor" means an individual or body charged with duties to conduct criminal prosecutions,

"qualifying offence" has the meaning given by section 75(8).

(2) Subject to rules of court made under section 53(1) of the Supreme Court Act 1981 (c. 54) (power by rules to distribute business of Court of Appeal between its civil and criminal divisions)—

(a) the jurisdiction of the Court of Appeal under this Part is to be exercised by the criminal division of that court, and

(b) references in this Part to the Court of Appeal are to be construed as references to that division.

(3) References in this Part to an officer of a specified rank or above are, in the case of a customs and excise officer, references to an officer of such description as—

    (a) appears to the Commissioners of Customs and Excise to comprise officers of equivalent rank or above, and

    (b) is specified by the Commissioners for the purposes of the provision concerned.

96. Application of Part 10 to Northern Ireland

(1) In its application to Northern Ireland this Part is to have effect subject to the modifications in this section.

(2) In sections 75(1)(a) and (b), 76(2)(a), 79(3) and 85(2)(a) for "England and Wales" substitute "Northern Ireland".

(3) For section 75(2)(c) substitute—

    "(c) in respect of which, in proceedings where he has been found to be unfit to be tried in accordance with Article 49 of the Mental Health (Northern Ireland) Order 1986 (S.I. 1986/595 (N.I. 4)), a finding has been made that he did the act or made the omission charged against him."

(4) In section 75(8) for "Part 1" substitute "Part 2"

(5) In section 81(1) for "Criminal Appeal Act 1968 (c. 19)" substitute "Criminal Appeal (Northern Ireland) Act 1980 (c. 47)"

(6) In section 81(2)—

    (a) for "33" substitute "31", and

    (b) for "An" substitute "Subject to the provisions of this Part of this Act, an"

(7) In section 81(4)—

    (a) for "34(2)" substitute "32(2)", and

    (b) for "33(1B)" substitute "31(1B)"

(8) In section 82(10) after "enactment" in each place insert "(including any provision of Northern Ireland legislation)"

(9) In section 84(1) and (2) for "preferred" substitute "presented".

(10) Section 84(6) has effect—

    (a) as if any reference to a provision of Part 11 were a reference to any corresponding provision contained in an Order in Council to which section 334(1) applies, at any time when such corresponding provision is in force;

    (b) at any other time, with the omission of paragraphs (b) and (c).

(11) After section 84(6) insert—

    "(6A) Article 29 of the Legal Aid, Advice and Assistance (Northern Ireland) Order 1981 (S.I. 1981/228 (N.I. 8)) applies in the case of a person who is to be tried in accordance with subsection (1) as if—

        (a) he had been returned for trial for the offence in question, and

        (b) the reference in paragraph (2)(a) of that Article to a magistrates' court included a reference to the Court of Appeal."

(12) In section 87—

    (a) in subsection (3), for "Part 4 of the 1984 Act" substitute "Part 5 of the Police and Criminal Evidence (Northern Ireland) Order 1989 (S. I. 1989/1341 (N. I. 12)) ("the 1989 Order")",

    (b) in paragraph (b) of that subsection, for "section 34(7) of that Act" substitute "Article 35(8) of that Order",

    (c) in subsection (6)—

(i) for the words from the beginning to "40(8) of that Act)" substitute "Article 38 of that Order (including any provision of that Article as applied by Article 41(8) of that Order)",

(ii) for "subsection" in each place substitute "paragraph",

(iii) in paragraph (e), for "subsections (7A), (7B) and (8)" substitute "paragraph (8)", and

(iv) in paragraph (f), in the inserted paragraph (10A) omit "above",

(d) for subsection (7) substitute—

"(7) Article 41 of that Order has effect as if in paragraphs (8) and (9) of that Article after "(6)" there were inserted "and (10A)".",

(e) in subsection (8)—

(i) for "Section 42 of that Act" substitute "Article 43 of that Order", and

(ii) for "subsection (1) of that section" substitute "paragraph (1) of that Article".

(13) For section 88(1) substitute—

"(1) In relation to a person charged in accordance with section 87(4)—

(a) Article 39 of the 1989 Order (including any provision of that Article as applied by Article 41(10) of that Order) has effect as if, in paragraph (1), for "either on bail or without bail" there were substituted "on bail",

(b) Article 48 of that Order has effect as if for paragraphs (1) to (11) there were substituted—

"(1) A person who is released on bail shall be subject to a duty to appear before the Crown Court at such place as the custody officer may appoint and at such time, not later than 24 hours after the person is released, as that officer may appoint.

(2) The custody officer may require a person who is to be released on bail to enter into a recognisance conditioned upon his subsequent appearance before the Crown Court in accordance with paragraph (1).

(3) A recognisance under paragraph (2) may be taken before the custody officer.", and

(c) Article 132A of the Magistrates' Courts (Northern Ireland) Order 1981 (S.I. 1981/1675 (N.I. 26)) does not apply."

(14) In section 88(2)—

(a) for paragraph (b) substitute—

"(b) detained in a place of safety in pursuance of arrangements made under Article 39(6) of the 1989 Order,", and

(b) for "section 46 of the 1984 Act" substitute "Article 47 of the 1989 Order".

(15) In section 89(6) for "section 81(5) of the Supreme Court Act 1981 (c. 54)" substitute "section 51(8) of the Judicature (Northern Ireland) Act 1978 (c. 23)".

(16) For section 90(4) substitute—

"(4) The court may at any time, as it sees fit, vary the conditions of bail granted under this section."

(17) In section 92(1) for the words from the beginning to "does" substitute "Sections 30(4) and 36 of the Justice (Northern Ireland) Act 2002 (c. 26) do".

(18) Until the coming into force of section 36 of that Act of 2002 the reference to that section in subsection (17) is to be read as a reference to Article 4(8) of the Prosecution of Offences (Northern Ireland) Order 1972 (S.I. 1972/538 (N.I. 1)).

(19) In section 93(2) for "the Criminal Appeal Rules and the Crown Court Rules" substitute "rules under section 55 of the Judicature (Northern Ireland) Act 1978 and Crown Court Rules".

(20) In section 93(3) after "enactment" insert "(including any provision of Northern Ireland legislation)".

(21) In section 95(1) for the definition of "police force" substitute—

" "police force" means—

(a) the Police Service of Northern Ireland or the Police Service of Northern Ireland Reserve,

(b) the Ministry of Defence Police,

(c) any body of constables appointed under Article 19 of the Airports (Northern Ireland) Order 1994 (S.I. 1994/426 (N.I. 1)), or

(d) any body of special constables appointed in Northern Ireland under section 79 of the Harbours, Docks and Piers Clauses Act 1847 (c. 27) or section 57 of the Civil Aviation Act 1982 (c. 16),".

(22) Omit section 95(2).

97. Application of Criminal Appeal Acts to proceedings under Part 10

Subject to the provisions of this Part, the Secretary of State may make an order containing provision, in relation to proceedings before the Court of Appeal under this Part, which corresponds to any provision, in relation to appeals or other proceedings before that court, which is contained in the Criminal Appeal Act 1968 (c. 19) or the Criminal Appeal (Northern Ireland) Act 1980 (c. 47) (subject to any specified modifications).

PART 11. EVIDENCE

CHAPTER 1
EVIDENCE OF BAD CHARACTER

Introductory

98. "Bad character"

References in this Chapter to evidence of a person's "bad character" are to evidence of, or of a disposition towards, misconduct on his part, other than evidence which—

(a) has to do with the alleged facts of the offence with which the defendant is charged, or

(b) is evidence of misconduct in connection with the investigation or prosecution of that offence.

99. Abolition of common law rules

(1) The common law rules governing the admissibility of evidence of bad character in criminal proceedings are abolished.

(2) Subsection (1) is subject to section 118(1) in so far as it preserves the rule under which in criminal proceedings a person's reputation is admissible for the purposes of proving his bad character.

Persons other than defendants

100. Non-defendant's bad character

(1) In criminal proceedings evidence of the bad character of a person other than the defendant is admissible if and only if—

(a) it is important explanatory evidence,

(b) it has substantial probative value in relation to a matter which—

    (i) is a matter in issue in the proceedings, and

    (ii) is of substantial importance in the context of the case as a whole, or

(c) all parties to the proceedings agree to the evidence being admissible.

(2) For the purposes of subsection (1)(a) evidence is important explanatory evidence if—

    (a) without it, the court or jury would find it impossible or difficult properly to understand other evidence in the case, and

    (b) its value for understanding the case as a whole is substantial.

(3) In assessing the probative value of evidence for the purposes of subsection (1)(b) the court must have regard to the following factors (and to any others it considers relevant)—

    (a) the nature and number of the events, or other things, to which the evidence relates;

    (b) when those events or things are alleged to have happened or existed;

    (c) where—

        (i) the evidence is evidence of a person's misconduct, and

        (ii) it is suggested that the evidence has probative value by reason of similarity between that misconduct and other alleged misconduct,

    the nature and extent of the similarities and the dissimilarities between each of the alleged instances of misconduct;

    (d) where—

        (i) the evidence is evidence of a person's misconduct,

        (ii) it is suggested that that person is also responsible for the misconduct charged, and

        (iii) the identity of the person responsible for the misconduct charged is disputed,

    the extent to which the evidence shows or tends to show that the same person was responsible each time.

(4) Except where subsection (1)(c) applies, evidence of the bad character of a person other than the defendant must not be given without leave of the court.

Defendants

101. Defendant's bad character

(1) In criminal proceedings evidence of the defendant's bad character is admissible if, but only if—

    (a) all parties to the proceedings agree to the evidence being admissible,

    (b) the evidence is adduced by the defendant himself or is given in answer to a question asked by him in cross-examination and intended to elicit it,

    (c) it is important explanatory evidence,

    (d) it is relevant to an important matter in issue between the defendant and the prosecution,

    (e) it has substantial probative value in relation to an important matter in issue between the defendant and a co-defendant,

    (f) it is evidence to correct a false impression given by the defendant, or

    (g) the defendant has made an attack on another person's character.

(2) Sections 102 to 106 contain provision supplementing subsection (1).

(3) The court must not admit evidence under subsection (1)(d) or (g) if, on an application by the defendant to exclude it, it appears to the court that the admission of the evidence would have such an adverse effect on the fairness of the proceedings that the court ought not to admit it.

(4) On an application to exclude evidence under subsection (3) the court must have regard, in particular, to the length of time between the matters to which that evidence relates and the matters which form the subject of the offence charged.

102. "Important explanatory evidence"

For the purposes of section 101(1)(c) evidence is important explanatory evidence if—
(a) without it, the court or jury would find it impossible or difficult properly to understand other evidence in the case, and
(b) its value for understanding the case as a whole is substantial.

103. "Matter in issue between the defendant and the prosecution

(1) For the purposes of section 101(1)(d) the matters in issue between the defendant and the prosecution include—
   (a) the question whether the defendant has a propensity to commit offences of the kind with which he is charged, except where his having such a propensity makes it no more likely that he is guilty of the offence;
   (b) the question whether the defendant has a propensity to be untruthful, except where it is not suggested that the defendant's case is untruthful in any respect.
(2) Where subsection (1)(a) applies, a defendant's propensity to commit offences of the kind with which he is charged may (without prejudice to any other way of doing so) be established by evidence that he has been convicted of—
   (a) an offence of the same description as the one with which he is charged, or
   (b) an offence of the same category as the one with which he is charged.
(3) Subsection (2) does not apply in the case of a particular defendant if the court is satisfied, by reason of the length of time since the conviction or for any other reason, that it would be unjust for it to apply in his case.
(4) For the purposes of subsection (2)—
   (a) two offences are of the same description as each other if the statement of the offence in a written charge or indictment would, in each case, be in the same terms;
   (b) two offences are of the same category as each other if they belong to the same category of offences prescribed for the purposes of this section by an order made by the Secretary of State.
(5) A category prescribed by an order under subsection (4)(b) must consist of offences of the same type.
(6) Only prosecution evidence is admissible under section 101(1)(d).

104. "Matter in issue between the defendant and a co-defendant"

(1) Evidence which is relevant to the question whether the defendant has a propensity to be untruthful is admissible on that basis under section 101(1)(e) only if the nature or conduct of his defence is such as to undermine the co-defendant's defence.
(2) Only evidence—
   (a) which is to be (or has been) adduced by the co-defendant, or
   (b) which a witness is to be invited to give (or has given) in cross-examination by the co-defendant,
   is admissible under section 101(1)(e).

105. "Evidence to correct a false impression"

(1) For the purposes of section 101(1)(f)—

    (a) the defendant gives a false impression if he is responsible for the making of an express or implied assertion which is apt to give the court or jury a false or misleading impression about the defendant;

    (b) evidence to correct such an impression is evidence which has probative value in correcting it.

(2) A defendant is treated as being responsible for the making of an assertion if—

    (a) the assertion is made by the defendant in the proceedings (whether or not in evidence given by him),

    (b) the assertion was made by the defendant—

      (i) on being questioned under caution, before charge, about the offence with which he is charged, or

      (ii) on being charged with the offence or officially informed that he might be prosecuted for it, and evidence of the assertion is given in the proceedings,

    (c) the assertion is made by a witness called by the defendant,

    (d) the assertion is made by any witness in cross-examination in response to a question asked by the defendant that is intended to elicit it, or is likely to do so, or

    (e) the assertion was made by any person out of court, and the defendant adduces evidence of it in the proceedings.

(3) A defendant who would otherwise be treated as responsible for the making of an assertion shall not be so treated if, or to the extent that, he withdraws it or disassociates himself from it.

(4) Where it appears to the court that a defendant, by means of his conduct (other than the giving of evidence) in the proceedings, is seeking to give the court or jury an impression about himself that is false or misleading, the court may if it appears just to do so treat the defendant as being responsible for the making of an assertion which is apt to give that impression.

(5) In subsection (4) "conduct" includes appearance or dress.

(6) Evidence is admissible under section 101(1)(f) only if it goes no further than is necessary to correct the false impression.

(7) Only prosecution evidence is admissible under section 101(1)(f).

106. "Attack on another person's character"

(1) For the purposes of section 101(1)(g) a defendant makes an attack on another person's character if—

    (a) he adduces evidence attacking the other person's character,

    (b) he (or any legal representative appointed under section 38(4) of the Youth Justice and Criminal Evidence Act 1999 (c. 23) to cross-examine a witness in his interests) asks questions in cross-examination that are intended to elicit such evidence, or are likely to do so, or

    (c) evidence is given of an imputation about the other person made by the defendant—

      (i) on being questioned under caution, before charge, about the offence with which he is charged, or

      (ii) on being charged with the offence or officially informed that he might be prosecuted for it.

(2) In subsection (1) "evidence attacking the other person's character" means evidence to the effect that the other person—

    (a) has committed an offence (whether a different offence from the one with which the defendant is charged or the same one), or

    (b) has behaved, or is disposed to behave, in a reprehensible way;

and "imputation about the other person" means an assertion to that effect.

(3) Only prosecution evidence is admissible under section 101(1)(g).

107. Stopping the case where evidence contaminated

(1) If on a defendant's trial before a judge and jury for an offence—

    (a) evidence of his bad character has been admitted under any of paragraphs (c) to (g) of section 101(1), and

    (b) the court is satisfied at any time after the close of the case for the prosecution that—

        (i) the evidence is contaminated, and

        (ii) the contamination is such that, considering the importance of the evidence to the case against the defendant, his conviction of the offence would be unsafe,

    the court must either direct the jury to acquit the defendant of the offence or, if it considers that there ought to be a retrial, discharge the jury.

(2) Where—

    (a) a jury is directed under subsection (1) to acquit a defendant of an offence, and

    (b) the circumstances are such that, apart from this subsection,

    the defendant could if acquitted of that offence be found guilty of another offence, the defendant may not be found guilty of that other offence if the court is satisfied as mentioned in subsection (1)(b) in respect of it.

(3) If—

    (a) a jury is required to determine under section 4A(2) of the Criminal Procedure (Insanity) Act 1964 (c. 84) whether a person charged on an indictment with an offence did the act or made the omission charged,

    (b) evidence of the person's bad character has been admitted under any of paragraphs (c) to (g) of section 101(1), and

    (c) the court is satisfied at any time after the close of the case for the prosecution that—

        (i) the evidence is contaminated, and

        (ii) the contamination is such that, considering the importance of the evidence to the case against the person, a finding that he did the act or made the omission would be unsafe,

    the court must either direct the jury to acquit the defendant of the offence or, if it considers that there ought to be a rehearing, discharge the jury.

(4) This section does not prejudice any other power a court may have to direct a jury to acquit a person of an offence or to discharge a jury.

(5) For the purposes of this section a person's evidence is contaminated where—

    (a) as a result of an agreement or understanding between the person and one or more others, or

    (b) as a result of the person being aware of anything alleged by one or more others whose evidence may be, or has been, given in the proceedings,

    the evidence is false or misleading in any respect, or is different from what it would otherwise have been.

108. Offences committed by defendant when a child

(1) Section 16(2) and (3) of the Children and Young Persons Act 1963 (c. 37) (offences committed by person under 14 disregarded for purposes of evidence relating to previous convictions) shall cease to have effect.

(2) In proceedings for an offence committed or alleged to have been committed by the defendant when aged 21 or over, evidence of his conviction for an offence when under the age of 14 is not admissible unless—

    (a) both of the offences are triable only on indictment, and

    (b) the court is satisfied that the interests of justice require the evidence to be admissible.

(3) Subsection (2) applies in addition to section 101.

General

109. Assumption of truth in assessment of relevance or probative value

(1) Subject to subsection (2), a reference in this Chapter to the relevance or probative value of evidence is a reference to its relevance or probative value on the assumption that it is true.

(2) In assessing the relevance or probative value of an item of evidence for any purpose of this Chapter, a court need not assume that the evidence is true if it appears, on the basis of any material before the court (including any evidence it decides to hear on the matter), that no court or jury could reasonably find it to be true.

110. Court's duty to give reasons for rulings

(1) Where the court makes a relevant ruling—

    (a) it must state in open court (but in the absence of the jury, if there is one) its reasons for the ruling;

    (b) if it is a magistrates' court, it must cause the ruling and the reasons for it to be entered in the register of the court's proceedings.

(2) In this section "relevant ruling" means—

    (a) a ruling on whether an item of evidence is evidence of a person's bad character;

    (b) a ruling on whether an item of such evidence is admissible under section 100 or 101 (including a ruling on an application under section 101(3));

    (c) a ruling under section 107.

111. Rules of court

(1) Rules of court may make such provision as appears to the appropriate authority to be necessary or expedient for the purposes of this Act; and the appropriate authority is the authority entitled to make the rules.

(2) The rules may, and, where the party in question is the prosecution, must, contain provision requiring a party who—

    (a) proposes to adduce evidence of a defendant's bad character, or

    (b) proposes to cross-examine a witness with a view to eliciting such evidence,

to serve on the defendant such notice, and such particulars of or relating to the evidence, as may be prescribed.

(3) The rules may provide that the court or the defendant may, in such circumstances as may be prescribed, dispense with a requirement imposed by virtue of subsection (2).

(4) In considering the exercise of its powers with respect to costs, the court may take into account any failure by a party to comply with a requirement imposed by virtue of subsection (2) and not dispensed with by virtue of subsection (3).

(5) The rules may—

    (a) limit the application of any provision of the rules to prescribed circumstances;

    (b) subject any provision of the rules to prescribed exceptions;

    (c) make different provision for different cases or circumstances.

(6) Nothing in this section prejudices the generality of any enactment conferring power to make rules of court; and no particular provision of this section prejudices any general provision of it.

(7) In this section—

"prescribed" means prescribed by rules of court;

"rules of court" means—

(a) Crown Court Rules;

(b) Criminal Appeal Rules;

(c) rules under section 144 of the Magistrates' Courts Act 1980 (c. 43).

112. Interpretation of Chapter 1

(1) In this Chapter—

"bad character" is to be read in accordance with section 98;

"criminal proceedings" means criminal proceedings in relation to which the strict rules of evidence apply;

"defendant", in relation to criminal proceedings, means a person charged with an offence in those proceedings; and "co-defendant", in relation to a defendant, means a person charged with an offence in the same proceedings;

"important matter" means a matter of substantial importance in the context of the case as a whole;

"misconduct" means the commission of an offence or other reprehensible behaviour;

"offence" includes a service offence;

"probative value", and "relevant" (in relation to an item of evidence), are to be read in accordance with section 109;

"prosecution evidence" means evidence which is to be (or has been) adduced by the prosecution, or which a witness is to be invited to give (or has given) in cross-examination by the prosecution;

"service offence" means an offence under the Army Act 1955 (3 & 4 Eliz. 2 c. 18), the Air Force Act 1955 (3 & 4 Eliz. 2 c. 19) or the Naval Discipline Act 1957 (c. 53);

"written charge" has the same meaning as in section 29 and also includes an information.

(2) Where a defendant is charged with two or more offences in the same criminal proceedings, this Chapter (except section 101(3)) has effect as if each offence were charged in separate proceedings; and references to the offence with which the defendant is charged are to be read accordingly.

(3) Nothing in this Chapter affects the exclusion of evidence—

(a) under the rule in section 3 of the Criminal Procedure Act 1865 (c. 18) against a party impeaching the credit of his own witness by general evidence of bad character,

(b) under section 41 of the Youth Justice and Criminal Evidence Act 1999 (c. 23) (restriction on evidence or questions about complainant's sexual history), or

(c) on grounds other than the fact that it is evidence of a person's bad character.

113. Armed forces

Schedule 6 (armed forces) has effect.

CHAPTER 2

HEARSAY EVIDENCE

Hearsay: main provisions

114. Admissibility of hearsay evidence

(1) In criminal proceedings a statement not made in oral evidence in the proceedings is admissible as evidence of any matter stated if, but only if—

(a) any provision of this Chapter or any other statutory provision makes it admissible,

(b) any rule of law preserved by section 118 makes it admissible,

(c) all parties to the proceedings agree to it being admissible, or

(d) the court is satisfied that it is in the interests of justice for it to be admissible.

(2) In deciding whether a statement not made in oral evidence should be admitted under subsection (1)(d), the court must have regard to the following factors (and to any others it considers relevant)—

(a) how much probative value the statement has (assuming it to be true) in relation to a matter in issue in the proceedings, or how valuable it is for the understanding of other evidence in the case;

(b) what other evidence has been, or can be, given on the matter or evidence mentioned in paragraph (a);

(c) how important the matter or evidence mentioned in paragraph (a) is in the context of the case as a whole;

(d) the circumstances in which the statement was made;

(e) how reliable the maker of the statement appears to be;

(f) how reliable the evidence of the making of the statement appears to be;

(g) whether oral evidence of the matter stated can be given and, if not, why it cannot;

(h) the amount of difficulty involved in challenging the statement;

(i) the extent to which that difficulty would be likely to prejudice the party facing it.

(3) Nothing in this Chapter affects the exclusion of evidence of a statement on grounds other than the fact that it is a statement not made in oral evidence in the proceedings.

115. Statements and matters stated

(1) In this Chapter references to a statement or to a matter stated are to be read as follows.

(2) A statement is any representation of fact or opinion made by a person by whatever means; and it includes a representation made in a sketch, photofit or other pictorial form.

(3) A matter stated is one to which this Chapter applies if (and only if) the purpose, or one of the purposes, of the person making the statement appears to the court to have been—

(a) to cause another person to believe the matter, or

(b) to cause another person to act or a machine to operate on the basis that the matter is as stated.

Principal categories of admissibility

116. Cases where a witness is unavailable

(1) In criminal proceedings a statement not made in oral evidence in the proceedings is admissible as evidence of any matter stated if—

(a) oral evidence given in the proceedings by the person who made the statement would be admissible as evidence of that matter,

(b) the person who made the statement (the relevant person) is identified to the court's satisfaction, and

(c) any of the five conditions mentioned in subsection (2) is satisfied.

(2) The conditions are—

(a) that the relevant person is dead;

(b) that the relevant person is unfit to be a witness because of his bodily or mental condition;

(c) that the relevant person is outside the United Kingdom and it is not reasonably practicable to secure his attendance;

347

(d) that the relevant person cannot be found although such steps as it is reasonably practicable to take to find him have been taken;

(e) that through fear the relevant person does not give (or does not continue to give) oral evidence in the proceedings, either at all or in connection with the subject matter of the statement, and the court gives leave for the statement to be given in evidence.

(3) For the purposes of subsection (2)(e) "fear" is to be widely construed and (for example) includes fear of the death or injury of another person or of financial loss.

(4) Leave may be given under subsection (2)(e) only if the court considers that the statement ought to be admitted in the interests of justice, having regard—

(a) to the statement's contents,

(b) to any risk that its admission or exclusion will result in unfairness to any party to the proceedings (and in particular to how difficult it will be to challenge the statement if the relevant person does not give oral evidence),

(c) in appropriate cases, to the fact that a direction under section 19 of the Youth Justice and Criminal Evidence Act 1999 (c. 23) (special measures for the giving of evidence by fearful witnesses etc) could be made in relation to the relevant person, and

(d) to any other relevant circumstances.

(5) A condition set out in anyparagraph of subsection (2) which is in fact satisfied is to be treated as not satisfied if it is shown that the circumstances described in that paragraph are caused—

(a) by the person in support of whose case it is sought to give the statement in evidence, or

(b) by a person acting on his behalf,

in order to prevent the relevant person giving oral evidence in the proceedings (whether at all or in connection with the subject matter of the statement).

117. Business and other documents

(1) In criminal proceedings a statement contained in a document is admissible as evidence of any matter stated if—

(a) oral evidence given in the proceedings would be admissible as evidence of that matter

(b) the requirements of subsection (2) are satisfied, and

(c) the requirements of subsection (5) are satisfied, in a case where subsection (4) requires them to be.

(2) The requirements of this subsection are satisfied if—

(a) the document or the part containing the statement was created or received by a person in the course of a trade, business, profession or other occupation, or as the holder of a paid or unpaid office,

(b) the person who supplied the information contained in the statement (the relevant person) had or may reasonably be supposed to have had personal knowledge of the matters dealt with, and

(c) each person (if any) through whom the information was supplied from the relevant person to the person mentioned in paragraph (a) received the information in the course of a trade, business, profession or other occupation, or as the holder of a paid or unpaid office.

(3) The persons mentioned in paragraphs (a) and (b) of subsection (2) may be the same person.

(4) The additional requirements of subsection (5) must be satisfied if the statement—

(a) was prepared for the purposes of pending or contemplated criminal proceedings, or for a criminal investigation, but

(b) was not obtained pursuant to a request under section 7 of the Crime (International Co-operation) Act 2003 (c. 32) or an order under paragraph 6 of Schedule 13 to the Criminal Justice Act 1988 (c. 33) (which relate to overseas evidence).

(5) The requirements of this subsection are satisfied if—

    (a) any of the five conditions mentioned in section 116(2) is satisfied (absence of relevant person etc), or

    (b) the relevant person cannot reasonably be expected to have any recollection of the matters dealt with in the statement (having regard to the length of time since he supplied the information and all other circumstances).

(6) A statement is not admissible under this section if the court makes a direction to that effect under subsection (7).

(7) The court may make a direction under this subsection if satisfied that the statement's reliability as evidence for the purpose for which it is tendered is doubtful in view of—

    (a) its contents,

    (b) the source of the information contained in it,

    (c) the way in which or the circumstances in which the information was supplied or received, or

    (d) the way in which or the circumstances in which the document concerned was created or received.

118. Preservation of certain common law categories of admissibility

(1) The following rules of law are preserved.

Public information etc

1 Any rule of law under which in criminal proceedings—

    (a) published works dealing with matters of a public nature (such as histories, scientific works, dictionaries and maps) are admissible as evidence of facts of a public nature stated in them,

    (b) public documents (such as public registers, and returns made under public authority with respect to matters of public interest) are admissible as evidence of facts stated in them,

    (c) records (such as the records of certain courts, treaties, Crown grants, pardons and commissions) are admissible as evidence of facts stated in them, or

    (d) evidence relating to a person's age or date or place of birth may be given by a person without personal knowledge of the matter.

Reputation as to character

2 Any rule of law under which in criminal proceedings evidence of a person's reputation is admissible for the purpose of proving his good or bad character.

Note

The rule is preserved only so far as it allows the court to treat such evidence as proving the atter concerned.

349

Reputation or family tradition

3 Any rule of law under which in criminal proceedings evidence of reputation or family tradition is admissible for the purpose of proving or disproving—

(a) pedigree or the existence of a marriage,

(b) the existence of any public or general right, or

(c) the identity of any person or thing.

Note

The rule is preserved only so far as it allows the court to treat such evidence as proving or disproving the matter concerned.

Res gestae

4 Any rule of law under which in criminal proceedings a statement is admissible as evidence of any matter stated if—

(a) the statement was made by a person so emotionally overpowered by an event that the possibility of concoction or distortion can be disregarded,

(b) the statement accompanied an act which can be properly evaluated as evidence only if considered in conjunction with the statement, or

(c) the statement relates to a physical sensation or a mental state (such as intention or emotion).

Confessions etc

5 Any rule of law relating to the admissibility of confessions or mixed statements in criminal proceedings.

Admissions by agents etc

6 Any rule of law under which in criminal proceedings—

(a) an admission made by an agent of a defendant is admissible against the defendant as evidence of any matter stated, or

(b) a statement made by a person to whom a defendant refers a person for information is admissible against the defendant as evidence of any matter stated.

Common enterprise

7 Any rule of law under which in criminal proceedings a statement made by a party to a common enterprise is admissible against another party to the enterprise as evidence of any matter stated.

Expert evidence

8 Any rule of law under which in criminal proceedings an expert witness may draw on the body of expertise relevant to his field.

(2) With the exception of the rules preserved by this section, the common law rules governing the admissibility of hearsay evidence in criminal proceedings are abolished.

119. Inconsistent statements

(1) If in criminal proceedings a person gives oral evidence and—
   (a) he admits making a previous inconsistent statement, or
   (b) a previous inconsistent statement made by him is proved by virtue of section 3, 4 or 5 of the Criminal Procedure Act 1865 (c. 18),
   the statement is admissible as evidence of any matter stated of which oral evidence by him would be admissible.
(2) If in criminal proceedings evidence of an inconsistent statement by any person is given under section 124(2)(c), the statement is admissible as evidence of any matter stated in it of which oral evidence by that person would be admissible.

120. Other previous statements of witnesses

(1) This section applies where a person (the witness) is called to give evidence in criminal proceedings.
(2) If a previous statement by the witness is admitted as evidence to rebut a suggestion that his oral evidence has been fabricated, that statement is admissible as evidence of any matter stated of which oral evidence by the witness would be admissible.
(3) A statement made by the witness in a document—
   (a) which is used by him to refresh his memory while giving evidence,
   (b) on which he is cross-examined, and
   (c) which as a consequence is received in evidence in the proceedings,
   is admissible as evidence of any matter stated of which oral evidence by him would be admissible.
(4) A previous statement by the witness is admissible as evidence of any matter stated of which oral evidence by him would be admissible, if—
   (a) any of the following three conditions is satisfied, and
   (b) while giving evidence the witness indicates that to the best of his belief he made the statement, and that to the best of his belief it states the truth.
(5) The first condition is that the statement identifies or describes a person, object or place.
(6) The second condition is that the statement was made by the witness when the matters stated were fresh in his memory but he does not remember them, and cannot reasonably be expected to remember them, well enough to give oral evidence of them in the proceedings.
(7) The third condition is that—
   (a) the witness claims to be a person against whom an offence has been committed,
   (b) the offence is one to which the proceedings relate,
   (c) the statement consists of a complaint made by the witness (whether to a person in authority or not) about conduct which would, if proved, constitute the offence or part of the offence,
   (d) the complaint was made as soon as could reasonably be expected after the alleged conduct,
   (e) the complaint was not made as a result of a threat or a promise, and
   (f) before the statement is adduced the witness gives oral evidence in connection with its subject matter.
(8) For the purposes of subsection (7) the fact that the complaint was elicited (for example, by a leading question) is irrelevant unless a threat or a promise was involved.

Supplementary

121. Additional requirement for admissibility of multiple hearsay

(1) A hearsay statement is not admissible to prove the fact that an earlier hearsay statement was made unless—

    (a) either of the statements is admissible under section 117, 119 or 120,

    (b) all parties to the proceedings so agree, or

    (c) the court is satisfied that the value of the evidence in question, taking into account how reliable the statements appear to be, is so high that the interests of justice require the later statement to be admissible for that purpose.

(2) In this section "hearsay statement" means a statement, not made in oral evidence, that is relied on as evidence of a matter stated in it.

122. Documents produced as exhibits

(1) This section applies if on a trial before a judge and jury for an offence—

    (a) a statement made in a document is admitted in evidence under section 119 or 120, and

    (b) the document or a copy of it is produced as an exhibit.

(2) The exhibit must not accompany the jury when they retire to consider their verdict unless—

    (a) the court considers it appropriate, or

    (b) all the parties to the proceedings agree that it should accompany the jury.

123. Capability to make statement

(1) Nothing in section 116, 119 or 120 makes a statement admissible as evidence if it was made by a person who did not have the required capability at the time when he made the statement.

(2) Nothing in section 117 makes a statement admissible as evidence if any person who, in order for the requirements of section 117(2) to be satisfied, must at any time have supplied or received the information concerned or created or received the document or part concerned—

    (a) did not have the required capability at that time, or

    (b) cannot be identified but cannot reasonably be assumed to have had the required capability at that time.

(3) For the purposes of this section a person has the required capability if he is capable of—

    (a) understanding questions put to him about the matters stated, and

    (b) giving answers to such questions which can be understood.

(4) Where by reason of this section there is an issue as to whether a person had the required capability when he made a statement—

    (a) proceedings held for the determination of the issue must take place in the absence of the jury (if there is one);

    (b) in determining the issue the court may receive expert evidence and evidence from any person to whom the statement in question was made;

    (c) the burden of proof on the issue lies on the party seeking to adduce the statement, and the standard of proof is the balance of probabilities.

124. Credibility

(1) This section applies if in criminal proceedings—

    (a) a statement not made in oral evidence in the proceedings is admitted as evidence of a matter stated, and

    (b) the maker of the statement does not give oral evidence in connection with the subject matter of the statement.

(2) In such a case—

    (a) any evidence which (if he had given such evidence) would have been admissible as relevant to his credibility as a witness is so admissible in the proceedings;

    (b) evidence may with the court's leave be given of any matter which (if he had given such evidence) could have been put to him in cross-examination as relevant to his credibility as a witness but of which evidence could not have been adduced by the cross-examining party;

    (c) evidence tending to prove that he made (at whatever time) any other statement inconsistent with the statement admitted as evidence is admissible for the purpose of showing that he contradicted himself.

(3) If as a result of evidence admitted under this section an allegation is made against the maker of a statement, the court may permit a party to lead additional evidence of such description as the court may specify for the purposes of denying or answering the allegation.

(4) In the case of a statement in a document which is admitted as evidence under section 117 each person who, in order for the statement to be admissible, must have supplied or received the information concerned or created or received the document or part concerned is to be treated as the maker of the statement for the purposes of subsections (1) to (3) above.

125. Stopping the case where evidence is unconvincing

(1) If on a defendant's trial before a judge and jury for an offence the court is satisfied at any time after the close of the case for the prosecution that—

    (a) the case against the defendant is based wholly or partly on a statement not made in oral evidence in the proceedings, and

    (b) the evidence provided by the statement is so unconvincing that, considering its importance to the case against the defendant, his conviction of the offence would be unsafe,

the court must either direct the jury to acquit the defendant of the offence or, if it considers that there ought to be a retrial, discharge the jury.

(2) Where—

    (a) a jury is directed under subsection (1) to acquit a defendant of an offence, and

    (b) the circumstances are such that, apart from this subsection, the defendant could if acquitted of that offence be found guilty of another offence,

the defendant may not be found guilty of that other offence if the court is satisfied as mentioned in subsection (1) in respect of it.

(3) If—

    (a) a jury is required to determine under section 4A(2) of the Criminal Procedure (Insanity) Act 1964 (c. 84) whether a person charged on an indictment with an offence did the act or made the omission charged, and

    (b) the court is satisfied as mentioned in subsection (1) above at any time after the close of the case for the prosecution that—

        (i) the case against the defendant is based wholly or partly on a statement not made in oral evidence in the proceedings, and

        (ii) the evidence provided by the statement is so unconvincing that, considering its importance to the case against the person, a finding that he did the act or made the omission would be unsafe,

the court must either direct the jury to acquit the defendant of the offence or, if it considers that there ought to be a rehearing, discharge the jury.

(4) This section does not prejudice any other power a court may have to direct a jury to acquit a person of an offence or to discharge a jury.

126. Court's general discretion to exclude evidence

(1) In criminal proceedings the court may refuse to admit a statement as evidence of a matter stated if—

    (a) the statement was made otherwise than in oral evidence in the proceedings, and

    (b) the court is satisfied that the case for excluding the statement, taking account of the danger that to admit it would result in undue waste of time, substantially outweighs the case for admitting it, taking account of the value of the evidence.

(2) Nothing in this Chapter prejudices—

    (a) any power of a court to exclude evidence under section 78 of the Police and Criminal Evidence Act 1984 (c. 60) (exclusion of unfair evidence), or

    (b) any other power of a court to exclude evidence at its discretion (whether by preventing questions from being put or otherwise).

Miscellaneous

127. Expert evidence: preparatory work

(1) This section applies if—

    (a) a statement has been prepared for the purposes of criminal proceedings,

    (b) the person who prepared the statement had or may reasonably be supposed to have had personal knowledge of the matters stated,

    (c) notice is given under the appropriate rules that another person (the expert) will in evidence given in the proceedings orally or under section 9 of the Criminal Justice Act 1967 (c. 80) base an opinion or inference on the statement, and

    (d) the notice gives the name of the person who prepared the statement and the nature of the matters stated.

(2) In evidence given in the proceedings the expert may base an opinion or inference on the statement.

(3) If evidence based on the statement is given under subsection (2) the statement is to be treated as evidence of what it states.

(4) This section does not apply if the court, on an application by a party to the proceedings, orders that it is not in the interests of justice that it should apply.

(5) The matters to be considered by the court in deciding whether to make an order under subsection (4) include—

    (a) the expense of calling as a witness the person who prepared the statement;

    (b) whether relevant evidence could be given by that person which could not be given by the expert;

    (c) whether that person can reasonably be expected to remember the matters stated well enough to give oral evidence of them.

(6) Subsections (1) to (5) apply to a statement prepared for the purposes of a criminal investigation as they apply to a statement prepared for the purposes of criminal proceedings, and in such a case references to the proceedings are to criminal proceedings arising from the investigation.

(7) The appropriate rules are rules made—

    (a) under section 81 of the Police and Criminal Evidence Act 1984 (advance notice of expert evidence in Crown Court), or

    (b) under section 144 of the Magistrates' Courts Act 1980 (c. 43) by virtue of section 20(3) of the Criminal Procedure and Investigations Act 1996 (c. 25) (advance notice of expert evidence in magistrates' courts).

128. Confessions

(1) In the Police and Criminal Evidence Act 1984 (c. 60) the following section is inserted after section 76—

"76A Confessions may be given in evidence for co-accused

(1) In any proceedings a confession made by an accused person may be given in evidence for another person charged in the same proceedings (a co-accused) in so far as it is relevant to any matter in issue in the proceedings and is not excluded by the court in pursuance of this section.

(2) If, in any proceedings where a co-accused proposes to give in evidence a confession made by an accused person, it is represented to the court that the confession was or may have been obtained—

(a) by oppression of the person who made it; or

(b) in consequence of anything said or done which was likely, in the circumstances existing at the time, to render unreliable any confession which might be made by him in consequence thereof,

the court shall not allow the confession to be given in evidence for the co-accused except in so far as it is proved to the court on the balance of probabilities that the confession (notwithstanding that it may be true) was not so obtained.

(3) Before allowing a confession made by an accused person to be given in evidence for a co-accused in any proceedings, the court may of its own motion require the fact that the confession was not obtained as mentioned in subsection (2) above to be proved in the proceedings on the balance of probabilities.

(4) The fact that a confession is wholly or partly excluded in pursuance of this section shall not affect the admissibility in evidence—

(a) of any facts discovered as a result of the confession; or

(b) where the confession is relevant as showing that the accused speaks, writes or expresses himself in a particular way, of so much of the confession as is necessary to show that he does so.

(5) Evidence that a fact to which this subsection applies was discovered as a result of a statement made by an accused person shall not be admissible unless evidence of how it was discovered is given by him or on his behalf.

(6) Subsection (5) above applies—

(a) to any fact discovered as a result of a confession which is wholly excluded in pursuance of this section; and

(b) to any fact discovered as a result of a confession which is partly so excluded, if the fact is discovered as a result of the excluded part of the confession.

(7) In this section "oppression" includes torture, inhuman or degrading treatment, and the use or threat of violence (whether or not amounting to torture)."

(2) Subject to subsection (1), nothing in this Chapter makes a confession by a defendant admissible if it would not be admissible under section 76 of the Police and Criminal Evidence Act 1984 (c. 60).

(3) In subsection (2) "confession" has the meaning given by section 82 of that Act.

129. Representations other than by a person

(1) Where a representation of any fact

(a) is made otherwise than by a person, but

355

(b) depends for its accuracy on information supplied (directly or indirectly) by a person,

the representation is not admissible in cirminal proceedings as evidence of the fact unless it is proved that the information was accurate.

(2) Subsection (1) does not affect the operation of the presumption that a mechanical device has been properly set or calibrated.

130. Depositions

In Schedule 3 to the Crime and Disorder Act 1998 (c. 37), sub-paragraph (4) of paragraph 5 is omitted (power of the court to overrule an objection to a deposition being read as evidence by virtue of that paragraph).

131. Evidence at retrial

For paragraphs 1 and 1A of Schedule 2 to the Criminal Appeal Act 1968 (c. 19) (oral evidence and use of transcripts etc at retrials under that Act) there is substituted—

"Evidence

(1) Evidence given at a retrial must be given orally if it was given orally at the original trial, unless—
   (a) all the parties to the retrial agree otherwise;
   (b) section 116 of the Criminal Justice Act 2003 applies (admissibility of hearsay evidence where a witness is unavailable); or
   (c) the witness is unavailable to give evidence, otherwise than as mentioned in subsection (2) of that section, and section 114(1)(d) of that Act applies (admission of hearsay evidence under residual discretion).
(2) Paragraph 5 of Schedule 3 to the Crime and Disorder Act 1998 (use of depositions) does not apply at a retrial to a deposition read as evidence at the original trial."

General

132. Rules of court

(1) Rules of court may make such provision as appears to the appropriate authority to be necessary or expedient for the purposes of this Chapter; and the appropriate authority is the authority entitled to make the rules.
(2) The rules may make provision about the procedure to be followed and other conditions to be fulfilled by a party proposing to tender a statement in evidence under any provision of this Chapter.
(3) The rules may require a party proposing to tender the evidence to serve on each party to the proceedings such notice, and such particulars of or relating to the evidence, as may be prescribed.
(4) The rules may provide that the evidence is to be treated as admissible by agreement of the parties if—
   (a) a notice has been served in accordance with provision made under subsection (3), and
   (b) no counter-notice in the prescribed form objecting to the admission of the evidence has been served by a party.
(5) If a party proposing to tender evidence fails to comply with a prescribed requirement applicable to it—

(a) the evidence is not admissible except with the court's leave;

(b) where leave is given the court or jury may draw such inferences from the failure as appear proper;

(c) the failure may be taken into account by the court in considering the exercise of its powers with respect to costs.

(6) In considering whether or how to exercise any of its powers under subsection (5) the court shall have regard to whether there is any justification for the failure to comply with the requirement.

(7) A person shall not be convicted of a offence solely on an inference drawn under subsection (5)(b).

(8) Rules under this section may—

(a) limit the application of any provision of the rules to prescribed circumstances;

(b) subject any provison of the rules to prescribed exceptions;

(c) make different provision for different cases or circumstances.

(9) Nothing in this section prejudices the generaltiy of any enactment conferring power to make rules of court; and no particular provision of this section prejudices any general provision of it.

(10) In this section—

"prescribed" means prescribed by rules of court;

"rules of court" means—

(a) Crown Court Rules;

(b) Criminal Appeal Rules;

(c) rules under section 144 of the Magistrates' Courts Act 1980 (c. 43).

133. Proof of statements in documents

Where a statement in a document is admissible as evidence in criminal proceedings, the statement may be proved by producing either—

(a) the document, or

(b) (whether or not the document exists) a copy of the document or of the material part of it, authenticated in whatever way the court may approve.

134. Interpretation of Chapter 2

(1) In this Chapter—

"copy", in relation to a document, means anything on to which information recorded in the document has been copied, by whatever means and whether directly or indirectly;

"criminal proceedings" means criminal proceedings in relation to which the strick rules of evidence apply;

"defendant", in relation to criminal proceedings, means a person charged with an offence in those proceedings;

"document" means anything in which information of any description is recorded;

"oral evidence" includes evidence which, by reason of any disability, disorder or other impairment, a person called as a witness gives in writing or by signs or by way of any device;

"statutory provision" means any provision contained in, or in an instrument made under, this or any other Act, including any Act passed after this Act.

(2) Section 115 (statements and matters stated) contains other general interpretative provisions.

(3) Where a defendant is charged with two or more offences in the same criminal proceedings, this Chapter has effect as if each offence were charged in separate proceedings.

135. Armed forces

Schedule 7 (hearsay evidence: armed forces) has effect.

136. Repeals etc

In the Criminal Justice Act 1988 (c. 33), the following provisions (which are to some extent superseded by provisions of this Chapter) are repealed—
(a) Part 2 and Schedule 2 (which relate to documentary evidence);
(b) in Schedule 13, paragraph 2 to 5 (which relate to documentary evidence in service courts etc).

CHAPTER 3
MISCELLANEOUS AND SUPPLEMENTAL

137. Evidence by video recording

(1) This section applies where—
  (a) a person is called as a witness in proceedings for an offence triable only on indictment, or for a prescribed offence triable either way,
  (b) the person claims to have witnessed (whether visually or in any other way)—
    (i) events alleged by the prosecution to include conduct constituting the offence or part of the offence, or
    (ii) events closely connected with such events,
  (c) he has previously given an account of the events in question (whether in response to questions asked or otherwise),
  (d) the account was given at a time when those events were fresh in the person's memory (or would have been, assuming the truth of the claim mentioned in paragraph (b)),
  (e) a video recording was made of the account,
  (f) the court has made a direction that the recording sould be admitted as evidence in chief of the witness, and the direction has not been rescinded, and
  (g) the recording is played in the proceedings in accordance with the direction.
(2) If, or to the extent that, the witness in his oral evidence in the proceedings asserts the truth of the statements made by him in the recorded account, they shall be treated as if made by him in that evidence.
(3) A direction under subsection (1)(f)—
  (a) may not be made in relation to a recorded account given by the defendant;
  (b) may be made only if it appears to the court that—
    (i) the witness's recollection of the events in question is likely to have been significantly better when he gave the recorded account than it will be when he gives oral evidence in the proceedings, and
    (ii) it is in the interests of justice for the recording to be admitted, having regard in particular to the matters mentioned in subsection (4).
(4) Those matters are—
  (a) the interval between the time of the events in question and the time when the recorded account was made;
  (b) any other factors that might affect the reliability of what the witness said in that account;
  (c) the quality of the recording;
  (d) any views of the witness as to whether his evidence in chief should be given orally or by means of the recording.

(5) For the purposes of subsection (2) it does not matter if the statements in the recorded account were not made on oath.

(6) In this section "prescribed" means of a description specified in an order made by the Secretary of State.

138. Video evidence: further provisions

(1) Where a video recording is admitted under section 137, the witness may not give evidence in chief otherwise than by means of the recording as to any matter which, in the opinion of the court, has been dealt with adequately in the recorded account.

(2) The reference in subsection (1)(f) of section 137 to the admission of a recording includes a reference to the admission of part of the recording; and references in that section and this one to the video recording or to the witness's recorded account shall, where appropriate, be read accordingly.

(3) In considering whether any part of a recording should be not admitted under section 137, the court must consider—
   (a) whether admitting that part would carry a risk of prejudice to the defendant, and
   (b) if so, whether the interests of justice nevertheless require it to be admitted in view of the desirability of showing the whole, or substantially the whole, of the recorded interview.

(4) A court may not make a direction under section 137(1)(f) in relation to any proceedings unless—
   (a) the Secretary of State has notified the court that arrangements can be made, in the area in which it appears to the court that the proceedings will take place, for implementing directions under that section, and
   (b) the notice has not been withdrawn.

(5) Nothing in section 137 affects the admissibility of any video recording which would be admissible apart from that section.

139. Use of documents to refresh memory

(1) A person giving oral evidence in criminal proceedings about any matter may, at any stage in the course of doing so, refresh his memory of it from a document made or verified by him at an earlier time if—
   (a) he states in his oral evidence that the document records his recollection of the matter at that earlier time, and
   (b) his recollection of the matter is likely to have been significantly better at that time than it is at the time of his oral evidence.

(2) Where—
   (a) a person giving oral evidence in criminal proceedings about any matter has previously given an oral account, of which a sound recording was made, and he states in that evidence that the account represented his recollection of the matter at that time,
   (b) his recollection of the matter is likely to have been significantly better at the time of the previous account than it is at the time of his oral evidence, and
   (c) a transcript has been made of the sound recording,
   he may, at any stage in the course of giving his evidence, refresh his memory of the matter from that transcript.

140. Interpretation of Chapter 3

In this Chapter—
   "criminal proceedings" means criminal proceedings in relation to which the strict rules of evidence apply;

"defendant", in relation to criminal proceedings, means a person charged with an offence in those proceedings;

"document" means anything in which information of any description is recorded, but not including any recording of sounds or moving images;

"oral evidence" includes evidence which, by reason of any disability, disorder or other impairment, a person called as a witness gives in writing or by signs or by way of any device;

"video recording" means any recording, on any medium, from which a moving image may by any means be produced, and includes the accompanying sound-track.

141. Saving

No provision of this Part has effect in realtion to criminal
Proceedings begun before the commencement of that provision.

PART 12. SENTENCING

CHAPTER 1
GENERAL PROVISIONS ABOUT SENTENCING

Matters to be taken into account in sentencing

142. Purposes of sentencing

(1) Any court dealing with an offender in respect of his offence must have regard to the following purposes of sentencing—

(a) the punishment of offenders,

(b) the reduction of crime (including its reduction by deterrence),

(c) the reform and rehabilitation of offenders,

(d) the protection of the public, and

(e) the making of reparation by offenders to persons affected by their offences.

(2) Subsection (1) does not apply—

(a) in relation to an offender who is aged under 18 at the time of conviction,

(b) to an offence the sentence for which is fixed by law,

(c) to an offence the sentence for which falls to be imposed under section 51A(2) of the Firearms Act 1968 (c. 27) (minimum sentence for certain firearms offences), under subsection (2) of section 110 or 111 of the Sentencing Act (required custodial sentences) or under any of sections 225 to 228 of this Act (dangerous offenders), or

(d) in relation to the making under Part 3 of the Mental Health Act 1983 (c. 20) of a hospital order (with or without a restriction order), an interim hospital order, a hospital direction or a limitation direction.

(3) In this Chapter "sentence", in relation to an offence, includes any order made by a court when dealing with the offender in respect of his offence; and "sentencing" is to be construed accordingly.

143. Determining the seriousness of an offence

(1) In considering the seriousness of any offence, the court must consider the offender's culpability in committing the offence and any harm which the offence caused, was intended to cause or might forseeably have caused.

(2) In considering the seriousness of an offence ("the current offence") committed by an offender who has one or more previous convictions, the court must treat each previous conviction as an aggravating factor if (in the case of that conviction) the court considers that it can reasonably be so treated having regard, in particular, to—

(a) the nature of the offence to which the conviction relates and its relevance to the current offence, and

(b) the time that has elapsed since the conviction.

(3) In considering the seriousness of any offence committed while the offender was on bail, the court must treat the fact that it was committed in those circumstances as an aggravating factor.

(4) Any reference in subsection (2) to a previous conviction is to be read as a reference to—

(a) a previous conviction by a court in the United Kingdom, or

(b) a previous finding of guilt in service disciplinary proceedings.

(5) Subsections (2) and (4) do not prevent the court from treating a previous conviction by a court outside the United Kingdom as an aggravating factor in any case where the court considers it appropriate to do so.

144. Reduction in sentences for guilty pleas

(1) In determining what sentence to pass on an offender who has pleaded guilty to an offence in proceedings before that or another court, a court must take into account—

(a) the stage in the proceedings for the offence at which the offender indicated his intention to plead guilty, and

(b) the circumstances in which this indication was given.

(2) In the case of an offence the sentence for which falls to be imposed under subsection (2) of section 110 or 111 of the Sentencing Act, nothing in that subsection prevents the court, after taking into account any matter referred to in subsection (1) of this section, from imposing any sentence which is not less than 80 per cent of that specified in that subsection.

145. Increase in sentences for racial or religious aggravation

(1) This section applies where a court is considering the seriousness of an offence other than one under sections 29 to 32 of the Crime and Disorder Act 1998 (c. 37) (racially or religiously aggravated assaults, criminal damage, public order offences and harassment etc).

(2) If the offence was racially or religiously aggravated, the court—

(a) must treat that fact as an aggravating factor, and

(b) must state in open court that the offence was so aggravated.

(3) Section 28 of the Crime and Disorder Act 1998 (meaning of "racially or religiously aggravated") applies for the purposes of this section as it applies for the purposes of sections 29 to 32 of that Act.

146. Increase in sentences for aggravation related to disability or sexual orientation

(1) This section applies where the court is considering the seriousness of an offence committed in any of the circumstances mentioned in subsection (2).

(2) Those circumstances are—

(a) that, at the time of committing the offence, or immediately before or after doing so, the offender demonstrated towards the victim of the offence hostility based on—

(i) the sexual orientation (or presumed sexual orientation) of the victim, or

(ii) a disability (or presumed disability) of the victim, or

(b) that the offence is motivated (wholly or partly)—
    (i) by hostility towards persons who are of a particular sexual orientation, or
    (ii) by hostility towards persons who have a disability or a particular disability.

(3) The court—
    (a) must treat the fact that the offence was committed in any of those circumstances as an aggravating factor, and
    (b) must state in open court that the offence was committed in such circumstances.

(4) It is immaterial for the purposes of paragraph (a) or (b) of subsection (2) whether or not the offender's hostility is also based, to any extent, on any other factor not mentioned in that paragraph.

(5) In this section "disability" means any physical or mental impairment.

General restrictions on community sentences

147. Meaning of "community sentence" etc.

(1) In this Part "community sentence" means a sentence which consists of or includes—
    (a) a community order (as defined by section 177), or
    (b) one or more youth community orders.

(2) In this Chapter "youth community order" means—
    (a) a curfew order as defined by section 163 of the Sentencing Act,
    (b) an exclusion order under section 40A(1) of that Act,
    (c) an attendance centre order as defined by section 163 of that Act,
    (d) a supervision order under section 63(1) of that Act, or
    (e) an action plan order under section 69(1) of that Act.

148. Restrictions on imposing community sentences

(1) A court must not pass a community sentence on an offender unless it is of the opinion that the offence, or the combination of the offence and one or more offences associated with it, was serious enough to warrant such a sentence.

(2) Where a court passes a community sentence which consists of or includes a community order
    (a) the particular requirement or requirements forming part of the community order must be such as, in the opinion of the court, is, or taken together are, the most suitable for the offender, and
    (b) the restrictions on liberty imposed by the order must be such as in the opinion of the court are commensurate with the seriousness of the offence, or the combination of the offence and one or more offences associated with it.

(3) Where a court passes a community sentence which consists of or includes one or more youth community orders—
    (a) the particular order or orders forming part of the sentence must be such as, in the opinion of the court, is, or taken together are, the most suitable for the offender, and
    (b) the restrictions on liberty imposed by the order or orders must be such as in the opinion of the court are commensurate with the seriousness of the offence, or the combination of the offence and one or more offences associated with it.

(4) Subsections (1) and (2)(b) have effect subject to section 151(2).

149. Passing of community sentence on offender remanded in custody

(1) In determining the restrictions on liberty to be imposed by a community order or youth community order in respect of an offence, the court may have regard to any period for which the offender has been remanded in custody in connection with the offence or any other offence the charge for which was founded on the same facts or evidence.

(2) In subsection (1) "remanded in custody" has the meaning given by section 242(2).

150. Community sentence not available where sentence fixed by law etc.

The power to make a community order or youth community order is not exercisable in respect of an offence for which the sentence—

    (a) is fixed by law,

    (b) falls to be imposed under section 51A(2) of the Firearms Act 1968 (c. 27) (required custodial sentence for certain firearms offences),

    (c) falls to be imposed under section 110(2) or 111(2) of the Sentencing Act (requirement to impose custodial sentences for certain repeated offences committed by offenders aged 18 or over), or

    (d) falls to be imposed under any of sections 225 to 228 of this Act (requirement to impose custodial sentences for certain offences committed by offenders posing risk to public).

151. Community order for persistent offender previously fined

(1) Subsection (2) applies where—

    (a) a person aged 16 or over is convicted of an offence ("the current offence"),

    (b) on three or more previous occasions he has, on conviction by a court in the United Kingdom of any offence committed by him after attaining the age of 16, had passed on him a sentence consisting only of a fine, and

    (c) despite the effect of section 143(2), the court would not (apart from this section) regard the current offence, or the combination of the current offence and one or more offences associated with it, as being serious enough to warrant a community sentence.

(2) The court may make a community order in respect of the current offence instead of imposing a fine if it considers that, having regard to all the circumstances including the matters mentioned in subsection (3), it would be in the interests of justice to make such an order.

(3) The matters referred to in subsection (2) are—

    (a) the nature of the offences to which the previous convictions mentioned in subsection (1)(b) relate and their relevance to the current offence, and

    (b) the time that has elapsed since the offender's conviction of each of those offences.

(4) In subsection (1)(b), the reference to conviction by a court in the United Kingdom includes a reference to the finding of guilt in service disciplinary proceedings; and, in relation to any such finding of guilt, the reference to the sentence passed is a reference to the punishment awarded.

(5) For the purposes of subsection (1)(b), a compensation order does not form part of an offender's sentence.

(6) For the purposes of subsection (1)(b), it is immaterial whether on other previous occasions a court has passed on the offender a sentence not consisting only of a fine.

(7) This section does not limit the extent to which a court may, in accordance with section 143(2), treat any previous convictions of the offender as increasing the seriousness of an offence.

General restrictions on discretionary custodial sentences

152. General restrictions on imposing discretionary custodial sentences

(1) This section applies where a person is convicted of an offence punishable with a custodial sentence other than one—
  (a) fixed by law, or
  (b) falling to be imposed under section 51A(2) of the Firearms Act 1968 (c. 27), under 110(2) or 111(2) of the Sentencing Act or under any of sections 225 to 228 of this Act.

(2) The court must not pass a custodial sentence unless it is of the opinion that the offence, or the combination of the offence and one or more offences associated with it, was so serious that neither a fine alone nor a community sentence can be justified for the offence.

(3) Nothing in subsection (2) prevents the court from passing a custodial sentence on the offender if—
  (a) he fails to express his willingness to comply with a requirement which is proposed by the court to be included in a community order and which requires an expression of such willingness, or
  (b) he fails to comply with an order under section 161(2) (pre-sentence drug testing).

153. Length of discretionary custodial sentences: general provision

(1) This section applies where a court passes a custodial sentence other than one fixed by law or falling to be imposed under section 225 or 226.

(2) Subject to section 51A(2) of the Firearms Act 1968 (c. 27), sections 110(2) and 111(2) of the Sentencing Act and sections 227(2) and 228(2) of this Act, the custodial sentence must be for the shortest term (not exceeding the permitted maximum) that in the opinion of the court is commensurate with the seriousness of the offence, or the combination of the offence and one or more offences associated with it.

General limit on magistrates' court's power to impose imprisonment

154. General limit on magistrates' court's power to impose imprisonment

(1) A magistrates' court does not have power to impose imprisonment for more than 12 months in respect of any one offence.

(2) Unless expressly excluded, subsection (1) applies even if the offence in question is one for which a person would otherwise be liable on summary conviction to imprisonment for more than 12 months.

(3) Subsection (1) is without prejudice to section 133 of the Magistrates' Courts Act 1980 (c. 43) (consecutive terms of imprisonment).

(4) Any power of a magistrates' court to impose a term of imprisonment for non-payment of a fine, or for want of sufficient distress to satisfy a fine, is not limited by virtue of subsection (1).

(5) In subsection (4) "fine" includes a pecuniary penalty but does not include a pecuniary forfeiture or pecuniary compensation.

(6) In this section "impose imprisonment" means pass a sentence of imprisonment or fix a term of imprisonment for failure to pay any sum of money, or for want of sufficient distress to satisfy any sum of money, or for failure to do or abstain from doing anything required to be done or left undone.

(7) Section 132 of the Magistrates' Courts Act 1980 contains provisions about the minimum term of imprisonment which may be imposed by a magistrates' court.

155. Consecutive terms of imprisonment

(1) Section 133 of the Magistrates' Courts Act 1980 (consecutive terms of imprisonment) is amended as follows.
(2) In subsection (1), for "6 months" there is substituted "65 weeks".
(3) Subsection (2) is omitted.
(4) In subsection (3) for "the preceding subsections" there is substituted "subsection (1) above".

Procedural requirements for imposing community sentences and discretionary custodial sentences

156. Pre-sentence reports and other requirements

(1) In forming any such opinion as is mentioned in section 148(1), (2)(b) or (3)(b), section 152(2) or section 153(2), a court must take into account all such information as is available to it about the circumstances of the offence or (as the case may be) of the offence and the offence or offences associated with it, including any aggravating or mitigating factors.
(2) In forming any such opinion as is mentioned in section 148(2)(a) or (3)(a), the court may take into account any information about the offender which is before it.
(3) Subject to subsection (4), a court must obtain and consider a pre-sentence report before—
  (a) in the case of a custodial sentence, forming any such opinion as is mentioned in section 152(2), section 153(2), section 225(1)(b), section 226(1)(b), section 227(1)(b) or section 228(1)(b)(i), or
  (b) in the case of a community sentence, forming any such opinion as is mentioned in section 148(1), (2)(b) or (3)(b) or any opinion as to the suitability for the offender of the particular requirement or requirements to be imposed by the community order.
(4) Subsection (3) does not apply if, in the circumstances of the case, the court is of the opinion that it is unnecessary to obtain a pre-sentence report.
(5) In a case where the offender is aged under 18, the court must not form the opinion mentioned in subsection (4) unless—
  (a) there exists a previous pre-sentence report obtained in respect of the offender, and
  (b) the court has had regard to the information contained in that report, or, if there is more than one such report, the most recent report.
(6) No custodial sentence or community sentence is invalidated by the failure of a court to obtain and consider a pre-sentence report before forming an opinion referred to in subsection (3), but any court on an appeal against such a sentence—
  (a) must, subject to subsection (7), obtain a pre-sentence report if none was obtained by the court below, and
  (b) must consider any such report obtained by it or by that court.
(7) Subsection (6) (a) does not apply if the court is of the opinion—
  (a) that the court below was justified in forming an opinion that it was unnecessary to obtain a pre-sentence report, or
  (b) that, although the court below was not justified in forming that opinion, in the circumstances of the case at the time it is before the court, it is unnecessary to obtain a pre-sentence report.

(8) In a case where the offender is aged under 18, the court must not form the opinion mentioned in subsection (7) unless—

(a) there exists a previous pre-sentence report obtained in respect of the offender, and

(b) the court has had regard to the information contained in that report, or, if there is more than one such report, the most recent report.

157. Additional requirements in case of mentally disordered offender

(1) Subject to subsection (2), in any case where the offender is or appears to be mentally disordered, the court must obtain and consider a medical report before passing a custodial sentence other than one fixed by law.

(2) Subsection (1) does not apply if, in the circumstances of the case, the court is of the opinion that it is unnecessary to obtain a medical report.

(3) Before passing a custodial sentence other than one fixed by law on an offender who is or appears to be mentally disordered, a court must consider—

(a) any information before it which relates to his mental condition (whether given in a medical report, a pre-sentence report or otherwise), and

(b) the likely effect of such a sentence on that condition and on any treatment which may be available for it.

(4) No custodial sentence which is passed in a case to which subsection (1) applies is invalidated by the failure of a court to comply with that subsection, but any court on an appeal against such a sentence—

(a) must obtain a medical report if none was obtained by the court below, and

(b) must consider any such report obtained by it or by that court.

(5) In this section "mentally disordered", in relation to any person, means suffering from a mental disorder within the meaning of the Mental Health Act 1983 (c. 20).

(6) In this section "medical report" means a report as to an offender's mental condition made or submitted orally or in writing by a registered medical practitioner who is approved for the purposes of section 12 of the Mental Health Act 1983 by the Secretary of State as having special experience in the diagnosis or treatment of mental disorder.

(7) Nothing in this section is to be taken to limit the generality of section 156.

158. Meaning of "pre-sentence report"

(1) In this Part "pre-sentence report" means a report which—

(a) with a view to assisting the court in determining the most suitable method of dealing with an offender, is made or submitted by an appropriate officer, and

(b) contains information as to such matters, presented in such manner, as may be prescribed by rules made by the Secretary of State.

(2) In subsection (1) "an appropriate officer" means—

(a) where the offender is aged 18 or over, an officer of a local probation board, and

(b) where the offender is aged under 18, an officer of a local probation board, a social worker of a local authority social services department or a member of a youth offending team.

Disclosure of pre-sentence reports etc

159. Disclosure of pre-sentence reports

(1) This section applies where the court obtains a pre-sentence report, other than a report given orally in open court.

(2) Subject to subsections (3) and (4), the court must give a copy of the report—
   (a) to the offender or his counsel or solicitor,
   (b) if the offender is aged under 18, to any parent or guardian of his who is present in court, and
   (c) to the prosecutor, that is to say, the person having the conduct of the proceedings in respect of the offence.

(3) If the offender is aged under 18 and it appears to the court that the disclosure to the offender or to any parent or guardian of his of any information contained in the report would be likely to create a risk of significant harm to the offender, a complete copy of the report need not be given to the offender or, as the case may be, to that parent or guardian.

(4) If the prosecutor is not of a description prescribed by order made by the Secretary of State, a copy of the report need not be given to the prosecutor if the court considers that it would be inappropriate for him to be given it.

(5) No information obtained by virtue of subsection (2)(c) may be used or disclosed otherwise than for the purpose of—
   (a) determining whether representations as to matters contained in the report need to be made to the court, or
   (b) making such representations to the court.

(6) In relation to an offender aged under 18 for whom a local authority have parental responsibility and who—
   (a) is in their care, or
   (b) is provided with accommodation by them in the exercise of any social services functions,
   references in this section to his parent or guardian are to be read as references to that authority.

(7) In this section and section 160—
   "harm" has the same meaning as in section 31 of the Children Act 1989 (c. 41);
   "local authority" and "parental responsibility" have the same meanings as in that Act;
   "social services functions", in relation to a local authority, has the meaning given by section 1A of the Local Authority Social Services Act 1970 (c. 42).

160. Other reports of local probation boards and members of youth offending teams

(1) This section applies where—
   (a) a report by an officer of a local probation board or a member of a youth offending team is made to any court (other than a youth court) with a view to assisting the court in determining the most suitable method of dealing with any person in respect of an offence, and
   (b) the report is not a pre-sentence report.

(2) Subject to subsection (3), the court must give a copy of the report—
   (a) to the offender or his counsel or solicitor, and
   (b) if the offender is aged under 18, to any parent or guardian of his who is present in court.

(3) If the offender is aged under 18 and it appears to the court that the disclosure to the offender or to any parent or guardian of his of any information contained in the report

would be likely to create a risk of significant harm to the offender, a complete copy of the report need not be given to the offender, or as the case may be, to that parent or guardian.

(4) In relation to an offender aged under 18 for whom a local authority have parental responsibility and who—

(a) is in their care, or

(b) is provided with accommodation by them in the exercise of any social services functions, references in this section to his parent or guardian are to be read as references to that authority.

Pre-sentence drug testing

161. Pre-sentence drug testing

(1) Where a person aged 14 or over is convicted of an offence and the court is considering passing a community sentence or a suspended sentence, it may make an order under subsection (2) for the purpose of ascertaining whether the offender has any specified Class A drug in his body.

(2) The order requires the offender to provide, in accordance with the order, samples of any description specified in the order.

(3) Where the offender has not attained the age of 17, the order must provide for the samples to be provided in the presence of an appropriate adult.

(4) If it is proved to the satisfaction of the court that the offender has, without reasonable excuse, failed to comply with the order it may impose on him a fine of an amount not exceeding level 4.

(5) In subsection (4) "level 4" means the amount which, in relation to a fine for a summary offence, is level 4 on the standard scale.

(6) The court may not make an order under subsection (2) unless it has been notified by the Secretary of State that the power to make such orders is exercisable by the court and the notice has not been withdrawn.

(7) The Secretary of State may by order amend subsection (1) by substituting for the age for the time being specified there a different age specified in the order.

(8) In this section—

"appropriate adult", in relation to a person under the age of 17, means—

(a) his parent or guardian or, if he is in the care of a local authority or voluntary organisation, a person representing that authority or organisation,

(b) a social worker of a local authority social services department, or

(c) if no person falling within paragraph (a) or (b) is available, any responsible person aged 18 or over who is not a police officer or a person employed by the police;

"specified Class A drug" has the same meaning as in Part 3 of the Criminal Justice and Court Services Act 2000 (c. 43).

Fines

162. Powers to order statement as to offender's financial circumstances

(1) Where an individual has been convicted of an offence, the court may, before sentencing him, make a financial circumstances order with respect to him.

(2) Where a magistrates' court has been notified in accordance with section 12(4) of the Magistrates' Courts Act 1980 (c. 43) that an individual desires to plead guilty without appearing before the court, the court may make a financial circumstances order with respect to him.

(3) In this section "a financial circumstances order" means, in relation to any individual, an order requiring him to give to the court, within such period as may be specified in the order, such a statement of his financial circumstances as the court may require.

(4) An individual who without reasonable excuse fails to comply with a financial circumstances order is liable on summary conviction to a fine not exceeding level 3 on the standard scale.

(5) If an individual, in furnishing any statement in pursuance of a financial circumstances order—

(a) makes a statement which he knows to be false in a material particular,

(b) recklessly furnishes a statement which is false in a material particular, or

(c) knowingly fails to disclose any material fact,

he is liable on summary conviction to a fine not exceeding level 4 on the standard scale.

(6) Proceedings in respect of an offence under subsection (5) may, notwithstanding anything in section 127(1) of the Magistrates' Courts Act 1980 (c. 43) (limitation of time), be commenced at any time within two years from the date of the commission of the offence or within six months from its first discovery by the prosecutor, whichever period expires the earlier.

163. General power of Crown Court to fine offender convicted on indictment

Where a person is convicted on indictment of any offence, other than an offence for which the sentence is fixed by law or falls to be imposed under section 110(2) or 111(2) of the Sentencing Act or under any of sections 225 to 228 of this Act, the court, if not precluded from sentencing an offender by its exercise of some other power, may impose a fine instead of or in addition to dealing with him in any other way in which the court has power to deal with him, subject however to any enactment requiring the offender to be dealt with in a particular way.

164. Fixing of fines

(1) Before fixing the amount of any fine to be imposed on an offender who is an individual, a court must inquire into his financial circumstances.

(2) The amount of any fine fixed by a court must be such as, in the opinion of the court, reflects the seriousness of the offence.

(3) In fixing the amount of any fine to be imposed on an offender (whether an individual or other person), a court must take into account the circumstances of the case including, among other things, the financial circumstances of the offender so far as they are known, or appear, to the court.

(4) Subsection (3) applies whether taking into account the financial circumstances of the offender has the effect of increasing or reducing the amount of the fine.

(5) Where—

(a) an offender has been convicted in his absence in pursuance of section 11 or 12 of the Magistrates' Courts Act 1980 (c. 43) (non-appearance of accused), or

(b) an offender—

(i) has failed to furnish a statement of his financial circumstances in response to a request which is an official request for the purposes of section 20A of the Criminal Justice Act 1991 (c.53) (offence of making false statement as to financial circumstances),

(ii) has failed to comply with an order under section 162(1), or

(iii) has otherwise failed to co-operate with the court in its inquiry into his financial circumstances,

and the court considers that it has insufficient information to make a proper determination of the financial circumstances of the offender, it may make such determination as it thinks fit.

165. Remission of fines

(1) This section applies where a court has, in fixing the amount of a fine, determined the offender's financial circumstances under section 164(5).

(2) If, on subsequently inquiring into the offender's financial circumstances, the court is satisfied that had it had the results of that inquiry when sentencing the offender it would—

    (a) have fixed a smaller amount, or

    (b) not have fined him,

it may remit the whole or part of the fine.

(3) Where under this section the court remits the whole or part of a fine after a term of imprisonment has been fixed under section 139 of the Sentencing Act (powers of Crown Court in relation to fines) or section 82(5) of the Magistrates' Courts Act 1980 (magistrates' powers in relation to default) it must reduce the term by the corresponding proportion.

(4) In calculating any reduction required by subsection (3), any fraction of a day is to be ignored.

Savings for power to mitigate etc

166. Savings for powers to mitigate sentences and deal appropriately with mentally disordered offenders

(1) Nothing in—

    (a) section 148 (imposing community sentences),

    (b) section 152, 153 or 157 (imposing custodial sentences),

    (c) section 156 (pre-sentence reports and other requirements),

    (d) section 164 (fixing of fines),

prevents a court from mitigating an offender's sentence by taking into account any such matters as, in the opinion of the court, are relevant in mitigation of sentence.

(2) Section 152(2) does not prevent a court, after taking into account such matters, from passing a community sentence even though it is of the opinion that the offence, or the combination of the offence and one or more offences associated with it, was so serious that a community sentence could not normally be justified for the offence.

(3) Nothing in the sections mentioned in subsection (1)(a) to (d) prevents a court—

    (a) from mitigating any penalty included in an offender's sentence by taking into account any other penalty included in that sentence, and

    (b) in the case of an offender who is convicted of one or more other offences, from mitigating his sentence by applying any rule of law as to the totality of sentences.

(4) Subsections (2) and (3) are without prejudice to the generality of subsection (1).

(5) Nothing in the sections mentioned in subsection (1)(a) to (d) is to be taken—

    (a) as requiring a court to pass a custodial sentence, or any particular custodial sentence, on a mentally disordered offender, or

    (b) as restricting any power (whether under the Mental Health Act 1983 (c. 20) or otherwise) which enables a court to deal with such an offender in the manner it considers to be most appropriate in all the circumstances.

(6) In subsection (5) "mentally disordered", in relation to a person, means suffering from a mental disorder within the meaning of the Mental Health Act 1983.

Sentencing and allocation guidelines

167. The Sentencing Guidelines Council

(1) There shall be a Sentencing Guidelines Council (in this Chapter referred to as the Council) consisting of—

   (a) the Lord Chief Justice, who is to be chairman of the Council,

   (b) seven members (in this section and section 168 referred to as "judicial members") appointed by the Lord Chancellor after consultation with the Secretary of State and the Lord Chief Justice, and

   (c) four members (in this section and section 168 referred to as "non-judicial members") appointed by the Secretary of State after consultation with the Lord Chancellor and the Lord Chief Justice.

(2) A person is eligible to be appointed as a judicial member if he is—

   (a) a Lord Justice of Appeal,

   (b) a judge of the High Court,

   (c) a Circuit judge,

   (d) a District Judge (Magistrates' Courts), or

   (e) a lay justice.

(3) The judicial members must include a Circuit judge, a District Judge (Magistrates' Courts) and a lay justice.

(4) A person is eligible for appointment as a non-judicial member if he appears to the Secretary of State to have experience in one or more of the following areas—

   (a) policing,

   (b) criminal prosecution,

   (c) criminal defence, and

   (d) the promotion of the welfare of victims of crime.

(5) The persons eligible for appointment as a non-judicial member by virtue of experience of criminal prosecution include the Director of Public Prosecutions.

(6) The non-judicial members must include at least one person appearing to the Secretary of State to have experience in each area.

(7) The Lord Chief Justice must appoint one of the judicial members or non-judicial members to be deputy chairman of the Council.

(8) In relation to any meeting of the Council from which the Lord Chief Justice is to be absent, he may nominate any person eligible for appointment as a judicial member to act as a member on his behalf at the meeting.

(9) The Secretary of State may appoint a person appearing to him to have experience of sentencing policy and the administration of sentences to attend and speak at any meeting of the Council.

(10) In this section and section 168 "lay justice" means a justice of the peace who is not a District Judge (Magistrates' Courts).

168. Sentencing Guidelines Council: supplementary provisions

(1) In relation to the Council, the Lord Chancellor may by order make provision—

   (a) as to the term of office, resignation and re-appointment of judicial members and non-judicial members,

   (b) enabling the appropriate Minister to remove a judicial member or non-judicial member from office on grounds of incapacity or misbehaviour, and

   (c) as to the proceedings of the Council.

(2) In subsection (1) (b) "the appropriate Minister" means—
- (a) in relation to a judicial member, the Lord Chancellor, and
- (b) in relation to a non-judicial member, the Secretary of State.

(3) The validity of anything done by the Council is not affected by any vacancy among its members, by any defect in the appointment of a member or by any failure to comply with section 167(3), (6) or (7).

(4) The Lord Chancellor may pay—
- (a) to any judicial member who is appointed by virtue of being a lay justice, such remuneration or expenses as he may determine, and
- (b) to any other judicial member or the Lord Chief Justice, such expenses as he may determine.

(5) The Secretary of State may pay to any non-judicial member such remuneration or expenses as he may determine.

169. The Sentencing Advisory Panel

(1) There shall continue to be a Sentencing Advisory Panel (in this Chapter referred to as "the Panel") constituted by the Lord Chancellor after consultation with the Secretary of State and the Lord Chief Justice.

(2) The Lord Chancellor must, after consultation with the Secretary of State and the Lord Chief Justice, appoint one of the members of the Panel to be its chairman.

(3) The Lord Chancellor may pay to any member of the Panel such remuneration or expenses as he may determine.

170. Guidelines relating to sentencing and allocation

(1) In this Chapter—
- (a) "sentencing guidelines" means guidelines relating to the sentencing of offenders, which may be general in nature or limited to a particular category of offence or offender, and
- (b) "allocation guidelines" means guidelines relating to decisions by a magistrates' court under section 19 of the Magistrates' Courts Act 1980 (c. 43) as to whether an offence is more suitable for summary trial or trial on indictment.

(2) The Secretary of State may at any time propose to the Council—
- (a) that sentencing guidelines be framed or revised by the Council—
  - (i) in respect of offences or offenders of a particular category, or
  - (ii) in respect of a particular matter affecting sentencing, or
- (b) that allocation guidelines be framed or revised by the Council.

(3) The Council may from time to time consider whether to frame sentencing guidelines or allocation guidelines and, if it receives—
- (a) a proposal under section 171(2) from the Panel, or
- (b) a proposal under subsection (2) from the Secretary of State,

must consider whether to do so.

(4) Where sentencing guidelines or allocation guidelines have been issued by the Council as definitive guidelines, the Council must from time to time (and, in particular, if it receives a proposal under section 171(2) from the Panel or under subsection (2) from the Secretary of State) consider whether to revise them.

(5) Where the Council decides to frame or revise sentencing guidelines, the matters to which the Council must have regard include—
- (a) the need to promote consistency in sentencing,
- (b) the sentences imposed by courts in England and Wales for offences to which the guidelines relate,

(c) the cost of different sentences and their relative effectiveness in preventing re-offending,

(d) the need to promote public confidence in the criminal justice system, and

(e) the views communicated to the Council, in accordance with section 171(3)(b), by the Panel.

(6) Where the Council decides to frame or revise allocation guidelines, the matters to which the Council must have regard include—

(a) the need to promote consistency in decisions under section 19 of the Magistrates' Courts Act 1980 (c. 43), and

(b) the views communicated to the Council, in accordance with section 171(3)(b), by the Panel.

(7) Sentencing guidelines in respect of an offence or category of offences must include criteria for determining the seriousness of the offence or offences, including (where appropriate) criteria for determining the weight to be given to any previous convictions of offenders.

(8) Where the Council has prepared or revised any sentencing guidelines or allocation guidelines, it must—

(a) publish them as draft guidelines, and

(b) consult about the draft guidelines—

(i) the Secretary of State,

(ii) such persons as the Lord Chancellor, after consultation with the Secretary of State, may direct, and

(iii) such other persons as the Council considers appropriate.

(9) The Council may, after making any amendment of the draft guidelines which it considers appropriate, issue the guidelines as definitive guidelines.

171. Functions of Sentencing Advisory Panel in relation to guidelines

(1) Where the Council decides to frame or revise any sentencing guidelines or allocation guidelines, otherwise than in response to a proposal from the Panel under subsection (2), the Council must notify the Panel.

(2) The Panel may at any time propose to the Council—

(a) that sentencing guidelines be framed or revised by the Council—

(i) in respect of offences or offenders of a particular category, or

(ii) in respect of a particular matter affecting sentencing, or

(b) that allocation guidelines be framed or revised by the Council.

(3) Where the Panel receives a notification under subsection (1) or makes a proposal under subsection (2), the Panel must—

(a) obtain and consider the views on the matters in issue of such persons or bodies as may be determined, after consultation with the Secretary of State and the Lord Chancellor, by the Council, and

(b) formulate its own views on those matters and communicate them to the Council.

(4) Paragraph (a) of subsection (3) does not apply where the Council notifies the Panel of the Council's view that the urgency of the case makes it impracticable for the Panel to comply with that paragraph.

172. Duty of court to have regard to sentencing guidelines

(1) Every court must—

(a) in sentencing an offender, have regard to any guidelines which are relevant to the offender's case, and

(b) in exercising any other function relating to the sentencing of offenders, have regard to any guidelines which are relevant to the exercise of the function.

(2) In subsection (1) "guidelines" means sentencing guidelines issued by the Council under section 170(9) as definitive guidelines, as revised by subsequent guidelines so issued.

173. Annual report by Council

(1) The Council must as soon as practicable after the end of each financial year make to the Ministers a report on the exercise of the Council's functions during the year.

(2) If section 167 comes into force after the beginning of a financial year, the first report may relate to a period beginning with the day on which that section comes into force and ending with the end of the next financial year.

(3) The Ministers must lay a copy of the report before each House of Parliament.

(4) The Council must publish the report once the copy has been so laid.

(5) In this section—

"financial year" means a period of 12 months ending with 31st March;

"the Ministers" means the Secretary of State and the Lord Chancellor.

Duty of court to explain sentence

174. Duty to give reasons for, and explain effect of, sentence

(1) Subject to subsections (3) and (4), any court passing sentence on an offender—

    (a) must state in open court, in ordinary language and in general terms, its reasons for deciding on the sentence passed, and

    (b) must explain to the offender in ordinary language—

        (i) the effect of the sentence,

        (ii) where the offender is required to comply with any order of the court forming part of the sentence, the effects of non-compliance with the order,

        (iii) any power of the court, on the application of the offender or any other person, to vary or review any order of the court forming part of the sentence, and

        (iv) where the sentence consists of or includes a fine, the effects of failure to pay the fine.

(2) In complying with subsection (1)(a), the court must—

    (a) where guidelines indicate that a sentence of a particular kind, or within a particular range, would normally be appropriate for the offence and the sentence is of a different kind, or is outside that range, state the court's reasons for deciding on a sentence of a different kind or outside that range,

    (b) where the sentence is a custodial sentence and the duty in subsection (2) of section 152 is not excluded by subsection (1)(a) or (b) or (3) of that section, state that it is of the opinion referred to in section 152(2) and why it is of that opinion,

    (c) where the sentence is a community sentence and the case does not fall within section 151(2), state that it is of the opinion that section 148(1) applies and why it is of that opinion,

    (d) where as a result of taking into account any matter referred to in section 144(1), the court imposes a punishment on the offender which is less severe than the punishment it would otherwise have imposed, state that fact, and

    (e) in any case, mention any aggravating or mitigating factors which the court has regarded as being of particular importance.

(3) Subsection (1)(a) does not apply—

    (a) to an offence the sentence for which is fixed by law (provision relating to sentencing for such an offence being made by section 270), or

    (b) to an offence the sentence for which falls to be imposed under section 51A(2) of the Firearms Act 1968 (c. 27) or under subsection (2) of section 110 or 111 of the Sentencing Act (required custodial sentences).

(4) The Secretary of State may by order—
  (a) prescribe cases in which subsection (1)(a) or (b) does not apply, and
  (b) prescribe cases in which the statement referred to in subsection (1) (a) or the explanation referred to in subsection (1)(b) may be made in the absence of the offender, or may be provided in written form.
(5) Where a magistrates' court passes a custodial sentence, it must cause any reason stated by virtue of subsection (2)(b) to be specified in the warrant of commitment and entered on the register.
(6) In this section—
  "guidelines" has the same meaning as in section 172;
  "the register" has the meaning given by section 163 of the Sentencing Act.

Publication of information by Secretary of State

175. Duty to publish information about sentencing

In section 95 of the Criminal Justice Act 1991 (c. 53) (information for financial and other purposes) in subsection (1) before the "or" at the end of paragraph (a) there is inserted—
  "(aa) enabling such persons to become aware of the relative effectiveness of different sentences—
    (i) in preventing re-offending, and
    (ii) in promoting public confidence in the criminal justice system;".

Interpretation of Chapter

176. Interpretation of Chapter 1

In this Chapter—
  "allocation guidelines" has the meaning given by section 170(1)(b);
  "the Council" means the Sentencing Guidelines Council;
  "the Panel" means the Sentencing Advisory Panel;
  "sentence" and "sentencing" are to be read in accordance with section 142(3);
  "sentencing guidelines" has the meaning given by section 170(1)(a);
  "youth community order" has the meaning given by section 147(2).

CHAPTER 2
COMMUNITY ORDERS: OFFENDERS AGED 16 OR OVER

177. Community orders

(1) Where a person aged 16 or over is convicted of an offence, the court by or before which he is convicted may make an order (in this Part referred to as a "community order") imposing on him any one or more of the following requirements—
  (a) an unpaid work requirement (as defined by section 199),
  (b) an activity requirement (as defined by section 201),
  (c) a programme requirement (as defined by section 202),
  (d) a prohibited activity requirement (as defined by section 203),
  (e) a curfew requirement (as defined by section 204),
  (f) an exclusion requirement (as defined by section 205),

(g) a residence requirement (as defined by section 206),

(h) a mental health treatment requirement (as defined by section 207),

(i) a drug rehabilitation requirement (as defined by section 209),

(j) an alcohol treatment requirement (as defined by section 212),

(k) a supervision requirement (as defined by section 213), and

(l) in a case where the offender is aged under 25, an attendance centre requirement (as defined by section 214).

(2) Subsection (1) has effect subject to sections 150 and 218 and to the following provisions of Chapter 4 relating to particular requirements—

(a) section 199(3) (unpaid work requirement),

(b) section 201(3) and (4) (activity requirement),

(c) section 202(4) and (5) (programme requirement),

(d) section 203(2) (prohibited activity requirement),

(e) section 207(3) (mental health treatment requirement),

(f) section 209(2) (drug rehabilitation requirement), and

(g) section 212(2) and (3) (alcohol treatment requirement).

(3) Where the court makes a community order imposing a curfew requirement or an exclusion requirement, the court must also impose an electronic monitoring requirement (as defined by section 215) unless—

(a) it is prevented from doing so by section 215(2) or 218(4), or

(b) in the particular circumstances of the case, it considers it inappropriate to do so.

(4) Where the court makes a community order imposing an unpaid work requirement, an activity requirement, a programme requirement, a prohibited activity requirement, a residence requirement, a mental health treatment requirement, a drug rehabilitation requirement, an alcohol treatment requirement, a supervision requirement or an attendance centre requirement, the court may also impose an electronic monitoring requirement unless prevented from doing so by section 215(2) or 218(4).

(5) A community order must specify a date, not more than three years after the date of the order, by which all the requirements in it must have been complied with; and a community order which imposes two or more different requirements falling within subsection (1) may also specify an earlier date or dates in relation to compliance with any one or more of them.

(6) Before making a community order imposing two or more different requirements falling within subsection (1), the court must consider whether, in the circumstances of the case, the requirements are compatible with each other.

178. Power to provide for court review of community orders

(1) The Secretary of State may by order—

(a) enable or require a court making a community order to provide for the community order to be reviewed periodically by that or another court,

(b) enable a court to amend a community order so as to include or remove a provision for review by a court, and

(c) make provision as to the timing and conduct of reviews and as to the powers of the court on a review.

(2) An order under this section may, in particular, make provision in relation to community orders corresponding to any provision made by sections 191 and 192 in relation to suspended sentence orders.

(3) An order under this section may repeal or amend any provision of this Part.

179. Breach, revocation or amendment of community order

Schedule 8 (which relates to failures to comply with the requirements of community orders and to the revocation or amendment of such orders) shall have effect.

180. Transfer of community orders to Scotland or Northern Ireland

Schedule 9 (transfer of community orders to Scotland or Northern Ireland) shall have effect.

CHAPTER 3
PRISON SENTENCES OF LESS THAN 12 MONTHS

Prison sentences of less than twelve months

181. Prison sentences of less than 12 months

(1) Any power of a court to impose a sentence of imprisonment for a term of less than 12 months on an offender may be exercised only in accordance with the following provisions of this section unless the court makes an intermittent custody order (as defined by section 183).

(2) The term of the sentence—

    (a) must be expressed in weeks,

    (b) must be at least 28 weeks,

    (c) must not be more than 51 weeks in respect of any one offence, and

    (d) must not exceed the maximum term permitted for the offence.

(3) The court, when passing sentence, must—

    (a) specify a period (in this Chapter referred to as "the custodial period") at the end of which the offender is to be released on a licence, and

    (b) by order require the licence to be granted subject to conditions requiring the offender's compliance during the remainder of the term (in this Chapter referred to as "the licence period") or any part of it with one or more requirements falling within section 182(1) and specified in the order.

(4) In this Part "custody plus order" means an order under subsection (3) (b).

(5) The custodial period—

    (a) must be at least 2 weeks, and

    (b) in respect of any one offence, must not be more than 13 weeks.

(6) In determining the term of the sentence and the length of the custodial period, the court must ensure that the licence period is at least 26 weeks in length.

(7) Where a court imposes two or more terms of imprisonment in accordance with this section to be served consecutively—

    (a) the aggregate length of the terms of imprisonment must not be more than 65 weeks, and

    (b) the aggregate length of the custodial periods must not be more than 26 weeks.

(8) A custody plus order which specifies two or more requirements may, in relation to any requirement, refer to compliance within such part of the licence period as is specified in the order.

(9) Subsection (3) (b) does not apply where the sentence is a suspended sentence.

182. Licence conditions

(1) The requirements falling within this subsection are—

    (a) an unpaid work requirement (as defined by section 199),

    (b) an activity requirement (as defined by section 201),

    (c) a programme requirement (as defined by section 202),

    (d) a prohibited activity requirement (as defined by section 203),

    (e) a curfew requirement (as defined by section 204),

    (f) an exclusion requirement (as defined by section 205),

    (g) a supervision requirement (as defined by section 213), and

    (h) in a case where the offender is aged under 25, an attendance centre requirement (as defined by section 214).

(2) The power under section 181(3)(b) to determine the conditions of the licence has effect subject to section 218 and to the following provisions of Chapter 4 relating to particular requirements—

    (a) section 199(3) (unpaid work requirement),

    (b) section 201(3) and (4) (activity requirement),

    (c) section 202(4) and (5) (programme requirement), and

    (d) section 203(2) (prohibited activity requirement).

(3) Where the court makes a custody plus order requiring a licence to contain a curfew requirement or an exclusion requirement, the court must also require the licence to contain an electronic monitoring requirement (as defined by section 215) unless—

    (a) the court is prevented from doing so by section 215(2) or 218(4), or

    (b) in the particular circumstances of the case, it considers it inappropriate to do so.

(4) Where the court makes a custody plus order requiring a licence to contain an unpaid work requirement, an activity requirement, a programme requirement, a prohibited activity requirement, a supervision requirement or an attendance centre requirement, the court may also require the licence to contain an electronic monitoring requirement unless the court is prevented from doing so by section 215(2) or 218(4).

(5) Before making a custody plus order requiring a licence to contain two or more different requirements falling within subsection (1), the court must consider whether, in the circumstances of the case, the requirements are compatible with each other.

Intermittent custody

183. Intermittent custody

(1) A court may, when passing a sentence of imprisonment for a term complying with subsection (4)—

    (a) specify the number of days that the offender must serve in prison under the sentence before being released on licence for the remainder of the term, and

    (b) by order—

        (i) specify periods during which the offender is to be released temporarily on licence before he has served that number of days in prison, and

        (ii) require any licence to be granted subject to conditions requiring the offender's compliance during the licence periods with one or more requirements falling within section 182(1) and specified in the order.

(2) In this Part "intermittent custody order" means an order under subsection (1)(b).

(3) In this Chapter—

"licence period", in relation to a term of imprisonment to which an intermittent custody order relates, means any period during which the offender is released on licence by virtue of subsection (1)(a) or (b)(i);

"the number of custodial days", in relation to a term of imprisonment to which an intermittent custody order relates, means the number of days specified under subsection (1)(a).

(4) The term of the sentence—
  (a) must be expressed in weeks,
  (b) must be at least 28 weeks,
  (c) must not be more than 51 weeks in respect of any one offence, and
  (d) must not exceed the maximum term permitted for the offence.

(5) The number of custodial days—
  (a) must be at least 14, and
  (b) in respect of any one offence, must not be more than 90.

(6) A court may not exercise its powers under subsection (1) unless the offender has expressed his willingness to serve the custodial part of the proposed sentence intermittently, during the parts of the sentence that are not to be licence periods.

(7) Where a court exercises its powers under subsection (1) in respect of two or more terms of imprisonment that are to be served consecutively—
  (a) the aggregate length of the terms of imprisonment must not be more than 65 weeks, and
  (b) the aggregate of the numbers of custodial days must not be more than 180.

(8) The Secretary of State may by order require a court, in specifying licence periods under subsection (1)(b)(i), to specify only—
  (a) periods of a prescribed duration,
  (b) periods beginning or ending at prescribed times, or
  (c) periods including, or not including, specified parts of the week.

(9) An intermittent custody order which specifies two or more requirements may, in relation to any requirement, refer to compliance within such licence period or periods, or part of a licence period, as is specified in the order.

184. Restrictions on power to make intermittent custody order

(1) A court may not make an intermittent custody order unless it has been notified by the Secretary of State that arrangements for implementing such orders are available in the area proposed to be specified in the intermittent custody order and the notice has not been withdrawn.

(2) The court may not make an intermittent custody order in respect of any offender unless—
  (a) it has consulted an officer of a local probation board,
  (b) it has received from the Secretary of State notification that suitable prison accommodation is available for the offender during the custodial periods, and
  (c) it appears to the court that the offender will have suitable accommodation available to him during the licence periods.

(3) In this section "custodial period", in relation to a sentence to which an intermittent custody order relates, means any part of the sentence that is not a licence period.

185. Intermittent custody: licence conditions

(1) Section 183(1)(b) has effect subject to section 218 and to the following provisions of Chapter 4 limiting the power to require the licence to contain particular requirements—
  (a) section 199(3) (unpaid work requirement),
  (b) section 201(3) and (4) (activity requirement),
  (c) section 202(4) and (5) (programme requirement), and
  (d) section 203(2) (prohibited activity requirement).

(2) Subsections (3) to (5) of section 182 have effect in relation to an intermittent custody order as they have effect in relation to a custody plus order.

186. Further provisions relating to intermittent custody

(1) Section 21 of the 1952 Act (expenses of conveyance to prison) does not apply in relation to the conveyance to prison at the end of any licence period of an offender to whom an intermittent custody order relates.

(2) The Secretary of State may pay to any offender to whom an intermittent custody order relates the whole or part of any expenses incurred by the offender in travelling to and from prison during licence periods.

(3) In section 49 of the 1952 Act (persons unlawfully at large) after subsection (4) there is inserted—

"(4A) For the purposes of this section a person shall also be deemed to be unlawfully at large if, having been temporarily released in pursuance of an intermittent custody order made under section 183 of the Criminal Justice Act 2003, he remains at large at a time when, by reason of the expiry of the period for which he was temporarily released, he is liable to be detained in pursuance of his sentence."

(4) In section 23 of the Criminal Justice Act 1961 (c. 39) (prison rules), in subsection (3) for "The days" there is substituted "Subject to subsection (3A), the days" and after subsection (3) there is inserted—

"(3A) In relation to a prisoner to whom an intermittent custody order under section 183 of the Criminal Justice Act 2003 relates, the only days to which subsection (3) applies are Christmas Day, Good Friday and any day which under the Banking and Financial Dealings Act 1971 is a bank holiday in England and Wales."

(5) In section 1 of the Prisoners (Return to Custody) Act 1995 (c. 16) (remaining at large after temporary release) after subsection (1) there is inserted—

"(1A) A person who has been temporarily released in pursuance of an intermittent custody order made under section 183 of the Criminal Justice Act 2003 is guilty of an offence if, without reasonable excuse, he remains unlawfully at large at any time after becoming so at large by virtue of the expiry of the period for which he was temporarily released."

(6) In this section "the 1952 Act" means the Prison Act 1952 (c. 52).

Further provision about custody plus orders and intermittent custody orders

187. Revocation or amendment of order

Schedule 10 (which contains provisions relating to the revocation or amendment of custody plus orders and the amendment of intermittent custody orders) shall have effect.

**188. Transfer of custody plus orders and intermittent custody orders
to Scotland or Northern Ireland**

Schedule 11 (transfer of custody plus orders and intermittent custody orders to Scotland or Northern Ireland) shall have effect.

Suspended sentences

189. Suspended sentences of imprisonment

(1) A court which passes a sentence of imprisonment for a term of at least 28 weeks but not more than 51 weeks in accordance with section 181 may—

(a) order the offender to comply during a period specified for the purposes of this paragraph in the order (in this Chapter referred to as "the supervision period") with one or more requirements falling within section 190(1) and specified in the order, and

   (b) order that the sentence of imprisonment is not to take effect unless either—
        (i) during the supervision period the offender fails to comply with a requirement imposed under paragraph (a), or
      (ii) during a period specified in the order for the purposes of this sub-paragraph (in this Chapter referred to as "the operational period") the offender commits in the United Kingdom another offence (whether or not punishable with imprisonment),

       and (in either case) a court having power to do so subsequently orders under paragraph 8 of Schedule 12 that the original sentence is to take effect.

(2) Where two or more sentences imposed on the same occasion are to be served consecutively, the power conferred by subsection (1) is not exercisable in relation to any of them unless the aggregate of the terms of the sentences does not exceed 65 weeks.

(3) The supervision period and the operational period must each be a period of not less than six months and not more than two years beginning with the date of the order.

(4) The supervision period must not end later than the operational period.

(5) A court which passes a suspended sentence on any person for an offence may not impose a community sentence in his case in respect of that offence or any other offence of which he is convicted by or before the court or for which he is dealt with by the court.

(6) Subject to any provision to the contrary contained in the Criminal Justice Act 1967 (c. 80), the Sentencing Act or any other enactment passed or instrument made under any enactment after 31st December 1967, a suspended sentence which has not taken effect under paragraph 8 of Schedule 12 is to be treated as a sentence of imprisonment for the purposes of all enactments and instruments made under enactments.

(7) In this Part—
   (a) "suspended sentence order" means an order under subsection (1),
   (b) "suspended sentence" means a sentence to which a suspended sentence order relates, and
   (c) "community requirement", in relation to a suspended sentence order, means a requirement imposed under subsection (1)(a).

190. Imposition of requirements by suspended sentence order

(1) The requirements falling within this subsection are—
   (a) an unpaid work requirement (as defined by section 199),
   (b) an activity requirement (as defined by section 201),
   (c) a programme requirement (as defined by section 202),
   (d) a prohibited activity requirement (as defined by section 203),
   (e) a curfew requirement (as defined by section 204),
   (f) an exclusion requirement (as defined by section 205),
   (g) a residence requirement (as defined by section 206),
   (h) a mental health treatment requirement (as defined by section 207),
   (i) a drug rehabilitation requirement (as defined by section 209),
   (j) an alcohol treatment requirement (as defined by section 212),
   (k) a supervision requirement (as defined by section 213), and
   (l) in a case where the offender is aged under 25, an attendance centre requirement (as defined by section 214).

(2) Section 189(1)(a) has effect subject to section 218 and to the following provisions of Chapter 4 relating to particular requirements—
   (a) section 199(3) (unpaid work requirement),
   (b) section 201(3) and (4) (activity requirement),

    (c) section 202(4) and (5) (programme requirement),

    (d) section 203(2) (prohibited activity requirement),

    (e) section 207(3) (mental health treatment requirement),

    (f) section 209(2) (drug rehabilitation requirement), and

    (g) section 212(2) and (3) (alcohol treatment requirement).

(3) Where the court makes a suspended sentence order imposing a curfew requirement or an exclusion requirement, it must also impose an electronic monitoring requirement (as defined by section 215) unless—

    (a) the court is prevented from doing so by section 215(2) or 218(4), or

    (b) in the particular circumstances of the case, it considers it inappropriate to do so.

(4) Where the court makes a suspended sentence order imposing an unpaid work requirement, an activity requirement, a programme requirement, a prohibited activity requirement, a residence requirement, a mental health treatment requirement, a drug rehabilitation requirement, an alcohol treatment requirement, a supervision requirement or an attendance centre requirement, the court may also impose an electronic monitoring requirement unless the court is prevented from doing so by section 215(2) or 218(4).

(5) Before making a suspended sentence order imposing two or more different requirements falling within subsection (1), the court must consider whether, in the circumstances of the case, the requirements are compatible with each other.

191. Power to provide for review of suspended sentence order

(1) A suspended sentence order may—

    (a) provide for the order to be reviewed periodically at specified intervals,

    (b) provide for each review to be made, subject to section 192(4), at a hearing held for the purpose by the court responsible for the order (a "review hearing"),

    (c) require the offender to attend each review hearing, and

    (d) provide for the responsible officer to make to the court responsible for the order, before each review, a report on the offender's progress in complying with the community requirements of the order.

(2) Subsection (1) does not apply in the case of an order imposing a drug rehabilitation requirement (provision for such a requirement to be subject to review being made by section 210).

(3) In this section references to the court responsible for a suspended sentence order are references—

    (a) where a court is specified in the order in accordance with subsection (4), to that court;

    (b) in any other case, to the court by which the order is made.

(4) Where the area specified in a suspended sentence order made by a magistrates' court is not the area for which the court acts, the court may, if it thinks fit, include in the order provision specifying for the purpose of subsection (3) a magistrates' court which acts for the area specified in the order.

(5) Where a suspended sentence order has been made on an appeal brought from the Crown Court or from the criminal division of the Court of Appeal, it is to be taken for the purposes of subsection (3) (b) to have been made by the Crown Court.

192. Periodic reviews of suspended sentence order

(1) At a review hearing (within the meaning of subsection (1) of section 191) the court may, after considering the responsible officer's report referred to in that subsection, amend the

community requirements of the suspended sentence order, or any provision of the order which relates to those requirements.

(2) The court—

    (a) may not amend the community requirements of the order so as to impose a requirement of a different kind unless the offender expresses his willingness to comply with that requirement,

    (b) may not amend a mental health treatment requirement, a drug rehabilitation requirement or an alcohol treatment requirement unless the offender expresses his willingness to comply with the requirement as amended,

    (c) may amend the supervision period only if the period as amended complies with section 189(3) and (4),

    (d) may not amend the operational period of the suspended sentence, and

    (e) except with the consent of the offender, may not amend the order while an appeal against the order is pending.

(3) For the purposes of subsection (2)(a)—

    (a) a community requirement falling within any paragraph of section 190(1) is of the same kind as any other community requirement falling within that paragraph, and

    (b) an electronic monitoring requirement is a community requirement of the same kind as any requirement falling within section 190(1) to which it relates.

(4) If before a review hearing is held at any review the court, after considering the responsible officer's report, is of the opinion that the offender's progress in complying with the community requirements of the order is satisfactory, it may order that no review hearing is to be held at that review; and if before a review hearing is held at any review, or at a review hearing, the court, after considering that report, is of that opinion, it may amend the suspended sentence order so as to provide for each subsequent review to be held without a hearing.

(5) If at a review held without a hearing the court, after considering the responsible officer's report, is of the opinion that the offender's progress under the order is no longer satisfactory, the court may require the offender to attend a hearing of the court at a specified time and place.

(6) If at a review hearing the court is of the opinion that the offender has without reasonable excuse failed to comply with any of the community requirements of the order, the court may adjourn the hearing for the purpose of dealing with the case under paragraph 8 of Schedule 12.

(7) At a review hearing the court may amend the suspended sentence order so as to vary the intervals specified under section 191(1).

(8) In this section any reference to the court, in relation to a review without a hearing, is to be read—

    (a) in the case of the Crown Court, as a reference to a judge of the court, and

    (b) in the case of a magistrates' court, as a reference to a justice of the peace acting for the commission area for which the court acts.

193. Breach, revocation or amendment of suspended sentence order, and effect of further conviction

Schedule 12 (which relates to the breach, revocation or amendment of the community requirements of suspended sentence orders, and to the effect of any further conviction) shall have effect.

194. Transfer of suspended sentence orders to Scotland or Northern Ireland

Schedule 13 (transfer of suspended sentence orders to Scotland or Northern Ireland) shall have effect.

Interpretation of Chapter

195. Interpretation of Chapter 3

In this Chapter—

"custodial period", in relation to a term of imprisonment imposed in accordance with section 181, has the meaning given by subsection (3)(a) of that section;

"licence period"—

(a) in relation to a term of imprisonment imposed in accordance with section 181, has the meaning given by subsection (3)(b) of that section, and

(b) in relation to a term of imprisonment to which an intermittent custody order relates, has the meaning given by section 183(3);

"the number of custodial days", in relation to a term of imprisonment to which an intermittent custody order relates, has the meaning given by section 183(3);

"operational period" and "supervision period", in relation to a suspended sentence, are to be read in accordance with section 189(1);

"sentence of imprisonment" does not include a committal for contempt of court or any kindred offence.

CHAPTER 4
FURTHER PROVISIONS ABOUT ORDERS UNDER CHAPTERS 2 AND 3

Introductory

196. Meaning of "relevant order"

(1) In this Chapter "relevant order" means—

(a) a community order,

(b) a custody plus order,

(c) a suspended sentence order, or

(d) an intermittent custody order.

(2) In this Chapter any reference to a requirement being imposed by, or included in, a relevant order is, in relation to a custody plus order or an intermittent custody order, a reference to compliance with the requirement being required by the order to be a condition of a licence.

197. Meaning of "the responsible officer"

(1) For the purposes of this Part, "the responsible officer", in relation to an offender to whom a relevant order relates, means—

(a) in a case where the order—

(i) imposes a curfew requirement or an exclusion requirement but no other requirement mentioned in section 177(1) or, as the case requires, section 182(1) or 190(1), and

(ii) imposes an electronic monitoring requirement,

the person who under section 215(3) is responsible for the electronic monitoring required by the order;

    (b) in a case where the offender is aged 18 or over and the only requirement imposed by the order is an attendance centre requirement, the officer in charge of the attendance centre in question;

    (c) in any other case, the qualifying officer who, as respects the offender, is for the time being responsible for discharging the functions conferred by this Part on the responsible officer.

(2) The following are qualifying officers for the purposes of subsection (1)(c)—

    (a) in a case where the offender is aged under 18 at the time when the relevant order is made, an officer of a local probation board appointed for or assigned to the petty sessions area for the time being specified in the order or a member of a youth offending team established by a local authority for the time being specified in the order;

    (b) in any other case, an officer of a local probation board appointed for or assigned to the petty sessions area for the time being specified in the order.

(3) The Secretary of State may by order—

    (a) amend subsections (1) and (2), and

    (b) make any other amendments of this Part that appear to him to be necessary or expedient in consequence of any amendment made by virtue of paragraph (a).

(4) An order under subsection (3) may, in particular, provide for the court to determine which of two or more descriptions of "responsible officer" is to apply in relation to any relevant order.

198. Duties of responsible officer

(1) Where a relevant order has effect, it is the duty of the responsible officer—

    (a) to make any arrangements that are necessary in connection with the requirements imposed by the order,

    (b) to promote the offender's compliance with those requirements, and

    (c) where appropriate, to take steps to enforce those requirements.

(2) In this section "responsible officer" does not include a person falling within section 197(1) (a).

Requirements available in case of all offenders

199. Unpaid work requirement

(1) In this Part "unpaid work requirement", in relation to a relevant order, means a requirement that the offender must perform unpaid work in accordance with section 200.

(2) The number of hours which a person may be required to work under an unpaid work requirement must be specified in the relevant order and must be in the aggregate—

    (a) not less than 40, and

    (b) not more than 300.

(3) A court may not impose an unpaid work requirement in respect of an offender unless after hearing (if the courts thinks necessary) an appropriate officer, the court is satisfied that the offender is a suitable person to perform work under such a requirement.

(4) In subsection (3) "an appropriate officer" means—

    (a) in the case of an offender aged 18 or over, an officer of a local probation board, and

    (b) in the case of an offender aged under 18, an officer of a local probation board, a social worker of a local authority social services department or a member of a youth offending team.

(5) Where the court makes relevant orders in respect of two or more offences of which the offender has been convicted on the same occasion and includes unpaid work requirements in each of them, the court may direct that the hours of work specified in any of those requirements is to be concurrent with or additional to those specified in any other of those orders, but so that the total number of hours which are not concurrent does not exceed the maximum specified in subsection (2)(b).

200. Obligations of person subject to unpaid work requirement

(1) An offender in respect of whom an unpaid work requirement of a relevant order is in force must perform for the number of hours specified in the order such work at such times as he may be instructed by the responsible officer.

(2) Subject to paragraph 20 of Schedule 8 and paragraph 18 of Schedule 12 (power to extend order), the work required to be performed under an unpaid work requirement of a community order or a suspended sentence order must be performed during a period of twelve months.

(3) Unless revoked, a community order imposing an unpaid work requirement remains in force until the offender has worked under it for the number of hours specified in it.

(4) Where an unpaid work requirement is imposed by a suspended sentence order, the supervision period as defined by section 189(1)(a) continues until the offender has worked under the order for the number of hours specified in the order, but does not continue beyond the end of the operational period as defined by section 189(1)(b)(ii).

201. Activity requirement

(1) In this Part "activity requirement", in relation to a relevant order, means a requirement that the offender must do either or both of the following—

    (a) present himself to a person or persons specified in the relevant order at a place or places so specified on such number of days as may be so specified;

    (b) participate in activities specified in the order on such number of days as may be so specified.

(2) The specified activities may consist of or include activities whose purpose is that of reparation, such as activities involving contact between offenders and persons affected by their offences.

(3) A court may not include an activity requirement in a relevant order unless—

    (a) it has consulted—

        (i) in the case of an offender aged 18 or over, an officer of a local probation board,

        (ii) in the case of an offender aged under 18, either an officer of a local probation board or a member of a youth offending team, and

    (b) it is satisfied that it is feasible to secure compliance with the requirement.

(4) A court may not include an activity requirement in a relevant order if compliance with that requirement would involve the co-operation of a person other than the offender and the offender's responsible officer, unless that other person consents to its inclusion.

(5) The aggregate of the number of days specified under subsection (1)(a) and (b) must not exceed 60.

(6) A requirement such as is mentioned in subsection (1)(a) operates to require the offender—

    (a) in accordance with instructions given by his responsible officer, to present himself at a place or places on the number of days specified in the order, and

    (b) while at any place, to comply with instructions given by, or under the authority of, the person in charge of that place.

(7) A place specified under subsection (1)(a) must be—

    (a) a community rehabilitation centre, or

    (b) a place that has been approved by the local probation board for the area in which the premises are situated as providing facilities suitable for persons subject to activity requirements.

(8) Where the place specified under subsection (1)(a) is a community rehabilitation centre, the reference in subsection (6)(a) to the offender presenting himself at the specified place includes a reference to him presenting himself elsewhere than at the centre for the purpose of participating in activities in accordance with instructions given by, or under the authority of, the person in charge of the centre.

(9) A requirement to participate in activities operates to require the offender—

    (a) in accordance with instructions given by his responsible officer, to participate in activities on the number of days specified in the order, and

    (b) while participating, to comply with instructions given by, or under the authority of, the person in charge of the activities.

(10) In this section "community rehabilitation centre" means premises—

    (a) at which non-residential facilities are provided for use in connection with the rehabilitation of offenders, and

    (b) which are for the time being approved by the Secretary of State as providing facilities suitable for persons subject to relevant orders.

202. Programme requirement

(1) In this Part "programme requirement", in relation to a relevant order, means a requirement that the offender must participate in an accredited programme specified in the order at a place so specified on such number of days as may be so specified.

(2) In this Part "accredited programme" means a programme that is for the time being accredited by the accreditation body.

(3) In this section—

    (a) "programme" means a systematic set of activities, and

    (b) "the accreditation body" means such body as the Secretary of State may designate for the purposes of this section by order.

(4) A court may not include a programme requirement in a relevant order unless—

    (a) the accredited programme which the court proposes to specify in the order has been recommended to the court as being suitable for the offender—

        (i) in the case of an offender aged 18 or over, by an officer of a local probation board, or

        (ii) in the case of an offender aged under 18, either by an officer of a local probation board or by a member of a youth offending team, and

    (b) the court is satisfied that the programme is (or, where the relevant order is a custody plus order or an intermittent custody order, will be) available at the place proposed to be specified.

387

(5) A court may not include a programme requirement in a relevant order if compliance with that requirement would involve the co-operation of a person other than the offender and the offender's responsible officer, unless that other person consents to its inclusion.

(6) A requirement to attend an accredited programme operates to require the offender—

(a) in accordance with instructions given by the responsible officer, to participate in the accredited programme at the place specified in the order on the number of days specified in the order, and

(b) while at that place, to comply with instructions given by, or under the authority of, the person in charge of the programme.

(7) A place specified in an order must be a place that has been approved by the local probation board for the area in which the premises are situated as providing facilities suitable for persons subject to programme requirements.

203. Prohibited activity requirement

(1) In this Part "prohibited activity requirement", in relation to a relevant order, means a requirement that the offender must refrain from participating in activities specified in the order—

(a) on a day or days so specified, or

(b) during a period so specified.

(2) A court may not include a prohibited activity requirement in a relevant order unless it has consulted—

(a) in the case of an offender aged 18 or over, an officer of a local probation board;

(b) in the case of an offender aged under 18, either an officer of a local probation board or a member of a youth offending team.

(3) The requirements that may by virtue of this section be included in a relevant order include a requirement that the offender does not possess, use or carry a firearm within the meaning of the Firearms Act 1968 (c. 27).

204. Curfew requirement

(1) In this Part "curfew requirement", in relation to a relevant order, means a requirement that the offender must remain, for periods specified in the relevant order, at a place so specified

(2) A relevant order imposing a curfew requirement may specify different places or different periods for different days, but may not specify periods which amount to less than two hours or more than twelve hours in any day.

(3) A community order or suspended sentence order which imposes a curfew requirement may not specify periods which fall outside the period of six months beginning with the day on which it is made.

(4) A custody plus order which imposes a curfew requirement may not specify a period which falls outside the period of six months beginning with the first day of the licence period as defined by section 181(3)(b).

(5) An intermittent custody order which imposes a curfew requirement must not specify a period if to do so would cause the aggregate number of days on which the offender is subject to the requirement for any part of the day to exceed 182.

(6) Before making a relevant order imposing a curfew requirement, the court must obtain and consider information about the place proposed to be specified in the order (including information as to the attitude of persons likely to be affected by the enforced presence there of the offender).

205. Exclusion requirement

(1) In this Part "exclusion requirement", in relation to a relevant order, means a provision prohibiting the offender from entering a place specified in the order for a period so specified.

(2) Where the relevant order is a community order, the period specified must not be more than two years.

(3) An exclusion requirement—

    (a) may provide for the prohibition to operate only during the periods specified in the order, and

    (b) may specify different places for different periods or days.

(4) In this section "place" includes an area.

206. Residence requirement

(1) In this Part, "residence requirement", in relation to a community order or a suspended sentence order, means a requirement that, during a period specified in the relevant order, the offender must reside at a place specified in the order.

(2) If the order so provides, a residence requirement does not prohibit the offender from residing, with the prior approval of the responsible officer, at a place other than that specified in the order.

(3) Before making a community order or suspended sentence order containing a residence requirement, the court must consider the home surroundings of the offender.

(4) A court may not specify a hostel or other institution as the place where an offender must reside, except on the recommendation of an officer of a local probation board.

207. Mental health treatment requirement

(1) In this Part, "mental health treatment requirement", in relation to a community order or suspended sentence order, means a requirement that the offender must submit, during a period or periods specified in the order, to treatment by or under the direction of a registered medical practitioner or a chartered psychologist (or both, for different periods) with a view to the improvement of the offender's mental condition.

(2) The treatment required must be such one of the following kinds of treatment as may be specified in the relevant order—

    (a) treatment as a resident patient in an independent hospital or care home within the meaning of the Care Standards Act 2000 (c. 14) or a hospital within the meaning of the Mental Health Act 1983 (c. 20), but not in hospital premises where high security psychiatric services within the meaning of that Act are provided;

    (b) treatment as a non-resident patient at such institution or place as may be specified in the order;

    (c) treatment by or under the direction of such registered medical practitioner or chartered psychologist (or both) as may be so specified;

but the nature of the treatment is not to be specified in the order except as mentioned in paragraph (a), (b) or (c).

(3) A court may not by virtue of this section include a mental health treatment requirement in a relevant order unless—

    (a) the court is satisfied, on the evidence of a registered medical practitioner approved for the purposes of section 12 of the Mental Health Act 1983, that the mental condition of the offender—

        (i) is such as requires and may be susceptible to treatment, but

        (ii) is not such as to warrant the making of a hospital order or guardianship order within the meaning of that Act;

    (b) the court is also satisfied that arrangements have been or can be made for the treatment intended to be specified in the order (including arrangements for the reception of the offender where he is to be required to submit to treatment as a resident patient); and

    (c) the offender has expressed his willingness to comply with such a requirement.

(4) While the offender is under treatment as a resident patient in pursuance of a mental health requirement of a relevant order, his responsible officer shall carry out the supervision of the offender to such extent only as may be necessary for the purpose of the revocation or amendment of the order.

(5) Subsections (2) and (3) of section 54 of the Mental Health Act 1983 (c. 20) have effect with respect to proof for the purposes of subsection (3)(a) of an offender's mental condition as they have effect with respect to proof of an offender's mental condition for the purposes of section 37(2)(a) of that Act.

(6) In this section and section 208, "chartered psychologist" means a person for the time being listed in the British Psychological Society's Register of Chartered Psychologists.

208. Mental health treatment at place other than that specified in order

(1) Where the medical practitioner or chartered psychologist by whom or under whose direction an offender is being treated for his mental condition in pursuance of a mental health treatment requirement is of the opinion that part of the treatment can be better or more conveniently given in or at an institution or place which—

    (a) is not specified in the relevant order, and

    (b) is one in or at which the treatment of the offender will be given by or under the direction of a registered medical practitioner or chartered psychologist,

he may, with the consent of the offender, make arrangements for him to be treated accordingly.

(2) Such arrangements as are mentioned in subsection (1) may provide for the offender to receive part of his treatment as a resident patient in an institution or place notwithstanding that the institution or place is not one which could have been specified for that purpose in the relevant order.

(3) Where any such arrangements as are mentioned in subsection (1) are made for the treatment of an offender—

    (a) the medical practitioner or chartered psychologist by whom the arrangements are made shall give notice in writing to the offender's responsible officer, specifying the institution or place in or at which the treatment is to be carried out; and

    (b) the treatment provided for by the arrangements shall be deemed to be treatment to which he is required to submit in pursuance of the relevant order.

209. Drug rehabilitation requirement

(1) In this Part "drug rehabilitation requirement", in relation to a community order or suspended sentence order, means a requirement that during a period specified in the order ("the treatment and testing period") the offender—

    (a) must submit to treatment by or under the direction of a specified person having the necessary qualifications or experience with a view to the reduction or elimination of the offender's dependency on or propensity to misuse drugs, and

    (b) for the purpose of ascertaining whether he has any drug in his body during that period, must provide samples of such description as may be so determined, at such times or in such circumstances as may (subject to the provisions of the order) be determined by the responsible officer or by the person specified as the person by or under whose direction the treatment is to be provided.

(2) A court may not impose a drug rehabilitation requirement unless—
   (a) it is satisfied—
      (i) that the offender is dependent on, or has a propensity to misuse, drugs, and
      (ii) that his dependency or propensity is such as requires and may be susceptible to treatment,
   (b) it is also satisfied that arrangements have been or can be made for the treatment intended to be specified in the order (including arrangements for the reception of the offender where he is to be required to submit to treatment as a resident),
   (c) the requirement has been recommended to the court as being suitable for the offender—
      (i) in the case of an offender aged 18 or over, by an officer of a local probation board, or
      (ii) in the case of an offender aged under 18, either by an officer of a local probation board or by a member of a youth offending team, and
   (d) the offender expresses his willingness to comply with the requirement.

(3) The treatment and testing period must be at least six months.

(4) The required treatment for any particular period must be—
   (a) treatment as a resident in such institution or place as may be specified in the order, or
   (b) treatment as a non-resident in or at such institution or place, and at such intervals, as may be so specified;
but the nature of the treatment is not to be specified in the order except as mentioned in paragraph (a) or (b) above.

(5) The function of making a determination as to the provision of samples under provision included in the community order or suspended sentence order by virtue of subsection (1) (b) is to be exercised in accordance with guidance given from time to time by the Secretary of State.

(6) A community order or suspended sentence order imposing a drug rehabilitation requirement must provide that the results of tests carried out on any samples provided by the offender in pursuance of the requirement to a person other than the responsible officer are to be communicated to the responsible officer.

(7) In this section "drug" means a controlled drug as defined by section 2 of the Misuse of Drugs Act 1971 (c. 38).

210. Drug rehabilitation requirement: provision for review by court

(1) A community order or suspended sentence order imposing a drug rehabilitation requirement may (and must if the treatment and testing period is more than 12 months)—
   (a) provide for the requirement to be reviewed periodically at intervals of not less than one month,
   (b) provide for each review of the requirement to be made, subject to section 211(6), at a hearing held for the purpose by the court responsible for the order (a "review hearing"),
   (c) require the offender to attend each review hearing,
   (d) provide for the responsible officer to make to the court responsible for the order, before each review, a report in writing on the offender's progress under the requirement, and
   (e) provide for each such report to include the test results communicated to the responsible officer under section 209(6) or otherwise and the views of the treatment provider as to the treatment and testing of the offender.

391

(2) In this section references to the court responsible for a community order or suspended sentence order imposing a drug rehabilitation requirement are references—

(a) where a court is specified in the order in accordance with subsection (3), to that court;

(b) in any other case, to the court by which the order is made.

(3) Where the area specified in a community order or suspended sentence order which is made by a magistrates' court and imposes a drug rehabilitation requirement is not the area for which the court acts, the court may, if it thinks fit, include in the order provision specifying for the purposes of subsection (2) a magistrates' court which acts for the area specified in the order.

(4) Where a community order or suspended sentence order imposing a drug rehabilitation requirement has been made on an appeal brought from the Crown Court or from the criminal division of the Court of Appeal, for the purposes of subsection (2)(b) it shall be taken to have been made by the Crown Court.

211. Periodic review of drug rehabilitation requirement

(1) At a review hearing (within the meaning given by subsection (1) of section 210) the court may, after considering the responsible officer's report referred to in that subsection, amend the community order or suspended sentence order, so far as it relates to the drug rehabilitation requirement.

(2) The court—

(a) may not amend the drug rehabilitation requirement unless the offender expresses his willingness to comply with the requirement as amended,

(b) may not amend any provision of the order so as to reduce the period for which the drug rehabilitation requirement has effect below the minimum specified in section 209(3), and

(c) except with the consent of the offender, may not amend any requirement or provision of the order while an appeal against the order is pending.

(3) If the offender fails to express his willingness to comply with the drug rehabilitation requirement as proposed to be amended by the court, the court may—

(a) revoke the community order, or the suspended sentence order and the suspended sentence to which it relates, and

(b) deal with him, for the offence in respect of which the order was made, in any way in which he could have been dealt with for that offence by the court which made the order if the order had not been made.

(4) In dealing with the offender under subsection (3)(b), the court—

(a) shall take into account the extent to which the offender has complied with the requirements of the order, and

(b) may impose a custodial sentence (where the order was made in respect of an offence punishable with such a sentence) notwithstanding anything in section 152(2).

(5) Where the order is a community order made by a magistrates' court in the case of an offender under 18 years of age in respect of an offence triable only on indictment in the case of an adult, any powers exercisable under subsection (3)(b) in respect of the offender after he attains the age of 18 are powers to do either or both of the following—

(a) to impose a fine not exceeding £5,000 for the offence in respect of which the order was made;

(b) to deal with the offender for that offence in any way in which the court could deal with him if it had just convicted him of an offence punishable with imprisonment for a term not exceeding twelve months.

(6) If at a review hearing (as defined by section 210(1)(b)) the court, after considering the responsible officer's report, is of the opinion that the offender's progress under the requirement is satisfactory, the court may so amend the order as to provide for each subsequent review to be made by the court without a hearing.

(7) If at a review without a hearing the court, after considering the responsible officer's report, is of the opinion that the offender's progress under the requirement is no longer satisfactory, the court may require the offender to attend a hearing of the court at a specified time and place.

(8) At that hearing the court, after considering that report, may—

(a) exercise the powers conferred by this section as if the hearing were a review hearing, and

(b) so amend the order as to provide for each subsequent review to be made at a review hearing.

(9) In this section any reference to the court, in relation to a review without a hearing, is to be read—

(a) in the case of the Crown Court, as a reference to a judge of the court;

(b) in the case of a magistrates' court, as a reference to a justice of the peace acting for the commission area for which the court acts.

212. Alcohol treatment requirement

(1) In this Part "alcohol treatment requirement", in relation to a community order or suspended sentence order, means a requirement that the offender must submit during a period specified in the order to treatment by or under the direction of a specified person having the necessary qualifications or experience with a view to the reduction or elimination of the offender's dependency on alcohol.

(2) A court may not impose an alcohol treatment requirement in respect of an offender unless it is satisfied—

(a) that he is dependent on alcohol,

(b) that his dependency is such as requires and may be susceptible to treatment, and

(c) that arrangements have been or can be made for the treatment intended to be specified in the order (including arrangements for the reception of the offender where he is to be required to submit to treatment as a resident).

(3) A court may not impose an alcohol treatment requirement unless the offender expresses his willingness to comply with its requirements.

(4) The period for which the alcohol treatment requirement has effect must be not less than six months.

(5) The treatment required by an alcohol treatment requirement for any particular period must be—

(a) treatment as a resident in such institution or place as may be specified in the order,

(b) treatment as a non-resident in or at such institution or place, and at such intervals, as may be so specified, or

(c) treatment by or under the direction of such person having the necessary qualification or experience as may be so specified;

but the nature of the treatment shall not be specified in the order except as mentioned in paragraph (a), (b) or (c) above.

393

213. Supervision requirement

(1) In this Part "supervision requirement", in relation to a relevant order, means a requirement that, during the relevant period, the offender must attend appointments with the responsible officer or another person determined by the responsible officer, at such time and place as may be determined by the officer.

(2) The purpose for which a supervision requirement may be imposed is that of promoting the offender's rehabilitation.

(3) In subsection (1) "the relevant period" means—

    (a) in relation to a community order, the period for which the community order remains in force,

    (b) in relation to a custody plus order, the licence period as defined by section 181(3)(b),

    (c) in relation to an intermittent custody order, the licence periods as defined by section 183(3), and

    (d) in relation to a suspended sentence order, the supervision period as defined by section 189(1)(a).

Requirements available only in case of offenders aged under 25

214. Attendance centre requirement

(1) In this Part "attendance centre requirement", in relation to a relevant order, means a requirement that the offender must attend at an attendance centre specified in the relevant order for such number of hours as may be so specified.

(2) The aggregate number of hours for which the offender may be required to attend at an attendance centre must not be less than 12 or more than 36.

(3) The court may not impose an attendance centre requirement unless the court is satisfied that the attendance centre to be specified in it is reasonably accessible to the offender concerned, having regard to the means of access available to him and any other circumstances.

(4) The first time at which the offender is required to attend at the attendance centre is a time notified to the offender by the responsible officer.

(5) The subsequent hours are to be fixed by the officer in charge of the centre, having regard to the offender's circumstances.

(6) An offender may not be required under this section to attend at an attendance centre on more than one occasion on any day, or for more than three hours on any occasion.

Electronic monitoring

215. Electronic monitoring requirement

(1) In this Part "electronic monitoring requirement", in relation to a relevant order, means a requirement for securing the electronic monitoring of the offender's compliance with other requirements imposed by the order during a period specified in the order, or determined by the responsible officer in accordance with the relevant order.

(2) Where—

    (a) it is proposed to include in a relevant order a requirement for securing electronic monitoring in accordance with this section, but

    (b) there is a person (other than the offender) without whose co-operation it will not be practicable to secure the monitoring,

the requirement may not be included in the order without that person's consent.

(3) A relevant order which includes an electronic monitoring requirement must include provision for making a person responsible for the monitoring; and a person who is made so responsible must be of a description specified in an order made by the Secretary of State.

(4) Where an electronic monitoring requirement is required to take effect during a period determined by the responsible officer in accordance with the relevant order, the responsible officer must, before the beginning of that period, notify—

   (a) the offender,

   (b) the person responsible for the monitoring, and

   (c) any person falling within subsection (2)(b),

of the time when the period is to begin.

Provisions applying to relevant orders generally

216. Petty sessions area to be specified in relevant order

(1) A community order or suspended sentence order must specify the petty sessions area in which the offender resides or will reside.

(2) A custody plus order or an intermittent custody order must specify the petty sessions area in which the offender will reside—

   (a) in the case of a custody plus order, during the licence period as defined by section 181(3)(b), or

   (b) in the case of an intermittent custody order, during the licence periods as defined by section 183(3).

217. Requirement to avoid conflict with religious beliefs, etc

(1) The court must ensure, as far as practicable, that any requirement imposed by a relevant order is such as to avoid—

   (a) any conflict with the offender's religious beliefs or with the requirements of any other relevant order to which he may be subject; and

   (b) any interference with the times, if any, at which he normally works or attends school or any other educational establishment.

(2) The responsible officer in relation to an offender to whom a relevant order relates must ensure, as far as practicable, that any instruction given or requirement imposed by him in pursuance of the order is such as to avoid the conflict or interference mentioned in subsection (1).

(3) The Secretary of State may by order provide that subsection (1) or (2) is to have effect with such additional restrictions as may be specified in the order.

218. Availability of arrangements in local area

(1) A court may not include an unpaid work requirement in a relevant order unless the court is satisfied that provision for the offender to work under such a requirement can be made under the arrangements for persons to perform work under such a requirement which exist in the petty sessions area in which he resides or will reside.

(2) A court may not include an activity requirement in a relevant order unless the court is satisfied that provision for the offender to participate in the activities proposed to be specified in the order can be made under the arrangements for persons to participate in such activities which exist in the petty sessions area in which he resides or will reside.

(3) A court may not include an attendance centre requirement in a relevant order in respect of an offender unless the court has been notified by the Secretary of State that an attendance centre is available for persons of his description.

(4) A court may not include an electronic monitoring requirement in a relevant order in respect of an offender unless the court—

    (a) has been notified by the Secretary of State that electronic monitoring arrangements are available in the relevant areas mentioned in subsections (5) to (7), and

    (b) is satisfied that the necessary provision can be made under those arrangements.

(5) In the case of a relevant order containing a curfew requirement or an exclusion requirement, the relevant area for the purposes of subsection (4) is the area in which the place proposed to be specified in the order is situated.

(6) In the case of a relevant order containing an attendance centre requirement, the relevant area for the purposes of subsection (4) is the area in which the attendance centre proposed to be specified in the order is situated.

(7) In the case of any other relevant order, the relevant area for the purposes of subsection (4) is the petty sessions area proposed to be specified in the order.

(8) In subsection (5) "place", in relation to an exclusion requirement, has the same meaning as in section 205.

219. Provision of copies of relevant orders

(1) The court by which any relevant order is made must forthwith provide copies of the order—

    (a) to the offender,

    (b) if the offender is aged 18 or over, to an officer of a local probation board assigned to the court,

    (c) if the offender is aged 16 or 17, to an officer of a local probation board assigned to the court or to a member of a youth offending team assigned to the court, and

    (d) where the order specifies a petty sessions area for which the court making the order does not act, to the local probation board acting for that area.

(2) Where a relevant order imposes any requirement specified in the first column of Schedule 14, the court by which the order is made must also forthwith provide the person specified in relation to that requirement in the second column of that Schedule with a copy of so much of the order as relates to that requirement.

(3) Where a relevant order specifies a petty sessions area for which the court making the order does not act, the court making the order must provide to the magistrates's court acting for that area—

    (a) a copy of the order, and

    (b) such documents and information relating to the case as it considers likely to be of assistance to a court acting for that area in the exercise of its functions in relation to the order.

220. Duty of offender to keep in touch with responsible officer

(1) An offender in respect of whom a community order or a suspended sentence order is in force—

    (a) must keep in touch with the responsible officer in accordance with such instructions as he may from time to time be given by that officer, and

    (b) must notify him of any change of address.

(2) The obligation imposed by subsection (1) is enforceable as if it were a requirement imposed by the order.

Powers of Secretary of State

221. Provision of attendance centres

(1) The Secretary of State may continue to provide attendance centres.

(2) In this Part "attendance centre" means a place at which offenders aged under 25 may be required to attend and be given under supervision appropriate occupation or instruction in pursuance of—

(a) attendance centre requirements of relevant orders, or

(b) attendance centre orders under section 60 of the Sentencing Act.

(3) For the purpose of providing attendance centres, the Secretary of State may make arrangements with any local authority or police authority for the use of premises of that authority.

222. Rules

(1) The Secretary of State may make rules for regulating—

(a) the supervision of persons who are subject to relevant orders,

(b) without prejudice to the generality of paragraph (a), the functions of responsible officers in relation to offenders subject to relevant orders,

(c) the arrangements to be made by local probation boards for persons subject to unpaid work requirements to perform work and the performance of such work,

(d) the provision and carrying on of attendance centres and community rehabilitation centres,

(e) the attendance of persons subject to activity requirements or attendance centre requirements at the places at which they are required to attend, including hours of attendance, reckoning days of attendance and the keeping of attendance records,

(f) electronic monitoring in pursuance of an electronic monitoring requirement, and

(g) without prejudice to the generality of paragraph (f), the functions of persons made responsible for securing electronic monitoring in pursuance of such a requirement.

(2) Rules under subsection (1) (c) may, in particular, make provision—

(a) limiting the number of hours of work to be done by a person on any one day,

(b) as to the reckoning of hours worked and the keeping of work records, and

(c) for the payment of travelling and other expenses in connection with the performance of work.

223. Power to amend limits

(1) The Secretary of State may by order amend—

(a) subsection (2) of section 199 (unpaid work requirement), or

(b) subsection (2) of section 204 (curfew requirement),

by substituting, for the maximum number of hours for the time being specified in that subsection, such other number of hours as may be specified in the order.

(2) The Secretary of State may by order amend any of the provisions mentioned in subsection (3) by substituting, for any period for the time being specified in the provision, such other period as may be specified in the order.

(3) Those provisions are—
  (a) section 204(3) (curfew requirement);
  (b) section 205(2) (exclusion requirement);
  (c) section 209(3) (drug rehabilitation requirement);
  (d) section 212(4) (alcohol treatment requirement).

CHAPTER 5
DANGEROUS OFFENDERS

224. Meaning of "specified offence" etc.

(1) An offence is a "specified offence" for the purposes of this Chapter if it is a specified violent offence or a specified sexual offence.

(2) An offence is a "serious offence" for the purposes of this Chapter if and only if—
  (a) it is a specified offence, and
  (b) it is, apart from section 225, punishable in the case of a person aged 18 or over by—
    (i) imprisonment for life, or
    (ii) imprisonment for a determinate period of ten years or more.

(3) In this Chapter—
  "relevant offence" has the meaning given by section 229(4);
  "serious harm" means death or serious personal injury, whether physical or psychological;
  "specified violent offence" means an offence specified in Part 1 of Schedule 15;
  "specified sexual offence" means an offence specified in Part 2 of that Schedule.

225. Life sentence or imprisonment for public protection for serious offences

(1) This section applies where—
  (a) a person aged 18 or over is convicted of a serious offence committed after the commencement of this section, and
  (b) the court is of the opinion that there is a significant risk to members of the public of serious harm occasioned by the commission by him of further specified offences.

(2) If—
  (a) the offence is one in respect of which the offender would apart from this section be liable to imprisonment for life, and
  (b) the court considers that the seriousness of the offence, or of the offence and one or more offences associated with it, is such as to justify the imposition of a sentence of imprisonment for life,
  the court must impose a sentence of imprisonment for life.

(3) In a case not falling within subsection (2), the court must impose a sentence of imprisonment for public protection.

(4) A sentence of imprisonment for public protection is a sentence of imprisonment for an indeterminate period, subject to the provisions of Chapter 2 of Part 2 of the Crime (Sentences) Act 1997 (c. 43) as to the release of prisoners and duration of licences.

(5) An offence the sentence for which is imposed under this section is not to be regarded as an offence the sentence for which is fixed by law.

226. Detention for life or detention for public protection for serious offences committed by those under 18

(1) This section applies where—
    (a) a person aged under 18 is convicted of a serious offence committed after the commencement of this section, and
    (b) the court is of the opinion that there is a significant risk to members of the public of serious harm occasioned by the commission by him of further specified offences.

(2) If—
    (a) the offence is one in respect of which the offender would apart from this section be liable to a sentence of detention for life under section 91 of the Sentencing Act, and
    (b) the court considers that the seriousness of the offence, or of the offence and one or more offences associated with it, is such as to justify the imposition of a sentence of detention for life,
the court must impose a sentence of detention for life under that section.

(3) If, in a case not falling within subsection (2), the court considers that an extended sentence under section 228 would not be adequate for the purpose of protecting the public from serious harm occasioned by the commission by the offender of further specified offences, the court must impose a sentence of detention for public protection.

(4) A sentence of detention for public protection is a sentence of detention for an indeterminate period, subject to the provisions of Chapter 2 of Part 2 of the Crime (Sentences) Act 1997 (c. 43) as to the release of prisoners and duration of licences.

(5) An offence the sentence for which is imposed under this section is not to be regarded as an offence the sentence for which is fixed by law.

227. Extended sentence for certain violent or sexual offences: persons 18 or over

(1) This section applies where—
    (a) a person aged 18 or over is convicted of a specified offence, other than a serious offence, committed after the commencement of this section, and
    (b) the court considers that there is a significant risk to members of the public of serious harm occasioned by the commission by the offender of further specified offences.

(2) The court must impose on the offender an extended sentence of imprisonment, that is to say, a sentence of imprisonment the term of which is equal to the aggregate of—
    (a) the appropriate custodial term, and
    (b) a further period ("the extension period") for which the offender is to be subject to a licence and which is of such length as the court considers necessary for the purpose of protecting members of the public from serious harm occasioned by the commission by him of further specified offences.

(3) In subsection (2) "the appropriate custodial term" means a term of imprisonment (not exceeding the maximum term permitted for the offence) which—
    (a) is the term that would (apart from this section) be imposed in compliance with section 153(2), or
    (b) where the term that would be so imposed is a term of less than 12 months, is a term of 12 months.

(4) The extension period must not exceed—
    (a) five years in the case of a specified violent offence, and
    (b) eight years in the case of a specified sexual offence.

(5) The term of an extended sentence of imprisonment passed under this section in respect of an offence must not exceed the maximum term permitted for the offence.

228. Extended sentence for certain violent or sexual offences: persons under 18

(1) This section applies where—

    (a) a person aged under 18 is convicted of a specified offence committed after the commencement of this section, and

    (b) the court considers—

        (i) that there is a significant risk to members of the public of serious harm occasioned by the commission by the offender of further specified offences, and

        (ii) where the specified offence is a serious offence, that the case is not one in which the court is required by section 226(2) to impose a sentence of detention for life under section 91 of the Sentencing Act or by section 226(3) to impose a sentence of detention for public protection.

(2) The court must impose on the offender an extended sentence of detention, that is to say, a sentence of detention the term of which is equal to the aggregate of—

    (a) the appropriate custodial term, and

    (b) a further period ("the extension period") for which the offender is to be subject to a licence and which is of such length as the court considers necessary for the purpose of protecting members of the public from serious harm occasioned by the commission by him of further specified offences.

(3) In subsection (2) "the appropriate custodial term" means such term as the court considers appropriate, which—

    (a) must be at least 12 months, and

    (b) must not exceed the maximum term of imprisonment permitted for the offence.

(4) The extension period must not exceed—

    (a) five years in the case of a specified violent offence, and

    (b) eight years in the case of a specified sexual offence.

(5) The term of an extended sentence of detention passed under this section in respect of an offence must not exceed the maximum term of imprisonment permitted for the offence.

(6) Any reference in this section to the maximum term of imprisonment permitted for an offence is a reference to the maximum term of imprisonment that is, apart from section 225, permitted for the offence in the case of a person aged 18 or over.

229. The assessment of dangerousness

(1) This section applies where—

    (a) a person has been convicted of a specified offence, and

    (b) it falls to a court to assess under any of sections 225 to 228 whether there is a significant risk to members of the public of serious harm occasioned by the commission by him of further such offences.

(2) If at the time when that offence was committed the offender had not been convicted in any part of the United Kingdom of any relevant offence or was aged under 18, the court in making the assessment referred to in subsection (1)(b)—

    (a) must take into account all such information as is available to it about the nature and circumstances of the offence,

    (b) may take into account any information which is before it about any pattern of behaviour of which the offence forms part, and

    (c) may take into account any information about the offender which is before it.

(3) If at the time when that offence was committed the offender was aged 18 or over and had been convicted in any part of the United Kingdom of one or more relevant offences, the court must assume that there is such a risk as is mentioned in subsection (1)(b) unless, after taking into account—

(a) all such information as is available to it about the nature and circumstances of each of the offences,

(b) where appropriate, any information which is before it about any pattern of behaviour of which any of the offences forms part, and

(c) any information about the offender which is before it,

the court considers that it would be unreasonable to conclude that there is such a risk.

(4) In this Chapter "relevant offence" means—

(a) a specified offence,

(b) an offence specified in Schedule 16 (offences under the law of Scotland), or

(c) an offence specified in Schedule 17 (offences under the law of Northern Ireland).

230. Imprisonment or detention for public protection: release on licence

Schedule 18 (release of prisoners serving sentences of imprisonment or detention for public protection) shall have effect.

231. Appeals where previous convictions set aside

(1) This section applies where —

(a) a sentence has been imposed on any person under section 225 or 227, and

(b) any previous conviction of his without which the court would not have been required to make the assumption mentioned in section 229(3) has been subsequently set aside on appeal.

(2) Notwithstanding anything in section 18 of the Criminal Appeal Act 1968 (c. 19), notice of appeal against the sentence may be given at any time within 28 days from the date on which the previous conviction was set aside.

232. Certificates of convictions for purposes of section 229

Where—

(a) on any date after the commencement of this section a person is convicted in England and Wales of a relevant offence, and

(b) the court by or before which he is so convicted states in open court that he has been convicted of such an offence on that date, and

(c) that court subsequently certifies that fact,

that certificate shall be evidence, for the purposes of section 229, that he was convicted of such an offence on that date.

233. Offences under service law

Where—

(a) a person has at any time been convicted of an offence under section 70 of the Army Act 1955 (3 & 4 Eliz. 2 c. 18), section 70 of the Air Force Act 1955 (3 & 4 Eliz. 2 c. 19) or section 42 of the Naval Discipline Act 1957 (c. 53), and

(b) the corresponding civil offence (within the meaning of that Act) was a relevant offence,

section 229 shall have effect as if he had at that time been convicted in England and Wales of the corresponding civil offence.

234. Determination of day when offence committed

Where an offence is found to have been committed over a period of two or more days, or at some time during a period of two or more days, it shall be taken for the purposes of section 229 to have been committed on the last of those days.

235. Detention under sections 226 and 228

A person sentenced to be detained under section 226 or 228 is liable to be detained in such place, and under such conditions, as may be determined by the Secretary of State or by such other person as may be authorised by him for the purpose.

236. Conversion of sentences of detention into sentences of imprisonment

For section 99 of the Sentencing Act (conversion of sentence of detention and custody into sentence of imprisonment) there is substituted—

"Conversion of sentence of detention to sentence of imprisonment

99. Conversion of sentence of detention to sentence of imprisonment

(1) Subject to the following provisions of this section, where an offender has been sentenced by a relevant sentence of detention to a term of detention and either—

  (a) he has attained the age of 21, or

  (b) he has attained the age of 18 and has been reported to the Secretary of State by the board of visitors of the institution in which he is detained as exercising a bad influence on the other inmates of the institution or as behaving in a disruptive manner to the detriment of those inmates,

the Secretary of State may direct that he shall be treated as if he had been sentenced to imprisonment for the same term.

(2) Where the Secretary of State gives a direction under subsection (1) above in relation to an offender, the portion of the term of detention imposed under the relevant sentence of detention which he has already served shall be deemed to have been a portion of a term of imprisonment.

(3) Where the Secretary of State gives a direction under subsection (1) above in relation to an offender serving a sentence of detention for public protection under section 226 of the Criminal Justice Act 2003 the offender shall be treated as if he had been sentenced under section 225 of that Act; and where the Secretary of State gives such a direction in relation to an offender serving an extended sentence of detention under section 228 of that Act the offender shall be treated as if he had been sentenced under section 227 of that Act.

(4) Rules under section 47 of the Prison Act 1952 may provide that any award for an offence against discipline made in respect of an offender serving a relevant sentence of detention shall continue to have effect after a direction under subsection (1) has been given in relation to him.

(5) In this section "relevant sentence of detention" means—

  (a) a sentence of detention under section 90 or 91 above,

  (b) a sentence of detention for public protection under section 226 of the Criminal Justice Act 2003, or

  (c) an extended sentence of detention under section 228 of that Act."

CHAPTER 6
RELEASE ON LICENCE

Preliminary

237. Meaning of "fixed-term prisoner"

(1) In this Chapter "fixed-term prisoner" means—

    (a) a person serving a sentence of imprisonment for a determinate term, or

    (b) a person serving a determinate sentence of detention under section 91 of the Sentencing Act or under section 228 of this Act.

(2) In this Chapter, unless the context otherwise requires, "prisoner" includes a person serving a sentence falling within subsection (1)(b); and "prison" includes any place where a person serving such a sentence is liable to be detained.

Power of court to recommend licence conditions

238. Power of court to recommend licence conditions for certain prisoners

(1) A court which sentences an offender to a term of imprisonment of twelve months or more in respect of any offence may, when passing sentence, recommend to the Secretary of State particular conditions which in its view should be included in any licence granted to the offender under this Chapter on his release from prison

(2) In exercising his powers under section 250(4)(b) in respect of an offender, the Secretary of State must have regard to any recommendation under subsection (1).

(3) A recommendation under subsection (1) is not to be treated for any purpose as part of the sentence passed on the offender.

(4) This section does not apply in relation to a sentence of detention under section 91 of the Sentencing Act or section 228 of this Act.

239. The Parole Board

(1) The Parole Board is to continue to be, by that name, a body corporate and as such is—

    (a) to be constituted in accordance with this Chapter, and

    (b) to have the functions conferred on it by this Chapter in respect of fixed-term prisoners and by Chapter 2 of Part 2 of the Crime (Sentences) Act 1997 (c. 43) (in this Chapter referred to as "the 1997 Act") in respect of life prisoners within the meaning of that Chapter.

(2) It is the duty of the Board to advise the Secretary of State with respect to any matter referred to it by him which is to do with the early release or recall of prisoners.

(3) The Board must, in dealing with cases as respects which it makes recommendations under this Chapter or under Chapter 2 of Part 2 of the 1997 Act, consider—

    (a) any documents given to it by the Secretary of State, and

    (b) any other oral or written information obtained by it;

and if in any particular case the Board thinks it necessary to interview the person to whom the case relates before reaching a decision, the Board may authorise one of its members to interview him and must consider the report of the interview made by that member.

(4) The Board must deal with cases as respects which it gives directions under this Chapter or under Chapter 2 of Part 2 of the 1997 Act on consideration of all such evidence as may be adduced before it.

(5) Without prejudice to subsections (3) and (4), the Secretary of State may make rules with respect to the proceedings of the Board, including proceedings authorising cases to be

dealt with by a prescribed number of its members or requiring cases to be dealt with at prescribed times.

(6) The Secretary of State may also give to the Board directions as to the matters to be taken into account by it in discharging any functions under this Chapter or under Chapter 2 of Part 2 of the 1997 Act; and in giving any such directions the Secretary of State must have regard to—
    (a) the need to protect the public from serious harm from offenders, and
    (b) the desirability of preventing the commission by them of further offences and of securing their rehabilitation.

(7) Schedule 19 shall have effect with respect to the Board.

Effect of remand in custody

240. Crediting of periods of remand in custody: terms of imprisonment and detention

(1) This section applies where—
    (a) a court sentences an offender to imprisonment for a term in respect of an offence committed after the commencement of this section, and
    (b) the offender has been remanded in custody (within the meaning given by section 242) in connection with the offence or a related offence, that is to say, any other offence the charge for which was founded on the same facts or evidence.

(2) It is immaterial for that purpose whether the offender—
    (a) has also been remanded in custody in connection with other offences; or
    (b) has also been detained in connection with other matters.

(3) Subject to subsection (4), the court must direct that the number of days for which the offender was remanded in custody in connection with the offence or a related offence is to count as time served by him as part of the sentence.

(4) Subsection (3) does not apply if and to the extent that—
    (a) rules made by the Secretary of State so provide in the case of—
        (i) a remand in custody which is wholly or partly concurrent with a sentence of imprisonment, or
        (ii) sentences of imprisonment for consecutive terms or for terms which are wholly or partly concurrent, or
    (h) it is in the opinion of the court just in all the circumstances not to give a direction under that subsection.

(5) Where the court gives a direction under subsection (3), it shall state in open court—
    (a) the number of days for which the offender was remanded in custody, and
    (b) the number of days in relation to which the direction is given.

(6) Where the court does not give a direction under subsection (3), or gives such a direction in relation to a number of days less than that for which the offender was remanded in custody, it shall state in open court—
    (a) that its decision is in accordance with rules made under paragraph (a) of subsection (4), or
    (b) that it is of the opinion mentioned in paragraph (b) of that subsection and what the circumstances are.

(7) For the purposes of this section a suspended sentence—
    (a) is to be treated as a sentence of imprisonment when it takes effect under paragraph 8(2)(a) or (b) of Schedule 12, and
    (b) is to be treated as being imposed by the order under which it takes effect.

(8) For the purposes of the reference in subsection (3) to the term of imprisonment to which a person has been sentenced (that is to say, the reference to his "sentence"), consecutive terms and terms which are wholly or partly concurrent are to be treated as a single term if—

(a) the sentences were passed on the same occasion, or

(b) where they were passed on different occasions, the person has not been released under this Chapter at any time during the period beginning with the first and ending with the last of those occasions.

(9) Where an offence is found to have been committed over a period of two or more days, or at some time during a period of two or more days, it shall be taken for the purposes of subsection (1) to have been committed on the last of those days.

(10) This section applies to a determinate sentence of detention under section 91 of the Sentencing Act or section 228 of this Act as it applies to an equivalent sentence of imprisonment.

241. Effect of direction under section 240 on release on licence

(1) In determining for the purposes of this Chapter or Chapter 3 (prison sentences of less than twelve months) whether a person to whom a direction under section 240 relates—

(a) has served, or would (but for his release) have served, a particular proportion of his sentence, or

(b) has served a particular period,

the number of days specified in the direction are to be treated as having been served by him as part of that sentence or period.

(2) In determining for the purposes of section 183 (intermittent custody) whether any part of a sentence to which an intermittent custody order relates is a licence period, the number of custodial days, as defined by subsection (3) of that section, is to be taken to be reduced by the number of days specified in a direction under section 240.

242. Interpretation of sections 240 and 241

(1) For the purposes of sections 240 and 241, the definition of "sentence of imprisonment" in section 305 applies as if for the words from the beginning of the definition to the end of paragraph (a) there were substituted—

"'sentence of imprisonment' does not include a committal—

(a) in default of payment of any sum of money, other than one adjudged to be paid on a conviction,";

and references in those sections to sentencing an offender to imprisonment, and to an offender's sentence, are to be read accordingly.

(2) References in sections 240 and 241 to an offender's being remanded in custody are references to his being—

(a) remanded in or committed to custody by order of a court,

(b) remanded or committed to local authority accommodation under section 23 of the Children and Young Persons Act 1969 (c. 54) and kept in secure accommodation or detained in a secure training centre pursuant to arrangements under subsection (7A) of that section, or

(c) remanded, admitted or removed to hospital under section 35, 36, 38 or 48 of the Mental Health Act 1983 (c. 20).

(3) In subsection (2), "secure accommodation" has the same meaning as in section 23 of the Children and Young Persons Act 1969.

243. Persons extradited to the United Kingdom

(1) A fixed-term prisoner is an extradited prisoner for the purposes of this section if—
    (a) he was tried for the offence in respect of which his sentence was imposed—
        (i) after having been extradited to the United Kingdom, and
        (ii) without having first been restored or had an opportunity of leaving the United Kingdom, and
    (b) he was for any period kept in custody while awaiting his extradition to the United Kingdom as mentioned in paragraph (a).

(2) In the case of an extradited prisoner, section 240 has effect as if the days for which he was kept in custody while awaiting extradition were days for which he was remanded in custody in connection with the offence, or any other offence the charge for which was founded on the same facts or evidence.

(3) In this section—
"extradited to the United Kingdom" means returned to the United Kingdom—
    (a) in pursuance of extradition arrangements,
    (b) under any law of a designated Commonwealth country corresponding to the Extradition Act 1989 (c. 33),
    (c) under that Act as extended to a British overseas territory or under any corresponding law of a British overseas territory,
    (d) in pursuance of a warrant of arrest endorsed in the Republic of Ireland under the law of that country corresponding to the Backing of Warrants (Republic of Ireland) Act 1965 (c. 45), or
    (e) in pursuance of arrangements with a foreign state in respect of which an Order in Council under section 2 of the Extradition Act 1870 (c. 52) is in force;
"extradition arrangements" has the meaning given by section 3 of the Extradition Act 1989;
"designated Commonwealth country" has the meaning given by section 5(1) of that Act.

Release on licence

244. Duty to release prisoners

(1) As soon as a fixed-term prisoner, other than a prisoner to whom section 247 applies, has served the requisite custodial period, it is the duty of the Secretary of State to release him on licence under this section.

(2) Subsection (1) is subject to section 245.

(3) In this section "the requisite custodial period" means—
    (a) in relation to a person serving a sentence of imprisonment for a term of twelve months or more or any determinate sentence of detention under section 91 of the Sentencing Act, one-half of his sentence,
    (b) in relation to a person serving a sentence of imprisonment for a term of less than twelve months (other than one to which an intermittent custody order relates), the custodial period within the meaning of section 181,
    (c) in relation to a person serving a sentence of imprisonment to which an intermittent custody order relates, any part of the term which is not a licence period as defined by section 183(3), and
    (d) in relation to a person serving two or more concurrent or consecutive sentences, the period determined under sections 263(2) and 264(2).

245. Restrictions on operation of section 244(1) in relation to intermittent custody prisoners

(1) Where an intermittent custody prisoner returns to custody after being unlawfully at large within the meaning of section 49 of the Prison Act 1952 (c. 52) at any time during the currency of his sentence, section 244(1) does not apply until—

    (a) the relevant time (as defined in subsection (2)), or

    (b) if earlier, the date on which he has served in prison the number of custodial days required by the intermittent custody order.

(2) In subsection (1)(a) "the relevant time" means—

    (a) in a case where, within the period of 72 hours beginning with the return to custody of the intermittent custody prisoner, the Secretary of State or the responsible officer has applied to the court for the amendment of the intermittent custody order under paragraph 6(1)(b) of Schedule 10, the date on which the application is withdrawn or determined, and

    (b) in any other case, the end of that 72-hour period.

(3) Section 244(1) does not apply in relation to an intermittent custody prisoner at any time after he has been recalled under section 254, unless after his recall the Board has directed his further release on licence.

246. Power to release prisoners on licence before required to do so

(1) Subject to subsections (2) to (4), the Secretary of State may—

    (a) release on licence under this section a fixed-term prisoner, other than an intermittent custody prisoner, at any time during the period of 135 days ending with the day on which the prisoner will have served the requisite custodial period, and

    (b) release on licence under this section an intermittent custody prisoner when 135 or less of the required custodial days remain to be served.

(2) Subsection (1)(a) does not apply in relation to a prisoner unless—

    (a) the length of the requisite custodial period is at least 6 weeks,

    (b) he has served—

        (i) at least 4 weeks of his sentence, and

        (ii) at least one-half of the requisite custodial period.

(3) Subsection (1)(b) does not apply in relation to a prisoner unless—

    (a) the number of required custodial days is at least 42, and

    (b) the prisoner has served—

        (i) at least 28 of those days, and

        (ii) at least one-half of the total number of those days.

(4) Subsection (1) does not apply where—

    (a) the sentence is imposed under section 227 or 228,

    (b) the sentence is for an offence under section 1 of the Prisoners (Return to Custody) Act 1995 (c. 16),

    (c) the prisoner is subject to a hospital order, hospital direction or transfer direction under section 37, 45A or 47 of the Mental Health Act 1983 (c. 20),

    (d) the sentence was imposed by virtue of paragraph 9(1)(b) or (c) or 10(1)(b) or (c) of Schedule 8 in a case where the prisoner has failed to comply with a curfew requirement of a community order,

(e) the prisoner is subject to the notification requirements of Part 2 of the Sexual Offences Act 2003 (c. 42),

(f) the prisoner is liable to removal from the United Kingdom,

(g) the prisoner has been released on licence under this section during the currency of the sentence, and has been recalled to prison under section 255(1)(a),

(h) the prisoner has been released on licence under section 248 during the currency of the sentence, and has been recalled to prison under section 254, or

(i) in the case of a prisoner to whom a direction under section 240 relates, the interval between the date on which the sentence was passed and the date on which the prisoner will have served the requisite custodial period is less than 14 days or, where the sentence is one of intermittent custody, the number of the required custodial days remaining to be served is less than 14.

(5) The Secretary of State may by order—

(a) amend the number of days for the time being specified in subsection (1)(a) or (b), (3) or (4) (i),

(b) amend the number of weeks for the time being specified in subsection (2)(a) or (b)(i), and

(c) amend the fraction for the time being specified in subsection (2)(b)(ii) or (3)(b)(ii).

(6) In this section—

"the required custodial days", in relation to an intermittent custody prisoner, means—

(a) the number of custodial days specified under section 183, or

(b) in the case of two or more sentences of intermittent custody, the aggregate of the numbers so specified;

"the requisite custodial period" in relation to a person serving any sentence other than a sentence of intermittent custody, has the meaning given by paragraph (a), (b) or (d) of section 244(3);

"sentence of intermittent custody" means a sentence to which an intermittent custody order relates.

247. Release on licence of prisoner serving extended sentence under section 227 or 228

(1) This section applies to a prisoner who is serving an extended sentence imposed under section 227 or 228.

(2) As soon as—

(a) a prisoner to whom this section applies has served one-half of the appropriate custodial term, and

(b) the Parole Board has directed his release under this section, it is the duty of the Secretary of State to release him on licence.

(3) The Parole Board may not give a direction under subsection (2) unless the Board is satisfied that it is no longer necessary for the protection of the public that the prisoner should be confined.

(4) As soon as a prisoner to whom this section applies has served the appropriate custodial term, it is the duty of the Secretary of State to release him on licence unless the prisoner has previously been recalled under section 254.

(5) Where a prisoner to whom this section applies is released on a licence, the Secretary of State may not by virtue of section 250(4)(b) include, or subsequently insert, a condition in the licence, or vary or cancel a condition in the licence, except after consultation with the Board.

(6) For the purposes of subsection (5), the Secretary of State is to be treated as having consulted the Board about a proposal to include, insert, vary or cancel a condition in any

case if he has consulted the Board about the implementation of proposals of that description generally or in that class of case.

(7) In this section "the appropriate custodial term" means the period determined by the court as the appropriate custodial term under section 227 or 228.

248. Power to release prisoners on compassionate grounds

(1) The Secretary of State may at any time release a fixed-term prisoner on licence if he is satisfied that exceptional circumstances exist which justify the prisoner's release on compassionate grounds.

(2) Before releasing under this section a prisoner to whom section 247 applies, the Secretary of State must consult the Board, unless the circumstances are such as to render such consultation impracticable.

249. Duration of licence

(1) Subject to subsections (2) and (3), where a fixed-term prisoner is released on licence, the licence shall, subject to any revocation under section 254 or 255, remain in force for the remainder of his sentence.

(2) Where an intermittent custody prisoner is released on licence under section 244, the licence shall, subject to any revocation under section 254, remain in force—
   (a) until the time when he is required to return to prison at the beginning of the next custodial period of the sentence, or
   (b) where it is granted at the end of the last custodial period, for the remainder of his sentence.

(3) Subsection (1) has effect subject to sections 263(2) (concurrent terms) and 264(3) and (4) (consecutive terms).

(4) In subsection (2) "custodial period", in relation to a sentence to which an intermittent custody order relates, means any period which is not a licence period as defined by 183(3).

250. Licence conditions

(1) In this section—
   (a) "the standard conditions" means such conditions as may be prescribed for the purposes of this section as standard conditions, and
   (b) "prescribed" means prescribed by the Secretary of State by order.

(2) Subject to subsection (6) and section 251, any licence under this Chapter in respect of a prisoner serving one or more sentences of imprisonment of less than twelve months and no sentence of twelve months or more—
   (a) must include—
      (i) the conditions required by the relevant court order, and
      (ii) so far as not inconsistent with them, the standard conditions, and
   (b) may also include—
      (i) any condition which is authorised by section 62 of the Criminal Justice and Court Services Act 2000 (c. 43) (electronic monitoring) or section 64 of that Act (drug testing requirements) and which is compatible with the conditions required by the relevant court order, and
      (ii) such other conditions of a kind prescribed for the purposes of this paragraph as the Secretary of State may for the time being consider to be necessary for the protection of the public and specify in the licence.

(3) For the purposes of subsection (2)(a)(i), any reference in the relevant court order to the licence period specified in the order is, in relation to a prohibited activity requirement, exclusion requirement, residence requirement or supervision requirement, to be taken to include a reference to any other period during which the prisoner is released on licence under section 246 or 248.

(4) Any licence under this Chapter in respect of a prisoner serving a sentence of imprisonment for a term of twelve months or more (including such a sentence imposed under section 227) or any sentence of detention under section 91 of the Sentencing Act or section 228 of this Act—

    (a) must include the standard conditions, and

    (b) may include—

        (i) any condition authorised by section 62 or 64 of the Criminal Justice and Court Services Act 2000, and

        (ii) such other conditions of a kind prescribed by the Secretary of State for the purposes of this paragraph as the Secretary of State may for the time being specify in the licence.

(5) A licence under section 246 must also include a curfew condition complying with section 253.

(6) Where—

    (a) a licence under section 246 is granted to a prisoner serving one or more sentences of imprisonment of less than 12 months and no sentence of 12 months or more, and

    (b) the relevant court order requires the licence to be granted subject to a condition requiring his compliance with a curfew requirement (as defined by section 204), that condition is not to be included in the licence at any time while a curfew condition required by section 253 is in force.

(7) The preceding provisions of this section have effect subject to section 263(3) (concurrent terms) and section 264(3) and (4) (consecutive terms).

(8) In exercising his powers to prescribe standard conditions or the other conditions referred to in subsection (4)(b)(ii), the Secretary of State must have regard to the following purposes of the supervision of offenders while on licence under this Chapter—

    (a) the protection of the public,

    (b) the prevention of re-offending, and

    (c) securing the successful re-integration of the prisoner into the community.

251. Licence conditions on re-release of prisoner serving sentence of less than 12 months

(1) In relation to any licence under this Chapter which is granted to a prisoner serving one or more sentences of imprisonment of less than twelve months and no sentence of twelve months or more on his release in pursuance of a decision of the Board under section 254 or 256, subsections (2) and (3) apply instead of section 250(2).

(2) The licence—

    (a) must include the standard conditions, and

    (b) may include—

        (i) any condition authorised by section 62 or 64 of the Criminal Justice and Court Services Act 2000 (c. 43), and

        (ii) such other conditions of a kind prescribed by the Secretary of State for the purposes of section 250(4)(b)(ii) as the Secretary of State may for the time being specify in the licence.

(3) In exercising his powers under subsection (2)(b)(ii), the Secretary of State must have regard to the terms of the relevant court order.

(4) In this section "the standard conditions" has the same meaning as in section 250.

252. Duty to comply with licence conditions

A person subject to a licence under this Chapter must comply with such conditions as may for the time being be specified in the licence.

253. Curfew condition to be included in licence under section 246

(1) For the purposes of this Chapter, a curfew condition is a condition which—
  (a) requires the released person to remain, for periods for the time being specified in the condition, at a place for the time being so specified (which may be premises approved by the Secretary of State under section 9 of the Criminal Justice and Court Services Act 2000 (c. 43)), and
  (b) includes requirements for securing the electronic monitoring of his whereabouts during the periods for the time being so specified.

(2) The curfew condition may specify different places or different periods for different days, but may not specify periods which amount to less than 9 hours in any one day (excluding for this purpose the first and last days of the period for which the condition is in force).

(3) The curfew condition is to remain in force until the date when the released person would (but for his release) fall to be released on licence under section 244.

(4) Subsection (3) does not apply in relation to a released person to whom an intermittent custody order relates; and in relation to such a person the curfew condition is to remain in force until the number of days during which it has been in force is equal to the number of the required custodial days, as defined in section 246(6), that remained to be served at the time when he was released under section 246.

(5) The curfew condition must include provision for making a person responsible for monitoring the released person's whereabouts during the periods for the time being specified in the condition; and a person who is made so responsible shall be of a description specified in an order made by the Secretary of State.

(6) Nothing in this section is to be taken to require the Secretary of State to ensure that arrangements are made for the electronic monitoring of released persons' whereabouts in any particular part of England and Wales.

Recall after release

254. Recall of prisoners while on licence

(1) The Secretary of State may, in the case of any prisoner who has been released on licence under this Chapter, revoke his licence and recall him to prison.

(2) A person recalled to prison under subsection (1)—
  (a) may make representations in writing with respect to his recall, and
  (b) on his return to prison, must be informed of the reasons for his recall and of his right to make representations.

(3) The Secretary of State must refer to the Board the case of a person recalled under subsection (1).

(4) Where on a reference under subsection (3) relating to any person the Board recommends his immediate release on licence under this Chapter, the Secretary of State must give effect to the recommendation.

(5) In the case of an intermittent custody prisoner who has not yet served in prison the number of custodial days specified in the intermittent custody order, any recommendation by the Board as to immediate release on licence is to be a recommendation as to his release on

licence until the end of one of the licence periods specified by virtue of section 183(1)(b) in the intermittent custody order.

(6) On the revocation of the licence of any person under this section, he shall be liable to be detained in pursuance of his sentence and, if at large, is to be treated as being unlawfully at large.

(7) Nothing in subsections (2) to (6) applies in relation to a person recalled under section 255.

255. Recall of prisoners released early under section 246

(1) If it appears to the Secretary of State, as regards a person released on licence under section 246—
  (a) that he has failed to comply with any condition included in his licence, or
  (b) that his whereabouts can no longer be electronically monitored at the place for the time being specified in the curfew condition included in his licence,

the Secretary of State may, if the curfew condition is still in force, revoke the licence and recall the person to prison under this section.

(2) A person whose licence under section 246 is revoked under this section—
  (a) may make representations in writing with respect to the revocation, and
  (b) on his return to prison, must be informed of the reasons for the revocation and of his right to make representations.

(3) The Secretary of State, after considering any representations under subsection (2)(b) or any other matters, may cancel a revocation under this section.

(4) Where the revocation of a person's licence is cancelled under subsection (3), the person is to be treated for the purposes of section 246 as if he had not been recalled to prison under this section.

(5) On the revocation of a person's licence under section 246, he is liable to be detained in pursuance of his sentence and, if at large, is to be treated as being unlawfully at large.

256. Further release after recall

(1) Where on a reference under section 254(3) in relation to any person, the Board does not recommend his immediate release on licence under this Chapter, the Board must either—
  (a) fix a date for the person's release on licence, or
  (b) fix a date as the date for the next review of the person's case by the Board.

(2) Any date fixed under subsection (1)(a) or (b) must not be later than the first anniversary of the date on which the decision is taken.

(3) The Board need not fix a date under subsection (1)(a) or (b) if the prisoner will fall to be released unconditionally at any time within the next 12 months.

(4) Where the Board has fixed a date under subsection (1)(a), it is the duty of the Secretary of State to release him on licence on that date.

(5) On a review required by subsection (1)(b) in relation to any person, the Board may—
  (a) recommend his immediate release on licence, or
  (b) fix a date under subsection (1)(a) or (b).

Additional days

257. Additional days for disciplinary offences

(1) Prison rules, that is to say, rules made under section 47 of the Prison Act 1952 (c. 52), may include provision for the award of additional days—
   (a) to fixed-term prisoners, or
   (b) conditionally on their subsequently becoming such prisoners, to persons on remand, who (in either case) are guilty of disciplinary offences.

(2) Where additional days are awarded to a fixed-term prisoner, or to a person on remand who subsequently becomes such a prisoner, and are not remitted in accordance with prison rules—
   (a) any period which he must serve before becoming entitled to or eligible for release under this Chapter,
   (b) any period which he must serve before he can be removed from prison under section 260, and
   (c) any period for which a licence granted to him under this Chapter remains in force,
   is extended by the aggregate of those additional days.

Fine defaulters and contemnors

258. Early release of fine defaulters and contemnors

(1) This section applies in relation to a person committed to prison—
   (a) in default of payment of a sum adjudged to be paid by a conviction, or
   (b) for contempt of court or any kindred offence.

(2) As soon as a person to whom this section applies has served one-half of the term for which he was committed, it is the duty of the Secretary of State to release him unconditionally.

(3) Where a person to whom this section applies is also serving one or more sentences of imprisonment, nothing in this section requires the Secretary of State to release him until he is also required to release him in respect of that sentence or each of those sentences.

(4) The Secretary of State may at any time release unconditionally a person to whom this section applies if he is satisfied that exceptional circumstances exist which justify the person's release on compassionate grounds.

Persons liable to removal from the United Kingdom

259. Persons liable to removal from the United Kingdom

For the purposes of this Chapter a person is liable to removal from the United Kingdom if—
(a) he is liable to deportation under section 3(5) of the Immigration Act 1971 (c. 77) and has been notified of a decision to make a deportation order against him,
(b) he is liable to deportation under section 3(6) of that Act,
(c) he has been notified of a decision to refuse him leave to enter the United Kingdom,
(d) he is an illegal entrant within the meaning of section 33(1) of that Act, or
(e) he is liable to removal under section 10 of the Immigration and Asylum Act 1999 (c. 33).

260. Early removal of prisoners liable to removal from United Kingdom

(1) Subject to subsections (2) and (3), where a fixed-term prisoner is liable to removal from the United Kingdom, the Secretary of State may remove him from prison under this

section at any time during the period of 135 days ending with the day on which the prisoner will have served the requisite custodial period.

(2) Subsection (1) does not apply in relation to a prisoner unless—

    (a) the length of the requisite custodial period is at least 6 weeks, and

    (b) he has served—

        (i) at least 4 weeks of his sentence, and

        (ii) at least one-half of the requisite custodial period.

(3) Subsection (1) does not apply where—

    (a) the sentence is imposed under section 227 or 228,

    (b) the sentence is for an offence under section 1 of the Prisoners (Return to Custody) Act 1995 (c. 16),

    (c) the prisoner is subject to a hospital order, hospital direction or transfer direction under section 37, 45A or 47 of the Mental Health Act 1983 (c. 20),

    (d) the prisoner is subject to the notification requirements of Part 2 of the Sexual Offences Act 2003 (c. 42), or

    (e) in the case of a prisoner to whom a direction under section 240 relates, the interval between the date on which the sentence was passed and the date on which the prisoner will have served the requisite custodial period is less than 14 days.

(4) A prisoner removed from prison under this section—

    (a) is so removed only for the purpose of enabling the Secretary of State to remove him from the United Kingdom under powers conferred by—

        (i) Schedule 2 or 3 to the Immigration Act 1971, or

        (ii) section 10 of the Immigration and Asylum Act 1999 (c. 33), and

    (b) so long as remaining in the United Kingdom, remains liable to be detained in pursuance of his sentence until he has served the requisite custodial period.

(5) So long as a prisoner removed from prison under this section remains in the United Kingdom but has not been returned to prison, any duty or power of the Secretary of State under section 244 or 248 is exercisable in relation to him as if he were in prison.

(6) The Secretary of State may by order—

    (a) amend the number of days for the time being specified in subsection (1) or (3)(e),

    (b) amend the number of weeks for the time being specified in subsection (2)(a) or (b)(i), and

    (c) amend the fraction for the time being specified in subsection (2)(b)(ii).

(7) In this section "the requisite custodial period" has the meaning given by paragraph (a), (b) or (d) of section 244(3).

261. Re-entry into United Kingdom of offender removed from prison early

(1) This section applies in relation to a person who, after being removed from prison under section 260, has been removed from the United Kingdom before he has served the requisite custodial period.

(2) If a person to whom this section applies enters the United Kingdom at any time before his sentence expiry date, he is liable to be detained in pursuance of his sentence from the time of his entry into the United Kingdom until whichever is the earlier of the following—

    (a) the end of a period ("the further custodial period") beginning with that time and equal in length to the outstanding custodial period, and

    (b) his sentence expiry date.

(3) A person who is liable to be detained by virtue of subsection (2) is, if at large, to be taken for the purposes of section 49 of the Prison Act 1952 (c. 52) (persons unlawfully at large) to be unlawfully at large.

(4) Subsection (2) does not prevent the further removal from the United Kingdom of a person falling within that subsection.

(5) Where, in the case of a person returned to prison by virtue of subsection (2), the further custodial period ends before the sentence expiry date, section 244 has effect in relation to him as if the reference to the requisite custodial period were a reference to the further custodial period.

(6) In this section—

"further custodial period" has the meaning given by subsection (2)(a);

"outstanding custodial period", in relation to a person to whom this section applies, means the period beginning with the date of his removal from the United Kingdom and ending with the date on which he would, but for his removal, have served the requisite custodial period;

"requisite custodial period" has the meaning given by paragraph (a), (b) or (d) of section 244(3);

"sentence expiry date", in relation to a person to whom this section applies, means the date on which, but for his removal from the United Kingdom, he would have ceased to be subject to a licence.

262. Prisoners liable to removal from United Kingdom: modifications of Criminal Justice Act 1991

Part 2 of the Criminal Justice Act 1991 (c. 53) (early release of prisoners) shall (until the coming into force of its repeal by this Act) have effect subject to the modifications set out in Schedule 20 (which relate to persons liable to removal from the United Kingdom).

Consecutive or concurrent terms

263. Concurrent terms

(1) This section applies where—

(a) a person ("the offender") has been sentenced by any court to two or more terms of imprisonment which are wholly or partly concurrent, and

(b) the sentences were passed on the same occasion or, where they were passed on different occasions, the person has not been released under this Chapter at any time during the period beginning with the first and ending with the last of those occasions.

(2) Where this section applies—

(a) nothing in this Chapter requires the Secretary of State to release the offender in respect of any of the terms unless and until he is required to release him in respect of each of the others,

(b) section 244 does not authorise the Secretary of State to release him on licence under that section in respect of any of the terms unless and until that section authorises the Secretary of State to do so in respect of each of the others,

(c) on and after his release under this Chapter the offender is to be on licence for so long, and subject to such conditions, as is required by this Chapter in respect of any of the sentences.

(3) Where the sentences include one or more sentences of twelve months or more and one or more sentences of less than twelve months, the terms of the licence may be determined by the Secretary of State in accordance with section 250(4)(b), without regard to the requirements of any custody plus order or intermittent custody order.

(4) In this section "term of imprisonment" includes a determinate sentence of detention under section 91 of the Sentencing Act or under section 228 of this Act.

264. Consecutive terms

(1) This section applies where—
  (a) a person ("the offender") has been sentenced to two or more terms of imprisonment which are to be served consecutively on each other, and
  (b) the sentences were passed on the same occasion or, where they were passed on different occasions, the person has not been released under this Chapter at any time during the period beginning with the first and ending with the last of those occasions.

(2) Nothing in this Chapter requires the Secretary of State to release the offender on licence until he has served a period equal in length to the aggregate of the length of the custodial periods in relation to each of the terms of imprisonment.

(3) Where any of the terms of imprisonment is a term of twelve months or more, the offender is, on and after his release under this Chapter, to be on licence—
  (a) until he would, but for his release, have served a term equal in length to the aggregate length of the terms of imprisonment, and
  (b) subject to such conditions as are required by this Chapter in respect of each of those terms of imprisonment.

(4) Where each of the terms of imprisonment is a term of less than twelve months, the offender is, on and after his release under this Chapter, to be on licence until the relevant time, and subject to such conditions as are required by this Chapter in respect of any of the terms of imprisonment, and none of the terms is to be regarded for any purpose as continuing after the relevant time.

(5) In subsection (4) "the relevant time" means the time when the offender would, but for his release, have served a term equal in length to the aggregate of—
  (a) all the custodial periods in relation to the terms of imprisonment, and
  (b) the longest of the licence periods in relation to those terms.

(6) In this section—
  (a) "custodial period"—
    (i) in relation to an extended sentence imposed under section 227 or 228, means the appropriate custodial term determined under that section,
    (ii) in relation to a term of twelve months or more, means one-half of the term, and
    (iii) in relation to a term of less than twelve months complying with section 181, means the custodial period as defined by subsection (3)(a) of that section;
  (b) "licence period", in relation to a term of less than twelve months complying with section 181, has the meaning given by subsection (3)(b) of that section.

(7) This section applies to a determinate sentence of detention under section 91 of the Sentencing Act or under section 228 of this Act as it applies to a term of imprisonment of 12 months or more.

Restriction on consecutive sentences for released prisoners

265. Restriction on consecutive sentences for released prisoners

(1) A court sentencing a person to a term of imprisonment may not order or direct that the term is to commence on the expiry of any other sentence of imprisonment from which he has been released early under this Chapter.

(2) In this section "sentence of imprisonment" includes a sentence of detention under section 91 of the Sentencing Act or section 228 of this Act, and "term of imprisonment" is to be read accordingly.

Drug testing requirements

266. Release on licence etc: drug testing requirements

(1) Section 64 of the Criminal Justice and Court Services Act 2000 (c. 43) (release on licence etc: drug testing requirements) is amended as follows.

(2) In subsection (1) for paragraph (a) there is substituted—

"(a) the Secretary of State releases from prison a person aged 14 or over on whom a sentence of imprisonment has been imposed,

(aa) a responsible officer is of the opinion—

(i) that the offender has a propensity to misuse specified Class A drugs, and

(ii) that the misuse by the offender of any specified Class A drug caused or contributed to any offence of which he has been convicted, or is likely to cause or contribute to the commission of further offences, and".

(3) After subsection (4) there is inserted—

"(4A) A person under the age of 17 years may not be required by virtue of this section to provide a sample otherwise than in the presence of an appropriate adult."

(4) In subsection (5), after paragraph (e) there is inserted "and

(f) a sentence of detention under section 226 or 228 of the Criminal Justice Act 2003".

(5) After subsection (5) there is inserted—

"(6) In this section—

"appropriate adult", in relation to a person aged under 17, means –

(a) his parent or guardian or, if he is in the care of a local authority or voluntary organisation, a person representing that authority or organisation,

(b) a social worker of a local authority social services department, or

(c) if no person falling within paragraph (a) or (b) is available, any responsible person aged 18 or over who is not a police officer or a person employed by the police;

"responsible officer" means—

(a) in relation to an offender aged under 18, an officer of a local probation board or a member of a youth offending team;

(b) in relation to an offender aged 18 or over, an officer of a local probation board."

Supplemental

267. Alteration by order of relevant proportion of sentence

The Secretary of State may by order provide that any reference in section 244(3)(a), section 247(2) or section 264(6)(a)(ii) to a particular proportion of a prisoner's sentence is to be read as a reference to such other proportion of a prisoner's sentence as may be specified in the order.

268. Interpretation of Chapter 6

In this Chapter—

"the 1997 Act" means the Crime (Sentences) Act 1997 (c. 43);

"the Board" means the Parole Board;

"fixed-term prisoner" has the meaning given by section 237(1);

"intermittent custody prisoner" means a prisoner serving a sentence of imprisonment to which an intermittent custody order relates;

"prison" and "prisoner" are to be read in accordance with section 237(2);

"release", in relation to a prisoner serving a sentence of imprisonment to which an intermittent custody order relates, includes temporary release;

"relevant court order", in relation to a person serving a sentence of imprisonment to which a custody plus order or intermittent custody order relates, means that order.

CHAPTER 7
EFFECT OF LIFE SENTENCE

269. Determination of minimum term in relation to mandatory life sentence

(1) This section applies where after the commencement of this section a court passes a life sentence in circumstances where the sentence is fixed by law.

(2) The court must, unless it makes an order under subsection (4), order that the provisions of section 28(5) to (8) of the Crime (Sentences) Act 1997 (referred to in this Chapter as "the early release provisions") are to apply to the offender as soon as he has served the part of his sentence which is specified in the order.

(3) The part of his sentence is to be such as the court considers appropriate taking into account—

    (a) the seriousness of the offence, or of the combination of the offence and any one or more offences associated with it, and

    (b) the effect of any direction which it would have given under section 240 (crediting periods of remand in custody) if it had sentenced him to a term of imprisonment.

(4) If the offender was 21 or over when he committed the offence and the court is of the opinion that, because of the seriousness of the offence, or of the combination of the offence and one or more offences associated with it, no order should be made under subsection (2), the court must order that the early release provisions are not to apply to the offender.

(5) In considering under subsection (3) or (4) the seriousness of an offence (or of the combination of an offence and one or more offences associated with it), the court must have regard to—

    (a) the general principles set out in Schedule 21, and

    (b) any guidelines relating to offences in general which are relevant to the case and are not incompatible with the provisions of Schedule 21.

(6) The Secretary of State may by order amend Schedule 21.

(7) Before making an order under subsection (6), the Secretary of State shall consult the Sentencing Guidelines Council.

270. Duty to give reasons

(1) Any court making an order under subsection (2) or (4) of section 269 must state in open court, in ordinary language, its reasons for deciding on the order made.

(2) In stating its reasons the court must, in particular—

    (a) state which of the starting points in Schedule 21 it has chosen and its reasons for doing so, and

    (b) state its reasons for any departure from that starting point.

271. Appeals

(1) In section 9 of the Criminal Appeal Act 1968 (c. 19) (appeal against sentence following conviction on indictment), after subsection (1) there is inserted—

    "(1A) In subsection (1) of this section, the reference to a sentence fixed by law does not include a reference to an order made under subsection (2) or (4) of section 269 of the Criminal Justice Act 2003 in relation to a life sentence (as defined in section 277 of that Act) that is fixed by law.".

(2) In section 8 of the Courts-Martial (Appeals) Act 1968 (c. 20) (right of appeal from court-martial to Courts-Martial Appeal Court) after subsection (1) there is inserted—

    "(1ZA) In subsection (1) above, the reference to a sentence fixed by law does not include a reference to an order made under subsection (2) or (4) of section 269 of the Criminal Justice Act 2003 in relation to a life sentence (as defined in section 277 of that Act) that is fixed by law."

272. Review of minimum term on a reference by Attorney General

(1) In section 36 of the Criminal Justice Act 1988 (c. 33) (review of sentencing) after subsection (3) there is inserted—

    "(3A) Where a reference under this section relates to an order under subsection (2) of section 269 of the Criminal Justice Act 2003 (determination of minimum term in relation to mandatory life sentence), the Court of Appeal shall not, in deciding what order under that section is appropriate for the case, make any allowance for the fact that the person to whom it relates is being sentenced for a second time.".

(2) Each of the following sections (which relate to the review by the Courts-Martial Appeal Court of sentences passed by courts-martial)—

    (a) section 113C of the Army Act 1955 (3 & 4 Eliz. 2 c. 18),

    (b) section 113C of the Air Force Act 1955 (3 & 4 Eliz. 2 c. 19), and

    (c) section 71AC of the Naval Discipline Act 1957 (c. 53),

is amended as follows.

(3) After subsection (3) there is inserted—

    "(3A) Where a reference under this section relates to an order under subsection (2) of section 269 of the Criminal Justice Act 2003 (determination of minimum term in relation to mandatory life sentence), the Courts-Martial Appeal Court shall not, in deciding what order under that section is appropriate for the case, make any allowance for the fact that the person to whom it relates is being sentenced for a second time.".

273. Life prisoners transferred to England and Wales

(1) The Secretary of State must refer the case of any transferred life prisoner to the High Court for the making of one or more relevant orders.

(2) In subsection (1) "transferred life prisoner" means a person—

    (a) on whom a court in a country or territory outside the British Islands has imposed one or more sentences of imprisonment or detention for an indeterminate period, and

    (b) who has been transferred to England and Wales after the commencement of this section in pursuance of—

        (i) an order made by the Secretary of State under section 2 of the Colonial Prisoners Removal Act 1884 (c. 31), or

        (ii) a warrant issued by the Secretary of State under the Repatriation of Prisoners Act 1984 (c. 47),

    there to serve his sentence or sentences or the remainder of his sentence or sentences.

(3) In subsection (1) "a relevant order" means—

    (a) in the case of an offence which appears to the court to be an offence for which, if it had been committed in England and Wales, the sentence would have been fixed by law, an order under subsection (2) or (4) of section 269, and

    (b) in any other case, an order under subsection (2) or (4) of section 82A of the Sentencing Act.

(4) In section 34(1) of the Crime (Sentences) Act 1997 (c. 43) (meaning of "life prisoner" in Chapter 2 of Part 2 of that Act) at the end there is inserted "and includes a transferred life prisoner as defined by section 273 of the Criminal Justice Act 2003".

274. Further provisions about references relating to transferred life prisoners

(1) A reference to the High Court under section 273 is to be determined by a single judge of that court without an oral hearing.

(2) In relation to a reference under that section, any reference to "the court" in subsections (2) to (5) of section 269, in Schedule 21 or in section 82A(2) to (4) of the Sentencing Act is to be read as a reference to the High Court.

(3) A person in respect of whom a reference has been made under section 273 may with the leave of the Court of Appeal appeal to the Court of Appeal against the decision of the High Court on the reference.

(4) Section 1(1) of the Administration of Justice Act 1960 (c. 65) (appeal to House of Lords from decision of High Court in a criminal cause or matter) and section 18(1)(a) of the Supreme Court Act 1981 (c. 54) (exclusion of appeal from High Court to Court of Appeal in a criminal cause or matter) do not apply in relation to a decision to which subsection (3) applies.

(5) The jurisdiction conferred on the Court of Appeal by subsection (3) is to be exercised by the criminal division of that court.

(6) Section 33(3) of the Criminal Appeal Act 1968 (c. 19) (limitation on appeal from criminal division of Court of Appeal) does not prevent an appeal to the House of Lords under this section.

(7) In relation to appeals to the Court of Appeal or the House of Lords under this section, the Secretary of State may make an order containing provision corresponding to any provision in the Criminal Appeal Act 1968 (subject to any specified modifications).

275. Duty to release certain life prisoners

(1) Section 28 of the Crime (Sentences) Act 1997 (c. 43) (duty to release certain life prisoners) is amended as follows.

(2) For subsection (1A) there is substituted—

"(1A) This section applies to a life prisoner in respect of whom a minimum term order has been made; and any reference in this section to the relevant part of such a prisoner's sentence is a reference to the part of the sentence specified in the order."

(3) In subsection (1B)(a)—

(a) for the words from the beginning to "applies" there is substituted "this section does not apply to him", and

(b) for the words from "such an order" to "appropriate stage" there is substituted "a minimum term order has been made in respect of each of those sentences".

(4) After subsection (8) there is inserted—

"(8A) In this section "minimum term order" means an order under—

(a) subsection (2) of section 82A of the Powers of Criminal Courts (Sentencing) Act 2000 (determination of minimum term in respect of life sentence that is not fixed by law), or

(b) subsection (2) of section 269 of the Criminal Justice Act 2003 (determination of minimum term in respect of mandatory life sentence)."

276. Mandatory life sentences: transitional cases

Schedule 22 (which relates to the effect in transitional cases of mandatory life sentences) shall have effect.

277. Interpretation of Chapter 7

In this Chapter—

"court" includes a court-martial;

"guidelines" has the same meaning as in section 172(1);

"life sentence" means—

(a) a sentence of imprisonment for life,

(b) a sentence of detention during Her Majesty's pleasure, or

(c) a sentence of custody for life passed before the commencement of section 61(1) of the Criminal Justice and Court Services Act 2000 (c. 43) (which abolishes that sentence).

CHAPTER 8
OTHER PROVISIONS ABOUT SENTENCING

Deferment of sentence

278. Deferment of sentence

Schedule 23 (deferment of sentence) shall have effect.

Power to include drug treatment and testing requirement in certain orders in respect of young offenders

279. Drug treatment and testing requirement in action plan order or supervision order

Schedule 24 (which enables a requirement as to drug treatment and testing to be included in an action plan order or a supervision order) shall have effect.

Alteration of penalties for offences

280. Alteration of penalties for specified summary offences

(1) The summary offences listed in Schedule 25 are no longer punishable with imprisonment.

(2) Schedule 26 (which contains amendments increasing the maximum term of imprisonment for certain summary offences from 4 months or less to 51 weeks) shall have effect.

(3) This section does not affect the penalty for any offence committed before the commencement of this section.

281. Alteration of penalties for other summary offences

(1) Subsection (2) applies to any summary offence which—
   (a) is an offence under a relevant enactment,
   (b) is punishable with a maximum term of imprisonment of five months or less, and
   (c) is not listed in Schedule 25 or Schedule 26.

(2) The Secretary of State may by order amend any relevant enactment so as to—
   (a) provide that any summary offence to which this subsection applies is no longer punishable with imprisonment, or
   (b) increase to 51 weeks the maximum term of imprisonment to which a person is liable on conviction of the offence.

(3) An order under subsection (2) may make such supplementary, incidental or consequential provision as the Secretary of State considers necessary or expedient, including provision amending any relevant enactment.

(4) Subsection (5) applies to any summary offence which—
   (a) is an offence under a relevant enactment, and
   (b) is punishable with a maximum term of imprisonment of six months.

(5) The maximum term of imprisonment to which a person is liable on conviction of an offence to which this subsection applies is, by virtue of this subsection, 51 weeks (and the relevant enactment in question is to be read as if it had been amended accordingly).

(6) Neither of the following—
   (a) an order under subsection (2), or
   (b) subsection (5),
   affects the penalty for any offence committed before the commencement of that order or subsection (as the case may be).

(7) In this section and section 282 "relevant enactment" means any enactment contained in—
   (a) an Act passed before or in the same Session as this Act, or
   (b) any subordinate legislation made before the passing of this Act.

(8) In subsection (7) "subordinate legislation" has the same meaning as in the Interpretation Act 1978 (c. 30).

282. Increase in maximum term that may be imposed on summary conviction of offence triable either way

(1) In section 32 of the Magistrates' Courts Act 1980 (c. 43) (penalties on summary conviction for offences triable either way) in subsection (1) (offences listed in Schedule 1 to that Act) for "not exceeding 6 months" there is substituted "not exceeding 12 months".

(2) Subsection (3) applies to any offence triable either way which—
   (a) is an offence under a relevant enactment,
   (b) is punishable with imprisonment on summary conviction, and
   (c) is not listed in Schedule 1 to the Magistrates' Courts Act 1980.

(3) The maximum term of imprisonment to which a person is liable on summary conviction of an offence to which this subsection applies is by virtue of this subsection 12 months (and the relevant enactment in question is to be read as if it had been amended accordingly).

(4) Nothing in this section affects the penalty for any offence committed before the commencement of this section.

283. Enabling powers: power to alter maximum penalties

(1) The Secretary of State may by order, in accordance with subsection (2) or (3), amend any relevant enactment which confers a power (however framed or worded) by subordinate legislation to make a person—

(a) as regards a summary offence, liable on conviction to a term of imprisonment;

(b) as regards an offence triable either way, liable on summary conviction to a term of imprisonment.

(2) An order made by virtue of paragraph (a) of subsection (1) may amend the relevant enactment in question so as to—

(a) restrict the power so that a person may no longer be made liable on conviction of a summary offence to a term of imprisonment, or

(b) increase to 51 weeks the maximum term of imprisonment to which a person may be made liable on conviction of a summary offence under the power.

(3) An order made by virtue of paragraph (b) of that subsection may amend the relevant enactment in question so as to increase the maximum term of imprisonment to which a person may be made liable on summary conviction of an offence under the power to 12 months.

(4) Schedule 27 (which amends the maximum penalties which may be imposed by virtue of certain enabling powers) shall have effect.

(5) The power conferred by subsection (1) shall not apply to the enactments amended under Schedule 27.

(6) An order under subsection (1) may make such supplementary, incidental or consequential provision as the Secretary of State considers necessary or expedient, including provision amending any relevant enactment.

(7) None of the following—

(a) an order under subsection (1), or

(b) Schedule 27,

affects the penalty for any offence committed before the commencement of that order or Schedule (as the case may be).

(8) In subsection (1) "subordinate legislation" has the same meaning as in the Interpretation Act 1978 (c. 30).

(9) In this section "relevant enactment" means any enactment contained in an Act passed before or in the same Session as this Act.

284. Increase in penalties for drug-related offences

(1) Schedule 28 (increase in penalties for certain drug-related offences) shall have effect.

(2) That Schedule does not affect the penalty for any offence committed before the commencement of that Schedule.

285. Increase in penalties for certain driving-related offences

(1) In section 12A of the Theft Act 1968 (c. 60) (aggravated vehicle-taking), in subsection (4), for "five years" there is substituted "fourteen years".

(2) Part 1 of Schedule 2 to the Road Traffic Offenders Act 1988 (c. 53) (prosecution and punishment of offences) is amended in accordance with subsections (3) and (4).

(3) In the entry relating to section 1 of the Road Traffic Act 1988 (c. 52) (causing death by dangerous driving), in column 4, for "10 years" there is substituted "14 years".

(4) In the entry relating to section 3A of that Act (causing death by careless driving when under influence of drink or drugs), in column 4, for "10 years" there is substituted "14 years".

(5) Part I of Schedule 1 to the Road Traffic Offenders (Northern Ireland) Order 1996 (S.I. 1996/1320 (N.I. 10)) (prosecution and punishment of offences) is amended in accordance with subsections (6) and (7).

(6) In the entry relating to Article 9 of the Road Traffic (Northern Ireland) Order 1995 (S.I. 1995/2994 (N.I. 18)) (causing death or grievous bodily injury by dangerous driving), in column 4, for "10 years" there is substituted "14 years".

(7) In the entry relating to Article 14 of that Order (causing death or grievous bodily injury by careless driving when under the influence of drink or drugs), in column 4, for "10 years" there is substituted "14 years".

(8) This section does not affect the penalty for any offence committed before the commencement of this section.

286. Increase in penalties for offences under section 174 of Road Traffic Act 1988

(1) In Part 1 of Schedule 2 to the Road Traffic Offenders Act 1988 (c. 53) (prosecution and punishment of offences), in the entry relating to section 174 of the Road Traffic Act 1988 (c. 52) (false statements and withholding material information), for columns (3) and (4) there is substituted—

"(a) Summarily   (a) 6 months or the statutory maximum or both
(b) On indictment   (b) 2 years or a fine or both."

(2) Section 282(3) (increase in maximum term that may be imposed on summary conviction of offence triable either way) has effect in relation to the entry amended by subsection (1) as it has effect in relation to any other enactment contained in an Act passed before this Act.

(3) This section does not apply in relation to any offence committed before the commencement of this section.

Firearms offences

287. Minimum sentence for certain firearms offences

After section 51 of the Firearms Act 1968 (c. 27) there is inserted the following section—

"51A Minimum sentence for certain offences under s 5

(1) This section applies where—

    (a) an individual is convicted of—

      (i) an offence under section 5(1)(a), (ab), (aba), (ac), (ad), (ae), (af) or (c) of this Act, or

      (ii) an offence under section 5(1A)(a) of this Act, and

  (b) the offence was committed after the commencement of this section and at a time when he was aged 16 or over.

(2) The court shall impose an appropriate custodial sentence (or order for detention) for a term of at least the required minimum term (with or without a fine) unless the court is of the opinion that there are exceptional circumstances relating to the offence or to the offender which justify its not doing so.

(3) Where an offence is found to have been committed over a period of two or more days, or at some time during a period of two or more days, it shall be taken for the purposes of this section to have been committed on the last of those days.

(4) In this section "appropriate custodial sentence (or order for detention)" means—

  (a) in relation to England and Wales—

      (i) in the case of an offender who is aged 18 or over when convicted, a sentence of imprisonment, and

      (ii) in the case of an offender who is aged under 18 at that time, a sentence of detention under section 91 of the Powers of Criminal Courts (Sentencing) Act 2000;

  (b) in relation to Scotland—

      (i) in the case of an offender who is aged 21 or over when convicted, a sentence of imprisonment,

      (ii) in the case of an offender who is aged under 21 at that time (not being an offender mentioned in sub-paragraph (iii)), a sentence of detention under section 207 of the Criminal Procedure (Scotland) Act 1995, and

      (iii) in the case of an offender who is aged under 18 at that time and is subject to a supervision requirement, an order for detention under section 44, or sentence of detention under section 208, of that Act.

(5) In this section "the required minimum term" means—

  (a) in relation to England and Wales—

      (i) in the case of an offender who was aged 18 or over when he committed the offence, five years, and

      (ii) in the case of an offender who was under 18 at that time, three years, and

  (b) in relation to Scotland—

      (i) in the case of an offender who was aged 21 or over when he committed the offence, five years, and

      (ii) in the case of an offender who was aged under 21 at that time, three years."

288. Certain firearms offences to be triable only on indictment

In Part 1 of Schedule 6 to the Firearms Act 1968 (c. 27) (prosecution and punishment of offences) for the entries relating to offences under section 5(1) (possessing or distributing prohibited weapons or ammunition) and section 5(1A) (possessing or distributing other prohibited weapons) there is substituted—

"Section 5(1)(a), (ab), (aba), (ac), (ad), (ae), (af) or (c)	Possessing or distributing prohibited weapons or ammunition.	On indictment	10 years or a fine, or both.
Section 5(1)(b)	Possessing or distributing prohibited weapon designed for discharge of noxious liquid etc.	(a) Summary	6 months or a fine of the statutory maximum, or both.
		(b) On indictment	10 years or a fine or both
Section 5(1A)(a)	Possessing or distributing firearm disguised as other object.	On indictment	10 years or a fine, or both.
Section 5(1A)(b), (c), (d), (e), (f) or (g)	Possessing or distributing other prohibited weapons.	(a) Summary	6 months or a fine of the statutory maximum, or both.
		(b) On indictment	10 years or a fine, or both."

289. Power to sentence young offender to detention in respect of certain firearms offences: England and Wales

(1) Section 91 of the Sentencing Act (offenders under 18 convicted of certain serious offences: power to detain for specified period) is amended as follows.

(2) After subsection (1) there is inserted—

"(1A) Subsection (3) below also applies where—

    (a) a person aged under 18 is convicted on indictment of an offence—

        (i) under subsection (1)(a), (ab), (aba), (ac), (ad), (ae), (af) or (c) of section 5 of the Firearms Act 1968 (prohibited weapons), or

        (ii) under subsection (1A)(a) of that section,

    (b) the offence was committed after the commencement of section 51A of that Act and at a time when he was aged 16 or over, and

    (c) the court is of the opinion mentioned in section 51A(2) of that Act (exceptional circumstances which justify its not imposing required custodial sentence)."

(3) After subsection (4) there is inserted—

"(5) Where subsection (2) of section 51A of the Firearms Act 1968 requires the imposition of a sentence of detention under this section for a term of at least the required minimum term (within the meaning of that section), the court shall sentence the offender to be detained for such period, of at least that term but not exceeding the maximum term of imprisonment with which the offence is punishable in the case of a person aged 18 or over, as may be specified in the sentence.".

290. Power to sentence young offender to detention in respect of certain firearms offences: Scotland

(1) The Criminal Procedure (Scotland) Act 1995 (c. 46) is amended as follows.

(2) In section 49(3) (children's hearing for purpose of obtaining advice as to treatment of child), at the end there is added "except that where the circumstances are such as are

mentioned in paragraphs (a) and (b) of section 51A(1) of the Firearms Act 1968 it shall itself dispose of the case".

(3) In section 208 (detention of children convicted on indictment), the existing provisions become subsection (1); and after that subsection there is added—

"(2) Subsection (1) does not apply where the circumstances are such as are mentioned in paragraphs (a) and (b) of section 51A(1) of the Firearms Act 1968.".

291. Power by order to exclude application of minimum sentence to those under 18

(1) The Secretary of State may by order—

(a) amend section 51A(1)(b) of the Firearms Act 1968 (c. 27) by substituting for the word "16" the word "18",

(b) repeal section 91(1A)(c) and (5) of the Sentencing Act,

(c) amend subsection (3) of section 49 of the Criminal Procedure (Scotland) Act 1995 by repealing the exception to that subsection,

(d) repeal section 208(2) of that Act, and

(e) make such other provision as he considers necessary or expedient in consequence of, or in connection with, the provision made by virtue of paragraphs (a) to (d).

(2) The provision that may be made by virtue of subsection (1)(e) includes, in particular, provision amending or repealing any provision of an Act (whenever passed), including any provision of this Act.

292. Sentencing for firearms offences in Northern Ireland

Schedule 29 (which contains amendments of the Firearms (Northern Ireland) Order 1981 (S.I. 1981/155 (N.I. 2)) relating to sentencing) shall have effect.

293. Increase in penalty for offences relating to importation or exportation of certain firearms

(1) The Customs and Excise Management Act 1979 (c. 2) is amended as follows.

(2) In section 50 (penalty for improper importation of goods), for subsection (5A) there is substituted—

"(5A) In the case of—

(a) an offence under subsection (2) or (3) above committed in Great Britain in connection with a prohibition or restriction on the importation of any weapon or ammunition that is of a kind mentioned in section 5(1)(a), (ab), (aba), (ac), (ad), (ae), (af) or (c) or (1A)(a) of the Firearms Act 1968,

(b) any such offence committed in Northern Ireland in connection with a prohibition or restriction on the importation of any weapon or ammunition that is of a kind mentioned in Article 6(1)(a), (ab), (ac), (ad), (ae) or (c) or (1A)(a) of the Firearms (Northern Ireland) Order 1981, or

(c) any such offence committed in connection with the prohibition contained in section 20 of the Forgery and Counterfeiting Act 1981,

subsection (4)(b) above shall have effect as if for the words "7 years" there were substituted the words "10 years"."

(3) In section 68 (offences in relation to exportation of prohibited or restricted goods) for subsection (4A) there is substituted—

"(4A) In the case of—

 (a) an offence under subsection (2) or (3) above committed in Great Britain in connection with a prohibition or restriction on the exportation of any weapon or ammunition that is of a kind mentioned in section 5(1)(a), (ab), (aba), (ac), (ad), (ae), (af) or (c) or (1A)(a) of the Firearms Act 1968,

 (b) any such offence committed in Northern Ireland in connection with a prohibition or restriction on the exportation of any weapon or ammunition that is of a kind mentioned in Article 6(1)(a), (ab), (ac), (ad), (ae) or (c) or (1A)(a) of the Firearms (Northern Ireland) Order 1981, or

 (c) any such offence committed in connection with the prohibition contained in section 21 of the Forgery and Counterfeiting Act 1981,

subsection (3)(b) above shall have effect as if for the words "7 years" there were substituted the words "10 years"."

(4) In section 170 (penalty for fraudulent evasion of duty, etc), for subsection (4A) there is substituted—

"(4A) In the case of—

 (a) an offence under subsection (2) or (3) above committed in Great Britain in connection with a prohibition or restriction on the importation or exportation of any weapon or ammunition that is of a kind mentioned in section 5(1)(a), (ab), (aba), (ac), (ad), (ae), (af) or (c) or (1A)(a) of the Firearms Act 1968,

 (b) any such offence committed in Northern Ireland in connection with a prohibition or restriction on the importation or exportation of any weapon or ammunition that is of a kind mentioned in Article 6(1)(a), (ab), (ac), (ad), (ae) or (c) or (1A)(a) of the Firearms (Northern Ireland) Order 1981, or

 (c) any such offence committed in connection with the prohibitions contained in sections 20 and 21 of the Forgery and Counterfeiting Act 1981,

subsection (3)(b) above shall have effect as if for the words "7 years" there were substituted the words "10 years"."

(5) This section does not affect the penalty for any offence committed before the commencement of this section.

Offenders transferred to mental hospital

294. Duration of directions under Mental Health Act 1983 in relation to offenders

(1) Section 50 of the Mental Health Act 1983 (c. 20) (further provisions as to prisoners under sentence) is amended as follows.

(2) In subsection (1), for "the expiration of that person's sentence" there is substituted "his release date".

(3) For subsections (2) and (3) there is substituted—

"(2) A restriction direction in the case of a person serving a sentence of imprisonment shall cease to have effect, if it has not previously done so, on his release date.

(3) In this section, references to a person's release date are to the day (if any) on which he would be entitled to be released (whether unconditionally or on licence) from any prison or other institution in which he might have been detained if the transfer direction had not

428

been given; and in determining that day there shall be disregarded—

(a) any powers that would be exercisable by the Parole Board if he were detained in such a prison or other institution, and

(b) any practice of the Secretary of State in relation to the early release under discretionary powers of persons detained in such a prison or other institution."

295. Access to Parole Board for certain patients serving prison sentences

In section 74 of the Mental Health Act 1983 (restricted patients subject to restriction directions) after subsection (5) there is inserted—

"(5A) Where the tribunal have made a recommendation under subsection (1)(b) above in the case of a patient who is subject to a restriction direction or a limitation direction—

(a) the fact that the restriction direction or limitation direction remains in force does not prevent the making of any application or reference to the Parole Board by or in respect of him or the exercise by him of any power to require the Secretary of State to refer his case to the Parole Board, and

(b) if the Parole Board make a direction or recommendation by virtue of which the patient would become entitled to be released (whether unconditionally or on licence) from any prison or other institution in which he might have been detained if he had not been removed to hospital, the restriction direction or limitation direction shall cease to have effect at the time when he would become entitled to be so released."

296. Duration of directions under Mental Health (Northern Ireland) Order 1986 in relation to offenders

(1) Article 56 of the Mental Health (Northern Ireland) Order 1986 (S.I. 1986/ 595 (N.I. 4)) (further provisions as to prisoners under sentence) is amended as follows.

(2) In paragraph (1), for "the expiration of that person's sentence" there is substituted "his release date".

(3) For paragraphs (2) and (3) there is substituted—

"(2) A restriction direction in the case of a person serving a sentence of imprisonment shall cease to have effect, if it has not previously done so, on his release date.

(3) In this Article, references to a person's release date are to the day (if any) on which he would be entitled to be released (whether unconditionally or on licence) from any prison or juvenile justice centre in which he might have been detained if the transfer direction had not been given; and in determining that day any powers that would be exercisable by the Sentence Review Commissioners or the Life Sentence Review Commissioners if he were detained in such a prison or juvenile justice centre shall be disregarded."

297. Access to Sentence Review Commissioners and Life Sentence Review Commissioners for certain Northern Ireland patients

In Article 79 of the Mental Health (Northern Ireland) Order 1986 (restricted patients subject to restriction directions) after paragraph (5) there is inserted—

"(5A) Where the tribunal have made a recommendation under paragraph (1)(b) in the case of a patient who is subject to a restriction direction—

(a) the fact that the restriction direction remains in force does not prevent—

(i) the making of any application or reference to the Life Sentence Review Commissioners by or in respect of him or the exercise by him of any power to require the Secretary of State to refer his case to those Commissioners, or

(ii) the making of any application by him to the Sentence Review Commissioners, and

(b) if—

(i) the Life Sentence Review Commissioners give a direction by virtue of which the patient would become entitled to be released (whether unconditionally or on licence) from any prison or juvenile justice centre in which he might have been detained if the transfer direction had not been given, or

(ii) the Sentence Review Commissioners grant a declaration by virtue of which he would become so entitled,

the restriction direction shall cease to have effect at the time at which he would become so entitled.".

Term of detention and training order

298. Term of detention and training order

(1) Section 101 of the Sentencing Act (which relates to detention and training orders) is amended as follows.

(2) In subsection (1), for "subsection (2)" there is substituted "subsections (2) and (2A)".

(3) After subsection (2) there is inserted—

"(2A) Where—

(a) the offence is a summary offence,

(b) the maximum term of imprisonment that a court could (in the case of an offender aged 18 or over) impose for the offence is 51 weeks,

the term of a detention and training order may not exceed 6 months."

Disqualification from working with children

299. Disqualification from working with children

Schedule 30 (which contains amendments of Part 2 of the Criminal Justice and Court Services Act 2000 (c. 43) relating to disqualification orders under that Part) shall have effect.

Fine defaulters

300. Power to impose unpaid work requirement or curfew requirement on fine defaulter

(1) Subsection (2) applies in any case where, in respect of a person aged 16 or over, a magistrates' court—

(a) has power under Part 3 of the Magistrates' Courts Act 1980 (c. 43) to issue a warrant of commitment for default in paying a sum adjudged to be paid by a conviction (other than a sum ordered to be paid under section 6 of the Proceeds of Crime Act 2002 (c. 29)), or

(b) would, but for section 89 of the Sentencing Act (restrictions on custodial sentences for persons under 18), have power to issue such a warrant for such default.

(2) The magistrates' court may, instead of issuing a warrant of commitment or, as the case may be, proceeding under section 81 of the Magistrates' Courts Act 1980 (enforcement of fines imposed on young offender), order the person in default to comply with—

(a) an unpaid work requirement (as defined by section 199), or

(b) a curfew requirement (as defined by section 204).

(3) In this Part "default order" means an order under subsection (2).

(4) Subsections (3) and (4) of section 177 (which relate to electronic monitoring) have effect in relation to a default order as they have effect in relation to a community order.

(5) Where a magistrates' court has power to make a default order, it may, if it thinks it expedient to do so, postpone the making of the order until such time and on such conditions (if any) as it thinks just.

(6) Schedule 8 (breach, revocation or amendment of community order), Schedule 9 (transfer of community orders to Scotland or Northern Ireland) and Chapter 4 (further provisions about orders under Chapters 2 and 3) have effect in relation to default orders as they have effect in relation to community orders, but subject to the modifications contained in Schedule 31.

(7) Where a default order has been made for default in paying any sum—

(a) on payment of the whole sum to any person authorised to receive it, the order shall cease to have effect, and

(b) on payment of a part of the sum to any such person, the total number of hours or days to which the order relates is to be taken to be reduced by a proportion corresponding to that which the part paid bears to the whole sum.

(8) In calculating any reduction required by subsection (7)(b), any fraction of a day or hour is to be disregarded.

301. Fine defaulters: driving disqualification

(1) Subsection (2) applies in any case where a magistrates' court—

(a) has power under Part 3 of the Magistrates' Courts Act 1980 (c. 43) to issue a warrant of commitment for default in paying a sum adjudged to be paid by a conviction (other than a sum ordered to be paid under section 6 of the Proceeds of Crime Act 2002 (c. 29)), or

(b) would, but for section 89 of the Sentencing Act (restrictions on custodial sentences for persons under 18), have power to issue such a warrant for such default.

(2) The magistrates' court may, instead of issuing a warrant of commitment or, as the case may be, proceeding under section 81 of the Magistrates' Courts Act 1980 (enforcement of fines imposed on young offenders), order the person in default to be disqualified, for such period not exceeding twelve months as it thinks fit, for holding or obtaining a driving licence.

(3) Where an order has been made under subsection (2) for default in paying any sum—

(a) on payment of the whole sum to any person authorised to receive it, the order shall cease to have effect, and

(b) on payment of part of the sum to any such person, the total number of weeks or months to which the order relates is to be taken to be reduced by a proportion corresponding to that which the part paid bears to the whole sum.

(4) In calculating any reduction required by subsection (3)(b) any fraction of a week or month is to be disregarded.

(5) The Secretary of State may by order amend subsection (2) by substituting, for the period there specified, such other period as may be specified in the order.

(6) A court which makes an order under this section disqualifying a person for holding or obtaining a driving licence shall require him to produce—

(a) any such licence held by him together with its counterpart; or

(b) in the case where he holds a Community licence (within the meaning of Part 3 of the Road Traffic Act 1988 (c. 52)), his Community licence and its counterpart (if any).

(7) In this section—

"driving licence" means a licence to drive a motor vehicle granted under Part 3 of the Road Traffic Act 1988;

"counterpart"—

(a) in relation to a driving licence, has the meaning given in relation to such a licence by section 108(1) of that Act; and

(b) in relation to a Community licence, has the meaning given by section 99B of that Act.

CHAPTER 9
SUPPLEMENTARY

302. Execution of process between England and Wales and Scotland

Section 4 of the Summary Jurisdiction (Process) Act 1881 (c. 24) (execution of process of English and Welsh courts in Scotland) applies to any process issued by a magistrates' court under—

paragraph 7(2) or (4), 13(6) or 25(1) of Schedule 8,

paragraph 12 of Schedule 9,

paragraph 8(1) of Schedule 10, or

paragraph 6(2) or (4), 12(1) or 20(1) of Schedule 12,

as it applies to process issued under the Magistrates' Courts Act 1980 by a magistrates' court.

303. Sentencing: repeals

The following enactments (which are superseded by the provisions of this Part) shall cease to have effect—

(a) Part 2 of the Criminal Justice Act 1991 (c. 53) (early release of prisoners),

(b) in the Crime (Sentences) Act 1997 (c. 43)—

(i) section 29 (power of Secretary of State to release life prisoners to whom section 28 of that Act does not apply),

(ii) section 33 (transferred prisoners), and

(iii) sections 35 and 40 (fine defaulters),

(c) sections 80 and 81 of the Crime and Disorder Act 1998 (c. 37) (sentencing guidelines), and

(d) in the Sentencing Act—

(i) Chapter 3 of Part 4 (community orders available only where offender 16 or over),

(ii) section 85 (sexual or violent offences: extension of custodial term for licence purposes),

(iii) sections 87 and 88 (remand in custody),

(iv) section 109 (life sentence for second serious offence), and

(v) Chapter 5 of Part 5 (suspended sentences).

304. Amendments relating to sentencing

Schedule 32 (which contains amendments related to the provisions of this Part) shall have effect.

305. Interpretation of Part 12

(1) In this Part, except where the contrary intention appears—

"accredited programme" has the meaning given by section 202(2);

"activity requirement", in relation to a community order, custody plus order, intermittent custody order or suspended sentence order, has the meaning given by section 201;

"alcohol treatment requirement", in relation to a community order or suspended sentence order, has the meaning given by section 212;

"the appropriate officer of the court" means, in relation to a magistrates' court, the clerk of the court;

"associated", in relation to offences, is to be read in accordance with section 161(1) of the Sentencing Act;

"attendance centre" has the meaning given by section 221(2);

"attendance centre requirement", in relation to a community order, custody plus order, intermittent custody order or suspended sentence order, has the meaning given by section 214;

"community order" has the meaning given by section 177(1);

"community requirement", in relation to a suspended sentence order, has the meaning given by section 189(7);

"community sentence" has the meaning given by section 147(1);

"court" (without more), except in Chapter 7, does not include a service court;

"curfew requirement", in relation to a community order, custody plus order, intermittent custody order or suspended sentence order, has the meaning given by section 204;

"custodial sentence" has the meaning given by section 76 of the Sentencing Act;

"custody plus order" has the meaning given by section 181(4);

"default order" has the meaning given by section 300(3);

"drug rehabilitation requirement", in relation to a community order or suspended sentence order, has the meaning given by section 209;

"electronic monitoring requirement", in relation to a community order, custody plus order, intermittent custody order or suspended sentence order, has the meaning given by section 215;

"exclusion requirement", in relation to a community order, custody plus order, intermittent custody order or suspended sentence order, has the meaning given by section 205;

"guardian" has the same meaning as in the Children and Young Persons Act 1933 (c. 12);

"intermittent custody order" has the meaning given by section 183(2);

"licence" means a licence under Chapter 6;

"local probation board" means a local probation board established under section 4 of the Criminal Justice and Court Services Act 2000 (c. 43);

"mental health treatment requirement", in relation to a community order or suspended sentence order, has the meaning given by section 207;

"pre-sentence report" has the meaning given by section 158(1);

"programme requirement", in relation to a community order, custody plus order, intermittent custody order or suspended sentence order, has the meaning given by section 202;

"prohibited activity requirement", in relation to a community order, custody plus order, intermittent custody order or suspended sentence order, has the meaning given by section 203;

"residence requirement", in relation to a community order or suspended sentence order, has the meaning given by section 206;

"responsible officer", in relation to an offender to whom a community order, a custody plus order, an intermittent custody order or a suspended sentence order relates, has the meaning given by section 197;

"sentence of imprisonment" does not include a committal—

(a) in default of payment of any sum of money,

(b) for want of sufficient distress to satisfy any sum of money, or

(c) for failure to do or abstain from doing anything required to be done or left undone,

and references to sentencing an offender to imprisonment are to be read accordingly;

"the Sentencing Act" means the Powers of Criminal Courts (Sentencing) Act 2000 (c. 6);

"service court" means—

(a) a court-martial constituted under the Army Act 1955 (3 & 4 Eliz. 2 c. 18), the Air Force Act 1955 (3 & 4 Eliz. 2 c. 19) or the Naval Discipline Act 1957 (c. 53);

(b) a summary appeal court constituted under section 83ZA of the Army Act 1955, section 83ZA of the Air Force Act 1955 or section 52FF of the Naval Discipline Act 1957;

(c) the Courts-Martial Appeal Court; or

(d) a Standing Civilian Court;

"service disciplinary proceedings" means—

(a) any proceedings under the Army Act 1955, the Air Force Act 1955 or the Naval Discipline Act 1957 (whether before a court-martial or any other court or person authorised under any of those Acts to award a punishment in respect of any offence), and

(b) any proceedings before a Standing Civilian Court;

"supervision requirement", in relation to a community order, custody plus order, intermittent custody order or suspended sentence order, has the meaning given by section 213;

"suspended sentence" and "suspended sentence order" have the meaning given by section 189(7);

"unpaid work requirement", in relation to a community order, custody plus order, intermittent custody order or suspended sentence order, has the meaning given by section 199;

"youth offending team" means a team established under section 39 of the Crime and Disorder Act 1998 (c. 37).

(2) For the purposes of any provision of this Part which requires the determination of the age of a person by the court or the Secretary of State, his age is to be taken to be that which it appears to the court or (as the case may be) the Secretary of State to be after considering any available evidence.

(3) Any reference in this Part to an offence punishable with imprisonment is to be read without regard to any prohibition or restriction imposed by or under any Act on the imprisonment of young offenders.

(4) For the purposes of this Part—

(a) a sentence falls to be imposed under subsection (2) of section 51A of the Firearms Act 1968 (c. 27) if it is required by that subsection and the court is not of the opinion there mentioned,

(b) a sentence falls to be imposed under section 110(2) or 111(2) of the Sentencing Act if it is required by that provision and the court is not of the opinion there mentioned,

(c) a sentence falls to be imposed under section 225 or 227 if, because the court is of the opinion mentioned in subsection (1) (b) of that section, the court is obliged to pass a sentence complying with that section,

(d) a sentence falls to be imposed under section 226 if, because the court is of the opinion mentioned in subsection (1) (b) of that section and considers that the case falls within subsection (2) or (3) of that section, the court is obliged to pass a sentence complying with that section, and

(e) a sentence falls to be imposed under section 228 if, because the court is of the opinion mentioned in subsection (1) (b) (i) and (ii) of that section, the court is obliged to pass a sentence complying with that section.

PART 13. MISCELLANEOUS

Detention of suspected terrorists

306. Limit on period of detention without charge of suspected terrorists

(1) Schedule 8 to the Terrorism Act 2000 (c. 11) (detention) is amended as follows.

(2) At the beginning of paragraph 29(3) (duration of warrants of further detention) there is inserted "Subject to paragraph 36(3A),"

(3) In sub-paragraph (3) of paragraph 36 (extension of warrants)—

(a) at the beginning there is inserted "Subject to sub-paragraph (3A),", and

(b) for the words from "beginning" onwards there is substituted "beginning with the relevant time".

(4) After that sub-paragraph there is inserted—

"(3A) Where the period specified in a warrant of further detention—

(a) ends at the end of the period of seven days beginning with the relevant time, or

(b) by virtue of a previous extension (or further extension) under this sub-paragraph, ends after the end of that period, the specified period may, on an application under this paragraph, be extended or further extended to a period ending not later than the end of the period of fourteen days beginning with the relevant time.

(3B) In this paragraph "the relevant time", in relation to a person, means—

(a) the time of his arrest under section 41, or

(b) if he was being detained under Schedule 7 when he was arrested under section 41, the time when his examination under that Schedule began."

Enforcement of legislation on endangered species

307. Enforcement of regulations implementing Community legislation on endangered species

(1) In this section—

"the 1972 Act" means the European Communities Act 1972 (c. 68);

"relevant Community instrument" means—

(a) Council Regulation 338/97/EC on the protection of species of wild fauna and flora by regulating the trade therein, and

(b) Commission Regulation 1808/01/EC on the implementation of the Council Regulation mentioned in paragraph (a).

(2) Regulations made under section 2(2) of the 1972 Act for the purpose of implementing any relevant Community instrument may, notwithstanding paragraph 1(1)(d) of Schedule 2 to the 1972 Act, create offences punishable on conviction on indictment with imprisonment for a term not exceeding five years.

(3) In relation to Scotland and Northern Ireland, regulations made under section 2(2) of the 1972 Act for the purpose of implementing any relevant Community instrument may, notwithstanding paragraph 1(1)(d) of Schedule 2 to the 1972 Act, create offences punishable on summary conviction with imprisonment for a term not exceeding six months.

(4) In Scotland, a constable may arrest without a warrant a person—

(a) who has committed or attempted to commit an offence under regulations made under section 2(2) of the 1972 Act for the purpose of implementing any relevant Community instrument, or

(b) whom he has reasonable grounds for suspecting to have committed or to have attempted to commit such an offence.

(5) Until the coming into force of paragraph 3 of Schedule 27 (which amends paragraph 1 of Schedule 2 to the 1972 Act), subsection (3) has effect—

(a) with the omission of the words "in relation to Scotland and Northern Ireland", and

(b) as if, in relation to England and Wales, the definition of "relevant Community instrument" also included Council Directive 92/43/EEC on the conservation of natural habitats and wild fauna and flora as amended by the Act of Accession to the European Union of Austria, Finland and Sweden and by Council Directive 97/62/EC.

(6) Any reference in this section to a Community instrument is to be read—

(a) as a reference to that instrument as amended from time to time, and

(b) where any provision of that instrument has been repealed, as including a reference to any instrument that re-enacts the repealed provision (with or without amendment).

Miscellaneous provisions about criminal proceedings

308. Non-appearance of defendant: plea of guilty

In section 12 of the Magistrates' Courts Act 1980 (c. 43) (non-appearance of accused: plea of guilty) subsection (1)(a)(i) (which excludes offences punishable with imprisonment for term exceeding 3 months) is omitted.

309. Preparatory hearings for serious offences not involving fraud

In section 29 of the Criminal Procedure and Investigations Act 1996 (c. 25) (power to order preparatory hearings) in subsection (1) (preparatory hearing may be held in complex or lengthy trial) after "complexity" there is inserted "a case of such seriousness".

310. Preparatory hearings to deal with severance and joinder of charges

(1) In section 7(1) of the Criminal Justice Act 1987 (c. 38) (which sets out the purposes of preparatory hearings in fraud cases) after paragraph (d) there is inserted "or

(e) considering questions as to the severance or joinder of charges."

(2) In section 9(3) of that Act (determinations as to the admissibility of evidence etc) after paragraph (c) there is inserted "and

(d) any question as to the severance or joinder of charges."

(3) In section 9(11) of that Act (appeals against orders or rulings under section 9(3)(b) or (c)) for "or (c)" there is substituted "(c) or (d)".

(4) In section 29(2) of the Criminal Procedure and Investigations Act 1996 (purposes of preparatory hearings in non-fraud cases) after paragraph (d) there is inserted—

"(e) considering questions as to the severance or joinder of charges,"

(5) In section 31(3) of that Act (rulings as to the admissibility of evidence etc) after paragraph (b) there is inserted—

"(c) any question as to the severance or joinder of charges."

311. Reporting restrictions for preparatory hearings

(1)   The Criminal Justice Act 1987 is amended as follows.

(2)   In paragraphs (a) and (b) of section 11(1) (restrictions on reporting) for "Great Britain" there is substituted "the United Kingdom".

(3)   In section 11A (offences in connection with reporting) after subsection (3) there is inserted—

"(3A)   Proceedings for an offence under this section shall not be instituted in Northern Ireland otherwise than by or with the consent of the Attorney General for Northern Ireland."

(4)   In section 17(3) (extent) after "sections 2 and 3;" there is inserted "sections 11 and 11A;".

(5)   The Criminal Procedure and Investigations Act 1996 (c. 25) is amended as follows.

(6)   In paragraphs (a) and (b) of section 37(1) (restrictions on reporting) for "Great Britain" there is substituted "the United Kingdom".

(7)   In section 38 (offences in connection with reporting) after subsection (3) there is inserted—

"(3A)   Proceedings for an offence under this section shall not be instituted in Northern Ireland otherwise than by or with the consent of the Attorney General for Northern Ireland."

(8)   In paragraphs (a) and (b) of section 41(1) (restrictions on reporting) for "Great Britain" there is substituted "the United Kingdom".

(9)   In section 79(3) (extent) after "Parts III" there is inserted "(other than sections 37 and 38)".

(10)   In Schedule 4 (modifications for Northern Ireland) paragraph 16 is omitted.

312. Awards of costs

(1)   The Prosecution of Offences Act 1985 (c. 23) is amended as follows.

(2)   In section 16(4A) (defence costs on an appeal under section 9(11) of Criminal Justice Act 1987 (c. 38) may be met out of central funds) after "1987" there is inserted "or section 35(1) of the Criminal Procedure and Investigations Act 1996".

(3)   In section 18(2) (award of costs against accused in case of dismissal of appeal under section 9(11) of the Criminal Justice Act 1987 etc) after paragraph (c) there is inserted "or

(d) an appeal or application for leave to appeal under section 35(1) of the Criminal Procedure and Investigations Act 1996."

313. Extension of investigations by Criminal Cases Review Commission in England and Wales

(1)   Section 23A of the Criminal Appeal Act 1968 (c. 19) (power to order investigations by Criminal Cases Review Commission) is amended as follows.

(2)   In subsection (1) after "conviction" there is inserted "or an application for leave to appeal against conviction,".

(3)   In paragraph (a) of that subsection—

(a)   at the beginning there is inserted "in the case of an appeal," and

(b)   for "case", in both places where it occurs, there is substituted "appeal".

(4)   After paragraph (a) of that subsection there is inserted—

437

"(aa) in the case of an application for leave to appeal, the matter is relevant to the determination of the application and ought, if possible, to be resolved before the application is determined;".

(5) After that subsection there is inserted—

"(1A) A direction under subsection (1) above may not be given by a single judge, notwithstanding that, in the case of an application for leave to appeal, the application may be determined by a single judge as provided for by section 31 of this Act."

(6) After subsection (4) there is inserted—

"(5) In this section "respondent" includes a person who will be a respondent if leave to appeal is granted."

314. Extension of investigations by Criminal Cases Review Commission in Northern Ireland

(1) Section 25A of the Criminal Appeal (Northern Ireland) Act 1980 (c. 47) (power to order investigations by Criminal Cases Review Commission) is amended as follows.

(2) In subsection (1) after "conviction" there is inserted "or an application for leave to appeal against conviction,".

(3) In paragraph (a) of that subsection—

(a) at the beginning there is inserted "in the case of an appeal,", and

(b) for "case", in both places where it occurs, there is substituted "appeal".

(4) After paragraph (a) of that subsection there is inserted—

"(aa) in the case of an application for leave to appeal, the matter is relevant to the determination of the application and ought, if possible, to be resolved before the application is determined;".

(5) After that subsection there is inserted—

"(1A) A direction under subsection (1) above may not be given by a single judge, notwithstanding that, in the case of an application for leave to appeal, the application may be determined by a single judge as provided for by section 45 below."

(6) After subsection (4) there is inserted—

"(5) In this section "respondent" includes a person who will be a respondent if leave to appeal is granted."

315. Appeals following reference by Criminal Cases Review Commission

(1) Section 14 of the Criminal Appeal Act 1995 (c. 35) (further provision about references by Criminal Cases Review Commission) is amended as follows.

(2) After subsection (4) there is inserted—

"(4A) Subject to subsection (4B), where a reference under section 9 or 10 is treated as an appeal against any conviction, verdict, finding or sentence, the appeal may not be on any ground which is not related to any reason given by the Commission for making the reference.

(4B) The Court of Appeal may give leave for an appeal mentioned in subsection (4A) to be on a ground relating to the conviction, verdict, finding or sentence which is not related to any reason given by the Commission for making the reference."

(3) In subsection (5) for "any of sections 9 to" there is substituted "section 11 or".

316. Power to substitute conviction of alternative offence on appeal in England and Wales

(1) The Criminal Appeal Act 1968 (c. 19) is amended as follows.

(2) In section 3 (power to substitute conviction of alternative offence) in subsection (1) after "an offence" there is inserted "to which he did not plead guilty"

(3) After section 3 there is inserted—

"3A. Power to substitute conviction of alternative offence after guilty plea

(1) This section applies on an appeal against conviction where—
   (a) an appellant has been convicted of an offence to which he pleaded guilty,
   (b) if he had not so pleaded, he could on the indictment have pleaded, or been found, guilty of some other offence, and
   (c) it appears to the Court of Appeal that the plea of guilty indicates an admission by the appellant of facts which prove him guilty of the other offence.

(2) The Court of Appeal may, instead of allowing or dismissing the appeal, substitute for the appellant's plea of guilty a plea of guilty of the other offence and pass such sentence in substitution for the sentence passed at the trial as may be authorised by law for the other offence, not being a sentence of greater severity."

317. Power to substitute conviction of alternative offence on appeal in Northern Ireland

(1) The Criminal Appeal (Northern Ireland) Act 1980 (c. 47) is amended as follows.

(2) In section 3 (power to substitute conviction of alternative offence) in subsection (1) after "an offence" there is inserted "to which he did not plead guilty"

(3) After section 3 there is inserted—

"3A. Power to substitute conviction of alternative offence after guilty plea

(1) This section applies where—
   (a) an appellant has been convicted of an offence to which he pleaded guilty,
   (b) if he had not so pleaded, he could on the indictment have pleaded, or been found, guilty of some other offence, and
   (c) it appears to the Court of Appeal that the plea of guilty indicates an admission by the appellant of facts which prove him guilty of that other offence.

(2) The Court may, instead of allowing or dismissing the appeal, substitute for the appellant's plea of guilty a plea of guilty of that other offence and pass such sentence in substitution for the sentence passed at the trial as may be warranted in law by the plea so substituted."

318. Substitution of conviction on different charge on appeal from court-martial

(1) The Courts-Martial (Appeals) Act 1968 (c. 20) is amended as follows.

(2) In section 14 (substitution of conviction on different charge) in subsection (1) after "an offence" there is inserted "to which he did not plead guilty".

(3) After section 14 there is inserted—

"14A. Substitution of conviction on different charge after guilty plea

(1) This section applies where—
   (a) an appellant has been convicted of an offence to which he pleaded guilty,
   (b) if he had not so pleaded, he could lawfully have pleaded, or been found, guilty of some other offence, and

(c) it appears to the Appeal Court on an appeal against conviction that the plea of guilty indicates an admission by the appellant of facts which prove him guilty of that other offence.

(2) The Appeal Court may, instead of allowing or dismissing the appeal, substitute for the appellant's plea of guilty a plea of guilty of the other offence, and may pass on the appellant, in substitution for the sentence passed on him by the court-martial, such sentence as they think proper, being a sentence warranted by the relevant Service Act for that other offence, but not a sentence of greater severity."

319. Appeals against sentences in England and Wales

(1) The Criminal Appeal Act 1968 (c. 19) is amended as follows.

(2) In section 10 (appeal against sentence in certain cases) for subsection (3) there is substituted—

"(3) An offender dealt with for an offence before the Crown Court in a proceeding to which subsection (2) of this section applies may appeal to the Court of Appeal against any sentence passed on him for the offence by the Crown Court."

(3) In section 11 (supplementary provisions as to appeal against sentence) after subsection (6) there is inserted—

"(7) For the purposes of this section, any two or more sentences are to be treated as passed in the same proceeding if—

(a) they are passed on the same day; or

(b) they are passed on different days but the court in passing any one of them states that it is treating that one together with the other or others as substantially one sentence."

Outraging public decency

320. Offence of outraging public decency triable either way

(1) After paragraph 1 of Schedule 1 to the Magistrates' Courts Act 1980 (c. 43) (offences triable either way by virtue of section 17) there is inserted—

"1A An offence at common law of outraging public decency."

(2) This section does not apply in relation to any offence committed before the commencement of this section.

Jury service

321. Jury service

Schedule 33 (jury service) shall have effect.

Individual support orders

322. Individual support orders

After section 1A of the Crime and Disorder Act 1998 (c. 37) there is inserted—

"1AA. Individual support orders

(1) Where a court makes an anti-social behaviour order in respect of a defendant who is a child or young person when that order is made, it must consider whether the individual support conditions are fulfilled.

(2) If it is satisfied that those conditions are fulfilled, the court must make an order under this section ("an individual support order") which—
  (a) requires the defendant to comply, for a period not exceeding six months, with such requirements as are specified in the order; and
  (b) requires the defendant to comply with any directions given by the responsible officer with a view to the implementation of the requirements under paragraph (a) above.

(3) The individual support conditions are—
  (a) that an individual support order would be desirable in the interests of preventing any repetition of the kind of behaviour which led to the making of the anti-social behaviour order;
  (b) that the defendant is not already subject to an individual support order; and
  (c) that the court has been notified by the Secretary of State that arrangements for implementing individual support orders are available in the area in which it appears to it that the defendant resides or will reside and the notice has not been withdrawn.

(4) If the court is not satisfied that the individual support conditions are fulfilled, it shall state in open court that it is not so satisfied and why it is not.

(5) The requirements that may be specified under subsection (2)(a) above are those that the court considers desirable in the interests of preventing any repetition of the kind of behaviour which led to the making of the anti-social behaviour order.

(6) Requirements included in an individual support order, or directions given under such an order by a responsible officer, may require the defendant to do all or any of the following things—
  (a) to participate in activities specified in the requirements or directions at a time or times so specified;
  (b) to present himself to a person or persons so specified at a place or places and at a time or times so specified;
  (c) to comply with any arrangements for his education so specified.

(7) But requirements included in, or directions given under, such an order may not require the defendant to attend (whether at the same place or at different places) on more than two days in any week; and "week" here means a period of seven days beginning with a Sunday.

(8) Requirements included in, and directions given under, an individual support order shall, as far as practicable, be such as to avoid—
  (a) any conflict with the defendant's religious beliefs; and
  (b) any interference with the times, if any, at which he normally works or attends school or any other educational establishment.

(9) Before making an individual support order, the court shall obtain from a social worker of a local authority social services department or a member of a youth offending team any information which it considers necessary in order—
  (a) to determine whether the individual support conditions are fulfilled, or
  (b) to determine what requirements should be imposed by an individual support order if made,
  and shall consider that information.

(10) In this section and section 1AB below "responsible officer", in relation to an individual support order, means one of the following who is specified in the order, namely—
  (a) a social worker of a local authority social services department;
  (b) a person nominated by a person appointed as chief education officer under section 532 of the Education Act 1996 (c. 56);
  (c) a member of a youth offending team.

1AB. Individual support orders: explanation, breach, amendment etc

(1) Before making an individual support order, the court shall explain to the defendant in ordinary language—

    (a) the effect of the order and of the requirements proposed to be included in it;

    (b) the consequences which may follow (under subsection (3) below) if he fails to comply with any of those requirements; and

    (c) that the court has power (under subsection (6) below) to review the order on the application either of the defendant or of the responsible officer.

(2) The power of the Secretary of State under section 174(4) of the Criminal Justice Act 2003 includes power by order to—

    (a) prescribe cases in which subsection (1) above does not apply; and

    (b) prescribe cases in which the explanation referred to in that subsection may be made in the absence of the defendant, or may be provided in written form.

(3) If the person in respect of whom an individual support order is made fails without reasonable excuse to comply with any requirement included in the order, he is guilty of an offence and liable on summary conviction to a fine not exceeding—

    (a) if he is aged 14 or over at the date of his conviction, £1,000;

    (b) if he is aged under 14 then, £250.

(4) No referral order under section 16(2) or (3) of the Powers of Criminal Courts (Sentencing) Act 2000 (referral of young offenders to youth offender panels) may be made in respect of an offence under subsection (3) above.

(5) If the anti-social behaviour order as a result of which an individual support order was made ceases to have effect, the individual support order (if it has not previously ceased to have effect) ceases to have effect when the anti-social behaviour order does.

(6) On an application made by complaint by—

    (a) the person subject to an individual support order, or

    (b) the responsible officer,

the court which made the individual support order may vary or discharge it by a further order.

(7) If the anti-social behaviour order as a result of which an individual support order was made is varied, the court varying the anti-social behaviour order may by a further order vary or discharge the individual support order."

323. Individual support orders: consequential amendments

(1) The Crime and Disorder Act 1998 (c. 37) is amended as mentioned in subsections (2) to (5).

(2) In section 4 of that Act (appeals against orders)—

    (a) in subsection (1) after "an anti-social behaviour order" there is inserted ", an individual support order", and

    (b) in subsection (3) after "1(8)" there is inserted ", 1AB(6)".

(3) In section 18(1) of that Act (interpretation of Chapter 1)—

    (a) after the definition of "curfew notice" there is inserted—

    " " individual support order" has the meaning given by section 1AA(2) above;", and

    (b) in the definition of "responsible officer", before paragraph (a) there is inserted—

    "(za) in relation to an individual support order, has the meaning given by section 1AA(10) above;".

(4) In section 18(4) of that Act (cases where social worker or member of a youth offending team to give supervision or directions)—

    (a) after "directions under" there is inserted "an individual support order or", and

    (b) for "the child or, as the case may be, the parent" there is substituted "the child, defendant or parent, as the case may be,".

(5) In section 38 of that Act (local provision of youth justice services), in subsection (4)(f) after "in relation to" there is inserted "individual support orders,".

(6) In section 143(2) (provisions in which sums may be altered) of the Magistrates' Courts Act 1980 (c. 43), after paragraph (d) there is inserted—

    "(da) section 1AB(3) of the Crime and Disorder Act 1998 (failure to comply with individual support order);".

Parenting orders and referral orders

324. Parenting orders and referral orders

Schedule 34 (parenting orders and referral orders) shall have effect.

Assessing etc. risks posed by sexual or violent offenders

325. Arrangements for assessing etc risks posed by certain offenders

(1) In this section—

"relevant sexual or violent offender" has the meaning given by section 327;

"responsible authority", in relation to any area, means the chief officer of police, the local probation board for that area and the Minister of the Crown exercising functions in relation to prisons, acting jointly.

(2) The responsible authority for each area must establish arrangements for the purpose of assessing and managing the risks posed in that area by—

    (a) relevant sexual and violent offenders, and

    (b) other persons who, by reason of offences committed by them (wherever committed), are considered by the responsible authority to be persons who may cause serious harm to the public.

(3) In establishing those arrangements, the responsible authority must act in co-operation with the persons specified in subsection (6); and it is the duty of those persons to co-operate in the establishment by the responsible authority of those arrangements, to the extent that such co-operation is compatible with the exercise by those persons of their functions under any other enactment.

(4) Co-operation under subsection (3) may include the exchange of information.

(5) The responsible authority for each area ("the relevant area") and the persons specified in subsection (6) must together draw up a memorandum setting out the ways in which they are to co-operate.

(6) The persons referred to in subsections (3) and (5) are—

    (a) every youth offending team established for an area any part of which falls within the relevant area,

    (b) the Ministers of the Crown exercising functions in relation to social security, child support, war pensions, employment and training,

    (c) every local education authority any part of whose area falls within the relevant area,

    (d) every local housing authority or social services authority any part of whose area falls within the relevant area,

(e) every registered social landlord which provides or manages residential accommodation in the relevant area in which persons falling within subsection (2)(a) or (b) reside or may reside,

(f) every Health Authority or Strategic Health Authority any part of whose area falls within the relevant area,

(g) every Primary Care Trust or Local Health Board any part of whose area falls within the relevant area,

(h) every NHS trust any part of whose area falls within the relevant area, and

(i) every person who is designated by the Secretary of State by order for the purposes of this paragraph as a provider of electronic monitoring services.

(7) The Secretary of State may by order amend subsection (6) by adding or removing any person or description of person.

(8) The Secretary of State may issue guidance to responsible authorities on the discharge of the functions conferred by this section and section 326.

(9) In this section—

"local education authority" has the same meaning as in the Education Act 1996 (c. 56);

"local housing authority" has the same meaning as in the Housing Act 1985 (c. 68);

"Minister of the Crown" has the same meaning as in the Ministers of the Crown Act 1975 (c. 26);

"NHS trust" has the same meaning as in the National Health Service Act 1977 (c. 49);

"prison" has the same meaning as in the Prison Act 1952 (c. 52);

"registered social landlord" has the same meaning as in Part 1 of the Housing Act 1996 (c.52);

"social services authority" means a local authority for the purposes of the Local Authority Social Services Act 1970 (c. 42).

326. Review of arrangements

(1) The responsible authority for each area must keep the arrangements established by it under section 325 under review with a view to monitoring their effectiveness and making any changes to them that appear necessary or expedient.

(2) The responsible authority for any area must exercise their functions under subsection (1) in consultation with persons appointed by the Secretary of State as lay advisers in relation to that authority.

(3) The Secretary of State must appoint two lay advisers under subsection (2) in relation to each responsible authority.

(4) The responsible authority must pay to or in respect of the persons so appointed such allowances as the Secretary of State may determine.

(5) As soon as practicable after the end of each period of 12 months beginning with 1st April, the responsible authority for each area must—

(a) prepare a report on the discharge by it during that period of the functions conferred by section 325 and this section, and

(b) publish the report in that area.

(6) The report must include—

(a) details of the arrangements established by the responsible authority, and

(b) information of such descriptions as the Secretary of State has notified to the responsible authority that he wishes to be included in the report.

327. Section 325: interpretation

(1) For the purposes of section 325, a person is a relevant sexual or violent offender if he falls within one or more of subsections (2) to (5)

(2) A person falls within this subsection if he is subject to the notification requirements of Part 2 of the Sexual Offences Act 2003 (c. 42).

(3) A person falls within this subsection if—

    (a) he is convicted by a court in England or Wales of murder or an offence specified in Schedule 15, and

    (b) one of the following sentences is imposed on him in respect of the conviction—

        (i) a sentence of imprisonment for a term of 12 months or more,

        (ii) a sentence of detention in a young offender institution for a term of 12 months or more,

        (iii) a sentence of detention during Her Majesty's pleasure,

        (iv) a sentence of detention for public protection under section 226,

        (v) a sentence of detention for a period of 12 months or more under section 91 of the Sentencing Act (offenders under 18 convicted of certain serious offences),

        (vi) a sentence of detention under section 228,

        (vii) a detention and training order for a term of 12 months or more, or

        (viii) a hospital or guardianship order within the meaning of the Mental Health Act 1983 (c. 20).

(4) A person falls within this subsection if—

    (a) he is found not guilty by a court in England and Wales of murder or an offence specified in Schedule 15 by reason of insanity or to be under a disability and to have done the act charged against him in respect of such an offence, and

    (b) one of the following orders is made in respect of the act charged against him as the offence—

        (i) an order that he be admitted to hospital, or

        (ii) a guardianship order within the meaning of the Mental Health Act 1983.

(5) A person falls within this subsection if—

    (a) the first condition set out in section 28(2) or 29(2) of the Criminal Justice and Court Services Act 2000 (c. 43) or the second condition set out in section 28(3) or 29(3) of that Act is satisfied in his case, or

    (b) an order under section 29A of that Act has been made in respect of him.

(6) In this section "court" does not include a service court, as defined by section 305(1).

Criminal record certificates

328. Criminal record certificates: amendments of Part 5 of Police Act 1997

Schedule 35 (which contains amendments of Part 5 of the Police Act 1997 (c. 50)) shall have effect.

Civil proceedings brought by offenders

329. Civil proceedings for trespass to the person brought by offender

(1) This section applies where—

    (a) a person ("the claimant") claims that another person ("the defendant") did an act amounting to trespass to the claimant's person, and

    (b) the claimant has been convicted in the United Kingdom of an imprisonable offence committed on the same occasion as that on which the act is alleged to have been done.

(2) Civil proceedings relating to the claim may be brought only with the permission of the court.

(3) The court may give permission for the proceedings to be brought only if there is evidence that either—

    (a) the condition in subsection (5) is not met, or

    (b) in all the circumstances, the defendant's act was grossly disproportionate.

(4) If the court gives permission and the proceedings are brought, it is a defence for the defendant to prove both—

    (a) that the condition in subsection (5) is met, and

    (b) that, in all the circumstances, his act was not grossly disproportionate.

(5) The condition referred to in subsection (3)(a) and (4)(a) is that the defendant did the act only because—

    (a) he believed that the claimant—

        (i) was about to commit an offence,

        (ii) was in the course of committing an offence, or

        (iii) had committed an offence immediately beforehand; and

    (b) he believed that the act was necessary to—

        (i) defend himself or another person,

        (ii) protect or recover property,

        (iii) prevent the commission or continuation of an offence, or

        (iv) apprehend, or secure the conviction, of the claimant after he had committed an offence;

    or was necessary to assist in achieving any of those things.

(6) Subsection (4) is without prejudice to any other defence.

(7) Where—

    (a) in service disciplinary proceedings, as defined by section 305(1), a person has been found guilty of an offence under section 70 of the Army Act 1955 (3 & 4 Eliz. 2 c. 18), section 70 of the Air Force Act 1955 (3 & 4 Eliz. 2 c. 19) or section 42 of the Naval Discipline Act 1957 (c. 53), and

    (b) the corresponding civil offence (within the meaning of that Act) was an imprisonable offence,

    he is to be treated for the purposes of this section as having been convicted in the United Kingdom of the corresponding civil offence.

(8) In this section—

    (a) the reference to trespass to the person is a reference to—

        (i) assault,

        (ii) battery, or

        (iii) false imprisonment;

    (b) references to a defendant's belief are to his honest belief, whether or not the belief was also reasonable;

    (c) "court" means the High Court or a county court; and

    (d) "imprisonable offence" means an offence which, in the case of a person aged 18 or over, is punishable by imprisonment.

PART 14. GENERAL

330. Orders and rules

(1) This section applies to—
    (a) any power conferred by this Act on the Secretary of State to make an order or rules;
    (b) the power conferred by section 168 on the Lord Chancellor to make an order.

(2) The power is exercisable by statutory instrument.

(3) The power—
    (a) may be exercised so as to make different provision for different purposes or different areas, and
    (b) may be exercised either for all the purposes to which the power extends, or for those purposes subject to specified exceptions, or only for specified purposes.

(4) The power includes power to make—
    (a) any supplementary, incidental or consequential provision, and
    (b) any transitory, transitional or saving provision,
which the Minister making the instrument considers necessary or expedient.

(5) A statutory instrument containing—
    (a) an order under any of the following provisions—
        section 25(5),
        section 103,
        section 161(7),
        section 178,
        section 197(3),
        section 223,
        section 246(5),
        section 260,
        section 267,
        section 269(6),
        section 281(2),
        section 283(1),
        section 291,
        section 301(5),
        section 325(7), and
        paragraph 5 of Schedule 31,
    (b) an order under section 336(3) bringing section 43 into force,
    (c) an order making any provision by virtue of section 333(2)(b) which adds to, replaces or omits any part of the text of an Act, or
    (d) rules under section 240(4)(a),
may only be made if a draft of the statutory instrument has been laid before, and approved by a resolution of, each House of Parliament.

(6) Any other statutory instrument made in the exercise of a power to which this section applies is subject to annulment in pursuance of a resolution of either House of Parliament.

(7) Subsection (6) does not apply to a statutory instrument containing only an order made under one or more of the following provisions—
section 202(3)(b),

section 215(3),
section 253(5),
section 325(6)(i), and
section 336.

331. Further minor and consequential amendments

Schedule 36 (further minor and consequential amendments) shall have effect.

332. Repeals

Schedule 37 (repeals) shall have effect.

333. Supplementary and consequential provision, etc.

(1) The Secretary of State may by order make—
    (a) any supplementary, incidental or consequential provision, and
    (b) any transitory, transitional or saving provision,
which he considers necessary or expedient for the purposes of, in consequence of, or for giving full effect to any provision of this Act.

(2) An order under subsection (1) may, in particular—
    (a) provide for any provision of this Act which comes into force before another such provision has come into force to have effect, until that other provision has come into force, with such modifications as are specified in the order, and
    (b) amend or repeal—
        (i) any Act passed before, or in the same Session as, this Act, and
        (ii) subordinate legislation made before the passing of this Act.

(3) Nothing in this section limits the power by virtue of section 330(4)(b) to include transitional or saving provision in an order under section 336.

(4) The amendments that may be made under subsection (2)(b) are in addition to those made by or under any other provision of this Act.

(5) In this section "subordinate legislation" has the same meaning as in the Interpretation Act 1978 (c. 30).

(6) Schedule 38 (which contains transitory and transitional provisions and savings) shall have effect.

334. Provision for Northern Ireland

(1) An Order in Council under section 85 of the Northern Ireland Act 1998 (c. 47) (provision dealing with certain reserved matters) which contains a statement that it is made only for purposes corresponding to those of any provisions of this Act specified in subsection (2)—
    (a) shall not be subject to subsections (3) to (9) of that section (affirmative resolution of both Houses of Parliament), but
    (b) shall be subject to annulment in pursuance of a resolution of either House of Parliament.

(2) The provisions are—
    (a) in Part 1, sections 1, 3(3), 4, 7 to 10 and 12 and paragraphs 1, 2, 5 to 10 and 20 of Schedule 1, and

(b) Parts 8, 9 and 11.

(3) In relation to any time when section 1 of the Northern Ireland Act 2000 (c. 1) is in force (suspension of devolved government in Northern Ireland)—

    (a) the reference in subsection (1) above to section 85 of the Northern Ireland Act 1998 shall be read as a reference to paragraph 1 of the Schedule to the Northern Ireland Act 2000 (legislation by Order in Council during suspension), and

    (b) the reference in subsection (1)(a) above to subsections (3) to (9) of that section shall be read as a reference to paragraph 2 of that Schedule.

(4) The reference in section 41(2) of the Justice (Northern Ireland) Act 2002 (c. 26) (transfer of certain functions to Director of Public Prosecutions for Northern Ireland) to any function of the Attorney General for Northern Ireland of consenting to the institution of criminal proceedings includes any such function which is conferred by an amendment made by this Act.

(5) Any reference to any provision of the Criminal Appeal (Northern Ireland) Act 1980 (c. 47) in the Access to Justice (Northern Ireland) Order 2003 (S.I. 2003/435 (N.I. 10)) is to be read as a reference to that provision as amended by this Act.

335. Expenses

There shall be paid out of money provided by Parliament—

(a) any expenditure incurred by a Minister of the Crown by virtue of this Act, and

(b) any increase attributable to this Act in the sums payable out of money so provided under any other enactment.

336. Commencement

(1) The following provisions of this Act come into force on the passing of this Act—

    section 168(1) and (2),

    section 183(8),

    section 307(1) to (3), (5) and (6),

    section 330,

    section 333(1) to (5),

    sections 334 and 335,

    this section and sections 337, 338 and 339, and

    the repeal in Part 9 of Schedule 37 of section 81(2) and (3) of the Countryside and Rights of Way Act 2000 (c. 37) (and section 332 so far as relating to that repeal), and

    paragraphs 1 and 6 of Schedule 38 (and section 333(6) so far as relating to those paragraphs).

(2) The following provisions of this Act come into force at the end of the period of four weeks beginning with the day on which this Act is passed—

    Chapter 7 of Part 12 (and Schedules 21 and 22);

    section 303(b)(i) and (ii);

    paragraphs 42, 43(3), 66, 83(1) to (3), 84 and 109(2), (3)(b), (4) and (5) of Schedule 32 (and section 304 so far as relating to those provisions);

    Part 8 of Schedule 37 (and section 332 so far as relating to that Part of that Schedule).

(3) The remaining provisions of this Act come into force in accordance with provision made by the Secretary of State by order.

(4) Different provision may be made for different purposes and different areas.

337. Extent

(1) Subject to the following provisions of this section and to section 338, this Act extends to England and Wales only.

(2) The following provisions extend also to Scotland and Northern Ireland—

    sections 71 and 72;

    sections 82 and 83;

    section 180 and Schedule 9;

    section 188 and Schedule 11;

    section 194 and Schedule 13;

    section 293;

    section 306;

    section 307;

    section 311;

    this Part, except sections 331, 332 and 334(5);

    paragraphs 19, 70 and 71 of Schedule 3;

    paragraph 12(3) of Schedule 12;

    paragraphs 3, 6, 7 and 8 of Schedule 27;

    paragraphs 6 to 8 of Schedule 31.

(3) The following provisions extend also to Scotland—

    section 50(14);

    section 286;

    sections 287, 288, and 291;

    section 302;

    paragraph 2 of Schedule 23;

    paragraphs 1, 2 and 5 of Schedule 27;

    paragraph 7 of Schedule 38.

(4) Section 290 extends to Scotland only.

(5) The following provisions extend also to Northern Ireland—

    Part 5;

    Part 7;

    sections 75 to 81;

    sections 84 to 93;

    sections 95 to 97;

    section 315;

    Schedule 5.

(6) The following provisions extend to Northern Ireland only—

    section 292 and Schedule 29;

    sections 296 and 297;

    section 314;

    section 317;

    section 334(5).

(7) The amendment or repeal of any enactment by any provision of—

    (a) Part 1,

    (b) section 285,

    (c) Part 2 of Schedule 3 (except as mentioned in subsection (8)),

    (d) Schedule 27,

    (e) Schedule 28,

    (f) Part 1 of Schedule 32,

(g) Parts 1 to 4 and 6 of Schedule 36, and

(h) Parts 1 to 4, 6 to 8, 10 and 12 of Schedule 37 (except as mentioned in subsection (9)),

extends to the part or parts of the United Kingdom to which the enactment extends.

(8) Paragraphs 29, 30, 31, 39, 41, 50, 53 and 63 of Schedule 3 do not extend to Northern Ireland.

(9) The repeals in Part 4 of Schedule 37 relating to—

(a) the Bankers' Books Evidence Act 1879 (c. 11),

(b) the Explosive Substances Act 1883 (c. 3),

(c) the Backing of Warrants (Republic of Ireland) Act 1965 (c. 45),

(d) the Customs and Excise Management Act 1979 (c. 2), and

(e) the Contempt of Court Act 1981 (c. 49),

do not extend to Northern Ireland.

(10) The provisions mentioned in subsection (11), so far as relating to proceedings before a particular service court, have the same extent as the Act under which the court is constituted.

(11) Those provisions are—

section 113 and Schedule 6;

section 135 and Schedule 7.

(12) Nothing in subsection (1) affects—

(a) the extent of Chapter 7 of Part 12 so far as relating to sentences passed by a court-martial, or

(b) the extent of section 299 and Schedule 30 so far as relating to the making of orders by, or orders made by, courts-martial or the Courts-Martial Appeal Court.

(13) Any provision of this Act which—

(a) relates to any enactment contained in—

(i) the Army Act 1955 (3 & 4 Eliz. 2 c. 18),

(ii) the Air Force Act 1955 (3 & 4 Eliz. 2 c. 19),

(iii) the Naval Discipline Act 1957 (c. 53),

(iv) the Courts-Martial (Appeals) Act 1968 (c. 20),

(v) the Armed Forces Act 1976 (c. 52),

(vi) section 113 of the Police and Criminal Evidence Act 1984 (c. 60),

(vii) the Reserve Forces Act 1996 (c. 14), or

(viii) the Armed Forces Act 2001 (c. 19), and

(b) is not itself contained in Schedule 25 or Part 9 of Schedule 37,

has the same extent as the enactment to which it relates.

338. Channel Islands and Isle of Man

(1) Subject to subsections (2) and (3), Her Majesty may by Order in Council extend any provision of this Act, with such modifications as appear to Her Majesty in Council to be appropriate, to any of the Channel Islands or the Isle of Man.

(2) Subsection (1) does not authorise the extension to any place of a provision of this Act so far as the provision amends an enactment that does not itself extend there and is not itself capable of being extended there in the exercise of a power conferred on Her Majesty in Council.

(3) Subsection (1) does not apply in relation to any provision that extends to the Channel Islands or the Isle of Man by virtue of any of subsections (10) to (13) of section 337.

(4) Subsection (4) of section 330 applies to the power to make an Order in Council under subsection (1) as it applies to any power of the Secretary of State to make an order under

this Act, but as if references in that subsection to the Minister making the instrument were references to Her Majesty in Council.

339. Short title

This Act may be cited as the Criminal Justice Act 2003.

SCHEDULES

SCHEDULE 1
AMENDMENTS RELATED TO PART 1

Section 12

The 1984 Act

1. The 1984 Act is amended as follows.
2. In section 18 (entry and search after arrest), for subsection (5) there is substituted—
   "(5) A constable may conduct a search under subsection (1)—
      (a) before the person is taken to a police station or released on bail under section 30A, and
      (b) without obtaining an authorisation under subsection (4),
      if the condition in subsection (5A) is satisfied.
   (5A) The condition is that the presence of the person at a place (other than a police station) is necessary for the effective investigation of the offence."
3. In section 21 (access and copying), at the end there is inserted—
   "(9) The references to a constable in subsections (1), (2), (3)(a) and (5) include a person authorised under section 16(2) to accompany a constable executing a warrant."
4. In section 22 (retention), at the end there is inserted—
   "(7) The reference in subsection (1) to anything seized by a constable includes anything seized by a person authorised under section 16(2) to accompany a constable executing a warrant."
5. In section 34 (limitation on police detention), for subsection (7) there is substituted—
   "(7) For the purposes of this Part a person who—
      (a) attends a police station to answer to bail granted under section 30A,
      (b) returns to a police station to answer to bail granted under this Part, or
      (c) is arrested under section 30D or 46A,
      is to be treated as arrested for an offence and that offence is the offence in connection with which he was granted bail."
6. In section 35(1) (designated police stations), for "section 30(3) and (5) above" there is substituted "sections 30(3) and (5), 30A(5) and 30D(2)".
7. In section 36 (custody officers at police stations), after subsection (7) there is inserted—
   "(7A) Subject to subsection (7B), subsection (7) applies where a person attends a police station which is not a designated station to answer to bail granted under section 30A as it applies where a person is taken to such a station.
   (7B) Where subsection (7) applies because of subsection (7A), the reference in subsection (7)(b) to the officer who took him to the station is to be read as a reference to the officer who granted him bail."
8. In section 41(2) (calculation of periods of time), after paragraph (c) there is inserted—
   "(ca) in the case of a person who attends a police station to answer to bail granted under section 30A, the time when he arrives at the police station;".

9. In section 45A(2)(a) (functions which may be performed by video-conferencing), after "taken to" there is inserted ", or answering to bail at,".
10. In section 47 (bail after arrest)—
    (a) in subsection (6), after "granted bail" there is inserted "under this Part", and
    (b) in subsection (7), after "released on bail" there is inserted "under this Part".

Criminal Justice Act 1987 (c. 38)

11. In section 2 of the Criminal Justice Act 1987 (director's investigation powers), after subsection (6) there is inserted—
    "(6A) Where an appropriate person accompanies a constable, he may exercise the powers conferred by subsection (5) but only in the company, and under the supervision, of the constable."
12. In subsection (7) of that section (meaning of appropriate person), for "subsection (6) above" there is substituted "this section".
13. In subsection (8D) of that section (references to evidence obtained by Director), after "by a constable" there is inserted "or by an appropriate person".

Criminal Justice and Police Act 2001 (c. 16)

14. In section 56 of the Criminal Justice and Police Act 2001 (property seized by constables etc.), after subsection (4) there is inserted—
    "(4A) Subsection (1)(a) includes property seized on any premises—
    (a) by a person authorised under section 16(2) of the 1984 Act to accompany a constable executing a warrant, or
    (b) by a person accompanying a constable under section 2(6) of the Criminal Justice Act 1987 in the execution of a warrant under section 2(4) of that Act."

Armed Forces Act 2001 (c. 19)

15. In section 2(9) of the Armed Forces Act 2001 (offences for purpose of definition of prohibited article), at the end of paragraph (d) there is inserted "; and
    (e) offences under section 1 of the Criminal Damage Act 1971 (destroying or damaging property)."

Police Reform Act 2002 (c. 30)

16. Schedule 4 to the Police Reform Act 2002 (powers exercisable by police civilians) is amended as follows.
17. In paragraph 17 (access to excluded and special procedure material) after paragraph (b) there is inserted—
    "(bb) section 15 of that Act (safeguards) shall have effect in relation to the issue of any warrant under paragraph 12 of that Schedule to that person as it has effect in relation to the issue of a warrant under that paragraph to a constable;
    (bc) section 16 of that Act (execution of warrants) shall have effect in relation to any warrant to enter and search premises that is issued under paragraph 12 of that Schedule (whether to that person or to any other person) in respect of premises in the relevant police area as if references in that section to a constable included references to that person;".

18. In paragraph 20 (access and copying in case of things seized by constables) after "by a constable" there is inserted "or by a person authorised to accompany him under section 16(2) of that Act".

19. After paragraph 24 (extended powers of seizure) there is inserted—

"Persons accompanying investigating officers

24A(1) This paragraph applies where a person ("an authorised person") is authorised by virtue of section 16(2) of the 1984 Act to accompany an investigating officer designated for the purposes of paragraph 16 (or 17) in the execution of a warrant.

(2) The reference in paragraph 16(h) (or 17(e)) to the seizure of anything by a designated person in exercise of a particular power includes a reference to the seizure of anything by the authorised person in exercise of that power by virtue of section 16(2A) of the 1984 Act.

(3) In relation to any such seizure, paragraph 16(h) (or 17(e)) is to be read as if it provided for the references to a constable and to an officer in section 21(1) and (2) of the 1984 Act to include references to the authorised person.

(4) The reference in paragraph 16(i) (or 17(f)) to anything seized by a designated person in exercise of a particular power includes a reference to anything seized by the authorised person in exercise of that power by virtue of section 16(2A) of the 1984 Act.

(5) In relation to anything so seized, paragraph 16(i)(ii) (or 17(f)(ii)) is to be read as if it provided for—

(a) the references to the supervision of a constable in subsections (3) and (4) of section 21 of the 1984 Act to include references to the supervision of a person designated for the purposes of paragraph 16 (or paragraph 17), and

(b) the reference to a constable in subsection (5) of that section to include a reference to such a person or an authorised person accompanying him.

(6) Where an authorised person accompanies an investigating officer who is also designated for the purposes of paragraph 24, the references in sub-paragraphs (a) and (b) of that paragraph to the designated person include references to the authorised person."

20. In paragraph 34 (powers of escort officer to take arrested person to prison), in sub-paragraph (1)(a), for "subsection (1) of section 30" there is substituted "subsection (1A) of section 30".

SCHEDULE 2

Section 28

CHARGING OR RELEASE OF PERSONS IN POLICE DETENTION

1. The Police and Criminal Evidence Act 1984 (c. 60) is amended as follows.

2. (1) Section 37 (duties of custody officers before charge) is amended as follows.

(2) In subsection (7) for paragraphs (a) and (b) there is substituted—

"(a) shall be released without charge and on bail for the purpose of enabling the Director of Public Prosecutions to make a decision under section 37B below,

(b) shall be released without charge and on bail but not for that purpose,

(c) shall be released without charge and without bail, or

(d) shall be charged."

(3) After that subsection there is inserted—

"(7A) The decision as to how a person is to be dealt with under subsection (7) above shall be that of the custody officer.

(7B) Where a person is released under subsection (7)(a) above, it shall be the duty of the custody officer to inform him that he is being released to enable the Director of Public Prosecutions to make a decision under section 37B below."

(4) In subsection (8)(a) after "(7)(b)" there is inserted "or (c)".

3. After that section there is inserted—

"37A Guidance

(1) The Director of Public Prosecutions may issue guidance—
   (a) for the purpose of enabling custody officers to decide how persons should be dealt with under section 37(7) above or 37C(2) below, and
   (b) as to the information to be sent to the Director of Public Prosecutions under section 37B(1) below.

(2) The Director of Public Prosecutions may from time to time revise guidance issued under this section.

(3) Custody officers are to have regard to guidance under this section in deciding how persons should be dealt with under section 37(7) above or 37C(2) below.

(4) A report under section 9 of the Prosecution of Offences Act 1985 (report by DPP to Attorney General) must set out the provisions of any guidance issued, and any revisions to guidance made, in the year to which the report relates.

(5) The Director of Public Prosecutions must publish in such manner as he thinks fit—
   (a) any guidance issued under this section, and
   (b) any revisions made to such guidance.

(6) Guidance under this section may make different provision for different cases, circumstances or areas.

37B. Consultation with the Director of Public Prosecutions

(1) Where a person is released on bail under section 37(7)(a) above, an officer involved in the investigation of the offence shall, as soon as is practicable, send to the Director of Public Prosecutions such information as may be specified in guidance under section 37A above.

(2) The Director of Public Prosecutions shall decide whether there is sufficient evidence to charge the person with an offence.

(3) If he decides that there is sufficient evidence to charge the person with an offence, he shall decide—
   (a) whether or not the person should be charged and, if so, the offence with which he should be charged, and
   (b) whether or not the person should be given a caution and, if so, the offence in respect of which he should be given a caution.

(4) The Director of Public Prosecutions shall give written notice of his decision to an officer involved in the investigation of the offence.

(5) If his decision is—
   (a) that there is not sufficient evidence to charge the person with an offence, or
   (b) that there is sufficient evidence to charge the person with an offence but that the person should not be charged with an offence or given a caution in respect of an offence,
   a custody officer shall give the person notice in writing that he is not to be prosecuted.

(6) If the decision of the Director of Public Prosecutions is that the person should be charged with an offence, or given a caution in respect of an offence, the person shall be charged or cautioned accordingly.

(7) But if his decision is that the person should be given a caution in respect of the offence and it proves not to be possible to give the person such a caution, he shall instead be charged with the offence.

(8) For the purposes of this section, a person is to be charged with an offence either—

(a) when he is in police detention after returning to a police station to answer bail or is otherwise in police detention at a police station, or

(b) in accordance with section 29 of the Criminal Justice Act 2003.

(9) In this section "caution" includes—

(a) a conditional caution within the meaning of Part 3 of the Criminal Justice Act 2003, and

(b) a warning or reprimand under section 65 of the Crime and Disorder Act 1998.

37C Breach of bail following release under section 37(7)(a)

(1) This section applies where—

(a) a person released on bail under section 37(7)(a) above or subsection (2)(b) below is arrested under section 46A below in respect of that bail, and

(b) at the time of his detention following that arrest at the police station mentioned in section 46A(2) below, notice under section 37B(4) above has not been given.

(2) The person arrested—

(a) shall be charged, or

(b) shall be released without charge, either on bail or without bail.

(3) The decision as to how a person is to be dealt with under subsection (2) above shall be that of a custody officer.

(4) A person released on bail under subsection (2)(b) above shall be released on bail subject to the same conditions (if any) which applied immediately before his arrest.

37D Release under section 37(7)(a): further provision

(1) Where a person is released on bail under section 37(7)(a) or section 37C(2)(b) above, a custody officer may subsequently appoint a different time, or an additional time, at which the person is to attend at the police station to answer bail.

(2) The custody officer shall give the person notice in writing of the exercise of the power under subsection (1).

(3) The exercise of the power under subsection (1) shall not affect the conditions (if any) to which bail is subject.

(4) Where a person released on bail under section 37(7)(a) or 37C(2)(b) above returns to a police station to answer bail or is otherwise in police detention at a police station, he may be kept in police detention to enable him to be dealt with in accordance with section 37B or 37C above or to enable the power under subsection (1) above to be exercised.

(5) If the person is not in a fit state to enable him to be so dealt with or to enable that power to be exercised, he may be kept in police detention until he is.

(6) Where a person is kept in police detention by virtue of subsection (4) or (5) above, section 37(1) to (3) and (7) above (and section 40(8) below so far as it relates to section 37(1) to (3)) shall not apply to the offence in connection with which he was released on bail under section 37(7)(a) or 37C(2)(b) above."

4. In section 40 (review of police detention) in subsection (9) after "37(9)" there is inserted "or 37D(5)".

5. In section 46A (power of arrest for failure to answer police bail) after subsection (1) insert—

"(1A) A person who has been released on bail under section 37(7)(a) or 37C(2)(b) above may be arrested without warrant by a constable if the constable has reasonable grounds for suspecting that the person has broken any of the conditions of bail."

6. (1) Section 47 (bail after arrest) is amended as follows.

(2) In subsection (1) (release on bail under Part 4 shall be release on bail granted in accordance with certain provisions of the Bail Act 1976) for "Subject to subsection (2) below" there is substituted "Subject to the following provisions of this section".

(3) In subsection (1A) (bail conditions may be imposed when a person is released under section 38(1)) after "section", in the first place where it occurs, there is inserted "37(7)(a) above or section".

(4) After that subsection there is inserted—

"(1B) No application may be made under section 5B of the Bail Act 1976 if a person is released on bail under section 37(7)(a) or 37C(2)(b) above.

(1C) Subsections (1D) to (1F) below apply where a person released on bail under section 37(7)(a) or 37C(2)(b) above is on bail subject to conditions.

(1D) The person shall not be entitled to make an application under section 43B of the Magistrates' Courts Act 1980.

(1E) A magistrates' court may, on an application by or on behalf of the person, vary the conditions of bail; and in this subsection "vary" has the same meaning as in the Bail Act 1976.

(1F) Where a magistrates' court varies the conditions of bail under subsection (1E) above, that bail shall not lapse but shall continue subject to the conditions as so varied."

SCHEDULE 3
ALLOCATION OF CASES TRIABLE EITHER WAY, AND SENDING CASES TO THE CROWN COURT ETC

Section 41

PART 1
PRINCIPAL AMENDMENTS

Magistrates' Courts Act 1980 (c. 43)

1. The Magistrates' Courts Act 1980 is amended as follows.

2. (1) Section 17A (initial indication as to plea) is amended as follows.

(2) For paragraph (b) of subsection (4) there is substituted—

"(b) he may (unless section 17D(2) below were to apply) be committed to the Crown Court under section 3 or (if applicable) 3A of the Powers of Criminal Courts (Sentencing) Act 2000 if the court is of such opinion as is mentioned in subsection (2) of the applicable section."

(3) After subsection (9) there is inserted—

"(10) If in respect of the offence the court receives a notice under section 51B or 51C of the Crime and Disorder Act 1998 (which relate to serious or complex fraud cases and to certain cases involving children respectively), the preceding provisions of this section and the provisions of section 17B below shall not apply, and the court shall proceed in relation to the offence in accordance with section 51 or, as the case may be, section 51A of that Act."

3. After section 17C there is inserted—

"17D Maximum penalty under section 17A(6) or 17B(2)(c) for certain offences

(1) If—
   (a) the offence is a scheduled offence (as defined in section 22(1) below);
   (b) the court proceeds in relation to the offence in accordance with section 17A(6) or 17B(2)(c) above; and
   (c) the court convicts the accused of the offence, the court shall consider whether, having regard to any representations made by him or by the prosecutor, the value involved (as defined in section 22(10) below) appears to the court to exceed the relevant sum (as specified for the purposes of section 22 below).

(2) If it appears to the court clear that the value involved does not exceed the relevant sum, or it appears to the court for any reason not clear whether the value involved does or does not exceed the relevant sum—
   (a) subject to subsection (4) below, the court shall not have power to impose on the accused in respect of the offence a sentence in excess of the limits mentioned in section 33(1)(a) below; and
   (b) sections 3 and 4 of the Powers of Criminal Courts (Sentencing) Act 2000 shall not apply as regards that offence.

(3) Subsections (9) to (12) of section 22 below shall apply for the purposes of this section as they apply for the purposes of that section (reading the reference to subsection (1) in section 22(9) as a reference to subsection (1) of this section).

(4) Subsection (2)(a) above does not apply to an offence under section 12A of the Theft Act 1968 (aggravated vehicle-taking).

17E Functions under sections 17A to 17D capable of exercise by single justice

(1) The functions of a magistrates' court under sections 17A to 17D above may be discharged by a single justice.

(2) Subsection (1) above shall not be taken as authorising—
   (a) the summary trial of an information (otherwise than in accordance with section 17A(6) or 17B(2)(c) above); or
   (b) the imposition of a sentence, by a magistrates' court composed of fewer than two justices."

4. In section 18 (initial procedure on information against adult for offence triable either way), for subsection (5) there is substituted—
   "(5) The functions of a magistrates' court under sections 19 to 23 below may be discharged by a single justice, but this subsection shall not be taken as authorising—
   (a) the summary trial of an information (otherwise than in accordance with section 20(7) below); or
   (b) the imposition of a sentence, by a magistrates' court composed of fewer than two justices."

5. For section 19 (court to begin by considering which mode of trial appears more suitable) there is substituted—

"19 Decision as to allocation

(1) The court shall decide whether the offence appears to it more suitable for summary trial or for trial on indictment.

(2) Before making a decision under this section, the court—

    (a) shall give the prosecution an opportunity to inform the court of the accused's previous convictions (if any); and

    (b) shall give the prosecution and the accused an opportunity to make representations as to whether summary trial or trial on indictment would be more suitable.

(3) In making a decision under this section, the court shall consider—

    (a) whether the sentence which a magistrates' court would have power to impose for the offence would be adequate; and

    (b) any representations made by the prosecution or the accused under subsection (2)(b) above,

and shall have regard to any allocation guidelines (or revised allocation guidelines) issued as definitive guidelines under section 170 of the Criminal Justice Act 2003.

(4) Where—

    (a) the accused is charged with two or more offences; and

    (b) it appears to the court that the charges for the offences could be joined in the same indictment or that the offences arise out of the same or connected circumstances,

subsection (3)(a) above shall have effect as if references to the sentence which a magistrates' court would have power to impose for the offence were a reference to the maximum aggregate sentence which a magistrates' court would have power to impose for all of the offences taken together.

(5) In this section any reference to a previous conviction is a reference to—

    (a) a previous conviction by a court in the United Kingdom; or

    (b) a previous finding of guilt in—

        (i) any proceedings under the Army Act 1955, the Air Force Act 1955 or the Naval Discipline Act 1957 (whether before a court-martial or any other court or person authorised under any of those Acts to award a punishment in respect of any offence); or

        (ii) any proceedings before a Standing Civilian Court.

(6) If, in respect of the offence, the court receives a notice under section 51B or 51C of the Crime and Disorder Act 1998 (which relate to serious or complex fraud cases and to certain cases involving children respectively), the preceding provisions of this section and sections 20, 20A and 21 below shall not apply, and the court shall proceed in relation to the offence in accordance with section 51(1) of that Act."

6. For section 20 (procedure where summary trial appears more suitable) there is substituted—

"20 Procedure where summary trial appears more suitable

(1) If the court decides under section 19 above that the offence appears to it more suitable for summary trial, the following provisions of this section shall apply (unless they are excluded by section 23 below).

(2) The court shall explain to the accused in ordinary language—

    (a) that it appears to the court more suitable for him to be tried summarily for the offence;

    (b) that he can either consent to be so tried or, if he wishes, be tried on indictment; and

    (c) in the case of a specified offence (within the meaning of section 224 of the Criminal Justice Act 2003), that if he is tried summarily and is convicted by the court, he may be committed for sentence to the Crown Court under section 3A of the Powers of Criminal Courts (Sentencing) Act 2000 if the committing court is of such opinion as is mentioned in subsection (2) of that section.

(3) The accused may then request an indication ("an indication of sentence") of whether a custodial sentence or non-custodial sentence would be more likely to be imposed if he were to be tried summarily for the offence and to plead guilty.

(4) If the accused requests an indication of sentence, the court may, but need not, give such an indication.

(5) If the accused requests and the court gives an indication of sentence, the court shall ask the accused whether he wishes, on the basis of the indication, to reconsider the indication of plea which was given, or is taken to have been given, under section 17A or 17B above.

(6) If the accused indicates that he wishes to reconsider the indication under section 17A or 17B above, the court shall ask the accused whether (if the offence were to proceed to trial) he would plead guilty or not guilty.

(7) If the accused indicates that he would plead guilty the court shall proceed as if—
   (a) the proceedings constituted from that time the summary trial of the information; and
   (b) section 9(1) above were complied with and he pleaded guilty under it.

(8) Subsection (9) below applies where—
   (a) the court does not give an indication of sentence (whether because the accused does not request one or because the court does not agree to give one);
   (b) the accused either—
       (i) does not indicate, in accordance with subsection (5) above, that he wishes; or
       (ii) indicates, in accordance with subsection (5) above, that he does not wish, to reconsider the indication of plea under section 17A or 17B above; or
   (c) the accused does not indicate, in accordance with subsection (6) above, that he would plead guilty.

(9) The court shall ask the accused whether he consents to be tried summarily or wishes to be tried on indictment and—
   (a) if he consents to be tried summarily, shall proceed to the summary trial of the information; and
   (b) if he does not so consent, shall proceed in relation to the offence in accordance with section 51(1) of the Crime and Disorder Act 1998.

20A Procedure where summary trial appears more suitable: supplementary

(1) Where the case is dealt with in accordance with section 20(7) above, no court (whether a magistrates' court or not) may impose a custodial sentence for the offence unless such a sentence was indicated in the indication of sentence referred to in section 20 above.

(2) Subsection (1) above is subject to sections 3A(4), 4(8) and 5(3) of the Powers of Criminal Courts (Sentencing) Act 2000.

(3) Except as provided in subsection (1) above—
   (a) an indication of sentence shall not be binding on any court (whether a magistrates' court or not); and
   (b) no sentence may be challenged or be the subject of appeal in any court on the ground that it is not consistent with an indication of sentence.

(4) Subject to section 20(7) above, the following shall not for any purpose be taken to constitute the taking of a plea—
   (a) asking the accused under section 20 above whether (if the offence were to proceed to trial) he would plead guilty or not guilty; or
   (b) an indication by the accused under that section of how he would plead.

(5) Where the court gives an indication of sentence under section 20 above, it shall cause each such indication to be entered in the register.

(6) In this section and in section 20 above, references to a custodial sentence are to a custodial sentence within the meaning of section 76 of the Powers of Criminal Courts (Sentencing) Act 2000, and references to a non-custodial sentence shall be construed accordingly."

7. For section 21 (procedure where trial on indictment appears more suitable) there is substituted—

"21 Procedure where trial on indictment appears more suitable

If the court decides under section 19 above that the offence appears to it more suitable for trial on indictment, the court shall tell the accused that the court has decided that it is more suitable for him to be tried on indictment, and shall proceed in relation to the offence in accordance with section 51(1) of the Crime and Disorder Act 1998."

8. (1) Section 23 (power of court, with consent of legally represented accused, to proceed in his absence) is amended as follows.

(2) In subsection (4)—

(a) for the words preceding paragraph (a) there is substituted "If the court decides under section 19 above that the offence appears to it more suitable for trial on indictment then- ", and

(b) in paragraph (b), for the words from "to inquire" to the end there is substituted "in relation to the offence in accordance with section 51(1) of the Crime and Disorder Act 1998.".

(3) For subsection (5) there is substituted—

"(5) If the court decides under section 19 above that the offence appears to it more suitable for trial on indictment, section 21 above shall not apply and the court shall proceed in relation to the offence in accordance with section 51(1) of the Crime and Disorder Act 1998."

9. (1) Section 24 (summary trial of information against child or young persons for indictable offence), as amended by section 42 of this Act, is amended as follows.

(2) For subsection (1) there is substituted—

"(1) Where a person under the age of 18 years appears or is brought before a magistrates' court on an information charging him with an indictable offence he shall, subject to sections 51 and 51A of the Crime and Disorder Act 1998 and to sections 24A and 24B below, be tried summarily."

(3) Subsections (1A) and (2) are omitted.

10. After section 24 there is inserted—

"24A Child or young person to indicate intention as to plea in certain cases

(1) This section applies where—

(a) a person under the age of 18 years appears or is brought before a magistrates' court on an information charging him with an offence other than one falling within section 51A(12) of the Crime and Disorder Act 1998 ("the 1998 Act"); and

(b) but for the application of the following provisions of this section, the court would be required at that stage, by virtue of section 51(7) or (8) or 51A(3)(b), (4) or (5) of the 1998 Act to determine, in relation to the offence, whether to send the person to the Crown Court for trial (or to determine any matter, the effect of which would be to determine whether he is sent to the Crown Court for trial).

(2) Where this section applies, the court shall, before proceeding to make any such determination as is referred to in subsection (1)(b) above (the "relevant determination"), follow the procedure set out in this section.

(3) Everything that the court is required to do under the following provisions of this section must be done with the accused person in court.

461

(4)   The court shall cause the charge to be written down, if this has not already been done, and to be read to the accused.

(5)   The court shall then explain to the accused in ordinary language that he may indicate whether (if the offence were to proceed to trial) he would plead guilty or not guilty, and that if he indicates that he would plead guilty—

    (a) the court must proceed as mentioned in subsection (7) below; and

    (b) (in cases where the offence is one mentioned in section 91(1) of the Powers of Criminal Courts (Sentencing) Act 2000) he may be sent to the Crown Court for sentencing under section 3B or (if applicable) 3C of that Act if the court is of such opinion as is mentioned in subsection (2) of the applicable section.

(6)   The court shall then ask the accused whether (if the offence were to proceed to trial) he would plead guilty or not guilty.

(7)   If the accused indicates that he would plead guilty, the court shall proceed as if—

    (a) the proceedings constituted from the beginning the summary trial of the information; and

    (b) section 9(1) above was complied with and he pleaded guilty under it, and, accordingly, the court shall not (and shall not be required to) proceed to make the relevant determination or to proceed further under section 51 or (as the case may be) section 51A of the 1998 Act in relation to the offence.

(8)   If the accused indicates that he would plead not guilty, the court shall proceed to make the relevant determination and this section shall cease to apply.

(9)   If the accused in fact fails to indicate how he would plead, for the purposes of this section he shall be taken to indicate that he would plead not guilty.

(10) Subject to subsection (7) above, the following shall not for any purpose be taken to constitute the taking of a plea—

    (a) asking the accused under this section whether (if the offence were to proceed to trial) he would plead guilty or not guilty;

    (b) an indication by the accused under this section of how he would plead.

24B Intention as to plea by child or young person: absence of accused

(1)   This section shall have effect where—

    (a) a person under the age of 18 years appears or is brought before a magistrates' court on an information charging him with an offence other than one falling within section 51A(12) of the Crime and Disorder Act 1998;

    (b) but for the application of the following provisions of this section, the court would be required at that stage to make one of the determinations referred to in paragraph (b) of section 24A(1) above ("the relevant determination");

    (c) the accused is represented by a legal representative;

    (d) if court considers that by reason of the accused's disorderly conduct before the court it is not practicable for proceedings under section 24A above to be conducted in his presence; and

    (e) the court considers that it should proceed in the absence of the accused.

(2)   In such a case—

    (a) the court shall cause the charge to be written down, if this has not already been done, and to be read to the representative;

    (b) the court shall ask the representative whether (if the offence were to proceed to trial) the accused would plead guilty or not guilty;

(c) if the representative indicates that the accused would plead guilty the court shall proceed as if the proceedings constituted from the beginning the summary trial of the information, and as if section 9(1) above was complied with and the accused pleaded guilty under it;

(d) if the representative indicates that the accused would plead not guilty the court shall proceed to make the relevant determination and this section shall cease to apply.

(3) If the representative in fact fails to indicate how the accused would plead, for the purposes of this section he shall be taken to indicate that the accused would plead not guilty.

(4) Subject to subsection (2)(c) above, the following shall not for any purpose be taken to constitute the taking of a plea—

(a) asking the representative under this section whether (if the offence were to proceed to trial) the accused would plead guilty or not guilty;

(b) an indication by the representative under this section of how the accused would plead.

24C Intention as to plea by child or young person: adjournment

(1) A magistrates' court proceeding under section 24A or 24B above may adjourn the proceedings at any time, and on doing so on any occasion when the accused is present may remand the accused.

(2) Where the court remands the accused, the time fixed for the resumption of proceedings shall be that at which he is required to appear or be brought before the court in pursuance of the remand or would be required to be brought before the court but for section 128(3A) below.

24D Functions under sections 24A to 24C capable of exercise by single justice

(1) The functions of a magistrates' court under sections 24A to 24C above may be discharged by a single justice.

(2) Subsection (1) above shall not be taken as authorising—

(a) the summary trial of an information (other than a summary trial by virtue of section 24A(7) or 24B(2)(c) above); or

(b) the imposition of a sentence, by a magistrates' court composed of fewer than two justices."

11. (1) Section 25 (power to change from summary trial to committal proceedings and vice versa), as amended by section 42 of this Act, is amended as follows.

(2) In subsection (1), for "(2) to (4)" there is substituted "(2) to (2D)".

(3) For subsection (2) there is substituted—

"(2) Where the court is required under section 20(9) above to proceed to the summary trial of the information, the prosecution may apply to the court for the offence to be tried on indictment instead.

(2A) An application under subsection (2) above—

(a) must be made before the summary trial begins; and

(b) must be dealt with by the court before any other application or issue in relation to the summary trial is dealt with.

(2B) The court may grant an application under subsection (2) above but only if it is satisfied that the sentence which a magistrates' court would have power to impose for the offence would be inadequate.

(2C) Where—

(a) the accused is charged on the same occasion with two or more offences; and

    (b) it appears to the court that they constitute or form part of a series of two or more offences of the same or a similar character,

subsection (2B) above shall have effect as if references to the sentence which a magistrates' court would have power to impose for the offence were a reference to the maximum aggregate sentence which a magistrates' court would have power to impose for all of the offences taken together.

   (2D) Where the court grants an application under subsection (2) above, it shall proceed in relation to the offence in accordance with section 51(1) of the Crime and Disorder Act 1998."

  (4) Subsections (3) to (8) are omitted.

12. For subsections (1) and (2) of section 26 (power to issue summons to accused in certain circumstances) there is substituted—

  "(1) Where, in the circumstances mentioned in section 23(1)(a) above, the court is not satisfied that there is good reason for proceeding in the absence of the accused, the justice or any of the justices of which the court is composed may issue a summons directed to the accused requiring his presence before the court.

  (2) In a case within subsection (1) above, if the accused is not present at the time and place appointed for the proceedings under section 19 or section 22(1) above, the court may issue a warrant for his arrest."

13. In section 33 (maximum penalties on summary conviction in pursuance of section 22), in subsection (1), paragraph (b) and the word "and" immediately preceding it are omitted.

14. Section 42 (restriction on justices sitting after dealing with bail) shall cease to have effect.

Crime and Disorder Act 1998 (c. 37)

15. The Crime and Disorder Act 1998 is amended as follows.

16. In section 50 (early administrative hearings), in subsection (1) (court may consist of single justice unless accused falls to be dealt with under section 51), the words "unless the accused falls to be dealt with under section 51 below" are omitted.

17. After section 50 there is inserted—

"50A Order of consideration for either-way offences

  (1) Where an adult appears or is brought before a magistrates' court charged with an either-way offence (the "relevant offence"), the court shall proceed in the manner described in this section.

  (2) If notice is given in respect of the relevant offence under section 51B or 51C below, the court shall deal with the offence as provided in section 51 below.

  (3) Otherwise—

    (a) if the adult (or another adult with whom the adult is charged jointly with the relevant offence) is or has been sent to the Crown Court for trial for an offence under section 51(2)(a) or 51(2)(c) below—

      (i) the court shall first consider the relevant offence under subsection (3), (4), (5) or, as the case may be, (6) of section 51 below and, where applicable, deal with it under that subsection;

     (ii) if the adult is not sent to the Crown Court for trial for the relevant offence by virtue of sub-paragraph (i) above, the court shall then proceed to deal with the relevant offence in accordance with sections 17A to 23 of the 1980 Act;

(b) in all other cases—

    (i)   the court shall first consider the relevant offence under sections 17A to 20 (excluding subsections (8) and (9) of section 20) of the 1980 Act;

    (ii) if, by virtue of sub-paragraph (i) above, the court would be required to proceed in relation to the offence as mentioned in section 17A(6), 17B(2)(c) or 20(7) of that Act (indication of guilty plea), it shall proceed as so required (and, accordingly, shall not consider the offence under section 51 or 51A below);

    (iii) if sub-paragraph (ii) above does not apply—

        (a) the court shall consider the relevant offence under sections 51 and 51A below and, where applicable, deal with it under the relevant section;

        (b) if the adult is not sent to the Crown Court for trial for the relevant offence by virtue of paragraph (a) of this sub-paragraph, the court shall then proceed to deal with the relevant offence as contemplated by section 20(9) or, as the case may be, section 21 of the 1980 Act.

(4) Subsection (3) above is subject to any requirement to proceed as mentioned in subsections (2) or (6)(a) of section 22 of the 1980 Act (certain offences where value involved is small).

(5) Nothing in this section shall prevent the court from committing the adult to the Crown Court for sentence pursuant to any enactment, if he is convicted of the relevant offence."

18. For section 51 (no committal proceedings for indictable-only offences) there is substituted—

"51 Sending cases to the Crown Court: adults

(1) Where an adult appears or is brought before a magistrates' court ("the court") charged with an offence and any of the conditions mentioned in subsection (2) below is satisfied, the court shall send him forthwith to the Crown Court for trial for the offence.

(2) Those conditions are—

    (a) that the offence is an offence triable only on indictment other than one in respect of which notice has been given under section 51B or 51C below;

    (b) the offence is an either-way offence and the court is required under section 20(9)(b), 21, 23(4)(b) or (5) or 25(2D) of the Magistrates' Courts Act 1980 to proceed in relation to the offence in accordance with subsection (1) above;

    (c) that notice is given to the court under section 51B or 51C below in respect of the offence.

(3) Where the court sends an adult for trial under subsection (1) above, it shall at the same time send him to the Crown Court for trial for any either-way or summary offence with which he is charged and which—

    (a) (if it is an either-way offence) appears to the court to be related to the offence mentioned in subsection (1) above; or

    (b) (if it is a summary offence) appears to the court to be related to the offence mentioned in subsection (1) above or to the either-way offence, and which fulfils the requisite condition (as defined in subsection (11) below).

(4) Where an adult who has been sent for trial under subsection (1) above subsequently appears or is brought before a magistrates' court charged with an either-way or summary offence which—

    (a) appears to the court to be related to the offence mentioned in subsection (1) above; and

    (b) (in the case of a summary offence) fulfils the requisite condition, the court may send him forthwith to the Crown Court for trial for the either-way or summary offence.

(5) Where—
   (a) the court sends an adult ("A") for trial under subsection (1) or (3) above;
   (b) another adult appears or is brought before the court on the same or a subsequent occasion charged jointly with A with an either-way offence; and
   (c) that offence appears to the court to be related to an offence for which A was sent for trial under subsection (1) or (3) above,
the court shall where it is the same occasion, and may where it is a subsequent occasion, send the other adult forthwith to the Crown Court for trial for the either-way offence.

(6) Where the court sends an adult for trial under subsection (5) above, it shall at the same time send him to the Crown Court for trial for any either-way or summary offence with which he is charged and which—
   (a) (if it is an either-way offence) appears to the court to be related to the offence for which he is sent for trial; and
   (b) (if it is a summary offence) appears to the court to be related to the offence for which he is sent for trial or to the either-way offence, and which fulfils the requisite condition.

(7) Where—
   (a) the court sends an adult ("A") for trial under subsection (1), (3) or (5) above; and
   (b) a child or young person appears or is brought before the court on the same or a subsequent occasion charged jointly with A with an indictable offence for which A is sent for trial under subsection (1), (3) or (5) above, or an indictable offence which appears to the court to be related to that offence,
the court shall, if it considers it necessary in the interests of justice to do so, send the child or young person forthwith to the Crown Court for trial for the indictable offence.

(8) Where the court sends a child or young person for trial under subsection (7) above, it may at the same time send him to the Crown Court for trial for any indictable or summary offence with which he is charged and which—
   (a) (if it is an indictable offence) appears to the court to be related to the offence for which he is sent for trial; and
   (b) (if it is a summary offence) appears to the court to be related to the offence for which he is sent for trial or to the indictable offence, and which fulfils the requisite condition.

(9) Subsections (7) and (8) above are subject to sections 24A and 24B of the Magistrates' Courts Act 1980 (which provide for certain cases involving children and young persons to be tried summarily).

(10) The trial of the information charging any summary offence for which a person is sent for trial under this section shall be treated as if the court had adjourned it under section 10 of the 1980 Act and had not fixed the time and place for its resumption.

(11) A summary offence fulfils the requisite condition if it is punishable with imprisonment or involves obligatory or discretionary disqualification from driving.

(12) In the case of an adult charged with an offence—
   (a) if the offence satisfies paragraph (c) of subsection (2) above, the offence shall be dealt with under subsection (1) above and not under any other provision of this section or section 51A below;
   (b) subject to paragraph (a) above, if the offence is one in respect of which the court is required to, or would decide to, send the adult to the Crown Court under—
     (i) subsection (5) above; or
     (ii) subsection (6) of section 51A below, the offence shall be dealt with under that subsection and not under any other provision of this section or section 51A below.

(13) The functions of a magistrates' court under this section, and its related functions under section 51D below, may be discharged by a single justice.

51A Sending cases to the Crown Court: children and young persons

(1) This section is subject to sections 24A and 24B of the Magistrates' Courts Act 1980 (which provide for certain offences involving children or young persons to be tried summarily).

(2) Where a child or young person appears or is brought before a magistrates' court ("the court") charged with an offence and any of the conditions mentioned in subsection (3) below is satisfied, the court shall send him forthwith to the Crown Court for trial for the offence.

(3) Those conditions are—
   (a) that the offence falls within subsection (12) below;
   (b) that the offence is such as is mentioned in subsection (1) of section 91 of the Powers of Criminal Courts (Sentencing) Act 2000 (other than one mentioned in paragraph (d) below in relation to which it appears to the court as mentioned there) and the court considers that if he is found guilty of the offence it ought to be possible to sentence him in pursuance of subsection (3) of that section;
   (c) that notice is given to the court under section 51B or 51C below in respect of the offence;
   (d) that the offence is a specified offence (within the meaning of section 224 of the Criminal Justice Act 2003) and it appears to the court that if he is found guilty of the offence the criteria for the imposition of a sentence under section 226(3) or 228(2) of that Act would be met.

(4) Where the court sends a child or young person for trial under subsection (2) above, it may at the same time send him to the Crown Court for trial for any indictable or summary offence with which he is charged and which—
   (a) (if it is an indictable offence) appears to the court to be related to the offence mentioned in subsection (2) above; or
   (b) (if it is a summary offence) appears to the court to be related to the offence mentioned in subsection (2) above or to the indictable offence, and which fulfils the requisite condition (as defined in subsection (9) below).

(5) Where a child or young person who has been sent for trial under subsection (2) above subsequently appears or is brought before a magistrates' court charged with an indictable or summary offence which—
   (a) appears to the court to be related to the offence mentioned in subsection (2) above; and
   (b) (in the case of a summary offence) fulfils the requisite condition, the court may send him forthwith to the Crown Court for trial for the indictable or summary offence.

(6) Where—
   (a) the court sends a child or young person ("C") for trial under subsection (2) or (4) above; and
   (b) an adult appears or is brought before the court on the same or a subsequent occasion charged jointly with C with an either-way offence for which C is sent for trial under subsection (2) or (4) above, or an either-way offence which appears to the court to be related to that offence,
   the court shall where it is the same occasion, and may where it is a subsequent occasion, send the adult forthwith to the Crown Court for trial for the either-way offence.

(7) Where the court sends an adult for trial under subsection (6) above, it shall at the same time send him to the Crown Court for trial for any either-way or summary offence with which he is charged and which—

    (a) (if it is an either-way offence) appears to the court to be related to the offence for which he was sent for trial; and

    (b) (if it is a summary offence) appears to the court to be related to the offence for which he was sent for trial or to the either-way offence, and which fulfils the requisite condition.

(8) The trial of the information charging any summary offence for which a person is sent for trial under this section shall be treated as if the court had adjourned it under section 10 of the 1980 Act and had not fixed the time and place for its resumption.

(9) A summary offence fulfils the requisite condition if it is punishable with imprisonment or involves obligatory or discretionary disqualification from driving.

(10) In the case of a child or young person charged with an offence—

    (a) if the offence satisfies any of the conditions in subsection (3) above, the offence shall be dealt with under subsection (2) above and not under any other provision of this section or section 51 above;

    (b) subject to paragraph (a) above, if the offence is one in respect of which the requirements of subsection (7) of section 51 above for sending the child or young person to the Crown Court are satisfied, the offence shall be dealt with under that subsection and not under any other provision of this section or section 51 above.

(11) The functions of a magistrates' court under this section, and its related functions under section 51D below, may be discharged by a single justice.

(12) An offence falls within this subsection if—

    (a) it is an offence of homicide; or

    (b) each of the requirements of section 51A(1) of the Firearms Act 1968 would be satisfied with respect to—

        (i) the offence; and

        (ii) the person charged with it, if he were convicted of the offence.

51B Notices in serious or complex fraud cases

(1) A notice may be given by a designated authority under this section in respect of an indictable offence if the authority is of the opinion that the evidence of the offence charged—

    (a) is sufficient for the person charged to be put on trial for the offence; and

    (b) reveals a case of fraud of such seriousness or complexity that it is appropriate that the management of the case should without delay be taken over by the Crown Court.

(2) That opinion must be certified by the designated authority in the notice.

(3) The notice must also specify the proposed place of trial, and in selecting that place the designated authority must have regard to the same matters as are specified in paragraphs (a) to (c) of section 51D(4) below.

(4) A notice under this section must be given to the magistrates' court at which the person charged appears or before which he is brought.

(5) Such a notice must be given to the magistrates' court before any summary trial begins.

(6) The effect of such a notice is that the functions of the magistrates' court cease in relation to the case, except—

    (a) for the purposes of section 51D below;

    (b) as provided by paragraph 2 of Schedule 3 to the Access to Justice Act 1999; and

    (c) as provided by section 52 below.

(7) The functions of a designated authority under this section may be exercised by an officer of the authority acting on behalf of the authority.

(8) A decision to give a notice under this section shall not be subject to appeal or liable to be questioned in any court (whether a magistrates' court or not).

(9) In this section "designated authority" means—

    (a) the Director of Public Prosecutions;

    (b) the Director of the Serious Fraud Office;

    (c) the Commissioners of the Inland Revenue;

    (d) the Commissioners of Customs and Excise; or

    (e) the Secretary of State.

51C Notices in certain cases involving children

(1) A notice may be given by the Director of Public Prosecutions under this section in respect of an offence falling within subsection (3) below if he is of the opinion—

    (a) that the evidence of the offence would be sufficient for the person charged to be put on trial for the offence;

    (b) that a child would be called as a witness at the trial; and

    (c) that, for the purpose of avoiding any prejudice to the welfare of the child, the case should be taken over and proceeded with without delay by the Crown Court.

(2) That opinion must be certified by the Director of Public Prosecutions in the notice.

(3) This subsection applies to an offence—

    (a) which involves an assault on, or injury or a threat of injury to, a person;

    (b) under section 1 of the Children and Young Persons Act 1933 (cruelty to persons under 16);

    (c) under the Sexual Offences Act 1956, the Protection of Children Act 1978 or the Sexual Offences Act 2003;

    (d) of kidnapping or false imprisonment, or an offence under section 1 or 2 of the Child Abduction Act 1984;

    (e) which consists of attempting or conspiring to commit, or of aiding, abetting, counselling, procuring or inciting the commission of, an offence falling within paragraph (a), (b), (c) or (d) above.

(4) Subsections (4), (5) and (6) of section 51B above apply for the purposes of this section as they apply for the purposes of that.

(5) The functions of the Director of Public Prosecutions under this section may be exercised by an officer acting on behalf of the Director.

(6) A decision to give a notice under this section shall not be subject to appeal or liable to be questioned in any court (whether a magistrates' court or not).

(7) In this section "child" means—

    (a) a person who is under the age of 17; or

    (b) any person of whom a video recording (as defined in section 63(1) of the Youth Justice and Criminal Evidence Act 1999) was made when he was under the age of 17 with a view to its admission as his evidence in chief in the trial referred to in subsection (1) above.

51D Notice of offence and place of trial

(1) The court shall specify in a notice—

    (a) the offence or offences for which a person is sent for trial under section 51 or 51A above; and

    (b) the place at which he is to be tried (which, if a notice has been given under section 51B above, must be the place specified in that notice).

(2) A copy of the notice shall be served on the accused and given to the Crown Court sitting at that place.

(3) In a case where a person is sent for trial under section 51 or 51A above for more than one offence, the court shall specify in that notice, for each offence—

    (a) the subsection under which the person is so sent; and

    (b) if applicable, the offence to which that offence appears to the court to be related.

(4) Where the court selects the place of trial for the purposes of subsection (1) above, it shall have regard to—

    (a) the convenience of the defence, the prosecution and the witnesses;

    (b) the desirability of expediting the trial; and

    (c) any direction given by or on behalf of the Lord Chief Justice with the concurrence of the Lord Chancellor under section 75(1) of the Supreme Court Act 1981.

51E Interpretation of sections 50A to 51D

For the purposes of sections 50A to 51D above—

    (a) "adult" means a person aged 18 or over, and references to an adult include a corporation;

    (b) "either-way offence" means an offence triable either way;

    (c) an either-way offence is related to an indictable offence if the charge for the either-way offence could be joined in the same indictment as the charge for the indictable offence;

    (d) a summary offence is related to an indictable offence if it arises out of circumstances which are the same as or connected with those giving rise to the indictable offence."

19. (1) After section 52 there is inserted—

"52A Restrictions on reporting

(1) Except as provided by this section, it shall not be lawful—

    (a) to publish in the United Kingdom a written report of any allocation or sending proceedings in England and Wales; or

    (b) to include in a relevant programme for reception in the United Kingdom a report of any such proceedings, if (in either case) the report contains any matter other than that permitted by this section.

(2) Subject to subsections (3) and (4) below, a magistrates' court may, with reference to any allocation or sending proceedings, order that subsection (1) above shall not apply to reports of those proceedings.

(3) Where there is only one accused and he objects to the making of an order under subsection (2) above, the court shall make the order if, and only if, it is satisfied, after hearing the representations of the accused, that it is in the interests of justice to do so.

(4) Where in the case of two or more accused one of them objects to the making of an order under subsection (2) above, the court shall make the order if, and only if, it is satisfied, after hearing the representations of the accused, that it is in the interests of justice to do so.

(5) An order under subsection (2) above shall not apply to reports of proceedings under subsection (3) or (4) above, but any decision of the court to make or not to make such an order may be contained in reports published or included in a relevant programme before the time authorised by subsection (6) below.

(6) It shall not be unlawful under this section to publish or include in a relevant programme a report of allocation or sending proceedings containing any matter other than that permitted by subsection (7) below—

    (a) where, in relation to the accused (or all of them, if there are more than one), the magistrates' court is required to proceed as mentioned in section 20(7) of the 1980 Act, after the court is so required;

    (b) where, in relation to the accused (or any of them, if there are more than one), the court proceeds other than as mentioned there, after conclusion of his trial or, as the case may be, the trial of the last to be tried.

(7) The following matters may be contained in a report of allocation or sending proceedings published or included in a relevant programme without an order under subsection (2) above before the time authorised by subsection (6) above—

    (a) the identity of the court and the name of the justice or justices;

    (b) the name, age, home address and occupation of the accused;

    (c) in the case of an accused charged with an offence in respect of which notice has been given to the court under section 51B above, any relevant business information;

    (d) the offence or offences, or a summary of them, with which the accused is or are charged;

    (e) the names of counsel and solicitors engaged in the proceedings;

    (f) where the proceedings are adjourned, the date and place to which they are adjourned;

    (g) the arrangements as to bail;

    (h) whether a right to representation funded by the Legal Services Commission as part of the Criminal Defence Service was granted to the accused or any of the accused.

(8) The addresses that may be published or included in a relevant programme under subsection (7) above are addresses—

    (a) at any relevant time; and

    (b) at the time of their publication or inclusion in a relevant programme.

(9) The following is relevant business information for the purposes of subsection (7) above—

    (a) any address used by the accused for carrying on a business on his own account;

    (b) the name of any business which he was carrying on on his own account at any relevant time;

    (c) the name of any firm in which he was a partner at any relevant time or by which he was engaged at any such time;

    (d) the address of any such firm;

    (e) the name of any company of which he was a director at any relevant time or by which he was otherwise engaged at any such time;

    (f) the address of the registered or principal office of any such company;

    (g) any working address of the accused in his capacity as a person engaged by any such company; and here "engaged" means engaged under a contract of service or a contract for services.

(10) Subsection (1) above shall be in addition to, and not in derogation from, the provisions of any other enactment with respect to the publication of reports of court proceedings.

(11) In this section—

"allocation or sending proceedings" means, in relation to an information charging an indictable offence—

471

(a) any proceedings in the magistrates' court at which matters are considered under any of the following provisions—
  (i) sections 19 to 23 of the 1980 Act;
  (ii) section 51, 51A or 52 above;
(b) any proceedings in the magistrates' court before the court proceeds to consider any matter mentioned in paragraph (a) above; and
(c) any proceedings in the magistrates' court at which an application under section 25(2) of the 1980 Act is considered;

"publish", in relation to a report, means publish the report, either by itself or as part of a newspaper or periodical, for distribution to the public;

"relevant programme" means a programme included in a programme service (within the meaning of the Broadcasting Act 1990);

"relevant time" means a time when events giving rise to the charges to which the proceedings relate occurred.

52B Offences in connection with reporting

(1) If a report is published or included in a relevant programme in contravention of section 52A above, each of the following persons is guilty of an offence—
  (a) in the case of a publication of a written report as part of a newspaper or periodical, any proprietor, editor or publisher of the newspaper or periodical;
  (b) in the case of a publication of a written report otherwise than as part of a newspaper or periodical, the person who publishes it;
  (c) in the case of the inclusion of a report in a relevant programme, any body corporate which is engaged in providing the service in which the programme is included and any person having functions in relation to the programme corresponding to those of the editor of a newspaper.
(2) A person guilty of an offence under this section is liable on summary conviction to a fine not exceeding level 5 on the standard scale.
(3) Proceedings for an offence under this section shall not, in England and Wales, be instituted otherwise than by or with the consent of the Attorney General.
(4) Proceedings for an offence under this section shall not, in Northern Ireland, be instituted otherwise than by or with the consent of the Attorney General for Northern Ireland.
(5) Subsection (11) of section 52A above applies for the purposes of this section as it applies for the purposes of that section.".
  (2) In section 121 (short title, commencement and extent)—
    (a) in subsection (6), after paragraph (b) there is inserted—
      "(bb) sections 52A and 52B;", and
    (b) in subsection (8), after "(5) above," there is inserted "sections 52A and 52B above,".
20. (1) Schedule 3 (procedure where persons are sent for trial under section 51 of the Crime and Disorder Act 1998) is amended as follows.
  (2) In paragraph 1(1)—
    (a) after "51" there is inserted "or 51A", and
    (b) in paragraph (b), for "subsection (7) of that section" there is substituted "section 51D(1) of this Act".
  (3) In paragraph 2—
    (a) in sub-paragraph (1)—
      (i) after "51" there is inserted "or 51A", and
      (ii) for "subsection (7) of that section" there is substituted "section 51D(1) of this Act", and

    (b) sub-paragraphs (4) and (5) are omitted.

(4) In paragraph 4, in sub-paragraph (1)(a), after "51" there is inserted "or 51A".

(5) In paragraph 5, in sub-paragraph (2), after "51" there is inserted "or 51A".

(6) Paragraph 6 is amended as follows—

    (a) in sub-paragraph (1), after "51" there is inserted "or 51A",

    (b) in sub-paragraph (2), for the words from the second "offence" to the end there is substituted "indictable offence for which he was sent for trial or, as the case may be, any of the indictable offences for which he was so sent", and

    (c) in sub-paragraph (9), for "indictable-only" there is substituted "indictable".

(7) In paragraph 7—

    (a) in sub-paragraph (1)(a), after "51" there is inserted "or 51A",

    (b) in sub-paragraph (1)(b), for "offence that is triable only on indictment" there is substituted "main offence",

    (c) in sub-paragraph (3), after "each" there is inserted "remaining",

    (d) in sub-paragraph (7), for "consider" there is substituted "decide", and

    (e) after sub-paragraph (8) there is inserted—

       "(9) In this paragraph, a "main offence" is—

          (a) an offence for which the person has been sent to the Crown Court for trial under section 51(1) of this Act; or

          (b) an offence—

             (i) for which the person has been sent to the Crown Court for trial under subsection (5) of section 51 or subsection (6) of section 51A of this Act ("the applicable subsection"); and

             (ii) in respect of which the conditions for sending him to the Crown Court for trial under the applicable subsection (as set out in paragraphs (a) to (c) of section 51(5) or paragraphs (a) and (b) of section 51A(6)) continue to be satisfied."

(8) In paragraph 8—

    (a) in sub-paragraph (1)(a), after "51" there is inserted "or 51A",

    (b) in sub-paragraph (1)(b), for "offence that is triable only on indictment" there is substituted "main offence (within the meaning of paragraph 7 above)",

    (c) in sub-paragraph (2)(a), after "each" there is inserted "remaining", and

    (d) in sub-paragraph (2)(d), for "consider" there is substituted "decide".

(9) In paragraph 9—

    (a) in sub-paragraph (1), for "consider" there is substituted "decide", and

    (b) for sub-paragraphs (2) and (3), there is substituted—

       "(2) Before deciding the question, the court—

          (a) shall give the prosecution an opportunity to inform the court of the accused's previous convictions (if any); and

          (b) shall give the prosecution and the accused an opportunity to make representations as to whether summary trial or trial on indictment would be more suitable.

      (3) In deciding the question, the court shall consider—

          (a) whether the sentence which a magistrates' court would have power to impose for the offence would be adequate; and

          (b) any representations made by the prosecution or the accused under sub-paragraph (2)(b) above, and shall have regard to any allocation guidelines (or revised allocation guidelines) issued as definitive guidelines under section 170 of the Criminal Justice Act 2003.

(4) Where—

    (a) the accused is charged on the same occasion with two or more offences; and

    (b) it appears to the court that they constitute or form part of a series of two or more offences of the same or a similar character;

sub-paragraph (3)(a) above shall have effect as if references to the sentence which a magistrates' court would have power to impose for the offence were a reference to the maximum aggregate sentence which a magistrates' court would have power to impose for all of the offences taken together.

(5) In this paragraph any reference to a previous conviction is a reference to—

    (a) a previous conviction by a court in the United Kingdom, or

    (b) a previous finding of guilt in—

        (i) any proceedings under the Army Act 1955, the Air Force Act 1955 or the Naval Discipline Act 1957 (whether before a court-martial or any other court or person authorised under any of those Acts to award a punishment in respect of any offence), or

        (ii) any proceedings before a Standing Civilian Court."

(10) In paragraph 10—

    (a) for sub-paragraph (2), there is substituted—

    "(2) The court shall explain to the accused in ordinary language—

        (a) that it appears to the court more suitable for him to be tried summarily for the offence;

        (b) that he can either consent to be so tried or, if he wishes, be tried on indictment; and

        (c) in the case of a specified offence (within the meaning of section 224 of the Criminal Justice Act 2003), that if he is tried summarily and is convicted by the court, he may be committed for sentence to the Crown Court under section 3A of the Powers of Criminal Courts (Sentencing) Act 2000 if the committing court is of such opinion as is mentioned in subsection (2) of that section.", and

    (b) in sub-paragraph (3), for "by a jury" there is substituted "on indictment".

(11) In paragraph 11, in sub-paragraph (a), for "by a jury" there is substituted "on indictment".

(12) Paragraph 12 shall cease to have effect.

(13) In paragraph 13—

    (a) in sub-paragraph (1)(a), after "51" there is inserted "or 51A",

    (b) in sub-paragraph (1)(b), for "offence that is triable only on indictment" there is substituted "main offence",

    (c) in sub-paragraph (2), the words from "unless" to the end are omitted, and

    (d) for sub-paragraph (3) there is substituted—

    "(3) In this paragraph, a "main offence" is—

        (a) an offence for which the child or young person has been sent to the Crown Court for trial under section 51A(2) of this Act; or

        (b) an offence—

            (i) for which the child or young person has been sent to the Crown Court for trial under subsection (7) of section 51 of this Act; and

            (ii) in respect of which the conditions for sending him to the Crown Court for trial under that subsection (as set out in paragraphs (a) and (b) of that subsection) continue to be satisfied."

(14) In paragraph 15, in each of sub-paragraphs (3) and (4), for "considered" there is substituted "decided".

Powers of Criminal Courts (Sentencing) Act 2000 (c. 6)

21. The Powers of Criminal Courts (Sentencing) Act 2000 is amended as follows.

22. For section 3 (committal for sentence on summary trial of offence triable either way) there is substituted—

"3 Committal for sentence on indication of guilty plea to serious offence triable either way

(1) Subject to subsection (4) below, this section applies where—

    (a) a person aged 18 or over appears or is brought before a magistrates' court ("the court") on an information charging him with an offence triable either way ("the offence");

    (b) he or his representative indicates under section 17A or (as the case may be) 17B of the Magistrates' Courts Act 1980 (initial procedure: accused to indicate intention as to plea), but not section 20(7) of that Act, that he would plead guilty if the offence were to proceed to trial; and

    (c) proceeding as if section 9(1) of that Act were complied with and he pleaded guilty under it, the court convicts him of the offence.

(2) If the court is of the opinion that—

    (a) the offence; or

    (b) the combination of the offence and one or more offences associated with it,

was so serious that the Crown Court should, in the court's opinion, have the power to deal with the offender in any way it could deal with him if he had been convicted on indictment, the court may commit him in custody or on bail to the Crown Court for sentence in accordance with section 5(1) below.

(3) Where the court commits a person under subsection (2) above, section 6 below (which enables a magistrates' court, where it commits a person under this section in respect of an offence, also to commit him to the Crown Court to be dealt with in respect of certain other offences) shall apply accordingly.

(4) This section does not apply in relation to an offence as regards which this section is excluded by section 17D of the Magistrates' Courts Act 1980 (certain offences where value involved is small).

(5) The preceding provisions of this section shall apply in relation to a corporation as if—

    (a) the corporation were an individual aged 18 or over; and

    (b) in subsection (2) above, the words "in custody or on bail" were omitted."

23. After section 3 there is inserted—

"3A Committal for sentence of dangerous adult offenders

(1) This section applies where on the summary trial of a specified offence triable either way a person aged 18 or over is convicted of the offence.

(2) If, in relation to the offence, it appears to the court that the criteria for the imposition of a sentence under section 225(3) or 227(2) of the Criminal Justice Act 2003 would be met, the court must commit the offender in custody or on bail to the Crown Court for sentence in accordance with section 5(1) below.

(3) Where the court commits a person under subsection (2) above, section 6 below (which enables a magistrates' court, where it commits a person under this section in respect of an offence, also to commit him to the Crown Court to be dealt with in respect of certain other offences) shall apply accordingly.

(4) In reaching any decision under or taking any step contemplated by this section—

(a) the court shall not be bound by any indication of sentence given in respect of the offence under section 20 of the Magistrates' Courts Act 1980 (procedure where summary trial appears more suitable); and

(b) nothing the court does under this section may be challenged or be the subject of any appeal in any court on the ground that it is not consistent with an indication of sentence.

(5) Nothing in this section shall prevent the court from committing a specified offence to the Crown Court for sentence under section 3 above if the provisions of that section are satisfied.

(6) In this section, references to a specified offence are to a specified offence within the meaning of section 224 of the Criminal Justice Act 2003.

3B Committal for sentence on indication of guilty plea by child or young person

(1) This section applies where—

(a) a person aged under 18 appears or is brought before a magistrates' court ("the court") on an information charging him with an offence mentioned in subsection (1) of section 91 below ("the offence");

(b) he or his representative indicates under section 24A or (as the case may be) 24B of the Magistrates' Courts Act 1980 (child or young person to indicate intention as to plea in certain cases) that he would plead guilty if the offence were to proceed to trial; and

(c) proceeding as if section 9(1) of that Act were complied with and he pleaded guilty under it, the court convicts him of the offence.

(2) If the court is of the opinion that—

(a) the offence; or

(b) the combination of the offence and one or more offences associated with it, was such that the Crown Court should, in the court's opinion, have power to deal with the offender as if the provisions of section 91(3) below applied, the court may commit him in custody or on bail to the Crown Court for sentence in accordance with section 5A(1) below.

(3) Where the court commits a person under subsection (2) above, section 6 below (which enables a magistrates' court, where it commits a person under this section in respect of an offence, also to commit him to the Crown Court to be dealt with in respect of certain other offences) shall apply accordingly.

3C Committal for sentence of dangerous young offenders

(1) This section applies where on the summary trial of a specified offence a person aged under 18 is convicted of the offence.

(2) If, in relation to the offence, it appears to the court that the criteria for the imposition of a sentence under section 226(3) or 228(2) of the Criminal Justice Act 2003 would be met, the court must commit the offender in custody or on bail to the Crown Court for sentence in accordance with section 5A(1) below.

(3) Where the court commits a person under subsection (2) above, section 6 below (which enables a magistrates' court, where it commits a person under this section in respect of an offence, also to commit him to the Crown Court to be dealt with in respect of certain other offences) shall apply accordingly.

(4) Nothing in this section shall prevent the court from committing a specified offence to the Crown Court for sentence under section 3B above if the provisions of that section are satisfied.

(5) In this section, references to a specified offence are to a specified offence within the meaning of section 224 of the Criminal Justice Act 2003."

24. (1) Section 4 (committal for sentence on indication of guilty plea to offence triable either way) is amended as follows.

(2) For subsection (1)(b), there is substituted—

"(b) he or (where applicable) his representative indicates under section 17A, 17B or 20(7) of the Magistrates' Courts Act 1980 that he would plead guilty if the offence were to proceed to trial; and".

(3) In subsection (1)(c), for "the Magistrates' Courts Act 1980" there is substituted "that Act".

(4) After subsection (1) there is inserted—

"(1A) But this section does not apply to an offence as regards which this section is excluded by section 17D of that Act (certain offences where value involved is small)."

(5) For subsection (3), there is substituted—

"(3) If the power conferred by subsection (2) above is not exercisable but the court is still to determine to, or to determine whether to, send the offender to the Crown Court for trial under section 51 or 51A of the Crime and Disorder Act 1998 for one or more related offences—

(a) it shall adjourn the proceedings relating to the offence until after it has made those determinations; and

(b) if it sends the offender to the Crown Court for trial for one or more related offences, it may then exercise that power."

(6) In subsection (4)(b), after "section 3(2)" there is inserted "or, as the case may be, section 3A(2)".

(7) After subsection (7) there is inserted—

"(8) In reaching any decision under or taking any step contemplated by this section—

(a) the court shall not be bound by any indication of sentence given in respect of the offence under section 20 of the Magistrates' Courts Act 1980 (procedure where summary trial appears more suitable); and

(b) nothing the court does under this section may be challenged or be the subject of any appeal in any court on the ground that it is not consistent with an indication of sentence."

25. After section 4 there is inserted—

"4A Committal for sentence on indication of guilty plea by child or young person with related offences

(1) This section applies where—

(a) a person aged under 18 appears or brought before a magistrates' court ("the court") on an information charging him with an offence mentioned in subsection (1) of section 91 below ("the offence");

(b) he or his representative indicates under section 24A or (as the case may be) 24B of the Magistrates' Courts Act 1980 (child or young person to indicate intention as to plea in certain cases) that he would plead guilty if the offence were to proceed to trial; and

(c) proceeding as if section 9(1) of that Act were complied with and he pleaded guilty under it, the court convicts him of the offence.

(2) If the court has sent the offender to the Crown Court for trial for one or more related offences, that is to say one or more offences which, in its opinion, are related to the offence, it may commit him in custody or on bail to the Crown Court to be dealt with in respect of the offence in accordance with section 5A(1) below.

(3) If the power conferred by subsection (2) above is not exercisable but the court is still to determine to, or to determine whether to, send the offender to the Crown Court for trial

under section 51 or 51A of the Crime and Disorder Act 1998 for one or more related offences—

(a) it shall adjourn the proceedings relating to the offence until after it has made those determinations; and

(b) if it sends the offender to the Crown Court for trial for one or more related offences, it may then exercise that power.

(4) Where the court—

(a) under subsection (2) above commits the offender to the Crown Court to be dealt with in respect of the offence; and

(b) does not state that, in its opinion, it also has power so to commit him under section 3B(2) or, as the case may be, section 3C(2) above,

section 5A(1) below shall not apply unless he is convicted before the Crown Court of one or more of the related offences.

(5) Where section 5A(1) below does not apply, the Crown Court may deal with the offender in respect of the offence in any way in which the magistrates' court could deal with him if it had just convicted him of the offence.

(6) Where the court commits a person under subsection (2) above, section 6 below (which enables a magistrates' court, where it commits a person under this section in respect of an offence, also to commit him to the Crown Court to be dealt with in respect of certain other offences) shall apply accordingly.

(7) Section 4(7) above applies for the purposes of this section as it applies for the purposes of that

26. For section 5 (power of Crown Court on committal for sentence under sections 3 and 4) there is substituted—

"5 Power of Crown Court on committal for sentence under sections 3, 3A and 4

(1) Where an offender is committed by a magistrates' court for sentence under section 3, 3A or 4 above, the Crown Court shall inquire into the circumstances of the case and may deal with the offender in any way in which it could deal with him if he had just been convicted of the offence on indictment before the court.

(2) In relation to committals under section 4 above, subsection (1) above has effect subject to section 4(4) and (5) above.

(3) Section 20A(1) of the Magistrates' Courts Act 1980 (which relates to the effect of an indication of sentence under section 20 of that Act) shall not apply in respect of any specified offence (within the meaning of section 224 of the Criminal Justice Act 2003)—

(a) in respect of which the offender is committed under section 3A(2) above; or

(b) in respect of which—

(i) the offender is committed under section 4(2) above; and

(ii) the court states under section 4(4) above that, in its opinion, it also has power to commit the offender under section 3A(2) above."

27. After section 5 there is inserted—

"5A Power of Crown Court on committal for sentence under section 3B, 3C and 4A

(1) Where an offender in committed by a magistrates' court for sentence under section 3B, 3C or 4A above, the Crown Court shall inquire into the circumstances of the case and may deal with the offender in any way in which it could deal with him in he had just been convicted of the offence on indictment before the court.

(2) In relation to committals under section 4A above, subsection(1) above has effect subject to section 4A(4) and (5) above."

28. In section 6 (committal for sentence in certain cases where offender committed in respect of another offence), in subsection (4)(b), for "3 and 4" there is substituted "3 to 4A".

PART 2
MINOR AND CONSEQUENTIAL AMENDMENTS

Territorial Waters Jurisdiction Act 1878 (c. 73)

29. In section 4 of the Territorial Waters Jurisdiction Act 1878 (provisions as to procedure), in the paragraph beginning "Proceedings before a justice of the peace", for the words from the beginning to "his trial" there is substituted—
"Any stage of proceedings—
(a) before the summary trial of the offence; or
(b) before the offender has been sent for trial for the offence,".

Bankers' Books Evidence Act 1879 (c. 11)

30. (1) The Bankers' Books Evidence Act 1879 is amended as follows.
(2) In section 4 (proof that book is a banker's book), the paragraph beginning "Where the proceedings" is omitted.
(3) In section 5 (verification of copy), the paragraph beginning "Where the proceedings" is omitted.

Explosive Substances Act 1883 (c. 3)

31. In section 6 of the Explosive Substances Act 1883 (inquiry by Attorney-General, and apprehension of absconding witnesses), subsection (3) is omitted.

Criminal Justice Act 1925 (c. 86)

32. In section 49 of the Criminal Justice Act 1925 (interpretation, etc), subsection (2) is omitted.

Children and Young Persons Act 1933 (c. 12)

33. In section 42 of the Children and Young Persons Act 1933 (extension of power to take deposition of child or young person), in subsection (2)(a), for "committed" in both places there is substituted "sent".

Administration of Justice (Miscellaneous Provisions) Act 1933 (c. 36)

34. (1) Section 2 of the Administration of Justice (Miscellaneous Provisions) Act 1933 (procedure for indictment of offenders) is amended as follows.
(2) In subsection (2)—
(a) in paragraph (a), for "committed" there is substituted "sent",

    (b) paragraphs (aa) to (ac) are omitted,

    (c) for paragraph (i) there is substituted—

        "(i) where the person charged has been sent for trial, the bill of indictment against him may include, either in substitution for or in addition to any count charging an offence specified in the notice under section 57D(1) of the Crime and Disorder Act 1998, any counts founded on material which, in pursuance of regulations made under paragraph 1 of Schedule 3 to that Act, was served on the person charged, being counts which may lawfully be joined in the same indictment;",

    (d) paragraphs (iA) and (iB) are omitted,

    (e) in paragraph (ii), for "the committal" there is substituted "such notice", and

    (f) the words from "and in paragraph (iA)" to the end are omitted.

  (3) In subsection (3)(b), for "committed" there is substituted "sent".

Criminal Justice Act 1948 (c. 58)

35. (1) The Criminal Justice Act 1948 is amended as follows.

  (2) In section 27 (remand and committal of persons aged 17 to 20), in subsection (1), for "commits him for trial or" there is substituted "sends him to the Crown Court for trial or commits him there for".

  (3) In section 41 (evidence by certificate), subsection (5A) is omitted.

  (4) In section 80 (interpretation), the definition of "Court of summary jurisdiction" is omitted.

Prison Act 1952 (c. 52)

36. Until their repeal by (respectively) section 59 of, and paragraph 10(a)(ii) of Schedule 7 to, the Criminal Justice and Court Services Act 2000, paragraph (a) of subsection (1), and paragraphs (b) and (c) of subsection (2), of section 43 of the Prison Act 1952 (remand centres, detention centres and youth custody centres) are to have effect as if references to being committed for trial were references to being sent for trial.

Army Act 1955 (3 & 4 Eliz. 2 c. 18)

37. In section 187 of the Army Act 1955 (proceedings before a civil court where persons suspected of illegal absence), at the end of subsection (4) there is inserted—

"The references in this subsection to provisions of the Magistrates' Courts Act 1980 and to corresponding enactments are to be taken to refer to those provisions and enactments as if no amendment to them had been made by the Criminal Justice Act 2003."

Air Force Act 1955 (3 & 4 Eliz. 2 c. 19)

38. In section 187 of the Air Force Act 1955 (proceedings before a civil court where persons suspected of illegal absence), at the end of subsection (4) there is inserted—

"The references in this subsection to provisions of the Magistrates' Courts Act 1980 and to corresponding enactments are to be taken to refer to those provisions and enactments as if no amendment to them had been made by the Criminal Justice Act 2003."

Geneva Conventions Act 1957 (c. 52)

39. In section 5 of the Geneva Conventions Act 1957 (reduction of sentence and custody of protected persons)—
    (a) in subsection (1), for "committal" there is substituted "having been sent",
    (b) in subsection (2), for "committal", where it first appears, there is substituted "having been sent".

Naval Discipline Act 1957 (c. 53)

40. In section 109 of the Naval Discipline Act 1957 (proceedings before summary courts), at the end of subsection (4) there is inserted—
    "The references in this subsection to provisions are to be taken to refer to those provisions as if no amendment to them had been made by the Criminal Justice Act 2003."

Backing of Warrants (Republic of Ireland) Act 1965 (c. 45)

41. In paragraph 4 of the Schedule to the Backing of Warrants (Republic of Ireland) Act 1965 (supplementary procedures as to proceedings under section 2)—
    (a) the words "and section 2 of the Poor Prisoners Defence Act 1930 (legal aid before examining justices)" are omitted, and
    (b) for "it had determined not to commit for trial" there is substituted "the offence were to be dealt with summarily and the court had dismissed the information".

Criminal Procedure (Attendance of Witnesses) Act 1965 (c. 69)

42. In section 2 of the Criminal Procedure (Attendance of Witnesses) Act 1965 (issue of witness summons on application to Crown Court)—
    (a) for subsection (4) there is substituted—
        "(4) Where a person has been sent for trial for any offence to which the proceedings concerned relate, an application must be made as soon as is reasonably practicable after service on that person, in pursuance of regulations made under paragraph 1 of Schedule 3 to the Crime and Disorder Act 1998, of the documents relevant to that offence.", and
    (b) subsection (5) is omitted.

Criminal Justice Act 1967 (c. 80)

43. (1) The Criminal Justice Act 1967 is amended as follows.
    (2) In section 9 (proof by written statement), in subsection (1), the words ", other than committal proceedings," are omitted.
    (3) In section 36 (interpretation), in subsection (1), the definition of "committal proceedings" is omitted.

Criminal Appeal Act 1968 (c. 19)

44. (1) The Criminal Appeal Act 1968 is amended as follows.

(2) In section 1 (right of appeal), in subsection (3), for "committed him" there is substituted "sent him to the Crown Court".

(3) In section 9 (appeal against sentence following conviction on indictment), in subsection (2), the words from "section 41" to "either way offence" are omitted.

Firearms Act 1968 (c. 27)

45. In Schedule 6 to the Firearms Act 1968 (prosecution and punishment of offences), in Part 2, paragraph 3 is omitted.

Theft Act 1968 (c. 60)

46. In section 27 of the Theft Act 1968 (evidence and procedure on charge of theft or handling stolen goods), subsection (4A) is omitted.

Criminal Justice Act 1972 (c. 71)

47. In section 46 of the Criminal Justice Act 1972 (admissibility of written statements outside England and Wales), subsections (1A) to (1C) are omitted.

Bail Act 1976 (c. 63)

48. (1) The Bail Act 1976 is amended as follows.

(2) In section 3 (general provisions)—

(a) in subsection (8)—

(i) for "committed" there is substituted "sent", and

(ii) after "for trial or" there is inserted "committed him on bail to the Crown Court", and

(b) subsections (8A) and (8B), and the subsection (10) inserted by paragraph 12(b) of Schedule 9 to the Criminal Justice and Public Order Act 1994 (c. 33), are omitted.

(3) In section 5 (supplementary provisions about decisions on bail)—

(a) in subsection (6)(a), for "committing" there is substituted "sending", and

(b) in subsection (6A)(a)—

(i) after "under" there is inserted "section 52(5) of the Crime and Disorder Act 1998,",

(ii) sub-paragraph (i) is omitted,

(iii) after sub-paragraph (ii) there is inserted—

"(iia) section 17C (intention as to plea: adjournment);", and

(iv) at the end of sub-paragraph (iii) there is inserted "or

(iv) section 24C (intention as to plea by child or young person: adjournment),".

(4) In section 6 (offence of absconding by person released on bail), in subsection (6)(b), for "commits" there is substituted "sends".

(5) In section 9 (offence of agreeing to indemnify sureties in criminal proceedings), in subsection (3)(b), for "commits" there is substituted "sends".

Interpretation Act 1978 (c. 30)

49. In Schedule 1 to the Interpretation Act 1978 (words and expressions defined)—

(a) in the definition of "Committed for trial", paragraph (a) is omitted,

(b) after the entry for "Secretary of State" there is inserted—
""Sent for trial" means, in relation to England and Wales, sent by a magistrates' court to the Crown Court for trial pursuant to section 51 or 51A of the Crime and Disorder Act 1998."

Customs and Excise Management Act 1979 (c. 2)

50. In section 147 of the Customs and Excise Management Act 1979 (proceedings for offences), subsection (2) is omitted.

Magistrates' Courts Act 1980 (c. 43)

51. (1) The Magistrates' Courts Act 1980 is amended as follows.
   (2) In section 2, as substituted by the Courts Act 2003 (trial of summary offences), in sub-section (2), for "as examining justices over" there is substituted "under sections 51 and 51A of the Crime and Disorder Act 1998 in respect of".
   (3) Sections 4 to 8 (which relate to committal proceedings) shall cease to have effect and the cross-heading preceding section 4 is omitted.
   (4) In section 8B, as inserted by the Courts Act 2003 (effect of rulings at pre-trial hearing), in subsection (6), the words "commits or" are omitted.
   (5) In section 29 (power of magistrates' court to remit a person under 17 for trial to a juve-nile court in certain circumstances), in subsection (2)(b)(i), for the words from "pro-ceeds" to the end there is substituted "sends him to the Crown Court for trial under section 51 or 51A of the Crime and Disorder Act 1998; and".
   (6) The following sections shall cease to have effect—
      (a) section 97A (summons or warrant as to committal proceedings),
      (b) section 103 (evidence of persons under 14 in committal proceedings for assault, sexual offences etc), and
      (c) section 106 (false written statements tendered in evidence).
   (7) In section 128 (remand in custody or on bail)—
      (a) in subsection (1)(b), the words "inquiring into or" are omitted,
      (b) in subsection (1A)(a)—
         (i) "5," is omitted, and
         (ii) for "or 18(4)" there is substituted ", 18(4) or 24C",
      (c) in subsection (3A)—
         (i) "5," is omitted, and
         (ii) for "or 18(4)" there is substituted ", 18(4) or 24C",
      (d) in subsection (3C)(a)—
         (i) "5," is omitted, and
         (ii) for "or 18(4)" there is substituted ", 18(4) or 24C", and
      (e) in subsection (3E)(a)—
         (i) "5," is omitted, and
         (ii) for "or 18(4)" there is substituted ", 18(4) or 24C".
   (8) In section 129 (further remand), in subsection (4)—
      (a) for "commits a person" there is substituted "sends a person to the Crown Court", and
      (b) for "committed" there is substituted "sent".
   (9) In section 130 (transfer of remand hearings), in subsection (1)—
      (a) "5," is omitted, and

    (b) for "or 18(4)" there is substituted ", 18(4) or 24C".

(10) In section 145 (rules: supplementary provisions), in subsection (1), paragraph (f) is omitted.

(11) In section 150 (interpretation of other terms), in subsection (1), the definition of "committal proceedings" is omitted.

(12) In section 155 (short title, extent and commencement), in subsection (2)(a), the words "8 (except subsection (9))" are omitted.

(13) In Schedule 3 (corporations)—

    (a) in paragraph 2, sub-paragraph (a) is omitted,

    (b) in paragraph 6, for "inquiry into, and trial of," there is substituted "trial of".

(14) In Schedule 5 (transfer of remand hearings)—

    (a) paragraph 2 is omitted, and

    (b) in paragraph 5, for "5, 10 or 18(4)" there is substituted "10, 17C, 18(4) or 24C".

Criminal Attempts Act 1981 (c. 47)

52. In section 2 of the Criminal Attempts Act 1981 (application of procedures and other provisions to offences under section 1), in subsection (2)(g), the words "or committed for trial" are omitted.

Contempt of Court Act 1981 (c. 49)

53. In section 4 of the Contempt of Court Act 1981 (contemporary reports of proceedings), in subsection (3), for paragraph (b) there is substituted—

"(b) in the case of a report of allocation or sending proceedings of which publication is permitted by virtue only of subsection (6) of section 52A of the Crime and Disorder Act 1998 ("the 1998 Act"), if published as soon as practicable after publication is so permitted;

(c) in the case of a report of an application of which publication is permitted by virtue only of sub-paragraph (5) or (7) of paragraph 3 of Schedule 3 to the 1998 Act, if published as soon as practicable after publication is so permitted."

Supreme Court Act 1981 (c. 54)

54. (1) The Supreme Court Act 1981 is amended as follows.

(2) In section 76 (committal for trial: alteration of place of trial)—

    (a) in subsection (1), for the words from "varying" (where it first appears) to "to Crown Court)" there is substituted "substituting some other place for the place specified in a notice under section 51D(1) of the Crime and Disorder Act 1998 (a "section 51D notice")",

    (b) in subsection (3), for the words "fixed by the magistrates' court, as specified in a notice under a relevant transfer provision" there is substituted "specified in a section 51D notice",

    (c) subsection (5) is omitted, and

    (d) in the heading, for "Committal" there is substituted "Sending".

(3) In section 77 (committal for trial: date of trial)—

    (a) in subsection (1), for "committal for trial or the giving of a notice of transfer under a relevant transfer provision" there is substituted "being sent for trial",

    (b) in subsection (2), for "committed by a magistrates' court or in respect of whom a notice of transfer under a relevant transfer provision has been given" there is substituted "sent for trial",

    (c) in subsection (3), for "of committal for trial or of a notice of transfer" there is substituted "when the defendant is sent for trial",

    (d) subsection (4) is omitted, and

    (e) in the heading, for "Committal" there is substituted "Sending".

(4) In section 80 (process to compel appearance), in subsection (2), for "committed" there is substituted "sent".

(5) In section 81—

    (a) in subsection (1)—

        (i) in paragraph (a)—

            (a) the words "who has been committed in custody for appearance before the Crown Court or in relation to whose case a notice of transfer has been given under a relevant transfer provision or" are omitted, and

            (b) after "51" there is inserted "or 51A",

        (ii) in paragraph (g), sub-paragraph (i) is omitted, and

        (b) subsection (7) is omitted.

Mental Health Act 1983 (c. 20)

55. (1) The Mental Health Act 1983 is amended as follows.

(2) In section 43 (power of magistrates' court to commit for restriction order), for subsection (4) there is substituted—

    "(4) The powers of a magistrates' court under section 3 or 3B of the Powers of Criminal Courts (Sentencing) Act 2000 (which enable such a court to commit an offender to the Crown Court where the court is of the opinion, or it appears to the court, as mentioned in the section in question) shall also be exercisable by a magistrates' court where it is of that opinion (or it so appears to it) unless a hospital order is made in the offender's case with a restriction order."

(3) In section 52 (further provisions as to persons remanded by magistrates' courts)—

    (a) in subsection (2), for "committed" there is substituted "sent",

    (b) in subsection (5), for "committed" there is substituted "sent",

    (c) in subsection (6), for "committed" there is substituted "sent", and

    (d) in subsection (7), for the words from "inquire" to "1980" there is substituted "send him to the Crown Court for trial under section 51 or 51A of the Crime and Disorder Act 1998", and in paragraph (b) of that subsection, the words "where the court proceeds under subsection (1) of that section" are omitted.

Police and Criminal Evidence Act 1984 (c. 60)

56. (1) The Police and Criminal Evidence Act 1984 is amended as follows.

(2) In section 62 (intimate samples), in subsection (10)—

    (a) sub-paragraph (i) of paragraph (a) is omitted, and

    (b) in paragraph (aa), for sub-paragraphs (i) and (ii) there is substituted "paragraph 2 of Schedule 3 to the Crime and Disorder Act 1998 (applications for dismissal); and".

(3) In section 71 (microfilm copies), the paragraph beginning "Where the proceedings" is omitted.

(4) In section 76 (confessions), subsection (9) is omitted.

(5) In section 78 (exclusion of unfair evidence), subsection (3) is omitted.

Prosecution of Offences Act 1985 (c. 23)

57. (1) The Prosecution of Offences Act 1985 is amended as follows.

(2) In section 7A (powers of non-legal staff), for subsection (6) there is substituted—

"(6) This section applies to an offence if it is triable only on indictment or is an offence for which the accused has been sent for trial."

(3) In section 16 (defence costs)—

(a) in subsection (1), paragraph (b) is omitted, and

(b) in subsection (2)—

(i) in paragraph (a), for "committed" there is substituted "sent", and

(ii) paragraph (aa) is omitted, and

(c) subsection (12) is omitted.

(4) In section 21 (interpretation), in subsection (6)(b), for "committed" there is substituted "sent".

(5) In section 22 (power of Secretary of State to set time limits in relation to preliminary stages of criminal proceedings), in subsection (11)—

(a) in paragraph (a) of the definition of "appropriate court", for "committed for trial, sent for trial under section 51 of the Crime and Disorder Act 1998" there is substituted "sent for trial",

(b) for the definition of "custody of the Crown Court" there is substituted—

" "custody of the Crown Court" includes custody to which a person is committed in pursuance of—

(a) section 43A of the Magistrates' Courts Act 1980 (magistrates' court dealing with a person brought before it following his arrest in pursuance of a warrant issued by the Crown Court); or

(b) section 52 of the Crime and Disorder Act 1998 (provisions supplementing section 51);".

(6) In section 23 (discontinuance of proceedings in magistrates' court), in subsection (2), for paragraphs (a) to (c) there is substituted—

"(a) any stage of the proceedings after the court has begun to hear evidence for the prosecution at a summary trial of the offence; or

(b) any stage of the proceedings after the accused has been sent for trial for the offence."

(7) In section 23A (discontinuance of proceedings after accused has been sent for trial)—

(a) in paragraph (b) of subsection (1), the words from "under" to "1998" are omitted, and

(b) in subsection (2), for "51(7)" there is substituted "51D(1)".

Criminal Justice Act 1987 (c. 38)

58. (1) The Criminal Justice Act 1987 is amended as follows.

(2) Sections 4 to 6 (which relate to the transfer of cases to the Crown Court) shall cease to have effect.

(3) In section 11 (restrictions on reporting)—

(a) in subsection (2), paragraph (a) is omitted,

(b) subsection (3) is omitted,

(c) in subsection (7), "(3)," is omitted,

    (d) in subsection (8), "(3)," is omitted,

    (e) subsections (9) and (10) are omitted,

    (f) in subsection (11), paragraphs (a) and (d) are omitted.

Coroners Act 1988 (c. 13)

59. (1) The Coroners Act 1988 is amended as follows.

   (2) In section 16 (adjournment of inquest in event of criminal proceedings)—

    (a) in subsection (1)(b), for "charged before examining justices with" there is substituted "sent for trial for", and

    (b) for subsection (8) there is substituted—

       "(8) In this section, the "relevant criminal proceedings" means the proceedings—

         (a) before a magistrates' court to determine whether the person charged is to be sent to the Crown Court for trial; or

         (b) before any court to which that person is sent for trial."

   (3) In section 17 (provisions supplementary to section 16)—

    (a) in subsection (2), for "committed" there is substituted "sent", and

    (b) in subsection (3)(b), for "committed" there is substituted "sent".

Criminal Justice Act 1988 (c. 33)

60. (1) The Criminal Justice Act 1988 is amended as follows.

   (2) In section 23 (first-hand hearsay), subsection (5) is omitted.

   (3) In section 24 (business etc documents), subsection (5) is omitted.

   (4) In section 26 (statements in certain documents), the paragraph beginning "This section shall not apply" is omitted.

   (5) In section 27 (proof of statements contained in documents), the paragraph beginning "This section shall not apply" is omitted.

   (6) In section 30 (expert reports), subsection (4A) is omitted.

   (7) In section 40 (power to join in indictment count for common assault etc), in subsection (1)—

    (a) the words "were disclosed to a magistrates' court inquiring into the offence as examining justices or" are omitted,

    (b) after "51" there is inserted "or 51A".

   (8) Section 41 (power of Crown Court to deal with summary offence where person committed for either way offence) shall cease to have effect.

Road Traffic Offenders Act 1988 (c. 53)

61. (1) The Road Traffic Offenders Act 1988 is amended as follows.

   (2) In section 11 (evidence by certificate as to driver, user or owner), subsection (3A) is omitted.

   (3) In section 13 (admissibility of records as evidence), subsection (7) is omitted.

   (4) In section 16 (documentary evidence as to specimens), subsection (6A) is omitted.

   (5) In section 20 (speeding offences etc), subsection (8A) is omitted.

Criminal Justice Act 1991 (c. 53)

62. (1) The Criminal Justice Act 1991 is amended as follows.

   (2) Section 53 (notices of transfer in certain cases involving children) shall cease to have effect.

(3) Schedule 6 (notices of transfer: procedures in lieu of committal) shall cease to have effect.

Sexual Offences (Amendment) Act 1992 (c. 34)

63. In section 6 of the Sexual Offences (Amendment) Act 1992 (interpretation), in subsection (3)(c), for "commits him" there is substituted "sends him to the Crown Court".

Criminal Justice and Public Order Act 1994 (c. 33)

64. (1) The Criminal Justice and Public Order Act 1994 is amended as follows.
    (2) In section 34 (effect of accused's failure to mention facts when questioned or charged), in subsection (2)—
      (a) paragraph (a) is omitted, and
      (b) in paragraph (b), for sub-paragraphs (i) and (ii), there is substituted "paragraph 2 of Schedule 3 to the Crime and Disorder Act 1998".
    (3) In section 36 (effect of accused's failure or refusal to account for objects, substances or marks), in subsection (2)—
      (a) paragraph (a) is omitted, and
      (b) in paragraph (b), for sub-paragraphs (i) and (ii), there is substituted "paragraph 2 of Schedule 3 to the Crime and Disorder Act 1998".
    (4) In section 37 (effect of accused's failure or refusal to account for presence at a particular place), in subsection (2)—
      (a) paragraph (a) is omitted, and
      (b) in paragraph (b), for sub-paragraphs (i) and (ii), there is substituted "paragraph 2 of Schedule 3 to the Crime and Disorder Act 1998".

Reserve Forces Act 1996 (c. 14)

65. In Schedule 2 to the Reserve Forces Act 1996 (deserters and absentees without leave), in paragraph 3, after sub-paragraph (2) there is inserted—
    "(2A) The reference in sub-paragraph (2) to provisions of the Magistrates' Courts Act 1980 is to be taken to refer to those provisions as if no amendment to them had been made by the Criminal Justice Act 2003."

Criminal Procedure and Investigations Act 1996 (c. 25)

66. (1) The Criminal Procedure and Investigations Act 1996 is amended as follows.
    (2) In section 1 (application of this Part), in subsection (2)—
      (a) paragraphs (a) to (c) are omitted, and
      (b) in paragraph (cc), the words from "under" to the end are omitted.
    (3) In section 5 (compulsory disclosure by accused)—
      (a) in subsection (1), for "(2) to" there is substituted "(3A) and",
      (b) subsections (2) and (3) are omitted, and
      (c) in subsection (3A), in paragraph (b), for "subsection (7) of section 51" there is substituted "subsection (1) of section 51D".
    (4) In section 13 (time limits: transitional), in subsection (1), paragraphs (a) to (c) of the modified section 3(8) are omitted.
    (5) In section 21 (common law rules as to disclosure), in subsection (3), for paragraphs (b) and (c) there is substituted—
      "(b) the accused is sent for trial (where this Part applies by virtue of section 1(2)(cc)),".

(6) In section 28 (introduction to Part 3), in subsection (1)—
    (a) for paragraph (a) there is substituted—
        "(a) on or after the appointed day the accused is sent for trial for the offence concerned,", and
    (b) paragraph (b) is omitted.

(7) In section 39 (meaning of pre-trial hearing), in subsection (1), for paragraph (a) there is substituted—
    "(a) after the accused has been sent for trial for the offence, and".

(8) Section 68 (use of written statements and depositions at trial) and Schedule 2 (statements and depositions) shall cease to have effect.

Sexual Offences (Protected Material) Act 1997 (c. 39)

67. In section 9 of the Sexual Offences (Protected Material) Act 1997 (modification and amendment of certain enactments), subsection (1) is omitted.

Crime and Disorder Act 1998 (c. 37)

68. The Crime and Disorder Act 1998 is amended as follows.
69. In section 52 (provisions supplementing section 51)—
    (a) in subsection (1), after "51" there is inserted "or 51A",
    (b) in subsection (3), after "51" there is inserted "or 51A",
    (c) in subsection (5), after "51" there is inserted "or 51A",
    (d) in subsection (6), after "51" there is inserted "or 51A", and
    (e) in the heading, after "51" there is inserted "and 51A".
70. In section 121 (short title, commencement and extent), in subsection (8), before "paragraphs 7(1)" there is inserted "paragraph 3 of Schedule 3 to this Act, section 52(6) above so far as relating to that paragraph,".
71. In paragraph 3 of Schedule 3 (reporting restrictions)—
    (a) in each of paragraphs (a) and (b) of sub-paragraph (1), for "Great Britain" there is substituted "the United Kingdom",
    (b) sub-paragraph (8), after paragraph (b) there is inserted—
        "(bb) where the application made by the accused under paragraph 2(1) above relates to a charge for an offence in respect of which notice has been given to the court under section 51B of this Act, any relevant business information;",
    (c) after sub-paragraph (9) there is inserted—
        "(9A) The following is relevant business information for the purposes of sub-paragraph (8) above—
            (a) any address used by the accused for carrying on a business on his own account;
            (b) the name of any business which he was carrying on on his own account at any relevant time;
            (c) the name of any firm in which he was a partner at any relevant time or by which he was engaged at any such time;
            (d) the address of any such firm;
            (e) the name of any company of which he was a director at any relevant time or by which he was otherwise engaged at any such time;
            (f) the address of the registered or principal office of any such company;
            (g) any working address of the accused in his capacity as a person engaged by any such company; and here "engaged" means engaged under a contract of service or a contract for services.", and

    (d) after sub-paragraph (11) there is inserted—

       "(11A) Proceedings for an offence under this paragraph shall not, in Northern Ireland, be instituted otherwise than by or with the consent of the Attorney General for Northern Ireland."

72. In paragraph 4 of Schedule 3 (power of justice to take depositions etc), in sub-paragraph (12), for the definition of "the relevant date" there is substituted—

    " "the relevant date" means the expiry of the period referred to in paragraph 1(1) above.

Youth Justice and Criminal Evidence Act 1999 (c. 23)

73. (1) The Youth Justice and Criminal Evidence Act 1999 is amended as follows.

    (2) In section 27 (video recorded evidence in chief), subsection (10) is omitted.

    (3) In section 42 (interpretation and application of section 41), in subsection (3)—

      (a) paragraphs (a) and (b) are omitted, and

      (b) in paragraph (c), after "51" there is inserted "or 51A".

Powers of Criminal Courts (Sentencing) Act 2000 (c. 6)

74. (1) The Powers of Criminal Courts (Sentencing) Act 2000 is amended as follows.

    (2) In section 8 (power and duty to remit young offenders to youth courts for sentence), in subsection (2), for paragraph (a) there is substituted—

      "(a) if the offender was sent to the Crown Court for trial under section 51 or 51A of the Crime and Disorder Act 1998, to a youth court acting for the place where he was sent to the Crown Court for trial;".

    (3) In section 89 (restriction on imposing imprisonment), in subsection (2)—

      (a) in paragraph (b), the words "trial or" are omitted, and

      (b) in paragraph (c), after "51" there is inserted "or 51A".

    (4) In section 140 (enforcement of fines etc), in subsection (1)(b)—

      (a) the words "was committed to the Crown Court to be tried or dealt with or by which he" are omitted, and

      (b) after "51" there is inserted "or 51A".

    (5) In section 148 (restitution orders), in subsection (6), for paragraph (b) there is substituted—

      "(b) such documents as were served on the offender in pursuance of regulations made under paragraph 1 of Schedule 3 to the Crime and Disorder Act 1998."

    (6) In Schedule 11, paragraph 9 is omitted.

Proceeds of Crime Act 2002 (c. 29)

75. (1) The Proceeds of Crime Act 2002 is amended as follows.

    (2) In section 6 (making of confiscation order), in subsection (2)(b), for "section 3, 4 or 6" there is substituted "section 3, 3A, 3B, 3C, 4, 4A or 6".

    (3) In section 27 (defendant absconds after being convicted or committed), in subsection (2)(b), for "section 3, 4 or 6" there is substituted "section 3, 3A, 3B, 3C, 4, 4A or 6".

    (4) In section 70 (committal by magistrates' court), in subsection (5), after "way)" there is inserted "or under section 3B(2) of that Act (committal of child or young person)".

SCHEDULE 4
QUALIFYING OFFENCES FOR PURPOSES OF SECTION 62   Section 62

PART 1
LIST OF OFFENCES

Offences Against the Person
Murder

1. Murder.

Attempted murder

2. An offence under section 1 of the Criminal Attempts Act 1981 (c. 47) of attempting to commit murder.

Soliciting murder

3. An offence under section 4 of the Offences against the Person Act 1861 (c. 100).

Manslaughter

4. Manslaughter.

Wounding or causing grievous bodily harm with intent

5. An offence under section 18 of the Offences against the Person Act 1861 (c. 100).

Kidnapping

6. Kidnapping.

Sexual Offences
Rape

7. An offence under section 1 of the Sexual Offences Act 1956 (c. 69) or section 1 of the Sexual Offences Act 2003 (c. 42).

Attempted rape

8. An offence under section 1 of the Criminal Attempts Act 1981 (c. 47) of attempting to commit an offence under section 1 of the Sexual Offences Act 1956 or section 1 of the Sexual Offences Act 2003.

Intercourse with a girl under thirteen

9. An offence under section 5 of the Sexual Offences Act 1956.

491

Incest by a man with a girl under thirteen

10. An offence under section 10 of the Sexual Offences Act 1956 alleged to have been committed with a girl under thirteen.

Assault by penetration

11. An offence under section 2 of the Sexual Offences Act 2003.

Causing a person to engage in sexual activity without consent

12. An offence under section 4 of the Sexual Offences Act 2003 where it is alleged that the activity caused involved penetration within subsection (4)(a) to (d) of that section.

Rape of a child under thirteen

13. An offence under section 5 of the Sexual Offences Act 2003.

Attempted rape of a child under thirteen

14. An offence under section 1 of the Criminal Attempts Act 1981 of attempting to commit an offence under section 5 of the Sexual Offences Act 2003.

Assault of a child under thirteen by penetration

15. An offence under section 6 of the Sexual Offences Act 2003.

Causing a child under thirteen to engage in sexual activity

16. An offence under section 8 of the Sexual Offences Act 2003 (c. 42) where it is alleged that an activity involving penetration within subsection (2)(a) to (d) of that section was caused.

Sexual activity with a person with a mental disorder impeding choice

17. An offence under section 30 of the Sexual Offences Act 2003 where it is alleged that the touching involved penetration within subsection (3)(a) to (d) of that section.

Causing or inciting a person with a mental disorder impeding choice to engage in sexual activity

18. An offence under section 31 of the Sexual Offences Act 2003 where it is alleged that an activity involving penetration within subsection (3)(a) to (d) of that section was caused.

Drugs Offences
Unlawful importation of Class A drug

19. An offence under section 50(2) of the Customs and Excise Management Act 1979 (c. 2) alleged to have been committed in respect of a Class A drug (as defined by section 2 of the Misuse of Drugs Act 1971 (c. 38)).

Unlawful exportation of Class A drug

20. An offence under section 68(2) of the Customs and Excise Management Act 1979 alleged to have been committed in respect of a Class A drug (as defined by section 2 of the Misuse of Drugs Act 1971).

Fraudulent evasion in respect of Class A drug

21. An offence under section 170(1) or (2) of the Customs and Excise Management Act 1979 alleged to have been committed in respect of a Class A drug (as defined by section 2 of the Misuse of Drugs Act 1971).

Producing or being concerned in production of Class A drug

22. An offence under section 4(2) of the Misuse of Drugs Act 1971 alleged to have been committed in relation to a Class A drug (as defined by section 2 of that Act).

Supplying or offering to supply Class A drug

23. An offence under section 4(3) of the Misuse of Drugs Act 1971 alleged to have been committed in relation to a Class A drug (as defined by section 2 of that Act).

Theft Offences
Robbery

24. An offence under section 8(1) of the Theft Act 1968 (c. 60) where it is alleged that, at some time during the commission of the offence, the defendant had in his possession a firearm or imitation firearm (as defined by section 57 of the Firearms Act 1968 (c. 27)).

Criminal Damage Offences
Arson endangering life

25. An offence under section 1(2) of the Criminal Damage Act 1971 (c. 48) alleged to have been committed by destroying or damaging property by fire.

Causing explosion likely to endanger life or property

26. An offence under section 2 of the Explosive Substances Act 1883 (c. 3).

Intent or conspiracy to cause explosion likely to endanger life or property

27. An offence under section 3(1)(a) of the Explosive Substances Act 1883.

War Crimes and Terrorism
Genocide, crimes against humanity and war crimes

28. An offence under section 51 or 52 of the International Criminal Court Act 2001 (c. 17).

Grave breaches of the Geneva Conventions

29. An offence under section 1 of the Geneva Conventions Act 1957 (c. 52).

Directing terrorist organisation

30. An offence under section 56 of the Terrorism Act 2000 (c. 11).

Hostage-taking

31. An offence under section 1 of the Taking of Hostages Act 1982 (c. 28).

Hijacking and Other Offences Relating to Aviation, Maritime and Rail Security
Hijacking of aircraft

32. An offence under section 1 of the Aviation Security Act 1982 (c. 36).

Destroying, damaging or endangering the safety of an aircraft

33. An offence under section 2 of the Aviation Security Act 1982.

Hijacking of ships

34. An offence under section 9 of the Aviation and Maritime Security Act 1990 (c. 31).

Seizing or exercising control of fixed platforms

35. An offence under section 10 of the Aviation and Maritime Security Act 1990.

Destroying ships or fixed platforms or endangering their safety

36. An offence under section 11 of the Aviation and Maritime Security Act 1990.

Hijacking of Channel Tunnel trains

37. An offence under article 4 of the Channel Tunnel (Security) Order 1994 (S.I.1994/570).

Seizing or exercising control of the Channel Tunnel system

38. An offence under article 5 of the Channel Tunnel (Security) Order 1994 (S.I.1994/570).

Conspiracy
Conspiracy

39. An offence under section 1 of the Criminal Law Act 1977 (c. 45) of conspiracy to commit an offence listed in this Part of this Schedule.

PART 2
SUPPLEMENTARY

40. A reference in Part 1 of this Schedule to an offence includes a reference to an offence of aiding, abetting, counselling or procuring the commission of the offence.
41. A reference in Part 1 of this Schedule to an enactment includes a reference to the enactment as enacted and as amended from time to time.

SCHEDULE 5
QUALIFYING OFFENCES FOR PURPOSES OF PART 10   Section 75

PART 1
LIST OF OFFENCES FOR ENGLAND AND WALES

Offences Against the Person
Murder

1. Murder.

Attempted murder

2. An offence under section 1 of the Criminal Attempts Act 1981 (c. 47) of attempting to commit murder.

Soliciting murder

3. An offence under section 4 of the Offences against the Person Act 1861 (c. 100).

Manslaughter

4. Manslaughter.

Kidnapping

5. Kidnapping.

Sexual Offences
Rape

6. An offence under section 1 of the Sexual Offences Act 1956 (c. 69) or section 1 of the Sexual Offences Act 2003 (c. 42).

Attempted rape

7. An offence under section 1 of the Criminal Attempts Act 1981 of attempting to commit an offence under section 1 of the Sexual Offences Act 1956 or section 1 of the Sexual Offences Act 2003.

Intercourse with a girl under thirteen

8. An offence under section 5 of the Sexual Offences Act 1956.

Incest by a man with a girl under thirteen

9. An offence under section 10 of the Sexual Offences Act 1956 alleged to have been committed with a girl under thirteen.

Assault by penetration

10. An offence under section 2 of the Sexual Offences Act 2003 (c. 42).

Causing a person to engage in sexual activity without consent

11. An offence under section 4 of the Sexual Offences Act 2003 where it is alleged that the activity caused involved penetration within subsection (4)(a) to (d) of that section.

Rape of a child under thirteen

12. An offence under section 5 of the Sexual Offences Act 2003.

Attempted rape of a child under thirteen

13. An offence under section 1 of the Criminal Attempts Act 1981 (c. 47) of attempting to commit an offence under section 5 of the Sexual Offences Act 2003.

Assault of a child under thirteen by penetration

14. An offence under section 6 of the Sexual Offences Act 2003.

Causing a child under thirteen to engage in sexual activity

15. An offence under section 8 of the Sexual Offences Act 2003 where it is alleged that an activity involving penetration within subsection (2)(a) to (d) of that section was caused.

Sexual activity with a person with a mental disorder impeding choice

16. An offence under section 30 of the Sexual Offences Act 2003 where it is alleged that the touching involved penetration within subsection (3)(a) to (d) of that section.

Causing a person with a mental disorder impeding choice to engage in sexual activity

17. An offence under section 31 of the Sexual Offences Act 2003 where it is alleged that an activity involving penetration within subsection (3)(a) to (d) of that section was caused.

Drugs Offences
Unlawful importation of Class A drug

18. An offence under section 50(2) of the Customs and Excise Management Act 1979 (c. 2) alleged to have been committed in respect of a Class A drug (as defined by section 2 of the Misuse of Drugs Act 1971 (c. 38)).

Unlawful exportation of Class A drug

19. An offence under section 68(2) of the Customs and Excise Management Act 1979 alleged to have been committed in respect of a Class A drug (as defined by section 2 of the Misuse of Drugs Act 1971).

Fraudulent evasion in respect of Class A drug

20. An offence under section 170(1) or (2) of the Customs and Excise Management Act 1979 (c. 2) alleged to have been committed in respect of a Class A drug (as defined by section 2 of the Misuse of Drugs Act 1971 (c. 38)).

Producing or being concerned in production of Class A drug

21. An offence under section 4(2) of the Misuse of Drugs Act 1971 alleged to have been committed in relation to a Class A drug (as defined by section 2 of that Act).

Criminal Damage Offences
Arson endangering life

22. An offence under section 1(2) of the Criminal Damage Act 1971 (c. 48) alleged to have been committed by destroying or damaging property by fire.

Causing explosion likely to endanger life or property

23. An offence under section 2 of the Explosive Substances Act 1883 (c. 3).

Intent or conspiracy to cause explosion likely to endanger life or property

24. An offence under section 3(1)(a) of the Explosive Substances Act 1883.

War Crimes and Terrorism
Genocide, crimes against humanity and war crimes

25. An offence under section 51 or 52 of the International Criminal Court Act 2001 (c. 17).

Grave breaches of the Geneva Conventions

26. An offence under section 1 of the Geneva Conventions Act 1957 (c. 52).

Directing terrorist organisation

27. An offence under section 56 of the Terrorism Act 2000 (c. 11).

Hostage-taking

28. An offence under section 1 of the Taking of Hostages Act 1982 (c. 28).

Conspiracy
Conspiracy

29. An offence under section 1 of the Criminal Law Act 1977 (c. 45) of conspiracy to commit an offence listed in this Part of this Schedule.

PART 2
LIST OF OFFENCES FOR NORTHERN IRELAND

Offences Against the Person
Murder

30. Murder.

Attempted murder

31. An offence under Article 3 of the Criminal Attempts and Conspiracy (Northern Ireland) Order 1983 of attempting to commit murder.

Soliciting murder

32. An offence under section 4 of the Offences against the Person Act 1861 (c. 100).

Manslaughter

33. Manslaughter.

Kidnapping

34. Kidnapping.

Sexual Offences
Rape

35. Rape.

Attempted rape

36. An offence under section 2 of the Attempted Rape, etc., Act (Northern Ireland) 1960.

Intercourse with a girl under fourteen

37. An offence under section 4 of the Criminal Law Amendment Act 1885 (c. 69) of unlawfully and carnally knowing a girl under fourteen.

Incest by a man with a girl under fourteen

38. An offence under section 1(1) of the Punishment of Incest Act 1908 (c.45) alleged to have been committed with a girl under fourteen.

Drugs Offences
Unlawful importation of Class A drug

39. An offence under section 50(2) of the Customs and Excise Management Act 1979 (c. 2) alleged to have been committed in respect of a Class A drug (as defined by section 2 of the Misuse of Drugs Act 1971 (c. 38)).

Unlawful exportation of Class A drug

40. An offence under section 68(2) of the Customs and Excise Management Act 1979 alleged to have been committed in respect of a Class A drug (as defined by section 2 of the Misuse of Drugs Act 1971).

Fraudulent evasion in respect of Class A drug

41. An offence under section 170(1) or (2) of the Customs and Excise Management Act 1979 alleged to have been committed in respect of a Class A drug (as defined by section 2 of the Misuse of Drugs Act 1971).

Producing or being concerned in production of Class A drug

42. An offence under section 4(2) of the Misuse of Drugs Act 1971 alleged to have been committed in respect of a Class A drug (as defined by section 2 of that Act).

Criminal Damage Offences
Arson endangering life

43. An offence under Article 3(2) of the Criminal Damage (Northern Ireland) Order 1977 alleged to have been committed by destroying or damaging property by fire.

Causing explosion likely to endanger life or property

44. An offence under section 2 of the Explosive Substances Act 1883 (c. 3).

Intent or conspiracy to cause explosion likely to endanger life or property

45. An offence under section 3(1)(a) of the Explosive Substances Act 1883.

War Crimes and Terrorism
Genocide, crimes against humanity and war crimes

46. An offence under section 51 or 52 of the International Criminal Court Act 2001 (c. 17).

Grave breaches of the Geneva Conventions

47. An offence under section 1 of the Geneva Conventions Act 1957 (c. 52).

Directing terrorist organisation

48. An offence under section 56 of the Terrorism Act 2000 (c. 11).

Hostage-taking

49. An offence under section 1 of the Taking of Hostages Act 1982 (c. 28).

Conspiracy
Conspiracy

50. An offence under Article 9 of the Criminal Attempts and Conspiracy (Northern Ireland) Order 1983 of conspiracy to commit an offence listed in this Part of this Schedule.

PART 3
SUPPLEMENTARY

51. A reference in this Schedule to an offence includes a reference to an offence of aiding, abetting, counselling or procuring the commission of the offence.
52. A reference in this Schedule to an enactment includes a reference to the enactment as enacted and as amended from time to time.

SCHEDULE 6
EVIDENCE OF BAD CHARACTER: ARMED FORCES

Section 113

1. Sections 98 to 106, 109, 110 and 112, in so far as they are not applied in relation to proceedings before service courts by provision contained in or made under any other Act, have effect in relation to such proceedings (whether in the United Kingdom or elsewhere) as they have effect in relation to criminal proceedings.

2. Section 103, as it applies in relation to proceedings before service courts, has effect with the substitution in subsection (4)(a) of "charge sheet" for "written charge or indictment".

3. (1) Section 107 has effect in relation to proceedings before courts-martial (whether in the United Kingdom or elsewhere) with the following modifications.

   (2) In subsection (1)—

      (a) for "judge and jury" substitute "court-martial";

      (b) for "the court is satisfied" substitute "the judge advocate is satisfied";

      (c) for the words after paragraph (b) substitute "the judge advocate must either direct the court to acquit the defendant of the offence or, if he considers that there ought to be a retrial, dissolve the court."

   (3) In subsection (2)—

      (a) for "jury" substitute "court";

      (b) for "the court is satisfied" substitute "the judge advocate is satisfied".

   (4) In subsection (3)—

      (a) for paragraph (a) substitute—

         "(a) a court is required to determine under section 115B(2) of the Army Act 1955, section 115B(2) of the Air Force Act 1955 or section 62B(2) of the Naval Discipline Act 1957 whether a person charged with an offence did the act or made the omission charged,";

      (b) for "the court is satisfied" substitute "the judge advocate is satisfied";

      (c) for the words after paragraph (c) substitute "the judge advocate must either direct the court to acquit the defendant of the offence or, if he considers that there ought to be a rehearing, dissolve the court."

   (5) For subsection (4) substitute—

      "(4) This section does not prejudice any other power a judge advocate may have to direct a court to acquit a person of an offence or to dissolve a court."

4. Section 110, as it applies in relation to proceedings before service courts, has effect with the substitution of the following for subsection (1)—

   "(1) Where the court makes a relevant ruling—

      (a) it must state in open court (but, in the case of a ruling by a judge advocate in proceedings before a court-martial, in the absence of the other members of the court) its reasons for the ruling;

      (b) if it is a Standing Civilian Court, it must cause the ruling and the reasons for it to be entered in the note of the court's proceedings."

5. Section 111 has effect as if, in subsection (7), the definition of "rules of court" included rules regulating the practice and procedure of service courts.

6. (1) In this Schedule, and in section 107 as applied by this Schedule, "court-martial" means a court-martial constituted under the Army Act 1955 (3 & 4 Eliz. 2 c. 18), the Air Force Act 1955 (3 & 4 Eliz. 2 c. 19) or the Naval Discipline Act 1957 (c. 53).

(2) In this Schedule "service court" means—
  (a) a court-martial;
  (b) a summary appeal court constituted under section 83ZA of the Army Act 1955, section 83ZA of the Air Force Act 1955 or section 52FF of the Naval Discipline Act 1957;
  (c) the Courts-Martial Appeal Court;
  (d) a Standing Civilian Court.

ection 135

SCHEDULE 7
HEARSAY EVIDENCE: ARMED FORCES

Application to proceedings before service courts

1. Sections 114 to 121, 123, 124, 126, 127 to 129 and 133 and 134, in so far as they are not applied in relation to proceedings before service courts by provision contained in or made under any other Act, have effect in relation to such proceedings (whether in the United Kingdom or elsewhere) as they have effect in relation to criminal proceedings.

2. (1) In their application to such proceedings those sections have effect with the following modifications.
  (2) In section 116(2)(c) for "United Kingdom" substitute "country where the court is sitting".
  (3) In section 117 insert after subsection (7)—
    "(8) In subsection (4) "criminal proceedings" includes summary proceedings under section 76B of the Army Act 1955, section 76B of the Air Force Act 1955 or section 52D of the Naval Discipline Act 1957; and the definition of "criminal proceedings" in section 134(1) has effect accordingly."
  (4) In section 123(4) for paragraph (a) substitute—
    "(a) in the case of proceedings before a court-martial, proceedings held for the determination of the issue must take place before the judge advocate in the absence of the other members of the court;".
  (5) In section 127, for subsection (7) substitute—
    "(7) The appropriate rules are those regulating the practice and procedure of service courts."
  (6) In section 132(10), at the end of the definition of "rules of court" insert—
    "(d) rules regulating the practice and procedure of service courts."
  (7) In section 134 insert after subsection (1)—
    "(1A) In this Part "criminal investigation" includes any investigation which may lead—
      (a) to proceedings before a court-martial or Standing Civilian Court, or
      (b) to summary proceedings under section 76B of the Army Act 1955, section 76B of the Air Force Act 1955 or section 52D of the Naval Discipline Act 1957."

3. (1) Section 122 has effect in relation to proceedings before courts-martial (whether in the United Kingdom or elsewhere) with the following modifications.
  (2) In subsection (1) for "judge and jury" substitute "court-martial".
  (3) In subsection (2)—

   (a) for "jury when they retire to consider their" substitute "court when it retires to consider its".

   (b) for "the court" in paragraph (a) substitute "the judge advocate";

   (c) for "the jury" in paragraph (b) substitute "the court".

4. (1) Section 125 has effect in relation to proceedings before courts-martial (whether in the United Kingdom or elsewhere) with the following modifications.

   (2) In subsection (1)—

      (a) for "judge and jury" substitute "court-martial";

      (b) for "the court is satisfied" substitute "the judge advocate is satisfied";

      (c) for the words after paragraph (b) substitute "the judge advocate must either direct the court to acquit the defendant of the offence or, if he considers that there ought to be a retrial, dissolve the court."

   (3) In subsection (2)—

      (a) for "jury" substitute "court";

      (b) for "the court is satisfied" substitute "the judge advocate is satisfied".

   (4) In subsection (3)—

      (a) for paragraph (a) substitute—

         "(a) a court is required to determine under section 115B(2) of the Army Act 1955, section 115B(2) of the Air Force Act 1955 or section 62B(2) of the Naval Discipline Act 1957 whether a person charged with an offence did the act or made the omission charged,";

      (b) for "the court is satisfied" substitute "the judge advocate is satisfied";

      (c) for the words after paragraph (b) substitute "the judge advocate must either direct the court to acquit the defendant of the offence or, if he considers that there ought to be a rehearing, dissolve the court."

   (5) For subsection (4) substitute—

      "(4) This section does not prejudice any other power a judge advocate may have to direct a court to acquit a person of an offence or to dissolve a court."

Amendments

5. For paragraph 1 of Schedule 1 to the Courts-Martial (Appeals) Act 1968 (c. 20) (use at retrial under Naval Discipline Act 1957 of record of evidence given at original trial) substitute—

   "1 Evidence given at the retrial of any person under section 19 of this Act shall be given orally if it was given orally at the original trial, unless—

      (a) all the parties to the retrial agree otherwise;

      (b) section 116 of the Criminal Justice Act 2003 applies (admissibility of hearsay evidence where a witness is unavailable); or

      (c) the witness is unavailable to give evidence, otherwise than as mentioned in subsection (2) of that section, and section 114(1)(d) of that Act applies (admission of hearsay evidence under residual discretion)."

6. For paragraph 3 of that Schedule (use at retrial under Army Act 1955 of record of evidence given at original trial) substitute—

   "3 Evidence given at the retrial of any person under section 19 of this Act shall be given orally if it was given orally at the original trial, unless—

      (a) all the parties to the retrial agree otherwise;

      (b) section 116 of the Criminal Justice Act 2003 applies (admissibility of hearsay evidence where a witness is unavailable); or

    (c) the witness is unavailable to give evidence, otherwise than as mentioned in subsection (2) of that section, and section 114(1)(d) of that Act applies (admission of hearsay evidence under residual discretion)."

7. For paragraph 5 of that Schedule (use at retrial under Air Force Act 1955 of record of evidence given at original trial) substitute—

"5 Evidence given at the retrial of any person under section 19 of this Act shall be given orally if it was given orally at the original trial, unless—

    (a) all the parties to the retrial agree otherwise;

    (b) section 116 of the Criminal Justice Act 2003 applies (admissibility of hearsay evidence where a witness is unavailable); or

    (c) the witness is unavailable to give evidence, otherwise than as mentioned in subsection (2) of that section, and section 114(1)(d) of that Act applies (admission of hearsay evidence under residual discretion)."

Interpretation

8. In this Schedule, and in any provision of this Part as applied by this Schedule—

"court-martial" means a court-martial constituted under the Army Act 1955 (3 & 4 Eliz. 2 c. 18), the Air Force Act 1955 (3 & 4 Eliz. 2 c. 19) or the Naval Discipline Act 1957 (c. 53);

"service court" means—

    (a) a court-martial;

    (b) a summary appeal court constituted under section 83ZA of the Army Act 1955, section 83ZA of the Air Force Act 1955 or section 52FF of the Naval Discipline Act 1957;

    (c) the Courts-Martial Appeal Court;

    (d) a Standing Civilian Court.

SCHEDULE 8
Section 179   BREACH, REVOCATION OR AMENDMENT OF COMMUNITY ORDER

PART 1
PRELIMINARY

Interpretation

1. In this Schedule—

"the offender", in relation to a community order, means the person in respect of whom the order is made;

"the petty sessions area concerned", in relation to a community order, means the petty sessions area for the time being specified in the order;

"the responsible officer" has the meaning given by section 197.

2. In this Schedule—

    (a) references to a drug rehabilitation requirement of a community order being subject to review are references to that requirement being subject to review in accordance with section 210(1)(b);

    (b) references to the court responsible for a community order imposing a drug rehabilitation requirement which is subject to review are to be construed in accordance with section 210(2).

3. For the purposes of this Schedule—
   (a) a requirement falling within any paragraph of section 177(1) is of the same kind as any other requirement falling within that paragraph, and
   (b) an electronic monitoring requirement is a requirement of the same kind as any requirement falling within section 177(1) to which it relates.

Orders made on appeal

4. Where a community order has been made on appeal, it is to be taken for the purposes of this Schedule to have been made by the Crown Court.

PART 2
BREACH OF REQUIREMENT OF ORDER

Duty to give warning

5. (1) If the responsible officer is of the opinion that the offender has failed without reasonable excuse to comply with any of the requirements of a community order, the officer must give him a warning under this paragraph unless—
   (a) the offender has within the previous twelve months been given a warning under this paragraph in relation to a failure to comply with any of the requirements of the order, or
   (b) the officer causes an information to be laid before a justice of the peace in respect of the failure.
   (2) A warning under this paragraph must—
   (a) describe the circumstances of the failure,
   (b) state that the failure is unacceptable, and
   (c) inform the offender that, if within the next twelve months he again fails to comply with any requirement of the order, he will be liable to be brought before a court.
   (3) The responsible officer must, as soon as practicable after the warning has been given, record that fact.
   (4) In relation to any community order which was made by the Crown Court and does not include a direction that any failure to comply with the requirements of the order is to be dealt with by a magistrates' court, the reference in sub-paragraph (1)(b) to a justice of the peace is to be read as a reference to the Crown Court.

Breach of order after warning

6. (1) If—
   (a) the responsible officer has given a warning under paragraph 5 to the offender in respect of a community order, and
   (b) at any time within the twelve months beginning with the date on which the warning was given, the responsible officer is of the opinion that the offender has since that date failed without reasonable excuse to comply with any of the requirements of the order,
   the officer must cause an information to be laid before a justice of the peace in respect of the failure in question.
   (2) In relation to any community order which was made by the Crown Court and does not include a direction that any failure to comply with the requirements of the order is to be

dealt with by a magistrates' court, the reference in sub-paragraph (1) to a justice of the peace is to be read as a reference to the Crown Court.

Issue of summons or warrant by justice of the peace

7. (1) This paragraph applies to—
   (a) a community order made by a magistrates' court, or
   (b) any community order which was made by the Crown Court and includes a direction that any failure to comply with the requirements of the order is to be dealt with by a magistrates' court.

   (2) If at any time while a community order to which this paragraph applies is in force it appears on information to a justice of the peace acting for the petty sessions area concerned that the offender has failed to comply with any of the requirements of the order, the justice may—
   (a) issue a summons requiring the offender to appear at the place and time specified in it, or
   (b) if the information is in writing and on oath, issue a warrant for his arrest.

   (3) Any summons or warrant issued under this paragraph must direct the offender to appear or be brought—
   (a) in the case of a community order imposing a drug rehabilitation requirement which is subject to review, before the magistrates' court responsible for the order, or
   (b) in any other case, before a magistrates' court acting for the petty sessions area concerned.

   (4) Where a summons issued under sub-paragraph (2)(a) requires the offender to appear before a magistrates' court and the offender does not appear in answer to the summons, the magistrates' court may issue a warrant for the arrest of the offender.

Issue of summons or warrant by Crown Court

8. (1) This paragraph applies to a community order made by the Crown Court which does not include a direction that any failure to comply with the requirements of the order is to be dealt with by a magistrates' court.

   (2) If at any time while a community order to which this paragraph applies is in force it appears on information to the Crown Court that the offender has failed to comply with any of the requirements of the order, the Crown Court may—
   (a) issue a summons requiring the offender to appear at the place and time specified in it, or
   (b) if the information is in writing and on oath, issue a warrant for his arrest.

   (3) Any summons or warrant issued under this paragraph must direct the offender to appear or be brought before the Crown Court.

   (4) Where a summons issued under sub-paragraph (2)(a) requires the offender to appear before the Crown Court and the offender does not appear in answer to the summons, the Crown Court may issue a warrant for the arrest of the offender.

Powers of magistrates' court

9. (1) If it is proved to the satisfaction of a magistrates' court before which an offender appears or is brought under paragraph 7 that he has failed without reasonable excuse to comply

with any of the requirements of the community order, the court must deal with him in respect of the failure in any one of the following ways—

    (a) by amending the terms of the community order so as to impose more onerous requirements which the court could include if it were then making the order;

    (b) where the community order was made by a magistrates' court, by dealing with him, for the offence in respect of which the order was made, in any way in which the court could deal with him if he had just been convicted by it of the offence;

    (c) where—

        (i)   the community order was made by a magistrates' court,

        (ii)   the offence in respect of which the order was made was not an offence punishable by imprisonment,

        (iii)   the offender is aged 18 or over, and

        (iv)   the offender has wilfully and persistently failed to comply with the requirements of the order, by dealing with him, in respect of that offence,

    by imposing a sentence of imprisonment for a term not exceeding 51 weeks.

(2) In dealing with an offender under sub-paragraph (1), a magistrates' court must take into account the extent to which the offender has complied with the requirements of the community order.

(3) In dealing with an offender under sub-paragraph (1)(a), the court may extend the duration of particular requirements (subject to any limit imposed by Chapter 4 of Part 12 of this Act) but may not extend the period specified under section 177(5).

(4) In dealing with an offender under sub-paragraph (1)(b), the court may, in the case of an offender who has wilfully and persistently failed to comply with the requirements of the community order, impose a custodial sentence (where the order was made in respect of an offence punishable with such a sentence) notwithstanding anything in section 152(2).

(5) Where a magistrates' court deals with an offender under sub-paragraph (1)(b) or (c), it must revoke the community order if it is still in force.

(6) Where a community order was made by the Crown Court and a magistrates' court would (apart from this sub-paragraph) be required to deal with the offender under sub-paragraph (1)(a), (b) or (c), it may instead commit him to custody or release him on bail until he can be brought or appear before the Crown Court.

(7) A magistrates' court which deals with an offender's case under sub-paragraph (6) must send to the Crown Court—

    (a) a certificate signed by a justice of the peace certifying that the offender has failed to comply with the requirements of the community order in the respect specified in the certificate, and

    (b) such other particulars of the case as may be desirable; and a certificate purporting to be so signed is admissible as evidence of the failure before the Crown Court.

(8) A person sentenced under sub-paragraph (1)(b) or (c) for an offence may appeal to the Crown Court against the sentence.

Powers of Crown Court

10. (1) Where under paragraph 8 or by virtue of paragraph 9(6) an offender appears or is brought before the Crown Court and it is proved to the satisfaction of that court that he has failed without reasonable excuse to comply with any of the requirements of the community order, the Crown Court must deal with him in respect of the failure in any one of the following ways—

    (a) by amending the terms of the community order so as to impose more onerous require-
        ments which the Crown Court could impose if it were then making the order;

    (b) by dealing with him, for the offence in respect of which the order was made, in any
        way in which he could have been dealt with for that offence by the court which made
        the order if the order had not been made;

    (c) where—
        (i)   the offence in respect of which the order was made was not an offence punishable
            by imprisonment,
        (ii) the offender is aged 18 or over,
        (iii) the offender has wilfully and persistently failed to comply with the requirements
            of the order, by dealing with him, in respect of that offence,
        by imposing a sentence of imprisonment for a term not exceeding 51 weeks.

(2) In dealing with an offender under sub-paragraph (1), the Crown Court must take into
account the extent to which the offender has complied with the requirements of the community order.

(3) In dealing with an offender under sub-paragraph (1)(a), the court may extend the duration
of particular requirements (subject to any limit imposed by Chapter 4 of Part 12 of this Act)
but may not extend the period specified under section 177(5).

(4) In dealing with an offender under sub-paragraph (1)(b), the Crown Court may, in the case
of an offender who has wilfully and persistently failed to comply with the requirements of
the community order, impose a custodial sentence (where the order was made in respect of
an offence punishable with such a sentence) notwithstanding anything in section 152(2).

(5) Where the Crown Court deals with an offender under sub-paragraph (1)(b) or (c), it must
revoke the community order if it is still in force.

(6) In proceedings before the Crown Court under this paragraph any question whether the
offender has failed to comply with the requirements of the community order is to be determined by the court and not by the verdict of a jury.

Restriction of powers in paragraphs 9 and 10 where treatment required

11. (1) An offender who is required by any of the following requirements of a community
       order—
       (a) a mental health treatment requirement,
       (b) a drug rehabilitation requirement, or
       (c) an alcohol treatment requirement,
       to submit to treatment for his mental condition, or his dependency on or propensity to
       misuse drugs or alcohol, is not to be treated for the purposes of paragraph 9 or 10 as
       having failed to comply with that requirement on the ground only that he had refused
       to undergo any surgical, electrical or other treatment if, in the opinion of the court, his
       refusal was reasonable having regard to all the circumstances.

    (2) A court may not under paragraph 9(1)(a) or 10(1)(a) amend a mental health treatment
       requirement, a drug rehabilitation requirement or an alcohol treatment requirement unless
       the offender expresses his willingness to comply with the requirement as amended.

Supplementary

12. Where a community order was made by a magistrates' court in the case of an offender
    under 18 years of age in respect of an offence triable only on indictment in the case of an

adult, any powers exercisable under paragraph 9(1)(b) in respect of the offender after he attains the age of 18 are powers to do either or both of the following—

PART 3
REVOCATION OF ORDER

Revocation of order with or without re-sentencing: powers of magistrates' court

13. (1) This paragraph applies where a community order, other than an order made by the Crown Court and falling within paragraph 14(1)(a), is in force and on the application of the offender or the responsible officer it appears to the appropriate magistrates' court that, having regard to circumstances which have arisen since the order was made, it would be in the interests of justice—

    (a) for the order to be revoked, or

    (b) for the offender to be dealt with in some other way for the offence in respect of which the order was made.

  (2) The appropriate magistrates' court may—

    (a) revoke the order, or

    (b) both—

      (i) revoke the order, and

      (ii) deal with the offender, for the offence in respect of which the order was made, in any way in which it could deal with him if he had just been convicted by the court of the offence.

  (3) The circumstances in which a community order may be revoked under sub-paragraph (2) include the offender's making good progress or his responding satisfactorily to supervision or treatment (as the case requires).

  (4) In dealing with an offender under sub-paragraph (2)(b), a magistrates' court must take into account the extent to which the offender has complied with the requirements of the community order.

  (5) A person sentenced under sub-paragraph (2)(b) for an offence may appeal to the Crown Court against the sentence.

  (6) Where a magistrates' court proposes to exercise its powers under this paragraph otherwise than on the application of the offender, it must summon him to appear before the court and, if he does not appear in answer to the summons, may issue a warrant for his arrest.

  (7) In this paragraph "the appropriate magistrates' court" means—

    (a) in the case of an order imposing a drug rehabilitation requirement which is subject to review, the magistrates' court responsible for the order, and

    (b) in the case of any other community order, a magistrates' court acting for the petty sessions area concerned.

Revocation of order with or without re-sentencing: powers of Crown Court

14. (1) This paragraph applies where—

    (a) there is in force a community order made by the Crown Court which does not include a direction that any failure to comply with the requirements of the order is to be dealt with by a magistrates' court, and

    (b) the offender or the responsible officer applies to the Crown Court for the order to be revoked or for the offender to be dealt with in some other way for the offence in respect of which the order was made.

(2) If it appears to the Crown Court to be in the interests of justice to do so, having regard to circumstances which have arisen since the order was made, the Crown Court may—

    (a) revoke the order, or

    (b) both—

        (i) revoke the order, and

        (ii) deal with the offender, for the offence in respect of which the order was made, in any way in which he could have been dealt with for that offence by the court which made the order if the order had not been made.

(3) The circumstances in which a community order may be revoked under sub-paragraph (2) include the offender's making good progress or his responding satisfactorily to supervision or treatment (as the case requires).

(4) In dealing with an offender under sub-paragraph (2)(b), the Crown Court must take into account the extent to which the offender has complied with the requirements of the order.

(5) Where the Crown Court proposes to exercise its powers under this paragraph otherwise than on the application of the offender, it must summon him to appear before the court and, if he does not appear in answer to the summons, may issue a warrant for his arrest.

Supplementary

15. Paragraph 12 applies for the purposes of paragraphs 13 and 14 as it applies for the purposes of paragraph 9 above, but as if for the words "paragraph 9(1)(b)" there were substituted "paragraph 13(2)(b)(ii) or 14(2)(b)(ii)".

PART 4
AMENDMENT OF ORDER

Amendment by reason of change of residence

16. (1) This paragraph applies where, at any time while a community order is in force in respect of an offender, the appropriate court is satisfied that the offender proposes to change, or has changed, his residence from the petty sessions area concerned to another petty sessions area.

(2) Subject to sub-paragraphs (3) and (4), the appropriate court may, and on the application of the responsible officer must, amend the community order by substituting the other petty sessions area for the area specified in the order.

(3) The court may not under this paragraph amend a community order which contains requirements which, in the opinion of the court, cannot be complied with unless the offender continues to reside in the petty sessions area concerned unless, in accordance with paragraph 17, it either—

    (a) cancels those requirements, or

    (b) substitutes for those requirements other requirements which can be complied with if the offender ceases to reside in that area.

(4) The court may not amend under this paragraph a community order imposing a programme requirement unless it appears to the court that the accredited programme specified in the requirement is available in the other petty sessions area.

(5) In this paragraph "the appropriate court" means—

   (a) in relation to any community order imposing a drug rehabilitation requirement which is subject to review, the court responsible for the order,

   (b) in relation to any community order which was made by the Crown Court and does not include any direction that any failure to comply with the requirements of the order is to be dealt with by a magistrates' court, the Crown Court, and

   (c) in relation to any other community order, a magistrates' court acting for the petty sessions area concerned.

Amendment of requirements of community order

17. (1) The appropriate court may, on the application of the offender or the responsible officer, by order am end a community order—

   (a) by cancelling any of the requirements of the order, or

   (b) by replacing any of those requirements with a requirement of the same kind, which the court could include if it were then making the order.

   (2) The court may not under this paragraph amend a mental health treatment requirement, a drug rehabilitation requirement or an alcohol treatment requirement unless the offender expresses his willingness to comply with the requirement as amended.

   (3) If the offender fails to express his willingness to comply with a mental health treatment requirement, drug rehabilitation requirement or alcohol treatment requirement as proposed to be amended by the court under this paragraph, the court may—

   (a) revoke the community order, and

   (b) deal with him, for the offence in respect of which the order was made, in any way in which he could have been dealt with for that offence by the court which made the order if the order had not been made.

   (4) In dealing with the offender under sub-paragraph (3)(b), the court—

   (a) must take into account the extent to which the offender has complied with the requirements of the order, and

   (b) may impose a custodial sentence (where the order was made in respect of an offence punishable with such a sentence) notwithstanding anything in section 152(2).

   (5) Paragraph 12 applies for the purposes of this paragraph as it applies for the purposes of paragraph 9, but as if for the words "paragraph 9(1)(b)" there were substituted "paragraph 17(3)(b)".

   (6) In this paragraph "the appropriate court" has the same meaning as in paragraph 16.

Amendment of treatment requirements of community order on report of practitioner

18. (1) Where the medical practitioner or other person by whom or under whose direction an offender is, in pursuance of any requirement to which this sub-paragraph applies, being treated for his mental condition or his dependency on or propensity to misuse drugs or alcohol—

   (a) is of the opinion mentioned in sub-paragraph (3), or

   (b) is for any reason unwilling to continue to treat or direct the treatment of the offender,

   he must make a report in writing to that effect to the responsible officer and that officer must apply under paragraph 17 to the appropriate court for the variation or cancellation of the requirement.

(2) The requirements to which sub-paragraph (1) applies are—

    (a) a mental health treatment requirement,

    (b) a drug rehabilitation requirement, and

    (c) an alcohol treatment requirement.

(3) The opinion referred to in sub-paragraph (1) is—

    (a) that the treatment of the offender should be continued beyond the period specified in that behalf in the order,

    (b) that the offender needs different treatment,

    (c) that the offender is not susceptible to treatment, or

    (d) that the offender does not require further treatment.

(4) In this paragraph "the appropriate court" has the same meaning as in paragraph 16.

Amendment in relation to review of drug rehabilitation requirement

19. Where the responsible officer is of the opinion that a community order imposing a drug rehabilitation requirement which is subject to review should be so amended as to provide for each subsequent periodic review (required by section 211) to be made without a hearing instead of at a review hearing, or vice versa, he must apply under paragraph 17 to the court responsible for the order for the variation of the order.

Extension of unpaid work requirement

20. (1) Where—

    (a) a community order imposing an unpaid work requirement is in force in respect of any offender, and

    (b) on the application of the offender or the responsible officer, it appears to the appropriate court that it would be in the interests of justice to do so having regard to circumstances which have arisen since the order was made,

the court may, in relation to the order, extend the period of twelve months specified in section 200(2).

PART 5
POWERS OF COURT IN RELATION TO ORDER FOLLOWING SUBSEQUENT CONVICTION

Powers of magistrates' court following subsequent conviction

21. (1) This paragraph applies where—

    (a) an offender in respect of whom a community order made by a magistrates' court is in force is convicted of an offence by a magistrates' court, and

    (b) it appears to the court that it would be in the interests of justice to exercise its powers under this paragraph, having regard to circumstances which have arisen since the community order was made.

(2) The magistrates' court may—

    (a) revoke the order, or

    (b) both—

        (i) revoke the order, and

    (ii) deal with the offender, for the offence in respect of which the order was made, in any way in which he could have been dealt with for that offence by the court which made the order if the order had not been made.

(3) In dealing with an offender under sub-paragraph (2)(b), a magistrates' court must take into account the extent to which the offender has complied with the requirements of the community order.

(4) A person sentenced under sub-paragraph (2)(b) for an offence may appeal to the Crown Court against the sentence.

22. (1) Where an offender in respect of whom a community order made by the Crown Court is in force is convicted of an offence by a magistrates' court, the magistrates' court may commit the offender in custody or release him on bail until he can be brought before the Crown Court.

(2) Where the magistrates' court deals with an offender's case under sub-paragraph (1), it must send to the Crown Court such particulars of the case as may be desirable.

Powers of Crown Court following subsequent conviction

23. (1) This paragraph applies where—
    (a) an offender in respect of whom a community order is in force—
        (i) is convicted of an offence by the Crown Court, or
        (ii) is brought or appears before the Crown Court by virtue of paragraph 22 or having been committed by the magistrates' court to the Crown Court for sentence, and
    (b) it appears to the Crown Court that it would be in the interests of justice to exercise its powers under this paragraph, having regard to circumstances which have arisen since the community order was made.

(2) The Crown Court may—
    (a) revoke the order, or
    (b) both—
        (i) revoke the order, and
        (ii) deal with the offender, for the offence in respect of which the order was made, in any way in which he could have been dealt with for that offence by the court which made the order if the order had not been made.

(3) In dealing with an offender under sub-paragraph (2)(b), the Crown Court must take into account the extent to which the offender has complied with the requirements of the community order.

PART 6
SUPPLEMENTARY

24. (1) No order may be made under paragraph 16, and no application may be made under paragraph 13, 17 or 20, while an appeal against the community order is pending.

(2) Sub-paragraph (1) does not apply to an application under paragraph 17 which—
    (a) relates to a mental health treatment requirement, a drug rehabilitation requirement or an alcohol treatment requirement, and
    (b) is made by the responsible officer with the consent of the offender.

25. (1) Subject to sub-paragraph (2), where a court proposes to exercise its powers under Part 4 or 5 of this Schedule, otherwise than on the application of the offender, the court—
    (a) must summon him to appear before the court, and
    (b) if he does not appear in answer to the summons, may issue a warrant for his arrest.

    (2) This paragraph does not apply to an order cancelling a requirement of a community order or reducing the period of any requirement, or substituting a new petty sessions area or a new place for the one specified in the order.

26. Paragraphs 9(1)(a), 10(1)(a) and 17(1)(b) have effect subject to the provisions mentioned in subsection (2) of section 177, and to subsections (3) and (6) of that section.

27. (1) On the making under this Schedule of an order revoking or amending a community order, the proper officer of the court must—
    (a) provide copies of the revoking or amending order to the offender and the responsible officer,
    (b) in the case of an amending order which substitutes a new petty sessions area, provide a copy of the amending order to—
        (i) the local probation board acting for that area, and
        (ii) the magistrates' court acting for that area, and
    (c) in the case of an amending order which imposes or amends a requirement specified in the first column of Schedule 14, provide a copy of so much of the amending order as relates to that requirement to the person specified in relation to that requirement in the second column of that Schedule.

    (2) Where under sub-paragraph (1)(b) the proper officer of the court provides a copy of an amending order to a magistrates' court acting for a different area, the officer must also provide to that court such documents and information relating to the case as it considers likely to be of assistance to a court acting for that area in the exercise of its functions in relation to the order.

    (3) In this paragraph "proper officer" means—
    (a) in relation to a magistrates' court, the justices' chief executive for the court; and
    (b) in relation to the Crown Court, the appropriate officer.

SCHEDULE 9
TRANSFER OF COMMUNITY ORDERS TO SCOTLAND OR NORTHERN IRELAND

Section 180

PART 1
SCOTLAND

1. (1) Where the court considering the making of a community order is satisfied that the offender resides in Scotland, or will reside there when the order comes into force, the court may not make a community order in respect of the offender unless it appears to the court—
    (a) in the case of an order imposing a requirement mentioned in sub-paragraph (2), that arrangements exist for persons to comply with such a requirement in the locality in Scotland in which the offender resides, or will be residing when the order comes into force, and that provision can be made for him to comply with the requirement under those arrangements, and
    (b) in any case, that suitable arrangements for his supervision can be made by the council constituted under section 2 of the Local Government etc. (Scotland) Act

1994 (c. 39) in whose area he resides, or will be residing when the order comes into force.

(2) The requirements referred to in sub-paragraph (1)(a) are—

    (a) an unpaid work requirement,

    (b) an activity requirement,

    (c) a programme requirement,

    (d) a mental health treatment requirement,

    (e) a drug rehabilitation requirement,

    (f) an alcohol treatment requirement, and

    (g) an electronic monitoring requirement.

(3) Where—

    (a) the appropriate court for the purposes of paragraph 16 of Schedule 8 (amendment by reason of change of residence) is satisfied that an offender in respect of whom a community order is in force proposes to reside or is residing in Scotland, and

    (b) it appears to the court that the conditions in sub-paragraph (1)(a) and (b) are satisfied,

the power of the court to amend the order under Part 4 of Schedule 8 includes power to amend it by requiring it to be complied with in Scotland and the offender to be supervised in accordance with the arrangements referred to in subparagraph (1)(b).

(4) For the purposes of sub-paragraph (3), any reference in sub-paragraph (1)(a) and (b) to the time when the order comes into force is to be treated as a reference to the time when the amendment comes into force.

(5) The court may not by virtue of sub-paragraph (1) or (3) require an attendance centre requirement to be complied with in Scotland.

(6) A community order made or amended in accordance with this paragraph must—

    (a) specify the locality in Scotland in which the offender resides or will be residing when the order or amendment comes into force;

    (b) specify as the corresponding order for the purposes of this Schedule an order that may be made by a court in Scotland;

    (c) specify as the appropriate court for the purposes of subsection (4) of section 228 of the Criminal Procedure (Scotland) Act 1995 (c. 46) a court of summary jurisdiction (which, in the case of an offender convicted on indictment, must be the sheriff court) having jurisdiction in the locality specified under paragraph (a);

and section 216 (petty sessions area to be specified) does not apply in relation to an order so made or amended.

2. (1) Where a court is considering the making or amendment of a community order by virtue of paragraph 1, Chapter 4 of Part 12 of this Act has effect subject to the following modifications.

(2) Any reference to the responsible officer has effect as a reference to the officer of a council constituted under section 2 of the Local Government etc. (Scotland) Act 1994 (c. 39) responsible for the offender's supervision or, as the case may be, discharging in relation to him the functions in respect of community service orders assigned by sections 239 to 245 of the Criminal Procedure (Scotland) Act 1995.

(3) The following provisions are omitted—

    (a) subsection (7) of section 201 (activity requirement),

    (b) subsection (7) of section 202 (programme requirement),

    (c) subsection (4) of section 206 (residence requirement), and

    (d) subsection (4) of section 218 (availability of arrangements in local area).

(4) In section 207 (mental health treatment requirement), for subsection (2)(a) there is substituted—

"(a) treatment as a resident patient in a hospital within the meaning of the Mental Health (Care and Treatment) (Scotland) Act 2003, not being a State hospital within the meaning of that Act;".

(5) In section 215 (electronic monitoring requirement), in subsection (3), the words from "and" onwards are omitted.

PART 2
NORTHERN IRELAND

3. (1) Where the court considering the making of a community order is satisfied that the offender resides in Northern Ireland, or will reside there when the order comes into force, the court may not make a community order in respect of the offender unless it appears to the court—

(a) in the case of an order imposing a requirement mentioned in sub-paragraph (2), that arrangements exist for persons to comply with such a requirement in the petty sessions district in Northern Ireland in which the offender resides, or will be residing when the order comes into force, and that provision can be made for him to comply with the requirement under those arrangements, and

(b) in any case, that suitable arrangements for his supervision can be made by the Probation Board for Northern Ireland.

(2) The requirements referred to in sub-paragraph (1) are—

(a) an unpaid work requirement,

(b) an activity requirement,

(c) a programme requirement,

(d) a mental health treatment requirement,

(e) a drug rehabilitation requirement,

(f) an alcohol treatment requirement,

(g) an attendance centre requirement, and

(h) an electronic monitoring requirement.

(3) Where—

(a) the appropriate court for the purposes of paragraph 16 of Schedule 8 (amendment by reason of change of residence) is satisfied that the offender to whom a community order relates proposes to reside or is residing in Northern Ireland, and

(b) it appears to the court that the conditions in sub-paragraphs (1)(a) and (b) are satisfied,

the power of the court to amend the order under Part 4 of Schedule 8 includes power to amend it by requiring it to be complied with in Northern Ireland and the offender to be supervised in accordance with the arrangements referred to in sub-paragraph (1)(b).

(4) For the purposes of sub-paragraph (3), any reference in sub-paragraph (1)(a) and (b) to the time when the order comes into force is to be treated as a reference to the time when the amendment comes into force.

(5) A community order made or amended in accordance with this paragraph must specify the petty sessions district in Northern Ireland in which the offender resides or will be residing when the order or amendment comes into force; and section 216 (petty sessions area to be specified) does not apply in relation to an order so made or amended.

(6) A community order made or amended in accordance with this paragraph must also specify as the corresponding order for the purposes of this Schedule an order that may be made by a court in Northern Ireland.

4. (1) Where a court is considering the making or amendment of a community order by virtue of paragraph 3, Chapter 4 of Part 12 of this Act has effect subject to the following modifications.

(2) Any reference to the responsible officer has effect as a reference to the probation officer responsible for the offender's supervision or, as the case may be, discharging in relation to the offender the functions conferred by Part 2 of the Criminal Justice (Northern Ireland) Order 1996 (S.I. 1996/3160 (N.I. 24)).

(3) The following provisions are omitted—

(a) subsection (7) of section 201 (activity requirement),

(b) subsection (7) of section 202 (programme requirement),

(c) subsection (4) of section 206 (residence requirement), and

(d) subsection (4) of section 218 (availability of arrangements in local area).

(4) In section 207 (mental health treatment requirement), for subsection (2)(a) there is substituted—

"(a) treatment (whether as an in-patient or an out-patient) at such hospital as may be specified in the order, being a hospital within the meaning of the Health and Personal Social Services (Northern Ireland) Order 1972, approved by the Department of Health, Social Services and Public Safety for the purposes of paragraph 4(3) of Schedule 1 to the Criminal Justice (Northern Ireland) Order 1996 (S.I. 1996/3160 (N.I. 24));".

(5) In section 214 (attendance centre requirement), any reference to an attendance centre has effect as a reference to a day centre, as defined by paragraph 3(6) of Schedule 1 to the Criminal Justice (Northern Ireland) Order 1996 (S.I. 1996/3160 (N.I. 24)).

(6) In section 215 (electronic monitoring requirement), in subsection (3), the words from "and" onwards are omitted.

PART 3
GENERAL PROVISIONS

5. In this Part of this Schedule—

"corresponding order" means the order specified under paragraph 1(6)(b) or 3(6);

"home court" means—

(a) if the offender resides in Scotland, or will be residing there at the relevant time, the sheriff court having jurisdiction in the locality in which he resides or proposes to reside, and

(b) if he resides in Northern Ireland, or will be residing there at the relevant time, the court of summary jurisdiction acting for the petty sessions district in which he resides or proposes to reside;

"the local authority officer concerned", in relation to an offender, means the officer of a council constituted under section 2 of the Local Government etc. (Scotland) Act 1994 (c. 39) responsible for his supervision or, as the case may be, discharging in relation to him the functions in respect of community service orders assigned by sections 239 to 245 of the Criminal Procedure (Scotland) Act 1995 (c. 46);

"the probation officer concerned", in relation to an offender, means the probation officer responsible for his supervision or, as the case may be, discharging in relation to him the functions conferred by Part 2 of the Criminal Justice (Northern Ireland) Order 1996;

"the relevant time" means the time when the order or the amendment to it comes into force.

6. Where a community order is made or amended in accordance with paragraph 1 or 3, the court which makes or amends the order must provide the home court with a copy of the order as made or amended, together with such other documents and information relating to the case as it considers likely to be of assistance to that court; and paragraphs (b) to (d) of subsection (1) of section 219 (provision of copies of relevant orders) do not apply.

7. In section 220 (duty of offender to keep in touch with responsible officer) the reference to the responsible officer is to be read in accordance with paragraph 2(2) or 4(2).

8. Where a community order is made or amended in accordance with paragraph 1 or 3, then, subject to the following provisions of this Part of this Schedule—

   (a) the order is to be treated as if it were a corresponding order made in the part of the United Kingdom in which the offender resides, or will be residing at the relevant time, and

   (b) the legislation relating to such orders which has effect in that part of the United Kingdom applies accordingly.

9. Before making or amending a community order in those circumstances the court must explain to the offender in ordinary language—

   (a) the requirements of the legislation relating to corresponding orders which has effect in the part of the United Kingdom in which he resides or will be residing at the relevant time, and

   (b) the legislation relating to such orders which has effect in that part of the United Kingdom applies accordingly.

   (c) its own powers under this Part of this Schedule.

10. The home court may exercise in relation to the community order any power which it could exercise in relation to the corresponding order made by a court in the part of the United Kingdom in which the home court exercises jurisdiction, by virtue of the legislation relating to such orders which has effect in that part, except the following—

   (a) any power to discharge or revoke the order (other than a power to revoke the order where the offender has been convicted of a further offence and the court has imposed a custodial sentence),

   (b) any power to deal with the offender for the offence in respect of which the order was made,

   (c) in the case of a community order imposing an unpaid work requirement, any power to vary the order by substituting for the number of hours of work specified in it any greater number than the court which made the order could have specified, and

   (d) in the case of a community order imposing a curfew requirement, any power to vary the order by substituting for the period specified in it any longer period than the court which made the order could have specified.

11. If at any time while legislation relating to corresponding orders which has effect in Scotland or Northern Ireland applies by virtue of paragraph 7 to a community order made in England and Wales—

   (a) it appears to the home court—

      (i) if that court is in Scotland, on information from the local authority officer concerned, or

     (ii) if that court is in Northern Ireland, upon a complaint being made to a justice of the peace acting for the petty sessions district for the time being specified in the order, that the offender has failed to comply with any of the requirements of the order, or

  (b) it appears to the home court—

     (i) if that court is in Scotland, on the application of the offender or of the local authority officer concerned, or

     (ii) if it is in Northern Ireland, on the application of the offender or of the probation officer concerned,

that it would be in the interests of justice for a power conferred by paragraph 13 or 14 of Schedule 8 to be exercised,

the home court may require the offender to appear before the court which made the order or the court which last amended the order in England and Wales.

12. Where an offender is required by virtue of paragraph 11 to appear before a court in England and Wales that court—

  (a) may issue a warrant for his arrest, and

  (b) may exercise any power which it could exercise in respect of the community order if the offender resided in England and Wales,

and any enactment relating to the exercise of such powers has effect accordingly, and with any reference to the responsible officer being read as a reference to the local authority officer or probation officer concerned.

13. Paragraph 12(b) does not enable the court to amend the community order unless—

  (a) where the offender resides in Scotland, it appears to the court that the conditions in paragraph 1(1)(a) and (b) are satisfied in relation to any requirement to be imposed, or

  (b) where the offender resides in Northern Ireland, it appears to the court that the conditions in paragraph 3(1)(a) and (b) are satisfied in relation to any requirement to be imposed.

14. The preceding paragraphs of this Schedule have effect in relation to the amendment of a community order by virtue of paragraph 12(b) as they have effect in relation to the amendment of such an order by virtue of paragraph 1(3) or 3(3).

15. Where an offender is required by virtue of paragraph (a) of paragraph 11 to appear before a court in England and Wales—

  (a) the home court must send to that court a certificate certifying that the offender has failed to comply with such of the requirements of the order as may be specified in the certificate, together with such other particulars of the case as may be desirable, and

  (b) a certificate purporting to be signed by the clerk of the home court is admissible as evidence of the failure before the court which made the order.

SCHEDULE 10
REVOCATION OR AMENDMENT OF CUSTODY PLUS ORDERS AND AMENDMENT OF INTERMITTENT CUSTODY ORDERS

Section 187

Interpretation

1. (1) In this Schedule—

"the appropriate court" means—

  (a) where the custody plus order or intermittent custody order was made by the Crown Court, the Crown Court, and

  (b) in any other case, a magistrates' court acting for the petty sessions area concerned;

"the offender", in relation to a custody plus order or intermittent custody order, means the person in respect of whom the order is made;

"the petty sessions area concerned", in relation to a custody plus order or intermittent custody order, means the petty sessions area for the time being specified in the order;

"the responsible officer" has the meaning given by section 197.

(2) In this Schedule any reference to a requirement being imposed by, or included in, a custody plus order or intermittent custody order is to be read as a reference to compliance with the requirement being required by the order to be a condition of a licence.

Orders made on appeal

2. Where a custody plus order or intermittent custody order has been made on appeal, it is to be taken for the purposes of this Schedule to have been made by the Crown Court.

Revocation of custody plus order or removal from intermittent custody order of requirements as to licence conditions

3. (1) Where at any time while a custody plus order or intermittent custody order is in force, it appears to the appropriate court on the application of the offender or the responsible officer that, having regard to circumstances which have arisen since the order was made, it would be in the interests of justice to do so, the court may—

(a) in the case of a custody plus order, revoke the order, and

(b) in the case of an intermittent custody order, amend the order so that it contains only provision specifying periods for the purposes of section 183(1)(b)(i).

(2) The revocation under this paragraph of a custody plus order does not affect the sentence of imprisonment to which the order relates, except in relation to the conditions of the licence.

Amendment by reason of change of residence

4. (1) This paragraph applies where, at any time during the term of imprisonment to which a custody plus order or intermittent custody order relates, the appropriate court is satisfied that the offender proposes to change, or has changed, his residence during the licence period from the petty sessions area concerned to another petty sessions area.

(2) Subject to sub-paragraphs (3) and (4), the appropriate court may, and on the application of the Secretary of State or the responsible officer must, amend the custody plus order or intermittent custody order by substituting the other petty sessions area for the area specified in the order.

(3) The court may not amend under this paragraph a custody plus order or intermittent custody order which contains requirements which, in the opinion of the court, cannot be complied with unless the offender resides in the petty sessions area concerned unless, in accordance with paragraph 5, it either—

(a) cancels those requirements, or

(b) substitutes for those requirements other requirements which can be complied with if the offender does not reside in that area.

(4) The court may not amend under this paragraph any custody plus order or intermittent custody order imposing a programme requirement unless it appears to the court that the accredited programme specified in the requirement is available in the other petty sessions area.

Amendment of requirements of custody plus order or intermittent custody order

5. (1) At any time during the term of imprisonment to which a custody plus order or intermittent custody order relates, the appropriate court may, on the application of the offender, the Secretary of State or the responsible officer, by order amend any requirement of the custody plus order or intermittent custody order—

    (a) by cancelling the requirement, or

    (b) by replacing it with a requirement of the same kind imposing different obligations, which the court could include if it were then making the order.

  (2) For the purposes of sub-paragraph (1)—

    (a) a requirement falling within any paragraph of section 182(1) is of the same kind as any other requirement falling within that paragraph, and

    (b) an electronic monitoring requirement is a requirement of the same kind as any requirement falling within section 182(1) to which it relates.

  (3) Sub-paragraph (1)(b) has effect subject to the provisions mentioned in subsection (2) of section 182, and to subsections (3) and (5) of that section.

Alteration of pattern of temporary release

6. (1) At any time during the term of imprisonment to which an intermittent custody order relates, the appropriate court may, on the application of the offender, the Secretary of State or the responsible officer, amend the order—

    (a) so as to specify different periods for the purposes of section 183(1)(b)(i), or

    (b) so as to provide that he is to remain in prison until the number of days served by him in prison is equal to the number of custodial days.

  (2) The appropriate court may not by virtue of sub-paragraph (1) amend an intermittent custody order unless it has received from the Secretary of State notification that suitable prison accommodation is available for the offender during the periods which, under the order as amended, will be custodial periods.

  (3) In this paragraph "custodial period" has the same meaning as in section 184(3).

Supplementary

7. No application may be made under paragraph 3(1), 5(1) or 6(1) while an appeal against the sentence of which the custody plus or intermittent custody order forms part is pending.

8. (1) Subject to sub-paragraph (2), where a court proposes to exercise its powers under paragraph 5 or 6, otherwise than on the application of the offender, the court—

    (a) must summon him to appear before the court, and

    (b) if he does not appear in answer to the summons, may issue a warrant for his arrest.

  (2) This paragraph does not apply to an order cancelling any requirement of a custody plus or intermittent custody order.

9. (1) On the making under this Schedule of an order revoking or amending a custody plus order or amending an intermittent custody order, the proper officer of the court must—

    (a) provide copies of the revoking or amending order to the offender and the responsible officer,

    (b) in the case of an amending order which substitutes a new petty sessions area, provide a copy of the amending order to—

      (i) the local probation board acting for that area, and

       (ii) the magistrates' court acting for that area,

(c) in the case of an order which cancels or amends a requirement specified in the first column of Schedule 14, provide a copy of so much of the amending order as relates to that requirement to the person specified in relation to that requirement in the second column of that Schedule.

(2) Where under sub-paragraph (1)(b) the proper officer of the court provides a copy of an amending order to a magistrates' court acting for a different area, the officer must also provide to that court such documents and information relating to the case as it considers likely to be of assistance to a court acting for that area in the exercise of its functions in relation to the order.

SCHEDULE 11
TRANSFER OF CUSTODY PLUS ORDERS AND INTERMITTENT CUSTODY ORDERS TO SCOTLAND OR NORTHERN IRELAND

Section 188

PART 1
INTRODUCTORY

1. In this Schedule—
    (a) "the 1997 Act" means the Crime (Sentences) Act 1997 (c. 43), and
    (b) any reference to a requirement being imposed by, or included in a custody plus order or intermittent custody order is a reference to compliance with the requirement being required by the order to be a condition of a licence.

PART 2
SCOTLAND

2. (1) Where the court making a custody plus order is satisfied that the offender resides in Scotland, or will reside there during the licence period, the court may, subject to sub-paragraph (2), impose requirements that are to be complied with in Scotland and require the offender's compliance with the order to be supervised in accordance with arrangements made by the local authority in Scotland in whose area he resides or will reside.

(2) The court may not make an order by virtue of this paragraph unless it appears to the court—
    (a) in the case of an order imposing a requirement mentioned in sub-paragraph (3), that arrangements exist for persons to comply with such a requirement in the locality in Scotland in which the offender resides, or will be residing during the licence period, and that provision can be made for him to comply with the requirement under those arrangements, and
    (b) in any case, that suitable arrangements for supervising his compliance with the order can be made by the local authority in whose area he resides, or will be residing during the licence period.

(3) The requirements referred to in sub-paragraph (2)(a) are—
    (a) an unpaid work requirement,
    (b) an activity requirement,
    (c) a programme requirement, and

    (d) an electronic monitoring requirement.

  (4) If an order has been made in accordance with this paragraph in relation to an offender but—

    (a) the Secretary of State decides not to make an order under paragraph 1 or 4 of Schedule 1 to the 1997 Act in relation to him, and

    (b) the offender has not applied under paragraph 22 of this Schedule for the amendment of the custody plus order or intermittent custody order,

  the Secretary of State must apply to the court under paragraph 22 of this Schedule for the amendment of the order.

3. Where—

    (a) the appropriate court for the purposes of paragraph 4 of Schedule 10 (amendment by reason of change of residence) is satisfied that the offender in respect of whom a custody plus order or intermittent custody order is in force is residing in Scotland, or proposes to reside there during the licence period,

    (b) the Secretary of State has made, or has indicated his willingness to make, an order under paragraph 1 or 4 of Schedule 1 to the 1997 Act in relation to the offender, and

    (c) it appears to the court that the conditions in paragraph 2(2)(a) and (b) are satisfied,

  the power of the court to amend the order under Schedule 10 includes power to amend it by requiring the requirements included in the order to be complied with in Scotland and the offender's compliance with them to be supervised in accordance with the arrangements referred to in paragraph 2(2)(b).

4. A court may not by virtue of paragraph 2 or 3 require an attendance centre requirement to be complied with in Scotland.

5. A custody plus order made in accordance with paragraph 2 or a custody plus order or intermittent order amended in accordance with paragraph 3 must—

    (a) specify the local authority area in which the offender resides or will reside during the licence period, and

    (b) require the local authority for that area to appoint or assign an officer who will be responsible for discharging in relation to him the functions conferred on responsible officers by Part 12 of this Act;

  and section 216 (petty sessions area to be specified) does not apply in relation to an order so made or amended.

6. (1) Where a court makes a custody plus order in accordance with paragraph 2 or amends a custody plus order or intermittent custody order in accordance with paragraph 3, the court must provide the relevant documents to—

    (a) the local authority for the area specified in the order, and

    (b) the sheriff court having jurisdiction in the locality in which the offender resides or proposes to reside;

  and paragraphs (b) to (d) of subsection (1) of section 219 (which relate to the provision of copies) do not apply in relation to an order so made or amended.

  (2) In this paragraph, "the relevant documents" means—

    (a) a copy of the order as made or amended, and

    (b) such other documents and information relating to the case as the court making or amending the order considers likely to be of assistance.

7. (1) In relation to the making of a custody plus order by virtue of paragraph 2, in relation to the amendment of a custody plus order or intermittent custody order by virtue of paragraph 3, and (except for the purposes of paragraph 22) in relation to an order so

made or amended, Chapter 4 of Part 12 of this Act has effect subject to the following modifications.

(2) Any reference to the responsible officer has effect as a reference to the officer appointed or assigned under paragraph 5(b).

(3) The following provisions are omitted—

(a) subsection (7) of section 201 (activity requirement);

(b) subsection (7) of section 202 (programme requirement);

(c) subsection (4) of section 218 (availability of arrangements in local area).

(4) In section 215 (electronic monitoring requirement), in subsection (3), the words from "and" onwards are omitted.

8. In this Part of this Schedule "local authority" means a council constituted under section 2 of the Local Government etc. (Scotland) Act 1994 (c. 39); and any reference to the area of such an authority is a reference to the local government area within the meaning of that Act.

PART 3
NORTHERN IRELAND

9. (1) Where the court making a custody plus order is satisfied that the offender resides in Northern Ireland, or will reside there during the licence period, the court may, subject to sub-paragraph (2), impose requirements that are to be complied with in Northern Ireland and require the offender's compliance with the order to be supervised in accordance with arrangements made by the Probation Board for Northern Ireland.

(2) The court may not make an order by virtue of this paragraph unless it appears to the court—

(a) in the case of an order imposing a requirement mentioned in sub-paragraph (3), that arrangements exist for persons to comply with such a requirement in the petty sessions district in Northern Ireland in which the offender resides, or will be residing during the licence period, and that provision can be made for him to comply with the requirement under those arrangements, and

(b) in any case, that suitable arrangements for supervising his compliance with the order can be made by the Probation Board for Northern Ireland.

(3) The requirements referred to in sub-paragraph (1)(a) are—

(a) an unpaid work requirement,

(b) an activity requirement,

(c) a programme requirement,

(d) an attendance centre requirement, and

(e) an electronic monitoring requirement.

(4) If an order has been made in accordance with this paragraph in relation to an offender but—

(a) the Secretary of State decides not to make an order under paragraph 1 or 4 of Schedule 1 to the 1997 Act in relation to him, and

(b) the offender has not applied under paragraph 22 of this Schedule for the amendment of the custody plus order or intermittent custody order,

the Secretary of State must apply to the court under paragraph 22 for the amendment of the order.

10. Where—

(a) the appropriate court for the purposes of paragraph 4 of Schedule 10 (amendment by reason of change of residence) is satisfied that the offender in respect of whom a custody plus order or intermittent custody order is in force is residing in Northern Ireland, or proposes to reside there during the licence period,

(b) the Secretary of State has made, or has indicated his willingness to make, an order under paragraph 1 or 4 of Schedule 1 to the 1997 Act in relation to the offender, and

(c) it appears to the court that the conditions in paragraph 9(2)(a) and (b) are satisfied,

the power of the court to amend the order under Schedule 10 includes power to amend it by requiring the requirements included in the order to be complied with in Northern Ireland and the offender's compliance with them to be supervised in accordance with the arrangements referred to in paragraph 9(2)(b).

11. A custody plus order made in accordance with paragraph 9 or a custody plus order or intermittent custody order amended in accordance with paragraph 10 must—

(a) specify the petty sessions district in Northern Ireland in which the offender resides or will reside during the licence period, and

(b) require the Probation Board for Northern Ireland to appoint or assign a probation officer who will be responsible for discharging in relation to him the functions conferred on responsible officers by Part 11 of this Act;

and section 216 (petty sessions area to be specified) does not apply in relation to an order so made or amended.

12. (1) Where a court makes a custody plus order in accordance with paragraph 9 or amends a custody plus order or intermittent custody order in accordance with paragraph 10, the court must provide the relevant documents to—

(a) the Probation Board for Northern Ireland, and

(b) the court of summary jurisdiction acting for the petty sessions district in which the offender resides or proposes to reside;

and paragraphs (b) to (d) of subsection (1) of section 219 (which relate to the provision of copies) do not apply in relation to an order so made or amended.

(2) In this paragraph, "the relevant documents" means—

(a) a copy of the order as made or amended, and

(b) such other documents and information relating to the case as the court making or amending the order considers likely to be of assistance.

13. (1) In relation to the making of a custody plus order by virtue of paragraph 9, in relation to the amendment of a custody plus order or intermittent custody order by virtue of paragraph 10, and (except for the purposes of paragraph 22) in relation to an order so made or amended, Chapter 4 of Part 12 of this Act has effect subject to the following modifications.

(2) Any reference to the responsible officer has effect as a reference to the probation officer appointed or assigned under paragraph 11(b).

(3) The following provisions are omitted—

(a) subsection (7) of section 201 (activity requirement);

(b) subsection (7) of section 202 (programme requirement);

(c) subsection (4) of section 218 (availability of arrangements in local area).

(4) In section 214 (attendance centre requirement), any reference to an attendance centre has effect as a reference to a day centre, as defined by paragraph 3(6) of Schedule 1 to the Criminal Justice (Northern Ireland) Order 1996 (S.I. 1996/3160 (N.I. 24).

(5) In section 215 (electronic monitoring requirement), in subsection (3), the words from "and" onwards are omitted.

PART 4
GENERAL PROVISIONS

14. This Part of this Schedule applies at any time while a custody plus order made in accordance with paragraph 2 or 9 or amended in accordance with paragraph 3 or 10, or an intermittent custody order amended in accordance with paragraph 3 or 10, is in force in respect of an offender.

15. In this Part of this Schedule—

"home court" means—

 (a) if the offender resides in Scotland, or will be residing there during the licence period, the sheriff court having jurisdiction in the locality in which the offender resides or proposes to reside, and

 (b) if he resides in Northern Ireland, or will be residing there during the licence period, the court of summary jurisdiction acting for the petty sessions district in which he resides or proposes to reside;

"local authority" and "local authority area" are to be read in accordance with paragraph 8;

"original court" means the court in England and Wales which made or last amended the custody plus order or intermittent custody order;

"the relevant officer" means—

 (a) where the order specifies a local authority area in Scotland, the local authority officer appointed or assigned under paragraph 5(b), and

 (b) where the order specifies a local authority district in Northern Ireland, the probation officer appointed or assigned under paragraph 11(b).

16. (1) Where this Part of this Schedule applies, Schedule 10 has effect subject to the following modifications.

 (2) Any reference to the responsible officer has effect as a reference to the relevant officer.

 (3) Any reference to the appropriate court has effect as a reference to the original court.

 (4) Where the order specifies a local authority area in Scotland—

 (a) any reference to the petty sessions area concerned has effect as a reference to that local authority area, and

 (b) any other reference to a petty sessions area has effect as a reference to a local authority area.

 (5) Where the order specifies a petty sessions district in Northern Ireland—

 (a) any reference to the petty sessions area concerned has effect as a reference to that petty sessions district, and

 (b) any other reference to a petty sessions area has effect as a reference to a petty sessions district.

 (6) Paragraph 9 is omitted.

17. (1) The home court may exercise any power under paragraph 4 or 5 of Schedule 10 - (amendment of custody plus order or intermittent custody order) as if it were the original court.

 (2) Subject to sub-paragraph (3), where the home court proposes to exercise the power conferred by paragraph 5 of Schedule 10, otherwise than on the application of the offender, the court—

 (a) if it is in Scotland—

 (i) must issue a citation requiring the offender to appear before it, and

 (ii) if he does not appear in answer to the citation, may issue a warrant for the offender's arrest;

(b) if it is in Northern Ireland—
    (i) must issue a summons requiring the offender to appear before it, and
    (ii) if he does not appear in answer to the summons, may issue a warrant for the offender's arrest;
and paragraph 8 of Schedule 10 does not apply to the home court.

(3) Sub-paragraph (2) does not apply to any order cancelling any requirement of a custody plus order or intermittent custody order.

(4) Where the home court is considering amending a custody plus or intermittent custody order, any reference in Chapter 4 of Part 12 of this Act to a local probation board has effect as a reference to a local authority in Scotland or, as the case may be, the Probation Board for Northern Ireland.

18. Where by virtue of paragraph 17 any application is made to the home court under paragraph 4 or 5 of Schedule 10, the home court may (instead of dealing with the application) require the offender to appear before the original court.

19. No court may amend or further amend a custody plus order or an intermittent custody order unless it appears to the court that the conditions in paragraph 2(2)(a) and (b) or, as the case may be, the conditions in paragraph 9(2)(a) and (b) are satisfied in relation to any requirement to be imposed; but this paragraph does not apply to any amendment made by virtue of paragraph 22(1).

20. The preceding paragraphs of this Schedule have effect in relation to any amendment of a custody plus or intermittent custody order by any court as they have effect in relation to the amendment of such an order by virtue of paragraph 3 or 10.

21. On the making of an order amending a custody plus order or intermittent custody order—
(a) the court must provide copies of the amending order to the offender and the relevant officer, and
(b) in the case of an amending order which substitutes a new local authority area or petty sessions district, paragraphs 5 and 6, or as the case may be paragraphs 11 and 12, have effect in relation to the order as they have effect in relation to an order made or amended in accordance with paragraph 2 or 3, or as the case may be, 9 or 10.

22. (1) Where—
(a) a custody plus order has been made in accordance with paragraph 2 or 9 or a custody plus or intermittent custody order has been amended in accordance with paragraph 3 or 10, but (in any of those cases) the Secretary of State has not made an order under paragraph 1 or 4 of Schedule 1 to the 1997 Act in relation to the offender, or
(b) the Secretary of State has made, or indicated his willingness to make, an order under paragraph 7(1) of Schedule 1 to the 1997 Act transferring the offender or his supervision back to England and Wales,
the court may, on the application of the offender or the Secretary of State, amend the custody plus order or intermittent custody order by requiring it to be complied with in England and Wales.

(2) In sub-paragraph (1) "the court", in a case falling within paragraph (a) of that sub-paragraph, means the original court.

(3) In a case where paragraph 2(4) or 9(4) requires the Secretary of State to apply under this paragraph, the court must make an amending order under this paragraph.

(4) Where under this paragraph the court amends a custody plus order or intermittent custody order which contains requirements which, in the opinion of the court, cannot be complied with in the petty sessions area in which the offender is residing or proposes to reside, the court must, in accordance with paragraph 5 of Schedule 10, either—

    (a) cancel those requirements, or

    (b) substitute for those requirements other requirements which can be complied with if the offender resides in that area.

(5) Where the court amends under this paragraph any custody plus order or intermittent custody order imposing a programme requirement, the court must ensure that the requirement as amended specifies a programme which is available in the petty sessions area in England and Wales in which the offender is residing or proposes to reside.

(6) The custody plus order or intermittent custody order as amended under this paragraph must specify the petty sessions area in which the offender resides or proposes to reside in the licence period.

(7) On the making under this paragraph of an order amending a custody plus order or intermittent custody order, the court must—

    (a) provide copies of the amending order to the offender, the relevant officer and the local probation board acting for the new petty sessions area, and

    (b) provide the magistrates' court acting for that area with a copy of the amending order and such other documents and information relating to the case as the home court considers likely to be of assistance to the court acting for that area in the exercise of its functions in relation to the order.

(8) Where an order has been amended under this paragraph, the preceding paragraphs of this Schedule shall cease to apply to the order as amended.

PART 5
SUPPLEMENTARY

23. Subsections (1) and (3) of section 245C of the Criminal Procedure (Scotland) Act 1995 (c. 46) (provision of remote monitoring) have effect as if they included a reference to the electronic monitoring of the requirements of a custody plus order made in accordance with paragraph 2 or a custody plus order or intermittent custody order made in accordance with paragraph 3.

24. (1) Section 4 of the Summary Jurisdiction (Process) Act 1881 (c. 24) (which provides, among other things, for service in England and Wales of Scottish citations or warrants) applies to any citation or warrant issued under paragraph 17(2)(a) as it applies to a citation or warrant granted under section 134 of the Criminal Procedure (Scotland) Act 1995.

(2) A summons issued by a court in Northern Ireland under paragraph 17(2)(b) may, in such circumstances as may be prescribed by rules of court, be served in England and Wales or Scotland.

SCHEDULE 12
ction 193
BREACH OR AMENDMENT OF SUSPENDED SENTENCE ORDER, AND EFFECT OF FURTHER CONVICTION

PART 1
PRELIMINARY

Interpretation

1. In this Schedule—

"the offender", in relation to a suspended sentence order, means the person in respect of whom the order is made;

"the petty sessions area concerned", in relation to a suspended sentence order, means the petty sessions area for the time being specified in the order;

"the responsible officer" has the meaning given by section 197.

2. In this Schedule—

  (a) any reference to a suspended sentence order being subject to review is a reference to such an order being subject to review in accordance with section 191(1)(b) or to a drug rehabilitation requirement of such an order being subject to review in accordance with section 210(1)(b);

  (b) any reference to the court responsible for a suspended sentence order which is subject to review is to be construed in accordance with section 191(3) or, as the case may be, 210(2).

Orders made on appeal

3. Where a suspended sentence order is made on appeal it is to be taken for the purposes of this Schedule to have been made by the Crown Court.

PART 2

BREACH OF COMMUNITY REQUIREMENT OR CONVICTION OF FURTHER OFFENCE

Duty to give warning in relation to community requirement

4. (1) If the responsible officer is of the opinion that the offender has failed without reasonable excuse to comply with any of the community requirements of a suspended sentence order, the officer must give him a warning under this paragraph unless—

  (a) the offender has within the previous twelve months been given a warning under this paragraph in relation to a failure to comply with any of the community requirements of the order, or

  (b) the officer causes an information to be laid before a justice of the peace in respect of the failure.

(2) A warning under this paragraph must—

  (a) describe the circumstances of the failure,

  (b) state that the failure is unacceptable, and

  (c) inform the offender that if within the next twelve months he again fails to comply with any requirement of the order, he will be liable to be brought before a court.

(3) The responsible officer must, as soon as practicable after the warning has been given, record that fact.

(4) In relation to any suspended sentence order which is made by the Crown Court and does not include a direction that any failure to comply with the community requirements of the order is to be dealt with by a magistrates' court, the reference in subparagraph (1)(b) to a justice of the peace is to be read as a reference to the Crown Court.

Breach of order after warning

5. (1) If—

    (a) the responsible officer has given a warning under paragraph 4 to the offender in respect of a suspended sentence order, and

    (b) at any time within the twelve months beginning with the date on which the warning was given, the responsible officer is of the opinion that the offender has since that date failed without reasonable excuse to comply with any of the community requirements of the order,

the officer must cause an information to be laid before a justice of the peace in respect of the failure in question.

  (2) In relation to any suspended sentence order which is made by the Crown Court and does not include a direction that any failure to comply with the community requirements of the order is to be dealt with by a magistrates' court, the reference in sub-paragraph (1) to a justice of the peace is to be read as a reference to the Crown Court.

Issue of summons or warrant by justice of the peace

6. (1) This paragraph applies to—

    (a) a suspended sentence order made by a magistrates' court, or

    (b) any suspended sentence order which was made by the Crown Court and includes a direction that any failure to comply with the community requirements of the order is to be dealt with by a magistrates' court.

  (2) If at any time while a suspended sentence order to which this paragraph applies is in force it appears on information to a justice of the peace acting for the petty sessions area concerned that the offender has failed to comply with any of the community requirements of the order, the justice may—

    (a) issue a summons requiring the offender to appear at the place and time specified in it, or

    (b) if the information is in writing and on oath, issue a warrant for his arrest.

  (3) Any summons or warrant issued under this paragraph must direct the offender to appear or be brought—

    (a) in the case of a suspended sentence order which is subject to review, before the court responsible for the order,

    (b) in any other case, before a magistrates' court acting for the petty sessions area concerned.

  (4) Where a summons issued under sub-paragraph (2)(a) requires the offender to appear before a magistrates' court and the offender does not appear in answer to the summons, the magistrates' court may issue a warrant for the arrest of the offender.

Issue of summons or warrant by Crown Court

7. (1) This paragraph applies to a suspended sentence order made by the Crown Court which does not include a direction that any failure to comply with the community requirements of the order is to be dealt with by a magistrates' court.

(2) If at any time while a suspended sentence order to which this paragraph applies is in force it appears on information to the Crown Court that the offender has failed to comply with any of the community requirements of the order, the Crown Court may—

(a) issue a summons requiring the offender to appear at the place and time specified in it, or

(b) if the information is in writing and on oath, issue a warrant for his arrest.

(3) Any summons or warrant issued under this paragraph must direct the offender to appear or be brought before the Crown Court.

(4) Where a summons issued under sub-paragraph (1)(a) requires the offender to appear before the Crown Court and the offender does not appear in answer to the summons, the Crown Court may issue a warrant for the arrest of the offender.

Powers of court on breach of community requirement or conviction of further offence

8. (1) This paragraph applies where—

(a) it is proved to the satisfaction of a court before which an offender appears or is brought under paragraph 6 or 7 or by virtue of section 192(6) that he has failed without reasonable excuse to comply with any of the community requirements of the suspended sentence order, or

(b) an offender is convicted of an offence committed during the operational period of a suspended sentence (other than one which has already taken effect) and either—

(i) he is so convicted by or before a court having power under paragraph 11 to deal with him in respect of the suspended sentence, or

(ii) he subsequently appears or is brought before such a court.

(2) The court must consider his case and deal with him in one of the following ways—

(a) the court may order that the suspended sentence is to take effect with its original term and custodial period unaltered,

(b) the court may order that the sentence is to take effect with either or both of the following modifications—

(i) the substitution for the original term of a lesser term complying with section 181(2), and

(ii) the substitution for the original custodial period of a lesser custodial period complying with section 181(5) and (6),

(c) the court may amend the order by doing any one or more of the following—

(i) imposing more onerous community requirements which the court could include if it were then making the order,

(ii) subject to subsections (3) and (4) of section 189, extending the supervision period, or

(iii) subject to subsection (3) of that section, extending the operational period.

(3) The court must make an order under sub-paragraph (2)(a) or (b) unless it is of the opinion that it would be unjust to do so in view of all the circumstances, including the matters mentioned in sub-paragraph (4); and where it is of that opinion the court must state its reasons.

(4) The matters referred to in sub-paragraph (3) are—

(a) the extent to which the offender has complied with the community requirements of the suspended sentence order, and

(b) in a case falling within sub-paragraph (1)(b), the facts of the subsequent offence.

(5) Where a court deals with an offender under sub-paragraph (2) in respect of a suspended sentence, the appropriate officer of the court must notify the appropriate officer of the court which passed the sentence of the method adopted.

(6) Where a suspended sentence order was made by the Crown Court and a magistrates' court would (apart from this sub-paragraph) be required to deal with the offender under sub-paragraph (2)(a), (b) or (c) it may instead commit him to custody or release him on bail until he can be brought or appear before the Crown Court.

(7) A magistrates' court which deals with an offender's case under sub-paragraph (6) must send to the Crown Court—

(a) a certificate signed by a justice of the peace certifying that the offender has failed to comply with the community requirements of the suspended sentence order in the respect specified in the certificate, and

(b) such other particulars of the case as may be desirable;

and a certificate purporting to be so signed is admissible as evidence of the failure before the Crown Court.

(8) In proceedings before the Crown Court under this paragraph any question whether the offender has failed to comply with the community requirements of the suspended sentence order and any question whether the offender has been convicted of an offence committed during the operational period of the suspended sentence is to be determined by the court and not by the verdict of a jury.

Further provisions as to order that suspended sentence is to take effect

9. (1) When making an order under paragraph 8(2)(a) or (b) that a sentence is to take effect (with or without any variation of the original term and custodial period), the court—

(a) must also make a custody plus order, and

(b) may order that the sentence is to take effect immediately or that the term of that sentence is to commence on the expiry of another term of imprisonment passed on the offender by that or another court.

(2) The power to make an order under sub-paragraph (1)(b) has effect subject to section 265 (restriction on consecutive sentences for released prisoners).

(3) For the purpose of any enactment conferring rights of appeal in criminal cases, any order made by the court under paragraph 8(2)(a) or (b) is to be treated as a sentence passed on the offender by that court for the offence for which the suspended sentence was passed.

Restriction of powers in paragraph 8 where treatment required

10. (1) An offender who is required by any of the following community requirements of a suspended sentence order—

(a) a mental health treatment requirement,

(b) a drug rehabilitation requirement, or

(c) an alcohol treatment requirement,

to submit to treatment for his mental condition, or his dependency on or propensity to misuse drugs or alcohol, is not to be treated for the purposes of paragraph 8(1)(a) as having failed to comply with that requirement on the ground only that he had refused to undergo any surgical, electrical or other treatment if, in the opinion of the court, his refusal was reasonable having regard to all the circumstances.

(2) A court may not under paragraph 8(2)(c)(i) amend a mental health treatment requirement, a drug rehabilitation requirement or an alcohol treatment requirement unless the

offender expresses his willingness to comply with the requirement as amended.

Court by which suspended sentence may be dealt with under paragraph 8(1)(b)

11. (1) An offender may be dealt with under paragraph 8(1)(b) in respect of a suspended sentence by the Crown Court or, where the sentence was passed by a magistrates' court, by any magistrates' court before which he appears or is brought.

(2) Where an offender is convicted by a magistrates' court of any offence and the court is satisfied that the offence was committed during the operational period of a suspended sentence passed by the Crown Court—

   (a) the court may, if it thinks fit, commit him in custody or on bail to the Crown Court, and

   (b) if it does not, must give written notice of the conviction to the appropriate officer of the Crown Court.

Procedure where court convicting of further offence does not deal with suspended sentence

12. (1) If it appears to the Crown Court, where that court has jurisdiction in accordance with sub-paragraph (2), or to a justice of the peace having jurisdiction in accordance with that sub-paragraph—

   (a) that an offender has been convicted in the United Kingdom of an offence committed during the operational period of a suspended sentence, and

   (b) that he has not been dealt with in respect of the suspended sentence,

   that court or justice may, subject to the following provisions of this paragraph, issue a summons requiring the offender to appear at the place and time specified in it, or a warrant for his arrest.

(2) Jurisdiction for the purposes of sub-paragraph (1) may be exercised—

   (a) if the suspended sentence was passed by the Crown Court, by that court;

   (b) if it was passed by a magistrates' court, by a justice acting for the petty sessions area for which that court acted.

(3) Where—

   (a) offender is convicted in Scotland or Northern Ireland of an offence, and

   (b) the court is informed that the offence was committed during the operational period of a suspended sentence passed in England or Wales,

   the court must give written notice of the conviction to the appropriate officer of the court by which the suspended sentence was passed.

(4) Unless he is acting in consequence of a notice under sub-paragraph (3), a justice of the peace may not issue a summons under this paragraph except on information and may not issue a warrant under this paragraph except on information in writing and on oath.

(5) A summons or warrant issued under this paragraph must direct the offender to appear or be brought before the court by which the suspended sentence was passed.

PART 3
AMENDMENT OF SUSPENDED SENTENCE ORDER

Cancellation of community requirements of suspended sentence order

13. (1) Where at any time while a suspended sentence order is in force, it appears to the appropriate court on the application of the offender or the responsible officer that,

having regard to the circumstances which have arisen since the order was made, it would be in the interests of justice to do so, the court may cancel the community requirements of the suspended sentence order.

(2) The circumstances in which the appropriate court may exercise its power under sub-paragraph (1) include the offender's making good progress or his responding satisfactorily to supervision.

(3) In this paragraph "the appropriate court" means—

   (a) in the case of a suspended sentence order which is subject to review, the court responsible for the order,

   (b) in the case of a suspended sentence order which was made by the Crown Court and does not include any direction that any failure to comply with the community requirements of the order is to be dealt with by a magistrates' court, the Crown Court, and

   (c) in any other case, a magistrates' court acting for the petty sessions area concerned.

Amendment by reason of change of residence

14. (1) This paragraph applies where, at any time while a suspended sentence order is in force, the appropriate court is satisfied that the offender proposes to change, or has changed, his residence from the petty sessions area concerned to another petty sessions area.

   (2) Subject to sub-paragraphs (3) and (4), the appropriate court may, and on the application of the responsible officer must, amend the suspended sentence order by substituting the other petty sessions area for the area specified in the order.

   (3) The court may not amend under this paragraph a suspended sentence order which contains requirements which, in the opinion of the court, cannot be complied with unless the offender resides in the petty sessions area concerned unless, in accordance with paragraph 15 it either—

   (a) cancels those requirements, or

   (b) substitutes for those requirements other requirements which can be complied with if the offender does not reside in that area.

   (4) The court may not amend under this paragraph any suspended sentence order imposing a programme requirement unless it appears to the court that the accredited programme specified in the requirement is available in the other petty sessions area.

   (5) In this paragraph "the appropriate court" has the same meaning as in paragraph 13.

Amendment of community requirements of suspended sentence order

15. (1) At any time during the supervision period, the appropriate court may, on the application of the offender or the responsible officer, by order amend any community requirement of a suspended sentence order—

   (a) by cancelling the requirement, or

   (b) by replacing it with a requirement of the same kind, which the court could include if it were then making the order.

   (2) For the purposes of sub-paragraph (1)—

   (a) a requirement falling within any paragraph of section 190(1) is of the same kind as any other requirement falling within that paragraph, and

   (b) an electronic monitoring requirement is a requirement of the same kind as any requirement falling within section 190(1) to which it relates.

(3) The court may not under this paragraph amend a mental health treatment requirement, a drug rehabilitation requirement or an alcohol treatment requirement unless the offender expresses his willingness to comply with the requirement as amended.

(4) If the offender fails to express his willingness to comply with a mental health treatment requirement, drug rehabilitation requirement or alcohol treatment requirement as proposed to be amended by the court under this paragraph, the court may—

    (a) revoke the suspended sentence order and the suspended sentence to which it relates, and

    (b) deal with him, for the offence in respect of which the suspended sentence was imposed, in any way in which it could deal with him if he had just been convicted by or before the court of the offence.

(5) In dealing with the offender under sub-paragraph (4)(b), the court must take into account the extent to which the offender has complied with the requirements of the order.

(6) In this paragraph "the appropriate court" has the same meaning as in paragraph 13.

Amendment of treatment requirements on report of practitioner

16. (1) Where the medical practitioner or other person by whom or under whose direction an offender is, in pursuance of any requirement to which this sub-paragraph applies, being treated for his mental condition or his dependency on or propensity to misuse drugs or alcohol—

    (a) is of the opinion mentioned in sub-paragraph (3), or

    (b) is for any reason unwilling to continue to treat or direct the treatment of the offender,

he must make a report in writing to that effect to the responsible officer and that officer must apply under paragraph 15 to the appropriate court for the variation or cancellation of the requirement.

(2) The requirements to which sub-paragraph (1) applies are—

    (a) a mental health treatment requirement,

    (b) a drug rehabilitation requirement, and

    (c) an alcohol treatment requirement.

(3) The opinion referred to in sub-paragraph (1) is—

    (a) that the treatment of the offender should be continued beyond the period specified in that behalf in the order,

    (b) that the offender needs different treatment,

    (c) that the offender is not susceptible to treatment, or

    (d) that the offender does not require further treatment.

(4) In this paragraph "the appropriate court" has the same meaning as in paragraph 13.

Amendment in relation to review of drug rehabilitation requirement

17. Where the responsible officer is of the opinion that a suspended sentence order imposing a drug rehabilitation requirement which is subject to review should be so amended as to provide for each periodic review (required by section 211) to be made without a hearing instead of at a review hearing, or vice versa, he must apply under paragraph 15 to the court responsible for the order for the variation of the order.

Extension of unpaid work requirement

18. (1) Where—

    (a) a suspended sentence order imposing an unpaid work requirement is in force in respect of the offender, and

    (b) on the application of the offender or the responsible officer, it appears to the appropriate court that it would be in the interests of justice to do so having regard to circumstances which have arisen since the order was made,

the court may, in relation to the order, extend the period of twelve months specified in section 200(2).

  (2) In this paragraph "the appropriate court" has the same meaning as in paragraph 13.

Supplementary

19. (1) No application may be made under paragraph 13, 15 or 18, and no order may be made under paragraph 14, while an appeal against the suspended sentence is pending.

  (2) Sub-paragraph (1) does not apply to an application under paragraph 15 which—

    (a) relates to a mental health treatment requirement, a drug rehabilitation requirement or an alcohol treatment requirement, and

    (b) is made by the responsible officer with the consent of the offender.

20. (1) Subject to sub-paragraph (2), where a court proposes to exercise its powers under paragraph 15, otherwise than on the application of the offender, the court—

    (a) must summon him to appear before the court, and

    (b) if he does not appear in answer to the summons, may issue a warrant for his arrest.

  (2) This paragraph does not apply to an order cancelling any community requirement of a suspended sentence order.

21. Paragraphs 8(2)(c) and 15(1)(b) have effect subject to the provisions mentioned in subsection (2) of section 190, and to subsections (3) and (5) of that section.

22. (1) On the making under this Schedule of an order amending a suspended sentence order, the proper officer of the court must—

    (a) provide copies of the amending order to the offender and the responsible officer,

    (b) in the case of an amending order which substitutes a new petty sessions area, provide a copy of the amending order to—

      (i) the local probation board acting for that area, and

      (ii) the magistrates' court acting for that area, and

    (c) in the case of an amending order which imposes or amends a requirement specified in the first column of Schedule 14, provide a copy of so much of the amending order as relates to that requirement to the person specified in relation to that requirement in the second column of that Schedule.

  (2) Where under sub-paragraph (1)(b) the proper officer of the court provides a copy of an amending order to a magistrates' court acting for a different area, the officer must also provide to that court such documents and information relating to the case as it considers likely to be of assistance to a court acting for that area in the exercise of its functions in relation to the order.535

  (3) In this paragraph "proper officer" means—

    (a) in relation to a magistrates' court, the justices' chief executive for the court; and

    (b) in relation to the Crown Court, the appropriate officer.

SCHEDULE 13
TRANSFER OF SUSPENDED SENTENCE ORDERS TO SCOTLAND OR
NORTHERN IRELAND

Section 194

PART 1
SCOTLAND

1. (1) Where the court considering the making of a suspended sentence order is satisfied that the offender resides in Scotland, or will reside there when the order comes into force, the court may not make a suspended sentence order in respect of the offender unless it appears to the court—

(a) in the case of an order imposing a requirement mentioned in sub-paragraph (2), that arrangements exist for persons to comply with such a requirement in the locality in Scotland in which the offender resides, or will be residing when the order comes into force, and that provision can be made for him to comply with the requirement under those arrangements, and

(b) in any case, that suitable arrangements for his supervision can be made by the local authority in whose area he resides, or will be residing when the order comes into force.

(2) The requirements referred to in sub-paragraph (1)(a) are—

(a) an unpaid work requirement,

(b) an activity requirement,

(c) a programme requirement,

(d) a mental health treatment requirement,

(e) a drug rehabilitation requirement,

(f) an alcohol treatment requirement, and

(g) an electronic monitoring requirement.

(3) Where—

(a) the appropriate court for the purposes of paragraph 14 of Schedule 12 (amendment by reason of change of residence) is satisfied that an offender in respect of whom a suspended sentence order is in force proposes to reside or is residing in Scotland, and

(b) it appears to the court that the conditions in sub-paragraph (1)(a) and (b) are satisfied,

the power of the court to amend the order under Part 3 of Schedule 12 includes power to amend it by requiring it to be complied with in Scotland and the offender to be supervised in accordance with the arrangements referred to in sub-paragraph (1)(b).

(4) For the purposes of sub-paragraph (3), any reference in sub-paragraph (1)(a) and (b) to the time when the order comes into force is to be treated as a reference to the time when the amendment comes into force.

(5) The court may not by virtue of sub-paragraph (1) or (3) require an attendance centre requirement to be complied with in Scotland.

(6) The court may not provide for an order made in accordance with this paragraph to be subject to review under section 191 or 210; and where an order which is subject to review under either of those sections is amended in accordance with this paragraph, the order shall cease to be so subject.

2. A suspended sentence order made or amended in accordance with paragraph 1 must—

(a) specify the local authority area in which the offender resides or will be residing when the order or amendment comes into force, and

    (b) require the local authority for that area to appoint or assign an officer who will be responsible for discharging in relation to him the functions conferred on responsible officers by Part 12 of this Act;

and section 216 (petty sessions area to be specified) does not apply in relation to an order so made or amended.

3. (1) Where a court makes or amends a suspended sentence order in accordance with paragraph 1, the court must provide the relevant documents to—

    (a) the local authority for the area specified in the order, and

    (b) the sheriff court having jurisdiction in the locality in which the offender resides or proposes to reside;

and paragraphs (b) to (d) of subsection (1) of section 219 (provision of copies of relevant orders) do not apply in relation to an order so made or amended.

    (2) In this paragraph, "the relevant documents" means—

    (a) a copy of the order as made or amended, and

    (b) such other documents and information relating to the case as the court making or amending the order considers likely to be of assistance.

4. (1) In relation to the making or amendment of a suspended sentence order in accordance with paragraph 1, and (except for the purposes of paragraph 20) in relation to an order so made or amended, Chapter 4 of Part 12 of this Act has effect subject to the following modifications.

    (2) Any reference to the responsible officer has effect as a reference to the officer appointed or assigned under paragraph 2(b).

    (3) The following provisions are omitted—

    (a) subsection (7) of section 201 (activity requirement),

    (b) subsection (7) of section 202 (programme requirement),

    (c) subsection (4) of section 206 (residence requirement),

    (d) subsection (4) of section 218 (availability of arrangements in local area).

    (4) In section 207 (mental health treatment requirement), for subsection (2)(a) there is substituted—

      "(a) treatment as a resident patient in a hospital within the meaning of the Mental Health (Care and Treatment) (Scotland) Act 2003, not being a state hospital within the meaning of that Act;".

    (5) In section 215 (electronic monitoring requirement), in subsection (3), the words from "and" onwards are omitted.

5. In this Part of this Schedule "local authority" means a council constituted under section 2 of the Local Government etc. (Scotland) Act 1994 (c. 39); and any reference to the area of such an authority is a reference to the local government area within the meaning of that Act.

PART 2

NORTHERN IRELAND

6. (1) Where the court considering the making of a suspended sentence order is satisfied that the offender resides in Northern Ireland, or will reside there when the order comes into force, the court may not make a suspended sentence order in respect of the offender unless it appears to the court—

    (a) in the case of an order imposing a requirement mentioned in sub-paragraph (2), that arrangements exist for persons to comply with such a requirement in the petty sessions district in Northern Ireland in which the offender resides, or will be residing when the order comes into force, and that provision can be made for him to comply with the requirement under those arrangements, and

(b) in any case, that suitable arrangements for his supervision can be made by the Probation Board for Northern Ireland.

(2) The requirements referred to in sub-paragraph (1)(a) are—

(a) an unpaid work requirement,

(b) an activity requirement,

(c) a programme requirement,

(d) a mental health treatment requirement,

(e) a drug rehabilitation requirement,

(f) an alcohol treatment requirement,

(g) an attendance centre requirement, and

(h) an electronic monitoring requirement.

(3) Where—

(a) the appropriate court for the purposes of paragraph 14 of Schedule 12 (amendment by reason of change of residence) is satisfied that an offender in respect of whom a suspended sentence order is in force proposes to reside or is residing in Northern Ireland, and

(b) it appears to the court that the conditions in sub-paragraphs (1)(a) and (b) are satisfied,

the power of the court to amend the order under Part 3 of Schedule 12 includes power to amend it by requiring it to be complied with in Northern Ireland and the offender to be supervised in accordance with the arrangements referred to in sub-paragraph (1)(b).

(4) For the purposes of sub-paragraph (3), any reference in sub-paragraph (1)(a) and (b) to the time when the order comes into force is to be treated as a reference to the time when the amendment comes into force.

(5) The court may not provide for an order made in accordance with this paragraph to be subject to review under section 191 or 210; and where an order which is subject to review under either of those sections is amended in accordance with this paragraph, the order shall cease to be so subject.

7. A suspended sentence order made or amended in accordance with paragraph 6 must—

(a) specify the petty sessions district in Northern Ireland in which the offender resides or will be residing when the order or amendment comes into force, and

(b) require the Probation Board for Northern Ireland to appoint or assign a probation officer who will be responsible for discharging in relation to him the functions conferred on responsible officers by Part 12 of this Act;

and section 216 (petty sessions area to be specified) does not apply in relation to an order so made or amended.

8. (1) Where a court makes or amends a suspended sentence order in accordance with paragraph 6, the court must provide the relevant documents to—

(a) the Probation Board for Northern Ireland, and

(b) the court of summary jurisdiction acting for the petty sessions district in which the offender resides or proposes to reside;

and paragraphs (b) to (d) of subsection (1) of section 219 (provision of copies of relevant orders) do not apply in relation to an order so made or amended.

(2) In this paragraph, "the relevant documents" means—

(a) a copy of the order as made or amended, and

(b) such other documents and information relating to the case as the court making or amending the order considers likely to be of assistance.

9. (1) In relation to the making or amendment of a suspended sentence order in accordance with paragraph 6, and (except for the purposes of paragraph 20) in relation to an order so made or amended, Chapter 4 of Part 12 of this Act has effect subject to the following modifications.

(2) Any reference to the responsible officer has effect as a reference to the probation officer appointed or assigned under paragraph 7(b).

(3) The following provisions are omitted—

(a) subsection (7) of section 201 (activity requirement),

(b) subsection (7) of section 202 (programme requirement),

(c) subsection (4) of section 206 (residence requirement),

(d) subsection (4) of section 218 (availability of arrangements in local area).

(4) In section 207 (mental health treatment requirement), for subsection (2)(a) there is substituted—

"(a) treatment (whether as an in-patient or an out-patient) at such hospital as may be specified in the order, being a hospital within the meaning of the Health and Personal Social Services (Northern Ireland) Order 1972, approved by the Department of Health, Social Services and Public Safety for the purposes of paragraph 4(3) of Schedule 1 to the Criminal Justice (Northern Ireland) Order 1996 (S.I. 1996/ 3160 (N.I. 24));".

(5) In section 214 (attendance centre requirement), any reference to an attendance centre has effect as a reference to a day centre, as defined by paragraph 3(6) of Schedule 1 to the Criminal Justice (Northern Ireland) Order 1996 (S.I. 1996/3160 (N.I. 24).

(6) In section 215 (electronic monitoring requirement), in subsection (3), the words from "and" onwards are omitted.

PART 3
GENERAL PROVISIONS: BREACH OR AMENDMENT

10. This Part of this Schedule applies at any time while a suspended sentence order made or amended in accordance with paragraph 1 or 6 is in force in respect of an offender.

11. In this Part of this Schedule—

"home court" means—

(a) if the offender resides in Scotland, or will be residing there at the relevant time, the sheriff court having jurisdiction in the locality in which the offender resides or proposes to reside, and

(b) if he resides in Northern Ireland, or will be residing there at the relevant time, the court of summary jurisdiction acting for the petty sessions district in which he resides or proposes to reside;

"local authority" and "local authority area" are to be read in accordance with paragraph 5;

"original court" means the court in England and Wales which made or last amended the order;

"the relevant officer" means—

(a) where the order specifies a local authority area in Scotland, the local authority officer appointed or assigned under paragraph 2(b), and

(b) where the court specifies a petty sessions district in Northern Ireland, the probation officer appointed or assigned under paragraph 7(b);

"the relevant time" means the time when the order or the amendment to it comes into force.

12. (1) Where this Part of this Schedule applies, Schedule 12 has effect subject to the following modifications.

(2) Any reference to the responsible officer has effect as a reference to the relevant officer.

(3) Any reference to a magistrates' court acting for the petty sessions area concerned has effect as a reference to a magistrates' court acting for the same petty sessions area as the original court; and any reference to a justice of the peace acting for the petty sessions area concerned has effect as a reference to a justice of the peace acting for the same petty sessions area as that court.

(4) Any reference to the appropriate court has effect as a reference to the original court.

(5) In paragraphs 4 and 5, any reference to causing an information to be laid before a justice of the peace has effect—

(a) if the home court is in Scotland, as a reference to providing information to the home court with a view to it issuing a citation, and

(b) if the home court is in Northern Ireland, as a reference to making a complaint to a justice of the peace in Northern Ireland.

(6) In paragraph 14—

(a) if the home court is in Scotland—

(i) any reference to the petty sessions area concerned has effect as a reference to the local authority area specified in the order, and

(ii) any other reference to a petty sessions area has effect as a reference to a local authority area, and

(b) if the home court is in Northern Ireland—

(i) any reference to the petty sessions area concerned has effect as a reference to the petty sessions district specified in the order, and

(ii) any other reference to a petty sessions area has effect as a reference to a petty sessions district.

(7) Paragraph 22 is omitted.

(8) No court in England and Wales may—

(a) exercise any power in relation to any failure by the offender to comply with any community requirement of the order unless the offender has been required in accordance with paragraph 14(1)(b) or (2)(a) of this Schedule to appear before that court;

(b) exercise any power under Part 3 of Schedule 12 unless the offender has been required in accordance with paragraph 15(2) or 16 of this Schedule to appear before that court.

13. (1) Sub-paragraph (2) applies where it appears to the home court—

(a) if that court is in Scotland, on information from the relevant officer, or

(b) if that court is in Northern Ireland, upon a complaint being made by the relevant officer,

that the offender has failed without reasonable excuse to comply with any of the community requirements of the suspended sentence order.

(2) The home court may—

(a) if it is in Scotland—

(i) issue a citation requiring the offender to appear before it at the time specified in the citation, or

(ii) issue a warrant for the offender's arrest;

(b) if it is in Northern Ireland—

        (i) issue a summons requiring the offender to appear before it at the time specified in the summons, or

        (ii) issue a warrant for the offender's arrest.

14. (1) The court before which an offender appears or is brought by virtue of paragraph 13 must—

    (a) determine whether the offender has failed without reasonable excuse to comply with any of the community requirements of the suspended sentence order, or

    (b) require the offender to appear before the original court.

  (2) If the home court determines that the offender has failed without reasonable excuse to comply with any of the community requirements of the order—

    (a) the home court must require the offender to appear before the original court, and

    (b) when the offender appears before the original court, paragraph 8 of Schedule 12 applies as if it had already been proved to the satisfaction of the original court that the offender failed without reasonable excuse to comply with such of the community requirements of the order as may have been determined.

  (3) An offender who is required by any of the following community requirements of a suspended sentence order—

    (a) a mental health treatment requirement,

    (b) a drug rehabilitation requirement, or

    (c) an alcohol treatment requirement,

to submit to treatment for his mental condition, or his dependency on or propensity to misuse drugs or alcohol, is not to be treated for the purposes of sub-paragraph (2) as having failed to comply with that requirement on the ground only that he had refused to undergo any surgical, electrical or other treatment if, in the opinion of the court, his refusal was reasonable having regard to all the circumstances.

  (4) The evidence of one witness shall, for the purposes of sub-paragraph (2), be sufficient.

  (5) Where the home court is in Scotland and the order contains an electronic monitoring requirement, section 245H of the Criminal Procedure (Scotland) Act 1995 (c. 46) (documentary evidence) applies to proceedings under this paragraph as it applies to proceedings under section 245F of that Act (breach of restriction of liberty order).

  (6) Where an offender is required by virtue of sub-paragraph (2) to appear before the original court—

    (a) the home court must send to the original court a certificate certifying that the offender has failed without reasonable excuse to comply with the requirements of the order in the respect specified, and

    (b) such a certificate signed by the clerk of the home court is admissible before the original court as conclusive evidence of the matters specified in it.

15. (1) The home court may exercise any power under Part 3 of Schedule 12 (amendment of suspended sentence order) as if it were the original court, except that the home court may not exercise the power conferred by paragraph 15(4) of that Schedule.

  (2) Where paragraph 15(4) of Schedule 12 applies the home court must require the offender to appear before the original court.

  (3) Subject to sub-paragraph (4), where the home court proposes to exercise the power conferred by paragraph 15(1) of Schedule 12, otherwise than on the application of the offender, the court—

    (a) if it is in Scotland—

        (i) must issue a citation requiring the offender to appear before it, and

        (ii) if he does not appear in answer to the citation, may issue a warrant for the offender's arrest;

   (b) if it is in Northern Ireland—

        (i)   must issue a summons requiring the offender to appear before it, and

        (ii) if he does not appear in answer to the summons, may issue a warrant for the offender's arrest;

   and paragraph 20 of Schedule 12 does not apply to the home court.

(4) Sub-paragraph (3) does not apply to an order cancelling any community requirement of a suspended sentence order.

(5) Where the home court is considering amending a suspended sentence order, any reference in Chapter 4 of Part 12 of this Act to a local probation board has effect as a reference to a local authority in Scotland or, as the case may be, the Probation Board for Northern Ireland.

16. Where by virtue of paragraph 15 any application is made to the home court under Part 3 of Schedule 12, the home court may (instead of dealing with the application) require the offender to appear before the original court.

17. No court may amend or further amend a suspended sentence order unless it appears to the court that the conditions in paragraph 1(1)(a) and (b) or, as the case may be, paragraph 6(1)(a) and (b) are satisfied in relation to any requirement to be imposed; but this paragraph does not apply to any amendment by virtue of paragraph 20(2).

18. The preceding paragraphs of this Schedule have effect in relation to any amendment of a suspended order by any court as they have effect in relation to the amendment of such an order by virtue of paragraph 1(3) or 6(3).

19. On the making of an order amending a suspended sentence order—

   (a) the court must provide copies of the amending order to the offender and the relevant officer, and

   (b) in the case of an amending order which substitutes a new local authority area or petty sessions district, paragraphs 2 and 3 or, as the case may be, 7 and 8 have effect in relation to the order as they have effect in relation to an order made or amended in accordance with paragraph 1 or 6.

20. (1) This paragraph applies where the home court is satisfied that the offender is residing or proposes to reside in England and Wales.

   (2) Subject to sub-paragraphs (3) and (4), the home court may, and on the application of the relevant officer must, amend the suspended sentence order by requiring it to be complied with in England and Wales.

   (3) The court may not amend under this paragraph a suspended sentence order which contains requirements which, in the opinion of the court, cannot be complied with in the petty sessions area in which the offender is residing or proposes to reside unless, in accordance with paragraph 15 of Schedule 12 it either—

      (a) cancels those requirements, or

      (b) substitutes for those requirements other requirements which can be complied with if the offender resides in that area.

   (4) The court may not amend under this paragraph any suspended sentence order imposing a programme requirement unless it appears to the court that the accredited programme specified in the requirement is available in the petty sessions area in England and Wales in which the offender is residing or proposes to reside.

   (5) The suspended sentence order as amended must specify the petty sessions area in which the offender resides or proposes to reside.

(6) On the making under this paragraph of an order amending a suspended sentence order, the home court must—

(a) provide copies of the amending order to the offender, the relevant officer and the local probation board acting for the new petty sessions area, and

(b) provide the magistrates' court acting for that area with a copy of the amending order and such other documents and information relating to the case as the home court considers likely to be of assistance to a court acting for that area in the exercise of its functions in relation to the order.

(7) Where an order has been amended under this paragraph, the preceding paragraphs of this Schedule shall cease to apply to the order as amended.

PART 4
SUPPLEMENTARY

21. Subsections (1) and (3) of section 245C of the Criminal Procedure (Scotland) Act 1995 (c. 46) (provision of remote monitoring) have effect as if they included a reference to the electronic monitoring of the community requirements of a suspended sentence order made or amended in accordance with paragraph 1 of this Schedule.

22. (1) Section 4 of the Summary Jurisdiction (Process) Act 1881 (c. 24) (which provides, among other things, for service in England and Wales of Scottish citations or warrants) applies to any citation or warrant issued under paragraph 13(2)(a) or 15(3)(a) as it applies to a citation or warrant granted under section 134 of the Criminal Procedure (Scotland) Act 1995.

(2) A summons issued by a court in Northern Ireland under paragraph 13(2)(b) or 15(3)(b) may, in such circumstances as may be prescribed by rules of court, be served in England and Wales or Scotland.

SCHEDULE 14
PERSONS TO WHOM COPIES OF REQUIREMENTS TO BE PROVIDED IN PARTICULAR CASES

Section 219

Requirement	Person to whom copy of requirement is to be given
An activity requirement.	The person specified under section 201(1)(a).
An exclusion requirement imposed for the purpose (or partly for the purpose) of protecting a person from being approached by the offender.	The person intended to be protected.
A residence requirement relating to residence in an institution.	The person in charge of the institution.
A mental health treatment requirement.	The person specified under section 207(2)(c) or the person in

	charge of the institution or place specified under section 207(2)(a) or (b).
A drug rehabilitation requirement.	The person in charge of the institution or place specified under section 209(4)(a) or (b).
An alcohol treatment requirement.	The person specified under section 212(5)(c) or the person in charge of the institution or place specified under section 212(5)(a) or (b).
An attendance centre requirement.	The officer in charge of the attendance centre specified in the requirement.
An electronic monitoring requirement.	Any person who by virtue of section 215(3) will be responsible for the electronic monitoring. Any person by virtue of whose consent the requirement is included in the order.

SCHEDULE 15

SPECIFIED OFFENCES FOR PURPOSES OF CHAPTER 5 OF PART 12 Section 224

PART 1
SPECIFIED VIOLENT OFFENCES

1   Manslaughter.
2   Kidnapping.
3   False imprisonment.
4   An offence under section 4 of the Offences against the Person Act 1861 (c. 100) (soliciting murder).
5   An offence under section 16 of that Act (threats to kill).
6   An offence under section 18 of that Act (wounding with intent to cause grievous bodily harm).
7   An offence under section 20 of that Act (malicious wounding).
8   An offence under section 21 of that Act (attempting to choke, suffocate or strangle in order to commit or assist in committing an indictable offence).
9   An offence under section 22 of that Act (using chloroform etc. to commit or assist in the committing of any indictable offence).
10 An offence under section 23 of that Act (maliciously administering poison etc. so as to endanger life or inflict grievous bodily harm).
11 An offence under section 27 of that Act (abandoning children).
12 An offence under section 28 of that Act (causing bodily injury by explosives).
13 An offence under section 29 of that Act (using explosives etc. with intent to do grievous bodily harm).
14 An offence under section 30 of that Act (placing explosives with intent to do bodily injury).
15 An offence under section 31 of that Act (setting spring guns etc. with intent to do grievous bodily harm).

16 An offence under section 32 of that Act (endangering the safety of railway passengers).

17 An offence under section 35 of that Act (injuring persons by furious driving).

18 An offence under section 37 of that Act (assaulting officer preserving wreck).

19 An offence under section 38 of that Act (assault with intent to resist arrest).

20 An offence under section 47 of that Act (assault occasioning actual bodily harm).

21 An offence under section 2 of the Explosive Substances Act 1883 (c. 3) (causing explosion likely to endanger life or property).

22 An offence under section 3 of that Act (attempt to cause explosion, or making or keeping explosive with intent to endanger life or property).

23 An offence under section 1 of the Infant Life (Preservation) Act 1929 (c. 34) (child destruction).

24 An offence under section 1 of the Children and Young Persons Act 1933 (c. 12) (cruelty to children).

25 An offence under section 1 of the Infanticide Act 1938 (c. 36) (infanticide).

26 An offence under section 16 of the Firearms Act 1968 (c. 27) (possession of firearm with intent to endanger life).

27 An offence under section 16A of that Act (possession of firearm with intent to cause fear of violence).

28 An offence under section 17(1) of that Act (use of firearm to resist arrest).

29 An offence under section 17(2) of that Act (possession of firearm at time of committing or being arrested for offence specified in Schedule 1 to that Act).

30 An offence under section 18 of that Act (carrying a firearm with criminal intent).

31 An offence under section 8 of the Theft Act 1968 (c. 60) (robbery or assault with intent to rob).

32 An offence under section 9 of that Act of burglary with intent to—
    (a) inflict grievous bodily harm on a person, or
    (b) do unlawful damage to a building or anything in it.

33 An offence under section 10 of that Act (aggravated burglary).

34 An offence under section 12A of that Act (aggravated vehicle-taking) involving an accident which caused the death of any person.

35 An offence of arson under section 1 of the Criminal Damage Act 1971 (c. 48).

36 An offence under section 1(2) of that Act (destroying or damaging property) other than an offence of arson.

37 An offence under section 1 of the Taking of Hostages Act 1982 (c. 28) (hostage-taking).

38 An offence under section 1 of the Aviation Security Act 1982 (c. 36) (hijacking).

39 An offence under section 2 of that Act (destroying, damaging or endangering safety of aircraft).

40 An offence under section 3 of that Act (other acts endangering or likely to endanger safety of aircraft).

41 An offence under section 4 of that Act (offences in relation to certain dangerous articles).

42 An offence under section 127 of the Mental Health Act 1983 (c. 20) (ill-treatment of patients).

43 An offence under section 1 of the Prohibition of Female Circumcision Act 1985 (c. 38) (prohibition of female circumcision).

44 An offence under section 1 of the Public Order Act 1986 (c. 64) (riot).

45 An offence under section 2 of that Act (violent disorder).

46 An offence under section 3 of that Act (affray).

47 An offence under section 134 of the Criminal Justice Act 1988 (c. 33) (torture).

48 An offence under section 1 of the Road Traffic Act 1988 (c. 52) (causing death by dangerous driving).

49 An offence under section 3A of that Act (causing death by careless driving when under influence of drink or drugs).

50 An offence under section 1 of the Aviation and Maritime Security Act 1990 (c. 31) (endangering safety at aerodromes).

51 An offence under section 9 of that Act (hijacking of ships).

52 An offence under section 10 of that Act (seizing or exercising control of fixed platforms).

53 An offence under section 11 of that Act (destroying fixed platforms or endangering their safety).

54 An offence under section 12 of that Act (other acts endangering or likely to endanger safe navigation).

55 An offence under section 13 of that Act (offences involving threats).

56 An offence under Part II of the Channel Tunnel (Security) Order 1994 (S.I. 1994/570) (offences relating to Channel Tunnel trains and the tunnel system).

57 An offence under section 4 of the Protection from Harassment Act 1997 (c. 40) (putting people in fear of violence).

58 An offence under section 29 of the Crime and Disorder Act 1998 (c. 37) (racially or religiously aggravated assaults).

59 An offence falling within section 31(1)(a) or (b) of that Act (racially or religiously aggravated offences under section 4 or 4A of the Public Order Act 1986 (c. 64)).

60 An offence under section 51 or 52 of the International Criminal Court Act 2001 (c. 17) (genocide, crimes against humanity, war crimes and related offences), other than one involving murder.

61 An offence under section 1 of the Female Genital Mutilation Act 2003 (c. 31) (female genital mutilation).

62 An offence under section 2 of that Act (assisting a girl to mutilate her own genitalia).

63 An offence under section 3 of that Act (assisting a non-UK person to mutilate overseas a girl's genitalia).

64 An offence of—
  (a) aiding, abetting, counselling, procuring or inciting the commission of an offence specified in this Part of this Schedule,
  (b) conspiring to commit an offence so specified, or
  (c) attempting to commit an offence so specified.

65 An attempt to commit murder or a conspiracy to commit murder.

PART 2
SPECIFIED SEXUAL OFFENCES

66 An offence under section 1 of the Sexual Offences Act 1956 (c. 69) (rape).

67 An offence under section 2 of that Act (procurement of woman by threats).

68 An offence under section 3 of that Act (procurement of woman by false pretences).

69 An offence under section 4 of that Act (administering drugs to obtain or facilitate intercourse).

70 An offence under section 5 of that Act (intercourse with girl under thirteen).

71 An offence under section 6 of that Act (intercourse with girl under 16).

72 An offence under section 7 of that Act (intercourse with a defective).

73 An offence under section 9 of that Act (procurement of a defective).

74 An offence under section 10 of that Act (incest by a man).

75 An offence under section 11 of that Act (incest by a woman).

76 An offence under section 14 of that Act (indecent assault on a woman).

77 An offence under section 15 of that Act (indecent assault on a man).

78 An offence under section 16 of that Act (assault with intent to commit buggery).

79 An offence under section 17 of that Act (abduction of woman by force or for the sake of her property).

80 An offence under section 19 of that Act (abduction of unmarried girl under eighteen from parent or guardian).

81 An offence under section 20 of that Act (abduction of unmarried girl under sixteen from parent or guardian).

82 An offence under section 21 of that Act (abduction of defective from parent or guardian).

83 An offence under section 22 of that Act (causing prostitution of women).

84 An offence under section 23 of that Act (procuration of girl under twenty-one).

85 An offence under section 24 of that Act (detention of woman in brothel).

86 An offence under section 25 of that Act (permitting girl under thirteen to use premises for intercourse).

87 An offence under section 26 of that Act (permitting girl under sixteen to use premises for intercourse).

88 An offence under section 27 of that Act (permitting defective to use premises for intercourse).

89 An offence under section 28 of that Act (causing or encouraging the prostitution of, intercourse with or indecent assault on girl under sixteen).

90 An offence under section 29 of that Act (causing or encouraging prostitution of defective).

91 An offence under section 32 of that Act (soliciting by men).

92 An offence under section 33 of that Act (keeping a brothel).

93 An offence under section 128 of the Mental Health Act 1959 (c. 72) (sexual intercourse with patients).

94 An offence under section 1 of the Indecency with Children Act 1960 (c. 33) (indecent conduct towards young child).

95 An offence under section 4 of the Sexual Offences Act 1967 (c. 60) (procuring others to commit homosexual acts).

96 An offence under section 5 of that Act (living on earnings of male prostitution).

97 An offence under section 9 of the Theft Act 1968 (c. 60) of burglary with intent to commit rape.

98 An offence under section 54 of the Criminal Law Act 1977 (c. 45) (inciting girl under sixteen to have incestuous sexual intercourse).

99 An offence under section 1 of the Protection of Children Act 1978 (c. 37) (indecent photographs of children).

100 An offence under section 170 of the Customs and Excise Management Act 1979 (c. 2) (penalty for fraudulent evasion of duty etc.) in relation to goods prohibited to be imported under section 42 of the Customs Consolidation Act 1876 (c. 36) (indecent or obscene articles).

101 An offence under section 160 of the Criminal Justice Act 1988 (c. 33) (possession of indecent photograph of a child).

102 An offence under section 1 of the Sexual Offences Act 2003 (c. 42) (rape).

103 An offence under section 2 of that Act (assault by penetration).

104 An offence under section 3 of that Act (sexual assault).

105 An offence under section 4 of that Act (causing a person to engage in sexual activity without consent).

106 An offence under section 5 of that Act (rape of a child under 13).

107 An offence under section 6 of that Act (assault of a child under 13 by penetration).

108 An offence under section 7 of that Act (sexual assault of a child under 13).

109 An offence under section 8 of that Act (causing or inciting a child under 13 to engage in sexual activity).

110 An offence under section 9 of that Act (sexual activity with a child).

111 An offence under section 10 of that Act (causing or inciting a child to engage in sexual activity).

112 An offence under section 11 of that Act (engaging in sexual activity in the presence of a child).

113 An offence under section 12 of that Act (causing a child to watch a sexual act).

114 An offence under section 13 of that Act (child sex offences committed by children or young persons).

115 An offence under section 14 of that Act (arranging or facilitating commission of a child sex offence).

116 An offence under section 15 of that Act (meeting a child following sexual grooming etc.).

117 An offence under section 16 of that Act (abuse of position of trust: sexual activity with a child).

118 An offence under section 17 of that Act (abuse of position of trust: causing or inciting a child to engage in sexual activity).

119 An offence under section 18 of that Act (abuse of position of trust: sexual activity in the presence of a child).

120 An offence under section 19 of that Act (abuse of position of trust: causing a child to watch a sexual act).

121 An offence under section 25 of that Act (sexual activity with a child family member).

122 An offence under section 26 of that Act (inciting a child family member to engage in sexual activity).

123 An offence under section 30 of that Act (sexual activity with a person with a mental disorder impeding choice).

124 An offence under section 31 of that Act (causing or inciting a person with a mental-disorder impeding choice to engage in sexual activity).

125 An offence under section 32 of that Act (engaging in sexual activity in the presence of a person with a mental disorder impeding choice).

126 An offence under section 33 of that Act (causing a person with a mental disorder impeding choice to watch a sexual act).

127 An offence under section 34 of that Act (inducement, threat or deception to procure sexual activity with a person with a mental disorder).

128 An offence under section 35 of that Act (causing a person with a mental disorder to engage in or agree to engage in sexual activity by inducement, threat or deception).

129 An offence under section 36 of that Act (engaging in sexual activity in the presence, procured by inducement, threat or deception, of a person with a mental disorder).

130 An offence under section 37 of that Act (causing a person with a mental disorder to watch a sexual act by inducement, threat or deception).

131 An offence under section 38 of that Act (care workers: sexual activity with a person with a mental disorder).

132 An offence under section 39 of that Act (care workers: causing or inciting sexual activity).

133 An offence under section 40 of that Act (care workers: sexual activity in the presence of a person with a mental disorder).

134 An offence under section 41 of that Act (care workers: causing a person with a mental disorder to watch a sexual act).

135 An offence under section 47 of that Act (paying for sexual services of a child).

136 An offence under section 48 of that Act (causing or inciting child prostitution or pornography).

137 An offence under section 49 of that Act (controlling a child prostitute or a child involved in pornography).

138 An offence under section 50 of that Act (arranging or facilitating child prostitution or pornography).

139 An offence under section 52 of that Act (causing or inciting prostitution for gain).

140 An offence under section 53 of that Act (controlling prostitution for gain).

141 An offence under section 57 of that Act (trafficking into the UK for sexual exploitation).

142 An offence under section 58 of that Act (trafficking within the UK for sexual exploitation).

143 An offence under section 59 of that Act (trafficking out of the UK for sexual exploitation).

144 An offence under section 61 of that Act (administering a substance with intent).

145 An offence under section 62 of that Act (committing an offence with intent to commit a sexual offence).

146 An offence under section 63 of that Act (trespass with intent to commit a sexual offence).

147 An offence under section 64 of that Act (sex with an adult relative: penetration).

148 An offence under section 65 of that Act (sex with an adult relative: consenting to penetration).

149 An offence under section 66 of that Act (exposure).

150 An offence under section 67 of that Act (voyeurism).

151 An offence under section 69 of that Act (intercourse with an animal).

152 An offence under section 70 of that Act (sexual penetration of a corpse).

153 An offence of—

(a) aiding, abetting, counselling, procuring or inciting the commission of an offence specified in this Part of this Schedule,

(b) conspiring to commit an offence so specified, or

(c) attempting to commit an offence so specified.

SCHEDULE 16
SCOTTISH OFFENCES SPECIFIED FOR
Section 229   THE PURPOSES OF SECTION 229(4)

1 Rape.

2 Clandestine injury to women.

3 Abduction of woman or girl with intent to rape or ravish.

4 Assault with intent to rape or ravish.

5 Indecent assault.

6 Lewd, indecent or libidinous behaviour or practices.

7 Shameless indecency.

8 Sodomy.

9 An offence under section 170 of the Customs and Excise Management Act 1979 (c. 2) in relation to goods prohibited to be imported under section 42 of the Customs Consolidation

Act 1876 (c. 36), but only where the prohibited goods include indecent photographs of persons.

10 An offence under section 52 of the Civic Government (Scotland) Act 1982 (c. 45) (taking and distribution of indecent images of children).

11 An offence under section 52A of that Act (possession of indecent images of children).

12 An offence under section 1 of the Criminal Law (Consolidation) (Scotland) Act 1995 (c. 39) (incest).

13 An offence under section 2 of that Act (intercourse with a stepchild).

14 An offence under section 3 of that Act (intercourse with child under 16 by person in position of trust).

15 An offence under section 5 of that Act (unlawful intercourse with girl under 16).

16 An offence under section 6 of that Act (indecent behaviour towards girl between 12 and 16).

17 An offence under section 8 of that Act (detention of woman in brothel or other premises).

18 An offence under section 10 of that Act (person having parental responsibilities causing or encouraging sexual activity in relation to a girl under 16).

19 An offence under subsection (5) of section 13 of that Act (homosexual offences).

20 An offence under section 3 of the Sexual Offences (Amendment) Act 2000 (c. 44) (abuse of position of trust).

21 An offence of—
   (a) attempting, conspiring or inciting another to commit any offence specified in the preceding paragraphs, or
   (b) aiding, abetting, counselling or procuring the commission of any offence specified in paragraphs 9 to 20.

SCHEDULE 17
NORTHERN IRELAND OFFENCES SPECIFIED FOR
THE PURPOSES OF SECTION 229(4)   Section 229

PART 1
VIOLENT OFFENCES

1 Manslaughter.
2 Kidnapping.
3 Riot.
4 Affray.
5 False imprisonment.
6 An offence under section 4 of the Offences against the Person Act 1861 (c. 100) (soliciting murder).
7 An offence under section 16 of that Act (threats to kill).
8 An offence under section 18 of that Act (wounding with intent to cause grievous bodily harm).
9 An offence under section 20 of that Act (malicious wounding).
10 An offence under section 21 of that Act (attempting to choke, suffocate or strangle in order to commit or assist in committing an indictable offence).
11 An offence under section 22 of that Act (using chloroform etc. to commit or assist in the committing of any indictable offence).
12 An offence under section 23 of that Act (maliciously administering poison etc. so as to endanger life or inflict grievous bodily harm).

13 An offence under section 27 of that Act (abandoning children).

14 An offence under section 28 of that Act (causing bodily injury by explosives).

15 An offence under section 29 of that Act (using explosives etc. with intent to do grievous bodily harm).

16 An offence under section 30 of that Act (placing explosives with intent to do bodily injury).

17 An offence under section 31 of that Act (setting spring guns etc. with intent to do grievous bodily harm).

18 An offence under section 32 of that Act (endangering the safety of railway passengers).

19 An offence under section 35 of that Act (injuring persons by furious driving).

20 An offence under section 37 of that Act (assaulting officer preserving wreck).

21 An offence under section 47 of that Act of assault occasioning actual bodily harm.

22 An offence under section 2 of the Explosive Substances Act 1883 (c. 3) (causing explosion likely to endanger life or property).

23 offence under section 3 of that Act (attempt to cause explosion, or making or keeping explosive with intent to endanger life or property).

24 An offence under section 25 of the Criminal Justice (Northern Ireland) Act 1945 (c. 15) (child destruction).

25 An offence under section 1 of the Infanticide Act (Northern Ireland) 1939 (c. 5) (infanticide).

26 An offence under section 7(1)(b) of the Criminal Justice (Miscellaneous Provisions) Act (Northern Ireland) 1968 (c. 28) (assault with intent to resist arrest).

27 An offence under section 20 of the Children and Young Persons Act (Northern Ireland) 1968 (c. 34) (cruelty to children).

28 An offence under section 8 of the Theft Act (Northern Ireland) 1969 (c. 16) (robbery or assault with intent to rob).

29 An offence under section 9 of that Act of burglary with intent to—
    (a) inflict grievous bodily harm on a person, or
    (b) do unlawful damage to a building or anything in it.

30 An offence under section 10 of that Act (aggravated burglary).

31 An offence of arson under Article 3 of the Criminal Damage Northern Ireland) Order 1977 (S.I. 1977/426 (N.I. 4)).

32 An offence under Article 3(2) of that Order (destroying or damaging property) other than an offence of arson.

33 An offence under Article 17 of the Firearms (Northern Ireland) Order 1981 (S.I. 1981/155 (N.I. 2)) (possession of firearm with intent to endanger life).

34 An offence under Article 17A of that Order (possession of firearm with intent to cause fear of violence).

35 An offence under Article 18(1) of that Order (use of firearm to resist arrest).

36 An offence under Article 18(2) of that Order (possession of firearm at time of committing or being arrested for an offence specified in Schedule 1 to that Order).

37 An offence under Article 19 of that Order (carrying a firearm with criminal intent).

38 An offence under section 1 of the Taking of Hostages Act 1982 (c. 28) (hostage-taking).

39 An offence under section 1 of the Aviation Security Act 1982 (c. 36) (hijacking).

40 An offence under section 2 of that Act (destroying, damaging or endangering safety of aircraft).

41 An offence under section 3 of that Act (other acts endangering or likely to endanger safety of aircraft).

42 An offence under section 4 of that Act (offences in relation to certain dangerous articles).

43 An offence under section 1 of the Prohibition of Female Circumcision Act 1985 (c. 38) (prohibition of female circumcision).

44 An offence under Article 121 of the Mental Health (Northern Ireland) Order 1986 (S.I. 1986/595 (N.I.4) (ill-treatment of patients).

45 An offence under section 134 of the Criminal Justice Act 1988 (c. 33) (torture).

46 An offence under section 1 of the Aviation and Maritime Security Act 1990 (c. 31) (endangering safety at aerodromes).

47 An offence under section 9 of that Act (hijacking of ships).

48 An offence under section 10 of that Act (seizing or exercising control of fixed platforms).

49 An offence under section 11 of that Act (destroying fixed platforms or endangering their safety).

50 An offence under section 12 of that Act (other acts endangering or likely to endanger safe navigation).

51 An offence under section 13 of that Act (offences involving threats).

52 An offence under Part II of the Channel Tunnel (Security) Order 1994 (S.I. 1994/570) (offences relating to Channel Tunnel trains and the tunnel system).

53 An offence under Article 9 of the Road Traffic (Northern Ireland) Order 1995 (S.I. 1995/2994 (N.I. 18)) (causing death or grievous bodily injury by dangerous driving).

54 An offence under Article 14 of that Order (causing death or grievous bodily injury by careless driving when under the influence of drink or drugs).

55 An offence under Article 6 of the Protection from Harassment (Northern Ireland) Order 1997 (S.I. 1997/1180 (N.I. 9)) (putting people in fear of violence).

56 An offence under section 66 of the Police (Northern Ireland) Act 1998 (c. 32) (assaulting or obstructing a constable etc.)

57 An offence under section 51 or 52 of the International Criminal Court Act 2001 (c. 17) (genocide, crimes against humanity, war crimes and related offences), other than one involving murder.

58 An offence under section 1 of the Female Genital Mutilation Act 2003 (c. 31) (female genital mutilation).

59 An offence under section 2 of that Act (assisting a girl to mutilate her own genitalia).

60 An offence under section 3 of that Act (assisting a non-UK person to mutilate overseas a girl's genitalia).

61 An offence of—

(a) aiding, abetting, counselling, procuring or inciting the commission of an offence specified in this Part of this Schedule,

(b) conspiring to commit an offence so specified, or

(c) attempting to commit an offence so specified.

62 An attempt to commit murder or a conspiracy to commit murder.

PART 2
SEXUAL OFFENCES

63 Rape.

64 Indecent assault upon a female.

65 An offence under section 52 of the Offences against the Person Act 1861 (c. 100) (indecent assault upon a female).

66 An offence under section 53 of that Act (abduction of woman etc.).

67 An offence under section 54 of that Act (abduction of woman by force).

68 An offence under section 55 of that Act (abduction of unmarried girl under 16 from parent or guardian).

69 An offence under section 2 of the Criminal Law Amendment Act 1885 (c. 69) (procuration).

70 An offence under section 3 of that Act (procurement of woman or girl by threats etc. or administering drugs).

71 An offence under section 4 of that Act (intercourse or attempted intercourse with girl under 14).

72 An offence under section 5 of that Act (intercourse or attempted intercourse with girl under 17).

73 An offence under section 6 of that Act (permitting girl under 17 to use premises for intercourse).

74 An offence under section 7 of that Act (abduction of girl under 18 from parent or guardian).

75 An offence under section 8 of that Act (unlawful detention of woman or girl in brothel etc.).

76 An offence under section 1 of the Vagrancy Act 1898 (c. 39) (living on earnings of prostitution or soliciting or importuning in a public place).

77 An offence under section 1 of the Punishment of Incest Act 1908 (c. 45) (incest by a man).

78 An offence under section 2 of that Act (incest by a woman).

79 An offence under section 21 of the Children and Young Persons Act (Northern Ireland) 1968 (c. 34) (causing or encouraging seduction or prostitution of girl under 17).

80 An offence under section 22 of that Act (indecent conduct towards child).

81 An offence under section 9 of the Theft Act (Northern Ireland) 1969 (c. 16) of burglary with intent to commit rape.

82 An offence under Article 3 of the Protection of Children (Northern Ireland) Order 1978 (S.I. 1978/1047 (N.I. 17)) (indecent photographs of children).

83 An offence under section 170 of the Customs and Excise Management Act 1979 (c. 2) (penalty for fraudulent evasion of duty etc.) in relation to goods prohibited to be imported under section 42 of the Customs Consolidation Act 1876 (c. 36) (indecent or obscene articles).

84 An offence under Article 9 of the Criminal Justice (Northern Ireland) Order 1980 (S.I. 1980/704 (N.I. 6)) (inciting girl under 16 to have incestuous sexual intercourse).

85 An offence under Article 7 of the Homosexual Offences (Northern Ireland) Order 1982 (S.I. 1982/1536 (N.I. 19)) (procuring others to commit homosexual acts).

86 An offence under Article 8 of that Order (living on earnings of male prostitution).

87 An offence under Article 122 of the Mental Health (Northern Ireland) Order 1986 (S.I. 1986/595 (N.I. 4)) (protection of women suffering from severe mental handicap).

88 An offence under Article 123 of that Order (protection of patients).

89 An offence under Article 15 of the Criminal Justice (Evidence, etc.) (Northern Ireland) Order 1988 (S.I. 1988/1847 (N.I. 17) (possession of indecent photograph of a child).

90 An offence under section 15 of the Sexual Offences Act 2003 (c. 42) (meeting a child following sexual grooming etc.).

91 An offence under section 16 of that Act (abuse of position of trust: sexual activity with a child).

92 An offence under section 17 of that Act (abuse of position of trust: causing or inciting a child to engage in sexual activity).

93 An offence under section 18 of that Act (abuse of position of trust: sexual activity in the presence of a child).

94 An offence under section 19 of that Act (abuse of position of trust: causing a child to watch a sexual act).

95 An offence under section 47 of that Act (paying for sexual services of a child).

96 An offence under section 48 of that Act (causing or inciting child prostitution or pornography).
97 An offence under section 49 of that Act (controlling a child prostitute or a child involved in pornography).
98 An offence under section 50 of that Act (arranging or facilitating child prostitution or pornography).
99 An offence under section 52 of that Act (causing or inciting prostitution for gain).
100 An offence under section 53 of that Act (controlling prostitution for gain).
101 An offence under section 57 of that Act (trafficking into the UK for sexual exploitation).
102 An offence under section 58 of that Act (trafficking within the UK for sexual exploitation).
103 An offence under section 59 of that Act (trafficking out of the UK for sexual exploitation).
104 An offence under section 66 of that Act (exposure).
105 An offence under section 67 of that Act (voyeurism).
106 An offence under section 69 of that Act (intercourse with an animal).
107 An offence under section 70 of that Act (sexual penetration of a corpse).
108 An offence under Article 20 of the Criminal Justice (Northern Ireland) Order 2003 (S.I. 2003/1247 (N.I. 13)) (assault with intent to commit buggery).
109 An offence under Article 21 of that Order (indecent assault on a male).
110 An offence of—
    (a) aiding, abetting, counselling, procuring or inciting the commission of an offence specified in this Part of this Schedule,
    (b) conspiring to commit an offence so specified, or
    (c) attempting to commit an offence so specified.

SCHEDULE 18
RELEASE OF PRISONERS SERVING SENTENCES OF IMPRISONMENT OR DETENTION FOR PUBLIC PROTECTION

Section 230

Release on licence

1. (1) Section 31 of the Crime (Sentences) Act 1997 (c. 43) (duration and conditions of licences for life prisoners), is amended as follows.
   (2) In subsection (1) (licence to remain in force until death), after "life prisoner" there is inserted ", other than a prisoner to whom section 31A below applies,".
   (3) After that subsection there is inserted—
   "(1A) Where a prisoner to whom section 31A below applies is released on licence, the licence shall remain in force until his death unless—
    (a) it is previously revoked under section 32(1) or (2) below; or
    (b) it ceases to have effect in accordance with an order made by the Secretary of State under section 31A below."
2. After that section there is inserted—

"31A Imprisonment or detention for public protection: termination of licences

   (1) This section applies to a prisoner who—
    (a) is serving one or more preventive sentences, and
    (b) is not serving any other life sentence.
   (2) Where—
    (a) the prisoner has been released on licence under this Chapter; and
    (b) the qualifying period has expired,

555

the Secretary of State shall, if directed to do so by the Parole Board, order that the licence is to cease to have effect.

(3) Where—

(a) the prisoner has been released on licence under this Chapter;

(b) the qualifying period has expired; and

(c) if he has made a previous application under this subsection, a period of at least twelve months has expired since the disposal of that application,

the prisoner may make an application to the Parole Board under this subsection.

(4) Where an application is made under subsection (3) above, the Parole Board—

(a) shall, if it is satisfied that it is no longer necessary for the protection of the public that the licence should remain in force, direct the Secretary of State to make an order that the licence is to cease to have effect;

(b) shall otherwise dismiss the application.

(5) In this section—

"preventive sentence" means a sentence of imprisonment for public protection under section 225 of the Criminal Justice Act 2003 or a sentence of detention for public protection under section 226 of that Act;

"the qualifying period", in relation to a prisoner who has been released on licence, means the period of ten years beginning with the date of his release."

3. In section 34(2) of that Act (meaning of "life sentence"), after paragraph (c) there is inserted—

"(d) a sentence of imprisonment for public protection under section 225 of the Criminal Justice Act 2003, and

(e) a sentence of detention for public protection under section 226 of that Act."

Determination of tariffs

4. In section 82A of the Sentencing Act (determination of tariffs), after subsection (4) there is inserted—

"(4A) No order under subsection (4) above may be made where the life sentence is—

(a) a sentence of imprisonment for public protection under section 225 of the Criminal Justice Act 2003, or

(b) a sentence of detention for public protection under section 226 of that Act."

SCHEDULE 19

THE PAROLE BOARD: SUPPLEMENTARY PROVISIONS

Section 239(7)

Status and capacity

1. (1) The Board is not to be regarded as the servant or agent of the Crown or as enjoying any status, immunity or privilege of the Crown; and the Board's property is not to be regarded as property of, or held on behalf of, the Crown.

(2) It is within the capacity of the Board as a statutory corporation to do such things and enter into such transactions as are incidental to or conducive to the discharge of—

(a) its functions under Chapter 6 of Part 12 in respect of fixed-term prisoners, and

(b) its functions under Chapter 2 of Part 2 of the Crime (Sentences) Act 1997 (c. 43) in relation to life prisoners within the meaning of that Chapter.

Membership

2. (1) The Board is to consist of a chairman and not less than four other members appointed by the Secretary of State.

(2) The Board must include among its members—
   (a) a person who holds or has held judicial office;
   (b) a registered medical practitioner who is a psychiatrist;
   (c) a person appearing to the Secretary of State to have knowledge and experience of the supervision or after-care of discharged prisoners; and
   (d) a person appearing to the Secretary of State to have made a study of the causes of delinquency or the treatment of offenders.

(3) A member of the Board—
   (a) holds and vacates office in accordance with the terms of his appointment;
   (b) may resign his office by notice in writing addressed to the Secretary of State;
   and a person who ceases to hold office as a member of the Board is eligible for re-appointment.

Payments to members

3. (1) The Board may pay to each member such remuneration and allowances as the Secretary of State may determine.

(2) The Board may pay or make provision for paying to or in respect of any member such sums by way of pension, allowances or gratuities as the Secretary of State may determine.

(3) If a person ceases to be a member otherwise than on the expiry of his term of office and it appears to the Secretary of State that there are special circumstances that make it right that he should receive compensation, the Secretary of State may direct the Board to make to that person a payment of such amount as the Secretary of State may determine.

(4) A determination or direction of the Secretary of State under this paragraph requires the approval of the Treasury.

Proceedings

4. (1) Subject to the provisions of section 239(5), the arrangements relating to meetings of the Board are to be such as the Board may determine.

(2) The arrangements may provide for the discharge, under the general direction of the Board, of any of the Board's functions by a committee or by one or more of the members or employees of the Board.

(3) The validity of the proceedings of the Board are not to be affected by any vacancy among the members or by any defect in the appointment of a member.

Staff

5. (1) The Board may appoint such number of employees as it may determine.

(2) The remuneration and other conditions of service of the persons appointed under this paragraph are to be determined by the Board.

(3) Any determination under sub-paragraph (1) or (2) requires the approval of the Secretary of State given with the consent of the Treasury.

(4) The Employers' Liability (Compulsory Insurance) Act 1969 (c. 57) shall not require insurance to be effected by the Board.

6. (1) Employment with the Board shall continue to be included among the kinds of employment to which a scheme under section 1 of the Superannuation Act 1972 (c. 11) can apply, and accordingly in Schedule 1 to that Act (in which those kinds of employment are listed) at the end of the list of Other Bodies there shall continue to be inserted—
"Parole Board.".

(2) The Board shall pay to the Treasury, at such times as the Treasury may direct, such sums as the Treasury may determine in respect of the increase attributable to this paragraph in the sums payable under the Superannuation Act 1972 out of money provided by Parliament.

Financial provisions

7. (1) The Secretary of State shall pay to the Board—
   (a) any expenses incurred or to be incurred by the Board by virtue of paragraph 3 or 5; and
   (b) with the consent of the Treasury, such sums as he thinks fit for enabling the Board to meet other expenses.

(2) Any sums required by the Secretary of State for making payments under sub-paragraph (1) are to be paid out of money provided by Parliament.

Authentication of Board's seal

8. The application of the seal of the Board is to be authenticated by the signature of the Chairman or some other person authorised for the purpose.

Presumption of authenticity of documents issued by Board

9. Any document purporting to be an instrument issued by the Board and to be duly executed under the seal of the Board or to be signed on behalf of the Board shall be received in evidence and shall be deemed to be such an instrument unless the contrary is shown.

Accounts and audit

10. (1) It is the duty of the Board—
   (a) to keep proper accounts and proper records in relation to the accounts;
   (b) to prepare in respect of each financial year a statement of accounts in such form as the Secretary of State may direct with the approval of the Treasury; and
   (c) to send copies of each such statement to the Secretary of State and the Comptroller and Auditor General not later than 31st August next following the end of the financial year to which the statement relates.

(2) The Comptroller and Auditor General shall examine, certify and report on each statement of accounts sent to him by the Board and shall lay a copy of every such statement and of his report before each House of Parliament.

(3) In this paragraph and paragraph 11 "financial year" means a period of 12 months ending with 31st March.

Reports

11. The Board must as soon as practicable after the end of each financial year make to the Secretary of State a report on the performance of its functions during the year; and the Secretary of State must lay a copy of the report before each House of Parliament.

SCHEDULE 20
PRISONERS LIABLE TO REMOVAL FROM UNITED KINGDOM:
MODIFICATIONS OF CRIMINAL JUSTICE ACT 1991   Section 26

1. In this Schedule "the 1991 Act" means the Criminal Justice Act 1991 (c. 53).
2. In section 42 of the 1991 Act (additional days for disciplinary offences), in subsection (2) before the word "and" at the end of paragraph (a) there is inserted—
   "(aa) any period which he must serve before he can be removed under section 46A below;".
3. (1) In section 46 of the 1991 Act (persons liable to removal from the United Kingdom) in subsection (3) after paragraph (d) there is inserted "or
   (e) he is liable to removal under section 10 of the Immigration and Asylum Act 1999".
   (2) Sub-paragraph (1) does not apply to any prisoner whose sentence relates to an offence committed before the commencement of this Schedule.
4. After section 46 of the 1991 Act there is inserted—

"46A Early removal of persons liable to removal from United Kingdom

(1) Subject to subsection (2) below, where a short-term or long-term prisoner is liable to removal from the United Kingdom, the Secretary of State may under this section remove him from prison at any time after he has served the requisite period.
(2) Subsection (1) above does not apply where—
   (a) the sentence is an extended sentence within the meaning of section 85 of the Powers of Criminal Courts (Sentencing) Act 2000,
   (b) the sentence is for an offence under section 1 of the Prisoners (Return to Custody) Act 1995,
   (c) the prisoner is subject to a hospital order, hospital direction or transfer direction under section 37, 45A or 47 of the Mental Health Act 1983,
   (d) the prisoner is subject to the notification requirements of Part 2 of the Sexual Offences Act 2003, or
   (e) the interval between—
      (i) the date on which the prisoner will have served the requisite period for the term of the sentence, and
      (ii) the date on which he will have served one-half of the sentence, is less than 14 days.
(3) A prisoner removed from prison under this section—
   (a) is so removed only for the purpose of enabling the Secretary of State to remove him from the United Kingdom under powers conferred by—
      (i) Schedule 2 or 3 to the Immigration Act 1971, or
      (ii) section 10 of the Immigration and Asylum Act 1999, and
   (b) so long as remaining in the United Kingdom, remains liable to be detained in pursuance of his sentence until he falls to be released under section 33 or 35 above.

(4) So long as a prisoner removed from prison under this section remains in the United Kingdom but has not been returned to prison, any duty or power of the Secretary of State under section 33, 35 or 36 is exercisable in relation to him as if he were in prison.

(5) In this section "the requisite period" means—

    (a) for a term of three months or more but less than four months, a period of 30 days;

    (b) for a term of four months or more but less than 18 months, a period equal to one-quarter of the term;

    (c) for a term of 18 months or more, a period that is 135 days less than one-half of the term.

(6) The Secretary of State may by order made by statutory instrument—

    (a) amend the definition of "the requisite period" in subsection (5) above,

    (b) make such transitional provision as appears to him necessary or expedient in connection with the amendment.

(7) No order shall be made under subsection (6) above unless a draft of the order has been laid before and approved by a resolution of each House of Parliament.

(8) In relation to any time before the commencement of sections 80 and 81 of the Sexual Offences Act 2003, the reference in subsection (2)(d) above to Part 2 of that Act is to be read as a reference to Part 1 of the Sex Offenders Act 1997.

46B Early removal of persons liable to removal from United Kingdom

(1) This section applies in relation to a person who, after being removed from prison under section 46A above, has been removed from the United Kingdom before he has served one-half of his sentence.

(2) If a person to whom this section applies enters the United Kingdom at any time before his sentence expiry date, he is liable to be detained in pursuance of his sentence from the time of his entry into the United Kingdom until whichever is the earlier of the following—

    (a) the end of a period ("the further custodial period") beginning with that time and equal in length to the outstanding custodial period, and

    (b) his sentence expiry date.

(3) A person who is liable to be detained by virtue of subsection (2) above is, if at large, to be taken for the purposes of section 49 of the Prison Act 1952 (persons unlawfully at large) to be unlawfully at large.

(4) Subsection (2) above does not prevent the further removal from the United Kingdom of a person falling within that subsection.

(5) Where, in the case of a person returned to prison by virtue of subsection (2) above, the further custodial period ends before the sentence expiry date, subsections (1) and (2) of section 33 above apply in relation to him as if any reference to one-half or two-thirds of the prisoner's sentence were a reference to the further custodial period.

(6) If a person returned to prison by virtue of subsection (2) above falls by virtue of subsection (5) above to be released on licence under section 33(1) or (2) above after the date on which (but for his removal from the United Kingdom) he would have served three-quarters of his sentence, section 37(1) above has effect in relation to him as if for the reference to three-quarters of his sentence there were substituted a reference to the whole of his sentence.

(7) If a person who is released on licence under section 33(1) or (2) above at the end of the further custodial period is recalled to prison under section 39(1) or (2) above, section 33A(3) above shall not apply, but it shall be the duty of the Secretary of State—

    (a) if the person is recalled before the date on which (but for his removal from the United Kingdom) he would have served three-quarters of his sentence, to release him on licence on that date, and

(b) if he is recalled after that date, to release him on the sentence expiry date.

(8) A licence granted by virtue of subsection (7)(a) above shall remain in force until the sentence expiry date.

(9) In this section—

"further custodial period" has the meaning given by subsection (2)(a) above;

"outstanding custodial period", in relation to a person to whom this section applies, means the period beginning with the date on which he was removed from the United Kingdom and ending with the date on which (but for his removal) he would have served one-half of his sentence;

"sentence expiry date", in relation to a person to whom this section applies, means the date on which (but for his removal from the United Kingdom) he would have served the whole of this sentence."

SCHEDULE 21
DETERMINATION OF MINIMUM TERM IN RELATION TO MANDATORY LIFE SENTENCE

Section 269(5)

Interpretation

1. In this Schedule—

"child" means a person under 18 years;

"mandatory life sentence" means a life sentence passed in circumstances where the sentence is fixed by law;

"minimum term", in relation to a mandatory life sentence, means the part of the sentence to be specified in an order under section 269(2);

"whole life order" means an order under subsection (4) of section 269.

2. Section 28 of the Crime and Disorder Act 1998 (c. 37) (meaning of "racially or religiously aggravated") applies for the purposes of this Schedule as it applies for the purposes of sections 29 to 32 of that Act.

3. For the purposes of this Schedule an offence is aggravated by sexual orientation if it is committed in circumstances falling within subsection (2)(a)(i) or (b)(i) of section 146.

Starting points

4. (1) If—

(a) the court considers that the seriousness of the offence (or the combination of the offence and one or more offences associated with it) is exceptionally high, and

(b) the offender was aged 21 or over when he committed the offence,

the appropriate starting point is a whole life order.

(2) Cases that would normally fall within sub-paragraph (1)(a) include—

(a) the murder of two or more persons, where each murder involves any of the following—

(i) a substantial degree of premeditation or planning,

(ii) the abduction of the victim, or

(iii) sexual or sadistic conduct,

(b) the murder of a child if involving the abduction of the child or sexual or sadistic motivation,

    (c) a murder done for the purpose of advancing a political, religious or ideological cause, or

    (d) a murder by an offender previously convicted of murder.

5. (1) If—

    (a) the case does not fall within paragraph 4(1) but the court considers that the seriousness of the offence (or the combination of the offence and one or more offences associated with it) is particularly high, and

    (b) the offender was aged 18 or over when he committed the offence,

the appropriate starting point, in determining the minimum term, is 30 years.

  (2) Cases that (if not falling within paragraph 4(1)) would normally fall within sub-paragraph (1)(a) include—

    (a) the murder of a police officer or prison officer in the course of his duty,

    (b) a murder involving the use of a firearm or explosive,

    (c) a murder done for gain (such as a murder done in the course or furtherance of robbery or burglary, done for payment or done in the expectation of gain as a result of the death),

    (d) a murder intended to obstruct or interfere with the course of justice,

    (e) a murder involving sexual or sadistic conduct,

    (f) the murder of two or more persons,

    (g) a murder that is racially or religiously aggravated or aggravated by sexual orientation, or

    (h) a murder falling within paragraph 4(2) committed by an offender who was aged under 21 when he committed the offence.

6. If the offender was aged 18 or over when he committed the offence and the case does not fall within paragraph 4(1) or 5(1), the appropriate starting point, in determining the minimum term, is 15 years.

7. If the offender was aged under 18 when he committed the offence, the appropriate starting point, in determining the minimum term, is 12 years.

Aggravating and mitigating factors

8. Having chosen a starting point, the court should take into account any aggravating or mitigating factors, to the extent that it has not allowed for them in its choice of starting point.

9. Detailed consideration of aggravating or mitigating factors may result in a minimum term of any length (whatever the starting point), or in the making of a whole life order.

10. Aggravating factors (additional to those mentioned in paragraph 4(2) and 5(2)) that may be relevant to the offence of murder include—

    (a) a significant degree of planning or premeditation,

    (b) the fact that the victim was particularly vulnerable because of age or disability,

    (c) mental or physical suffering inflicted on the victim before death,

    (d) the abuse of a position of trust,

    (e) the use of duress or threats against another person to facilitate the commission of the offence,

    (f) the fact that the victim was providing a public service or performing a public duty, and

    (g) concealment, destruction or dismemberment of the body.

11. Mitigating factors that may be relevant to the offence of murder include—

    (a) an intention to cause serious bodily harm rather than to kill,

    (b) lack of premeditation,

(c) the fact that the offender suffered from any mental disorder or mental disability which (although not falling within section 2(1) of the Homicide Act 1957 (c. 11)), lowered his degree of culpability,

(d) the fact that the offender was provoked (for example, by prolonged stress) in a way not amounting to a defence of provocation,

(e) the fact that the offender acted to any extent in self-defence,

(f) a belief by the offender that the murder was an act of mercy, and

(g) the age of the offender.

12. Nothing in this Schedule restricts the application of—

(a) section 143(2) (previous convictions),

(b) section 143(3) (bail), or

(c) section 144 (guilty plea).

SCHEDULE 22
MANDATORY LIFE SENTENCES: TRANSITIONAL CASES

Section 276

Interpretation

1. In this Schedule—

"the commencement date" means the day on which section 269 comes into force;

"the early release provisions" means the provisions of section 28(5) to (8) of the Crime (Sentences) Act 1997 (c. 43);

"existing prisoner" means a person serving one or more mandatory life sentences passed before the commencement date (whether or not he is also serving any other sentence);

"life sentence" means a sentence of imprisonment for life or custody for life passed in England and Wales or by a court-martial outside England and Wales;

"mandatory life sentence" means a life sentence passed in circumstances where the sentence was fixed by law.

Existing prisoners notified by Secretary of State

2. Paragraph 3 applies in relation to any existing prisoner who, in respect of any mandatory life sentence, has before the commencement date been notified in writing by the Secretary of State (otherwise than in a notice that is expressed to be provisional) either—

(a) of a minimum period which in the view of the Secretary of State should be served before the prisoner's release on licence, or

(b) that the Secretary of State does not intend that the prisoner should ever be released on licence.

3. (1) On the application of the existing prisoner, the High Court must, in relation to the mandatory life sentence, either—

(a) order that the early release provisions are to apply to him as soon as he has served the part of the sentence which is specified in the order, which in a case falling within paragraph 2(a) must not be greater than the notified minimum term, or

(b) in a case falling within paragraph 2(b), order that the early release provisions are not to apply to the offender.

(2) In a case falling within paragraph 2(a), no application may be made under this paragraph after the end of the notified minimum term.

(3) Where no application under this paragraph is made in a case falling within paragraph 2(a), the early release provisions apply to the prisoner in respect of the sentence as soon as he has served the notified minimum term (or, if he has served that term before the commencement date but has not been released, from the commencement date).

(4) In this paragraph "the notified minimum term" means the minimum period notified as mentioned in paragraph 2(a), or where the prisoner has been so notified on more than one occasion, the period most recently so notified.

4. (1) In dealing with an application under paragraph 3, the High Court must have regard to—

  (a) the seriousness of the offence, or of the combination of the offence and one or more offences associated with it,

  (b) where the court is satisfied that, if the prisoner had been sentenced to a term of imprisonment, the length of his sentence would have been treated by section 67 of the Criminal Justice Act 1967 (c. 80) as being reduced by a particular period, the effect which that section would have had if he had been sentenced to a term of imprisonment, and

  (c) the length of the notified minimum term or, where a notification falling within paragraph 2(b) has been given to the prisoner, to the fact that such a notification has been given.

(2) In considering under sub-paragraph (1) the seriousness of the offence, or of the combination of the offence and one or more offences associated with it, the High Court must have regard to—

  (a) the general principles set out in Schedule 21, and

  (b) any recommendation made to the Secretary of State by the trial judge or the Lord Chief Justice as to the minimum term to be served by the offender before release on licence.

(3) In this paragraph "the notified minimum term" has the same meaning as in paragraph 3.

Existing prisoners not notified by Secretary of State

5. Paragraph 6 applies in relation to any existing prisoner who, in respect of any mandatory life sentence, has not before the commencement date been notified as mentioned in paragraph 2(a) or (b) by the Secretary of State.

6. The Secretary of State must refer the prisoner's case to the High Court for the making by the High Court of an order under subsection (2) or (4) of section 269 in relation to the mandatory life sentence.

7. In considering under subsection (3) or (4) of section 269 the seriousness of an offence (or the combination of an offence and one or more offences associated with it) in a case referred to the High Court under paragraph 6, the High Court must have regard not only to the matters mentioned in subsection (5) of that section but also to any recommendation made to the Secretary of State by the trial judge or the Lord Chief Justice as to the minimum term to be served by the offender before release on licence.

8. In dealing with a reference under paragraph 6, the High Court—

  (a) may not make an order under subsection (2) of section 269 specifying a part of the sentence which in the opinion of the court is greater than that which, under the practice followed by the Secretary of State before December 2002, the Secretary of State would have been likely to notify as mentioned in paragraph 2(a), and

(b) may not make an order under subsection (4) of section 269 unless the court is of the opinion that, under the practice followed by the Secretary of State before December 2002, the Secretary of State would have been likely to give the prisoner a notification falling within paragraph 2(b).

Sentences passed on or after commencement date in respect of offences committed before that date

9. Paragraph 10 applies where—
  (a) on or after the commencement date a court passes a life sentence in circumstances where the sentence is fixed by law, and
  (b) the offence to which the sentence relates was committed before the commencement date.
10. The court—
  (a) may not make an order under subsection (2) of section 269 specifying a part of the sentence which in the opinion of the court is greater than that which, under the practice followed by the Secretary of State before December 2002, the Secretary of State would have been likely to notify as mentioned in paragraph 2(a), and
  (b) may not make an order under subsection (4) of section 269 unless the court is of the opinion that, under the practice followed by the Secretary of State before December 2002, the Secretary of State would have been likely to give the prisoner a notification falling within paragraph 2(b).

Proceedings in High Court

11. (1) An application under paragraph 3 or a reference under paragraph 6 is to be determined by a single judge of the High Court without an oral hearing.
  (2) In relation to such an application or reference, any reference to "the court" in section 269(2) to (5) and Schedule 21 is to be read as a reference to the High Court.

Giving of reasons

12. (1) Where the High Court makes an order under paragraph 3(1)(a) or (b), it must state in open court, in ordinary language, its reasons for deciding on the order made.
  (2) Where the order is an order under paragraph 3(1)(a) specifying a part of the sentence shorter than the notified minimum term the High Court must, in particular, state its reasons for departing from the notified minimum term.
13. Where the High Court makes an order under subsection (2) or (4) of section 269 on a reference under paragraph 6, subsection (2) of section 270 does not apply.

Right of appeal

14. (1) A person who has made an application under paragraph 3 or in respect of whom a reference has been made under paragraph 6 may with the leave of the Court of Appeal appeal to the Court of Appeal against the decision of the High Court on the application or reference.

(2) Section 1(1) of the Administration of Justice Act 1960 (c. 65) (appeal to House of Lords from decision of High Court in a criminal cause or matter) and section 18(1)(a) of the Supreme Court Act 1981 (c. 54) (exclusion of appeal from High Court to Court of Appeal in a criminal cause or matter) do not apply in relation to a decision to which sub-paragraph (1) applies.

(3) The jurisdiction conferred on the Court of Appeal by this paragraph is to be exercised by the criminal division of that court.

(4) Section 33(3) of the Criminal Appeal Act 1968 (c. 19) (limitation on appeal from criminal division of Court of Appeal) does not prevent an appeal to the House of Lords under this paragraph.

(5) In relation to appeals to the Court of Appeal or the House of Lords under this paragraph, the Secretary of State may make an order containing provision corresponding to any provision in the Criminal Appeal Act 1968 (subject to any specified modifications).

Review of minimum term on reference by Attorney General

15. Section 36 of the Criminal Justice Act 1988 (c. 33) applies in relation to an order made by the High Court under paragraph 3(1)(a) as it applies in relation to an order made by the Crown Court under section 269(2).

Modification of early release provisions

16. (1) In relation to an existing prisoner, section 28 of the Crime (Sentences) Act 1997 (c. 43) has effect subject to the following modifications.

(2) Any reference to a life prisoner in respect of whom a minimum term order has been made includes a reference to—

(a) an existing prisoner in respect of whom an order under paragraph 3(1)(a) has been made, and

(b) an existing prisoner serving a sentence in respect of which paragraph 3(3) applies.

(3) Any reference to the relevant part of the sentence is to be read—

(a) in relation to a sentence in respect of which an order under paragraph 3(1)(a) has been made, as a reference to the part specified in the order, and

(b) in relation to a sentence in respect of which paragraph 3(3) applies, as a reference to the notified minimum term as defined by paragraph 3(4).

(4) In subsection (1B) (life prisoner serving two or more sentences), paragraph (a) is to be read as if it referred to each of the sentences being one—

(a) in respect of which a minimum term order or an order under paragraph 3(1)(a) has been made, or

(b) in respect of which paragraph 3(3) applies.

17. In section 34(1) of the Crime (Sentences) Act 1997 (c. 43) (interpretation of Chapter 2 of that Act), in the definition of "life prisoner", the reference to a transferred prisoner as defined by section 273 of this Act includes a reference to an existing prisoner who immediately before the commencement date is a transferred life prisoner for the purposes of section 33 of that Act.

Transferred life prisoners

18. In relation to an existing prisoner who immediately before the commencement date is a transferred life prisoner for the purposes of section 33 of the Crime (Sentences) Act 1997, this Schedule is to be read as if—

    (a) any certificate under subsection (2) of that section were a notification falling within paragraph 2(a) of this Schedule, and

    (b) references to any recommendation of the trial judge or the Lord Chief Justice were omitted.

SCHEDULE 23
DEFERMENT OF SENTENCE

Section 278

1. For sections 1 and 2 of the Sentencing Act (deferment of sentence) there is substituted—

"Deferment of sentence

1. Deferment of sentence

(1) The Crown Court or a magistrates' court may defer passing sentence on an offender for the purpose of enabling the court, or any other court to which it falls to deal with him, to have regard in dealing with him to—

    (a) his conduct after conviction (including, where appropriate, the making by him of reparation for his offence); or

    (b) any change in his circumstances;

    but this is subject to subsections (3) and (4) below.

(2) Without prejudice to the generality of subsection (1) above, the matters to which the court to which it falls to deal with the offender may have regard by virtue of paragraph (a) of that subsection include the extent to which the offender has complied with any requirements imposed under subsection (3)(b) below.

(3) The power conferred by subsection (1) above shall be exercisable only if—

    (a) the offender consents;

    (b) the offender undertakes to comply with any requirements as to his conduct during the period of the deferment that the court considers it appropriate to impose; and

    (c) the court is satisfied, having regard to the nature of the offence and the character and circumstances of the offender, that it would be in the interests of justice to exercise the power.

(4) Any deferment under this section shall be until such date as may be specified by the court, not being more than six months after the date on which the deferment is announced by the court; and, subject to section 1D(3) below, where the passing of sentence has been deferred under this section it shall not be further so deferred.

(5) Where a court has under this section deferred passing sentence on an offender, it shall forthwith give a copy of the order deferring the passing of sentence and setting out any requirements imposed under subsection (3)(b) above—

    (a) to the offender,

    (b) where an officer of a local probation board has been appointed to act as a supervisor in relation to him, to that board, and

(c) where a person has been appointed under section 1A(2)(b) below to act as a supervisor in relation to him, to that person.

(6) Notwithstanding any enactment, a court which under this section defers passing sentence on an offender shall not on the same occasion remand him.

(7) Where—

    (a) a court which under this section has deferred passing sentence on an offender proposes to deal with him on the date originally specified by the court, or

    (b) the offender does not appear on the day so specified,

the court may issue a summons requiring him to appear before the court at a time and place specified in the summons, or may issue a warrant to arrest him and bring him before the court at a time and place specified in the warrant.

(8) Nothing in this section or sections 1A to 1D below shall affect—

    (a) the power of the Crown Court to bind over an offender to come up for judgment when called upon; or

    (b) the power of any court to defer passing sentence for any purpose for which it may lawfully do so apart from this section.

1A. Further provision about undertakings

(1) Without prejudice to the generality of paragraph (b) of section 1(3) above, the requirements that may be imposed by virtue of that paragraph include requirements as to the residence of the offender during the whole or any part of the period of deferment.

(2) Where an offender has undertaken to comply with any requirements imposed under section 1(3)(b) above the court may appoint—

    (a) an officer of a local probation board, or

    (b) any other person whom the court thinks appropriate,

to act as a supervisor in relation to him.

(3) A person shall not be appointed under subsection (2)(b) above without his consent.

(4) It shall be the duty of a supervisor appointed under subsection (2) above—

    (a) to monitor the offender's compliance with the requirements; and

    (b) to provide the court to which it falls to deal with the offender in respect of the offence in question with such information as the court may require relating to the offender's compliance with the requirements.

1B. Breach of undertakings

(1) A court which under section 1 above has deferred passing sentence on an offender may deal with him before the end of the period of deferment if—

    (a) he appears or is brought before the court under subsection (3) below; and

    (b) the court is satisfied that he has failed to comply with one or more requirements imposed under section 1(3)(b) above in connection with the deferment.

(2) Subsection (3) below applies where—

    (a) a court has under section 1 above deferred passing sentence on an offender;

    (b) the offender undertook to comply with one or more requirements imposed under section 1(3)(b) above in connection with the deferment; and

    (c) a person appointed under section 1A(2) above to act as a supervisor in relation to the offender has reported to the court that the offender has failed to comply with one or more of those requirements.

(3) Where this subsection applies, the court may issue—

(a) a summons requiring the offender to appear before the court at a time and place specified in the summons; or

(b) a warrant to arrest him and bring him before the court at a time and place specified in the warrant.

1C. Conviction of offence during period of deferment

(1) A court which under section 1 above has deferred passing sentence on an offender may deal with him before the end of the period of deferment if during that period he is convicted in Great Britain of any offence.

(2) Subsection (3) below applies where a court has under section 1 above deferred passing sentence on an offender in respect of one or more offences and during the period of deferment the offender is convicted in England and Wales of any offence ("the later offence").

(3) Where this subsection applies, then (without prejudice to subsection (1) above and whether or not the offender is sentenced for the later offence during the period of deferment), the court which passes sentence on him for the later offence may also, if this has not already been done, deal with him for the offence or offences for which passing of sentence has been deferred, except that—

(a) the power conferred by this subsection shall not be exercised by a magistrates' court if the court which deferred passing sentence was the Crown Court; and

(b) the Crown Court, in exercising that power in a case in which the court which deferred passing sentence was a magistrates' court, shall not pass any sentence which could not have been passed by a magistrates' court in exercising that power.

(4) Where a court which under section 1 above has deferred passing sentence on an offender proposes to deal with him by virtue of subsection (1) above before the end of the period of deferment, the court may issue—

(a) a summons requiring him to appear before the court at a time and place specified in the summons; or

(b) a warrant to arrest him and bring him before the court at a time and place specified in the warrant.

1D. Deferment of sentence: supplementary

(1) In deferring the passing of sentence under section 1 above a magistrates' court shall be regarded as exercising the power of adjourning the trial conferred by section 10(1) of the Magistrates' Courts Act 1980, and accordingly sections 11(1) and 13(1) to (3A) and (5) of that Act (non-appearance of the accused) apply (without prejudice to section 1(7) above) if the offender does not appear on the date specified under section 1(4) above.

(2) Where the passing of sentence on an offender has been deferred by a court ("the original court") under section 1 above, the power of that court under that section to deal with the offender at the end of the period of deferment and any power of that court under section 1B(1) or 1C(1) above, or of any court under section 1C(3) above, to deal with the offender—

(a) is power to deal with him, in respect of the offence for which passing of sentence has been deferred, in any way in which the original court could have dealt with him if it had not deferred passing sentence; and

(b) without prejudice to the generality of paragraph (a) above, in the case of a magistrates' court, includes the power conferred by section 3 below to commit him to the Crown Court for sentence.

(3) Where—

    (a) the passing of sentence on an offender in respect of one or more offences has been deferred under section 1 above, and

    (b) a magistrates' court deals with him in respect of the offence or any of the offences by committing him to the Crown Court under section 3 below,

the power of the Crown Court to deal with him includes the same power to defer passing sentence on him as if he had just been convicted of the offence or offences on indictment before the court.

(4) Subsection (5) below applies where—

    (a) the passing of sentence on an offender in respect of one or more offences has been deferred under section 1 above;

    (b) it falls to a magistrates' court to determine a relevant matter; and

    (c) a justice of the peace is satisfied—

        (i) that a person appointed under section 1A(2)(b) above to act as a supervisor in relation to the offender is likely to be able to give evidence that may assist the court in determining that matter; and

        (ii) that that person will not voluntarily attend as a witness.

(5) The justice may issue a summons directed to that person requiring him to attend before the court at the time and place appointed in the summons to give evidence.

(6) For the purposes of subsection (4) above a court determines a relevant matter if it—

    (a) deals with the offender in respect of the offence, or any of the offences, for which the passing of sentence has been deferred; or

    (b) determines, for the purposes of section 1B(1)(b) above, whether the offender has failed to comply with any requirements imposed under section 1(3)(b) above."

2. In section 159 of the Sentencing Act (execution of process between England and Wales and Scotland), for "section 2(4)," there is substituted "section 1(7), 1B(3), 1C(4),".

SCHEDULE 24
DRUG TREATMENT AND TESTING REQUIREMENT IN ACTION PLAN
ORDER OR SUPERVISION ORDER

Section 279

1. (1) Section 70 of the Sentencing Act (requirements which may be included in action plan orders and directions) is amended as follows.

    (2) After subsection (4) there is inserted—

    "(4A) Subsection (4B) below applies where a court proposing to make an action plan order is satisfied—

        (a) that the offender is dependent on, or has a propensity to misuse, drugs, and

        (b) that his dependency or propensity is such as requires and may be susceptible to treatment.

    (4B) Where this subsection applies, requirements included in an action plan order may require the offender for a period specified in the order ("the treatment period") to submit to treatment by or under the direction of a specified person having the necessary qualifications and experience ("the treatment provider") with a view to the reduction or elimination of the offender's dependency on or propensity to misuse drugs.

(4C) The required treatment shall be—

(a) treatment as a resident in such institution or place as may be specified in the order, or

(b) treatment as a non-resident at such institution or place, and at such intervals, as may be so specified;

but the nature of the treatment shall not be specified in the order except as mentioned in paragraph (a) or (b) above.

(4D) A requirement shall not be included in an action plan order by virtue of subsection (4B) above—

(a) in any case, unless—

(i) the court is satisfied that arrangements have been or can be made for the treatment intended to be specified in the order (including arrangements for the reception of the offender where he is to be required to submit to treatment as a resident), and

(ii) the requirement has been recommended to the court as suitable for the offender by an officer of a local probation board or by a member of a youth offending team; and

(b) in the case of an order made or to be made in respect of a person aged 14 or over, unless he consents to its inclusion.

(4E) Subject to subsection (4F), an action plan order which includes a requirement by virtue of subsection (4B) above may, if the offender is aged 14 or over, also include a requirement ("a testing requirement") that, for the purpose of ascertaining whether he has any drug in his body during the treatment period, the offender shall during that period, at such times or in such circumstances as may (subject to the provisions of the order) be determined by the responsible officer or the treatment provider, provide samples of such description as may be so determined.

(4F) A testing requirement shall not be included in an action plan order by virtue of subsection (4E) above unless—

(a) the offender is aged 14 or over and consents to its inclusion, and

(b) the court has been notified by the Secretary of State that arrangements for implementing such requirements are in force in the area proposed to be specified in the order

(4G) A testing requirement shall specify for each month the minimum number of occasions on which samples are to be provided.

(4H) An action plan order including a testing requirement shall provide for the results of tests carried out on any samples provided by the offender in pursuance of the requirement to a person other than the responsible officer to be communicated to the responsible officer."

2. (1) Schedule 6 to the Sentencing Act (requirements which may be included in supervision orders) is amended as follows.

(2) In paragraph 1, after "6" there is inserted ", 6A".

(3) After paragraph 6 there is inserted—

"Requirements as to drug treatment and testing

6A. (1) This paragraph applies where a court proposing to make a supervision order is satisfied—

(a) that the offender is dependent on, or has a propensity to misuse, drugs, and

    (b) that his dependency or propensity is such as requires and may be susceptible to treatment.

(2) Where this paragraph applies, the court may include in the supervision order a requirement that the offender shall, for a period specified in the order ("the treatment period"), submit to treatment by or under the direction of a specified person having the necessary qualifications and experience ("the treatment provider") with a view to the reduction or elimination of the offender's dependency on or propensity to misuse drugs.

(3) The required treatment shall be—

    (a) treatment as a resident in such institution or place as may be specified in the order, or

    (b) treatment as a non-resident at such institution or place, and at such intervals, as may be so specified;

but the nature of the treatment shall not be specified in the order except as mentioned in paragraph (a) or (b) above.

(4) A requirement shall not be included in a supervision order by virtue of sub-paragraph (2) above—

    (a) in any case, unless—

        (i) the court is satisfied that arrangements have been or can be made for the treatment intended to be specified in the order (including arrangements for the reception of the offender where he is to be required to submit to treatment as a resident), and

        (ii) the requirement has been recommended to the court as suitable for the offender by an officer of a local probation board or by a member of a youth offending team; and

    (b) in the case of an order made or to be made in respect of a person aged 14 or over, unless he consents to its inclusion.

(5) Subject to sub-paragraph (6), a supervision order which includes a treatment requirement may also include a requirement ("a testing requirement") that, for the purpose of ascertaining whether he has any drug in his body during the treatment period, the offender shall during that period, at such times or in such circumstances as may (subject to the provisions of the order) be determined by the supervisor or the treatment provider, provide samples of such description as may be so determined.

(6) A testing requirement shall not be included in a supervision order by virtue of sub-paragraph (5) above unless—

    (a) the offender is aged 14 or over and consents to its inclusion, and

    (b) the court has been notified by the Secretary of State that arrangements for implementing such requirements are in force in the area proposed to be specified in the order.

(7) A testing requirement shall specify for each month the minimum number of occasions on which samples are to be provided.

(8) A supervision order including a testing requirement shall provide for the results of tests carried out on any samples provided by the offender in pursuance of the requirement to a person other than the supervisor to be communicated to the supervisor."

3. In Schedule 7 to the Sentencing Act (breach, revocation and amendment of supervision orders), in paragraph 2(1), before "or 7" there is inserted ", 6A".

SCHEDULE 25
SUMMARY OFFENCES NO LONGER PUNISHABLE WITH IMPRISONMENT

Vagrancy Act 1824 (c. 83)

1. The offence under section 3 of the Vagrancy Act 1824 (idle and disorderly persons) of causing or procuring or encouraging any child or children to wander abroad, or place himself or herself in any public place, street, highway, court, or passage, to beg or gather alms.
2. The following offences under section 4 of that Act (rogues and vagabonds)—
   (a) the offence of going about as a gatherer or collector of alms, or endeavouring to procure charitable contributions of any nature or kind, under any false or fraudulent pretence,
   (b) the offence of being found in or upon any dwelling house, warehouse, coach-house, stable, or outhouse, or in any inclosed yard, garden, or area, for any unlawful purpose, and
   (c) the offence of being apprehended as an idle and disorderly person, and violently resisting any constable, or other peace officer so apprehending him or her, and being subsequently convicted of the offence for which he or she shall have been so apprehended.

Railway Regulation Act 1842 (c. 55)

3. An offence under section 17 of the Railway Regulation Act 1842 (punishment of railway employees guilty of misconduct).

London Hackney Carriages Act 1843 (c. 86)

4. An offence under section 28 of the London Hackney Carriages Act 1843 (punishment for furious driving etc.).

Town Police Clauses Act 1847 (c. 89)

5. An offence under section 26 of the Town Police Clauses Act 1847 (unlawful release of impounded stray cattle).
6. An offence under section 28 of that Act (offences relating to obstructions and nuisances).
7. An offence under section 29 of that Act (drunken persons, etc. guilty of violent or indecent behaviour).
8. An offence under section 36 of that Act (keeping places for bear-baiting, cock-fighting etc.).

Ecclesiastical Courts Jurisdiction Act 1860 (c. 32)

9. An offence under section 2 of the Ecclesiastical Courts Jurisdiction Act 1860 (making a disturbance in churches, chapels, churchyards, etc.).

Town Gardens Protection Act 1863 (c. 13)

10. An offence under section 5 of the Town Gardens Protection Act 1863 (injuring gardens).

Public Stores Act 1875 (c. 25)

11. An offence under section 8 of the Public Stores Act 1875 (sweeping, etc., near dockyards, artillery ranges, etc.).

North Sea Fisheries Act 1893 (c. 17)

12. An offence under section 2 of the North Sea Fisheries Act 1893 (penalty for supplying, exchanging, or otherwise selling spirits).

13. An offence under section 3 of that Act (penalty for purchasing spirits by exchange or otherwise).

Seamen's and Soldiers' False Characters Act 1906 (c. 5)

14. An offence under section 1 of the Seamen's and Soldiers' False Characters Act 1906 (forgery of service or discharge certificate and personation).

Aliens Restriction (Amendment) Act 1919 (c. 92)

15. An offence under section 3(2) of the Aliens Restriction (Amendment) Act 1919 (promoting industrial unrest).

Children and Young Persons Act 1933 (c. 12)

16. An offence under section 4 of the Children and Young Persons Act 1933 (causing or allowing persons under sixteen to be used for begging).

Protection of Animals Act 1934 (c. 21)

17. An offence under section 2 of the Protection of Animals Act 1934 (offences relating to the prohibition of certain public contests, performances, and exhibitions with animals).

Public Health Act 1936 (c. 49)

18. An offence under section 287 of the Public Health Act 1936 (power to enter premises).

Essential Commodities Reserves Act 1938 (c. 51)

19. An offence under section 4(2) of the Essential Commodities Reserves Act 1938 (enforcement).

London Building Acts (Amendment) Act 1939 (c. xcvii)

20. An offence under section 142 of the London Building Acts (Amendment) Act 1939 (power of Council and others to enter buildings etc).

Cancer Act 1939 (c. 13)

21. An offence under section 4 of the Cancer Act 1939 (prohibition of certain advertisements).

Civil Defence Act 1939 (c. 31)

22. An offence under section 77 of the Civil Defence Act 1939 (penalty for false statements).

Hill Farming Act 1946 (c. 73)

23. An offence under section 19(2) or (3) of the Hill Farming Act 1946 (offences in relation to the control of rams).

Polish Resettlement Act 1947 (c. 19)

24. An offence under paragraph 7 of the Schedule to the Polish Resettlement Act 1947 (false representation or making a false statement).

Agriculture Act 1947 (c. 48)

25. An offence under section 14(7) of the Agriculture Act 1947, as remaining in force for the purposes of section 95 of that Act, (directions to secure good estate management and good husbandry).
26. An offence under section 95 of that Act (failure to comply with a direction to secure production).

Civil Defence Act 1948 (c. 5)

27. An offence under section 4 of the Civil Defence Act 1948 (powers as to land).

Agricultural Wages Act 1948 (c. 47)

28. An offence under section 12 of the Agricultural Wages Act 1948 (hindering investigation of complaints etc.).

Wireless Telegraphy Act 1949 (c. 54)

29. An offence under section 11(7) of the Wireless Telegraphy Act 1949 (enforcement of regulations as to use of apparatus), other than one within section 14(1A)(c) of that Act.

Prevention of Damage by Pests Act 1949 (c. 55)

30. An offence under section 22(5) of the Prevention of Damage by Pests Act 1949 (wrongful disclosure of information).

Coast Protection Act 1949 (c. 74)

31. An offence under section 25(9) of the Coast Protection Act 1949 (powers of entry and inspection).

Pet Animals Act 1951 (c. 35)

32. An offence under the Pet Animals Act 1951 (offences relating to licensing of pet shops and the sale of pets), other than one under section 4 of that Act.

Cockfighting Act 1952 (c. 59)

33. An offence under section 1 of the Cockfighting Act 1952 (possession of appliances for use in fighting of domestic fowl).

Agricultural Land (Removal of Surface Soil) Act 1953 (c. 10)

34. An offence under the Agricultural Land (Removal of Surface Soil) Act 1953 (removal of surface soil without planning permission).

Accommodation Agencies Act 1953 (c. 23)

35. An offence under section 1 of the Accommodation Agencies Act 1953 (illegal commissions and advertisements).

Army Act 1955 (3 & 4 Eliz. 2 c. 18)

36. An offence under section 19 of the Army Act 1955 (false answers in attestation paper).
37. An offence under section 161 of that Act (refusal to receive persons billeted, etc.).
38. An offence under section 171 of that Act (offences relating to the enforcement of provisions as to requisitioning).
39. An offence under section 191 of that Act (pretending to be a deserter).
40. An offence under section 193 of that Act (obstructing members of regular forces in execution of duty).
41. An offence under section 196 of that Act (illegal dealings in documents relating to pay, pensions, mobilisation etc.).
42. An offence under section 197 of that Act (unauthorised use of and dealing in decorations etc.).

Air Force Act 1955 (3 & 4 Eliz. 2 c. 19)

43. An offence under section 19 of the Air Force Act 1955 (false answers in attestation paper).
44. An offence under section 161 of that Act (refusal to receive persons billeted, etc.).
45. An offence under section 171 of that Act (offences relating to the enforcement of provisions as to requisitioning).
46. An offence under section 191 of that Act (pretending to be a deserter).
47. An offence under section 193 of that Act (obstructing members of regular air force in execution of duty).
48. An offence under section 196 of that Act (illegal dealings in documents relating to pay, pensions, mobilisation etc.).
49. An offence under section 197 of that Act (unauthorised use of and dealing in decorations etc.).

Naval Discipline Act 1957 (c. 53)

50. An offence under section 96 of the Naval Discipline Act 1957 (false pretence of desertion or absence without leave).
51. An offence under section 99 of that Act (illegal dealings in official documents).

Agricultural Marketing Act 1958 (c. 47)

52. An offence under section 45 of the Agricultural Marketing Act 1958 (failure to comply with demand for information or knowingly making any false statement in reply thereto).

Rivers (Prevention of Pollution) Act 1961 (c. 50)

53. An offence under section 12(1) of the Rivers (Prevention of Pollution) Act 1961 (restriction of disclosure of information).

Betting, Gaming and Lotteries Act 1963 (c. 2)

54. An offence under section 8 of the Betting, Gaming and Lotteries Act 1963 (betting in streets and public places).

Children and Young Persons Act 1963 (c. 37)

55. An offence under section 40 of the Children and Young Persons Act 1963 (offences relating to persons under 16 taking part in public performances etc.).

Animal Boarding Establishments Act 1963 (c. 43)

56. An offence under the Animal Boarding Establishments Act 1963 (offences in connection with the licensing and inspection of boarding establishments for animals), other than an offence under section 2 of that Act.

Agriculture and Horticulture Act 1964 (c. 28)

57. An offence under Part 3 of the Agriculture and Horticulture Act 1964 (offences relating to the grading and transport of fresh horticultural produce), other than an offence under section 15(1) of that Act.

Emergency Laws (Re-enactments and Repeals) Act 1964 (c. 60)

58. An offence under paragraph 1(3) or 2(4) of Schedule 1 to the Emergency Laws (Re-enactments and Repeals) Act 1964 (offences relating to the production of documents).

Riding Establishments Act 1964 (c. 70)

59. An offence under the Riding Establishments Act 1964 (offences relating to the keeping of riding establishments), other than an offence under section 2(4) of that Act.

Industrial and Provident Societies Act 1965 (c. 12)

60. An offence under section 16 of the Industrial and Provident Societies Act 1965 (cancellation of registration of society).
61. An offence under section 48 of that Act (production of documents and provision of information for certain purposes).

Cereals Marketing Act 1965 (c. 14)

62. An offence under section 17(1) of the Cereals Marketing Act 1965 (failure to comply with a requirement of a scheme).

Gas Act 1965 (c. 36)

63. An offence under paragraph 9 of Schedule 6 to the Gas Act 1965 (wrongful disclosure of information).

Armed Forces Act 1966 (c. 45)

64. An offence under section 8 of the Armed Forces Act 1966 (false statements on entry into Royal Navy).

Agriculture Act 1967 (c. 22)

65. An offence under section 6(9) of the Agriculture Act 1967 (compulsory use of systems of classification of carcases).
66. An offence under section 14(2) of that Act (levy schemes: requirements in relation to registration, returns and records).
67. An offence under section 69 of that Act (false statements to obtain grants etc).

Sea Fisheries (Shellfish) Act 1967 (c. 83)

68. An offence under section 14(2) of the Sea Fisheries (Shellfish) Act 1967 (offences relating to the deposit and importation of shellfish).

Theatres Act 1968 (c. 54)

69. An offence under section 13(1) or (2) of the Theatres Act 1968 (offences relating to licensing of premises for public performances of plays).

Theft Act 1968 (c. 60)

70. An offence under paragraph 2(1) of Schedule 1 to the Theft Act 1968 (taking or destroying fish).

Agriculture Act 1970 (c. 40)

71. An offence under section 106(8) of the Agriculture Act 1970 (eradication of brucellosis: obstructing or impeding an officer in the exercise of powers to obtain information).

Breeding of Dogs Act 1973 (c. 60)

72. An offence under the Breeding of Dogs Act 1973 (offences connected with the licensing of breeding establishments for dogs), other than under section 2 of that Act.

Slaughterhouses Act 1974 (c. 3)

73. An offence under section 4(5) of the Slaughterhouses Act 1974 (knacker's yard licences and applications for such licences).

National Health Service Act 1977 (c. 49)

74. An offence under paragraph 8(3) or 9(4) of Schedule 11 to the National Health Service Act 1977 (offences relating to the production of documents etc.).

Magistrates' Courts Act 1980 (c. 43)

75. An offence under section 84(3) of the Magistrates' Courts Act 1980 (making of false statement as to means).

Animal Health Act 1981 (c. 22)

76. An offence under paragraph 6 of Schedule 1 to the Animal Health Act 1981 (offences relating to the manufacture of veterinary therapeutic substances).

Fisheries Act 1981 (c. 29)

77. An offence under section 5(4) of the Fisheries Act 1981 (alteration of records or furnishing false information).

Civil Aviation Act 1982 (c. 16)

78. An offence under section 82 of the Civil Aviation Act 1982 (using an aircraft for advertising, etc.).

Mental Health Act 1983 (c. 20)

79. An offence under section 103 of the Mental Health Act 1983 (wrongful disclosure of a report made by a Visitor).
80. An offence under section 129 of that Act (obstruction).

Building Act 1984 (c. 55)

81. An offence under section 96(3) of the Building Act 1984 (wrongful disclosure of information).

Surrogacy Arrangements Act 1985 (c. 49)

82. An offence under section 2 of the Surrogacy Arrangements Act 1985 (negotiating surrogacy arrangements on a commercial basis, etc.).

Animals (Scientific Procedures) Act 1986 (c. 14)

83. An offence under section 22(3), 23 or 25(3) of the Animals (Scientific Procedures) Act 1986 (false statements and offences in relation to powers of entry).

Motor Cycle Noise Act 1987 (c. 34)

84. An offence under paragraph 1 of Schedule 1 to the Motor Cycle Noise Act 1987 (supply of exhaust systems etc. not complying with prescribed requirements).

Human Organ Transplants Act 1989 (c. 31)

85. An offence under section 2 of the Human Organ Transplants Act 1989 (restrictions on organ transplants).

Town and Country Planning Act 1990 (c. 8)

86. An offence under paragraph 14(4) of Schedule 15 to the Town and Country Planning Act 1990 (wrongful disclosure of information).

Environmental Protection Act 1990 (c. 43)

87. An offence under section 118(1)(g), (h) or (i) of the Environmental Protection Act 1990 (offences relating to inspection of genetically modified organisms).

Criminal Justice Act 1991 (c. 53)

88. An offence under section 20A of the Criminal Justice Act 1991 (false statements as to financial circumstances).

Deer Act 1991 (c. 54)

89. An offence under section 10(3) of the Deer Act 1991 (offences relating to sale and purchase etc. of venison).

Water Industry Act 1991 (c. 56)

90. An offence under section 206(2) of the Water Industry Act 1991 (wrongful disclosure of information).
91. An offence that falls within paragraph 5(5) of Schedule 6 to that Act (wrongful disclosure of information).

Social Security Administration Act 1992 (c. 5)

92. An offence under section 105 of the Social Security Administration Act 1992 (failure of person to maintain himself or another).
93. An offence under section 182 of that Act (illegal possession of documents).

Local Government Finance Act 1992 (c. 14)

94. An offence under section 27(5) of the Local Government Finance Act 1992 (false statements in relation to properties).

Trade Union and Labour Relations (Consolidation) Act 1992 (c. 52)

95. An offence under section 240 of the Trade Union and Labour Relations (Consolidation) Act 1992 (breach of contract involving injury to persons or property).

Merchant Shipping Act 1995 (c. 21)

96. An offence under section 57 of the Merchant Shipping Act 1995 (offences relating to merchant navy uniforms).

Reserve Forces Act 1996 (c. 14)

97. An offence under section 75(5) of the Reserve Forces Act 1996 (making false statements).
98. An offence under section 82(1) of that Act (offences in connection with regulations under sections 78 and 79 of that Act).
99. An offence under section 87(1) of that Act (offences in connection with claims for payment).
100. An offence under section 99 of that Act (false pretence of illegal absence).
101. An offence under paragraph 5(1) of Schedule 1 to that Act (false answers in attestation papers).

Housing Act 1996 (c. 52)

102. An offence under paragraph 23 or 24 of Schedule 1 to the Housing Act 1996 (contravening order not to part with money etc. held on behalf of a social landlord).

Broadcasting Act 1996 (c. 55)

103. An offence under section 144 of the Broadcasting Act 1996 (providing false information in connection with licences).

Breeding and Sale of Dogs (Welfare) Act 1999 (c. 11)

104. An offence under section 8 or 9(6) of the Breeding and Sale of Dogs (Welfare) Act 1999 (offences relating to the sale of dogs and connected matters).

Transport Act 2000 (c. 38)

105. An offence under section 82(2) of the Transport Act 2000 (wrongful disclosure of information).

SCHEDULE 26

INCREASE IN MAXIMUM TERM FOR CERTAIN SUMMARY OFFENCES   Section 28

Railway Regulation Act 1840 (c. 97)

1. In section 16 of the Railway Regulation Act 1840 (obstructing officers or trespassing upon railway), for "one month", there is substituted "51 weeks".

Licensing Act 1872 (c. 94)

2. In section 12 of the Licensing Act 1872 (penalty for being found drunk), for "one month" there is substituted "51 weeks".

Regulation of Railways Act 1889 (c. 57)

3. In section 5 of the Regulation of Railways Act 1889 (avoiding payment of fares, etc.), in subsection (3), for "three months" there is substituted "51 weeks".

Witnesses (Public Inquiries) Protection Act 1892 (c. 64)

4. In section 2 of the Witnesses (Public Inquiries) Protection Act 1892 (persons obstructing or intimidating witnesses), for "three months" there is substituted "51 weeks".

Licensing Act 1902 (c. 28)

5. In section 2 of the Licensing Act 1902 (penalty for being drunk while in charge of a child), in subsection (1), for "one month" there is substituted "51 weeks".

Emergency Powers Act 1920 (c. 55)

6. In section 2 of the Emergency Powers Act 1920 (emergency regulations), in subsection (3), for "three months" there is substituted "51 weeks".

Judicial Proceedings (Regulation of Reports) Act 1926 (c. 61)

7. In section 1 of the Judicial Proceedings (Regulation of Reports) Act 1926 (restriction on publication of reports of judicial proceedings), in subsection (2), for "four months" there is substituted "51 weeks".

Public Order Act 1936 (1 Edw. 8 & 1 Geo. 6 c. 6)

8. In section 7 of the Public Order Act 1936 (enforcement), in subsection (2), for "three months" there is substituted "51 weeks".

Cinematograph Films (Animals) Act 1937 (c. 59)

9. In section 1 of the Cinematograph Films (Animals) Act 1937 (prohibition of films involving cruelty to animals), in subsection (3), for "three months" there is substituted "51 weeks".

House to House Collections Act 1939 (c. 44)

10. In section 8 of the House to House Collections Act 1939, in subsection (2), for "three months" there is substituted "51 weeks".

Fire Services Act 1947 (c. 41)

11. In section 31 of the Fire Services Act 1947 (false alarms of fire), in subsection (1), for "three months" there is substituted "51 weeks".

National Assistance Act 1948 (c. 29)

12. (1) The National Assistance Act 1948 is amended as follows.

    (2) In section 51 (failure to maintain), in subsection (3)(a) and (b), for "three months" there is substituted "51 weeks".

    (3) In section 52 (false statements), in subsection (1), for "three months" there is substituted "51 weeks".

Docking and Nicking of Horses Act 1949 (c. 70)

13. (1) The Docking and Nicking of Horses Act 1949 is amended as follows.

    (2) In section 1 (prohibition of docking and nicking except in certain cases), in subsection (3), for "three months" there is substituted "51 weeks".

    (3) In section 2 (restriction on landing docked horses)—

      (a) in subsection (3), and

      (b) in subsection (4),

for "3 months" there is substituted "51 weeks".

Protection of Animals (Amendment) Act 1954 (c. 40)

14. In section 2 of the Protection of Animals (Amendment) Act 1954 (breach of disqualification order), for "three months" there is substituted "51 weeks".

Children and Young Persons (Harmful Publications) Act 1955 (c. 28)

15. In section 2 of the Children and Young Persons (Harmful Publications) Act 1955 (penalty for publishing certain works etc.), in subsection (1), for "four months" there is substituted "51 weeks".

Agriculture Act 1957 (c. 57)

16. In section 7 of the Agriculture Act 1957 (penalties)—

    (a) in subsection (1), for "three months" there is substituted "51 weeks", and

    (b) in subsection (2), for "one month" there is substituted "51 weeks".

Animals (Cruel Poisons) Act 1962 (c. 26)

17. In section 1 of the Animals (Cruel Poisons) Act 1962 (offences and penalties under regulations), in paragraph (b), for "three months" there is substituted "51 weeks".

Plant Varieties and Seeds Act 1964 (c. 14)

18. In section 27 of the Plant Varieties and Seeds Act 1964 (tampering with samples), in subsection (1), for "three months" there is substituted "51 weeks".

Agriculture Act 1967 (c. 22)

19. (1) The Agriculture Act 1967 is amended as follows.

(2) In section 6 (penalties), in subsection (4), for "three months" there is substituted "51 weeks".

(3) In section 21 (inquiry by Meat and Livestock Commission), in subsection (11), for "three months" there is substituted "51 weeks".

Firearms Act 1968 (c. 27)

20. (1) Part 1 of Schedule 6 to the Firearms Act 1968 (prosecution and punishment of offences) is amended as follows.

(2) In the entry relating to section 3(6) of that Act (business and other transactions with firearms and ammunition), in the fourth column, for "3 months" there is substituted "51 weeks".

(3) In the entry relating to section 6(3) of that Act (power to prohibit movement of arms and ammunition), in the fourth column, for "3 months" there is substituted "51 weeks".

(4) In the entry relating to section 20(2) of that Act (trespassing with firearm), in the fourth column, for "3 months" there is substituted "51 weeks".

(5) In the entry relating to section 22(1A) of that Act (acquisition and possession of firearms by minors), in the fourth column, for "3 months" there is substituted "51 weeks".

(6) In the entry relating to section 25 of that Act (supplying firearm to person drunk or insane), in the fourth column, for "3 months" there is substituted "51 weeks".

(7) In the entry relating to section 32C(6) of that Act (variation endorsement etc. of European documents), in the fourth column, for "3 months" there is substituted "51 weeks".

(8) In the entry relating to section 42A of that Act (information as to transactions under visitors' permits), in the fourth column, for "3 months" there is substituted "51 weeks".

(9) In the entry relating to section 47(2) of that Act (powers of constables to stop and search), in the fourth column, for "3 months" there is substituted "51 weeks".

(10) In the entry relating to section 49(3) of that Act (police powers in relation to arms traffic), in the fourth column, for "3 months" there is substituted "51 weeks".

Agriculture (Miscellaneous Provisions) Act 1968 (c. 34)

21. In section 7 of the Agriculture (Miscellaneous Provisions) Act 1968 (punishment of offences under Part 1), in subsection (1), for "three months" there is substituted "51 weeks".

Agriculture Act 1970 (c. 40)

22. (1) The Agriculture Act 1970 is amended as follows.

(2) In section 68 (duty to give statutory statement), in subsection (4), for "three months" there is substituted "51 weeks".

(3) In section 69 (marking of material prepared for sale), in subsection (4), for "three months" there is substituted "51 weeks".

(4) In section 70 (use of names or expressions with prescribed meanings), in subsection (2), for "three months" there is substituted "51 weeks".

(5) In section 71 (particulars to be given of attributes if claimed to be present), in subsection (2), for "three months" there is substituted "51 weeks".

(6) In section 73 (deleterious ingredients in feeding stuff), in subsection (4), for "three months" there is substituted "51 weeks".

(7) In section 73A (unwholesome feeding stuff), in subsection (4), for "three months" there is substituted "51 weeks".

(8)   In section 74A (regulations controlling the contents of feeding stuff), in subsection (3), for "three months" there is substituted "51 weeks".

(9)   In section 79 (supplementary provision relating to samples and analysis), in subsection (10), for "three months" there is substituted "51 weeks".

(10) In section 83 (exercise of powers by inspectors), in subsection (3), for "three months" there is substituted "51 weeks".

(11) In section 106 (eradication of brucellosis), in subsection (7), for "three months" there is substituted "51 weeks".

Slaughterhouses Act 1974 (c. 3)

23. (1) The Slaughterhouses Act 1974 is amended as follows.

(2)   In section 20 (wrongful disclosure of information), in subsection (4), for "three months" there is substituted "51 weeks".

(3)   In section 21 (obstruction), in subsection (1), for "one month" there is substituted "51 weeks".

(4)   In section 23 (prosecution and punishment of offences), in subsection (2)(a), for "three months" there is substituted "51 weeks".

Criminal Law Act 1977 (c. 45)

24.   In section 8 of the Criminal Law Act 1977 (trespassing with a weapon of offence), in subsection (3), for "three months" there is substituted "51 weeks".

Refuse Disposal (Amenity) Act 1978 (c. 3)

25.   In section 2 of the Refuse Disposal (Amenity) Act 1978 (penalty for unauthorised dumping), in subsection (1), for "three months" there is substituted "51 weeks".

Customs and Excise Management Act 1979 (c. 2)

26. (1) The Customs and Excise Management Act 1979 is amended as follows.

(2)   In section 21 (control of movement of aircraft), in subsection (6), for "3 months" there is substituted "51 weeks".

(3)   In section 33 (power to inspect aircraft etc.), in subsection (4), for "3 months" there is substituted "51 weeks".

(4)   In section 34 (power to prevent flight of aircraft)—
        (a) in subsection (2), and
        (b) in subsection (3),
        for "3 months" there is substituted "51 weeks".

Licensed Premises (Exclusion of Certain Persons) Act 1980 (c. 32)

27.   In section 2 of the Licensed Premises (Exclusion of Certain Persons) Act 1980 (penalty for non-compliance with an exclusion order), in subsection (1), for "one month" there is substituted "51 weeks".

Criminal Attempts Act 1981 (c. 47)

28.   In section 9 of the Criminal Attempts Act 1981 (interference with vehicles), in subsection (3), for "three months" there is substituted "51 weeks".

585

British Nationality Act 1981 (c. 61)

29. In section 46 of the British Nationality Act 1981 (offences and proceedings), in subsection (1) for "three months" there is substituted "51 weeks".

Civil Aviation Act 1982 (c. 16)

30. (1) The Civil Aviation Act 1982 is amended as follows.
    (2) In section 44 (offences relating to the power to obtain rights over land), in subsection (10), for "three months" there is substituted "51 weeks".
    (3) In section 75 (investigation of accidents), in subsection (5), for "three months" there is substituted "51 weeks".

Anatomy Act 1984 (c. 14)

31. In section 11 of the Anatomy Act 1984 (offences), in subsection (6), for "3 months" there is substituted "51 weeks".

Public Health (Control of Disease) Act 1984 (c. 22)

32. (1) The Public Health (Control of Disease) Act 1984 is amended as follows.
    (2) In section 29 (letting of house after recent case of notifiable disease), in subsection (1), for "one month" there is substituted "51 weeks".
    (3) In section 30 (duty on ceasing to occupy house after recent case of notifiable disease), in subsection (1), for "one month" there is substituted "51 weeks".
    (4) In section 62 (powers of entry), in subsection (3), for "3 months" there is substituted "51 weeks".

County Courts Act 1984 (c. 28)

33. (1) The County Courts Act 1984 is amended as follows.
    (2) In section 14 (penalty for assaulting officers), in subsection (1)(a), for "3 months" there is substituted "51 weeks".
    (3) In section 92 (penalty for rescuing goods seized), in subsection (1)(a), for "one month" there is substituted "51 weeks."

Animal Health and Welfare Act 1984 (c. 40)

34. In section 10 of the Animal Health and Welfare Act 1984 (artificial breeding of livestock), in subsection (6), for "three months" there is substituted "51 weeks".

Police and Criminal Evidence Act 1984 (c. 60)

35. In section 63C of the Police and Criminal Evidence Act 1984 (testing for presence of drugs), in subsection (1), for "three months" there is substituted "51 weeks".

Sporting Events (Control of Alcohol etc.) Act 1985 (c. 57)

36. In section 8 of the Sporting Events (Control of Alcohol etc.) Act 1985 (penalties for offences), in paragraph (b), for "three months" there is substituted "51 weeks".

Public Order Act 1986 (c. 64)

37. (1) The Public Order Act 1986 is amended as follows.
   (2) In section 12 (imposing conditions on public processions)—
   (a) in subsection (8), and
   (b) in subsection (10),
   for "3 months" there is substituted "51 weeks".
   (3) In section 13 (prohibiting public processions)—
   (a) in subsection (11), and
   (b) in subsection (13),
   for "3 months" there is substituted "51 weeks".
   (4) In section 14 (imposing conditions on public assemblies)—
   (a) in subsection (8), and
   (b) in subsection (10),
   for "3 months" there is substituted "51 weeks".
   (5) In section 14B (offences in connection with trespassory assemblies and arrest therefor)—
   (a) in subsection (5), and
   (b) in subsection (7),
   for "3 months" there is substituted "51 weeks".

Road Traffic Offenders Act 1988 (c. 53)

38. (1) Part 1 of Schedule 2 to the Road Traffic Offenders Act 1988 (prosecution and punishment of offenders) is amended as follows.
   (2) In the entry relating to section 4(2) of the Road Traffic Act 1988 (driving, or being in charge, when under the influence of drink or drugs), in column 4, for "3 months" there is substituted "51 weeks".
   (3) In the entry relating to section 5(1)(b) of that Act (driving or being in charge of a motor vehicle with alcohol concentration above prescribed limit), in column 4, for "3 months" there is substituted "51 weeks".
   (4) In the entry relating to section 7 of that Act (provision of specimens for analysis), in column 4, for "3 months" there is substituted "51 weeks".
   (5) In the entry relating to section 7A of that Act (failing to allow specimen to be subjected to analysis), in column 4, for "3 months" there is substituted "51 weeks".

Official Secrets Act 1989 (c. 6)

39. In section 10 of the Official Secrets Act 1989 (penalties), in subsection (2), for "three months" there is substituted "51 weeks".

Human Organ Transplants Act 1989 (c. 31)

40. In section 1 of the Human Organ Transplants Act 1989 (prohibition of commercial dealings in human organs), in subsection (5), for "three months" there is substituted "51 weeks".

Football Spectators Act 1989 (c. 37)

41. In section 2 of the Football Spectators Act 1989 (unauthorised attendance at designated football matches), in subsection (3), for "one month" there is substituted "51 weeks".

Food Safety Act 1990 (c. 16)

42. In section 35 of the Food Safety Act 1990 (punishment of offences), in subsection (1), for "three months" there is substituted "51 weeks".

Deer Act 1991 (c. 54)

43. In section 9 of the Deer Act 1991 (penalties for offences relating to deer), in subsection (1), for "three months" there is substituted "51 weeks".

Social Security Administration Act 1992 (c. 5)

44. In section 112 of the Social Security Administration Act 1992 (false representations for obtaining benefit etc.), in subsection (2), for "3 months" there is substituted "51 weeks".

Criminal Justice and Public Order Act 1994 (c. 33)

45. (1) The Criminal Justice and Public Order Act 1994 is amended as follows.
    (2) In section 60 (failing to stop), in subsection (8), for "one month" there is substituted "51 weeks".
    (3) In section 60AA (powers to require removal of disguises), in subsection (7), for "one month" there is substituted "51 weeks".
    (4) In section 61 (power to remove trespasser on land), in subsection (4), for "three months" there is substituted "51 weeks".
    (5) In section 62B (failure to comply with direction under section 62A: offences), in subsection (3), for "3 months" there is substituted "51 weeks".
    (6) In section 63 (powers to remove persons attending or preparing for a rave), in subsections (6) and (7B), for "three months" there is substituted "51 weeks".
    (7) In section 68 (offence of aggravated trespass), in subsection (3), for "three months" there is substituted "51 weeks".
    (8) In section 69 (powers to remove persons committing or participating in aggravated trespass), in subsection (3), for "three months" there is substituted "51 weeks".

London Local Authorities Act 1995 (c. x)

46. In section 24 of the London Local Authorities Act 1995 (enforcement), in subsection (1), for "three months" there is substituted "51 weeks".

Police Act 1996 (c. 16)

47. In section 89 of the Police Act 1996 (assaults on constables etc.), in subsection (2), for "one month" there is substituted "51 weeks".

Treasure Act 1996 (c. 24)

48. In section 8 of the Treasure Act 1996 (duty of finder of treasure to notify coroner), in subsection (3)(a), for "three months" there is substituted "51 weeks".

Education Act 1996 (c. 56)

49. (1) The Education Act 1996 is amended as follows.
    (2) In section 444 (failure to secure regular attendance at school), in subsection (8A)(b), for "three months" there is substituted "51 weeks".
    (3) In section 559 (prohibition or restriction on employment of children), in subsection (4)(b), for "one month" there is substituted "51 weeks".

Government of Wales Act 1998 (c. 38)

50. In section 75 of the Government of Wales Act 1998 (witnesses and documents: supplementary), in subsection (3)(b), for "three months" there is substituted "51 weeks".

Access to Justice Act 1999 (c. 22)

51. In section 21 of the Access to Justice Act 1999 (misrepresentation etc), in subsection (2)(b), for "three months" there is substituted "51 weeks".

Greater London Authority Act 1999 (c. 29)

52. In section 64 of the Greater London Authority Act 1999 (failure to attend proceedings etc), in subsection (2)(b), for "three months" there is substituted "51 weeks".

Immigration and Asylum Act 1999 (c. 33)

53. (1) The Immigration and Asylum Act 1999 is amended as follows.
    (2) In section 105 (false representation), in subsection (2), for "three months" there is substituted "51 weeks".
    (3) In section 108 (failure of sponsor to maintain), in subsection (2), for "3 months" there is substituted "51 weeks".

Financial Services and Markets Act 2000 (c. 8)

54. (1) The Financial Services and Markets Act 2000 is amended as follows.
    (2) In section 177 (offences), in subsection (6), for "three months" there is substituted "51 weeks".
    (3) In section 352 (offences), in subsection (5), for "three months" there is substituted "51 weeks".

Terrorism Act 2000 (c. 11)

55. (1) The Terrorism Act 2000 is amended as follows.
    (2) In section 36 (police powers), in subsection (4)(a), for "three months" there is substituted "51 weeks".

(3) In section 51 (offences in relation to parking), in subsection (6)(a), for "three months" there is substituted "51 weeks".

(4) In Schedule 5 (terrorist investigations: information)—
    (a) in paragraph 3(8)(a), and
    (b) in paragraph 15(5)(a),
for "three months" there is substituted "51 weeks".

(5) In Schedule 7 (ports and border controls), in paragraph 18(2)(a), for "three months" there is substituted "51 weeks".

Criminal Justice and Police Act 2001 (c. 16)

56. (1) The Criminal Justice and Police Act 2001 is amended as follows.

(2) In section 25 (enforcement of closure orders)—
    (a) in subsection (3)(a), for "one month" there is substituted "51 weeks", and
    (b) in subsections (4) and (5), for "three months" there is substituted "51 weeks".

(3) In section 42 (prevention of intimidation), in subsection (7), for "three months" there is substituted "51 weeks".

Police Reform Act 2002 (c. 30)

57. In section 46 of the Police Reform Act 2002 (offences against designated and accredited persons etc.), in subsection (2), for "one month" there is substituted "51 weeks".

Nationality, Immigration and Asylum Act 2002 (c. 41)

58. In section 137 of the Nationality, Immigration and Asylum Act 2002 (offences relating to the disclosure of information), in subsection (2)(a), for "three months" there is substituted "51 weeks".

Anti-social Behaviour Act 2003 (c. 38)

59. In section 40 of the Anti-social Behaviour Act 2003 (closure of noisy premises), in subsection (5)(a), for "three months" there is substituted "51 weeks".

SCHEDULE 27
Section 283
ENABLING POWERS: ALTERATION OF MAXIMUM PENALTIES ETC.

Plant Health Act 1967 (c. 8)

1. (1) Section 3 of the Plant Health Act 1967 (control of spread of pests in Great Britain) is amended as follows.

(2) In subsection (4A), for "three months" there is substituted "the prescribed term".

(3) After that subsection there is inserted—
    "(4B) In subsection (4A) above, "the prescribed term" means—
        (a) in relation to England and Wales, 51 weeks;
        (b) in relation to Scotland, three months."

Agriculture Act 1967 (c. 22)

2. (1) Section 9 of the Agriculture Act 1967 (powers to meet future developments in livestock and livestock products industries) is amended as follows.

   (2) In subsection (10), for "three months" there is substituted "the prescribed term".

   (3) After that subsection there is inserted—

   "(10A) In subsection (10), "the prescribed term" means—

       (a) in relation to England and Wales, 51 weeks;

       (b) in relation to Scotland, three months."

European Communities Act 1972 (c. 68)

3. (1) Paragraph 1 of Schedule 2 to the European Communities Act 1972 (provisions as to powers conferred by section 2(2)) is amended as follows.

   (2) In sub-paragraph (1)(d), for "three months" there is substituted "the prescribed term".

   (3) After sub-paragraph (2) there is inserted—

   "(3) In sub-paragraph (1)(d), "the prescribed term" means—

       (a) in relation to England and Wales, where the offence is a summary offence, 51 weeks;

       (b) in relation to England and Wales, where the offence is triable either way, twelve months;

       (c) in relation to Scotland and Northern Ireland, three months."

Slaughterhouses Act 1974 (c. 3)

4. In section 38(5) of the Slaughterhouses Act 1974 (maximum penalties to be prescribed by regulations), the words "or imprisonment for a term of three months or both" are omitted.

Anatomy Act 1984 (c. 14)

5. (1) Section 11 of the Anatomy Act 1984 (offences) is amended as follows.

   (2) In subsection (7), for "3 months" there is substituted "the prescribed term".

   (3) After that subsection there is inserted —

   "(7A) In subsection (7), "the prescribed term" means—

       (a) in relation to England and Wales, 51 weeks;

       (b) in relation to Scotland, 3 months."

Environmental Protection Act 1990 (c. 43)

6. (1) Section 141 of the Environmental Protection Act 1990 (power to prohibit or restrict the importation or exportation of waste) is amended as follows.

   (2) In paragraph (g) of subsection (5), for "six months" there is substituted "the prescribed term".

   (3) After that subsection there is inserted—

   "(5A) In subsection (5)(g), "the prescribed term" means—

       (a) in relation to England and Wales, where the offence is a summary offence, 51 weeks;

       (b) in relation to England and Wales, where the offence is triable either way, twelve months;

       (c) in relation to Scotland and Northern Ireland, six months."

Scotland Act 1998 (c. 46)

7. (1) Section 113 of the Scotland Act 1998 (subordinate legislation: scope of powers) is amended as follows.

(2) In paragraph (a) of subsection (10), for "three months" there is substituted "the prescribed term".

(3) After that subsection there is inserted—

"(10A) In subsection (10)(a), "the prescribed term" means—

(a) in relation to England and Wales, where the offence is a summary offence, 51 weeks;

(b) in relation to England and Wales, where the offence is triable either way, twelve months;

(c) in relation to Scotland and Northern Ireland, three months."

Regulatory Reform Act 2001 (c. 6)

8. (1) Section 3 of the Regulatory Reform Act 2001 (limitations on order-making power) is amended as follows.

(2) In paragraph (b) of subsection (3), for "six months" there is substituted "the prescribed term".

(3) After that subsection there is inserted—

"(3A) In subsection (3)(b), "the prescribed term" means—

(a) in relation to England and Wales, where the offence is a summary offence, 51 weeks;

(b) in relation to England and Wales, where the offence is triable either way, twelve months;

(c) in relation to Scotland and Northern Ireland, six months."

SCHEDULE 28
Section 284

INCREASE IN PENALTIES FOR DRUG-RELATED OFFENCES

Misuse of Drugs Act 1971 (c. 38)

1. (1) Schedule 4 to the Misuse of Drugs Act 1971 (prosecution and punishment of offences) is amended as follows.

(2) In column 6 of that Schedule (punishments for offences under that Act committed in relation to Class C drugs), in each of the following entries, for "5 years" there is substituted "14 years".

(3) Those entries are the entries relating to the punishment, on conviction on indictment, of offences under the following provisions of that Act—

(a) section 4(2) (production, or being concerned in the production, of a controlled drug),

(b) section 4(3) (supplying or offering to supply a controlled drug or being concerned in the doing of either activity by another),

(c) section 5(3) (having possession of a controlled drug with intent to supply it to another),

(d) section 8 (being the occupier, or concerned in the management, of premises and permitting or suffering certain activities to take place there),

(e) section 12(6) (contravention of direction prohibiting practitioner etc from possessing, supplying etc controlled drugs), and

(f) section 13(3) (contravention of direction prohibiting practitioner etc from prescribing, supplying etc controlled drugs).

Customs and Excise Management Act 1979 (c. 2)

2. In Schedule 1 to the Customs and Excise Management Act 1979 (controlled drugs: variation of punishments for certain offences under that Act), in paragraph 2(c) (punishment on conviction on indictment of offences under that Act committed in relation to Class C drugs), for "5 years" there is substituted "14 years".

Criminal Justice (International Co-operation) Act 1990 (c. 5)

3. In section 19 of the Criminal Justice (International Co-operation) Act 1990 (ships used for illicit traffic), in subsection (4)(c)(ii) (punishment on conviction on indictment of offences under that section committed in relation to Class C drugs), for "five years" there is substituted "fourteen years".

SCHEDULE 29
SENTENCING FOR FIREARMS OFFENCES IN NORTHERN IRELAND   Section 2

1. The Firearms (Northern Ireland) Order 1981 (S.I. 1981/155 (N.I. 2)) is amended as follows.
2. In Article 2(2) (interpretation) after the definition of "firearms dealer" there is inserted—
" "handgun" means any firearm which either has a barrel less than 30 centimetres in length or is less than 60 centimetres in length overall, other than an air weapon, a muzzle-loading gun or a firearm designed as signalling apparatus;".
3. In Article 3(1) (requirement of firearm certificate) for sub-paragraph (a) there is substituted—
"(aa) has in his possession, or purchases or acquires, a handgun without holding a firearm certificate in force at the time, or otherwise than as authorised by such a certificate;
(ab) has in his possession, or purchases or acquires, any firearm, other than a handgun, without holding a firearm certificate in force at the time, or otherwise than as authorised by such a certificate; or".
4. After Article 52 of that Order there is inserted—

"52A Minimum sentence for certain offences

(1) This Article applies where—
(a) an individual is convicted of—
(i) an offence under Article 3(1)(aa),
(ii) an offence under Article 6(1)(a), (ab), (ac), (ad), (ae) or (c), or
(iii) an offence under Article 6(1A)(a), and
(b) the offence was committed after the commencement of this Article and at a time when he was aged 16 or over.
(2) The court shall—
(a) in the case of an offence under Article 3(1)(aa) committed by a person who was aged 21 or over when he committed the offence, impose a sentence of imprisonment for a term of five years (with or without a fine), and
(b) in any other case, impose an appropriate custodial sentence for a term of at least the required minimum term (with or without a fine)
unless (in any of those cases) the court is of the opinion that there are exceptional circumstances relating to the offence or to the offender which justify its not doing so.

(3) Where an offence is found to have been committed over a period of two or more days, or at some time during a period of two or more days, it shall be taken for the purposes of this Article to have been committed on the last of those days.

(4) In this Article—

"appropriate custodial sentence" means—

(a) in the case of an offender who is aged 21 or over when convicted, a sentence of imprisonment, and

(b) in the case of an offender who is aged under 21 at that time, a sentence of detention under section 5(1) of the Treatment of Offenders Act (Northern Ireland) 1968;

"the required minimum term" means—

(a) in the case of an offender who was aged 21 or over when he committed the offence, five years, and

(b) in the case of an offender who was aged under 21 at that time, three years."

5. After Article 52A there is inserted—

"52B Power by order to exclude application of minimum sentence to those under 18

(1) The Secretary of State may by order—

(a) amend Article 52A(1)(b) by substituting for the word "16" the word "18", and

(b) make such other provision as he considers necessary or expedient in consequence of, or in connection with, the provision made by virtue of sub-paragraph (a).

(2) The provision that may be made by virtue of paragraph (1)(b) includes, in particular, provision amending or repealing any statutory provision within the meaning of section 1(f) of the Interpretation Act (Northern Ireland) 1954 (whenever passed or made).

(3) An order under paragraph (1) shall be subject to annulment in pursuance of a resolution of either House of Parliament in like manner as a statutory instrument and section 5 of the Statutory Instruments Act 1946 shall apply accordingly."

6. (1) Schedule 2 (table of punishments) is amended as follows.

(2) For the entry relating to offences under Article 3(1) (purchase, acquisition or possession of firearm or ammunition without firearm certificate) there is substituted—

"Article 3(1)(aa) Purchase, acquisition or possession of handgun without firearm certificate	Indictment	10 years or a fine, or both
Article 3(1)(ab) Purchase, acquisition or possession without firearm certificate of firearm other than handgun	(a) Summary	1 year or a fine of the statutory maximum, or both
	(b) Indictment	5 years or a fine, or both

Article 3(1)(b)	Purchase, acquisition or possession of ammunition without firearm certificate	(a) Summary	1 year or a fine of the statutory maximum, or both
		(b) Indictment	5 years or a fine, or both"

(3) For the entries relating to offences under Article 6(1) (manufacture, dealing in or possession of prohibited weapons) and Article 6(1A) (possession of or dealing in other prohibited weapons) there is substituted—

"Article 6(1), (a) (ab), (ac), (ad), (ae) and (c)	Manufacture, dealing in or possession of prohibited weapons.	Indictment	10 years or a fine, or both
Article 6(1) (b)	Manfacture, dealing in or possession of prohibited weapon designed for discharge of noxious liquid etc.	(a) Summary	1 year or a fine of the statutory maximum, or both
		(b) Indictment	10 years or a fine, or both
Article 6(1A) (a)	Possession of or dealing in firearm disguised as other object	Indictment	10 years or a fine, or both
Article 6(1A) (b), (c), (d), (e), (f) or (g)	Possession of or dealing in other prohibited weapons	(a) Summary	6 months or a fine of the statutory maximum, or both
		(b) Indictment	10 years or a fine, or both"

SCHEDULE 30
DISQUALIFICATION FROM WORKING WITH CHILDREN

Section 299

1. The Criminal Justice and Court Services Act 2000 (c. 43) is amended as follows.
2. After section 29 there is inserted—

"29A Disqualification at discretion of court: adults and juveniles

(1) This section applies where—
   (a) an individual is convicted of an offence against a child (whether or not committed when he was aged 18 or over),
   (b) the individual is sentenced by a senior court, and
   (c) no qualifying sentence is imposed in respect of the conviction.

(2) If the court is satisfied, having regard to all the circumstances, that it is likely that the individual will commit a further offence against a child, it may order the individual to be disqualified from working with children.

(3) If the court makes an order under this section, it must state its reasons for doing so and cause those reasons to be included in the record of the proceedings.

29B Subsequent application for order under section 28 or 29

(1) Where—

    (a) section 28 applies but the court has neither made an order under that section nor complied with subsection (6) of that section, or

    (b) section 29 applies but the court has not made an order under that section, and it appears to the prosecutor that the court has not considered the making of an order under that section,

the prosecutor may at any time apply to that court for an order under section 28 or 29.

(2) Subject to subsection (3), on an application under subsection (1)—

    (a) in a case falling within subsection (1)(a), the court—

        (i) must make an order under section 28 unless it is satisfied as mentioned in subsection (5) of that section, and

        (ii) if it does not make an order under that section, must comply with subsection (6) of that section,

    (b) in a case falling within subsection (1)(b), the court—

        (i) must make an order under section 29 if it is satisfied as mentioned in subsection (4) of that section, and

        (ii) if it does so, must comply with subsection (5) of that section.

(3) Subsection (2) does not enable or require an order under section 28 or 29 to be made where the court is satisfied that it had considered the making of an order under that section at the time when it imposed the qualifying sentence or made the relevant order."

3. (1) Section 30 (supplemental provisions) is amended as follows.

  (2) In the heading for "and 29" there is substituted "to 29B".

  (3) In subsection (1)—

    (a) for "and 29" there is substituted "to 29B", and

    (b) in the definition of "qualifying sentence", after paragraph (d) there is inserted—

      "(dd) a sentence of detention under section 226 or 228[a] of the Criminal Justice Act 2003,".

  (4) In subsection (5)—

    (a) in paragraph (a), for "or 29" there is substituted ", 29 or 29A",

    (b) after paragraph (b) there is inserted—

      "(c) in relation to an individual to whom section 29A applies and on whom a sentence has been passed, references to his sentence are to that sentence."

4. In section 31 (appeals), in subsection (1), after paragraph (b) there is inserted—

  "(c) where an order is made under section 29A, as if the order were a sentence passed on him for the offence of which he has been convicted."

5. (1) Section 33 (conditions for application under section 32) is amended as follows.

  (2) In subsection (6), after paragraph (d) there is inserted—

    "(e) in relation to an individual not falling within any of paragraphs (a) to (d), the day on which the disqualification order is made.".

  (3) For subsection (8) there is substituted—

    "(8) In subsection (7) "detention" means detention (or detention and training)—

      (a) under any sentence or order falling within paragraphs (b) to (f) of the definition of "qualifying sentence" in section 30(1), or

      (b) under any sentence or order which would fall within those paragraphs if it were for a term or period of 12 months or more.".

SCHEDULE 31
DEFAULT ORDERS: MODIFICATION OF PROVISIONS RELATING TO
COMMUNITY ORDERS

Section 300

General

1. Any reference to the offender is, in relation to a default order, to be read as a reference to the person in default.

Unpaid work requirement

2. (1) In its application to a default order, section 199 (unpaid work requirement) is modified as follows.
   (2) In subsection (2), for paragraphs (a) and (b) there is substituted—
   "(a) not less than 20 hours, and
   (b) in the case of an amount in default which is specified in the first column of the following Table, not more than the number of hours set out opposite that amount in the second column.

TABLE

Amount	Number of Hours
An amount not exceeding £200	40 hours
An amount exceeding £200 but not exceeding £500 60 hours	An amount exceeding £500 100 hours"

   (3) Subsection (5) is omitted.

Curfew requirement

3. (1) In its application to a default order, section 204 (curfew requirement) is modified as follows.
   (2) After subsection (2) there is inserted—
   "(2A) In the case of an amount in default which is specified in the first column of the following Table, the number of days on which the person in default is subject to the curfew requirement must not exceed the number of days set out opposite that amount in the second column.

TABLE

Amount	Number of days
An amount not exceeding £200	20 days
An amount exceeding £200 but not exceeding £500	30 days
An amount exceeding £500 but not exceeding £1,000	60 days
An amount exceeding £1,000 but not exceeding £2,500	90 days
An amount exceeding £2,500	180 days"

Enforcement, revocation and amendment of default order

4. (1) In its application to a default order, Schedule 8 (breach, revocation or amendment of community orders) is modified as follows.

   (2) Any reference to the offence in respect of which the community order was made is to be taken to be a reference to the default in respect of which the default order was made.

   (3) Any power of the court to revoke the community order and deal with the offender for the offence is to be taken to be a power to revoke the default order and deal with him in any way in which the court which made the default order could deal with him for his default in paying the sum in question.

   (4) In paragraph 4 the reference to the Crown Court is to be taken as a reference to a magistrates' court.

   (5) The following provisions are omitted—

   (a) paragraph 9(1)(c), (5) and (8),

   (b) paragraph 12,

   (c) paragraph 13(5),

   (d) paragraph 15,

   (e) paragraph 17(5),

   (f) paragraph 21(4), and

   (g) paragraph 23(2)(b).

Power to alter amount of money or number of hours or days

5. The Secretary of State may by order amend paragraph 2 or 3 by substituting for any reference to an amount of money or a number of hours or days there specified a reference to such other amount or number as may be specified in the order.

Transfer of default orders to Scotland or Northern Ireland

6. In its application to a default order, Schedule 9 (transfer of community orders to Scotland or Northern Ireland) is modified as follows.

7. After paragraph 8 there is inserted—

   "8A Nothing in paragraph 8 affects the application of section 300(7) to a default order made or amended in accordance with paragraph 1 or 3."

8. In paragraph 10, after paragraph (b) there is inserted—

   "(bb) any power to impose a fine on the offender."

Section 304

SCHEDULE 32
AMENDMENTS RELATING TO SENTENCING

PART 1
GENERAL

Piracy Act 1837 (c. 88)

1. Section 3 of the Piracy Act 1837 (punishment for offence under certain repealed Acts relating to piracy) shall cease to have effect.

Children and Young Persons Act 1933 (c. 12)

2. (1) Section 49 of the Children and Young Persons Act 1933 (restrictions on reports of proceedings in which young persons are concerned) is amended as follows.
   (2) In subsection (4A)(d), for "section 62(3) of the Powers of Criminal Courts (Sentencing) Act 2000" there is substituted "section 22?(1)(d) or (e) of the Criminal Justice Act 2003".
   (3) In subsection (11)—
      (a) in the definition of "sexual offence", for "has the same meaning as in the Powers of Criminal Courts (Sentencing) Act 2000" there is substituted "means an offence listed in Part 2 of Schedule 15 to the Criminal Justice Act 2003", and
      (b) in the definition of "violent offence", for "has the same meaning as in the Powers of Criminal Courts (Sentencing) Act 2000" there is substituted "means an offence listed in Part 1 of Schedule 15 to the Criminal Justice Act 2003".

Prison Act 1952 (c. 52)

3. In section 53 of the Prison Act 1952 (interpretation), for "section 62 of the Powers of Criminal Courts (Sentencing) Act 2000" there is substituted "section 221 of the Criminal Justice Act 2003".

Criminal Justice Act 1967 (c. 80)

4. The Criminal Justice Act 1967 is amended as follows.
5. In section 32 (amendments of Costs in Criminal Cases Act 1952), in subsection (3)(a), for "make an order under paragraph 5 of Schedule 2 to the Powers of Criminal Courts (Sentencing) Act 2000 (probation orders requiring treatment for mental condition) or" there is substituted "include in a community order (within the meaning of Part 12 of the Criminal Justice Act 2003) a mental health requirement under section 207 of that Act or make an order under".
6. In section 104 (general provisions as to interpretation)—
   (a) in subsection (1), the definition of "suspended sentence" is omitted, and
   (b) subsection (2) is omitted.

Criminal Appeal Act 1968 (c. 19)

7. The Criminal Appeal Act 1968 is amended as follows.
8. (1) Section 10 (appeal against sentence in cases dealt with by Crown Court otherwise than on conviction on indictment) is amended as follows.
   (2) In subsection (2) —
      (a) in paragraph (b), for "or a community order within the meaning of the Powers of Criminal Courts (Sentencing) Act 2000" there is substituted "a youth community order within the meaning of the Powers of Criminal Courts (Sentencing) Act 2000 or a community order within the meaning of Part 12 of the Criminal Justice Act 2003", and
      (b) paragraph (c) and the word "or" immediately preceding it are omitted.
9. In section 11 (supplementary provisions as to appeal against sentence), subsection (4) is omitted.
10. In Schedule 2 (procedural and other provisions applicable on order for retrial), in paragraph 2(4), for the words from the beginning to "apply" there is substituted "Section 240

of the Criminal Justice Act 2003 (crediting of periods of remand in custody: terms of imprisonment and detention) shall apply".

Firearms Act 1968 (c. 27)

11. The Firearms Act 1968 is amended as follows.
12. (1) Section 21 (possession of firearms by persons previously convicted of crime) is amended as follows.
    (2) In subsection (2A), after paragraph (c) there is inserted—
    "(d) in the case of a person who has been subject to a sentence of imprisonment to which an intermittent custody order under section 183(1)(b) of the Criminal Justice Act 2003 relates, the date of his final release."
    (3) After subsection (2A) there is inserted—
    "(2B) A person who is serving a sentence of imprisonment to which an intermittent custody order under section 183 of the Criminal Justice Act 2003 relates shall not during any licence period specified for the purposes of subsection (1)(b)(i) of that section have a firearm or ammunition in his possession.".
    (4) In subsection (3)(b), for "probation order" there is substituted "community order".
    (5) After subsection (3) there is inserted—
    "(3ZA) In subsection (3)(b) above, "community order" means—
    (a) a community order within the meaning of Part 12 of the Criminal Justice Act 2003 made in England and Wales, or
    (b) a probation order made in Scotland."
    (6) In subsection (6), after "(2)" there is inserted ", (2B)".
13. (1) Section 52 (forfeiture and disposal of firearms; cancellation of certificate by convicting court) is amended as follows.
    (2) In subsection (1)(c), for "probation order" there is substituted "community order".
    (3) After subsection (1) there is inserted —
    "(1A) In subsection (1)(c) "community order" means—
    (a) a community order within the meaning of Part 12 of the Criminal Justice Act 2003 made in England and Wales, or
    (b) a probation order made in Scotland."

Social Work (Scotland) Act 1968 (c. 49)

14. In section 94 of the Social Work (Scotland) Act 1968 (interpretation), in the definition of "probation order" in subsection (1), for "community rehabilitation order" there is substituted "community order within the meaning of Part 12 of the Criminal Justice Act 2003".

Children and Young Persons Act 1969 (c. 54)

15. In section 23 of the Children and Young Persons Act 1969 (remands and committals to local authority accommodation), for the definition of "sexual offence" and "violent offence" in subsection (12) there is substituted—
    " "sexual offence" means an offence specified in Part 2 of Schedule 15 to the Criminal Justice Act 2003;
    "violent offence" means murder or an offence specified in Part 1 of Schedule 15 to the Criminal Justice Act 2003;".

Immigration Act 1971 (c. 77)

16. In section 7 of the Immigration Act 1971 (exemption from deportation for certain existing residents), in subsection (4), for "section 67 of the Criminal Justice Act 1967" there is substituted "section 240 of the Criminal Justice Act 2003".

Thames Barrier and Flood Prevention Act 1972 (c. xiv)

17. In section 56 of the Thames Barrier and Flood Prevention Act 1972 (orders for carrying out certain defence works), in subsection (3)(a)(ii), for "six months" there is substituted "12 months".

Rehabilitation of Offenders Act 1974 (c. 53)

18. (1) Section 5 of the Rehabilitation of Offenders Act 1974 (rehabilitation periods for particular offences) is amended as follows.
   (2) In subsection (1)—
      (a) at the end of paragraph (e), there is inserted "and", and
      (b) after that paragraph, there is inserted the following paragraph—
         "(f) a sentence of imprisonment for public protection under section 225 of the Criminal Justice Act 2003, a sentence of detention for public protection under section 226 of that Act or an extended sentence under section 227 or 228 of that Act"
   (3) In subsection (4A), after the words "probation order" there is inserted "or a community order under section 177 of the Criminal Justice Act 2003".

Armed Forces Act 1976 (c. 52)

19. (1) Section 8 of the Armed Forces Act 1976 (powers of Standing Civilian Courts in relation to civilians) is amended as follows.
   (2) In subsection (1)(a), for "six months" there is substituted "twelve months".
   (3) In subsection (2), for "12 months" there is substituted "65 weeks".

Bail Act 1976 (c. 63)

20. The Bail Act 1976 is amended as follows.
21. (1) Section 2 (other definitions) is amended as follows.
   (2) In subsection (1)(d)—
      (a) the words "placing the offender on probation or" are omitted, and
      (b) for "him" there is substituted "the offender".
   (3) In subsection (2), in the definition of "probation hostel", for the words from "by" onwards there is substituted "by a community order under section 177 of the Criminal Justice Act 2003".
22. In section 4 (general right to bail of accused persons and others), in subsection (3), for the words from "to be dealt with" onwards there is substituted "or the Crown Court to be dealt with under—
      (a) Part 2 of Schedule 3 to the Powers of Criminal Courts (Sentencing) Act 2000 (breach of certain youth community orders), or

(b) Part 2 of Schedule 8 to the Criminal Justice Act 2003 (breach of requirement of community order)."

23. In Part 3 of Schedule 1 (interpretation), in the definition of "default" in paragraph 4, for the words from "Part II" onwards there is substituted "Part 2 of Schedule 8 to the Criminal Justice Act 2003 (breach of requirement of order)".

Criminal Law Act 1977 (c. 45)

24. In section 3 of the Criminal Law Act 1977 (penalties for conspiracy), in subsection (1), for "section 127 of the Powers of Criminal Courts (Sentencing) Act 2000" there is substituted "section 163 of the Criminal Justice Act 2003".

Magistrates' Courts Act 1980 (c. 43)

25. The Magistrates' Courts Act 1980 is amended as follows.

26. In section 11 (non appearance of accused), in subsection (3), for "section 119 of the Powers of Criminal Courts (Sentencing) Act 2000" there is substituted "paragraph 8(2)(a) or (b) of Schedule 12 to the Criminal Justice Act 2003".

27. In section 33 (maximum penalties on summary conviction in pursuance of section 22), in subsection (1)(a), for "3 months" there is substituted "51 weeks".

28. In section 85 (power to remit fine), in subsection (2A), for "section 35(2)(a) or (b) of the Crime (Sentences) Act 1997" there is substituted "section 300(2) of the Criminal Justice Act 2003".

29. In section 131 (remand of accused already in custody), after subsection (2) there is inserted—

"(2A) Where the accused person is serving a sentence of imprisonment to which an intermittent custody order under section 183 of the Criminal Justice Act 2003 relates, the reference in subsection (2) to the expected date of his release is to be read as a reference to the expected date of his next release on licence.".

30. In section 133 (consecutive terms of imprisonment), in subsection (1), for "Subject to section 84 of the Powers of Criminal Courts (Sentencing) Act 2000," there is substituted "Subject to section 265 of the Criminal Justice Act 2003,".

Law Reform (Miscellaneous Provisions) (Scotland) Act 1980 (c. 55)

31. In Schedule 1 to the Law Reform (Miscellaneous Provisions) (Scotland) Act 1980 (ineligibility for and disqualification and excusal from jury service), in Part 2, in paragraph (bb), for sub-paragraph (v) there is substituted—

"(v) a community order within the meaning of section 177 of the Criminal Justice Act 2003;

(va) a youth community order as defined by section 33 of the Powers of Criminal Courts (Sentencing) Act 2000;".

Public Passenger Vehicles Act 1981 (c. 14)

32. (1) In Schedule 3 to the Public Passenger Vehicles Act 1981 (supplementary provisions as to qualifications for PSV operators licence), paragraph 1 is amended as follows.

(2) In sub-paragraph (4)(a), for "a community service order for more than sixty hours" there is substituted "a community order requiring the offender to perform unpaid work for more than sixty hours".

(3) In sub-paragraph (6), for the words from ""a community" onwards there is substituted ""a community order" means an order under section 177 of the Criminal Justice Act 2003, a community punishment order made before the commencement of that section or a community service order under the Community Service by Offenders (Scotland) Act 1978".

Criminal Attempts Act 1981 (c. 47)

33. In section 4 of the Criminal Attempts Act 1981 (trials and penalties), in subsection (5)(b), for sub-paragraph (ii) there is substituted—

"(ii) in section 154(1) and (2) (general limit on magistrates' court's powers to impose imprisonment) of the Criminal Justice Act 2003.".

Criminal Justice Act 1982 (c. 48)

34. The Criminal Justice Act 1982 is amended as follows.

35. In section 32 (early release of prisoners), in subsection (1)(a), after "life" there is inserted ", imprisonment for public protection under section 225 of the Criminal Justice Act 2003 or an extended sentence under section 227 of that Act".

36. (1) Part 3 of Schedule 13 (reciprocal arrangements (Northern Ireland): persons residing in England and Wales or Scotland) is amended as follows.

(2) In paragraph 7—

(a) in sub-paragraph (2)(b), for "such orders" there is substituted "an unpaid work requirement of a community order (within the meaning of Part 12 of the Criminal Justice Act 2003)", and

(b) in sub-paragraph (3)(b), for the words from "community service orders" onwards there is substituted "community orders within the meaning of Part 12 of the Criminal Justice Act 2003 conferred on responsible officers by that Part of that Act.".

(3) For paragraph 9(3) there is substituted—

"(3) Subject to the following provisions of this paragraph—

(a) a community service order made or amended in the circumstances specified in paragraph 7 above shall be treated as if it were a community order made in England and Wales under section 177 of the Criminal Justice Act 2003 and the provisions of Part 12 of that Act (so far as relating to such orders) shall apply accordingly; and

(b) a community service order made or amended in the circumstances specified in paragraph 8 above shall be treated as if it were a community service order made in Scotland and the legislation relating to community service orders in Scotland shall apply accordingly."

(4) In paragraph 9(4)(a), after "community service orders" there is inserted "or, as the case may be, community orders (within the meaning of Part 12 of the Criminal Justice Act 2003)".

(5) In paragraph 9(5), after "a community service order" there is inserted "or, as the case may be, a community order (within the meaning of Part 12 of the Criminal Justice Act 2003)".

(6) In paragraph 9(6)—

    (a) after "community service orders", where first occurring, there is inserted "or, as the case may be, community orders (within the meaning of Part 12 of the Criminal Justice Act 2003)", and

    (b) in paragraph (b)(i), for "the Powers of Criminal Courts (Sentencing) Act 2000" there is substituted "Part 12 of the Criminal Justice Act 2003".

Mental Health Act 1983 (c. 20)

37. The Mental Health Act 1983 is amended as follows.

38. In section 37 (powers of courts to order hospital admission or guardianship)—

    (a) in subsection (1), the words "or falls to be imposed under section 109(2) of the Powers of Criminal Courts (Sentencing) Act 2000" are omitted,

    (b) for subsections (1A) and (1B) there is substituted —

      "(1A) In the case of an offence the sentence for which would otherwise fall to be imposed—

        (a) under section 51A(2) of the Firearms Act 1968,

        (b) under section 110(2) or 111(2) of the Powers of Criminal Courts (Sentencing) Act 2000, or

        (c) under any of sections 225 to 228 of the Criminal Justice Act 2003, nothing in those provisions shall prevent a court from making an order under subsection (1) above for the admission of the offender to a hospital.

      (1B) References in subsection (1A) above to a sentence falling to be imposed under any of the provisions mentioned in that subsection are to be read in accordance with section 305(4) of the Criminal Justice Act 2003."

    (c) in subsection (8), for "probation order" there is substituted "community order (within the meaning of Part 12 of the Criminal Justice Act 2003)".

39. In section 45A (powers of higher courts to direct hospital admission), in subsection (1)(b), the words from "except" to "1997" are omitted.

Repatriation of Prisoners Act 1984 (c. 47)

40. The Repatriation of Prisoners Act 1984 is amended as follows.

41. In section 2 (transfer out of the United Kingdom), in subsection (4)(b), for sub-paragraph (i) there is substituted—

    "(i) released on licence under section 28(5) of the Crime (Sentences) Act 1997 or under section 244 or 246 of the Criminal Justice Act 2003; or".

42. In section 3 (transfer into the United Kingdom), subsection (9) is omitted.

43. (1) The Schedule (operation of certain enactments in relation to the prisoner) is amended as follows in relation to prisoners repatriated to England and Wales.

    (2) In paragraph 2, for sub-paragraphs (1A) and (2) there is substituted—

      "(2) If the warrant specifies a period to be taken into account for the purposes of this paragraph, the amount of time the prisoner has served shall, so far only as the question whether he has served a particular part of a life sentence is concerned, be deemed to be increased by that period.

    (3) Where the prisoner's sentence is for a term of less than twelve months, Chapter 6 of Part 12 of the Criminal Justice Act 2003 shall apply as if the sentence were for a term of twelve months or more.

    (4) In this paragraph—

"the enactments relating to release on licence" means section 28(5) and (7) of the Crime (Sentences) Act 1997 and Chapter 6 of Part 12 of the Criminal Justice Act 2003; "sentence", means the provision included in the warrant which is equivalent to sentence.".

(3) Paragraph 3 is omitted.

Police and Criminal Evidence Act 1984 (c. 60)

44. In section 38 of the Police and Criminal Evidence Act 1984 (duties of custody officer after charge), for the definitions of "sexual offence" and "violent offence" in subsection (6A) there is substituted—

" "sexual offence" means an offence specified in Part 2 of Schedule 15 to the Criminal Justice Act 2003;

"violent offence" means murder or an offence specified in Part 1 of that Schedule;".

Criminal Justice Act 1988 (c. 33)

45. The Criminal Justice Act 1988 is amended as follows.

46. In section 36 (reviews of sentencing), in subsection (2), for the words from "erred in law" onwards there is substituted—

"(a) erred in law as to his powers of sentencing; or

(b) failed to impose a sentence required by—

(i) section 51A(2) of the Firearms Act 1968;

(ii) section 110(2) or 111(2) of the Powers of Criminal Courts (Sentencing) Act 2000; or

(iii) any of sections 225 to 228 of the Criminal Justice Act 2003."

47. In section 50 (suspended and partly suspended sentences on certain civilians in courts-martial and Standing Civilian Courts), in subsection (3)(b)(i), for "Powers of Criminal Courts (Sentencing) Act 2000" there is substituted "Criminal Justice Act 2003".

Firearms (Amendment) Act 1988 (c. 45)

48. The Firearms (Amendment) Act 1988 is amended as follows.

49. In section 1 (prohibited weapons and ammunition), in subsection (4A) after paragraph (b) there is inserted—

"(bb) may amend subsection (1A)(a) of section 91 of the Powers of Criminal Courts (Sentencing) Act 2000 (offenders under 18 convicted of certain serious offences: power to detain for specified period) so as to include a reference to any provision added by the order to section 5(1) of the principal Act,

(bc) may amend section 50(5A)(a), 68(4A)(a) or 170(4A)(a) of the Customs and Excise Management Act 1979 (offences relating to improper importation or export-ation) so as to include a reference to anything added by the order to section 5(1) of the principal Act,".

50. In section 27(4) (which relates to Northern Ireland), after "Except for" there is inserted "section 1, so far as enabling provision to be made amending the Customs and Excise Management Act 1979, and".

Road Traffic Act 1988 (c. 52)

51. In section 164 of the Road Traffic Act 1988 (power of constables to require production of driving licence and in certain cases statement of date of birth), in subsection (5), for "section 40 of the Crime (Sentences) Act 1997" there is substituted "section 301 of the Criminal Justice Act 2003".

Road Traffic Offenders Act 1988 (c. 53)

52. The Road Traffic Offenders Act 1988 is amended as follows.
53. In section 27 (production of licence), in subsection (3), for "section 40 of the Crime (Sentences) Act 1997" there is substituted "section 301 of the Criminal Justice Act 2003".
54. In section 46 (combination of disqualification and endorsement with probation orders and orders for discharge), in subsection (1), paragraph (a) and the word "or" following it shall cease to have effect.

Football Spectators Act 1989 (c. 37)

55. The Football Spectators Act 1989 is amended as follows.
56. In section 7 (disqualification for membership of scheme), subsection (9) is omitted.
57. In section 14E (banning orders: general), after subsection (6) there is inserted—
    "(7) A person serving a sentence of imprisonment to which an intermittent custody order under section 183 of the Criminal Justice Act 2003 relates is to be treated for the purposes of this section as having been detained in legal custody until his final release; and accordingly any reference in this section to release is, in relation to a person serving such a sentence, a reference to his final release."
58. In section 18 (information), after subsection (4) there is inserted—
    "(5) In relation to a person serving a sentence of imprisonment to which an intermittent custody order under section 183 of the Criminal Justice Act 2003 relates, any reference in this section to his detention or to his release shall be construed in accordance with section 14E(7)."

Children Act 1989 (c. 41)

59. The Children Act 1989 is amended as follows.
60. (1) Section 68 (persons disqualified from being foster parents) is amended as follows.
    (2) In subsection (2)(d), the words "a probation order has been made in respect of him or he has been" are omitted.
    (3) After subsection (2) there is inserted—
        "(2A) A conviction in respect of which a probation order was made before 1st October 1992 (which would not otherwise be treated as a conviction) is to be treated as a conviction for the purposes of subsection (2)(d)."
61. (1) In Schedule 9A (child minding and day care for young children), paragraph 4 is amended as follows.
    (2) In sub-paragraph (2)(g), the words "placed on probation or" are omitted.
    (3) At the end there is inserted—

"(7) A conviction in respect of which a probation order was made before 1st October 1992 (which would not otherwise be treated as a conviction) is to be treated as a conviction for the purposes of this paragraph.".

Criminal Justice Act 1991 (c. 53)

62. The Criminal Justice Act 1991 is amended as follows.
63. Section 65 (supervision of young offenders after release) is omitted.
64. (1) Schedule 3 (reciprocal enforcement of certain orders) is amended as follows.
    (2) In paragraph 10(3)(d), for the words from "paragraph 3 of Schedule 2" onwards there is substituted "section 201 of the Criminal Justice Act 2003".
    (3) In paragraph 11(2) —
        (a) in paragraph (a)—
            (i) for "probation order" there is substituted "community order", and
            (ii) after "England and Wales" there is inserted "under section 177 of the Criminal Justice Act 2003", and
        (b) for paragraph (b) there is substituted—
            "(b) the provisions of Part 12 of that Act (so far as relating to such orders) shall apply accordingly.".
    (4) In paragraph 11(3), for paragraphs (a) and (b) there is substituted—
        "(a) the requirements of Part 12 of the Criminal Justice Act 2003 relating to community orders (within the meaning of that Part);
        (b) the powers of the home court under Schedule 8 to that Act, as modified by this paragraph; and".
    (5) In paragraph 11(4), for the words from "probation order made by a court" onwards there is substituted "community order made by a court in England and Wales under section 177 of the Criminal Justice Act 2003, except a power conferred by paragraph 9(1)(b) or (c) or 13(2) of Schedule 8 to that Act".
    (6) In paragraph 11(5), for "the Powers of Criminal Courts (Sentencing) Act 2000" there is substituted "Part 12 of the Criminal Justice Act 2003".

Aggravated Vehicle-Taking Act 1992 (c. 11)

65. In section 1 of the Aggravated Vehicle-Taking Act 1992 (new offence of aggravated vehicle taking), in subsection (2)(a), for "section 127 of the Powers of Criminal Courts (Sentencing) Act 2000" there is substituted "section 163 of the Criminal Justice Act 2003".

Prisoners and Criminal Proceedings (Scotland) Act 1993 (c. 9)

66. In section 10 of the Prisoners and Criminal Proceedings (Scotland) Act 1993 (life prisoners transferred to Scotland)—
    (a) in subsection (1)—
        (i) in paragraph (a), sub-paragraph (i), and the succeeding "or", are omitted, and
        (ii) after paragraph (a)(ii) there is inserted "or
            (iii) subsections (5) to (8) of section 28 (early release of life prisoners to whom that section applies) of the Crime (Sentences) Act 1997 (c. 43) (in this section, the "1997 Act") apply by virtue of an order made under section 28(2)(b) of that Act (while that provision was in force) or an order made

607

under section 269(2) of, or paragraph 3(1)(a) of Schedule 22 to, the Criminal Justice Act 2003;", and

(iii) for "28(2)(b) or 82A(2) or paragraph" there is substituted "82A(2), 28(2)(b) or 269(2) or paragraph 3(1)(a) or";

(b) after subsection (1) there is inserted—

"(1AA) This Part of this Act, except section 2(9), applies also to a transferred life prisoner—

(a) who is transferred from England and Wales on or after the date on which section 269 of the Criminal Justice Act 2003 comes into force,

(b) in relation to whom paragraph 3 of Schedule 22 to that Act applies by virtue of paragraph 2(a) of that Schedule, but

(c) in respect of whom, under the paragraph so applying, no order has been made, as if the prisoner were a life prisoner within the meaning of section 2 of this Act and the punishment part of his sentence within the meaning of that section were the notified minimum term defined by paragraph 3(4) of that Schedule."; and

(c) in subsection (5)(b)—

(i) for "the Crime (Sentences) Act 1997" there is substituted "the 1997 Act", and

(ii) after the words "Powers of Criminal Courts (Sentencing) Act 2000 (c. 6)" there is inserted "section 269(2) of, or paragraph 3(1)(a) of Schedule 22 to, the Criminal Justice Act 2003,".

Criminal Justice and Public Order Act 1994 (c. 33)

67. In section 25 of the Criminal Justice and Public Order Act 1994 (no bail for defendants charged with or convicted of homicide or rape after previous conviction of such offences), in paragraph (c) of the definition of "conviction" in subsection (5)—

(a) the words "placing the offender on probation or" are omitted, and

(b) for "him" there is substituted "the offender".

Goods Vehicles (Licensing of Operators) Act 1995 (c. 23)

68. (1) In Schedule 3 to the Goods Vehicles (Licensing of Operators) Act 1995 (qualifications for standard licence), paragraph 3 is amended as follows.

(2) In sub-paragraph (2)(a), for "exceeding three months" there is substituted "of 12 months or more or, before the commencement of section 181 of the Criminal Justice Act 2003, a term exceeding 3 months".

(3) In sub-paragraph (2)(c), for "community service order" there is substituted "community order".

(4) For sub-paragraph (3)(b), there is substituted—

"(b) "community order" means a community order under section 177 of the Criminal Justice Act 2003, a community punishment order made under section 46 of the Powers of Criminal Courts (Sentencing) Act 2000 or a community service order under the Community Service by Offenders (Scotland) Act 1978."

Criminal Procedure (Scotland) Act 1995 (c. 46)

69. The Criminal Procedure (Scotland) Act 1995 is amended as follows.

70. (1) Section 234 (probation orders: persons residing in England and Wales) is amended as follows.

(2) In subsection (1), the words after paragraph (b) are omitted.

(3) For subsection (2) there is substituted—

"(2) Subsection (1) above applies to any probation order made under section 228 unless the order includes requirements which are more onerous than those which a court in England and Wales could impose on an offender under section 177 of the Criminal Justice Act 2003."

(4) In subsection (3), the words from "or to vary" to "one hundred" are omitted.

(5) In subsection (4)—

(a) in paragraph (a)—

(i) for "paragraph 5(3) of Schedule 2 to the 2000 Act" there is substituted "section 207(2) of the Criminal Justice Act 2003",

(ii) for "or, as the case may be, community rehabilitation orders" there is substituted "or, as the case may be, community orders under Part 12 of that Act", and

(iii) for "paragraph 5 of the said Schedule 2" there is substituted "section 207 of the Criminal Justice Act 2003", and

(b) in paragraph (b), for "sub-paragraphs (5) to (7) of the said paragraph 5" there is substituted "sections 207(4) and 208(1) and (2) of the Criminal Justice Act 2003".

(6) After subsection (4) there is inserted—

"(4A) A probation order made or amended under this section must specify as the corresponding requirements for the purposes of this section requirements which could be included in a community order made under section 177 of the Criminal Justice Act 2003."

(7) In subsection (5), for "Schedule 3" onwards there is substituted "Schedule 8 to the Criminal Justice Act 2003 shall apply as if it were a community order made by a magistrates' court under section 177 of that Act and imposing the requirements specified under subsection (4A) above".

(8) For subsection (6) there is substituted—

"(6) In its application to a probation order made or amended under this section, Schedule 8 to the Criminal Justice Act 2003 has effect subject to the following modifications—

(a) any reference to the responsible officer has effect as a reference to the person appointed or assigned under subsection (1)(a) above,

(b) in paragraph 9—

(i) paragraphs (b) and (c) of sub-paragraph (1) are omitted,

(ii) in sub-paragraph (6), the first reference to the Crown Court has effect as a reference to a court in Scotland, and

(iii) any other reference in sub-paragraphs (6) or (7) to the Crown Court has effect as a reference to the court in Scotland, and

(c) Parts 3 and 5 are omitted."

(9) In subsection (10)—

(a) for the words from "paragraph 6" to "community rehabilitation orders" there is substituted "paragraph 8 of Schedule 9 (which relates to community orders", and

(b) for "an order made under section 41" there is substituted "a community order made under Part 12".

71. In section 242 (community service orders: persons residing in England and Wales)—

(a) in subsection (1)—

    (i) in paragraph (a)(ii), for "a community punishment order" there is substituted "an unpaid work requirement imposed by a community order (within the meaning of Part 12 of the Criminal Justice Act 2003)", and

    (ii) in paragraph (a)(iii), for "community punishment orders made under section 46 of the Powers of Criminal Courts (Sentencing) Act 2000" there is substituted "unpaid work requirements imposed by community orders made under section 177 of the Criminal Justice Act 2003",

(b) in subsection (2)(b), for "community punishment orders made under section 46 of the Powers of Criminal Courts (Sentencing) Act 2000" there is substituted "unpaid work requirements imposed by community orders made under section 177 of the Criminal Justice Act 2003", and

(c) in subsection (3)(b), for "in respect of community punishment orders conferred on responsible officers by the Powers of Criminal Courts (Sentencing) Act 2000" there is substituted "conferred on responsible officers by Part 12 of the Criminal Justice Act 2003 in respect of unpaid work requirements imposed by community orders (within the meaning of that Part)".

72. In section 244 (community service orders: provisions relating to persons living in England and Wales or Northern Ireland)—

(a) in subsection (3)(a)—

    (i) for "community punishment order" there is substituted "community order (within the meaning of Part 12 of the Criminal Justice Act 2003)", and

    (ii) for "community punishment orders" there is substituted "such community orders",

(b) in subsection (4)(a), for "community punishment orders" there is substituted "community orders (within the meaning of Part 12 of the Criminal Justice Act 2003)",

(c) in subsection (5), for "community punishment order" there is substituted "a community order (within the meaning of Part 12 of the Criminal Justice Act 2003)", and

(d) in subsection (6)—

    (i) for "community punishment orders", where first occurring, there is substituted "community orders (within the meaning of Part 12 of the Criminal Justice Act 2003)", and

    (ii) in paragraph (b)(ii), for "the Powers of Criminal Courts (Sentencing) Act 2000" there is substituted "Part 12 of the Criminal Justice Act 2003".

Education Act 1996 (c. 56)

73. In section 562 of the Education Act 1996 (Act not to apply to persons detained under order of a court), for "probation order" there is substituted "community order under section 177 the Criminal Justice Act 2003".

Criminal Justice (Northern Ireland) Order 1996 (S.I. 1996/3160 (N.I.24))

74. The Criminal Justice (Northern Ireland) Order 1996 is amended as follows.

75. In Article 2 (interpretation) after paragraph (8) there is inserted—

"(9) For the purposes of this Order, a sentence falls to be imposed under paragraph (2) of Article 52A of the Firearms (Northern Ireland) Order 1981 if it is required by that paragraph and the court is not of the opinion there mentioned."

76. In Article 4 (absolute and conditional discharge), in paragraph (1), for "(not being an offence for which the sentence is fixed by law)" there is substituted "(not being an offence for which the sentence is fixed by law or falls to be imposed under Article 52A(2) of the Firearms (Northern Ireland) Order 1981)".

77. In Article 10 (probation orders), in paragraph (1) for "(not being an offence for which the sentence is fixed by law)" there is substituted "(not being an offence for which the sentence is fixed by law or falls to be imposed under Article 52A(2) of the Firearms (Northern Ireland) Order 1981)".

78. (1) Article 13 (community service orders) is amended as follows.

(2) In paragraph (1) for "(not being an offence for which the sentence is fixed by law)" there is substituted "(not being an offence for which the sentence is fixed by law or falls to be imposed under Article 52A(2) of the Firearms (Northern Ireland) Order 1981)".

(3) In paragraph (4)(b) as it has effect pursuant to paragraph 7(1) of Schedule 13 to the Criminal Justice Act 1982 (reciprocal arrangements), for "such orders" there is substituted "an unpaid work requirement of a community order (within the meaning of Part 12 of the Criminal Justice Act 2003)".

79. In Article 15 (orders combining probation and community service), in paragraph (1) for "(not being an offence for which the sentence is fixed by law)" there is substituted "(not being an offence for which the sentence is fixed by law or falls to be imposed under Article 52A(2) of the Firearms (Northern Ireland) Order 1981)".

80. In Article 19 (restrictions on imposing custodial sentences), at the end of paragraph (1) there is inserted "or falling to be imposed under Article 52A(2) of the Firearms (Northern Ireland) Order 1981".

81. (1) In Article 20 (length of custodial sentences), at the end of paragraph (1) there is inserted "or falling to be imposed under Article 52A(2) of the Firearms (Northern Ireland) Order 1981".

(2) In Article 24 (custody probation orders), in paragraph (1) for "other than one fixed by law" there is substituted ", other than an offence for which the sentence is fixed by law or falls to be imposed under Article 52A(2) of the Firearms (Northern Ireland) Order 1981,".

Crime (Sentences) Act 1997 (c. 43)

82. The Crime (Sentences) Act 1997 is amended as follows.

83. (1) Section 31 (duration and conditions of licences) is amended as follows.

(2) In subsection (3), for the words from "except" onwards there is substituted "except in accordance with recommendations of the Parole Board".

(3) Subsection (4) is omitted.

(4) In subsection (6), for "section 46(3) of the 1991 Act" there is substituted "section 259 of the Criminal Justice Act 2003".

84. In section 32 (recall of life prisoners while on licence) for subsection (5) there is substituted—

"(5) Where on a reference under subsection (4) above the Parole Board directs the immediate release on licence under this section of the life prisoner, the Secretary of State shall give effect to the direction."

85. (1) Schedule 1 (transfers of prisoners within the British Islands) is amended as follows.

(2) In paragraph 6, after sub-paragraph (3) there is inserted—

"(4) In this Part of this Schedule—

"the 2003 Act" means the Criminal Justice Act 2003;

"custody plus order" has the meaning given by section 181(4) of that Act;

"intermittent custody order" has the meaning given by section 183(2) of that Act."

(3) In paragraph 8 (restricted transfers from England and Wales to Scotland)—

(a) for sub-paragraph (2)(a) there is substituted—

"(a) sections 241, 244, 247 to 252 and 254 to 264 of the 2003 Act (fixed-term prisoners) or, as the case may require, sections 102 to 104 of the Powers of Criminal Courts (Sentencing) Act 2000 (detention and training orders) or sections 28 to 34 of this Act (life sentences) shall apply to him in place of the corresponding provisions of the law of Scotland;

(aa) sections 62 and 64 of the Criminal Justice and Court Services Act 2000 (which relate to licence conditions) shall apply to him in place of the corresponding provisions of the law of Scotland;

(ab) where a custody plus order or intermittent custody order has effect in relation to him, the provisions of Chapters 3 and 4 of Part 12 of the 2003 Act relating to such orders shall also apply to him (subject to Schedule 11 to that Act); and",

(b) for sub-paragraph (4)(a) there is substituted—

"(a) sections 241, 249 to 252 and 254 to 264 of the 2003 Act (fixed-term prisoners) or, as the case may require, sections 103 and 104 of the Powers of Criminal Courts (Sentencing) Act 2000 (detention and training orders) or sections 31 to 34 of this Act (life sentences) shall apply to him in place of the corresponding provisions of the law of Scotland;

(aa) sections 62 and 64 of the Criminal Justice and Court Services Act 2000 (which relate to licence conditions) shall apply to him in place of the corresponding provisions of the law of Scotland;

(ab) where a custody plus order or intermittent custody order has effect in relation to him, the provisions of Chapters 3 and 4 of Part 12 of the 2003 Act relating to such orders shall also apply to him (subject to Schedule 11 to that Act); and", and

(c) for sub-paragraphs (5) to (7) there is substituted—

"(5) Section 31(2A) of this Act (conditions as to supervision after release), as applied by sub-paragraph (2) or (4) above, shall have effect as if for paragraphs (a) to (c) there were substituted the words "a relevant officer of such local authority as may be specified in the licence".

"(6) Any provision of sections 102 to 104 of the Powers of Criminal Courts (Sentencing) Act 2000 which is applied by sub-paragraph (2) or (4) above shall have effect (as so applied) as if—

(a) any reference to secure accommodation were a reference to secure accommodation within the meaning of Part 2 of the Children (Scotland) Act 1995 or a young offenders institution provided under section 19(1)(b) of the Prisons (Scotland) Act 1989,

(b) except in section 103(2), any reference to the Secretary of State were a reference to the Scottish Ministers,

(c) any reference to an officer of a local probation board were a reference to a relevant officer as defined by section 27(1) of the Prisoners and Criminal Proceedings (Scotland) Act 1993,

  (d) any reference to a youth court were a reference to a sheriff court,
  (e) in section 103, any reference to a petty sessions area were a reference to a local government area within the meaning of the Local Government etc. (Scotland) Act 1994,
  (f) in section 103(3), for paragraphs (b) and (c) there were substituted a reference to an officer of a local authority constituted under that Act for the local government area in which the offender resides for the time being,
  (g) section 103(5) were omitted,
  (h) in section 104, for subsection (1) there were substituted—
       "(1) Where a detention and training order is in force in respect of an offender and it appears on information to a sheriff court having jurisdiction in the locality in which the offender resides that the offender has failed to comply with requirements under section 103(6)(b), the court may—
             (a) issue a citation requiring the offender to appear before it at the time specified in the citation, or
             (b) issue a warrant for the offender's arrest.",
  (i) section 104(2) were omitted, and
  (j) in section 104(6), the reference to the Crown Court were a reference to the High Court of Justiciary."
(4) In paragraph 9 (restricted transfers from England and Wales to Northern Ireland)—
  (a) for sub-paragraph (2)(a) there is substituted—
       "(a) sections 241, 244, 247 to 252 and 254 to 264 of the 2003 Act (fixed-term prisoners) or, as the case may require, sections 102 to 104 of the Powers of Criminal Courts (Sentencing) Act 2000 (detention and training orders) or sections 28 to 34 of this Act (life sentences) shall apply to him in place of the corresponding provisions of the law of Northern Ireland;
       (aa) sections 62 and 64 of the Criminal Justice and Court Services Act 2000 (which relate to licence conditions) shall apply to him in place of the corresponding provisions of the law of Northern Ireland;
       (ab) where a custody plus order or intermittent custody order has effect in relation to him, the provisions of Chapters 3 and 4 of Part 12 of the 2003 Act relating to such orders shall apply to him (subject to Schedule 11 to that Act); and",
  (b) for sub-paragraph (4)(a) there is substituted—
       "(a) sections 241, 249 to 252 and 254 to 264 of the 2003 Act (fixed-term prisoners) or, as the case may require, sections 103 and 104 of the Powers of Criminal Courts (Sentencing) Act 2000 (detention and training orders) or sections 31 to 34 of this Act (life sentences) shall apply to him in place of the corresponding provisions of the law of Northern Ireland;
       (aa) sections 62 and 64 of the Criminal Justice and Court Services Act 2000 (which relate to licence conditions) shall apply to him in place of the corresponding provisions of the law of Northern Ireland;
       (ab) where a custody plus order or intermittent custody order has effect in relation to him, the provisions of Chapters 3 and 4 of Part 12 of the 2003 Act relating to such orders shall apply to him (subject to Schedule 11 to that Act); and",
  (c) for sub-paragraphs (5) to (7) there is substituted—
       "(5) Section 31(2A) of this Act (conditions as to supervision after release), as applied by sub-paragraph (2) or (4) above, shall have effect as if for paragraphs (a) to (c)

there were substituted the words "a probation appointed for or assigned to the petty sessions district within which the prisoner for the time being resides"."

(5) In paragraph 15 (unrestricted transfers: general provisions), sub-paragraph (5) is omitted.

86. In Schedule 2 (repatriation of prisoners to the British Islands) paragraphs 2 and 3 are omitted.

Crime and Disorder Act 1998 (c. 37)

87. The Crime and Disorder Act 1998 is amended as follows.

88. In section 18 (interpretation etc. of Chapter 1)—

(a) after the definition of "responsible officer" in subsection (1) there is inserted— " "serious harm" shall be construed in accordance with section 224 of the Criminal Justice Act 2003;"; and

(b) subsection (2) is omitted.

89. (1) Section 38 (local provision of youth justice services) is amended as follows.

(2) In subsection (4)(g), for "probation order, a community service order or a combination order" there is substituted "community order under section 177 of the Criminal Justice Act 2003".

(3) In subsection (4)(i), after "1997 Act")" there is inserted "or by virtue of conditions imposed under section 250 of the Criminal Justice Act 2003".

Powers of Criminal Courts (Sentencing) Act 2000 (c. 6)

90. The Powers of Criminal Courts (Sentencing) Act 2000 is amended as follows.

91. (1) Section 6 (committal for sentence in certain cases where offender committed in respect of another offence) is amended as follows.

(2) In subsection (3)(b), for "section 120(1) below" there is substituted "paragraph 11(1) of Schedule 12 to the Criminal Justice Act 2003".

(3) For subsection (4)(e), there is substituted— "(e) paragraph 11(2) of Schedule 12 to the Criminal Justice Act 2003 (committal to Crown Court where offender convicted during operational period of suspended sentence).".

92. In section 7 (power of Crown Court on committal for sentence under section 6), in subsection (2), for "section 119 below" there is substituted "paragraphs 8 and 9 of Schedule 12 to the Criminal Justice Act 2003".

93. In section 12 (absolute and conditional discharge)—

(a) in subsection (1) for "109(2), 110(2) or 111(2) below" there is substituted "section 110(2) or 111(2) below, section 51A(2) of the Firearms Act 1968 or section 225, 226, 227 or 228 of the Criminal Justice Act 2003)", and

(b) subsection (4) (duty to explain effect of order for conditional discharge) is omitted.

94. In the heading to Part 4, and the heading to Chapter 1 of that Part, for "COMMUNITY ORDERS" there is substituted "YOUTH COMMUNITY ORDERS".

95. For section 33 there is substituted—

"33 Meaning of "youth community order" and "community sentence"

(1) In this Act "youth community order" means any of the following orders—

(a) a curfew order;

(b) an exclusion order;

(c) an attendance centre order;

    (d) a supervision order;

    (e) an action plan order.

  (2) In this Act "community sentence" means a sentence which consists of or includes—

    (a) a community order under section 177 of the Criminal Justice Act 2003, or

    (b) one or more youth community orders."

96. (1) Section 36B (electronic monitoring of requirements in community orders) is amended as follows.

  (2) In the heading for "community orders" there is substituted "youth community orders", and

  (3) In subsection (1)—

    (a) for "to (4)" there is substituted "and (3)", and

    (b) for "community order" there is substituted "youth community order".

  (4) In subsection (2) and (6)(a), for "community order" there is substituted "youth community order".

97. (1) Section 37 (curfew orders) is amended as follows.

  (2) In subsection (1)—

    (a) after the word "person" there is inserted "aged under 16", and

    (b) for "sections 34 to 36 above" there is substituted "sections 148, 150 and 156 of the Criminal Justice Act 2003".

  (3) In subsection (5), for "community order" there is substituted "youth community order".

  (4) Subsection (10) is omitted.

98. In section 39 (breach, revocation and amendment of curfew orders), for "community orders" there is substituted "youth community orders".

99. In section 40 (curfew orders: supplementary), in subsection (3), for "paragraphs 2A(4) and (5) and 19(3)" there is substituted "paragraph 16(2)".

100. (1) Section 40A (exclusion orders) is amended as follows.

  (2) In subsection (1)—

    (a) after "person" there is inserted "aged under 16",

    (b) for "sections 34 to 36 above" there is substituted "sections 148, 150 and 156 of the Criminal Justice Act 2003", and

    (c) for "two years" there is substituted "three months".

  (3) In subsection (5), for "community order" there is substituted "youth community order".

  (4) Subsection (10) is omitted.

101. In section 40B (breach, revocation and amendment of exclusion orders), for "community orders" there is substituted "youth community orders".

102. (1) Section 60 (attendance centre orders) is amended as follows.

  (2) In subsection (1)—

    (a) in paragraph (a), for "sections 34 to 36 above" there is substituted "sections 148, 150 and 156 of the Criminal Justice Act 2003" and for "21" there is substituted "16", and

    (b) in paragraph (b), for "21" there is substituted "16", and

    (c) paragraph (c) and the word "or" immediately preceding it are omitted.

  (3) In subsection (4), for paragraphs (a) and (b) there is substituted "shall not exceed 24".

  (4) In subsection (7), for "community order" there is substituted "youth community order".

103. In section 63 (supervision orders), in subsection (1), for "sections 34 to 36 above" there is substituted "sections 148, 150 and 156 of the Criminal Justice Act 2003".

104. (1) Section 69 (action plan orders) is amended as follows.

  (2) In subsection (1), for "sections 34 to 36 above" there is substituted "sections 148, 150 and 156 of the Criminal Justice Act 2003", and

(3) In subsection (5)(b), for "a community rehabilitation order, a community punishment order, a community punishment and rehabilitation order," there is substituted "a community order under section 177 of the Criminal Justice Act 2003".

(4) Subsection (11) is omitted.

105. In section 70 (requirements which may be included in action plan orders and directions), in subsection (5)(a), after the word "other" there is inserted "youth community order or any".

106. (1) Section 73 (reparation orders) is amended as follows.

(2) In subsection (4)(b), for "a community punishment order, a community punishment and rehabilitation order," there is substituted "a community order under section 177 of the Criminal Justice Act 2003".

(3) Subsection (7) is omitted.

107. In section 74 (requirements and provisions of reparation order, and obligations of person subject to it), in subsection (3)(a), after "community order" there is inserted "or any youth community order".

108. In section 76 (meaning of custodial sentence), in subsection (1) after paragraph (b) there is inserted—

"(bb) a sentence of detention for public protection under section 226 of the Criminal Justice Act 2003;

(bc) a sentence of detention under section 228 of that Act;".

109. (1) Section 82A (determination of tariffs) is amended as follows.

(2) In subsection (1), for the words from "where" onwards there is substituted "where the sentence is not fixed by law".

(3) In subsection (3)—

(a) in paragraph (b), for "section 87" there is substituted "section 240 of the Criminal Justice Act 2003", and

(b) in paragraph (c), for "sections 33(2) and 35(1) of the Criminal Justice Act 1991" there is substituted "section 244(1) of the Criminal Justice Act 2003".

(4) In subsection (4)—

(a) after "If" there is inserted "the offender was aged 21 or over when he committed the offence and", and

(b) the words "subject to subsection (5) below" are omitted.

(5) Subsections (5) and (6) are omitted.

110. (1) Section 91 (offenders under 18 convicted of certain serious offences) is amended as follows.

(2) In subsection (3), for "none of the other methods in which the case may legally be dealt with" there is substituted "neither a community sentence nor a detention and training order".

(3) In subsection (4), for "section 79 and 80 above" there is substituted "section 152 and 153 of the Criminal Justice Act 2003".

111. (1) Section 100 (detention and training orders) is amended as follows.

(2) In subsection (1)—

(a) for the words from the beginning to "subsection (2)" there is substituted "Subject to sections 90 and 91 above, sections 226 and 228 of the Criminal Justice Act 2003, and subsection (2)", and

(b) for paragraph (b) there is substituted—

"(b) the court is of the opinion that subsection (2) of section 152 of the Criminal Justice Act 2003 applies or the case falls within subsection (3) of that section,".

(3) Subsection (4) is omitted.

112. In section 106 (interaction of detention and training orders with sentences of detention in a young offender institution), subsections (2) and (3) are omitted.
113. After section 106 there is inserted—

"106A Interaction with sentences of detention

(1) In this section—
"the 2003 Act" means the Criminal Justice Act 2003;
"sentence of detention" means—
  (a) a sentence of detention under section 91 above, or
  (b) a sentence of detention under section 228 of the 2003 Act (extended sentence for certain violent or sexual offences: persons under 18).

(2) Where a court passes a sentence of detention in the case of an offender who is subject to a detention and training order, the sentence shall take effect as follows—
  (a) if the offender has at any time been released by virtue of subsection (2), (3), (4) or (5) of section 102 above, at the beginning of the day on which the sentence is passed, and
  (b) if not, either as mentioned in paragraph (a) above or, if the court so orders, at the time when the offender would otherwise be released by virtue of subsection (2), (3), (4) or (5) of section 102.

(3) Where a court makes a detention and training order in the case of an offender who is subject to a sentence of detention, the order shall take effect as follows—
  (a) if the offender has at any time been released under Chapter 6 of Part 12 of the 2003 Act (release on licence of fixed-term prisoners), at the beginning of the day on which the order is made, and
  (b) if not, either as mentioned in paragraph (a) above or, if the court so orders, at the time when the offender would otherwise be released under that Chapter.

(4) Where an order under section 102(5) above is made in the case of a person in respect of whom a sentence of detention is to take effect as mentioned in subsection (2)(b) above, the order is to be expressed as an order that the period of detention attributable to the detention and training order is to end at the time determined under section 102(5)(a) or (b) above.

(5) In determining for the purposes of subsection (3)(b) the time when an offender would otherwise be released under Chapter 6 of Part 12 of the 2003 Act, section 246 of that Act (power of Secretary of State to release prisoners on licence before he is required to do so) is to be disregarded.

(6) Where by virtue of subsection (3)(b) above a detention and training order made in the case of a person who is subject to a sentence of detention under section 228 of the 2003 Act is to take effect at the time when he would otherwise be released under Chapter 6 of Part 12 of that Act, any direction by the Parole Board under subsection (2)(b) of section 247 of that Act in respect of him is to be expressed as a direction that the Board would, but for the detention and training order, have directed his release under that section.

(7) Subject to subsection (9) below, where at any time an offender is subject concurrently—
  (a) to a detention and training order, and
  (b) to a sentence of detention, he shall be treated for the purposes of the provisions specified in subsection (8) below as if he were subject only to the sentence of detention.

(8) Those provisions are—
  (a) sections 102 to 105 above,
  (b) section 92 above and section 235 of the 2003 Act (place of detention, etc.), and
  (c) Chapter 6 of Part 12 of the 2003 Act.

(9) Nothing in subsection (7) above shall require the offender to be released in respect of either the order or the sentence unless and until he is required to be released in respect of each of them."

114. In section 110 (required custodial sentence for third class A drug trafficking offence), subsection (3) is omitted.

115. In section 111 (minimum of three years for third domestic burglary) subsection (3) is omitted.

116. Sections 116 and 117 (return to prison etc. where offence committed during original sentence) shall cease to have effect.

117. In section 130 (compensation orders against convicted persons), in subsection (2), for "109(2), 110(2) or 111(2) above," there is substituted "110(2) or 111(2) above, section 51A(2) of the Firearms Act 1968 or section 225, 226, 227 or 228 of the Criminal Justice Act 2003,".

118. In section 136 (power to order statement as to financial circumstances of parent or guardian) in subsection (2), for "section 126 above" there is substituted "section 162 of the Criminal Justice Act 2003".

119. (1) Section 138 (fixing of fine or compensation to be paid by parent or guardian) is amended as follows.

(2) In subsection (1)(a), for "section 128 above" there is substituted "section 164 of the Criminal Justice Act 2003".

(3) In subsection (2), for "sections 128(1) (duty to inquire into financial circumstances) and" there is substituted "section 164(1) of the Criminal Justice Act 2003 and section".

(4) In subsection (4)—
   (a) for "section 129 above" there is substituted "section 165 of the Criminal Justice Act 2003",
   (b) for "section 129(1)" there is substituted "section 165(1)", and
   (c) for "section 129(2)" there is substituted "section 165(2)".

120. In section 146 (driving disqualification for any offence), in subsection (2), for "109(2), 110(2) or 111(2) above" there is substituted "110(2) or 111(2) above, section 51A(2) of the Firearms Act 1968 or section 225, 226, 227 or 228 of the Criminal Justice Act 2003".

121. In section 154 (commencement of Crown Court sentence), in subsection (2), for "section 84 above" there is substituted "section 265 of the Criminal Justice Act 2003".

122. In section 159 (execution of process between England and Wales and Scotland), for "10(7) or 24(1)" there is substituted "10(6) or 18(1)".

123. (1) Section 163 (interpretation) is amended as follows.

(2) In the definition of "attendance centre" for "section 62(2) above" there is substituted "section 221(2) of the Criminal Justice Act 2003".

(3) In the definition of "attendance centre order" for the words from "by virtue of" to "Schedule 3" there is substituted "by virtue of paragraph 4(2)(b) or 5(2)(b) of Schedule 3".

(4) In the definition of "community order", for "section 33(1) above" there is substituted "section 177(1) of the Criminal Justice Act 2003".

(5) For the definition of "curfew order" there is substituted—
   " "curfew order" means an order under section 37(1) above (and, except where the contrary intention is shown by paragraph 7 of Schedule 3 or paragraph 3 of Schedule 7 or 8, includes orders made under section 37(1) by virtue of paragraph 4(2)(a) or 5(2)(a) of Schedule 3 or paragraph 2(2)(a) of Schedule 7 or 8).".

(6) In the definition of "operational period", for "section 118(3) above" there is substituted "section 189(1)(b)(ii) of the Criminal Justice Act 2003".

(7) In the definition of "suspended sentence", for "section 118(3) above" there is substituted "section 189(7) of the Criminal Justice Act 2003".

(8) At the end there is inserted—

" "youth community order" has the meaning given by section 33(1) above.".

124. In section 164 (further interpretative provision) for subsection (3) there is substituted—

"(3) References in this Act to a sentence falling to be imposed—

(a) under section 110(2) or 111(2) above,

(b) under section 51A(2) of the Firearms Act 1968, or

(c) under any of sections 225 to 228 of the Criminal Justice Act 2003, are to be read in accordance with section 305(4) of the Criminal Justice Act 2003."

125. For Schedule 3 (breach revocation and amendment of certain community orders) there is substituted—

"SCHEDULE 3
BREACH, REVOCATION AND AMENDMENT OF CURFEW ORDERS AND EXCLUSION ORDERS

PART 1
PRELIMINARY

Definitions

1. In this Schedule—

"the petty sessions area concerned" means—

(a) in relation to a curfew order, the petty sessions area in which the place for the time being specified in the order is situated; and

(b) in relation to an exclusion order, the petty sessions area for the time being specified in the order;

"relevant order" means a curfew order or an exclusion order.

Orders made on appeal

2. Where a relevant order has been made on appeal, for the purposes of this Schedule it shall be deemed—

(a) if it was made on an appeal brought from a magistrates' court, to have been made by a magistrates' court;

(b) if it was made on an appeal brought from the Crown Court or from the criminal division of the Court of Appeal, to have been made by the Crown Court.

PART 2
BREACH OF REQUIREMENT OF ORDER

Issue of summons or warrant

3. (1) If at any time while a relevant order is in force in respect of an offender it appears on information to a justice of the peace acting for the petty sessions area concerned

that the offender has failed to comply with any of the requirements of the order, the justice may—

(a) issue a summons requiring the offender to appear at the place and time specified in it; or

(b) if the information is in writing and on oath, issue a warrant for his arrest.

(2) Any summons or warrant issued under this paragraph shall direct the offender to appear or be brought—

(a) in the case of any relevant order which was made by the Crown Court and included a direction that any failure to comply with any of the requirements of the order be dealt with by the Crown Court, before the Crown Court; and

(b) in the case of a relevant order which is not an order to which paragraph (a) above applies, before a magistrates' court acting for the petty sessions area concerned.

(3) Where a summons issued under sub-paragraph (1)(a) above requires an offender to appear before the Crown Court and the offender does not appear in answer to the summons, the Crown Court may issue a further summons requiring the offender to appear at the place and time specified in it.

(4) Where a summons issued under sub-paragraph (1)(a) above or a further summons issued under sub-paragraph (3) above requires an offender to appear before the Crown Court and the offender does not appear in answer to the summons, the Crown Court may issue a warrant for the arrest of the offender.

Powers of magistrates' court

4. (1) This paragraph applies if it is proved to the satisfaction of a magistrates' court before which an offender appears or is brought under paragraph 3 above that he has failed without reasonable excuse to comply with any of the requirements of the relevant order.

(2) The magistrates' court may deal with the offender in respect of the failure in one of the following ways (and must deal with him in one of those ways if the relevant order is in force)—

(a) by making a curfew order in respect of him (subject to paragraph 7 below);

(b) by making an attendance centre order in respect of him (subject to paragraph 8 below); or

(c) where the relevant order was made by a magistrates' court, by dealing with him, for the offence in respect of which the order was made, in any way in which he could have been dealt with for that offence by the court which made the order if the order had not been made.

(3) In dealing with an offender under sub-paragraph (2)(c) above, a magistrates' court—

(a) shall take into account the extent to which the offender has complied with the requirements of the relevant order; and

(b) in the case of an offender who has wilfully and persistently failed to comply with those requirements, may impose a custodial sentence (where the relevant order was made in respect of an offence punishable with such a sentence) notwithstanding anything in section 152(2) of the Criminal Justice Act 2003.

(4) Where a magistrates' court deals with an offender under sub-paragraph (2)(c) above, it shall revoke the relevant order if it is still in force.

(5) Where a relevant order was made by the Crown Court and a magistrates' court has power to deal with the offender under sub-paragraph (2)(a) or (b) above, it may

instead commit him to custody or release him on bail until he can be brought or appear before the Crown Court.

(6) A magistrates' court which deals with an offender's case under sub-paragraph (5) above shall send to the Crown Court—

    (a) a certificate signed by a justice of the peace certifying that the offender has failed to comply with the requirements of the relevant order in the respect specified in the certificate; and

    (b) such other particulars of the case as may be desirable;

and a certificate purporting to be so signed shall be admissible as evidence of the failure before the Crown Court.

(7) A person sentenced under sub-paragraph (2)(c) above for an offence may appeal to the Crown Court against the sentence.

Powers of Crown Court

5. (1) This paragraph applies where under paragraph 3 or by virtue of paragraph 4(5) above an offender is brought or appears before the Crown Court and it is proved to the satisfaction of that court that he has failed without reasonable excuse to comply with any of the requirements of the relevant order.

(2) The Crown Court may deal with the offender in respect of the failure in one of the following ways (and must deal with him in one of those ways if the relevant order is in force)—

    (a) by making a curfew order in respect of him (subject to paragraph 7 below);

    (b) by making an attendance centre order in respect of him (subject to paragraph 8 below); or

    (c) by dealing with him, for the offence in respect of which the order was made, in any way in which he could have been dealt with for that offence by the court which made the order if the order had not been made.

(3) In dealing with an offender under sub-paragraph (2)(c) above, the Crown Court—

    (a) shall take into account the extent to which the offender has complied with the requirements of the relevant order; and

    (b) in the case of an offender who has wilfully and persistently failed to comply with those requirements, may impose a custodial sentence (where the relevant order was made in respect of an offence punishable with such a sentence) notwithstanding anything in section 152(2) of the Criminal Justice Act 2003.

(4) Where the Crown Court deals with an offender under sub-paragraph (2)(c) above, it shall revoke the relevant order if it is still in force.

(5) In proceedings before the Crown Court under this paragraph any question whether the offender has failed to comply with the requirements of the relevant order shall be determined by the court and not by the verdict of a jury.

Exclusions from paragraphs 4 and 5

6. Without prejudice to paragraphs 10 and 11 below, an offender who is convicted of a further offence while a relevant order is in force in respect of him shall not on that account be liable to be dealt with under paragraph 4 or 5 in respect of a failure to comply with any requirement of the order.

Curfew orders imposed for breach of relevant order

7. (1) Section 37 of this Act (curfew orders) shall apply for the purposes of paragraphs 4(2)(a) and 5(2)(a) above as if for the words from the beginning to "make" there were substituted "Where a court has power to deal with an offender under Part 2 of Schedule 3 to this Act for failure to comply with any of the requirements of a relevant order, the court may make in respect of the offender".

(2) The following provisions of this Act, namely—

(a) section 37(3) to (12), and

(b) so far as applicable, sections 36B and 40 and this Schedule so far as relating to curfew orders;

have effect in relation to a curfew order made by virtue of paragraphs 4(2)(a) and 5(2)(a) as they have effect in relation to any other curfew order, subject to sub-paragraph (3) below.

(3) This Schedule shall have effect in relation to such a curfew order as if—

(a) the power conferred on the court by each of paragraphs 4(2)(c), 5(2)(c) and 10(3)(b) to deal with the offender for the offence in respect of which the order was made were a power to deal with the offender, for his failure to comply with the relevant order, in any way in which the appropriate court could deal with him for that failure if it had just been proved to the satisfaction of the court;

(b) the reference in paragraph 10(1)(b) to the offence in respect of which the order was made were a reference to the failure to comply in respect of which the curfew order was made; and

(c) the power conferred on the Crown Court by paragraph 11(2)(b) to deal with the offender for the offence in respect of which the order was made were a power to deal with the offender, for his failure to comply with the relevant order, in any way in which the appropriate court (if the relevant order was made by the magistrates' court) or the Crown Court (if that order was made by the Crown Court) could deal with him for that failure if it had just been proved to its satisfaction.

(4) For the purposes of the provisions mentioned in paragraphs (a) and (c) of sub-paragraph (3) above, as applied by that sub-paragraph, if the relevant order is no longer in force the appropriate court's powers shall be determined on the assumption that it is still in force.

(5) Sections 148 and 156 of the Criminal Justice Act 2003 (restrictions and procedural requirements for community sentences) do not apply in relation to a curfew order made by virtue of paragraph 4(2)(a) or 5(2)(a) above.

Attendance centre orders imposed for breach of relevant order

8. (1) Section 60(1) of this Act (attendance centre orders) shall apply for the purposes of paragraphs 4(2)(b) and 5(2)(b) above as if for the words from the beginning to "the court may," there were substituted "Where a court has power to deal with an offender under Part 2 of Schedule 3 to this Act for failure to comply with any of the requirements of a relevant order, the court may,".

(2) The following provisions of this Act, namely—

(a) subsections (3) to (11) of section 60, and

(b) so far as applicable, section 36B and Schedule 5,

have effect in relation to an attendance centre order made by virtue of paragraph 4(2)(b) or 5(2)(b) above as they have effect in relation to any other attendance centre order, but as if there were omitted from each of paragraphs 2(1)(b), 3(1) and 4(3) of Schedule 5 the words ", for the offence in respect of which the order was made," and "for that offence".

(3) Sections 148 and 156 of the Criminal Justice Act 2003 (restrictions and procedural requirements for community sentences) do not apply in relation to an attendance centre order made by virtue of paragraph 4(2)(b) or 5(2)(b) above.

Supplementary

9. Any exercise by a court of its powers under paragraph 4(2)(a) or (b) or 5(2)(a) or (b) above shall be without prejudice to the continuance of the relevant order.

PART 3
REVOCATION OF ORDER

Revocation of order with or without re-sentencing:
powers of magistrates' court

10. (1) This paragraph applies where a relevant order made by a magistrates' court is in force in respect of any offender and on the application of the offender or the responsible officer it appears to the appropriate magistrates' court that, having regard to circumstances which have arisen since the order was made, it would be in the interests of justice—

(a) for the order to be revoked; or

(b) for the offender to be dealt with in some other way for the offence in respect of which the order was made.

(2) In this paragraph "the appropriate magistrates' court" means a magistrates' court acting for the petty sessions area concerned.

(3) The appropriate magistrates' court may—

(a) revoke the order; or

(b) both—

(i) revoke the order; and

(ii) deal with the offender for the offence in respect of which the order was made, in any way in which he could have been dealt with for that offence by the court which made the order if the order had not been made.

(4) In dealing with an offender under sub-paragraph (3)(b) above, a magistrates' court shall take into account the extent to which the offender has complied with the requirements of the relevant order.

(5) A person sentenced under sub-paragraph (3)(b) above for an offence may appeal to the Crown Court against the sentence.

(6) Where a magistrates' court proposes to exercise its powers under this paragraph otherwise than on the application of the offender, it shall summon him to appear before the court and, if he does not appear in answer to the summons, may issue a warrant for his arrest.

(7) No application may be made by the offender under sub-paragraph (1) above while an appeal against the relevant order is pending.

Revocation of order with or without re-sentencing: powers of
Crown Court on conviction etc.

11. (1) This paragraph applies where—

    (a) a relevant order made by the Crown Court is in force in respect of an offender and the offender or the responsible officer applies to the Crown Court for the order to be revoked or for the offender to be dealt with in some other way for the offence in respect of which the order was made; or

    (b) an offender in respect of whom a relevant order is in force is convicted of an offence before the Crown Court or, having been committed by a magistrates' court to the Crown Court for sentence, is brought or appears before the Crown Court.

  (2) If it appears to the Crown Court to be in the interests of justice to do so, having regard to circumstances which have arisen since the order was made, the Crown Court may—

    (a) revoke the order; or

    (b) both—

      (i) revoke the order; and

      (ii) deal with the offender for the offence in respect of which the order was made, in any way in which he could have been dealt with for that offence by the court which made the order if the order had not been made.

  (3) In dealing with an offender under sub-paragraph (2)(b) above, the Crown Court shall take into account the extent to which the offender has complied with the requirements of the relevant order.

Revocation following custodial sentence by magistrates' court unconnected with order

12. (1) This paragraph applies where—

    (a) an offender in respect of whom a relevant order is in force is convicted of an offence by a magistrates' court unconnected with the order;

    (b) the court imposes a custodial sentence on the offender; and

    (c) it appears to the court, on the application of the offender or the responsible officer, that it would be in the interests of justice to exercise its powers under this paragraph having regard to circumstances which have arisen since the order was made.

  (2) In sub-paragraph (1) above "a magistrates' court unconnected with the order" means a magistrates' court not acting for the petty sessions area concerned.

  (3) The court may—

    (a) if the order was made by a magistrates' court, revoke it;

    (b) if the order was made by the Crown Court, commit the offender in custody or release him on bail until he can be brought or appear before the Crown Court.

  (4) Where the court deals with an offender's case under sub-paragraph (3)(b) above, it shall send to the Crown Court such particulars of the case as may be desirable.

13. Where by virtue of paragraph 12(3)(b) above an offender is brought or appears before the Crown Court and it appears to the Crown Court to be in the interests of justice to do so, having regard to circumstances which have arisen since the relevant order was made, the Crown Court may revoke the order.

Supplementary

14. (1) On the making under this Part of this Schedule of an order revoking a relevant order, the proper officer of the court shall forthwith give copies of the revoking order to the responsible officer.

    (2) In sub-paragraph (1) above "proper officer" means —

        (a) in relation to a magistrates' court, the justices' chief executive for the court; and

        (b) in relation to the Crown Court, the appropriate officer.

    (3) A responsible officer to whom in accordance with sub-paragraph (1) above copies of a revoking order are given shall give a copy to the offender and to the person in charge of any institution in which the offender was required by the order to reside.

PART 4
AMENDMENT OF ORDER

Amendment by reason of change of residence

15. (1) This paragraph applies where, at any time while a relevant order is in force in respect of an offender, a magistrates' court acting for the petty sessions area concerned is satisfied that the offender proposes to change, or has changed, his residence from that petty sessions area to another petty sessions area.

    (2) Subject to sub-paragraph (3) below, the court may, and on the application of the responsible officer shall, amend the relevant order by substituting the other petty sessions area for the area specified in the order or, in the case of a curfew order, a place in that other area for the place so specified.

    (3) The court shall not amend under this paragraph a curfew order which contains requirements which, in the opinion of the court, cannot be complied with unless the offender continues to reside in the petty sessions area concerned unless, in accordance with paragraph 16 below, it either—

        (a) cancels those requirements; or

        (b) substitutes for those requirements other requirements which can be complied with if the offender ceases to reside in that area.

Amendment of requirements of order

16. (1) Without prejudice to the provisions of paragraph 15 above but subject to the following provisions of this paragraph, a magistrates' court acting for the petty sessions area concerned may, on the application of an eligible person, by order amend a relevant order—

        (a) by cancelling any of the requirements of the order; or

        (b) by inserting in the order (either in addition to or in substitution for any of its requirements) any requirement which the court could include if it were then making the order.

    (2) A magistrates' court shall not under sub-paragraph (1) above amend a curfew order by extending the curfew periods beyond the end of six months from the date of the original order.

    (3) A magistrates' court shall not under sub-paragraph (1) above amend an exclusion order by extending the period for which the offender is prohibited from entering the place in question beyond the end of three months from the date of the original order.

(4) For the purposes of this paragraph the eligible persons are—

   (a) the offender;

   (b) the responsible officer; and

   (c) in relation to an exclusion order, any affected person.

But an application under sub-paragraph (1) by a person such as is mentioned in paragraph (c) above must be for the cancellation of a requirement which was included in the order by virtue of his consent or for the purpose (or partly for the purpose) of protecting him from being approached by the offender, or for the· insertion of a requirement which will, if inserted, be such a requirement.

Supplementary

17. No order may be made under paragraph 15 above, and no application may be made under paragraph 16 above, while an appeal against the relevant order is pending.

18. (1) Subject to sub-paragraph (2) below, where a court proposes to exercise its powers under this Part of this Schedule, otherwise than on the application of the offender, the court—

   (a) shall summon him to appear before the court; and

   (b) if he does not appear in answer to the summons, may issue a warrant for his arrest.

  (2) This paragraph shall not apply to an order cancelling a requirement of a relevant order or reducing the period of any requirement, or to an order under paragraph 15 above substituting a new petty sessions area or a new place for the one specified in a relevant order.

19. (1) On the making under this Part of this Schedule of an order amending a relevant order, the justices' chief executive for the court shall forthwith—

   (a) if the order amends the relevant order otherwise than by substituting, by virtue of paragraph 15 above, a new petty session area or a new place for the one specified in the relevant order, give copies of the amending order to the responsible officer;

   (b) if the order amends the relevant order in the manner excepted by paragraph (a) above, send to the chief executive to the justices for the new petty sessions area or, as the case may be, for the petty sessions area in which the new place is situated—

     (i) copies of the amending order; and

     (ii) such documents and information relating to the case as he considers likely to be of assistance to a court acting for that area in the exercise of its functions in relation to the order;

   and in a case falling within paragraph (b) above the chief executive of the justices for that area shall give copies of the amending order to the responsible officer.

  (2) A responsible officer to whom in accordance with sub-paragraph (1) above copies of an order are given shall give a copy to the offender and to the person in charge of any institution in which the offender is or was required by the order to reside."

126. In Schedule 5 (breach, revocation and amendment of attendance centre orders)—

   (a) in paragraph 1(1)(b), for "section 62(3) of this Act" there is substituted "section 222(1)(d) or (e) of the Criminal Justice Act 2003",

   (b) in paragraph 2(5)(b), for "section 79(2) of this Act" there is substituted "section 152(2) of the Criminal Justice Act 2003", and

(c) in paragraph 3(3)(b), for "section 79(2) of this Act" there is substituted "section 152(2) of the Criminal Justice Act 2003".

127. In Schedule 6 (requirements which may be included in supervision orders)—

    (a) in paragraph 2(7)(a), after the word "other" there is inserted "youth community order or any", and

    (b) in paragraph 3(6)(a), for "community order" there is substituted "youth community order".

128. In Schedule 7 (breach, revocation and amendment of supervision orders)—

    (a) in paragraph 3—

      (i) in sub-paragraph (2), for "sub-paragraphs (4) and (5)" there is substituted "sub-paragraph (5)",

      (ii) in sub-paragraph (3), for "Sections 35 and 36 of this Act" there is substituted "Sections 148 and 156 of the Criminal Justice Act 2003",

      (iii) sub-paragraph (4) is omitted, and

      (iv) in sub-paragraph (5)(a), for the words from the beginning to "and" there is substituted "the power conferred on the court by each of paragraphs 4(2)(c) and", and

    (b) in paragraph 4(3), for "Sections 35 and 36 of this Act" there is substituted "Sections 148 and 156 of the Criminal Justice Act 2003".

129. In Schedule 8 (breach, revocation and amendment of action plan orders and reparation orders)—

    (a) in paragraph 3—

      (i) in sub-paragraph (2), for "sub-paragraphs (4) and (5)" there is substituted "sub-paragraph (5)",

      (ii) in sub-paragraph (3), for "Sections 35 and 36 of this Act" there is substituted "Sections 148 and 156 of the Criminal Justice Act 2003",

      (iii) sub-paragraph (4) is omitted, and

      (iv) in sub-paragraph (5)(a), for the words from the beginning to "and" there is substituted "The power conferred on the court by each of paragraphs 4(2)(c) and", and

    (b) in paragraph 4(3), for "Sections 35 and 36 of this Act" there is substituted "Sections 148 and 156 of the Criminal Justice Act 2003".

Child Support, Pensions and Social Security Act 2000 (c. 19)

130. The Child Support, Pensions and Social Security Act 2000 is amended as follows.

131. (1) Section 62 (loss of benefit for breach of community order) is amended as follows.

    (2) In subsection (8), for the definition of "relevant community order" there is substituted—

    " "relevant community order" means—

      (a) a community order made under section 177 of the Criminal Justice Act 2003; or

      (b) any order falling in England or Wales to be treated as such an order."

    (3) In subsection (11)(c)(ii), for "to (e)" there is substituted "and (b)".

132. In section 64 (information provision), in subsection (6)(a), after "community orders" there is inserted "(as defined by section 177 of the Criminal Justice Act 2003)".

Criminal Justice and Court Services Act 2000 (c. 43)

133. The Criminal Justice and Court Services Act 2000 is amended as follows.

134. In section 1 (purposes of Chapter 1 of Part 1 of the Act), in subsection (2)—

    (a) in paragraph (a), after "community orders" there is inserted "(as defined by section 177 of the Criminal Justice Act 2003)", and

    (b) after paragraph (c) there is inserted—

        "(d) giving effect to suspended sentence orders (as defined by section 189 of the Criminal Justice Act 2003)."

135. In section 42 (interpretation of Part 2), in subsection (2)(a), for "section 119 of the Powers of Criminal Court (Sentencing) Act 2000" there is substituted "paragraph 8(2)(a) or (b) of Schedule 12[a] of the Criminal Justice Act 2003".

136. (1) Section 62 (release on licence etc: conditions as to monitoring) is amended as follows.

    (2) For subsection (3) there is substituted—

        "(3) In relation to a prisoner released under section 246 of the Criminal Justice Act 2003 (power to release prisoners on licence before required to do so), the monitoring referred to in subsection (2)(a) does not include the monitoring of his compliance with conditions imposed under section 253 of that Act (curfew condition)."

    (3) In subsection (5) after paragraph (e) there is inserted ", and

        (f) a sentence of detention under section 226 or 228 of the Criminal Justice Act 2003".

137. In section 69 (duties of local probation boards in connection with victims of certain offences), in subsection (8), for paragraph (a) there is substituted—

    "(a) murder or an offence specified in Schedule 15 to the Criminal Justice Act 2003,"

138. In section 70 (general interpretation), in subsection (5), for the words "any community order" there is substituted "a curfew order, an exclusion order, a community rehabilitation order, a community punishment order, a community punishment and rehabilitation order, a drug treatment and testing order, a drug abstinence order, an attendance centre order, a supervision order or an action plan order".

International Criminal Court Act 2001 (c. 17)

139. (1) Schedule 7 to the International Criminal Court Act 2001 (domestic provisions not applicable to ICC prisoners), is amended as follows.

    (2) In paragraph 2(1), for paragraph (d) there is substituted—

        "(d) section 240 of the Criminal Justice Act 2003 (crediting of periods of remand in custody)."

    (3) In paragraph 3(1), for "Part 2 of the Criminal Justice Act 1991" there is substituted "sections 244 to 264 of the Criminal Justice Act 2003".

Armed Forces Act 2001 (c. 19)

140. In section 30 of the Armed Forces Act 2001 (conditional release from custody), in subsection (6)(a) for "six months" there is substituted "the term specified in subsection (1)(a) of section 8 of the Armed Forces Act 1976 (powers of courts in relation to civilians)".

Proceeds of Crime Act 2002 (c. 29)

141. In section 38 of the Proceeds of Crime Act 2002 (provisions about imprisonment or detention), in subsection (4)(a), for "section 118(1) of the Sentencing Act" there is substituted "section 189(1) of the Criminal Justice Act 2003".

Sexual Offences Act 2003 (c. 42)

142. The Sexual Offences Act 2003 is amended as follows.

143. In section 131 (application of Part 2 to young offenders), after paragraph (j) there is inserted—
   "(k) a sentence of detention for public protection under section 226 of the Criminal Justice Act 2003,
   (l) an extended sentence under section 228 of that Act,".

144. In section 133 (general interpretation), at the end of paragraph (a) of the definition of "community order" there is inserted "(as that Act had effect before the passing of the Criminal Justice Act 2003)".

PART 2
OFFENCES: ABOLITION OF IMPRISONMENT AND CONVERSION TO SUMMARY OFFENCE

Vagrancy Act 1824 (c. 83)

145. In section 3 of the Vagrancy Act 1824 (idle and disorderly persons), for the words from "subject to" to the end there is substituted "it shall be lawful for any justice of the peace to impose on such person (being thereof convicted before him by his own view, or by the confession of such person, or by the evidence on oath of one or more credible witnesses) a fine not exceeding level 3 on the standard scale".

146. (1) Section 4 of that Act (rogues and vagabonds) is amended as follows.
   (2) In that section, for the words from "shall be" to the end there is substituted "commits an offence under this section".
   (3) At the end of that section (which becomes subsection (1)) there is inserted—
      "(2) It shall be lawful for any justice of the peace to impose on any person who commits an offence under this section (being thereof convicted before him by the confession of such person, or by the evidence on oath of one or more credible witnesses)—
         (a) in the case of a person convicted of the offence of wandering abroad and lodging in any barn or outhouse, or in any deserted or unoccupied building, or in the open air, or under a tent, or in any cart or waggon, and not giving a good account of himself, a fine not exceeding level 1 on the standard scale, and
         (b) in the case of a person convicted of any other offence under this section, a fine not exceeding level 3 on the standard scale."

London Hackney Carriage Act 1843 (c. 86)

147. In section 28 of the London Hackney Carriages Act 1843, after "for every such offence", there is inserted "of which he is convicted before the justice".

Town Police Clauses Act 1847 (c. 89)

148. In section 26 of the Town Police Clauses Act 1847, for the words from "committed by them" to the end, there is substituted "liable to a fine not exceeding level 3 on the standard scale".

149. In section 28 of that Act, after "for each offence", there is inserted "of which he is convicted before the justice".

150. In section 29 of that Act, after "for each offence", there is inserted "of which he is convicted before the justice".

151. In section 36 of that Act, after "liable", there is inserted "on conviction before the justices".

Seamen's and Soldiers' False Characters Act 1906 (c. 5)

152. In section 1 of the Seamen's and Soldiers' False Characters Act 1906, for "imprisonment for a term not exceeding three months" there is substituted "a fine not exceeding level 2 on the standard scale".

Aliens Restriction (Amendment) Act 1919 (c. 92)

153. In section 3(2) of the Aliens Restriction (Amendment) Act 1919, for "imprisonment for a term not exceeding three months" there is substituted "a fine not exceeding level 3 on the standard scale".

Polish Resettlement Act 1947 (c. 19)

154. In the Schedule to the Polish Resettlement Act 1947, in paragraph 7, for "imprisonment for a term not exceeding three months" there is substituted "a fine not exceeding level 1 on the standard scale".

Army Act 1955 (3 & 4 Eliz. 2 c. 18)

155. In section 61 of the Army Act 1955, for the words from "the like" to "section nineteen of this Act" there is substituted "dismissal from Her Majesty's service with or without disgrace, to detention for a term not exceeding three months,".

Air Force Act 1955 (3 & 4 Eliz. 2 c. 19)

160. In section 61 of the Air Force Act 1955, for the words from "the like" to "section nineteen of this Act" there is substituted "dismissal from Her Majesty's service with or without disgrace, to detention for a term not exceeding three months,".

Naval Discipline Act 1957 (c. 53)

161. In section 34A of the Naval Discipline Act 1957, for the words "imprisonment for a term not exceeding three months" there is substituted "dismissal from Her Majesty's service with or without disgrace, detention for a term not exceeding three months,".

Slaughterhouses Act 1974 (c. 3)

158. In section 4 of the Slaughterhourses Act 1974, after subsection (5) there is inserted—
"(5A) A person guilty of an offence under subsection (5) above shall be liable to a fine not exceeding level 3 on the standard scale."

Water Industry Act 1991 (c. 56)

159. In Schedule 6 to the Water Industry Act 1991, in paragraph 5(4), for paragraphs (a) and (b) there is substituted", on summary conviction, to a fine not exceeding level 5 on the standard scale".

Water Resources Act 1991 (c. 57)

160. In section 205(6) of the Water Resources Act 1991, for paragraphs (a) and (b) there is substituted "on summary conviction to a fine not exceeding level 5 on the standard scale".

Transport Act 2000 (c. 38)

161. In section 82(4) of the Transport Act 2000, after "subsection (1)" there is inserted "or (2)".

Reserve Forces Act 1996 (c. 14)

162. In paragraph 5(3) of Schedule 1 to the Reserve Forces Act 1996, for the words "imprisonment for a term not exceeding three months" there is substituted "dismissal from Her Majesty's service with or without disgrace, to detention for a term not exceeding 3 months,".

SCHEDULE 33
JURY SERVICE

Section 321

1. The Juries Act 1974 (c. 23) is amended as follows.
2. For section 1 (qualification for jury service) there is substituted—

"1 Qualification for jury service

(1) Subject to the provisions of this Act, every person shall be qualified to serve as a juror in the Crown Court, the High Court and county courts and be liable accordingly to attend for jury service when summoned under this Act if—
  (a) he is for the time being registered as a parliamentary or local government elector and is not less than eighteen nor more than seventy years of age;
  (b) he has been ordinarily resident in the United Kingdom, the Channel Islands or the Isle of Man for any period of at least five years since attaining the age of thirteen;
  (c) he is not a mentally disordered person; and
  (d) he is not disqualified for jury service.
(2) In subsection (1) above "mentally disordered person" means any person listed in Part 1 of Schedule 1 to this Act.

(3) The persons who are disqualified for jury service are those listed in Part 2 of that Schedule."

3. Section 9(1) (certain persons entitled to be excused from jury service) shall cease to have effect.

4. In section 9(2) (discretionary excusal) after "may" there is inserted ", subject to section 9A(1A) of this Act,".

5. After section 9(2) (discretionary excusal) there is inserted—

"(2A) Without prejudice to subsection (2) above, the appropriate officer shall excuse a full-time serving member of Her Majesty's naval, military or air forces from attending in pursuance of a summons if—

(a) that member's commanding officer certifies to the appropriate officer that it would be prejudicial to the efficiency of the service if that member were to be required to be absent from duty, and

(b) subsection (2A) or (2B) of section 9A of this Act applies.

(2B) Subsection (2A) above does not affect the application of subsection (2) above to a full-time serving member of Her Majesty's naval, military or air forces in a case where he is not entitled to be excused under subsection (2A)."

6. In section 9(3) (discretionary excusal) after "above" there is inserted "or any failure by the appropriate officer to excuse him as required by subsection (2A) above".

7. In section 9A(1) (discretionary deferral) after "may" there is inserted ", subject to subsection (2) below,".

8. After section 9A(1) (discretionary deferral) there is inserted—

"(1A) Without prejudice to subsection (1) above and subject to subsection (2) below, the appropriate officer—

(a) shall defer the attendance of a full-time serving member of Her Majesty's naval, military or air forces in pursuance of a summons if subsection (1B) below applies, and

(b) for this purpose, shall vary the dates upon which that member is summoned to attend and the summons shall have effect accordingly.

(1B) This subsection applies if that member's commanding officer certifies to the appropriate officer that it would be prejudicial to the efficiency of the service if that member were to be required to be absent from duty.

(1C) Nothing in subsection (1A) or (1B) above shall affect the application of subsection (1) above to a full-time serving member of Her Majesty's naval, military or air forces in a case where subsection (1B) does not apply."

9. For section 9A(2) (discretionary deferral) there is substituted—

"(2) The attendance of a person in pursuance of a summons shall not be deferred under subsection (1) or (1A) above if subsection (2A) or (2B) below applies."

10. After section 9A(2) (discretionary deferral) there is inserted—

"(2A) This subsection applies where a deferral of the attendance of the person in pursuance of the summons has previously been made or refused under subsection (1) above or has previously been made under subsection (1A) above.

(2B) This subsection applies where—

(a) the person is a full-time serving member of Her Majesty's naval, military or air forces, and

(b) in addition to certifying to the appropriate officer that it would be prejudicial to the efficiency of the service if that member were to be required to be absent from duty, that member's commanding officer certifies that this position is likely to remain for any period specified for the purpose of this subsection in guidance issued under section 9AA of this Act."

11. In section 9A(3) (discretionary deferral) after "above" there is inserted "or any failure by the appropriate officer to defer his attendance as required by subsection (1A) above".

12. After section 9A (discretionary deferral) there is inserted—

"9AA Requirement to issue guidance

(1) The Lord Chancellor shall issue guidance as to the manner in which the functions of the appropriate officer under sections 9 and 9A of this Act are to be exercised.

(2) The Lord Chancellor shall—

(a) lay before each House of Parliament the guidance, and any revised guidance, issued under this section, and

(b) arrange for the guidance, or revised guidance, to be published in a manner which he considers appropriate."

13. In section 19 (payment for jury service), after subsection (1) there is inserted

"(1A) The reference in subsection (1) above to payments by way of allowance for subsistence includes a reference to vouchers and other benefits which may be used to pay for subsistence, whether or not their use is subject to any limitations."

14. In section 20 (offences), for subsection (5)(d) there is substituted—

"(d) knowing that he is disqualified under Part 2 of Schedule 1 to this Act, serves on a jury;"

15. For Schedule 1 (ineligibility and disqualification for and excusal from jury service) there is substituted—

"SCHEDULE 1
MENTALLY DISORDERED PERSONS AND PERSONS DISQUALIFIED FOR JURY SERVICE

PART 1
MENTALLY DISORDERED PERSONS

1. A person who suffers or has suffered from mental illness, psychopathic disorder, mental andicap or severe mental handicap and on account of that condition either—

(a) is resident in a hospital or similar institution; or

(b) regularly attends for treatment by a medical practitioner.

2. A person for the time being under guardianship under section 7 of the Mental Health Act 1983.

3. A person who, under Part 7 of that Act, has been determined by a judge to be incapable, by reason of mental disorder, of managing and administering his property and affairs.

4. (1) In this Part of this Schedule—

(a) "mental handicap" means a state of arrested or incomplete development of mind (not amounting to severe mental handicap) which includes significant impairment of intelligence and social functioning;

(b) "severe mental handicap" means a state of arrested or incomplete development of mind which includes severe impairment of intelligence and social functioning;

(c) other expressions are to be construed in accordance with the Mental Health Act 1983.

(2) For the purposes of this Part a person is to be treated as being under guardianship under section 7 of the Mental Health Act 1983 at any time while he is subject to guardianship pursuant to an order under section 116A(2)(b) of the Army Act 1955, section 116A(2)(b) of the Air Force Act 1955 or section 63A(2)(b) of the Naval Discipline Act 1957.

PART 2
PERSONS DISQUALIFIED

5. A person who is on bail in criminal proceedings (within the meaning of the Bail Act 1976).
6. A person who has at any time been sentenced in the United Kingdom, the Channel Islands or the Isle of Man—
   (a) to imprisonment for life, detention for life or custody for life,
   (b) to detention during her Majesty's pleasure or during the pleasure of the Secretary of State,
   (c) to imprisonment for public protection or detention for public protection,
   (d) to an extended sentence under section 227 or 228 of the Criminal Justice Act 2003 or section 210A of the Criminal Procedure (Scotland) Act 1995, or
   (e) to a term of imprisonment of five years or more or a term of detention of five years or more.
7. A person who at any time in the last ten years has—
   (a) in the United Kingdom, the Channel Islands or the Isle of Man—
      (i) served any part of a sentence of imprisonment or a sentence of detention, or
      (ii) had passed on him a suspended sentence of imprisonment or had made in respect of him a suspended order for detention,
   (b) in England and Wales, had made in respect of him a community order under section 177 of the Criminal Justice Act 2003, a community rehabilitation order, a community punishment order, a community punishment and rehabilitation order, a drug treatment and testing order or a drug abstinence order, or
   (c) had made in respect of him any corresponding order under the law of Scotland, Northern Ireland, the Isle of Man or any of the Channel Islands.
8. For the purposes of this Part of this Schedule—
   (a) a sentence passed by a court-martial is to be treated as having been passed in the United Kingdom, and
   (b) a person is sentenced to a term of detention if, but only if—
      (i) a court passes on him, or makes in respect of him on conviction, any sentence or order which requires him to be detained in custody for any period, and
      (ii) the sentence or order is available only in respect of offenders below a certain age, and any reference to serving a sentence of detention is to be construed accordingly."

SCHEDULE 34
PARENTING ORDERS AND REFERRAL ORDERS

Section 324

Crime and Disorder Act 1998 (c. 37)

1. In section 8 of the Crime and Disorder Act 1998 (parenting orders), in subsection (2) the words from "and to section 19(5)" to "2000" shall cease to have effect.

2. (1) Section 9 of that Act (parenting orders: supplemental) is amended as follows.

(2) For subsection (1A) there is substituted—

"(1A) The requirements of subsection (1) do not apply where the court makes a referral order in respect of the offence."

(3) After subsection (2) there is inserted—

"(2A) In a case where a court proposes to make both a referral order in respect of a child or young person convicted of an offence and a parenting order, before making the parenting order the court shall obtain and consider a report by an appropriate officer—

(a) indicating the requirements proposed by that officer to be included in the parenting order;

(b) indicating the reasons why he considers those requirements would be desirable in the interests of preventing the commission of any further offence by the child or young person; and

(c) if the child or young person is aged under 16, containing the information required by subsection (2) above.

(2B) In subsection (2A) above "an appropriate officer" means—

(a) an officer of a local probation board;

(b) a social worker of a local authority social services department; or

(c) a member of a youth offending team."

(4) After subsection (7) there is inserted—

"(7A) In this section "referral order" means an order under section 16(2) or (3) of the Powers of Criminal Courts (Sentencing) Act 2000 (referral of offender to youth offender panel)."

Powers of Criminal Courts (Sentencing) Act 2000 (c. 6)

3. In section 19(5) of the Powers of Criminal Courts (Sentencing) Act 2000 (orders that cannot be made with referral orders)—

(a) at the end of paragraph (a) there is inserted "or", and

(b) paragraph (c) (parenting orders) and the word "or" immediately preceding it shall cease to have effect.

4. In section 22 of that Act (referral orders: attendance at panel meetings), after subsection (2) there is inserted—

"(2A) If—

(a) a parent or guardian of the offender fails to comply with an order under section 20 above (requirement to attend the meetings of the panel), and

(b) the offender is aged under 18 at the time of the failure,

the panel may refer that parent or guardian to a youth court acting for the petty sessions area in which it appears to the panel that the offender resides or will reside."

5. (1) Section 28 of that Act (which introduces Schedule 1) is amended as follows.

(2) In the sidenote, for "Offender referred back to court or" there is substituted "Offender or parent referred back to court: offender".

(3) After paragraph (a) there is inserted—

"(aa) in Part 1A makes provision for what is to happen when a youth offender panel refers a parent or guardian to the court under section 22(2A) above, and".

6. In Schedule 1 to that Act (youth offender panels: further court proceedings), after Part 1 there is inserted—

"PART 1A
REFERRAL OF PARENT OR GUARDIAN FOR BREACH OF
SECTION 20 ORDER

Introductory

9A. (1) This Part of this Schedule applies where, under section 22(2A) of this Act, a youth offender panel refers an offender's parent or guardian to a youth court.

(2) In this Part of this Schedule—

(a) "the offender" means the offender whose parent or guardian is referred under section 22(2A);

(b) "the parent" means the parent or guardian so referred; and

(c) "the youth court" means a youth court as mentioned in section 22(2A).

Mode of referral to court

9B. The panel shall make the referral by sending a report to the youth court explaining why the parent is being referred to it.

Bringing the parent before the court

9C. (1) Where the youth court receives such a report it shall cause the parent to appear before it.

(2) For the purpose of securing the attendance of the parent before the court, a justice acting for the petty sessions area for which the court acts may—

(a) issue a summons requiring the parent to appear at the place and time specified in it; or

(b) if the report is substantiated on oath, issue a warrant for the parent's arrest.

(3) Any summons or warrant issued under sub-paragraph (2) above shall direct the parent to appear or be brought before the youth court.

Power of court to make parenting order: application of supplemental provisions

9D. (1) Where the parent appears or is brought before the youth court under paragraph 9C above, the court may make a parenting order in respect of the parent if—

(a) it is proved to the satisfaction of the court that the parent has failed without reasonable excuse to comply with the order under section 20 of this Act; and

(b) the court is satisfied that the parenting order would be desirable in the interests of preventing the commission of any further offence by the offender.

(2) A parenting order is an order which requires the parent—

(a) to comply, for a period not exceeding twelve months, with such requirements as are specified in the order, and

(b) subject to sub-paragraph (4) below, to attend, for a concurrent period not exceeding three months, such counselling or guidance programme as may be specified in directions given by the responsible officer.

(3) The requirements that may be specified under sub-paragraph (2)(a) above are those which the court considers desirable in the interests of preventing the commission of any further offence by the offender.

(4) A parenting order under this paragraph may, but need not, include a requirement mentioned in subsection (2)(b) above in any case where a parenting order under this paragraph or any other enactment has been made in respect of the parent on a previous occasion.

(5) A counselling or guidance programme which a parent is required to attend by virtue of subsection (2)(b) above may be or include a residential course but only if the court is satisfied—

(a) that the attendance of the parent at a residential course is likely to be more effective than his attendance at a non-residential course in preventing the commission of any further offence by the offender, and

(b) that any interference with family life which is likely to result from the attendance of the parent at a residential course is proportionate in all the circumstances.

(6) Before making a parenting order under this paragraph where the offender is aged under 16, the court shall obtain and consider information about his family circumstances and the likely effect of the order on those circumstances.

(7) Sections 8(3) and (8), 9(3) to (7) and 18(3) and (4) of the Crime and Disorder Act 1998 apply in relation to a parenting order made under this paragraph as they apply in relation to any other parenting order.

Appeal

9E. (1) An appeal shall lie to the Crown Court against the making of a parenting order under paragraph 9D above.

(2) Subsections (2) and (3) of section 10 of the Crime and Disorder Act 1998 (appeals against parenting orders) apply in relation to an appeal under this paragraph as they apply in relation to an appeal under subsection (1)(b) of that section.

Effect on section 20 order

9F. (1) The making of a parenting order under paragraph 9D above is without prejudice to the continuance of the order under section 20 of this Act.

(2) Section 63(1) to (4) of the Magistrates' Courts Act 1980 (power of magistrates' court to deal with person for breach of order, etc) apply (as well as section 22(2A) of this Act and this Part of this Schedule) in relation to an order under section 20 of this Act."

SCHEDULE 35

CRIMINAL RECORD CERTIFICATES: AMENDMENTS OF PART 5 OF POLICE ACT 1997

Section 328

1. The Police Act 1997 (c. 50) is amended as follows.

2. In section 112 (criminal conviction certificates), in subsection (1)(a), after "prescribed" there is inserted "manner and".

3. (1) Section 113 (criminal record certificates) is amended as follows.

(2) In subsection (1)—

(a) at the beginning there is inserted "Subject to subsection (4A)",

(b) in paragraph (a), after "prescribed" there is inserted "manner and", and

(c) in paragraph (b), after "pays" there is inserted "in the prescribed manner".

(3) After subsection (4) there is inserted—

"(4A) The Secretary of State may treat an application under this section as an application under section 115 if—

(a) in his opinion the certificate is required for a purpose prescribed under subsection (2) of that section,

(b) the registered person provides him with the statement required by subsection (2) of that section, and

(c) the applicant consents and pays to the Secretary of State the amount (if any) by which the fee payable in relation to an application under section 115 exceeds the fee paid in relation to the application under this section.".

4. (1) Section 115 (enhanced criminal record certificates) is amended as follows.

(2) In subsection (1)—

(a) at the beginning there is inserted "Subject to subsection (9A),",

(b) in paragraph (a), after "prescribed" there is inserted "manner and", and

(c) in paragraph (b), after "pays" there is inserted "in the prescribed manner".

(3) In subsection (2), for paragraphs (a) to (c) there is substituted "for such purposes as may be prescribed under this subsection".

(4) Subsections (3) to (5) and subsections (6C) to (6E) are omitted.

(5) After subsection (9) there is inserted—

"(9A) The Secretary of State may treat an application under this section as an application under section 113 if in his opinion the certificate is not required for a purpose prescribed under subsection (2).

(9B) Where by virtue of subsection (9A) the Secretary of State treats an application under this section as an application under section 113, he must refund to the applicant the amount (if any) by which the fee paid in relation to the application under this section exceeds the fee payable in relation to an application under section 113."

5. In section 116 (enhanced criminal record certificates: judicial appointments and Crown employment), in subsection (2)(b), for the words from "to which" onwards there is substituted "of such description as may be prescribed".

6. (1) Section 120 (registered persons) is amended as follows.

(2) For subsection (2) there is substituted—

"(2) Subject to regulations under section 120ZA and 120AA and to section 120A the Secretary of State shall include in the register any person who—

(a) applies to him in writing to be registered,

(b) satisfies the conditions in subsections (4) to (6), and

(c) has not in the period of two years ending with the date of the application been removed from the register under section 120A or 120AA."

(3) Subsection (3) is omitted.

7. After section 120 there is inserted—

"120ZA Regulations about registration

(1) The Secretary of State may by regulations make further provision about registration.

(2) Regulations under this section may in particular make provision for—

(a) the payment of fees,

(b) the information to be included in the register,

(c) the registration of any person to be subject to conditions,

   (d) the nomination by—
      (i) a body corporate or unincorporate, or
      (ii) a person appointed to an office by virtue of any enactment,
     of the individuals authorised to act for it or, as the case may be, him in relation to the countersigning of applications under this Part, and
   (e) the refusal by the Secretary of State, on such grounds as may be specified in or determined under the regulations, to accept or to continue to accept the nomination of a person as so authorised.
  (3) The provision which may be made by virtue of subsection (2)(c) includes provision—
   (a) for the registration or continued registration of any person to be subject to prescribed conditions or, if the regulations so provide, such conditions as the Secretary of State thinks fit, and
   (b) for the Secretary of State to vary or revoke those conditions.
  (4) The conditions imposed by virtue of subsection (2)(c) may in particular include conditions—
   (a) requiring a registered person, before he countersigns an application at an individual's request, to verify the identity of that individual in the prescribed manner,
   (b) requiring an application under section 113 or 115 to be transmitted by electronic means to the Secretary of State by the registered person who countersigns it, and
   (c) requiring a registered person to comply with any code of practice for the time being in force under section 122."
8. At the end of the sidenote to section 120A (refusal and cancellation of registration) there is inserted "on grounds related to disclosure".
9. After section 120A there is inserted—

"120AA Refusal, cancellation or suspension of registration on other grounds

  (1) Regulations may make provision enabling the Secretary of State in prescribed cases to refuse to register a person who, in the opinion of the Secretary of State, is likely to countersign fewer applications under this Part in any period of twelve months than a prescribed minimum number.
  (2) Subsection (3) applies where a registered person—
   (a) is, in the opinion of the Secretary of State, no longer likely to wish to countersign applications under this Part,
   (b) has, in any period of twelve months during which he was registered, countersigned fewer applications under this Part than the minimum number specified in respect of him by regulations under subsection (1), or
   (c) has failed to comply with any condition of his registration.
  (3) Subject to section 120AB, the Secretary of State may—
   (a) suspend that person's registration for such period not exceeding 6 months as the Secretary of State thinks fit, or
   (b) remove that person from the register.

120AB Procedure for cancellation or suspension under section 120AA

  (1) Before cancelling or suspending a person's registration by virtue of section 120AA, the Secretary of State must send him written notice of his intention to do so.
  (2) Every such notice must—

     (a) give the Secretary of State's reasons for proposing to cancel or suspend the registration, and

     (b) inform the person concerned of his right under subsection (3) to make representations.

(3) A person who receives such a notice may, within 21 days of service, make representations in writing to the Secretary of State as to why the registration should not be cancelled or suspended.

(4) After considering such representations, the Secretary of State must give the registered person written notice—

     (a) that at the end of a further period of six weeks beginning with the date of service, the person's registration will be cancelled or suspended, or

     (b) that he does not propose to take any further action.

(5) If no representations are received within the period mentioned in subsection (3) the Secretary of State may cancel or suspend the person's registration at the end of the period mentioned in that subsection.

(6) Subsection (1) does not prevent the Secretary of State from imposing on the registered person a lesser sanction than that specified in the notice under that subsection.

(7) Any notice under this section that is required to be given in writing may be given by being transmitted electronically.

(8) This section does not apply where—

     (a) the Secretary of State is satisfied, in the case of a registered person other than a body, that the person has died or is incapable, by reason of physical or mental impairment, of countersigning applications under this Part, or

     (b) the registered person has requested to be removed from the register.

(9) The Secretary of State may by regulations amend subsection (4)(a) by substituting for the period there specified, such other period as may be specified in the regulations."

10. After section 122 there is inserted—

"122A Delegation of functions of Secretary of State

(1) The Secretary of State may, to such extent and subject to such conditions as he thinks fit, delegate any relevant function of his under this Part to such person as he may determine.

(2) A function is relevant for the purposes of subsection (1) if it does not consist of a power—

     (a) to make regulations, or

     (b) to publish or revise a code of practice or to lay any such code before Parliament.

(3) A delegation under subsection (1) may be varied or revoked at any time."

11. After section 124 (offences: disclosure) there is inserted—

"124A Further offences: disclosure of information obtained in connection with delegated function

(1) Any person who is engaged in the discharge of functions conferred by this Part on the Secretary of State commits an offence if he discloses information which has been obtained by him in connection with those functions and which relates to a particular person unless he discloses the information, in the course of his duties,—

     (a) to another person engaged in the discharge of those functions,

     (b) to the chief officer of a police force in connection with a request under this Part to provide information to the Secretary of State, or

(c) to an applicant or registered person who is entitled under this Part to the information disclosed to him.

(2) Where information is disclosed to a person and the disclosure—

  (a) is an offence under subsection (1), or

  (b) would be an offence under subsection (1) but for subsection (3)(a), (d) or (e), the person to whom the information is disclosed commits an offence if he discloses it to any other person.

(3) Subsection (1) does not apply to a disclosure of information which is made—

  (a) with the written consent of the person to whom the information relates,

  (b) to a government department,

  (c) to a person appointed to an office by virtue of any enactment,

  (d) in accordance with an obligation to provide information under or by virtue of any enactment, or

  (e) for some other purpose specified in regulations made by the Secretary of State.

(4) A person who is guilty of an offence under this section shall be liable on summary conviction to imprisonment for a term not exceeding 51 weeks or to a fine not exceeding level 3 on the standard scale, or to both.

(5) In relation to an offence committed before the commencement of section 281(5) of the Criminal Justice Act 2003, the reference in subsection (4) to 51 weeks is to be read as a reference to 6 months."

12. In section 125 (regulations)—

  (a) subsection (3) is omitted, and

  (b) in subsection (4), the words "to which subsection (3) does not apply" are omitted.

SCHEDULE 36
FURTHER MINOR AND CONSEQUENTIAL AMENDMENTS
Section 331

PART 1
BAIL

Bail Act 1976 (c. 63)

1. The Bail Act 1976 is amended as follows.

2. (1) Section 5(6A)(a) (supplementary provisions about decisions on bail) is amended as follows.

  (2) After "examination)" there is inserted ", section 52(5) of the Crime and Disorder Act 1998 (adjournment of proceedings under section 51 etc)".

  (3) After sub-paragraph (ii) there is inserted—

    "(iia) section 17C (intention as to plea: adjournment), or"

  (4) After sub-paragraph (iii) there is inserted "or

    (iiia) section 24C (intention as to plea by child or young person: adjournment),".

3. In Part 3 of Schedule 1 (interpretation) for paragraph 2 there is substituted—

  "2 References in this Schedule to previous grants of bail include—

    (a) bail granted before the coming into force of this Act;

    (b) as respects the reference in paragraph 2A of Part 1 of this Schedule (as substituted by section 14(1) of the Criminal Justice Act 2003), bail granted before the coming into force of that paragraph;

(c) as respects the references in paragraph 6 of Part 1 of this Schedule (as substituted by section 15(1) of the Criminal Justice Act 2003), bail granted before the coming into force of that paragraph;

(d) as respects the references in paragraph 9AA of Part 1 of this Schedule, bail granted before the coming into force of that paragraph;

(e) as respects the references in paragraph 9AB of Part 1 of this Schedule, bail granted before the coming into force of that paragraph;

(f) as respects the reference in paragraph 5 of Part 2 of this Schedule (as substituted by section 13(4) of the Criminal Justice Act 2003), bail granted before the coming into force of that paragraph."

Supreme Court Act 1981 (c. 54)

4. (1) Section 81 of the Supreme Court Act 1981 (bail) is amended as follows.

(2) In subsection (1)(g) after "examination)" there is inserted ", section 52(5) of the Crime and Disorder Act 1998 (adjournment of proceedings under section 51 etc)".

(3) In subsection (1)(g) the word "or" at the end of sub-paragraph (ii) is omitted and after that sub-paragraph there is inserted—

"(iia) section 17C (intention as to plea: adjournment);".

(4) In subsection (1)(g) after sub-paragraph (iii) there is inserted "or

(iiia) section 24C (intention as to plea by child or young person: adjournment);".

Police and Criminal Evidence Act 1984 (c. 60)

5. In section 38(2A) of the Police and Criminal Evidence Act 1984 (bail granted by custody officer after charge)—

(a) for "2" there is substituted "2(1)", and

(b) after "1976" there is inserted "(disregarding paragraph 2(2) of that Part)".

PART 2
CHARGING ETC

Criminal Law Act 1977 (c. 45)

6. In section 39 of the Criminal Law Act 1977 (service of summons and citation throughout United Kingdom) for subsection (1) there is substituted—

"(1) The following documents, namely—

(a) a summons requiring a person charged with an offence to appear before a court in England or Wales,

(b) a written charge (within the meaning of section 29 of the Criminal Justice Act 2003) charging a person with an offence,

(c) a requisition (within the meaning of that section) requiring a person charged with an offence to appear before a court in England or Wales, and

(d) any other document which, by virtue of any enactment, may or must be served on a person with, or at the same time as, a document mentioned in paragraph (a), (b) or (c) above,

may, in such manner as may be prescribed by rules of court, be served on him in
Scotland or Northern Ireland."

Magistrates' Courts Act 1980 (c. 43)

7. The Magistrates' Courts Act 1980 is amended as follows.
8. (1) Section 1 (issue of summons to accused or warrant for his arrest) is amended as follows.
   (2) In subsection (3) after "section" there is inserted "upon an information being laid".
   (3) In subsection (4) after "summons" there is inserted ", or a written charge and requisition,".
   (4) In subsection (6) after "has" there is inserted ", or a written charge and requisition have,".
   (5) After subsection (6) there is inserted—
      "(6A) Where the offence charged is an indictable offence and a written charge and
      requisition have previously been issued, a warrant may be issued under this
      section by a justice of the peace upon a copy of the written charge (rather than
      an information) being laid before the justice by a public prosecutor."
   (6) After subsection (7) there is inserted—
      "(7A) For the purposes of subsection (6A) above, a copy of a written charge may be
      laid before, and a warrant under this section may be issued by, a single justice of
      the peace."
9. In section 150(1) (interpretation of other terms) after the definition of "prescribed" there is
   inserted—
   " "public prosecutor", "requisition" and "written charge" have the same meaning as in
   section 29 of the Criminal Justice Act 2003;".

Prosecution of Offences Act 1985 (c. 23)

10. (1) Section 15 of the Prosecution of Offences Act 1985 (interpretation) is amended as follows.
    (2) In subsection (1) after the definition of "public authority" there is inserted—
       " "public prosecutor", "requisition" and "written charge" have the same meaning as in
       section 29 of the Criminal Justice Act 2003;".
    (3) In subsection (2), after paragraph (b) there is inserted—
       "(ba) where a public prosecutor issues a written charge and requisition for the offence,
       when the written charge and requisition are issued;".

Criminal Justice and Public Order Act 1994 (c. 33)

11. (1) Section 51 of the Criminal Justice and Public Order Act 1994 (intimidation, etc, of
    witnesses, jurors and others) is amended as follows.
    (2) In subsection (9), for the word "and" at the end of the definition of "potential" there is
    substituted—
       " "public prosecutor", "requisition" and "written charge" have the same meaning as in
       section 29 of the Criminal Justice Act 2003;"
    (3) In subsection (10)(a), after sub-paragraph (i) there is inserted—
       "(ia) when a public prosecutor issues a written charge and requisition in respect of the
       offence;".

Drug Trafficking Act 1994 (c. 37)

12. (1) Section 60 of the Drug Trafficking Act 1994 (prosecution by order of Commissioners of Customs and Excise) is amended as follows.

(2) In subsection (6) for the word "and" at the end of the definition of "officer" there is substituted—

""public prosecutor", "requisition" and "written charge" have the same meaning as in section 29 of the Criminal Justice Act 2003;".

(3) In subsection (6A), after paragraph (a) there is inserted—

"(aa) when a public prosecutor issues a written charge and requisition in respect of the offence;".

Merchant Shipping Act 1995 (c. 21)

13. (1) Section 145 of the Merchant Shipping Act 1995 (interpretation of section 144) is amended as follows.

(2) In subsection (2)(a), after sub-paragraph (i) there is inserted—

"(ia) when a public prosecutor issues a written charge and requisition in respect of the offence;".

(3) After subsection (2) there is inserted—

"(2A) In subsection (2) above "public prosecutor", "requisition" and "written charge" have the same meaning as in section 29 of the Criminal Justice Act 2003."

Terrorism Act 2000 (c. 11)

14. (1) Paragraph 11 of Schedule 4 to the Terrorism Act 2000 (proceedings for an offence: timing) is amended as follows.

(2) In sub-paragraph (1), after paragraph (a) there is inserted—

"(aa) when a public prosecutor issues a written charge and requisition in respect of the offence;".

(3) After sub-paragraph (2) there is inserted—

"(2A) In sub-paragraph (1) "public prosecutor", "requisition" and "written charge" have the same meaning as in section 29 of the Criminal Justice Act 2003."

Proceeds of Crime Act 2002 (c. 29)

15. (1) Section 85 of the Proceeds of Crime Act 2002 (proceedings) is amended as follows.

(2) In subsection (1), after paragraph (a) there is inserted—

"(aa) when a public prosecutor issues a written charge and requisition in respect of the offence;".

(3) After subsection (8) there is inserted—

"(9) In this section "public prosecutor", "requisition" and "written charge" have the same meaning as in section 29 of the Criminal Justice Act 2003."

Crime (International Co-operation) Act 2003 (c. 32)

16. After section 4 of the Crime (International Co-operation) Act 2003 there is inserted—

"4A General requirements for service of written charge or requisition

(1) This section applies to the following documents issued for the purposes of criminal proceedings in England and Wales by a prosecutor-
  (a) a written charge (within the meaning of section 29 of the Criminal Justice Act 2003),
  (b) a requisition (within the meaning of that section).

(2) The written charge or requisition may be issued in spite of the fact that the person on whom it is to be served is outside the United Kingdom.

(3) Where the written charge or requisition is to be served outside the United Kingdom and the prosecutor believes that the person on whom it is to be served does not understand English, the written charge or requisition must be accompanied by a translation of it in an appropriate language.

(4) A written charge or requisition served outside the United Kingdom must be accompanied by a notice giving any information required to be given by rules of court.

(5) If a requisition is served outside the United Kingdom, no obligation under the law of England and Wales to comply with the requisition is imposed by virtue of the service.

(6) Accordingly, failure to comply with the requisition is not a ground for issuing a warrant to secure the attendance of the person in question.

(7) But the requisition may subsequently be served on the person in question in the United Kingdom (with the usual consequences for non-compliance).

4B Service of written charge or requisition otherwise than by post

(1) A written charge or requisition to which section 4A applies may, instead of being served by post, be served on a person outside the United Kingdom in accordance with arrangements made by the Secretary of State.

(2) But where the person is in a participating country, the written charge or requisition may be served in accordance with those arrangements only if one of the following conditions is met.

(3) The conditions are—
  (a) that the correct address of the person is unknown,
  (b) that it has not been possible to serve the written charge or requisition by post,
  (c) that there are good reasons for thinking that service by post will not be effective or is inappropriate."

PART 3
DISCLOSURE

Prosecution of Offences Act 1985 (c. 23)

17. In section 22B of the Prosecution of Offences Act 1985 (re-institution of proceedings stayed under section 22(4) or 22A(5)), in subsection (5)(a) for "section 3, 4, 7 or 9" there is substituted "section 3, 4 or 7A".

645

Criminal Justice Act 1987 (c. 38)

18. In section 9 of the Criminal Justice Act 1987 (preparatory hearings in serious fraud cases etc.), paragraphs (i) and (iii) of subsection (5) are omitted.

Criminal Justice (Serious Fraud) (Northern Ireland) Order 1988
(S.I. 1988/1846 (N.I. 16))

19. In Article 8 of the Criminal Justice (Serious Fraud) (Northern Ireland) Order 1988 (preparatory hearings in serious fraud cases etc.), sub-paragraphs (i) and (iii) of paragraph (5) are omitted.

Criminal Procedure and Investigations Act 1996 (c. 25)

20. The Criminal Procedure and Investigations Act 1996 is amended as follows.
21. In section 3 (primary disclosure by prosecutor), for the heading there is substituted **"Initial duty of prosecutor to disclose"**.
22. In section 4 (primary disclosure: further provisions), in the heading for **"Primary disclosure"** there is substituted **"Initial duty to disclose"**.
23. In section 5 (compulsory disclosure by accused), subsections (6) to (9) are omitted.
24. In section 6 (voluntary disclosure by accused), subsection (3) is omitted.
25. Section 7 (secondary disclosure by prosecutor) shall cease to have effect.
26. Section 9 (continuing duty of prosecutor to disclose) shall cease to have effect.
27. In section 10 (prosecutor's failure to observe time limits), in subsection (1), for paragraph (b) there is substituted—
"(b) purports to act under section 7A(5) after the end of the period which, by virtue of section 12, is the relevant period for section 7A."
28. In section 12 (time limits)—
    (a) in subsection (1), for "and 7" there is substituted", 6B, 6C and 7A(5)";
    (b) in subsection (5), for "7" there is substituted "7A(5)".
29. In section 13 (time limits: transitional), for subsection (2) there is substituted—
    "(2) As regards a case in relation to which no regulations under section 12 have come into force for the purposes of section 7A, section 7A(5) shall have effect as if—
    (a) in paragraph (a) for the words from "during the period" to the end, and
    (b) in paragraph (b) for "during that period",
    there were substituted "as soon as is reasonably practicable after the accused gives the statement in question"."
30. In section 14 (public interest: review for summary trials), in subsection (2)(a), for "7(5), 8(5) or 9(8)" there is substituted "7A(8) or 8(5)".
31. In section 15 (public interest: review in other cases), in subsection (2)(a), for "7(5), 8(5)" there is substituted "7A(8) or 8(5)".
32. In section 16 (applications: opportunity to be heard), in paragraph (a) and in the words after paragraph (c), for "7(5), 8(5), 9(8)" there is substituted "7A(8), 8(5)".
33. In section 17 (confidentiality of disclosed information), in subsection (1)(a), for "7, 9" there is substituted "7A".
34. In section 19 (rules of court) in subsection (2)(b) and (d), for "7(5), 8(2) or (5), 9(8)" there is substituted "5(5B), 6B(6), 6E(5), 7A(8), 8(2) or (5)".
35. In section 20 (other statutory rules as to disclosure)—
    (a) subsection (2) is omitted, and

    (b) in subsection (5)(a), for "sections 3 to 9" there is substituted "sections 3 to 8".

36. In section 31 (preparatory hearings in complex cases etc.), paragraphs (a) and (c) of subsection (6) are omitted.

37. (1) Section 77 (orders and regulations) is amended as follows.

    (2) In subsection (5)—

        (a) after "No" there is inserted "regulations or", and

        (b) after "section" there is inserted "6A or".

    (3) In subsection (6)(b) after "regulations" there is inserted "(other than regulations under section 6A)".

38. In Schedule 4 (modifications for Northern Ireland), in paragraph 7, for "3(6), 7(5), 8(5) or 9(8)" there is substituted "3(6), 7A(8) or 8(5)".

Sexual Offences (Protected Material) Act 1997 (c. 39)

39. In section 9(4) of the Sexual Offences (Protected Material) Act 1997 (which, when in force, will add a subsection (6) to section 1 of the Criminal Procedure and Investigations Act 1996), for "Section 3, 7 or 9" there is substituted "section 3 or 7A".

PART 4

TRIALS ON INDICTMENT WITHOUT A JURY

Indictments Act 1915 (c. 90)

40. (1) Section 5 of the Indictments Act 1915 (orders for amendment of indictment, separate trial and postponement of trial) is amended as follows.

    (2) In subsection (5)(a) for "are to" there is substituted "(if there is one)".

    (3) In subsection (5)(b) after "discharged" there is inserted "under paragraph (a)".

Criminal Law Act 1967 (c. 58)

41. In section 6(4) of the Criminal Law Act 1967 (trial of offences) after "jury" there is inserted "or otherwise act".

Criminal Justice Act 1967 (c. 80)

42. In section 17 of the Criminal Justice Act 1967 (entry of verdict of not guilty by order of a judge)—

    (a) for "the defendant being given in charge to a jury" there is substituted "any further steps being taken in the proceedings", and

    (b) after "verdict of a jury" there is inserted "or a court".

Criminal Law Act (Northern Ireland) 1967 (c. 18)

43. In section 6(3) of the Criminal Law Act (Northern Ireland) 1967 (trial of offences) after "jury" there is inserted "or otherwise act".

Criminal Appeal Act 1968 (c. 19)

44. In section 7(2)(c) of the Criminal Appeal Act 1968 (power to order retrial)—
    (a) for "the jury were discharged from giving a verdict" there is substituted "no verdict was given", and
    (b) for "convicting him" there is substituted "his being convicted".

Judicature (Northern Ireland) Act 1978 (c. 23)

45. (1) Section 48 of the Judicature (Northern Ireland) Act 1978 (committal for trial on indictment) is amended as follows.
    (2) In subsection (6A) for "the jury are sworn" there is substituted "the time when the jury are sworn".
    (3) After subsection (6A) there is inserted—
        "(6B) The reference in subsection (6A) to the time when the jury are sworn includes the time when the jury would be sworn but for—
            (a) the making of an order under Part 7 of the Criminal Justice Act 2003, or
            (b) the application of section 75 of the Terrorism Act 2000."

Criminal Appeal (Northern Ireland) Act 1980 (c. 47)

46. In section 6(3)(c) of the Criminal Appeal (Northern Ireland) Act 1980 (power to order retrial) for "the jury were discharged from giving a verdict" there is substituted "no verdict was given".

Supreme Court Act 1981 (c.54)

47. (1) Section 76 of the Supreme Court Act 1981 (committal for trial: alteration of place of trial) is amended as follows.
    (2) In subsection (2A) for "the jury are sworn" there is substituted "the time when the jury are sworn"
    (3) After subsection (2A) there is inserted—
        "(2B) The reference in subsection (2A) to the time when the jury are sworn includes the time when the jury would be sworn but for the making of an order under Part 7 of the Criminal Justice Act 2003."

Police and Criminal Evidence Act 1984 (c. 60)

48. (1) Section 77 of the Police and Criminal Evidence Act 1984 (confessions of mentally handicapped persons) is amended as follows.
    (2) In subsection (1) after "indictment" there is inserted "with a jury".
    (3) In subsection (2) after "indictment" there is inserted "with a jury".
    (4) After subsection (2) there is inserted—
        "(2A) In any case where at the trial on indictment without a jury of a person for an offence it appears to the court that a warning under subsection (1) above would be required if the trial were with a jury, the court shall treat the case as one in which there is a special need for caution before convicting the accused on his confession."

Prosecution of Offences Act 1985 (c.23)

49. The Prosecution of Offences Act 1985 is amended as follows.

50. In section 7A(6)(a) (powers of non-legal staff) for "by a jury" there is substituted "on indictment".

51. (1) Section 22 (power of Secretary of State to set time limits in relation to preliminary stages of criminal proceedings) is amended as follows.

   (2) In subsection (11A)—

      (a) for "when a jury is sworn" there is substituted "at the time when a jury is sworn",

      (b) for "a jury is sworn" there is substituted "the time when a jury is sworn".

   (3) After that subsection there is inserted—

      "(11AA) The references in subsection (11A) above to the time when a jury is sworn include the time when that jury would be sworn but for the making of an order under Part 7 of the Criminal Justice Act 2003."

Criminal Justice Act 1987 (c.38)

52. The Criminal Justice Act 1987 is amended as follows.

53. (1) Section 7 (power to order preparatory hearing) is amended as follows.

   (2) In subsection (1) for "the jury are sworn" there is substituted "the time when the jury are sworn".

   (3) After subsection (2) there is inserted—

      "(2A) The reference in subsection (1) above to the time when the jury are sworn includes the time when the jury would be sworn but for the making of an order under Part 7 of the Criminal Justice Act 2003."

54. (1) Section 9 (the preparatory hearing) is amended as follows.

   (2) In subsection (4)(b) for "the jury" there is substituted "a jury".

   (3) In subsection (13) for "no jury shall be sworn" there is substituted "the preparatory hearing shall not be concluded".

55. (1) Section 10 (later stages of trial) is amended as follows.

   (2) In subsection (2) after "jury" there is inserted "or, in the case of a trial without a jury, the judge".

   (3) In subsection (3) for "deciding whether to give leave" there is substituted "doing anything under subsection (2) above or in deciding whether to do anything under it".

   (4) In subsection (4) for "Except as provided by this section" there is substituted "Except as provided by this section, in the case of a trial with a jury".

Criminal Justice (Serious Fraud) (Northern Ireland) Order 1988
(S.I. 1988/1846 (N.I. 16))

56. The Criminal Justice (Serious Fraud) (Northern Ireland) Order 1988 is amended as follows.

57. (1) Article 6 (power to order preparatory hearing) is amended as follows.

   (2) In paragraph (1) for "the jury are sworn" there is substituted "the time when the jury are sworn".

   (3) After paragraph (2) there is inserted—

      "(2A) The reference in paragraph (1) to the time when the jury are sworn includes the time when the jury would be sworn but for—

    (a) the making of an order under Part 7 of the Criminal Justice Act 2003, or

    (b) the application of section 75 of the Terrorism Act 2000."

58. (1) Article 8 (the preparatory hearing) is amended as follows.

    (2) In paragraph (4)(b) for "the jury" there is substituted "a jury".

    (3) In paragraph (12) for "no jury shall be sworn" there is substituted "the preparatory hearing shall not be concluded".

59. (1) Article 9 (later stages of trial) (as originally enacted) is amended as follows.

    (2) In paragraph (1) after "jury" there is inserted "or, in the case of a trial without a jury, the judge".

    (3) In paragraph (2) for "deciding whether to give leave" there is substituted "doing anything under paragraph (1) or in deciding whether to do anything under it".

    (4) In paragraph (3) for "Except as provided by this Article" there is substituted "Except as provided by this Article, in the case of a trial with a jury".

60. (1) Article 9 (later stages of trial) (as substituted by paragraph 6 of Schedule 3 to the Criminal Procedure and Investigations Act 1996 (c. 25)) is amended as follows.

    (2) In paragraph (2) after "jury" there is inserted "or, in the case of a trial without a jury, the judge".

    (3) In paragraph (3) for "deciding whether to give leave" there is substituted "doing anything under paragraph (2) or in deciding whether to do anything under it".

    (4) In paragraph (4) for "Except as provided by this Article" there is substituted "Except as provided by this Article, in the case of a trial with a jury".

Police and Criminal Evidence (Northern Ireland) Order 1989
(S.I. 1989/1341 (N.I. 12))

61. (1) Article 75 of the Police and Criminal Evidence (Northern Ireland) Order 1989 (confessions of mentally handicapped persons) is amended as follows.

    (2) In paragraph (1) after "indictment" there is inserted "with a jury".

    (3) In paragraph (2) after "indictment" there is inserted "with a jury".

    (4) After paragraph (2) there is inserted—

       "(2A) In any case where at the trial on indictment without a jury of a person for an offence it appears to the court that a warning under paragraph (1) would be required if the trial were with a jury, the court shall treat the case as one in which there is a special need for caution before convicting the accused on his confession."

Criminal Justice and Public Order Act 1994 (c. 33)

62. The Criminal Justice and Public Order Act 1994 is amended as follows.

63. In section 35(2) (effect of accused's silence at trial) after "indictment" there is inserted "with a jury".

64. In section 51(10)(b) (intimidation of witnesses, jurors and others) after "finding" there is inserted "otherwise than in circumstances where the proceedings are continued without a jury".

Criminal Procedure and Investigations Act 1996 (c.25)

65. The Criminal Procedure and Investigations Act 1996 is amended as follows.

66. (1) Section 29 (power to order preparatory hearing) is amended as follows.

(2) In subsection (1)(a) for "the jury are sworn" there is substituted "the time when the jury are sworn".

(3) After subsection (4) there is inserted—

"(5) The reference in subsection (1)(a) to the time when the jury are sworn includes the time when the jury would be sworn but for the making of an order under Part 7 of the Criminal Justice Act 2003."

67. In section 31(4)(b) (the preparatory hearing) for "the jury" there is substituted "a jury".

68. (1) Section 34 (later stages of trial) is amended as follows.

(2) In subsection (2) after "jury" there is inserted "or, in the case of a trial without a jury, the judge".

(3) In subsection (3) for "deciding whether to give leave" there is substituted "doing anything under subsection (2) or in deciding whether to do anything under it".

(4) In subsection (4) for "Except as provided by this section" there is substituted "Except as provided by this section, in the case of a trial with a jury".

69. In section 35(2) (appeals to Court of Appeal) for "no jury shall be sworn" there is substituted "the preparatory hearing shall not be concluded".

70. In section 36(2) (appeals to House of Lords) for "no jury shall be sworn" there is substituted "the preparatory hearing shall not be concluded".

71. (1) Section 39 (meaning of pre-trial hearing) is amended as follows.

(2) In subsection (3)—

(a) for "when a jury is sworn" there is substituted "at the time when a jury is sworn",

(b) for "a jury is sworn" there is substituted "the time when a jury is sworn".

(3) After that subsection there is inserted—

"(4) The references in subsection (3) to the time when a jury is sworn include the time when that jury would be sworn but for the making of an order under Part 7 of the Criminal Justice Act 2003."

72. (1) Schedule 4 (modifications for Northern Ireland) is amended as follows.

(2) In paragraph 15 after the substituted version of section 39(2) there is inserted—

"(2A) But, for the purposes of this Part, a hearing of the kind mentioned in section 45(2)(b) of the Criminal Justice Act 2003 is not a pre-trial hearing."

(3) In paragraph 15 in paragraph (b) of the substituted version of section 39(3)—

(a) for "when a jury is sworn" there is substituted "at the time when a jury is sworn", and

(b) for "a jury is sworn" there is substituted "the time when a jury is sworn".

(4) After paragraph 15 there is inserted—

"15A In section 39(4) for "(3)" substitute "(3)(b)"."

Crime and Disorder Act 1998 (c. 37)

73. In paragraph 2(2) of Schedule 3 to the Crime and Disorder Act 1998 (applications for dismissal) for "a jury properly to convict him" there is substituted "him to be properly convicted".

Youth Justice and Criminal Evidence Act 1999 (c. 23)

74. The Youth Justice and Criminal Evidence Act 1999 is amended as follows.

75. In section 32 (warning to jury) after "indictment" there is inserted "with a jury".

76. In section 39(1) (warning to jury) after "indictment" there is inserted "with a jury".

Anti-terrorism, Crime and Security Act 2001 (c. 24)

77. In paragraph 19(6)(c) of Schedule 1 to the Anti-terrorism, Crime and Security Act 2001 (general interpretation) after "finding" there is inserted "otherwise than in circumstances where the proceedings are continued without a jury".

Proceeds of Crime Act 2002 (c. 29)

78. In section 316(9)(c) of the Proceeds of Crime Act 2002 (general interpretation) after "finding" there is inserted "otherwise than in circumstances where the proceedings are continued without a jury".

PART 5
EVIDENCE

Criminal Procedure Act 1865 (c. 18)

79. In section 6 of the Criminal Procedure Act 1865 (witness's conviction for offence may be proved if not admitted)—
(a) for "A witness may be" there is substituted "If, upon a witness being lawfully";
(b) the words "and upon being so questioned, if" are omitted.

Criminal Evidence Act 1898 (c. 36)

80. In section 1 of the Criminal Evidence Act 1898 (defendant as witness)—
(a) at the beginning of subsection (2) there is inserted "Subject to section 101 of the Criminal Justice Act 2003 (admissibility of evidence of defendant's bad character),";
(b) subsection (3) is omitted.

Army Act 1955 (c. 18)

81. In section 99(1) of the Army Act 1955 (rules of evidence) after "courts-martial etc)" there is inserted "to Schedules 6 and 7 to the Criminal Justice Act 2003".

Air Force Act 1955 (c. 19)

82. In section 99(1) of the Air Force Act 1955 (rules of evidence) after "courts-martial etc)" there is inserted "to Schedules 6 and 7 to the Criminal Justice Act 2003".

Naval Discipline Act 1957 (c. 53)

83. In section 64A(1) of the Naval Discipline Act 1957 (rules of evidence) after "courts-martial etc)" there is inserted "to Schedules 6 and 7 to the Criminal Justice Act 2003".

Armed Forces Act 1976 (c. 52)

84. In paragraph 11(1) of Schedule 3 to the Armed Forces Act 1976 (rules of evidence) after "paragraph 12 below" there is inserted "to Schedules 6 and 7 to the Criminal Justice Act 2003".

Police and Criminal Evidence Act 1984 (c. 60)

85. (1) Section 74 of the Police and Criminal Evidence Act 1984 (conviction as evidence of commission of offence) is amended as follows.
  (2) In subsection (1) (commission of offence by non-defendant) for the words from ", where to do so" to "committed that offence" there is substituted "that that person committed that offence, where evidence of his having done so is admissible".
  (3) In subsection (3) (commission of offence by defendant) the words from "in so far" to "he is charged," are omitted.

PART 6
MISCELLANEOUS

Criminal Appeal Act 1968 (c. 19)

86. The Criminal Appeal Act 1968 is amended as follows.
87. In section 31(1) (powers of Court of Appeal exercisable by single judge) after paragraph (a) there is inserted—
  "(aa) the power to give leave under section 14(4B) of the Criminal Appeal Act 1995;".
88. In section 31A (powers of Court of Appeal exercisable by registrar) after subsection (4) there is inserted—
  "(5) In this section "respondent" includes a person who will be a respondent if leave to appeal is granted."
89. In section 45 (construction of references to Court of Appeal)—
  (a) in subsection (1), for "section 44A" there is substituted "sections 44A and 51",
  (b) in subsection (2) after "sections" there is inserted "23A,".
90. (1) Section 51 (interpretation) is amended as follows.
  (2) In subsection (1) the definition of "the defendant" is omitted.
  (3) After that subsection there is inserted—
  "(1A) In Part 2 of this Act "the defendant"—
      (a) in relation to an appeal under section 33(1) of this Act against a decision of the Court of Appeal on an appeal under Part 1 of this Act, means the person who was the appellant before the Court of Appeal,
      (b) in relation to an appeal under section 33(1) of this Act against any other decision, means a defendant in the proceedings before the Crown Court who was a party to the proceedings before the Court of Appeal, and
      (c) in relation to an appeal under section 33(1B) of this Act, shall be construed in accordance with section 33(4) of this Act;
  and, subject to section 33(1A) of this Act, "prosecutor" shall be construed accordingly."

Criminal Appeal (Northern Ireland) Act 1980 (c. 47)

91. The Criminal Appeal (Northern Ireland) Act 1980 is amended as follows.

92. (1) Section 19 (legal aid) is amended as follows.

   (2) In subsection (1) after "an appeal" there is inserted "under this Part of this Act".

   (3) In subsection (1A) for "for the purpose" there is substituted "in respect".

   (4) In subsection (1A)(a)—

       (a) the words "application for leave to" are omitted, and

       (b) after "hearings)" there is inserted "or section 47 of the Criminal Justice Act 2003".

   (5) For subsection (1A)(b) there is substituted—

       "(b) any other appeal to the Court of Appeal under any Northern Ireland legislation (whenever passed or made) from proceedings before the Crown Court; or

       (c) an application for leave to appeal in relation to an appeal mentioned in paragraph (a) or (b) above."

   (6) After subsection (1A) there is inserted—

       "(1B) The Crown Court or the Court of Appeal may order that an acquitted person shall be given legal aid in respect of an application made in relation to him under section 76 of the Criminal Justice Act 2003."

   (7) In subsection (3) for "an appellant" there is substituted "a person".

93. (1) Section 28 (costs) is amended as follows.

   (2) In subsection (2)(a) for "this Part" there is substituted "section 19(1)".

   (3) After subsection (2) there is inserted—

       "(2AA) The expenses of any solicitor or counsel assigned to a person pursuant to a grant of legal aid under section 19(1A) or (1B) of this Act shall, up to an amount allowed by the Master (Taxing Office), be defrayed by the Lord Chancellor."

   (4) In subsection (2A) after "(2)(a)" there is inserted "or (2AA)".

   (5) In subsection (2G)—

       (a) after "(2)(a)" there is inserted "or (2AA)", and

       (b) for "subsection (2)" there is substituted "subsections (2) and (2AA)".

94. For section 31(3) (definition of defendant and prosecutor) there is substituted—

   "(3) In this Part of this Act "the defendant"—

       (a) in relation to an appeal under subsection (1) above against a decision of the Court on an appeal under Part 1 of this Act, means the person who was the appellant before the Court;

       (b) in relation to an appeal under subsection (1) above against any other decision, means a defendant in the proceedings before the Crown Court who was a party to the proceedings before the Court;

       (c) in relation to an appeal under subsection (1B) above, shall be construed in accordance with ubsection (4) below;

   and, subject to subsection (1A) above, "prosecutor" shall be construed accordingly."

95. In section 45 (powers of Court of Appeal exercisable by single judge) after subsection (3B) there is inserted—

   "(3C) Subject to section 44(4) above, the power of the Court of Appeal to give leave under section 14(4B) of the Criminal Appeal Act 1995 may be exercised by a single judge of the Court."

Criminal Justice Act 1988 (c. 33)

96. In section 36 of the Criminal Justice Act 1988 (reviews of sentencing)—

(a) in subsection (3), for "10" there is substituted "11",

(b) in subsection (9)(b), for "10 and 35(1)" there is substituted "11 and 35(1)".

Criminal Appeal Act 1995 (c. 35)

97. In section 15(2)(a) of the Criminal Appeal Act 1995 (investigations by Criminal Cases Review Commission for Court of Appeal) for "case", in both places where it occurs, there is substituted "appeal or application for leave to appeal".

Powers of Criminal Courts (Sentencing) Act 2000 (c. 6)

98. In section 159 of the Powers of Criminal Courts (Sentencing) Act 2000 (execution of process between England and Wales and Scotland), for "paragraph 3(2) of Schedule 1" there is substituted "paragraph 3(2) or 9C(2) of Schedule 1".

SCHEDULE 37
REPEALS

Section 332

PART 1
REPEALS RELATING TO AMENDMENTS OF POLICE AND CRIMINAL
EVIDENCE ACT 1984

Short title and chapter	*Extent of repeal*
Police and Criminal Evidence Act 1984 (c. 60)	In section 1(8), the word "and" at the end of paragraph (c).
	In section 54(1), the words "and record or . cause to be recorded"
	In section 63(3)(a), the words "is in police detention or".
	In section 67—
	(a) the word "such" in subsections (9), (10)(a),(b) and (c) and in both places where it occurs in subsection (11), and
	(b) the words "of practice to which this section applies" in subsection (9A).
	In section 113—
	(a) in subsection (4), the words "issued under that subsection",
	(b) in subsection (8), the words "of practice issued under this section", and
	(c) in subsection (10), the word "such" in both places where it occurs.
Criminal Justice and Public Order Act 1994 (c. 33)	Section 29(3).
Armed Forces Act 2001 (c. 19)	In section 2(9), the word "and" at the end

	of paragraph (c)
Police Reform Act 2002 (c. 30)	In Schedule 7, paragraph 9(1) and (6).

PART 2

BAIL

Short title and chapter	*Extent of repeal*
Criminal Justice Act 1967 (c. 80)	In section 22, in subsection (1) the words "subject to section 25 of the Criminal Justice and Public Order Act 1994" and in subsection (3) the words from "except that" to the end.
Courts Act 1971 (c. 23)	In Schedule 8, in paragraph 48(b), the word "22(3)".
Bail Act 1976 (c. 63)	In section 3(6), the words "to secure that".
	In section 3A(5), the words "for the purpose of preventing that person from".
	In section 5, in subsection (3), the words from "with a view" to "another court", and in subsection (6), in paragraph (a) the words "to the High Court or" and paragraph (b).
	In section 5A(2), in the substituted version of section 5(3), the words from "with a view" to "vary the conditions".
Supreme Court Act 1981 (c. 54)	In section 81(1)(g), the word "or" at the end of sub-paragraph (ii).
Criminal Justice Act 1991 (c. 53)	In Schedule 11, in paragraph 22(2), the words "and the words" onwards.
Criminal Justice and Public Order Act 1994 (c. 33)	Section 26. In Schedule 10, paragraphs 15 and 34.
Powers of Criminal Courts (Sentencing) Act 2000 (c. 6)	In Schedule 9, paragraph 87(b).

PART 3

DISCLOSURE

Short title and chapter	*Extent of repeal*
Criminal Justice Act 1987 (c. 38)	In section 9(5)(i) and (iii).
Criminal Justice (Serious Fraud) (Northern Ireland) Order 1988 (S.I. 1988/1846 (N.I. 16))	Article 8(5)(i) and (iii).
Criminal Procedure and Investigations Act 1996 (c. 25)	Section 5(6) to (9). Section 6(3). Section 7.

Section 9.
Section 20(2).
Section 31(6)(a) and (c).

PART 4

ALLOCATION AND SENDING OF OFFENCES

Short title and chapter	Extent of repeal
Bankers' Books Evidence Act 1879 (c. 11)	In section 4, the paragraph beginning "Where the proceedings". In section 5, the paragraph beginning "Where the proceedings".
Explosive Substances Act 1883 (c. 3)	Section 6(3).
Criminal Justice Act 1925 (c. 86)	Section 49(2).
Administration of Justice (Miscellaneous Provisions) Act 1933 (c. 36)	In section 2(2), paragraphs (aa) to (ac), paragraphs (iA) and (iB), and the words from "and in paragraph (iA)" to the end.
Criminal Justice Act 1948 (c. 58)	Section 41(5A). In section 80, the definition of "Court of summary jurisdiction".
Backing of Warrants (Republic of Ireland) Act 1965 (c. 45)	In the Schedule, in paragraph 4, the words "and section 2 of the Poor Prisoners Defence Act 1930 (legal aid before examining justices)".
Criminal Procedure (Attendance of Witnesses) Act 1965 (c. 69)	Section 2(5).
Criminal Justice Act 1967 (c. 80)	In section 9(1), the words ", other than committal proceedings". In section 36(1), the definition of "committal proceedings".
Criminal Appeal Act 1968 (c. 19)	In section 9(2), the words from "section 41" to "either way offence".
Firearms Act 1968 (c. 27)	In Schedule 6, in Part 2, paragraph 3.
Theft Act 1968 (c. 60)	Section 27(4A).
Criminal Justice Act 1972 (c. 71)	In section 46, subsections (1A) to (1C).
Bail Act 1976 (c. 63)	In section 3, subsections (8A) and (8B), and the subsection (10) inserted by paragraph 12(b) of Schedule 9 to the Criminal Justice and Public Order Act 1994 (c. 33). Section 5(6A)(a)(i).
Criminal Law Act 1977 (c. 45)	In Schedule 12, the entry relating to the Firearms Act 1968 (c. 27).
Interpretation Act 1978 (c. 30)	In Schedule 1, in the definition of "Committed for trial", paragraph (a).
Customs and Excise Management Act 1979 (c. 2)	Section 147(2).

Magistrates' Courts Act 1980 (c. 43)	Sections 4 to 8, and the cross-heading preceding section 4.
	In section 8B(6)(a), the words "commits or". Section 24(1A) and (2).
	In section 25, subsections (3) to (8).
	In section 33(1), paragraph (b) and the word "and" immediately preceding it.
	Section 42.
	Section 97A.
	Section 103.
	Section 106.
	In section 128, in subsection (1)(b), the words "inquiring into or", and in each of subsections (1A)(a), (3A), (3C)(a) and (3E)(a), the word "5,".
	In section 130(1), the word "5,".
	Section 145(1)(f).
	In section 150(1), the definition of "committal proceedings".
	In section 155(2)(a), the words "8 (except subsection (9))".
	In Schedule 3, paragraph 2(a).
	In Schedule 5, paragraph 2.
	In Schedule 7, paragraph 73.
Criminal Justice (Amendment) Act 1981 (c. 27)	The whole Act.
Criminal Attempts Act 1981 (c. 47)	In section 2(2)(g), the words "or committed for trial".
Contempt of Court Act 1981 (c. 49)	Section 4(4).
Supreme Court Act 1981 (c. 54)	Section 76(5).
	Section 77(4).
	In section 81—
	(a) in subsection (1)(a), the words "who has been committed in custody for appearance before the Crown Court or in relation to whose case a notice of transfer has been given under a relevant transfer provision or",
	(b) subsection (1)(g)(i),
	(c) subsection (7).
Criminal Justice Act 1982 (c. 48)	Section 61.
	In Schedule 9, paragraph 1(a).
Mental Health Act 1983 (c. 20)	In section 52(7)(b), the words "where the court proceeds under subsection (1) of that section,".
Police and Criminal Evidence Act 1984 (c. 60)	Section 62(10)(a)(i).
	In section 71, the paragraph beginning "Where the proceedings".

	Section 76(9).
	Section 78(3).
Prosecution of Offences Act 1985 (c. 23)	In section 16, subsections (1)(b), (2)(aa) and (12).
	In section 23A(1)(b), the words from "under" to "1998".
	In Schedule 1, paragraphs 2 and 3.
Criminal Justice Act 1987 (c. 38)	Sections 4 to 6.
	In section 11—
	(a) subsection (2)(a),
	(b) subsection (3),
	(c) in subsection (7), the word "(3),",
	(d) in subsection (8), the word "(3),",
	(e) subsections (9) and (10),
	(f) in subsection (11), paragraphs (a) and (d).
	In Schedule 2, paragraphs 1, 9 and 14.
Criminal Justice Act 1988 (c. 33)	Section 23(5).
	Section 24(5).
	In section 26, the paragraph beginning "This section shall not apply".
	In section 27, the paragraph beginning "This section shall not apply".
	Section 30(4A).
	Section 33.
	In section 40(1), the words "were disclosed to a magistrates' court inquiring into the offence as examining justices or".
	Section 41.
	Section 144.
	In Schedule 15, paragraphs 10, 66 and 104.
Road Traffic Offenders Act 1988 (c. 53)	Section 11(3A).
	Section 13(7).
	Section 16(6A).
	Section 20(8A).
Courts and Legal Services Act 1990 (c. 41)	In Schedule 18, paragraph 25(5).
Broadcasting Act 1990 (c. 42)	In Schedule 20, paragraph 29(1).
Criminal Justice Act 1991 (c. 53)	Section 53.
	Section 55(1).
	Schedule 6.
	In Schedule 11, paragraph 25.
Criminal Justice and Public Order Act 1994 (c. 33)	Section 34(2)(a).
	Section 36(2)(a).
	Section 37(2)(a).
	In Schedule 9, paragraphs 12, 17(c), 18(d), 25, 27, 29 and 49.

	In Schedule 10, paragraphs 40 and 71.
Criminal Procedure and Investigations Act 1996 (c. 25)	In section 1(2), paragraphs (a) to (c) and, in paragraph (cc), the words from "under" to the end. In section 5, subsections (2) and (3). In section 13(1), paragraphs (a) to (c) of the modified section 3(8). Section 28(1)(b). Section 44(3). Section 45. Section 49(4). Section 68. In Schedule 1, paragraphs 2 to 5, 8, 10, 12, 13, 15 to 19, 22(3), 24 to 26, 28 to 32, and 34 to 38. Schedule 2.
Sexual Offences (Protected Material) Act 1997 (c. 39)	Section 9(1).
Crime and Disorder Act 1998 (c. 37)	Section 47(6). In section 50(1), the words "unless the accused falls to be dealt with under section 51 below". In Schedule 3, in paragraph 2, sub-paragraphs (4) and (5), paragraph 12, and in paragraph 13(2), the words from "unless" to the end. In Schedule 8, paragraphs 8, 37, 40, 65 and 93.
Access to Justice Act 1999 (c. 22)	Section 67(3). In Schedule 4, paragraphs 16, 39 and 47. In Schedule 13, paragraphs 96, 111 and 137.
Youth Justice and Criminal Evidence Act 1999 (c. 23)	Section 27(10). In section 42(3), paragraphs (a) and (b).
Powers of Criminal Courts (Sentencing) Act 2000 (c. 6)	In section 89(2)(b), the words "trial or". In section 140(1)(b), the words "was committed to the Crown Court to be tried or dealt with or by which he". In Schedule 9, paragraphs 62, 63, 64(2), 65, 91 and 201. In Schedule 11, paragraph 9.

PART 5
EVIDENCE OF BAD CHARACTER

Short title and chapter	*Extent of repeal*
Criminal Procedure Act 1865 (c. 18)	In section 6, the words "and upon being

so questioned, if".

Criminal Evidence Act 1898 (c. 36)	Section 1(3).
Children and Young Persons Act 1963 (c. 37)	Section 16(2) and (3).
Criminal Evidence Act 1979 (c. 16)	In section 1, the words from "each of the following" to "1898, and".
Police and Criminal Evidence Act 1984 (c. 60)	In section 74(3), the words from "in so far" to "he is charged,".
Criminal Justice and Public Order Act 1994 (c. 33)	Section 31.
Crime (Sentences) Act 1997 (c. 43)	In Schedule 4, paragraph 4.
Youth Justice and Criminal Evidence Act 1999 (c. 23)	In Schedule 4, paragraph 1(5).

PART 6
HEARSAY EVIDENCE

Short title and chapter	*Extent of repeal*
Registered Designs Act 1949 (c. 88)	In section 17, in subsection (8) the words "Subject to subsection (11) below," and in subsection (10) the words ", subject to subsection (11) below,"
Patents Act 1977 (c. 37)	In section 32, in subsection (9) the words "Subject to subsection (12) below," and in subsection (11) the words ", subject to subsection (12) below,".
Criminal Justice Act 1988 (c. 33)	Part 2.
	Schedule 2.
	In Schedule 13, paragraphs 2 to 5.
	In Schedule 15, paragraph 32.
	In Schedule 4, paragraph 6(2).
Finance Act 1994 (c. 9)	Section 22(2)(b).
	In Schedule 7, paragraph 1(6)(b).
Value Added Tax Act 1994 (c. 23)	In Schedule 11, paragraph 6(6)(b).
Criminal Justice and Public Order Act 1994 (c. 33)	In Schedule 9, paragraph 31.
Civil Evidence Act 1995 (c. 38)	In Schedule 1, paragraph 12.
Finance Act 1996 (c. 8)	In Schedule 5, paragraph 2(6)(a).
Criminal Procedure and Investigations Act 1996 (c. 25)	In Schedule 1, paragraphs 28 to 31.
Crime and Disorder Act 1998 (c. 37)	In Schedule 3, paragraph 5(4).
Youth Justice and Criminal Evidence Act 1999 (c. 23)	In Schedule 4, paragraph 16.
Finance Act 2000 (c. 17)	In Schedule 6, paragraph 126(2)(a).
Finance Act 2001 (c. 9)	In Schedule 7, paragraph 3(2)(a).
Crime (International Co-operation)	In section 9(4), the words "section 25 of

Act 2003 (c. 32)   the Criminal Justice Act 1988 or".

PART 7

SENTENCING: GENERAL

Short title and chapter	*Extent of repeal*
Piracy Act 1837 (c. 88)	Section 3.
Children and Young Persons Act 1933 (c. 12)	In section 16(3), the words "mandatory and".
Criminal Justice Act 1967 (c. 80)	In section 104, in subsection (1) the definition of "suspended sentence" and subsection (2).
Criminal Appeal Act 1968 (c. 19)	In section 10 subsection (2)(c) and the word "or" immediately preceding it. Section 11(4).
Social Work (Scotland) Act 1968 (c. 49)	In section 94(1), the definition of "community rehabilitation order".
Bail Act 1976 (c. 63)	In section 2(1)(d), the words "placing the offender on probation or".
Magistrates' Courts Act 1980 (c. 43)	In section 82(4A), paragraph (e) and the word "or" immediately preceding it. Section 133(2). In Schedule 6A, the entry relating to section 123(3) of the Powers of Criminal Courts (Sentencing) Act 2000.
Forgery and Counterfeiting Act 1981 (c. 45)	Section 23(1)(b), (2)(b) and (3)(b).
Mental Health Act 1983 (c. 20)	In section 37(1B), the words "109(2),". In section 45A(1)(b), the words from "except" to "1997".
Road Traffic Offenders Act 1988 (c. 53)	In section 46(1), paragraph (a) and the word "or" following it.
Football Spectators Act 1989 (c. 37)	In section 7, subsection (9) and in sub-section (10)(b) the words from "(or" to the end.
Children Act 1989 (c. 41)	In section 68(2)(d), the words "a probation order has been made in respect of him or he has been". In Schedule 9A, in paragraph 4(2)(g), the words "placed on probation or".
Criminal Justice Act 1991 (c. 53)	Sections 32 to 51. Section 65. Schedule 5. In Schedule 12— (a) in paragraph 8(8), paragraph (d), and (b) in paragraph 9(3), paragraph (c).

Prisoners and Criminal Proceedings (Scotland) Act 1993 (c. 9)	In section 10(1)(a), sub-paragraph (i) and the succeeding "or".
Criminal Justice Act 1993 (c. 36)	Section 67(1).
Criminal Justice and Public Order Act 1994 (c. 33)	In section 25(3)(c), the words "placing the offender on probation or".
Criminal Procedure (Scotland) Act 1995 (c. 46)	In section 234—
	(a) in subsection (1), the words after paragraph (b),
	(b) in subsection (3), the words from "or to vary" to "one hundred", and
	(c) subsection (11).
Crime (Sentences) Act 1997 (c. 43)	Sections 35 and 40.
	In Schedule 1, paragraph 15(5).
	In Schedule 2, paragraphs 2 and 3.
	In Schedule 4, paragraphs 6(2), 7, 10(1), 12(1), 13 and 15(10).
Crime and Disorder Act 1998 (c. 37)	In section 18, subsection (2).
	In section 38(4)(i), the words "section 37(4A) or 65 of the 1991 Act or".
	Sections 59 and 60.
	Sections 80 and 81.
	Sections 99 and 100.
	Sections 101(1).
	Sections 103 to 105.
	In section 121(12), the words from the beginning to "paragraphs 56 to 60 of Schedule 8 to this Act;".
	In Schedule 7, paragraph 50.
	In Schedule 8, paragraphs 11, 13(2), 56, 58, 59, 79 to 84, 86 to 91, 94, 97, 132 and 135(3) and (4).
Criminal Justice (Children) (Northern Ireland) Order 1998 (S.I. 1998/1504 (N.I. 9))	In Schedule 5, paragraph 28(b).
Access to Justice Act 1999 (c. 22)	Section 58(5).
Powers of Criminal Courts (Sentencing) Act 2000 (c. 6)	Section 6(4)(d).
	Section 12(4).
	Sections 34 to 36A.
	In section 36B, subsections (4) and (8) and, in subsection (9), the words from "a community punishment order" to "a drug abstinence order".
	In section 37, in subsection (9) the words "who on conviction is under 16" and subsection (10).
	In section 40A, subsection (4), in sub-section (9) the words "who on conviction is under 16" and subsection (10). Sections 41 to 59.

In section 60, in subsection (1), paragraph (c) and the word "or" immediately preceding it.

Section 62.

Section 69(11).

Section 73(7).

Sections 78 to 82.

Section 84.

Section 85.

Sections 87 and 88.

Section 91(2).

Section 100(4).

Section 106(2) and (3).

Section 109.

Section 110(3).

Section 111(3).

In section 112(1)(a), the words "109,".

In section 113, in subsection (1)(a), the words "a serious offence or" and in sub-section (3), the words ""serious offence"," and "109,".

In section 114(1)(b), the words "a serious offence,".

In section 115, the word "109,".

Sections 116 and 117.

Sections 118 to 125.

Sections 126 to 129.

Sections 151 to 153.

Sections 156 to 158.

In section 159, the words ", 121(1) or 123(1)" and "paragraph 6(6) of Schedule 4 to this Act,".

In section 160—

(a) in subsection (2), in paragraph (a) the words from "42(2E)" to "Schedule 2" and in paragraph (b) the words from "122(7)" to the end,

(b) in subsection (3), in paragraph (a) the words "45, 50, 58, 58A(4), 85(7)", paragraph (b) and the word "or" immediately preceding it,

(c) subsection (4), and

Terrorism Act 2000 (c. 11)	In Schedule 15, paragraph 20.
Child Support, Pensions and Social Security Act 2000 (c. 19)	Section 62(10).
Criminal Justice and Court Services Act 2000 (c. 43)	Section 47 to 51.
	Sections 53 to 55.
	Section 63.
	Section 64(5)(e).
	In section 78(1), the definition of "community

664

order".

In Schedule 7, paragraphs 1 to 3, 104 to 107, 111(b), 123(a) and (c) to (f), 124(a) and (b), 133, 139, 140, 161, 162, 165 to 172, 177, 179, 189, 196(c)(ii) and (iii), 197(c) and (g)(ii), 198 to 200 and 206(a).

Short title and chapter	Extent of repeal
Anti-terrorism, Crime and Security Act 2001 (c. 24)	Section 39(7).
Proceeds of Crime Act 2002 (c. 29)	In Schedule 11, paragraph 32.

PART 8
LIFE SENTENCES

Short title and chapter	Extent of repeal
Murder (Abolition of Death Penalty) Act 1965 (c. 71)	Section 1(2).
Repatriation of Prisoners Act 1984 (c. 47)	In section 2(4)(b)(i), the words "or 29(1)". Section 3(9). Paragraph 3 of the Schedule.
Crime (Sentences) Act 1997 (c. 43)	Section 29. Section 31(4). Section 33. In section 34(3), the words from the beginning to "advocate; and".
Crime and Punishment (Scotland) Act 1977 (c. 48)	In Schedule 1, paragraph 10(3).
Crime and Disorder Act 1998 (c. 37)	In Schedule 8, paragraphs 57 and 60.
Powers of Criminal Courts (Sentencing) Act 2000 (c. 6)	In section 82A, in subsection (4) the words "subject to subsection (5) below", and subsections (5) and (6).

PART 9
ALTERATION OF PENALTIES FOR SUMMARY OFFENCES

Short title and chapter	Extent of repeal
Vagrancy Act 1824 (c. 83)	Section 5. Section 10.
Railway Regulation Act 1842 (c. 55)	In section 17, the words from "be imprisoned" (where first occurring) to "discretion of such justice, shall".
London Hackney Carriages Act 1843	In section 28, the words from "; or it

(c. 86)	shall be lawful" to the end.
Town Police Clauses Act 1847 (c. 89)	In section 28, the words from ", or, in the discretion" to "fourteen days".
	In section 29, the words from ", or, in the discretion" to the end.
	In section 36, the words from ", or, in the discretion" to "one month".
Ecclesiastical Courts Jurisdiction Act 1860 (c. 32)	In section 2, the words from ", or may, if the justices" to the end.
Town Gardens Protection Act 1863 (c. 13)	In section 5, the words ", or to imprisonment for any period not exceeding fourteen days".
Public Stores Act 1875 (c. 25)	In section 8, the words from ", or, in the discretion" to the end.
North Sea Fisheries Act 1893 (c. 17)	In section 2— (a) in paragraph (a), the words from ", or, in the discretion" to the end, and (b) in paragraph (b), the words from ", or in the discretion" to the end. In section 3(a), the words from ", or, in the discretion" to the end.
Children and Young Persons Act 1933 (c. 12)	In section 4(1), the words from ", or alternatively" to the end.
Protection of Animals Act 1934 (c. 21)	In section 2, the words from ", or, alternatively to the end.
Public Health Act 1936 (c. 49)	In section 287(5), the words from "or to imprisonment" to the end.
Essential Commodities Reserves Act 1938 (c. 51)	In section 4(2), the words from "or to imprisonment" to the end.
London Building Acts (Amendment) Act 1939 (c. xcvii)	In section 142(5), the words from "or to imprisonment" to the end.
Cancer Act 1939 (c. 13)	In section 4(2), the words from "or to imprisonment" to the end.
Civil Defence Act 1939 (c. 31)	In section 77, the words from "or to imprisonment" to the end.
Hill Farming Act 1946 (c. 73)	In section 19— (a) in subsection (2), the words from ", or to imprisonment" to the end, and (b) in subsection (3), the words from "or to imprisonment" to the end.
Agriculture Act 1947 (c. 48)	In section 14(7) (as remaining in force for the purposes of section 95), the words— (a) "to imprisonment for a term not exceeding three months or", and (b) "or to both such imprisonment and such fine". In section 95(3), the words— (a) "to imprisonment for a term not

	exceeding three months or", and (b) "or to both such imprisonment and such fine".
Civil Defence Act 1948 (c. 5)	In section 4(4), the words from "or to imprisonment" to the end.
Agricultural Wages Act 1948 (c. 47)	In section 12(7), the words from "or to imprisonment" to the end.
Wireless Telegraphy Act 1949 (c. 54)	In section 14(1B), the words— (a) "to imprisonment for a term not exceeding three months or", and (b) ", or both".
Prevention of Damage by Pests Act 1949 (c. 55)	In section 22(5), the words from "or to imprisonment" to the end.
Coast Protection Act 1949 (c. 74)	In section 25(9), the words from "or to imprisonment" to the end.
Pet Animals Act 1951 (c. 35)	In section 5— (a) in subsection (1), the words "other than the last foregoing section" and the words from "or to imprisonment" to the end, and (b) subsection (2).
Cockfighting Act 1952 (c. 59)	In section 1(1), the words— (a) "to imprisonment for a term not exceeding three months, or", and (b) ", or to both such imprisonment and such fine".
Agricultural Land (Removal of Surface Soil) Act 1953 (c. 10)	In section 2(1)— (a) paragraph (a) of the proviso, (b) the word "; or" immediately preceding paragraph (b) of the proviso, and (c) the words "or to both".
Accommodation Agencies Act 1953 (c. 23)	In section 1(5), the words from "or to imprisonment" to the end.
Army Act 1955 (3 & 4 Eliz. 2 c. 18)	In section 19(1), the words "to imprisonment for a term not exceeding three months or". In section 161, the words from ", or to imprisonment" to the end. In section 171(1), the words from ", or to imprisonment" to the end. In section 191, the words from "or to imprisonment" to the end. In section 193, the words from "or to imprisonment" to the end. In section 196(3), the words from "or to imprisonment" to the end. In section 197(3), the words from "or to imprisonment" to the end.Air Force Act 1955 (3 & 4 Eliz. 2 c. 19)In section

	19(1), the words "to imprisonment for a term not exceeding three months or".
	In section 161, the words from ", or to imprisonment" to the end.
	In section 171(1), the words from ", or to imprisonment" to the end.
	In section 191, the words from "or to imprisonment" to the end.
	In sections 193, the words from "or to imprisonment" to the end.
	In section 196(3), the words from "or to imprisonment" to the end.
	In section 197(3), the words from "or to imprisonment" to the end.
Naval Discipline Act 1957 (c. 53)	In section 96, the words from "or to imprisonment" to the end.
	In section 99(3), the words from "or to imprisonment" to the end.
Agricultural Marketing Act 1958 (c. 47)	In section 45(6), the words— (a) "to imprisonment for a term not exceeding one month, or", and (b) ", or to both such imprisonment and such fine".
Rivers (Prevention of Pollution) Act 1961 (c. 50)	In section 12(2), the words from "or to imprisonment" to the end.
Betting, Gaming and Lotteries Act 1963 (c. 2)	In section 8(1), the words— (a) "or to imprisonment for a term not exceeding three months, or to both", and (b) "in any case".
Children and Young Persons Act 1963 (c. 37)	In section 40— (a) in subsection (1), the words from "or imprisonment" to the end, and (b) in subsection (2), the words from "or imprisonment" to the end.
Animal Boarding Establishments Act 1963 (c. 43)	In section 3— (a) in subsection (1), the words "other than the last foregoing section" and the words from "or to imprisonment" to the end, and (b) subsection (2).
Agriculture and Horticulture Act 1964 (c. 28)	In section 20(2), the words from "or to imprisonment" to the end.
Emergency Laws (Re-enactments and Repeals) Act 1964 (c. 60)	In Schedule 1— (a) in paragraph 1(3), the words "to imprisonment for a term not exceeding three months or" and ", or to both", and (b) in paragraph 2(4), the words "to imprisonment for a term not exceeding

	three months or" and ", or to both".
Riding Establishments Act 1964 (c. 70)	In section 4(1), the words from "or to imprisonment" to the end.
Industrial and Provident Societies Act 1965 (c. 12)	In section 16(5), the words from "or to imprisonment" to the end.
	In section 48(2), the words from "or to imprisonment" to the end.
Cereals Marketing Act 1965 (c. 14)	In section 17(1), the words from "or to imprisonment" to the end.
Gas Act 1965 (c. 36)	In Schedule 6, in paragraph 9, the words from "or to imprisonment" to the end.
Armed Forces Act 1966 (c. 45)	In section 8, the words "to imprisonment for a term not exceeding three months or".
Agriculture Act 1967 (c. 22)	In section 6(9), the words from "or to imprisonment" to the end.
	In section 14(2), the words from "or to imprisonment" to the end.
	In section 69, the words from "or imprisonment" to the end.
Criminal Justice Act 1967 (c. 80)	Section 20.
Sea Fisheries (Shellfish) Act 1967 (c. 83)	In section 14(2), the words from "or to imprisonment" to the end.
Theatres Act 1968 (c. 54)	In section 13(3), the words from "or to imprisonment" to the end.
Theft Act 1968 (c. 60)	In Schedule 1, in paragraph 2(1), the words— (a) "to imprisonment for a term not exceeding three months or", and (b) "or to both".
Agriculture Act 1970 (c. 40)	In section 106(8), the words from "or imprisonment" to the end.
Breeding of Dogs Act 1973 (c. 60)	In section 3(1)— (a) paragraph (a), (b) the word "; or" immediately preceding paragraph (b), and (c) the words "or to both".
Slaughterhouses Act 1974 (c. 3)	In section 38(5), the words "or imprisonment for a term of three months or both".
National Health Service Act 1977 (c. 49)	In Schedule 11— (a) in paragraph 8(3), the words "to imprisonment for a term not exceeding three months or" and ", or to both", and (b) in paragraph 9(4), the words "to imprisonment for a term not exceeding three months or" and ", or to both".
Magistrates' Courts Act 1980 (c. 43)	In section 84(3), the words— (a) "imprisonment for a term not

	exceeding 4 months or", and
	(b) "to both".
Animal Health Act 1981 (c. 22)	In paragraph 6 of Schedule 1, the words—
	(a) "or to imprisonment for a term not exceeding 2 months,", and
	(b) "in either case".
Fisheries Act 1981 (c. 29)	In section 5(4), the words from "or to imprisonment" to the end.
Civil Aviation Act 1982 (c. 16)	In section 82(2), the words from "or to imprisonment" to the end.
Criminal Justice Act 1982 (c. 48)	Section 70.
Mental Health Act 1983 (c. 20)	Section 43(5).
	In section 103(9), the words—
	(a) "to imprisonment for a term not exceeding three months or", and
	(b) "or both".
	In section 129(3), the words—
	(a) "to imprisonment for a term not exceeding three months or", and
	(b) "or to both".
Building Act 1984 (c. 55)	In section 96(3), the words "or to imprisonment for a term not exceeding three months".
Surrogacy Arrangements Act 1985 (c. 49)	In section 4(1)—
	(a) paragraph (a), and
	(b) in paragraph (b), the words "in the case of an offence under section 3".
Animals (Scientific Procedures) Act 1986 (c. 14)	In section 22(3), the words—
	(a) "to imprisonment for a term not exceeding three months or", and
	(b) "or to both".
	In section 23(2), the words—
	(a) "to imprisonment for a term not exceeding three months or", and
	(b) "or to both".
	In section 25(3), the words—
	(a) "to imprisonment for a term not exceeding three months or", and
	(b) "or to both".
Motor Cycle Noise Act 1987 (c. 34)	In the Schedule, in paragraph 1(1), the words "to imprisonment for a term not exceeding three months or".
Human Organ Transplants Act 1989 (c. 31)	In section 2(5), the words—
	(a) "imprisonment for a term not exceeding three months or", and
	(b) "or both".
Town and Country Planning Act 1990	In Schedule 15, in paragraph 14(4), the

(c. 8)	words from "or to imprisonment" to the end.
Environmental Protection Act 1990 (c. 43)	In section 118(7), the words from "or to imprisonment" to the end.
Criminal Justice Act 1991 (c. 53)	Section 26(5).
Deer Act 1991 (c. 54)	In section 10(3), the words from "or to imprisonment" to the end.
Water Industry Act 1991 (c. 56)	In section 206(9), the words—
	(a) "to imprisonment for a term not exceeding three months or", and
	(b) "or to both".
	In Schedule 6, in paragraph 5(5), the words—
	(a) "to imprisonment for a term not exceeding three months or", and
	(b) "or to both".
Social Security Administration Act 1992 (c. 5)	In section 105(1), the words—
	(a) "to imprisonment for a term not exceeding 3 months or", and
	(b) "or to both".
	In section 182(3), the words—
	(a) "to imprisonment for a term not exceeding 3 months or", and
	(b) "or to both".
Local Government Finance Act 1992 (c. 14)	In section 27(5), the words—
	(a) "imprisonment for a term not exceeding three months or", and
	(b) "or both".
Trade Union and Labour Relations (Consolidation) Act 1992 (c. 52)	In section 240(3), the words—
	(a) "to imprisonment for a term not exceeding three months or", and
	(b) "or both".
Merchant Shipping Act 1995 (c. 21)	In section 57(2)—
	(a) in paragraph (a), the words "except in a case falling within paragraph (b) below,", and
	(b) paragraph (b).
Reserve Forces Act 1996 (c. 14)	In section 75(5), the words—
	(a) "imprisonment for a term not exceeding 3 months or", and
	(b) "(or both)".
	In section 82(1), the words—
	(a) "imprisonment for a term not exceeding 3 months", and
	(b) "(or both)".
	In section 87(1), the words—
	(a) "imprisonment for a term not exceeding 3 months or", and
	(b) "(or both)".

	In section 99, the words— (a) "imprisonment for a term not exceeding 3 months", and (b) "(or both)". In Schedule 1, in paragraph 5(2), the words— (a) "imprisonment for a term not exceeding 3 months or", and (b) "(or both)".
Housing Act 1996 (c. 52)	In Schedule 1— (a) in paragraph 23(6), the words from "or imprisonment" to "or both", and (b) in paragraph 24(6), the words from "or imprisonment" to "or both.
Broadcasting Act 1996 (c. 55)	In section 144(4), the words— (a) "to imprisonment for a term not exceeding three months or", and (b) "or to both".
Breeding and Sale of Dogs (Welfare) Act 1999 (c. 11)	In section 9— (a) in subsection (1), paragraph (a), the word ", or" immediately preceding paragraph (b) and the words "or to both", and (b) in subsection (7), paragraph (a), the word ", or" immediately preceding paragraph (b) and the words "or to both".
Powers of Criminal Courts (Sentencing) Act 2000 (c. 6)	In section 6(4), paragraph (a).
Countryside and Rights of Way Act 2000 (c. 37)	In section 81, subsections (2) and (3).
Transport Act 2000 (c. 38)	In section 82, subsection (5).

PART 10
JURY SERVICE

Short title and chapter	*Extent of repeal*
Juries Act 1974 (c. 23).	In section 2(5)(a), the word "9(1),". In section 9, subsection (1) and in subsection (2) the words from "and" to the end.
Criminal Law Act 1977 (c. 45).	In Schedule 12, the entry relating to the Juries Act 1974.
Criminal Justice Act 1982 (c. 48).	In Schedule 14, paragraph 35.
Mental Health (Amendment) Act 1982 (c. 51).	In Schedule 3, paragraph 48.
Mental Health Act 1983 (c. 20).	In Schedule 4, paragraph 37.
Juries (Disqualification) Act 1984 (c. 34).	The whole Act.
Coroners Act 1988 (c. 13).	Section 9(2).

Criminal Justice Act 1988 (c. 33).	Section 119.
	In Schedule 8, paragraph 8.
Courts and Legal Services Act 1990 (c. 41).	In Schedule 17, paragraph 7.
	In Schedule 18, paragraph 5.
Criminal Justice Act 1991 (c. 53).	In Schedule 11, paragraph 18.
Probation Service Act 1993 (c. 47).	In Schedule 3, paragraph 5.
Police and Magistrates' Courts Act 1994 (c. 29).	In Schedule 8, paragraph 28.
Criminal Justice and Public Order Act 1994 (c. 33).	Section 40.
	Section 42.
	In Schedule 10, paragraph 29.
Criminal Appeal Act 1995 (c. 35).	In Schedule 2, paragraph 8.
Police Act 1996 (c. 16).	In Schedule 7, paragraph 23.
Police Act 1997 (c. 50).	In Schedule 9, paragraph 27.
Government of Wales Act 1998 (c. 38).	In Schedule 12, paragraph 18.
Scotland Act 1998 (c. 46).	Section 85(1).
Access to Justice Act 1999 (c. 22).	In Schedule 11, paragraph 22.
Criminal Justice and Court Services Act 2000 (c. 43).	In Schedule 7, paragraph 47.
European Parliamentary Elections Act 2002 (c. 24).	In Schedule 3, paragraph 2.

PART 11
REPEALS RELATING TO AMENDMENTS OF PART 5 OF POLICE ACT 1997

Short title and chapter	*Extent of repeal*
Police Act 1997 (c. 50)	In section 115, subsections (3) to (5) and subsections (6C) to (6E).
	Section 120(3).
	In section 125, subsection (3) and, in subsection (4), the words "to which sub-section (3) does not apply".
Care Standards Act 2000 (c. 14)	Section 104(3)(a).
	In Schedule 4, paragraph 25(2)(a).
Private Security Industry Act 2001 (c. 12)	Section 21.
	Section 26(3)(a).
Health and Social Care Act 2001 (c. 15)	Section 19.
Criminal Justice and Police Act 2001 (c. 16)	Section 134(3) and (4).
National Health Service Reform and	Section 42(7).
Health Care Professions Act 2002 (c. 17)	In Schedule 2, paragraph 64.

Education Act 2002 (c. 32)	In Schedule 12, paragraph 15(2).
	In Schedule 13, paragraph 8(2).
Licensing Act 2003 (c. 17)	In Schedule 6, paragraph 116.

Section 333(6)

PART 12

MISCELLANEOUS

Short title and chapter	Extent of repeal
Criminal Appeal Act 1968 (c. 19)	Section 10(4).
	In section 11(2), the words from "(which expression" to "purposes of section 10)".
	In section 51(1), the definition of "the defendant".
Bail Act 1976 (c. 63)	In section 5(1)(c), the words "a court or officer of a court appoints".
Magistrates' Courts Act 1980 (c. 43)	In section 1(3), the words "and substantiated on oath".
	Section 12(1)(a)(i).
	In section 13(3)(a), the words "the information has been substantiated on oath and".
Criminal Appeal (Northern Ireland) Act 1980 (c. 47)	In section 19(1A)(a), the words "application for leave to".
Criminal Procedure and Investigations Act 1996 (c. 25)	In Schedule 4, paragraph 16.
Crime and Disorder Act 1998 (c. 37)	In section 8(2), the words from "and to section 19(5)" to "2000".
Youth Justice and Criminal Evidence Act 1999 (c. 23)	In Schedule 4, paragraphs 26 and 27.
Powers of Criminal Courts (Sentencing. Act 2000 (c. 6)	In section 19(5), paragraph (c) and the word "or" immediately preceding it.
	In Schedule 9, paragraphs 194 and 195.
Criminal Justice and Court Services Act 2000 (c. 43)	Sections 67 and 68.

SCHEDULE 38

Section 333(6)

TRANSITORY, TRANSITIONAL AND SAVING PROVISIONS

Sentencing of offenders aged 18 but under 21

1. If any provision of Part 12 ("the relevant provision") is to come into force before the day on which section 61 of the Criminal Justice and Court Services Act 2000 (abolition of sentences of detention in a young offender institution, custody for life, etc.) comes into force (or fully into force) the provision that may be made by order under section 333(1) includes

provision modifying the relevant provision with respect to sentences passed, or other things done, at any time before section 61 of that Act comes into force (or fully into force).

Sentencing guidelines

2. The repeal by this Act of sections 80 and 81 of the Crime and Disorder Act 1998 does not affect the authority of any guidelines with respect to sentencing which have been included in any judgment of the Court of Appeal given before the commencement of that repeal ("existing guidelines"), but any existing guidelines may be superseded by sentencing guidelines published by the Sentencing Guidelines Council under section 170 of this Act as definitive guidelines.

3. (1) Subject to sub-paragraph (2), the repeal by this Act of section 81 of the Crime and Disorder Act 1998 does not affect the operation of subsection (4) of that section in relation to any notification received by the Panel under subsection (2) of that section, or proposal made by the Panel under subsection (3) of that section, before the commencement of the repeal.

   (2) In its application by virtue of sub-paragraph (1) after the commencement of that repeal, section 81(4) of that Act is to have effect as if any reference to "the Court" were a reference to the Sentencing Guidelines Council.

   (3) In this paragraph "the Panel" means the Sentencing Advisory Panel.

Drug treatment and testing orders

4. A drug treatment and testing order made under section 52 of the Powers of Criminal Courts (Sentencing) Act 2000 before the repeal of that section by this Act is in force (or fully in force) need not include the provision referred to in subsection (6) of section 54 of that Act (periodic review by court) if the treatment and testing period (as defined by section 52(1) of that Act) is less than 12 months.

Drug testing as part of supervision of young offenders after release

5. (1) Until the coming into force of the repeal by this Act of section 65 of the Criminal Justice Act 1991 (c. 53) (supervision of young offenders after release), that section has effect subject to the following modifications.

   (2) In subsection (5B)—
      (a) in paragraph (a), for "18 years" there is substituted "14 years",
      (b) for paragraph (b) there is substituted—
         "(b) a responsible officer is of the opinion—
            (i) that the offender has a propensity to misuse specified Class A drugs, and
            (ii) that the misuse by the offender of any specified Class A drug caused or contributed to any offence of which he has been convicted, or is likely to cause or contribute to the commission by him of further offences; and".

   (3) After subsection (5D) there is inserted—
      "(5E) A person under the age of 17 years may not be required by virtue of subsection (5A) to provide a sample otherwise than in the presence of an appropriate adult." "

   (4) For subsection (10) there is substituted—
      "(10) In this section—
         "appropriate adult", in relation to a person aged under 17, means—

675

(a) his parent or guardian or, if he is in the care of a local authority or voluntary organisation, a person representing that authority or organisation,

(b) a social worker of a local authority social services department, or

(c) if no person falling within paragraph (a) or (b) is available, any responsible person aged 18 or over who is not a police officer or a person employed by the police;

"responsible officer" means—

(a) in relation to an offender aged under 18, an officer of a local probation board or a member of a youth offending team;

(b) in relation to an offender aged 18 or over, an officer of a local probation board;

"specified Class A drug" has the same meaning as in Part 3 of the Criminal Justice and Court Services Act 2000 (c. 43)."

Intermittent custody

6. If section 183 (intermittent custody) is to come into force for any purpose before the commencement of the repeal by this Act of section 78 of the Powers of Criminal Courts (Sentencing) Act 2000 (c. 6) (which imposes a general limit on the power of a magistrates' court to impose imprisonment), the provision that may be made by order under section 333(1) includes provision modifying any period or number of days specified in section 183 with respect to sentences passed by magistrates' courts before the commencement of that repeal.

Transfer to Scotland of community orders and suspended sentence orders

7. (1) Until the coming into force of the repeal by the Mental Health (Care and Treatment) (Scotland) Act 2003 of the Mental Health (Scotland) Act 1984 (c. 36), in the provisions mentioned in sub-paragraph (2) the reference to the Mental Health (Care and Treatment) (Scotland) Act 2003 has effect as a reference to the Mental Health (Scotland) Act 1984.

(2) Those provisions are—

(a) paragraph 2(4) of Schedule 9 (transfer of community orders to Scotland or Northern Ireland), and

(b) paragraph 4 of Schedule 13 (transfer of suspended sentence orders to Scotland or Northern Ireland).

Index

Prescription Drugs in Pregnancy

Your Pocket Guide to Fetal Risk for Hundreds of Drugs

by

D. Gary Benfield, M.D.
Cynthia S. Kelley, D.O.

Smart Start Press

To purchase copies of *Prescription Drugs in Pregnancy*,
use any of the following ways:

Go to www.atlasbooks.com
Phone: 800-247-6553
Fax: 419-281-6883

Copyright 2010, D. Gary Benfield, M.D.
Smart Start Press

ISBN: 978-0-9779848-3-1   Pocket Guide size version

LCCN: 2006909659   Pocket Guide size version

The information contained in this book is not intended to substitute for
your own doctor's medical advice. Readers should always consult their
doctors or other healthcare professionals for advice and treatment. If you
are pregnant or planning a pregnancy, always let your doctor know before
taking any drug, prescription or nonprescription, or herbal remedy. The
authors and the publisher disclaim any liability arising directly or indirectly
from the use of this book.

The listing of selected brand names in this book is intended only for ease of
reference. The inclusion of a brand name does not mean the authors or the
publisher have any particular knowledge that the brand listed has properties
different from other brands of the same drug, nor should it be interpreted
as an endorsement by the authors or the publisher. Similarly, the fact that
a particular brand has not been included does not indicate that the drug has
been judged to be unsatisfactory or unacceptable.

The use of a brand name in this book is not intended as a grant of authority
to exercise any right or privilege protected by a patent or trademark owned
by the drug's manufacturer.

Printed in the United States of America.